Personal Financial Planning

The Addison-Wesley Series in Finance

Campbell/Kracaw
Financial Institutions and Capital Markets

Chambers/Lacey
Modern Corporate Finance: Theory and Practice

Copeland/Weston
Financial Theory and Corporate Policy

Crawford/Sihler
Financial Service Organizations: Cases in Strategic Management

Davis/Pinches
Canadian Financial Management

Dufey/Giddy
Cases in International Finance

Eiteman/Stonehill/Moffett
Multinational Business Finance

Emery
Corporate Finance: Principles and Practice

Eng/Lees/Mauer
Global Finance

Gitman
Foundations of Managerial Finance

Gitman
Principles of Managerial Finance

Gitman
Principles of Managerial Finance —Brief Edition

Gitman/Joehnk
Fundamentals of Investing

Megginson
Corporate Finance Theory

Melvin
International Money and Finance

Mishkin/Eakins
Financial Markets and Institutions

Pinches
Essentials of Financial Management

Pinches
Financial Management

Radcliffe
Investment: Concepts-Analysis-Strategy

Rejda
Principles of Risk Management and Insurance

Rejda/McNamara
Personal Financial Planning

Ritchken
Derivative Markets: Theory, Strategy, and Applications

Sihler
Cases in Applied Corporate Finance

Solnik
International Investments

Thygerson
Management of Financial Institutions

Wagner
Financial Management with the Electronic Spreadsheet

Personal Financial Planning

First Edition

George E. Rejda and Michael J. McNamara

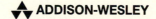 **ADDISON-WESLEY**

An Imprint of Addison Wesley Longman, Inc.

Reading, Massachusetts • Menlo Park, California • New York • Harlow, England
Don Mills, Ontario • Sydney • Mexico City • Madrid • Amsterdam

Personal Financial Planning
George E. Rejda
Michael J. McNamara

Senior Editor: Denise Clinton
Associate Editor: Julie Zasloff
Developmental Editor: Beverly Peavler
Supplements Editor: Joan Twining
Senior Production Supervisor: Nancy H. Fenton
Marketing Manager: Jodi Fazio
Manufacturing Supervisor: Hugh Crawford
Cover Designer: Regina Hagen
Project Coordination: Thompson Steele Production Services, Inc.

Library of Congress Cataloging-in-Publication Data

Rejda, George E., 1931–
    Personal financial planning / George E. Rejda, Michael J. McNamara.
    —1st ed.
        p.   cm.
      Includes index.
      ISBN 0-321-00927-4
      1. Finance, Personal. 2. Investments. I. McNamara, Michael J., 1961–.
    II. Title
        HG179.R392 1997
97-21669
        332.024—dc21
CIP

2 3 4 5 6 7 8 9 10 — DOC — 01 00 99 98

Contents

Chapter 5. Borrowing and Debt Management   144

Chapter 6. Tax Planning   182

Part Two

Protection Against Financial Insecurity

Chapter 8. Introduction to Risk Management and Insurance   266

Chapter 9. Life Insurance   288

Chapter 10. Health Insurance   330

Chapter 11. Property and Liability Insurance   374

Part Three

The Role of Investments In Financial Planning

Chapter 12. Fundamentals of Investing   420

Chapter 13. Investing in Stocks and Bonds   462

Part Four

Retirement Planning And Estate Planning

Preface

In recent months, headlines similar to the following have appeared in local newspapers:

"Stock market drops 247 points"

"Consumer debt reaches all-time high"

"Bankruptcies by Americans reach record levels"

"Federal Reserve leaves interest rates intact"

"Health insurance premiums reverse downward trend"

"Raging flood waters cause millions of dollars of property damage".

It is clear that money has an important impact on the lives of most Americans. Unfortunately, many Americans have little or no knowledge of money management and the necessary financial principles to attain their financial goals. This text attempts to remedy that problem.

Content

The text is specifically designed for a one-semester course in financial planning or personal finance at the undergraduate level with no prerequisites. It can also be used in courses that emphasize consumer economics, investments, or insurance. The goal is to take readers who have little or no knowledge of money and money management to the level where they are sophisticated and knowledgeable consumers in all major areas of personal finance.

The text is divided into four parts and covers all major areas in personal financial planning. Part One discusses the fundamentals of financial planning, financial goals and objectives, budgets and other tools of financial planning, money management, using credit wisely, borrowing and debt management, tax planning, and the housing decision.

Part Two deals with personal risk management and insurance, including the steps in the personal risk management process, methods for dealing with risk, life insurance, health insurance, and property and liability insurance.

Part Three treats the important role of investments in financial planning, which includes the fundamentals of investing and how to invest in stocks, bonds, mutual funds, and other investments.

Part Four examines retirement planning and estate planning. Topics discussed include saving for retirement, tax-deferred retirement plans, Section 401(k) plans, individual retirement accounts (IRAs), annuities, Social Security benefits, and strategies for minimizing federal estate taxes.

Unique Features

This text differs from competing textbooks in several important respects, which make it a superior product. There is a strong emphasis on pedagogy and ease of learning. The text emphasizes the following pedagogical features:

1. **Internet resources.** The Internet is becoming increasingly important as a marketing tool for financial institutions and a convenient source of financial information for consumers. Many mutual fund families, stock brokerage firms, insurers, banks, and other financial institutions have established World Wide Web sites. Each chapter contains Internet exercises and Web site addresses of financial institutions for students who are seeking current information on specific topics or who are doing research on financial planning subjects.

2. **Clarity in writing.** Financial planning as a subject can intimidate some students if set forth in a disjointed or abstract way. Since readability continues to be crucial, we are careful to present financial concepts clearly and directly, for the most user-friendly of texts.

3. **Boxed "Insights."** Each chapter contains one or more boxed "Insights" or mini-readings that provide students with a real-world application of the principle being discussed. These "Insights" are powerful learning tools. Each has been carefully edited and selected for its educational value. Additional timely materials appear in exhibits and appendices. Readers should look for these grabbers throughout the text:

- Ten Ways to Keep More of the Money You Earn
- To Build Portfolio Cheaply, Consider No-Load Stocks
- Investing through Dividend Reinvestment Plans
- Market Timing Can Be Painful
- You Should Consider the Big Gap Between Replacement Cost and Actual Cash Value
- Six Things Your Bank Won't Tell You. Listen Up—You'll Save Time and Money
- Getting the Most from Your IRA
- Students Can Learn a Lesson in Budgeting
- Determining the Rate of Return on Cash Value Policies
- How to Turn $10 Monthly into $22,000, or Even More
- Surfing Traps That Wipe Out Your Savings
- 10 Ways to Buy a Home with Bad Credit
- The 25 Facts Every Mutual Fund Investor Should Know
- Swamped by Debt? Here Are Six Ways to Get Out

- Paying Down Debt Can Boost Your Returns
- If You've Got Money to Squirrel Away, Sometimes There's No Place Like Home
- How to Borrow Like an Expert
- Increase Your Returns by Cutting Fund Expenses
- A Tip for Longer-Term Investors: Choosing Bonds Is Shortsighted
- For Novice Investors on Small Budgets, There Are Plenty of Ways to Start Out
- Word to 20-Somethings Aiming to Retire Rich: Start Saving Now
- How Much Emergency Cash Is Enough? Not Everyone Needs a Rainy-Day Umbrella
- Term Insurance Quotes: Online vs. By Mail
- Should You Replace a Life Insurance Policy?
- The Perils an Umbrella Policy Can Protect Against
- How Can Health Care Costs Be Controlled?

4. **Time value of money.** The time value of money is discussed more extensively than in competing texts. This is for the benefit of instructors who wish to teach this material in a more rigorous manner. However, for instructors who prefer to teach the time value of money in a minimum amount of class time, the fundamental concepts are clearly presented and are easily grasped by most students.

5. **Personal risk management.** Chapter 8 discusses protection against financial insecurity in the context of personal risk management. This section identifies the major risks that cause financial insecurity. The steps in the personal risk management process are clearly stated. Students can immediately apply the various methods of dealing with risk, including insurance, to their own personal risk management program.

6. **Insurance.** The text contains a number of insurance features seldom found in competing texts. Chapter 9 gets deeper into the financial impact of premature death and how it affects different types of families in the United States and their need for life insurance. Appendix E explains how to calculate the yearly rate-of-return on a cash-value life insurance policy.

Chapter 10 discusses clearly and concisely the health care problems in the United States and sets the stage for discussion of the various individual and group health insurance coverages. Because of their importance, managed care plans receive considerable treatment.

Finally, unlike competing texts, the appendix contains two specimen insurance contracts on homeowners insurance and the personal auto policy. These materials can be of great benefit to instructors who would like their students to read and understand an insurance contract in a financial planning course.

7. **Timely and up-to-date coverage.** Readers will find up-to-date coverage of current topics in financial planning throughout the text: new developments in managed care plans and health maintenance organizations (HMOs), analysis of the new Health Insurance and Portability Act of 1996, discussion of the new SIMPLE retirement plan, inflation-indexed bonds sold by the federal government, new changes in Series EE savings bonds, up-to-date treatment of employer-sponsored retirement plans and Section 401(k) plans, and numerous other topics.

Supplements

Instructor's Manual with Transparency Masters. Prepared by George E. Rejda, the University of Nebraska–Lincoln and Michael J. McNamara, The University of Memphis. Designed to reduce course start-up costs and to give instructors some fresh ideas, this comprehensive manual contains lecture outlines; answers to all end-of-chapter questions, problems, and cases; and a set of transparency masters that illustrate important points in the text.

Computerized Testing System. Prepared by C. Bruce Worsham, The American College. Instructors can use this high-quality test bank with confidence and a minimum of student friction. The computerized version of the test bank enables instructors to construct tests quickly and easily. Instructors can choose existing test items randomly by chapter, question type, and quantity, or manually by specific item number. The program allows instructors to edit test items or add their own questions; print tests in several formats; and incorporate graphs, charts, and tables. The test bank is designed for Macintosh, IBM-PC, and compatible computers and is available at no additional cost to text adopters.

Printed Test Bank. All tests questions from the computerized test bank are available in this bound supplement.

Study Guide. Prepared by Michael J. McNamara, The University of Memphis. This study tool is an improvement over traditional study guides and contains exercises that enable students to apply the various concepts to their own financial planning programs. The introductory section summarizes the benefits of the guide, and how to use the guide effectively as a learning tool. Each chapter contains practice items such as objective test questions similar to test bank questions; learning goals organized by objectives listed at the beginning of every text chapter; key-term exercises; worksheets where appropriate for solving end-of-chapter mini-cases; and step-by-step demonstration problems with rationales for each step. Solutions to all questions are found at the end of each chapter for quick reference and self-testing.

Personal Financial Planning Software Templates

This textbook contains a very special set of 39 *Personal Financial Planning* student software templates that supplement the text material. The templates help students solve personal financial planning problems that range from setting financial goals to allocating invested assets. The templates utilize Excel 5; Excel 7; or the latest version, Excel 97; software. Each template contains a custom toolbar that helps the user navigate through the Excel workbook, use a Windows calculator, review examples, print a report, and visit relevant World Wide Web personal finance sites. Every new copy of the text contains a CD-ROM bound in the back cover that contains all 39 PFP templates.

Acknowledgments

A successful textbook is seldom written alone. The authors owe an enormous intellectual debt to numerous financial planning experts and academicians for their kind and gracious assistance. Numerous educators have taken time out of their busy professional schedules to review part or all of the text, to contribute supplementary materials, or to offer valuable suggestions and comments. They include the following:

Tawny Aguirre, New Mexico State University

Burton T. Beam, Jr., The American College

Joseph M. Belth, Indiana University

Mary Ann Block, Tarleton State University

Stewart Bonem, Cincinnati Technical College

Claire S. Bronson, Western New England College

James Carson, Illinois State University

Cia Cheshier, California State University–Sacramento

Ronald Christner, Loyola University–New Orleans

Bobbie Corbett, Northern Virginia Community College

Raymond A. K. Cox, Central Michigan University

Carlene Creviston, Ball State University

Phillip Daves, University of Tennessee

William Demkey, Bakersfield College

Robert Drennan, Temple University

James Felton, Central Michigan University

Deborah Fowler, East Tennessee State University

Deborah Gaunt, Georgia State University

Joel Gold, University of Southern Maine

Linda J. Gorham, Northeastern University

Susan Alexander Greninger, University of Texas–Austin

Michael Griffin, University of Massachusetts–Dartmouth

Vickie Hampton, University of Texas

Donald Hardigree, University of Nevada–Las Vegas

Marianne Hite, University of Colorado–Denver

Arlene Holyoak, Oregon State University

Robert Hull, Washburn University

Harry M. Johnson, University of Connecticut

Jerry Jones, Spokane Community College

Ahmad Khurshid, Wright State University

Ernest W. King, University of Southern Mississippi

Daniel P. Klein, Bowling Green State University

Phillip T. Koble, The University of Memphis

Timothy Krehbiel, Oklahoma State University

Edward Krohn, Miami-Dade Community College

John T. Lee, Middle Tennessee State University

Linda Martin, Arizona State University

Thomas Mason, Brookdale Community College

Garth McCann, Colorado State University

Daniel McCarty, Florida Atlantic University

David Murphy, Madisonville Community College

Barbara Poole, University of Connecticut

Ann Rock, Wayne State University

Stephen Russell, Weber State University

Steven Scott, University of Oklahoma

Carl Shallenberger, Kent State University

Chris Swift, Lincoln Electric System

Ryland Syverson, University of North Dakota

Richard Whitaker, University of Houston

Deborah Wooldridge, Southeast Missouri State University

C. Bruce Worsham, The American College

The authors also wish to acknowledge the technical assistance of Beverly Peavler, who served as developmental editor, and Julie Zasloff, associate editor of finance at Addison-Wesley, who resolved numerous production problems in a first edition text. We also appreciate the feedback and observations of others who have helped us, including the supplements team of C. Bruce Worsham and Evelyn Rice.

Finally, the fundamental objective in writing this text remains unchanged—we have attempted to write an intellectually stimulating and visually attractive textbook from which students can learn and professors can teach.

George E. Rejda, Ph.D., CLU
V. J. Skutt Distinguished Professor of Insurance
University of Nebraska–Lincoln

Michael J. McNamara, Ph.D., CPCU, ARM, CLU
Assistant Professor of Finance and Insurance
The University of Memphis

Part One

Fundamentals of
Financial Planning

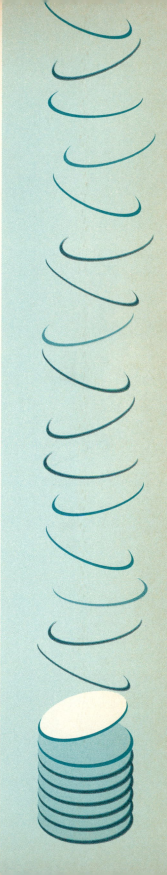

Chapter **1**

Introduction to Financial Planning

Learning Objectives

After studying this chapter, you should be able to:

- Explain the meaning of personal financial planning.

- Identify the major benefits of financial planning.

- Recognize the major obstacles to financial planning.

- Describe the five basic steps in the financial planning process.

- Identify important financial goals and objectives that should be considered in a financial plan.

- Design a financial plan that reflects your financial goals and objectives.

- Identify the important financial factors that individuals in different age brackets should consider.

Marry for money, my little sonny, a rich man's joke is always funny.

—Hebrew Proverb

There's only one thing money won't buy, and that's poverty.

—Joe E. Lewis

Welcome to the fascinating world of personal financial planning. Money is obviously important to you; if it weren't, you would not be reading this book. You need money to satisfy the immediate requirements of life, including food, clothing, housing, transportation, and college tuition. You also need money to attain your future financial goals, which may include starting a saving and investment program, accumulating a fund for early retirement, or purchasing a home or a new car. Financial planning can help you reach these goals. In addition, if you are in debt, financial planning can help you get out of debt and raise your standard of living.

This book is about how to use money and financial planning to attain your financial goals and objectives. It is designed to take readers who have little knowledge of money management and personal finance to the point at which they are sophisticated and knowledgeable consumers in the areas of money management, credit management, tax planning, investments, housing, insurance planning, retirement planning, and estate planning.

This chapter discusses the fundamentals of personal financial planning. It explains the meaning of financial planning, benefits of financial planning, obstacles to financial planning, steps in the financial planning process, and important financial goals and objectives. The chapter concludes with a discussion of important financial considerations for individuals in different age brackets.

Personal Financial Planning

Personal financial planning requires knowledge of certain principles, including (1) the meaning of financial planning, (2) the benefits of financial planning, and (3) the obstacles to financial planning.

The Meaning of Financial Planning

financial planning The process of developing a comprehensive plan that determines financial goals and objectives and the best strategies for obtaining them.

Financial planning is the development of a comprehensive plan in which you determine your financial goals and objectives, and select the best strategies for attaining them. In the process, you analyze your present financial position, determine your specific financial goals and objectives, and design a strategic plan for attaining these goals. You then review the plan periodically and revise it as your circumstances change.

To be effective, financial planning must start with well-defined financial goals. However, many consumers have not yet set such goals. In a recent national survey by Merrill Lynch, only about two in ten respondents (21 percent) stated they have specific and well-defined financial goals. Another 45 percent said they have general financial goals but have not established target amounts for attaining the goals, whereas a third of the respondents (34 percent) stated they have no clearly defined long-term goals.[1]

Just as setting financial goals is important, so is developing effective strategies for attaining these goals. However, most consumers do not have specific strategies for attaining their financial goals. The Merrill Lynch study showed that only about one in ten respondents (11 percent) have comprehensive strategies for attaining their financial goals. Slightly more than one third (36 percent) said they have strategies for some but not all of their goals, whereas about three in ten (31 percent) have a general plan but no strategies. The remaining 22 percent stated they have no strategies at all.[2]

The Benefits of Financial Planning

Financial planning offers numerous benefits to consumers. The major benefits include the following:

■ *Attainment of financial goals.* Financial planning can help you attain your financial goals. These goals, as noted, may include accumulating a fund for retirement, providing financial security for yourself and your family, establishing a college education fund for the children, buying your own business, or getting out of debt. Important financial goals are discussed in greater detail later in the chapter.

standard of living
The goods, services, and luxuries that a person can purchase.

■ *Higher standard of living.* Financial planning can also increase your standard of living. **Standard of living** refers to the goods, services, and luxuries that you can purchase with your present income. Obviously, raising your income is one way to raise your standard of living. For example, if you earn $50,000 annually, you can buy more food, clothes, housing, travel, entertainment, and other goods and services than someone who earns only $10,000 a year. However, financial planning can increase your standard of living even if your income does not increase substantially. Because of lack of financial knowledge, you may be spending more than is necessary for needed goods and services. For example, you may be paying an exorbitant rate of interest because of high credit card debts and impulse buying; you may be paying more for automobile, homeowners, life, and health insurance than is necessary; you may have to declare bankruptcy if you cannot pay catastrophic medical bills; and you may be paying higher-than-necessary federal and state income taxes. In addition, some people invest in highly speculative investments and incur substantial losses. Still others fail to plan for retirement and experience a reduced standard of living after retiring. Financial planning can help you avoid these mistakes and thus increase (or maintain) your standard of living.

■ *Protection against major risks.* Financial planning can give you the knowledge you need to protect yourself against major risks that can result in great economic insecurity. These risks include the risk of premature death, insufficient income during retirement, poor health, unemployment, destruction or damage to your home and personal property because of natural disasters, and a lawsuit for damages because you have injured someone. We discuss these risks in greater detail later in the chapter.

■ *Reduction or avoidance of problems with creditors.* Financial planning can help you reduce or avoid problems with creditors. Without a financial plan, you may experience serious credit problems. For example, if you do not have a budget to track your monthly cash flow and limit what you spend on food, clothing, entertainment, and so on, you may consistently overspend and go deeply into debt. Failure to make installment payments on time can seriously affect your credit rating, and the loss of a good credit rating can affect your ability to buy a house or car. In addition, if you fail to pay your bills on time, you may receive threatening letters or harassing phone calls from your creditors. Finally, continuous overspending and abuse of credit cards can result in personal bankruptcy. Declaring bankruptcy will remain on your credit record for 10 years and will severely limit your ability to obtain future credit. Financial planning can minimize such problems.

■ *Reduction in estate settlement costs.* When people die, certain costs are incurred, which include the costs of settling their estates. A large estate may shrink considerably because of such costs, but financial planning can reduce the costs of settling an estate.

The Obstacles to Financial Planning

Many consumers fail to make financial progress because of certain formidable obstacles that must be overcome. There are three major obstacles to financial planning:[3]

■ *Unwillingness to save.* Some consumers are simply unwilling to save or lack the financial discipline to save in order to attain their financial goals. Such consumers typically live beyond their means, habitually spend more than they earn, and are deeply in debt. As a result, they have little money available for saving and investing, and they never realize their financial goals.

■ *Natural tendency to procrastinate.* Consumers also ignore financial planning because of procrastination. In particular, many younger consumers believe they have plenty of time to prepare for retirement or to

Exhibit 1.1

Saving Sooner Is Always Better Than Starting Later

Assume Investor 1 invests $2,000 in a tax-deferred diversified portfolio for 10 years starting at age 25, and earns an 8 percent rate of return annually, then stops saving, but continues to earn an 8 percent annual investment return. Investor 2 doesn't start saving until age 35, then invests $2,000 each year for 30 years and receives an 8 percent annual return during the period. When both investors retire at age 65, the early saver comes out ahead, with $314,870 accumulated, whereas the late starter has accumulated only $244,692.

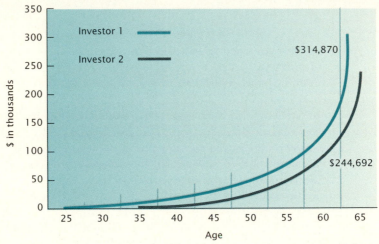

Source: Excerpted from Merrill Lynch, Pierce, Fenner & Smith, Inc. *Special Report: Saving and the American Family*, March 1994. Reprinted with permission.

save for their children's education. However, they may never undertake financial planning, and thus may never realize important financial goals. A delay in saving for retirement can be especially costly, as shown in Exhibit 1.1.

■ *Lack of knowledge about financial planning.* Some consumers never develop a financial plan because they lack knowledge about financial planning. In one nationwide study, for example, consumers were asked questions about checking and savings accounts, insurance, housing, food, product safety, and durable goods. *On average, consumers answered correctly only 54 percent of the questions asked, demonstrating huge gaps in consumer knowledge.*[4] Thus, because of the lack of knowledge, some consumers may never undertake financial planning.

Steps in the Financial Planning Process

Personal financial planning requires the development of an effective financial plan. There are five basic steps in the financial planning process (see Exhibit 1.2): (1) gather relevant financial information, (2)

Exhibit 1.2

Five Steps in the Financial Planning Process

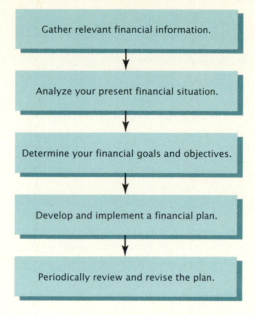

Gather relevant financial information.

Analyze your present financial situation.

Determine your financial goals and objectives.

Develop and implement a financial plan.

Periodically review and revise the plan.

analyze your present financial situation, (3) determine your financial goals and objectives, (4) develop and implement a financial plan, and (5) periodically review and revise the plan.

Gather Relevant Financial Information

The first step in financial planning is to gather relevant financial information. Necessary financial information includes the following:

- Monthly and annual gross earnings and net take-home pay

- Other sources of income, such as investment income

- Monthly or yearly cash-flow statement that shows how you spend your money, including the amounts you spend on food, housing, clothing, installment debts, and other necessary expenses

- Personal balance sheet that lists your assets and liabilities

- Summary of present insurance coverages, including life, health, homeowners, and auto insurance

- Value of your account in a private pension plan, profit sharing or thrift plan, or Section 401(k) plan

- Value of an individual retirement account (IRA)

■ Amounts in checking and savings accounts

■ A list of stocks, mutual funds, bonds, government securities, and other securities owned

■ Real estate or rental property owned

■ Number and ages of dependents

You should also indicate whether you have a will for the distribution of your property to your heirs. Chapter 2 provides several worksheets and financial statements that you can use to compile the necessary financial information.

Analyze Your Present Financial Position

The next step is to analyze the information to determine your present financial situation. You need to do this analysis to determine whether you can realistically attain your financial goals and objectives. Analysis of your present financial situation starts with the calculation of your net worth. **Net worth** is the difference between your assets and liabilities. You add up the value of all of your assets, including the value of your car, checking account, savings account, stocks, bonds, mutual funds, other financial assets, and other property. You then subtract your liabilities, which can include a car loan, student loan, credit card debts, and other debts. The difference between your assets and liabilities is your net worth. You should calculate your net worth at least once a year. This figure is important because it indicates whether you are making satisfactory financial progress over time.

net worth The difference between assets and liabilities.

Besides the calculation of your net worth, you should determine whether your present spending exceeds your monthly or annual income from all sources and whether you are living within your income. You need to determine the amount of your income, if any, that you currently save and how you invest the money. You should also state the amount of monthly payments on short-term debts (credit cards) and long-term debts (mortgage payment).

Determine Your Financial Goals and Objectives

After you have a clearer picture of your present financial situation, you need to determine your financial goals and objectives. This is an individual matter. Some consumers want to own sizable financial assets to feel financially secure; others want to save for a down payment for a home; still others want to save for retirement or establish a college education fund for their children. Finally, many consumers want to become knowledgeable and skilled in personal investing and accumulate a fund for investing.

Develop and Implement a Financial Plan

The next step is to develop and implement a financial plan to attain your financial goals. However, the plan should be realistic and have a time limit. For example, assume that Jennifer, age 26, earns $28,000 annually and wants to save $15,000 for a down payment on a home within the next three years. She needs a specific financial plan to attain her goal. In this case, Jennifer has $250 deducted from her salary each month, which is automatically deposited into a savings account. She has also cut back on the purchase of clothes, entertainment, and vacations, and saves the money instead. She avoids impulse buying and pays off her credit card balances each month to avoid paying exorbitant rates of interest. In addition, Jennifer used to spend an average of $5 daily to buy lunch at a nearby restaurant; to save money, she now takes her lunch to work ("brownbagging") rather than eating out. At the end of three years, Jennifer has accumulated $15,000 and has attained her goal. Her success is due to a realistic financial plan with a definite time limit.

In the preceding example, we discussed only one financial goal. A more comprehensive financial plan with numerous financial goals may require the assistance of professionals. A Chartered Life Underwriter (CLU), Certified Financial Planner (CFP), or Chartered Financial Consultant (ChFC) can provide valuable assistance to help you identify your financial goals and to develop effective strategies for attaining such goals. Competent insurance agents can recommend the right type and amount of life and health insurance, disability income insurance, homeowners insurance, and auto insurance to meet your insurance needs. A competent and ethical account executive of a brokerage firm can provide valuable advice on the various types of investments to meet your investment goals. Finally, you may need an attorney to draft a will or other trust documents, especially in estate planning.

Periodically Review and Revise the Plan

The final step is to review the plan periodically and revise it if necessary. Because financial circumstances change over time, you may have to change your financial plan. You should review your plan if there is a marriage, birth, death, divorce, disability, change of job or occupation, or acquisition or change in real estate. In addition, your financial plans may change quickly if you become involuntarily unemployed. You may be laid off during a business recession or be fired from your job. You may have to rely on relatively small state unemployment compensation benefits and personal savings to meet your expenses during the period of unemployment. You may have to postpone your plans for a new car or home or for an extended vacation.

Common Financial Goals and Objectives

Consumers are not identical, and individual financial goals and objectives differ widely with respect to specific details. (See Exhibit 1.3 for a worksheet on which you can list your financial goals and objectives.) However, certain financial goals and objectives are common to all financial plans. The most important financial goals fall into the following categories:

- Increase in personal wealth
- Higher standard of living
- Saving for specific needs
- Retirement planning
- Protection of family and property
- Getting out of debt
- Investment goals and objectives
- Minimizing taxes
- Estate planning

Increase in Personal Wealth

Increasing personal wealth is an important financial goal for most Americans. Almost all people would like to have more money in the bank and own additional financial assets in order to be financially more secure. However, some individuals and families are not doing well financially, and the amount of savings and financial assets they own is pitifully low. We will discuss this important point in greater detail later in the text.

Higher Standard of Living

real income Money income adjusted for inflation.

inflation An overall increase in prices throughout the economy.

One of the most important financial goals for all consumers is a higher standard of living. A higher standard of living means that your real income increases over time so that you can purchase additional goods and services. **Real income** refers to the goods and services that you can buy with your nominal or money income; stated differently, real income is money income adjusted for inflation. **Inflation** refers to an overall increase in prices throughout the economy. The rate of inflation is typically measured by the Consumer Price Index (CPI). For example, if the CPI increases 5 percent but your money income increases 10 percent, your real income is increased. As a result, your standard of living can

Exhibit 1.3

Personal Financial Goals

Use this worksheet to list several of your financial goals. Important goals for students might include getting out of debt, saving money for a car or house down payment or graduate school, increasing personal wealth, increasing net worth, and instituting an insurance program to protect against major risks. For each goal you list, include the date by which the goal should be reached and several strategies you can use to reach the goal.

Financial Goal	Goal Date	Strategies for Reaching Goal

rise. Financial planning can increase your future standard of living by a well-designed savings and investment program. Money that you save today can be invested to yield additional income at some future date.

Some studies show that many Americans do not attain a higher standard of living over time. The National Commission for Employment Policy analyzed the incomes and earnings of American families covering the period from 1967 through 1989. *The Commission concluded that only 67 percent of the individuals had a higher standard of living at the end of the 1980s than at the beginning of that decade.*[5]

real average weekly earnings Weekly earnings adjusted for inflation.

The failure of many Americans to attain a higher standard of living is due to several factors. First, real earnings of American workers have declined over time. Exhibit 1.4 shows the decline in **real average weekly earnings** (weekly earnings adjusted for inflation) since 1982. In addition, global competition from low-wage countries has reduced the bargaining ability of many American workers; employment in the United States has shifted from high-paying industries to low-paying industries; labor union membership has declined dramatically over time; and new technology has rewarded highly skilled workers at the expense of the less skilled.[6] In view of these trends, financial planning becomes even more important.

Exhibit 1.4

Real Average Weekly Earnings Have Declined Since 1982

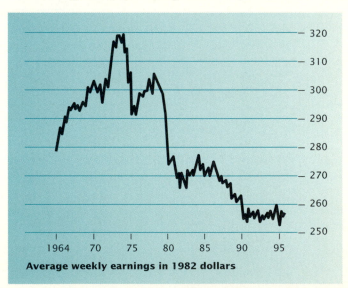

Average weekly earnings in 1982 dollars

Source: Alan Abelson, "Snake Oil," *Barron's*, February 19, 1996, p. 3. Reprinted by permission of Barron's, © 1996 Dow Jones & Co., Inc. All Rights Reserved Worldwide.

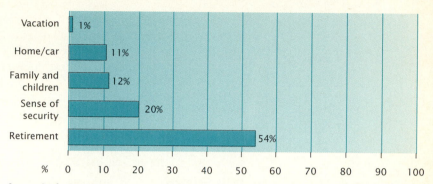

Exhibit 1.5

Reirement Is the No. 1 Savings Goal of Most Americans

Source: *Confronting the Savings Crisis, Perceptions and Attitudes About Retirement and Financial Planning,* The Seventh Annual Merrill Lynch Retirement and Financial Planning Survey, 1995, Chart 4, p. 4. Reprinted with permission.

Saving for Specific Needs

Another common financial goal is to save money for specific needs. Consumers typically save for a wide variety of reasons. A survey by Merrill Lynch showed that retirement is the major reason for saving, followed by a desire for financial security for the family and children (see Exhibit 1.5). Saving for college and a home or car are also important to many consumers.

It is also desirable to save for an unexpected emergency. Consumer experts typically recommend that you accumulate a liquid **emergency fund** equal to four to six months of take-home pay. Thus, if your monthly take-home pay is $1,500, you should have a liquid emergency fund of $6,000 to $9,000. An emergency fund is especially important with respect to the risk of unemployment. Most workers will become unemployed several times during their working careers. A liquid fund of four to six months of take-home pay can substantially reduce the painful financial shock and economic insecurity that result from unemployment.

Although saving for specific needs and having an emergency fund are extremely important, many Americans have little or no savings. Saving is a low-priority item for many Americans. Exhibit 1.6 shows that household savings in the United States as a percent of disposable personal income (personal income less personal taxes) averaged only 4.6 percent in 1993, last among our major international competitors.

emergency fund Liquid fund kept on hand in case of emergency.

Retirement Planning

Retirement planning is another important financial goal. Most workers want to be financially independent and have a comfortable retirement.

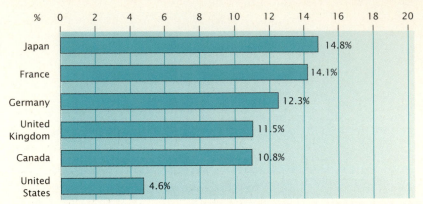

Exhibit 1.6

Net Household Savings Rates as a Percent of Disposable Personal Income

Source: *Confronting the Savings Crisis, Perceptions and Attitudes About Retirement and Financial Planning,* The Seventh Annual Merrill Lynch Retirement and Financial Planning Survey, 1995, Chart 3, p. 3. Reprinted with permission.

Although most workers are eligible for social security benefits, for average income workers, social security retirement benefits will replace only about 43 percent of their gross earnings in the year prior to retirement. Thus, most retired workers will need additional income just to maintain their present standard of living during retirement. You can obtain additional income by having a separate retirement program and, if available, by participating in a private pension plan sponsored by your employer. We will discuss private pension plans and other retirement plans in Chapter 16.

Although retirement planning is important, many workers are not saving enough to retire comfortably. A study by Merrill Lynch showed that the baby boom generation (those born between 1946 and 1964) has saved only about 35 percent of the amount needed just to maintain the standard of living in retirement that they have attained during their working years.[7]

In addition, the amount of financial assets accumulated by older workers on the threshold of retirement is relatively small, especially for minority workers. The Rand Corporation analyzed the amount of financial assets owned by older households and individuals ages 51–61. *The study showed that in 1993, the median amount of financial assets owned by middle-aged white households was only $17,300. For middle-aged black households, the median amount of financial assets owned was only $400, and for Hispanic households, only $150.*[8] These amounts are small. Thus, any supplemental retirement income will also be small. As a result, such workers will likely be faced with a reduced standard of living after retirement.

The preceding data show that many workers are inadequately prepared for retirement. Saving for retirement should receive greater emphasis in a financial plan even if the amounts saved are relatively small. *Because of the powerful effect of compound interest, small amounts saved regularly can accumulate to substantial amounts over a long period.* For example, if you save and invest only $10 monthly in a growth stock mutual fund in a tax-deferred retirement plan and earn an average annual return of 10 percent, you will accumulate more than $22,000 at the end of 30 years (see Insight 1.1).

Insight 1.1   How To Turn $10 Monthly Into $22,000, Or Even More

This table shows the growth of monthly deposits of $10 invested at various interest rates. For example, invest $10 monthly at 10 percent for 30 years, and you will have $22,793— the figure at the intersection of year 30 and the 10 percent interest column. If you can invest $100 each month, you will have ten times $22,793, or $227,930.

Year	5%	6%	7%	8%	9%	10%	11%	12%	13%	14%	15%
1	$123	$124	$125	$125	$126	$127	$127	$128	$129	$130	$130
2	253	256	258	261	264	267	270	272	275	278	281
3	389	395	402	408	415	421	428	435	442	449	457
4	532	544	555	567	580	592	605	618	632	646	660
5	683	701	720	740	760	781	802	825	848	872	897
6	841	868	897	926	957	989	1,023	1,058	1,094	1,132	1,171
7	1,008	1,046	1,086	1,129	1,173	1,220	1,268	1,320	1,374	1,430	1,490
8	1,182	1,234	1,289	1,348	1,409	1,474	1,543	1,615	1,692	1,773	1,859
9	1,366	1,435	1,507	1,585	1,667	1,755	1,849	1,948	2,054	2,168	2,288
10	1,559	1,647	1,741	1,842	1,950	2,066	2,190	2,323	2,467	2,621	2,787
15	2,684	2,923	3,188	3,483	3,812	4,179	4,589	5,046	5,557	6,129	6,769
20	4,128	4,644	5,240	5,929	6,729	7,657	8,736	9,991	11,445	13,163	15,160
25	5,980	6,965	8,148	9,574	11,295	13,379	15,906	18,976	22,714	27,273	32,841
30	8,357	10,095	12,271	15,003	18,445	22,793	28,302	35,299	44,206	55,571	70,098

Protection of Family and Property

risk Uncertainty concerning the occurrence of a loss.

Another important goal of financial planning is the protection of your family and your property against certain risks that create economic insecurity. **Risk** traditionally has been defined as uncertainty concerning the occurrence of a loss. Certain risks can create great economic insecurity for individuals and families. These risks include (1) premature death of a family head in which the family's share of the deceased breadwinner's earnings is lost forever; (2) insufficient income during retirement and a reduced standard of living; (3) poor health and catastrophic medical bills and the attendant loss of earned income; (4) involuntary unemployment and the loss of earned income; (5) damage or destruction of your home and personal property because of a fire, windstorm, tornado, hurricane, or other causes; and (6) a liability suit in which you are held legally liable and ordered to pay financial damages to someone you have injured.

Most consumers use insurance as the major way of handling risk, especially life and health insurance and homeowners and auto insurance. However, you can use other personal risk management choices to handle risk, including avoidance, retention, noninsurance transfers, loss control, as well as insurance. We will discuss personal risk management in greater detail in Chapter 8.

Getting Out of Debt

Another important financial goal is getting out of debt. Consumer installment debt has increased substantially in recent years (see Exhibit 1.7). Consumer loans include car loans, loans for appliances, personal loans, education loans, consolidation loans, and similar types of consumer installment debt. If you are deeply in debt and have high monthly payments, you substantially reduce the amount of discretionary income that you can spend on other goods and services.

A heavy debt load may also limit the amount of money you can save for retirement or for your children's education. In addition, if you use credit cards excessively and cannot pay off the balance each month, you may be charged an exorbitant interest rate of 18 percent or even higher on such debt.

Getting out of debt requires a financial plan. For example, you may have the goal of paying off all credit card debts within two years. The financial plan may require dropping all credit cards except one that you use only for emergency purposes; eliminating all nonessential spending and impulse buying; and analyzing your monthly expenditures to determine if you can reduce or eliminate any of them. You should also explore the possibility of replacing expensive credit card debt with a less costly personal loan from a commercial bank. Although the financial

Exhibit 1.7

Consumer Installment Debt as a Percentage of Disposable Income

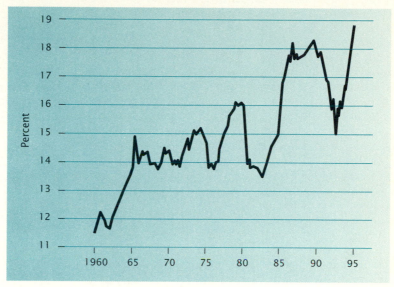

Source: Alan Abelson, "Snake Oil," *Barron's*, February 19, 1996. p. 3. Reprinted by permission of *Barron's*, © 1996 Dow Jones & Co., Inc. All Rights Reserved Worldwide.

adjustment is painful, the goal of eliminating all credit card debt within two years is realistic and usually attainable. Insight 1.2 shows how one innovative debtor developed a realistic plan for getting out of debt.

Investment Goals and Objectives

Investment goals and objectives are also important in financial planning. Many younger investors have long-term financial goals and invest primarily for the growth of principal over the long run; other investors are nearing retirement and invest primarily for steady income; still others invest for both growth and income. In addition, some investors are conservative and invest a higher proportion of their funds in conservative investments, such as savings accounts, money market funds, time certificates of deposit, Treasury bonds, and bond mutual funds. Other investors are aggressive risk takers and invest in highly speculative stocks where the potential return is high, but the probability of loss is also high. Finally, some investors are value investors who invest in common stocks that have declined sharply in price but have considerable potential for gain. Thus, your investment objectives should also be clearly defined in your financial plan.

Insight   1.2   Breaking Free of Bad Debt

During the summer of 1992, I was suffering through my seventh year of debt. Although I was earning almost $60,000 a year, I owed $12,025 in credit-card debt, $16,000 in loans and $3,700 to doctors—and I was paying as much as 21% interest on that total of $31,725. In addition, my credit reports were a mess.

Then my mother bought me a subscription to *Money*. Since I owed so much, I didn't need to read about investment and stock tips, but I found articles about ordinary people struggling with the same kinds of problems I had. I also read success stories of people who took one step at a time and accumulated small amounts of wealth. Rather than declare bankruptcy, I vowed to pay back every cent I owed and took the following steps to change my spending ways:

- Canceled my cable TV and stopped watching television and those commercials for products I didn't need that would cost money I didn't have to impress people I didn't know
- Canceled all catalogues coming to my home and removed my name from all mailing lists
- Stopped going to malls
- Started writing down every cent I spend—every cent
- Destroyed all my credit cards (my problems had started when I was issued a credit card during my third year of college and quickly ran up $1,000 in debt without any way to pay it off)
- Made a written inventory of everything I owned, then had a garage sale to liquidate everything I no longer wanted (the take was $455,

and I used it to pay down credit-card debt)
- Began a repayment program to all my debtors
- Signed up for my employer's 401(k) program ($100 a month)
- Hired a company to clean up my credit reports (successfully)

My financial situation is now strong and gaining momentum. I owe only $8,455 (an auto loan), and I have $40,421 in assets, including $9,766 in a 401(k) and $8,655 in mutual funds for a net worth of $31,966. And I still eagerly await every issue of *Money*. You helped save my financial life and gave me a future.

Source: Excerpted from "Your Letters, What You Say," *Money*, Vol. 24, No. 10 (October 1995), pp.11-12.

Minimizing Taxes

Another important financial goal is to minimize the taxes that you pay. Consumers pay a wide variety of taxes, many of which are hidden. These taxes typically include state and federal income tax, state and local sales tax, federal estate tax, property tax, gasoline tax, telephone tax, and numerous additional taxes. These taxes overall consume a large part of your total income. An average-income worker can easily spend 40 percent or more of his or her total annual income on taxes in all forms. Thus, an important financial planning goal is to minimize the amount of taxes that you must pay, which then increases the amount of income available for saving and investing.

The federal income tax is an important tax that most workers must pay. Although the federal income tax code is complex and difficult to understand, you can use certain legal tax strategies to reduce the amount of taxes payable. These tax strategies are discussed in Chapter 6.

Estate Planning

Estate planning is another important part of a total financial plan. Estate planning is a process for the conservation and distribution of a person's property and wealth after he or she dies. The general objectives of estate planning include conserving estate assets after death; distributing property according to the decedent's wishes; minimizing federal estate and state inheritance taxes; providing liquidity to pay the costs of estate settlement; and providing for the financial needs of surviving family members.

Estate planners use a variety of tools to attain the preceding objectives, including a will, marital deduction, gifts, trusts, and life insurance. We discuss these techniques in Chapter 17.

Overview of Financial Planning Over the Life Cycle

The following section provides a brief overview of some important financial factors that you should consider in the development of a financial plan over your life cycle. It sets the stage for specific financial planning recommendations that will be discussed in greater detail later in the text. Three age groups are discussed: ages 20–39, ages 40–59, and age 60 and over.[9]

Ages 20–39

After you finish college or school and are earning an income, get into the habit of saving money. *One basic rule is to save at least 10 percent of your gross income. You could save part or all of your next pay raise.* The money you save should be deducted automatically from your paycheck by payroll deduction; that way you reduce the temptation to spend the money. In addition, resist the temptation to spend money recklessly by the overuse of credit cards. Younger consumers tend to spend a disproportionate amount of their income on new clothes, costly vacations, and new technology (such as cellular phones). They typically finance such expenditures by using credit cards that carry high interest rates. In addition, you should carefully evaluate the decision to purchase a new automobile that has high monthly payments. High monthly payments on a car loan plus high-interest credit card payments will leave little or no discretionary income available for saving.

You should invest the money you save according to your financial goals. You should invest emergency funds and money for a down payment on a house in liquid investments and cash equivalents, such as checking and savings accounts, money market funds, Treasury bills, and short-term time certificates of deposit. Money for longer-term goals, such as retirement or the children's college education, should be invested in common stocks or growth stock mutual funds. Common stocks have historically earned about 10–12 percent annually over the past decades, outperforming both bonds and cash.

The proportion of your savings that you invest in common stocks will vary depending on your age and tolerance for risk. Some financial planners recommend that you subtract your age from 100 to determine the proportion of assets to invest in common stocks. Thus, someone age 25 might consider investing 75 percent of his or her financial assets in common stocks or growth mutual funds. You should invest the remainder in cash equivalents or in fixed-income investments, such as corporate or government bonds or bond funds.

When you invest for retirement, try to contribute the maximum amount into a tax-deferred Section 401(k) plan or private pension plan sponsored by your employer. The amounts contributed by your employer and the investment income earned on the principal are not currently taxable as income. Also consider investing in an individual retirement account (IRA), which receives favorable federal income tax treatment. *Finally, even if you are in your early 20s, start saving immediately for retirement even if you can save only small amounts.* Earlier, we noted how small amounts saved regularly can accumulate to sizable amounts over a long period. Because of compound interest, the earlier you start saving for retirement, the greater will be the amount of your retirement income and the higher the standard of living after retirement. Insight 1.3 provides some practical tips for keeping more of the money that you earn.

Financial planning becomes more complicated when younger children are present. If you are single or married and have dependents, you need life insurance to protect your family. Since younger family heads typically have limited amounts of money to spend on life insurance, term insurance is an attractive option. Term insurance provides only pure protection and has no cash value. You can purchase large amounts of term life insurance even if your income is limited. For example, based on the rates of one insurer, a male nonsmoker age 25 could buy $500,000 of term life insurance at an annual premium of $353. Females would pay less because of their longer life expectancy. Family heads with dependent children also need a will that names a guardian for the children; otherwise, a court of law will appoint a guardian if you die.

Younger consumers should consider other factors in a financial plan. You should review your auto insurance coverages, especially liability insurance, to determine if they are adequate. If you rent, you need a homeowners policy that protects your personal property and also provides a minimum of $100,000 of personal liability insurance if you injure someone. Consider purchasing an inexpensive personal umbrella policy that provides an additional $1 to $10 million of excess liability insurance on your home, cars, and boat.

Review your present health insurance coverages. *Two coverages are absolutely indispensable—a major medical policy that pays catastrophic medical bills and a high-quality individual disability income policy that pays at least 60 percent of your earnings if you should become totally disabled.* Both coverages provide considerable protection against the risk of poor health.

Ages 40–59

These years are typically high-earning years during which you can save substantially higher amounts for retirement. However, for couples who delay having children until they are in their 30s, the combined financial burden of financing a college education for the children and saving for retirement can be financially challenging. Parents have different views concerning the payment of a college education for the children. Some parents can afford to pay the entire cost, which leaves the children with little or no financial obligations or student loans. Other parents believe that the children should finance part or all of their college education by working and by student loans. Parents who hold the latter view should be able to save more of their income for retirement.

Money needed for college tuition within the next five years should be gradually shifted out of common stocks and growth stock mutual funds into low-risk liquid investments, such as money market funds, savings accounts, Treasury bills, and short-term time certificates of deposit.

Workers ages 40–59 should consider realistically whether or not they should retire early. In fact, the majority of American workers voluntarily retire before age 65. However, if the amounts saved during the working years are inadequate, early retirement can be an important cause of economic insecurity during the longer retirement period. Workers who retire before age 62 are ineligible for social security retirement benefits; private pension benefits may be actuarially reduced for early retirement; and the total contributions to a Section 401(k) plan or private pension plan will be less because of the shorter period of accumulation. In addition, many workers who retire early must pay a substantial part or all of the premiums under the employer's group health insurance plan. An increasing life span can also result in insufficient income during the longer retirement period.

In addition, workers ages 40–59 should make maximum contributions into an employer-sponsored retirement plan or Section 401(k) plan. If you have self-employment income, consider establishing a Keogh plan for the self-employed. As we noted earlier, tax-deferred plans receive favorable income tax treatment and are especially important for workers who plan to retire early. You should still invest a large percentage of the retirement contributions in common stocks or in growth mutual funds. Asset allocation prior to retirement is an important investment consideration that will be discussed in greater detail in Chapter 16.

Insight   1.3   Ten Ways to Keep More of the Money You Earn

Here are ten savvy tips to help you cut the cost of banking, borrowing, investing and more.

1. Cut the Cost of Bouncing a Check

Even the most responsible person may sometimes bounce a check, racking up a penalty of $15, $25, or more. Cut this cost to pennies by signing up for overdraft protection. If you have this service, the bank will lend you the shortfall (up to a set limit) if you bounce a check. Overdraft protection is free if you don't use it, and inexpensive if you do.

2. Pay No Annual Fee and Lower Interest Rates on Credit Cards

Competition among credit card companies means that issuers will waive the $20 to $35 annual fee for many cardholders. Call the issuer when the annual fee shows up on your bill (this may happen without warning when your introductory no-fee offer expires) and explain that you are unwilling to pay it when

there are so many no-fee cards available. In many cases they will remove the fee from your bill immediately, just because you asked.

3. Shop Around for the Best Checking-Account Deal

In some communities, checking-account fees have skyrocketed: At Barnett Bank in Florida, for example, it's $12 a month ($144 a year) if you fall below the minimum balance of $600. But a little research can usually turn up a better deal. For example, in New York City, where many banks require a minimum balance of $3,000 to avoid monthly fees, Republic National Bank of New York offers free checking—regardless of your checking account balance—as long as you keep a total of $1,500 in accounts with them, including IRAs or CDs. So moving your IRA from another bank to Republic would save you approximately $150 a year in checking fees. Bank of America on the West Coast provides a special no-fee, no-minimum-

balance account called Versatel to customers who have direct deposit and use ATM machines for all transactions. To find bargain checking deals in your community, check out small banks as well as big names and investigate credit unions or savings and loans associations.

4. Use a Discount Stockbroker

Buying and selling stocks through a full-service brokerage firm like Merrill Lynch & Co., Smith Barney, or Paine Webber can cost two or three times as much as a national discount brokerage, such as Muriel Siebert, Charles Schwab, or Quick & Reilly Inc. For example, at Siebert you'd pay a $45 commission to buy 100 shares of a $30 stock, compared with the $85.50 Merrill Lynch would charge. On 200 shares, Siebert would charge $61 versus Merrill Lynch's $149.

The caveat: Discounters do not provide advice on what or when to buy and sell. Also, you probably won't save on commis-

If you have neglected to save for retirement, you have a serious problem, since time is no longer on your side. *At this point, you have only two options: Increase your earned income or increase the amount that you can save for retirement.* Most workers cannot immediately increase their earned income, so they must save a higher percentage of their income for retirement purposes. One financial planner recommends that if you do not start saving for retirement until age 45, you should save at least 18 percent of your income. For those starting at age 55, the same planner

sions using a discounter to buy or sell small lots of stock (less than 100 shares).

5. Don't Pay Commissions on Mutual Funds

Mutual funds sold through stockbrokers or salespeople charge hefty commissions—typically 5 percent. For example, if you were putting the money in your IRA and invested $5,000 in mutual funds, you'd pay a $250 commission.

Today, however, about half of all mutual funds are no-load, meaning you buy directly from the fund, cutting out salespeople and commissions. These funds generally perform just as well as those with a commission.

6. Save When You Buy Checks

Buying checks directly from a check printing company is significantly cheaper than using the order form at the back of your bank-issued checkbook or buying checks at your bank. For example, 400 checks ordered through your bank might cost $16 or more; the identical checks ordered from Current Inc. (800-426-0822) cost around

$10 and meet all American Bankers Association standards.

7. Handle Your Tax Return Yourself

About half of all taxpayers hire a professional to do their tax returns, paying at least $50 to $100. In fact, the IRS reports that five percent of those who file the 1040EZ return pay someone to do it, even though it is a simple, one-page form with only 11 lines. Taxpayers with uncomplicated financial lives can probably fill out an accurate return on their own.

8. Pay No Fees When You Invest in U.S. Treasury Notes

Treasury bonds and notes are guaranteed, yield 6 to 7 percent, and can be bought in denominations as small as $1,000. A bank typically charges $50 to purchase them for you; brokers charge between $25 and $50. Avoid these costs by buying directly from the Federal Reserve. Any commercial bank can give you the address or phone number of the nearest Federal Reserve Bank, so you can phone or write for the necessary forms.

9. Consolidate High-Interest Loans

If you carry a balance on several credit cards and charge accounts, you are probably paying 18 to 21 percent interest. Talk to your banker about taking out a consolidation loan to pay off all these debts at a lower overall interest rate, typically around 16 percent. For example, if you are now paying 19 percent on $3,000 of debts, planning to repay over two years, you'll pay more than $600 in interest. With a consolidation loan at 16 percent, you might pay as little as $500.

10. Consider a Do-It-Yourself Will

Lawyer's fees to prepare the simplest will start at around $150. If your financial and personal life is straightforward (for example, if you are single, have limited assets and no children), consider preparing your own will using a kit or computer program from a stationery or office supply store.

Source: Adapted from Barbara Gilder Quint, "10 Ways to Keep More of the Money You Earn." Reprinted with permission. This article originally appeared in *Glamour* (July 1995).

recommends a stiff 35 percent.[10] Some workers are unable or unwilling to increase substantially the percentage of their income that they save for retirement. They must then be willing to accept a lower standard of living after retirement or find ways to cut their expenses substantially both before and during the retirement period.

Workers age 40–59 must also deal with the painful problem of unemployment. You may lose your job permanently because of a corporate downsizing or be laid off during a business cycle downswing. If you are eligible for state unemployment compensation benefits or have an emergency fund on which to draw, you reduce the painful financial shock of unemployment. If you are permanently laid off or if you voluntarily quit your job and have vested benefits under your employer's private pension or Section 40l(k) plan, you may receive a lump-sum retirement benefit. If the money is not rolled over into an IRA, you must pay an ordinary income tax on the distribution. If you are under age 59½, you must also pay an additional 10 percent penalty tax. If you ask your former employer to transfer the funds directly into an IRA rather than give the funds to you, you can avoid the unfavorable tax treatment and penalty. Moreover, if you do not receive the money directly, you will be less inclined to spend the distribution. *One study showed that about 90 percent of the employees who received lump-sum distributions or benefit cash-outs did not roll the money over into another retirement plan; only 35 percent used the funds for any kind of financial savings.*[11] Spending a sizable lump-sum distribution prior to retirement almost guarantees a reduced standard of living during retirement, especially for those workers who opt for early retirement.

Consumers age 40–59 should also review their financial safety net. This means a thorough review of life insurance, health insurance, homeowners insurance, and auto insurance to determine if the present coverages are appropriate and adequate. If you have not already done so, you should consider purchasing an individual disability income policy and a personal umbrella policy that provides an inexpensive liability supplement to your homeowner and auto insurance coverages.

Finally, most consumers do not have a will. If you are one of them, you should contact an attorney and have a will prepared. If you already have a will, be sure you update it to reflect your current wishes. Some middle-aged consumers have obsolete wills that were prepared years ago.

Age 60 and Over

Sufficient income during retirement is a major financial goal for consumers age 60 and over. If you plan to retire before age 65, make certain you have the necessary funds to do so. (Chapter 16 contains worksheets that will help you determine if you can retire comfortably before age 65.)

When you retire, you may receive a lump-sum retirement distribution from your employer. Since this money is probably the biggest sum you will receive in your remaining lifetime, you should invest it properly. Because of limited protection against inflation, the entire distribution should not be invested in fixed-income investments, such as bonds, Treasury notes, savings accounts, money market funds, or time certificates of deposit. You should invest part of the distribution in common stocks to stay ahead of inflation during the period of retirement. A male age 65 has an average life expectancy of another 15.3 years, whereas a female the same age has an average life expectancy of another 19 years. Thus, you should invest part of your portfolio in common stocks. Some financial planners recommend that older consumers, even those at age 70, should invest 20 to 40 percent of their portfolios in common stocks or mutual funds.

People age 65 and older might also consider purchasing a medigap policy to supplement the benefits available under the Medicare program. In addition, an estimated two in five people age 65 or over will spend some time in a nursing home. Such care is expensive and can easily cost more than $40,000 annually. Since Medicare does not cover long-term care in a nursing facility, you should consider purchasing a long-term care policy from a private insurer to cover this risk.

Four critical documents are needed if an older person dies or becomes disabled:

1. a current will that provides for the distribution of property;

2. a durable power of attorney that authorizes someone to manage your financial affairs if you become sick or disabled;

3. a living will that authorizes someone to make medical decisions on your behalf if you are incapable of doing so; and

4. a list of financial assets, insurance policies, location of safe deposit box and will, and names of your attorney, insurance agent, or professional advisor, as well as other relevant financial information.

The information should be readily available to the children or to the personal representative (also called an executor) who is responsible for settling your estate when you die. Ordinarily, the will should not be kept in a safe deposit box. Depending on the state in which you reside, the box may be sealed upon the decedent's death, and immediate access to its contents may be difficult.

Finally, financial planning for older consumers should include estate planning and any potential federal estate taxes that may have to be paid. A federal estate tax is payable if you should die and leave a taxable estate of more than $600,000 to someone other than a surviving spouse. Proper estate planning can reduce or even eliminate any federal estate taxes that may be payable.

SUMMARY

■ Financial planning is the development of a comprehensive plan that determines an individual's financial goals and objectives and selects the best strategies for attaining such goals.

■ Financial planning offers numerous benefits to consumers:
    Attainment of financial goals
    Higher standard of living
    Protection against major risks
    Reduction or avoidance of creditor problems
    Reduction in estate settlement costs

■ There are three major obstacles to financial planning:
    Unwillingness to save
    Natural tendency to procrastinate
    Lack of knowledge about financial planning

■ There are five basic steps in the financial planning process:
    Gather relevant financial information.
    Analyze your present financial position.
    Determine your financial goals and objectives.
    Develop and implement a financial plan.
    Periodically review and revise the plan.

■ Some common financial goals and objectives include the following:
    Increase in personal wealth
    Higher standard of living
    Saving for specific needs
    Retirement planning
    Protection of family and property
    Getting out of debt
    Investment goals and objectives
    Minimizing taxes
    Estate planning

■ The standard of living for many Americans has not increased over time. The majority of Americans have accumulated only modest amounts of financial assets.

■ Many Americans are saving an insufficient amount for a comfortable retirement. As a result, they may be faced with a reduced standard of living during the period of retirement.

■ Risk is traditionally defined as uncertainty concerning the occurrence of a loss. Major risks that can result in economic insecurity include the risk of premature death, insufficient income during retirement, poor health, unemployment, damage or destruction of real and personal property, and liability lawsuits.

■ Getting out of debt is an important financial goal. A large amount of debt reduces the amount of discretionary income available for other goods and services and makes it more difficult to save for your retirement or your children's college education. Exorbitant interest rates must also be paid on credit card debts.

■ Another important financial goal is to minimize the amount of taxes that you must pay, which then increases the amount of income available for saving and investing.

■ Investment or accumulation objectives include investing for safety of principal, for growth, for income, or for both growth and income.

■ Estate planning involves conservation of estate assets both before and after death, distribution of property according to the decedent's wishes, minimization of federal estate and state inheritance taxes, and providing for the financial needs of surviving family members.

■ Consumers in all age groups should consider certain financial factors in the development of a financial plan, including saving a sufficient amount of income on a regular basis, avoiding impulse buying and the excessive use of credit cards, and planning for both a comfortable retirement and settlement of an estate.

KEY CONCEPTS AND TERMS

Emergency fund
Financial planning
Inflation
Net worth
Real average weekly earnings

Real income
Risk
Standard of living
Steps in the financial planning
 process

QUESTIONS FOR REVIEW

1. Explain the meaning of financial planning.

2. Identify the major benefits of financial planning to consumers.

3. Describe the major obstacles to financial planning.

4. What are the five basic steps in the financial planning process?

5. Describe some individual investment objectives or goals.

6. Are Americans saving a sufficient amount of income to ensure a comfortable retirement? Explain your answer.

7. Identify the major risks that create economic insecurity.

8. Identify some common financial goals and objectives.

9. Why should the goal of minimizing taxes be considered in a financial plan?

10. What are the goals of estate planning?

11. Identify the important financial factors that should be considered by consumers in the following age groups:

    a. Ages 20–39   b. Ages 40–59   c. Age 60 and over

INTERNET EXERCISES

1. A World Wide Web site aimed at college students and recent graduates is Tripod. You'll find the site at:

    http://www.tripod.com/

    Once at the site, choose "Work and Money," and when you arrive at the "Work and Money" page, choose "Money Essentials." Browse through the information available on various money matters.

2. One way to find interesting sites on the World Wide Web is to use a search engine. Examples include Yahoo, Webcrawler, and Lycos, at:

    http://www.yahoo.com/

    http://www.webcrawler.com/

    http://www.lycos.com/

    Go to any or all of these sites, and type in a topic (such as credit card interest rates or home mortgages) in the space indicated. The search engine will list other sites relevant to that topic, which you can access directly by clicking on the site's name. Try it and see how many sites you can find on a personal finance topic of interest to you.

3. Information on college scholarships, grants, and loans can be found on the Financial Aid Information Page at:

    http://www.finaid.org/

    Check on what kinds of financial aid are available at your school or in your geographic area.

CASE APPLICATIONS

Case I

Megan, age 22, recently graduated from a large Midwestern university. She has accepted a job, with an annual salary of $26,000, as an underwriter trainee for a national insurance company. She owns a 1995 Ford sedan with a current market value of $8,000, personal property valued at $3,500, and a checking account with a current balance of $400. She also has the following debts:

> Student loans $25,000 (10 percent annual interest rate)
> Credit card debts $3,500 (18 percent annual interest rate)
> Car loan $6,500 (9½ percent annual interest rate)

1. Briefly explain the major steps in the financial planning process.

2. Based on the information given, calculate Megan's net worth. Is her financial situation satisfactory? Explain your answer.

3. Megan would like to get out of debt as soon as possible. Outline the details of a realistic plan that would enable her to reduce or eliminate her debts.

4. Megan's employer has a retirement plan that requires a contribution rate of 6 percent of salary. The employer also contributes 6 percent of salary into the plan. Although retirement is important, Megan believes she cannot afford to participate because of her current substantial debts. Should Megan participate in the employer's retirement plan even though she is deeply in debt? Explain your answer.

5. In addition to saving for retirement and getting out of debt, what other financial goals should Megan consider? Explain your answer.

Case II

Jennifer, age 32, and Mark, age 35, are married and have a son, age 1. Mark is an accountant for a local public utility company and earns $38,000 annually. Jennifer is a marketing analyst for a national public opinion firm and earns $45,000 annually. They are presently renting an apartment and pay monthly rent of $850. They seldom pay cash for any major purchase and routinely use credit cards to finance vacations, clothes, cosmetics, household furniture, and eating out weekly at local restaurants. They presently owe $3,500 on credit card debts, and they pay only the monthly minimum balance of $25. They also owe $9,000 on a car loan with monthly payments of $350, and student loans with a current balance of $8,000 and monthly payments of $100. In another six months, Jennifer will be eligible to participate in her employer's private pension plan. Mark is now participating in a retirement plan sponsored by his employer. Although the plan permits a maximum monthly contribution of 6 percent of salary, Mark is currently contributing only 4 percent of salary into the plan. In addition, the couple has $5,000 in a savings account at a nearby local bank that earns 3 percent annually. The couple has the following financial goals: (1) accumulate a down payment on a house, (2) provide for a comfortable retirement, (3) establish a college education fund for their son, and (4) get out of debt.

1. Based on the above facts, do Mark and Jennifer have a realistic plan for attaining their financial goals? In your answer, identify the major errors in current spending and saving that are obstacles to the attainment of their financial goals.

2. Recommend one strategy that will enable the couple to accumulate more easily the funds needed for a down payment on a house.

3. What strategies can you recommend that will make it easier for the couple to attain a comfortable retirement?

4. Outline the details of a realistic plan that will enable the couple to reduce or eliminate their credit card debts.

5. In addition to the preceding four financial goals, are there other important financial goals that the couple should consider? Explain your answer.

Case III

A Certified Financial Planner (CFP) recently stated that "although financial goals and objectives must be determined individually, certain financial goals are relatively more important to particular types of family situations than to others."

1. Do you agree or disagree with the CFP's statement? Explain your answer.

2. For each of the following household types, identify some relevant financial goals, and recommend appropriate strategies for attaining the goals:

   a. A single college student, age 21, who works part time to help pay tuition and other college expenses

   b. A single parent, age 32, who is the sole support of two minor children

   c. A married working couple, both age 28, with a son, age 1, who has been physically handicapped since birth

   d. A widow, age 48, who is presently supporting a teenage son and an elderly mother

   e. A working couple, both age 52, who plan to retire at age 62

SUGGESTIONS FOR ADDITIONAL READING

Crowe, Robert M. and Charles E. Hughes, eds. *Fundamentals of Financial Planning,* 2nd ed. Bryn Mawr, Pa.: The American College, 1993.

Damato, Karen Slater. "Financial Planning Through the Ages," *The Wall Street Journal,* June 4, 1993, p. C19.

Griffeth, Bill. *Bill Griffeth's 10 Steps to Financial Prosperity.* Chicago, Ill.: Probus Publishing Company, 1994.

Merrill Lynch & Co., Inc. *Confronting the Savings Crisis, Perceptions and Attitudes About Retirement and Financial Planning,* The Seventh Annual Merrill Lynch Retirement and Financial Planning Survey. Princeton, N.J.: Merrill Lynch & Co., Inc, 1995.

_____. *The Merrill Lynch Baby Boom Retirement Index,* July 14, 1994.

"New Study Tallies Assets, Net Worth of U.S. Families," *The Wall Street Journal,* December 21, 1994, p. C22.

Pasztor, Andy. "Middle-Age Have Fewer Assets Than Expected," *The Wall Street Journal,* July 25, 1995, p. B.1.

"The Retirement Security of the Baby Boom Generation," *Research Dialogues,* No. 43. New York: Teachers Insurance and Annuity Association, 1995.

Rose, Stephen J. *On Shaky Ground: Rising Fears About Incomes and Earnings, Research Report No. 94-02.* Washington, D.C.: National Commission for Employment Policy, 1994.

Smith, James P. *Documented Briefing, Unequal Wealth and Incentives to Save.* Santa Monica, Calif.: RAND, 1995.

NOTES

1. *Confronting the Savings Crisis, Perceptions and Attitudes About Retirement and Financial Planning,* The Seventh Annual Merrill Lynch Retirement and Financial Survey (Princeton, N.J.: Merrill Lynch & Co., Inc., 1995), p. 22.

2. Ibid.

3. Robert M. Crowe and Charles E. Hughes, eds. *Fundamentals of Financial Planning,* 2nd ed. (Bryn Mawr, Pa.: The American College, 1993), pp. 18–21.

4. Mary Jane Fisher, "Consumers Score Low On Financial Literacy Test," *The National Underwriter,* Life & Health/Financial Services edition, November 5, 1990, p. 26.

5. Stephen J. Rose, *On Shaky Ground: Rising Fears About Incomes and Earnings, Research Report No. 94-02* (Washington, D.C.: National Commission for Employment Policy, 1994), pp. iv–vii.

6. Ibid., p. 24.

7. *The Merrill Lynch Baby Boom Retirement Index,* July 14, 1994, p. 2.

8. James P. Smith, *Documented Briefing, Unequal Wealth and Incentives to Save* (Santa Monica, Calif.: RAND, 1995), p. 10.

9. The following section is based partly on Karen Slater Damato, "Financial Planning Through the Ages," *The Wall Street Journal,* June 4, 1993, p. C19.

10. Ibid.

11. United States General Accounting Office, *Women's Pensions, Recent Legislation Generally Improved Pension Entitlement and Increased Benefits,* GAO/T-HRD-92-90, Washington, D.C., March 1992, p. 3.

Chapter **2**

Tools of Financial Planning

Learning Objectives

After studying this chapter, you should be able to:

- Identify the major personal financial planning tools.

- Discuss the role of personal financial statements in financial planning, including the personal balance sheet and the personal income and expense statement.

- Explain the importance of budgeting, and describe the construction of a budget.

- Describe the importance of savings and liquidity analysis and explain how savings and liquidity ratios are calculated.

- Describe the importance of debt and debt service analysis and explain how debt and debt service ratios are calculated.

- Explain the importance of the time value of money in personal financial planning.

> *Annual income twenty pounds, annual expenditure nineteen nineteen six, result happiness. Annual income twenty pounds, annual expenditure twenty pounds ought and six, result misery.*
>
> —Charles Dickens' David Copperfield

> *Spend—that is what we hear at every turn. But when you save money before frittering it away, the money can build into impressive amounts because of the power of compounding. Saving is the bedrock of personal finance. Start now. Stay with it.*
>
> —Charles R. Schwab, Chairman and CEO, Charles Schwab Corporation

John and Carolyn Evans got married shortly after they graduated from college nine years ago. They are both in their early 30s. John is a middle-level manager at a manufacturing company and earns $40,000 per year. Carolyn is an accountant. In addition to serving as bookkeeper for a small drugstore chain, two years ago she started a tax preparation business. Between the two jobs, she earned $42,000 last year. John and Carolyn purchased a home several years ago and have repaid all of their educational loans. John and Carolyn have two children—Sarah, who is 5 years old, and Tyler, age 3.

After struggling to make ends meet after they got married, the couple now lives comfortably. They are bothered, however, by a recurring trend. Each month, after they pay their bills, there is less money left over than they thought there would be. They are not really sure how much "should" be left over, but with pretax work earnings of $82,000 last year, they believe they should be able to accumulate additional savings.

Obviously, income is not John and Carolyn's problem. Spending is the problem. In an effort to determine where the money goes, John and Carolyn decided to track their spending for one month. Each carried a small notepad, and whenever money was spent, it was logged. The results surprised John and Carolyn. They were spending much more on food, clothing, entertainment, and nonessential items than they realized. They resolved to take control of their finances. To that end, they constructed a table summarizing what they own and what they owe. A second table they prepared shows their sources and amounts of income, and where the money was spent last year. They are developing a schedule of income and expenditures for the next six months, and they will try to limit their spending to the predetermined level.

Chapter 1 discussed the steps in the financial planning process and the need for personal financial goals and objectives. Achieving your financial goals and objectives does not occur by accident. Although the financial planning process may seem daunting, a number of financial planning tools are available to assist you in your efforts. Financial planning tools are instruments and techniques designed to assist in personal financial planning. We discuss a number of financial planning tools in this chapter, including personal financial statements, the budgeting process, financial analysis, and the time value of money.

Personal Financial Statements

The first step in making financial plans is to assess your current financial position, and a convenient way to do that is by constructing personal financial statements. Personal financial statements summarize financial information in tabular form. Constructing personal financial statements helps you organize your financial data in a systematic way that simplifies analysis of your financial position. Personal financial statements include balance sheets and income and expense statements.[1]

The Balance Sheet

balance sheet A financial statement that summarizes the value of a person's assets, liabilities, and net worth position on a specific date.

The first important personal financial statement is the **balance sheet.** A personal balance sheet summarizes the value of your assets, liabilities, and net worth position on a specific date. The balance sheet is often described as a snapshot of your personal financial position. The balance sheet prepared by John and Carolyn Evans, the couple described in the introduction of this chapter, is displayed in Exhibit 2.1.

assets Items a person owns that have monetary value.

The first section of the balance sheet shows the Evanses' assets. **Assets** are items that they own that are of monetary value. To provide the most accurate assessment of financial position, assets are listed on the personal balance sheet at their current market value. **Current market value** is the price the asset would bring if sold in the open market at the present time. Current market value reflects today's value rather than historical information. For example, the current value of a home may differ from the original purchase price of a home. Total assets include three categories: current assets, property, and investments.

current market value The price an asset would bring if sold on the open market at the present time.

current assets Cash and cash equivalents.

Current assets consist of cash and cash equivalents. Examples of current assets include cash, deposits in savings and checking accounts, certificates of deposit, and money that is owed to you through short-term loans. Current assets are used to meet everyday living expenses and to serve as a safety fund should unexpected expenditures arise. You can see in Exhibit 2.1 that John and Carolyn Evans have total current assets of $9,640.

property Tangible objects that a person owns.

real property Land and permanent attachments to the land (primarily buildings).

personal property All property other than real property.

The second category of assets is property. **Property** consists of tangible objects that you own that are of value. Property can be divided into two categories: real property and personal property. **Real property** is land and permanent attachments to the land. Permanent attachments are things that cannot be readily moved—primarily buildings. Some examples of real property include undeveloped land, a home, a garage, and a tool shed. **Personal property** consists of all property that is not considered real property. Some examples of personal property include a car, clothing, furniture, a stereo system, a personal computer, tools, and sports equipment. The Evanses' balance sheet gives $157,000 as the total value of their property. The market value of their home accounts for most of this amount, which is not uncommon for homeowners.

investments Assets acquired for the purpose of earning a return, such as stocks and bonds.

The final category of assets is investments. **Investments** are assets that you acquire with the goal of earning a return. Investments can take the form of tangible property (such as artwork and gold coins) or intangibles (such as shares of common stock and bonds). Retirement plan assets and life insurance cash values are also included in investments. The Evanses' have total investments of $17,500.

Exhibit 2.1

Balance Sheet for John and Carolyn Evans, December 31, 1996

ASSETS

Current Assets

Cash	$ 140	
Savings Account	4,000	
Checking Account	3,000	
Certificate of Deposit	2,500	
Total Current Assets		$ 9,640

Property

Home Furnishings/Appliances	10,000	
Stereo System	800	
Clothing	4,000	
Television and VCR	1,200	
Personal Computer	3,000	
Market Value of Vehicles	18,000	
Market Value of Home	120,000	
Total Property		157,000

Investments

100 Shares of Stock	3,500	
Individual Retirement Account	12,000	
Retirement Plan Assets	2,000	
Total Investments		17,500
Total Assets		**$ 184,140**

LIABILITIES

Current Liabilities

Credit Card Debt	600	
Short-Term Personal Loan	1,200	
Total Current Liabilities		1,800

Long-Term Liabilities

Mortgage	101,000	
Car Loan	9,000	
Total Long-Term Liabilities		110,000
Total Liabilities		**$ 111,800**

NET WORTH

Total Assets – Total Liabilities		**$ 72,340**

liabilities The debts a person owes.

current liabilities, or short-term liabilities Short-term debts, such as short-term loans, credit card debt, and other debt for which repayment is due in one year or less.

Assets make up one "side" of the balance sheet. The other side comprises liabilities. **Liabilities** are debts that you owe. You can think of liabilities as claims against your assets. Liabilities can be divided into two categories: current liabilities and long-term liabilities.

Current liabilities, or **short-term liabilities,** consist of short-term obligations, such as short-term loans, credit card debt, and other debts

long-term liabilities
Debts for which repayment is due in more than one year.

for which repayment is due in one year or less. The Evanses' current liabilities, amounting to $1,800, include credit card debt and a short-term loan. **Long-term liabilities** are debts for which repayment is due in more than one year. Examples include a 4-year auto loan, a 30-year mortgage, and student loans requiring repayment over the next 5 years. The Evanses have long-term debt of $110,000, mostly made up of their home mortgage. Their other long-term debt consists of two car loans. These loans are both scheduled to be repaid during the next two years.

Notice the equation at the bottom of the Evanses' balance sheet:

Total Assets − Total Liabilities = Net Worth

As this equation indicates—and as we noted in Chapter 1—net worth is the difference between the total value of your assets and your liabilities. In other words, if you were forced to liquidate your assets—that is, convert them to cash by selling them—net worth is the amount you would have left after repaying what you owed.

Notice that net worth acts as a "balancing" figure. The balance sheet gets its name from the fact that the two sides—assets and liabilities plus net worth—are presented as equal. Obviously, your assets and your liabilities will not often be the same. Net worth balances the equation:

Total Liabilities + Net Worth = Total Assets

Net worth can be positive or negative. If the value of your assets is greater than the amount you owe, you have a positive net worth. The Evanses have a positive net worth of $72,340 ($184,140 − $111,800) as of December 31, 1996. If your liabilities exceed your assets, your net worth is negative. A personal balance sheet is provided in Exhibit 2.2 so that you can calculate your net worth.

Net worth is an important figure. Lenders, for example, consider your net worth position when deciding whether to extend credit. How can you improve your net worth? Some assets that you own may increase in value over time. Obviously, this appreciation will increase your net worth. As you pay off your debts, your liabilities will be reduced and your net worth will increase.

Another way in which your net worth can be increased is by earning more than you spend. For example, if you have take-home pay of $2,000 per month, but you spend only $1,400 per month, the $600 difference will be reflected in your total assets. Your earnings and expenditures are tracked in another financial statement, the income and expense statement.

The Income and Expense Statement

income and expense statement A financial statement that summarizes income received and expenses paid over a certain time period, such as the previous month or the previous year.

Another important personal financial statement is the income and expense statement. An **income and expense statement** summarizes income received and expenses paid over a certain period, such as the pre-

Exhibit 2.2

Balance Sheet for _____, _____, 199–

ASSETS

    Current Assets
        Cash $
        Savings Account
        Checking Account
        Certificate of Deposit
        Other Current Assets   _____
        Total Current Assets   (1)

    Property
        Home Furnishings/Appliances
        Clothing
        Electronic Equipment
        Vehicles
        Home
        Other Property   _____
        Total Property   (2)

    Investments
        Stocks and Bonds
        Retirement Plan Assets
        Other Investments   _____
        Total Investments   (3)

  Total Assets (1) + (2) + (3)   (4)

LIABILITIES

    Current Liabilities
        Credit Card Debt
        Short-Term Installment Loan
        Short-Term Personal Loan
        Other Current Liabilities   _____
        Total Current Liabilities   (5)

    Long-Term Liabilities
        Mortgage
        Long-Term Installment Loan
        Other Long-Term Liabilities _____
        Total Long-Term Liabilities   (6)

  Total Liabilities (5) + (6)   (7)

NET WORTH

  Total Assets (4) – Total Liabilities (7) $

vious month or the previous year. Whereas a balance sheet compares assets to liabilities on a specific day, an income and expense statement shows what income was received and how the income was used over a specified time. The income and expense statement for 1996 that John and Carolyn Evans prepared is provided in Exhibit 2.3.

Exhibit 2.3

**Income and Expense Statement for John and Carolyn Evans,
January 1, 1996–December 31, 1996**

INCOME

Regular Income:			
Salaries			
— John	$ 40,000		
— Carolyn	42,000		
Other Income:			
Dividends	60		
Interest	400		
Holiday Bonus— John	400		
Babysitting— Carolyn	80		
Total Income			**$ 82,940**

EXPENSES

Fixed Expenses			
Mortgage Payment	$ 12,960		
Car Payments	5,850		
Auto Insurance	850		
Homeowners Insurance	480		
Life Insurance	600		
Income Taxes (state and federal)	22,944		
Social Security Taxes	6,072		
Property Taxes	1,520		
Other Fixed Expenses	600		
Total Fixed Expenses		51,876	
Variable Expenses			
Food	4,800		
Clothing	3,600		
Car (fuel, oil, tires, etc.)	1,900		
Utilities (heat, electricity)	1,200		
Entertainment	2,000		
Telephone	960		
Medical Care/Medication	2,200		
Personal Care (hair, laundry)	720		
Church Donations	1,800		
Gifts	500		
Child Care	2,000		
Other Variable Expenses	600		
Total Variable Expenses		22,280	
Total Expenses			**$ 74,156**
Net Gain (+) or Net Loss (–)			**$ 8,784**

income Money received.

The first portion of the income and expense statement lists the type and amount of income. **Income** is money received. Common sources of income include the following:

- Wages and salaries
- Commissions
- Bonuses
- Income from self-employment
- Interest and dividends
- Proceeds from sale of investments
- Rental income
- Social security benefits
- Pension benefits and annuities
- Alimony and child support
- Grants and scholarships
- Royalties
- Tax refunds
- Loans received
- Public assistance (for example, Supplemental Security Income and Aid to Families with Dependent Children)

Sources of income vary with employment status, family situation, wealth, and life-cycle stage. For most individuals active in the workforce, wages and salaries are the largest component of total income. For retirees, however, social security old-age benefits, pension benefits, and annuity income are the primary sources of income.

gross pay The salary or total compensation earned for a given time period.

net pay, or disposable income Work earnings minus certain amounts that are withheld, such as taxes.

The total annual income for the Evanses in 1996 was $82,940. Almost all of their income is attributable to gross pay. **Gross pay** is the actual salary or total compensation earned for a given period. **Net pay** (also known as **disposable income**) is the income that remains after certain amounts have been withheld. Employers withhold a portion of gross pay for state and federal income taxes, social security taxes, and group insurance and pensions, for example. Gross pay is used in the income and expense exhibit.

Some sources of income are quite stable over time (for example, salaries, monthly social security benefits, quarterly dividend payments, semiannual bond interest payments, and monthly pension benefits). Other sources are more variable (such as proceeds from sale of investments, scholarships, royalties, and commissions). Income from all sources is summed, as in the upper portion of Exhibit 2.3, to determine the total income received during the period.

The second portion of the income and expense statement summarizes expenses. **Expenses** are cash outflows. Some expenses, called **fixed expenses,** do not vary over time. Examples of expenses that may be fixed include the following:

- Housing costs (rent or mortgage payments)

- Installment loan payments (such as payments on car or appliance loans)

- Insurance premiums (life, health, auto, homeowners)

- Taxes (income, property, social security)

- Pension contributions

Other expenses vary from period to period. Examples of these **variable expenses** include the following:

- Utilities (heat, electricity, telephone)

- Food (including dining out)

- Clothing

- Medical care

- Credit card payments

- Personal care (hair, laundry)

- Education expenses

- Child care

- Entertainment

- Contributions (religious, charitable)

The sum of the Evanses' fixed expenses ($51,876) is added to the sum of the variable expenses ($22,280) to arrive at the total expenses for the period. For the Evanses, total 1996 expenses equal $74,156. Exhibit 2.4 lists average annual expenditures for U.S. households.

The final step in preparing the income and expense statement is the calculation of the net gain or net loss. The **net gain** or **net loss** is the difference between total income and total expenses. A positive value, or net gain, reflects a cash surplus, meaning that income received during the period exceeded expenses for the period. This net gain can be saved, invested, or used for additional consumption. A negative value, or net loss, means that expenses exceeded income for the period. In this case, the excess expenditures were financed either with debt or by liquidating some savings or investments. The Evanses had a net gain of $8,784 ($82,940 − $74,156) for 1996.

How much did you earn and how much did you spend during the last six months or year? An income and expense statement is provided in

Exhibit 2.4

Are You Typical?

How do your household annual expenditures compare to national averages? A breakdown of average consumer unit expenditures by category is provided below.

Category	Percentage of Consumer Unit Total Expenditures	
Food	14.3	
At Home		8.9
Away from Home		5.4
Housing	31.4	
Shelter		17.6
Utilities, Fuel, etc.		6.9
Furnishings and Equipment		4.0
Operations/Housekeeping		2.9
Apparel and Services	5.5	
Transportation	17.8	
Vehicle Purchases		7.6
Gas and Motor Oil		3.2
Other Vehicle Expenses		6.0
Public Transportation		1.0
Health Care	5.8	
Personal Care Products/Services	1.3	
Entertainment	5.3	
Education	1.5	
Tobacco Products	0.9	
Alcoholic Beverages	0.9	
Cash Contributions	3.1	
Personal Insurance and Pensions	9.5	
Life and Other Insurance		1.3
Retirement/Pension/Social Security		8.2
Other Miscellaneous Expenditures	2.9	

Note: Average annual consumer unit expenditures were $30,692. The values expressed in the exhibit are percentages of that total. The percentages do not sum to 100 percent because of rounding.
Source: *Consumer Expenditure Survey, 1992–1993*. U.S. Department of Labor, Bureau of Labor Statistics, Bulletin 2462, September 1995, p. 2.

Exhibit 2.5. Complete this statement to determine if you had a net gain or a net loss for the period.

The Budget

budget A summary of projected income and expenses for a specified future period.

Another important financial planning tool is a budget. A **budget** is a summary of projected income and expenses for a specified future period. At first glance, a budget may appear similar to an income and expense statement. However, there is an important difference. The income and expense statement is prepared after a time period has ended, recording

Exhibit 2.5

Income and Expense Statement for _____, _____, 199__ to _____, 199__.

INCOME

Regular Income
  Salary $
  Salary $ _____
   Total Regular Income   (1)

Other Income:
  Dividends
  Interest
  Rent   _____
   Total Other Income   (2)

Total Income (1) + (2)   (3)

EXPENSES

Fixed Expenses
  Mortgage or Rent
  Car Payments
  Auto Insurance
  Homeowners Insurance
  Life Insurance
  Income Tax (state and federal)
  Social Security Taxes
  Other Fixed Expenses _____
   Total Fixed Expenses   (4)

Variable Expenses
  Food
  Clothing
  Vehicle Expenses
  Utilities (heat, electricity)
  Entertainment
  Telephone
  Medical Care
  Personal Care
  Church Donations
  Gifts
  Child Care
  Other Variable Expenses _____
   Total Variable Expenses   (5)

Total Expenses (4) + (5)   (6)

Net Gain (+) or Net Loss (–)   (3) – (6)

actual income and expenses for the period. A budget forecasts expected income and expenses for a future period. A budget may be developed for any period, such as a month or a year, and for individuals at any life-cycle stage. Some valuable lessons about budgeting for college students are discussed in Insight 2.1.

Insight   2.1   Students Can Learn a Lesson on Budgeting

When Erica Ford goes back to the University of Michigan at Ann Arbor next week, she'll be armed with new clothes, a new Indigo Girls compact disc and a fixed budget for the semester.

For the past three years, at the urging of her dad, the 21-year-old has avoided shopping sprees, kept her checkbook balanced and jotted down virtually every dollar she has spent at school. That way, the $2,000 or so from her father lasts the whole semester, covering off-campus rent of $320 a month, plus food, books and entertainment. "It's been a good experience," says the soon-to-be senior.

Unfortunately, many college kids are not nearly as disciplined. And too many families, weary after agonizing over financial aid forms, don't figure out how the family will pay for college staples like food outside the meal plan, entertainment and travel. But without budget limits or a plan for stretching college income, spending often skyrockets.

Credit cards are the quickest route to financial ruin, experts say. Gabrielle Mallol, a 21-year-old who attends Towson State University in Towson, Md., has been working full time this summer to pay off some $3,500 of debt she racked up on seven cards in her first two years of college. That's in addition to $1,400 of American Express debt her mom paid for her during her freshman year.

With credit-card marketers eagerly courting college students, stories like Ms. Mallol's are all too common. To be sure, some responsible college-age kids can get a head start on a good credit record by getting a credit card and paying off occasional, moderate charges over a couple of months. But students should be careful, because a history of late payments could torpedo attempts to borrow for a car or a house later in life.

College students also need to learn that paying only the minimum due each month is expensive and dangerous, says Ruth Susswein, executive director of the Salem, Va., group Bankcard Holders of America. She notes that if students owe $1,700—the national average debt per card—and pay only the minimum each month, it will take them as long to pay off the debt as it would to get three Bachelor's degrees and two master's degrees.

If you are counting on your kid's savings or work-study income for sizeable expenses like books, car insurance or food, make that clear before your child hits the campus. "Kids often think the money they make is extra," says Faye Kathryn Doria, a fee-only financial planner in Rochester, N.H.

Your best bet for keeping on track is to make a budget for all the expenses that are apt to come up during the year. A college's literature often includes a section listing likely expenses. Friends or acquaintances who have attended the school recently can help, too.

Be sure to factor in food, clothes, entertainment and things like phone bills, cable-TV bills and online computer services, where students can rack up steep hourly charges. As with any budget, such niggling costs can quickly add up and derail your plan.

Kids who tend to be reckless should keep track of their spending in a diary. Parents should review the diary at school breaks, and offer money-management tips if necessary. Also, if you send your kid's allowance directly to his checking account, advisers suggest you do so monthly or even weekly to minimize the amount your kid can blow at one time.

Should your college kid blow his monthly allowance in a week, you might do him a favor by not bailing him out. "My advice to parents is to let your kids suffer" if they waste money, says Michael Waldron, a financial adviser at fee-only planner L.J. Altfest Co., in New York.

Source: Adapted from Deborah Lohse, "Students Can Learn a Lesson on Budgeting," August 23, 1995, pp. C1, C19. Reprinted by permission of *The Wall Street Journal*, © 1995 Dow Jones & Company, Inc. All Rights Reserved Worldwide.

Why are budgets important? Because by constructing a budget, you can plan and control spending to match available income. Failure to accurately forecast income and spending can lead to poor use of funds and cash deficits. Since this will be their first attempt at budgeting, John and Carolyn have decided to start with a budget for the next six months. Their budget appears in Exhibit 2.6.

Exhibit 2.6

Planned Budget for John and Carolyn Evans, January 1997–June 1997

	January	February	March	April	May	June
INCOME:						
John	$ 2,300	$ 2,300	$ 2,300	$ 2,300	$ 2,300	$ 2,300
Carolyn						
Bookkeeping	2,100	2,100	2,100	2,100	2,100	2,100
Tax Service	700	1,050	1,750	1,400	140	350
Dividends			15			15
Interest	30	30	30	30	30	30
Babysitting	10	10			10	10
Total Income	$ 5,140	$ 5,490	$ 6,195	$ 5,830	$ 4,580	$ 4,805
EXPENSES:						
Mortgage	1,080	1,080	1,080	1,080	1,080	1,080
Car Payments	488	488	488	488	488	488
Loan Repayment	100	100	100	100	100	100
Auto Insurance	425					
Home Insurance	275					
Life Insurance					600	
Property Taxes					1,520	
Other Fixed Expenses	50	50	50	50	50	50
Food	350	350	350	350	350	350
Utilities	100	100	100	100	100	100
Phone	80	80	80	80	80	80
Personal Care	100	100	100	100	100	100
Car Fuel/Oil	125	125	125	125	125	125
Church Contrib.	150	150	150	150	150	150
Entertainment	125	125	125	125	125	125
Clothing	200	200	200	200	200	200
Child Care	150	250	400	300	200	150
Gifts	0	60	30	30	0	90
Other Variable Expenses	50	50	50	50	50	50
New Tires/Tune-up				250		
Uninsured Minor Surgery, Carolyn					600	
10th Anniversary Trip						1,000
Total Expenses	$ 3,848	$ 3,308	$ 3,428	$ 3,578	$ 5,918	$ 4,238
Monthly Surplus or Deficit	1,292	2,182	2,767	2,252	(1,338)	567
Cumulative Position	$ 1,292	$ 3,474	$ 6,241	$ 8,493	$ 7,155	$ 7,722

The Budgeting Process

Because budgeting is so important, we next examine the budgeting process. The steps involved, as shown in Exhibit 2.7, are setting goals, gathering financial information, constructing the budget, analyzing the budget, implementing the budget, and reviewing and controlling.

Set Goals

Exhibit 2.7

Budgeting Process

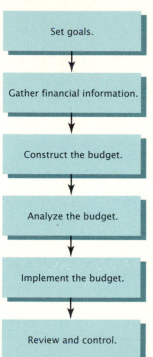

Set goals.

Gather financial information.

Construct the budget.

Analyze the budget.

Implement the budget.

Review and control.

The first step in the budgeting process is to set goals—what you hope to achieve by budgeting. The goal might be very simple, such as "finding out where my money goes," or more formal, such as "implementing a plan that will allow me to spend less so that I can invest more." Often budget goals are related to purchasing assets, such as saving enough for the down payment on a home or to purchase a new car. Your budget goals should be realistic and attainable.

John and Carolyn Evans hope to accomplish three goals through constructing and implementing a budget. First, they would like to identify and control spending. A review of expenses for the previous year showed several areas where they believe they are spending too much money. Second, by limiting spending, they hope to be able to put more money in savings and to be able to invest more. Finally, they would like to have enough money on hand to pay for any unexpected expenses that arise. The short-term loan listed on the balance sheet resulted from poor planning several years ago. Because of inadequate savings at that time, John and Carolyn were forced to borrow $3,600 from Carolyn's parents. They have been repaying the loan through $100 monthly installments and still owe Carolyn's parents $1,200.

Gather Information

The second step in the budgeting process is gathering financial information. Since a budget projects income and expenses for a future period, the income and expense statement for the previous period may be of great assistance. In addition, new sources of income and new expenses must be identified. You should also consider unexpected and emergency expenses that may develop during the budgeting period.

Estimates of the amount and the timing of cash flows are crucial in constructing a budget. Just because planned income exceeds planned expenses for the entire budgeting period does not guarantee a budget surplus each month. For example, the budget may project total available income for a 12-month period of $36,000 and total expenses of $2,000 per month, for a total of $24,000. Even though planned income exceeds planned expenses for the entire period, deficits will occur in some months if the income consists of two payments of $18,000, one at the end of six months and the other at the end of the year.

For the Evanses, John's income is stable whereas a portion of Carolyn's income is variable. Her tax preparation business generates additional income during "tax season," the period immediately before the income tax filing deadline of April 15. Additional income is also projected in months that end calendar quarters (for example, March and June) since some of Carolyn's clients pay their taxes quarterly and require her assistance in these months.

The couple's expenses are also estimated. Some of the expenses, such as the homeowners insurance premium, the cost of the anniversary trip, and the property tax bill are one-time outflows during the budgeting period, whereas other expenses recur. Some of the recurring expenses are constant across time; other expenses vary. For example, the mortgage payment is constant at $1,080 per month, whereas utilities vary with the cost to heat or cool the home, and child-care costs vary with John and Carolyn's work schedules.

Construct the Budget

The actual construction of the budget, bringing income and expense estimates together in tabular form, is the next step. John and Carolyn's expected net income is summarized in the top section of the budget in Exhibit 2.6. The middle section lists the couple's planned monthly expenditures. The first set of expenses are those that are fixed, and the second portion lists the expenses that are variable. The final section of the budget displays the monthly projected budget surplus or budget deficit and the cumulative position of the couple. A **budget surplus** is present when income exceeds expenses; a **budget deficit** occurs when expenses exceed income. The monthly surplus or deficit is simply the forecast total income minus the forecast total expenses. The cumulative position is a running total, representing the sum of the monthly surpluses or deficits, to date.

budget surplus Excess of income over expenses for a specific budget period.

budget deficit Excess of expenses over income for a specific budget period.

Analyze the Budget

After the budget is constructed, it must be examined carefully. The magnitude and timing of cash flows are considered, as is the monthly surplus or deficit. The budget that appears in Exhibit 2.6 is actually a revised budget. Under the first budget they constructed, Carolyn planned to have surgery in January, before tax season. John and Carolyn also planned to take a ski vacation for their tenth wedding anniversary in either January or February. A review of income and expenses in the early months of the budget convinced them to postpone both expenditures until later in the year when a planned surplus would be available.

Implement the Budget

The implementation step makes the budget operational. For John and Carolyn, implementation will bring about some changes in their spending. For example, the couple spent an average of $400 per month on food in 1996. They plan to try to save $50 per month by eating at home more often and by purchasing food on sale and in larger quantities. The monthly planned expenditure on entertainment has also been trimmed by about $40 per month. John and Carolyn were surprised to learn that the local public library also loans movies and compact discs. They plan to take advantage of this free service. When they do go out to a movie theater, they plan to attend shows at times when seats are available at a discount. The couple will also try to cut clothing expenditures by one third.

Exhibit 2.8

Ways to Cut Costs Every Day
Here are some simple things you can do to save money every day.

■ *Use Coupons.* The savings add up over time. But only use coupons on items that you purchase regularly.

■ *Buy on Sale.* Don't pay full price for anything you can buy on sale. You may have to wait for the item to go on sale, but the savings may be worth it.

■ *Buy Generic Products.* Many are of equal quality as the name brands, but they cost less.

■ *Call During Discount Hours.* Only make long-distance telephone calls during discount periods.

■ *Buy a Good Used Car.* A new car depreciates as soon as you drive it off the lot. Save money by purchasing a dependable used car.

■ *Use Credit Cards for Convenience.* Never charge more than you can afford to repay. Avoid interest charges by paying the entire balance due.

■ *Shop at Discount Stores.* These stores buy in volume and pass the savings along to you.

■ *Do Not Shop at Convenience Stores.* You pay extra for the convenience—take the time to shop elsewhere.

■ *Shop with a List.* Never go shopping without a list, and stick to the items on the list.

■ *Buy in Bulk.* It is less expensive per unit to buy in larger quantities.

■ *Shop Around for Insurance.* Prices vary from company to company. Make sure you are comparing similar coverages.

■ *Make a Budget and Follow It.* A budget is an excellent tool for planning and controlling spending.

■ *Conserve Energy.* Turn off lights, close vents in unused rooms, and purchase energy-efficient appliances.

■ *Wash Full Loads.* Do not run your dishwasher or washing machine unless it is full.

■ *Insulate Your Home.* The cost to insulate your home will be recouped through reduced heating and cooling costs.

■ *Reduce Entertainment Expenses.* Cancel cable television, attend movies during "discount hours," do not rent videos, and get a library card and use it.

■ *Pay Off Your Mortgage Early.* Early repayment can save thousands of dollars in interest.

■ *Do Not Gamble or Play the Lottery.* The odds are against you.

Source unknown.

John and Carolyn plan to purchase some children's clothing at garage sales. They also plan to limit spending for their own clothing and to take better care of their work clothes so that they will last longer. Some other simple steps that John and Carolyn can take to save money are provided in Exhibit 2.8.

Review and Control

Consider This

The Consumer Information Center in Pueblo, Colorado, has a site at:

http://www.pueblo.gsa.gov/

Choose "Browse the Consumer Information Catalog," and then select "Money" to see the many U.S. government publications available online that can help you in the budgeting process.

The final step in the budgeting process is review and control. John and Carolyn plan to monitor their income and expenses and attempt to remain "on budget" each month. They have agreed that any significant spending deviations from the budget will be made only if there is mutual agreement. If income is less than anticipated or some expenses are higher than predicted, the couple is willing to make further cuts in their clothing, entertainment, and personal care expenditures. If income is more than anticipated or some expenses are less than predicted, the couple will still attempt to hold spending to the predetermined level and to save or invest the surplus.

As we mentioned in the opening of this section, a budget can be developed for any period and for individuals at any life-cycle stage and family situation. The Evanses represent a double-income family, with both wage earners generating significant income. With more single adults in the United States than ever before, the budgeting challenges faced by singles should also be considered. How one single person took charge of her finances is discussed in Insight 2.2. A worksheet for constructing a budget is provided in Exhibit 2.9.

Financial Analysis

Once you have constructed the financial statements that describe your financial position, you should analyze them to determine the strengths and weaknesses of your current position. Then, if you detect problems, you can take corrective action. Using financial statements in this way can help you take control of your finances.

financial ratio A ratio that expresses the relationship between two financial values.

One way of analyzing financial statement data is through the construction of financial ratios. A **financial ratio** expresses the relationship between two values—for example, the relationship between savings and disposable income or between current assets and current liabilities. Although the ratio of any two values can be calculated, some ratios are more meaningful than others in analyzing your financial condition. Two areas of special concern in personal financial planning are savings and liquidity analysis, and debt and debt service analysis.

Insight

2.2   Budgeting For Singles

Singles face the same financial challenges that married couples do, but they face them alone—and often on less income. "Because they only have to think of themselves, singles tend to live in the present," says Kathryn Ioannides of the National Endowment for Financial Education. There's no spouse to answer to for splurges on cars or clothing—and no second income to contribute to a comfortable retirement. "That makes it more crucial for singles to get their financial picture in order," says Ioannides.

But the average single earns about $21,000 a year, less than half the average income of $48,919 that married couples earn. Only 66 percent of singles 21 and over are saving regularly for retirement, compared with 76 percent of married couples. Those who do save tuck away an average of $1,300 a year, much less than the $3,521 that couples manage to save, according to Census Bureau data.

It doesn't have to be that way. A little self-discipline, a painless savings plan, and an investment mix tailored to specific goals can get singles where they want to go.

Budgeting: The Future Is Now

Singles spend more than each member of a dual-income household—-an average of $15,300 a year, compared with $11,400 per person in a couple. (The rest of the average single's income goes to pay taxes and, if anything is left, into savings and investments.) That's partly because singles don't get the benefit of economies of scale couples enjoy by having someone to share the cost of the mortgage, utilities, and groceries. Relatively speaking, two can live more cheaply than one.

Sometimes singles have a deserved reputation for being footloose and free-spending, and sometimes they're overwhelmed by circumstances. A few years ago Gayla Davis, 33, was "wallowing in debt," snowed under by monthly bills, an illness that kept her out of work for months, and a small amount of disposable income that she sometimes overspent on clothes, travel, and eating out.

"Then it hit me," says Davis. "I'm in my thirties, I'm alone, and I have to take care of me." She became a self-described "budget demon," ditching her cable TV, cellular phone, call-waiting service, and voice messaging. That saved at least $100 a month.

She borrowed from her parents to help pay her debts; now her credit balances are down to zero, and she has paid back her parents. The only credit card she carries is a department store card.

Starting in 1994, Davis began socking away cash in a bank money-market account every payday and managed to save $12,000 in a year. Last August, she used some of that money to make a $6,000 down payment on a $120,000 house, keeping enough in reserve to cover six months' expenses. She contributes 6 percent of her salary to her 401(k) retirement plan and has about $3,700 in an IRA.

Davis is more comfortable financially since she got a new job as a mortgage broker in Albuquerque. But she still writes down her monthly expenses in a budgeting book and swears by automatic monthly transfers from a checking account into savings. "When I hit the $12,000 mark in my money-market account, I took my statement out and looked at it every night," she says.

Exhibit 2.9

Planned Budget for ___, ___, 199_, to ___, 199__

Month	1	2	3	4	5	6
INCOME						
Work Earnings						
Work Earnings						
Interest						
Other						
Total Income (1)						
EXPENSES						
Mortgage/Rent						
Car Payment						
Loan Repayment						
Auto Insurance						
Home Insurance						
Life Insurance						
Property Taxes						
Other Fixed Expenses						
Food						
Utilities						
Phone						
Personal Care						
Vehicle Expense						
Church Contributions						
Entertainment						
Clothing						
Child Care						
Gifts						
Medical Expenses						
Vacation						
Other Variable Expenses						
Total Expenses (2)						
Monthly Surplus or Deficit (3)						
(1) – (2) = (3)						
Cumulative Position						

Savings and Liquidity Analysis

savings Disposable income not used for current consumption.

Savings is disposable income that is not used for current consumption. In other words, it is the cash surplus that remains after taxes and all other expenditures have been paid. Savings is important since it provides a surplus that can be drawn upon to pay unexpected expenses. Surplus funds can also be used for investments. Unfortunately, many consumers do not have surplus funds available for savings or investment. As we noted in Chapter 1, household savings as a percent of disposable income in the United States is only around 4 to 5 percent—lower than any of our major international competitors.

A measure of the level of savings is the **savings ratio,** the ratio of net gain or net loss to total income after income taxes and social security taxes:

savings ratio The ratio of net gain or net loss to total income after income taxes and social security taxes.

$$\text{Savings Ratio} = \frac{\text{Net Gain or Net Loss}}{\text{Income After Taxes}}$$

We can compute this ratio for the Evanses by using figures from the income and expense statement in Exhibit 2.3. John and Carolyn Evans posted a net gain of $8,784 in 1996. Their total income was $82,940, of which $22,944 was paid in income taxes and $6,072 was paid in social security taxes. Substituting these values into the savings ratio equation, we have:

$$\text{Savings Ratio} = \frac{\$8,784}{\$82,940 - \$22,944 - \$6,072} = 16.3\%$$

The Evanses saved 16.3 percent of their income after taxes in 1996. It was their desire to control spending and increase savings that motivated John and Carolyn to construct the financial statements and the budget, and they are already doing well compared to the average U.S. household. The higher savings rate is partially attributable to the Evanses' higher-than-average household income.[2]

As noted earlier, income remaining after taxes can be used for two purposes: savings or consumption. Thus, subtracting the savings rate we just calculated from 1 (or 100 percent) tells you what percentage of after-tax income is used for consumption. The Evanses use 83.7 percent (100.0 percent − 16.3 percent) for consumption. The savings ratio and the consumption ratio are complementary—if you have a low savings ratio, you spend a greater percentage of your after-tax income on consumption. A high savings ratio indicates a lower percentage of after-tax income used for consumption.

liquidity The ability to meet short-term financial obligations with current assets.

Another important consideration is **liquidity**—the ability to meet short-term financial obligations through current assets. A measure of liquidity must consider both the magnitude of assets available to meet the short-term obligations, and the short-term obligations themselves. The **liquidity ratio** captures this information:

liquidity ratio The ratio of current assets to current liabilities plus current payments for long-term liabilities.

$$\text{Liquidity Ratio} = \frac{\text{Current Assets}}{\text{Current Liabilities} + \text{Current Payments for Long-Term Liabilities}}$$

The Evanses' current assets, $9,640, are listed at the top of the balance sheet in Exhibit 2.1. The current liabilities, $1,800, are also provided in the balance sheet in Exhibit 2.1. Current amounts payable for long-term liabilities, the amounts to be paid during the next year, can be determined from the income and expense statement in Exhibit 2.3 and from the budget in Exhibit 2.6. These payments include the next 12 monthly mortgage payments (12 × $1,080 = $12,960) plus the car payments for the next 12 months (12 × $488 = $5,856). Substituting this information into the equation, we have:

$$\text{Liquidity Ratio} = \frac{\$9,640}{\$1,800 + \$12,960 + \$5,856} = 46.8\%$$

The Evanses have a strong liquidity position. They have enough current assets on hand to cover almost half of their outstanding current obligations should their income stream be interrupted. In other words, the Evanses would be able to pay their debt obligations for almost six full months out of their current assets, with no additional income. This liquidity may give them enough time to search for alternative sources of income.

Debt and Debt Service Analysis

solvency The ability to pay all debts.

solvency ratio Net worth as a percentage of assets.

The relative level of debt and the ability to service the debt can be assessed through three ratios. The first of these ratios is the solvency ratio. **Solvency** means the ability to pay all one's debts. The **solvency ratio** expresses net worth as a percentage of assets:

$$\text{Solvency Ratio} = \frac{\text{Net Worth}}{\text{Total Assets}}$$

Although "debt" does not appear explicitly in the ratio, recall that net worth equals total assets minus total liabilities. Thus, the solvency ratio can be rewritten as:

$$\text{Solvency Ratio} = \frac{\text{Total Assets} - \text{Total Liabilities}}{\text{Total Assets}}$$

The solvency ratio indicates by what percentage the value of total assets could decrease before liabilities would exceed assets, indicating a negative net worth position.

The Evanses' net worth, $72,340, is listed on the final line of the balance sheet in Exhibit 2.1. The value of the Evanses' total assets, $184,140, is listed at the end of the first section of the balance sheet in Exhibit 2.1. Substituting these values into the equation, we have:

$$\text{Solvency Ratio} = \frac{\$72,340}{\$184,140} = 39.3\%$$

This ratio indicates that the Evanses could sustain a 39.3 percent decrease in the value of their assets and still remain solvent. This ratio is favorable, especially given the price volatility of their greatest asset, their home, which accounts for roughly two-thirds of their total assets. During economic downturns, housing markets are often hard hit. Given their level of cushion, the Evanses would continue to have a positive net worth position even if housing prices dipped significantly. In addition, they are using the income generated to repay their debts. Even if asset values remain constant, the solvency ratio will improve as debts are repaid.

The second important debt-related ratio is the debt-to-asset ratio:

$$\text{Debt-to-Asset Ratio} = \frac{\text{Total Liabilities}}{\text{Total Assets}}$$

debt-to-asset ratio The ratio of total liabilities to total assets.

The **debt-to-asset ratio** is the ratio of total liabilities to total assets. This ratio is closely related to the solvency ratio. A debt-to-asset ratio of one or 100 percent indicates that you owe as much as the value of your assets, whereas a ratio exceeding one indicates that you owe more than the value of your assets. Failure to correct this situation may eventually lead to personal bankruptcy. Obviously, consumers prefer debt-to-asset ratios less than one. The debt-to-asset ratio for the Evanses is:

$$\text{Debt-to-Asset Ratio} = \frac{\$111,800}{\$184,140} = 60.7\%$$

Thus the claims against existing assets are only 61 percent of the value of the assets. Mortgage debt accounts for more than 90 percent of their total liabilities.

debt service ratio The ratio of monthly debt payments to monthly gross income.

A third ratio that is used to analyze the debt position is the **debt service ratio,** which indicates your ability to "service," or pay, your long-term liabilities and personal loans. Open-account credit such as credit card debt is not considered in this ratio since payments on that type of debt are flexible. The debt service ratio is:

$$\text{Debt Service Ratio} = \frac{\text{Monthly Debt Payments}}{\text{Monthly Gross Income}}$$

The Evanses' monthly long-term debt (from Exhibit 2.1) includes their mortgage and car loans. Annual mortgage payments total $12,960, and annual car payments are $5,850, for a total of $18,810. In addition, the couple wants to repay the outstanding personal loan of $1,200 during the coming year, bringing the total debt payments for the next 12 months to $20,010. Converting this total to a monthly amount yields monthly payments of $1,668. Converting the Evanses' total income, $82,940, to a monthly amount yields $6,912. Thus, the debt service ratio for the Evanses is:

$$\text{Debt Service Ratio} = \frac{\$1,668}{\$6,912} = 24.1\%$$

This ratio indicates that currently about one-fourth of the Evanses' pretax monthly income is going to cover their long-term debts and to repay the personal loan. Viewed from the opposite perspective, the Evanses are currently earning four times the amount necessary to service their debts. Once again, this ratio indicates a strong position. Consumers should try to limit the ratio of debt service payments to gross income to less than 30 or 35 percent of gross income.

In summary, our financial analysis reveals that the Evans family is in a strong financial position. Their liquidity position is excellent, and they are generating a cash surplus. Although the couple has close to $112,000 in liabilities, their debt burden is quite manageable given the value of their assets, their net worth position, and their ability to service the debt.

Time Value of Money

time value of money The value of money when interest earned over time is taken into consideration.

One of the most important concepts in personal finance is the time value of money. When we refer to the **time value of money,** we mean that in valuing cash flows, we must consider time and interest. *A dollar received today is worth more than a dollar received one year from today because a dollar received today can start earning interest immediately.*

Three methods are commonly used to calculate the time value of money: time value of money equations, interest rate tables, and financial calculators. Here we consider the use of equations and tables.[3] The time value of money equations presented here are summarized in Exhibit 2.10. Numerical examples using equations, tables, and financial calculators are provided in Appendix 2.1 at the end of this chapter.

Single Amounts

Single amounts are individual cash flows. Examples include a single deposit of $1,000 to a savings account or the $10,000 that you believe you will need three years from today as a house down payment. Let's examine the valuation of these individual cash flows.

Compounding: Finding the Future Value. Suppose you place $1,000 in an account at your bank, and the bank agrees to credit your account with 6 percent interest calculated on an annual basis. What will your account balance equal at the end of the year? Obviously, you will have your original $1,000 plus an additional 6 percent of $1,000, or $1,060:

$$\text{Year 1 Ending Balance} = \$1,000 + (\$1,000 \times .06)$$
$$= \$1,000 + \$60$$
$$= \$1,060$$

Suppose you leave your money on deposit for another year. At the end of the second year, you will have the year-end balance at the end of the first year plus an additional 6 percent of that amount.

$$\text{Year 2 Ending Balance} = \$1,060 + (\$1,060 \times .06)$$
$$= \$1,060 + \$63.60$$
$$= \$1,123.60$$

Exhibit 2.10

Time Value of Money Equations

In all the equations, i = interest rate. In the first two equations, n is the number of periods. In the equation for annuities, 3 and 4, n is the number of payments.

1. Future Value of a Present Amount:

   Future Value = Present Value $\times (1 + i)^n$

   or

   Future Value = Present Value $\times$ Future Value Interest Factor

2. Present Value of a Future Amount:

   $$\text{Present Value} = \frac{\text{Future Value}}{(1 + i)^n}$$

   or

   Present Value = Future Value $\times$ Present Value Interest Factor

3. Future Value of an Annuity:

   $$\text{Future Value} = \text{Annuity Payment} \times \frac{(1 + i)^n - 1}{i}$$

   or

   Future Value = Annuity Payment $\times$ Future Value Interest Factor for an Annuity

   This equation can also be used when the future value is known to solve for the payment (for example, to calculate the equal periodic payment required to reach a savings goal).

4. Present Value of an Annuity:

   $$\text{Present Value} = \text{Annuity Payment} \times \frac{1 - \dfrac{1}{(1 + i)^n}}{i}$$

   or

   Present Value = Annuity Payment $\times$ Present Value Interest Factor for an Annuity

   This equation can also be used when the present value is known to solve for the payment (for example, to calculate installment loan payments).

Obviously, calculating the year-end balance in this way can be cumbersome when many years are involved. A simple equation for the future value of any present amount makes the process quicker. The equation is:

Future Value = Present Value $\times (1 + i)^n$

where i is the interest rate and n is the number of time periods. For example, let's recalculate the year 2 ending balance of our $1,000 deposit using this equation.[4] We use $1,000 as the present value (the amount we are depositing); .06 for i, the interest rate; and 2 for n, the number of time periods.

$$
\begin{aligned}
\text{Future Value} &= \text{Present Value} \times (1 + i)^n \\
&= \$1{,}000 \times (1 + .06)^2 \\
&= \$1{,}000 \times 1.1236 \\
&= \$1{,}123.60
\end{aligned}
$$

compounding Converting
the present value into a
future value.

If you want to know the future value of any present amount, simply multiply the present value by the quantity $(1 + i)^n$, where i is the interest rate, and n is the number of time periods. Converting a present value into a future value in this way is known as **compounding.**

We can simplify the mathematics of compounding somewhat by using a table value called the future value interest factor in place of the term $(1 + i)^n$. The equation then becomes:

Future Value = Present Value × Future Value Interest Factor

A table of future value interest factors is presented in Appendix B at the back of this book. Note that the table includes rows for periods (such as months or years) and columns for interest rates. Suppose we want to find the future value interest factor for the preceding problem, in which the number of time periods is 2 and the interest rate is 6 percent. We look in the row for 2 and the column for 6 percent and find the value 1.1236. We substitute this value into the equation along with $1,000, the present value:

Future Value = Present Value × Future Value Interest Factor

$\qquad\quad$ = $1,000 × 1.1236

$\qquad\quad$ = $1,123.60

In this case, the answer is identical to the one we calculated earlier. Sometimes, because the values in the tables are rounded off, the answers from the two methods will be slightly different.

How frequently interest is credited is an important consideration. Does compounding frequency really make a difference? Yes. With more frequent compounding, interest is credited earlier. When interest is credited earlier, you begin to earn interest on interest sooner.

A simple example will demonstrate this principle. Suppose you deposit $1,000 at a financial institution willing to pay 12 percent annual interest. The year-end balance will equal:

$1,000 × (1 + .12)^1 = $1,120

But suppose instead of crediting 12 percent interest annually, the financial institution is willing to pay 12 percent interest, compounded semiannually—that is, twice per year. To allow for more frequent compounding, our equation must be slightly adjusted:

Future Value = Present Value × $[1 + (i/m)]^{m \times n}$

where m is the number of compounding periods. For semiannual compounding, m equals 2 since interest is credited twice during the year. Substituting the values for i, m, and n into the equation yields:

Future Value = $1,000 × $[1 + (.12/2)]^{2 \times 1}$

$\qquad\qquad$ = $1,000 × $(1 + .06)^2$

$\qquad\qquad$ = $1,000 × 1.1236

$\qquad\qquad$ = $1,123.60

Exhibit 2.11

Compounding Frequency Makes a Difference

The table below shows the impact of compounding frequency upon future values. The example assumes that $1,000 is deposited in an account, 12 percent interest is paid, and the money is kept in the account for one year. Notice that with more frequent compounding, a higher effective annual interest rate is earned.

Compounding Frequency	Compounding Periods (m)	Interest Rate (i/m)	Year-End Balance	Effective Annual Rate*
Annual	1	.12000000	$1,120.00	.12000
Semiannual	2	.06000000	1,123.60	.12360
Quarterly	4	.03000000	1,125.51	.12551
Monthly	12	.01000000	1,126.83	.12683
Daily	365	.00032877	1,127.47	.12747

* The effective interest rate is simply the interest earned divided by the original investment.

With more frequent compounding, the interest earned in one year increases from $120 to $123.60. Exhibit 2.11 shows the results for various compounding periods. The final column in Exhibit 2.11 is of particular interest. Notice that when the compounding frequency is increased, the actual interest rate earned for the year—called the *effective annual interest rate*—is higher than the stated rate of 12 percent. The effective annual interest rate is the interest earned for the year divided by the initial investment. With more frequent compounding, interest can be earned on interest earlier, producing a higher effective annual rate.[5]

Discounting: Finding the Present Value. We have found the future value of a present amount. We can also find the present value of a future amount. To calculate present value, we can use the following equation:

$$\text{Present Value} = \frac{\text{Future Value}}{(1 + i)^n}$$

discounting Determining the present value of a future amount.

Determining the present value of a future amount is called **discounting.** There are many applications of discounting in personal financial planning. For example, you might want to know how much you must deposit today in an account that earns 6 percent interest, compounded annually, so that three years from today there will be $10,000 in the account. The future value is $10,000, the interest rate is 6 percent, and the number of periods is three. Thus, the amount required today (the present value) is equal to:

$$\text{Present Value} = \frac{\text{Future Value}}{(1 + i)^n}$$

$$= \frac{\$10,000}{(1 + .06)^3}$$

$$= \frac{\$10,000}{1.191016}$$

$$= \$8,396.19$$

The deposit of $8,396.19 grows to $10,000 over three years. The difference between $10,000 and the initial deposit is the interest earned on your account, which equals $1,603.81.

Again, we can use table values to simplify our calculations. In this case, we use a present value interest factor, and the equation is as follows:

Present Value = Future Value × Present Value Interest Factor

Present value interest factors appear in Appendix B. To perform the preceding calculation using a present value interest factor, we look in the table under 3 years and 6 percent. The factor is .8396. We substitute this value, along with $10,000 for the future value, into the equation as follows:

Present Value = Future Value × Present Value Interest Factor

= $10,000 × .8396

= $8,396

In this case, if you compare the results of the two calculations, you can see the effect of rounding, mentioned earlier.

Annuities

annuity A series of equal periodic payments.

The present value and future value of annuities can also be calculated. An **annuity** is a series of equal periodic payments. Annuities have many applications in personal finance. Monthly car payments, mortgage and rent payments, monthly retirement income benefits, and equal periodic contributions to a savings account are all examples of annuities.

Future Value of an Annuity. Let's examine the future value of a series of equal payments. Suppose you plan to make a series of equal savings deposits and you want to know how much money you will have in savings after a specific amount of time has passed. You could use the future value single amount equation to compute the future value of each of the individual deposits and then sum them together, but it's quicker to perform one calculation using the future value of an annuity formula. The equation is as follows:

$$\text{Future Value} = \text{Annuity Payment} \times \frac{(1 + i)^n - 1}{i}$$

where i is the interest rate, and n is the number of payments.

An example will demonstrate how to use the equation. Suppose you decide that you will save $2,000 at the end of each year for 30 years as a retirement fund. If your savings can earn 8 percent interest per year, how much will you have accumulated after 30 years? Substituting these values into the equation, we have:

$$\text{Future Value} = \$2,000 \times \frac{(1 + .08)^{30} - 1}{.08}$$

$$= \$2,000 \times \frac{9.062657}{.08}$$

$$= \$2,000 \times 113.28321$$

$$= \$226,566.42$$

Your savings will grow to $226,566 after 30 years. Notice that the amount you plan to deposit is only $60,000 ($2,000 × 30 years). The difference between the $60,000 that you will deposit and the $226,566 that you will have at the end of 30 years is $166,566. This amount is interest that will be credited to your account.

Once again, we can formulate a simpler version of the equation by using a table containing future value interest factors for annuities. Such a table appears in Appendix B. The equation then becomes:

| Future Value | = | Annuity Payment | × | Future Value Interest Factor for an Annuity |

Let's use the example worked earlier to illustrate. You know that you will save $2,000 per year (the annuity payment) for 30 years and will earn 8 percent interest per year. In the table, in the row for 30 payments and the column for 8 percent interest, you will find the value 113.2832, the future value interest factor for an annuity. Substituting these values into the equation yields the following:

| Future Value | = | Annuity Payment | × | Future Value Interest Factor for an Annuity |

$$= \$2,000 \times 113.2832$$

$$= \$226,566.40$$

Again, the small difference in the results is due to rounding in the table.

The future value equation also works in reverse. Situations often arise in which you know the future amount, but you do not know the corresponding payment. For example, suppose you want to save an equal amount each year so that you will have $10,000 after three years for the down payment on a house. Your bank will pay 6 percent interest on your account, compounded annually. How much would you have to save per year in order to accumulate $10,000 in three years? We start by rearranging the future value of an annuity equation to solve for the annuity payment. For simplicity, we will use the equation that includes the future value interest factor:

| Annuity Payment | × | Future Value Interest Factor for an Annuity | = | Future Value |

$$\text{Annuity Payment} = \frac{\text{Future Value}}{\text{Future Value Interest Factor for an Annuity}}$$

We know that the future value is $10,000. We find the future value interest factor for an annuity by looking in the row for three payments and the column for 6 percent. The factor is 3.1836. We substitute this value into the equation:

$$\text{Annuity Payment} = \frac{\$10,000}{3.1836}$$

$$= \$3,141.10$$

You need to save approximately $3,141 per year to accumulate $10,000 in three years, assuming an annual interest rate of 6 percent.

Present Value of an Annuity. You may also be in situations where you need to know the present value of a series of equal future payments. The equation for calculating the present value of an annuity is:

$$\text{Present Value} = \text{Annuity Payment} \times \frac{1 - \dfrac{1}{(1 + i)^n}}{i}$$

An example will demonstrate the application of the equation. Assume that you were injured in a car accident because of another person's negligence and that you have decided to sue the other person. The other person's lawyer has offered the following out-of-court settlement options: The other person will pay you $150,000 today or $50,000 per year for four years, with the first payment one year from today. If you decide to settle out-of-court, which option should you select? Would you rather have $150,000 today, or $200,000 ($50,000 × 4 years) over 4 years? Remember that money received today is worth more than money received in the future because you can begin earning interest immediately on money received today.

To determine which option is better, you need to convert the future dollars to today's dollars so that you can compare the amounts. In other words, you need to find the present value of the future payments. In substituting these values into the equation, we use $50,000 for the annuity payment and 4 for the number of payments. We will assume 8 percent (.08) is the appropriate interest rate.

$$\text{Present Value} = \$50,000 \times \frac{1 - \dfrac{1}{(1 + .08)^4}}{.08}$$

$$= \$50,000 \times \frac{1 - \dfrac{1}{1.360489}}{.08}$$

$$= \$50,000 \times \frac{1 - 0.7350298}{.08}$$

$$= \$50,000 \times \frac{0.2649702}{.08}$$

$$= \$50,000 \times 3.3121275$$

$$= \$165,606.38$$

The present value of the four payments of $50,000 is $165,606. Therefore, it would be better to accept the annuity rather than the $150,000 single amount today.

As you might expect, the present value of an annuity equation can be simplified by use of a table value:

Present Value	=	Annuity Payment	×	Present Value Interest Factor for an Annuity

Tables for present value interest factors appear in Appendix B at the back of the book. Using the table, let's recalculate the preceding problem. The annuity payment is $50,000, and the table value for four payments and 8 percent interest is 3.3121. Substituting these values and solving gives us the same answer as before (except for the small difference due to rounding):

Present Value	=	Annuity Payment	×	Present Value Interest Factor for an Annuity

$$= \$50,000 \times 3.3121$$

$$= \$165,605$$

Again, like the future value annuity equation, the present value equation can be reversed. Indeed, solving for the amount of the payment is a common use of the present value annuity equation in personal finance. An example involves installment loan agreements. An **installment loan** is a loan that is repaid through a series of equal periodic payments. Examples include home mortgages, auto loans, and furniture and appliance loans. Each payment includes a portion that repays the amount borrowed and a portion that is interest on the amount borrowed.

installment loan A loan repaid through a series of equal periodic payments.

Suppose that you would like to purchase a new car, and the cost is $24,000. Unfortunately, you do not have $24,000 on hand. You ask if the car dealer will accept $500 a month for 4 years, or 48 months ($500 × 48 = $24,000). The car dealer declines the offer because dollars received in the future are worth less than dollars received today, and the dealer must be compensated for not having use of the $24,000 immediately.

The dealer will, however, be willing to accept the promise of a stream of payments that has a present value equal to $24,000. We can use the present value of an annuity equation to determine the amount of each payment. Let's solve this problem using a table value. We rearrange the equation, supply values, and solve. We use the price of the car ($24,000) as the present value. In determining the present value interest factor, we use 48 because there will be 48 monthly payments. For simplicity, we will assume that the relevant interest rate is 1 percent (.01) per month (or 12 percent per year). Consulting the table for present value interest factors for an annuity in Appendix B, we find that the factor for 48 periods at 1 percent is 37.974.

$$\begin{array}{ccc} \text{Annuity} \\ \text{Payment} \end{array} \times \begin{array}{c} \text{Present Value Interest} \\ \text{Factor for an Annuity} \end{array} = \begin{array}{c} \text{Present} \\ \text{Value} \end{array}$$

$$\text{Annuity Payment} = \frac{\text{Present Value}}{\text{Present Value Interest Factor for an Annuity}}$$

$$= \frac{\$24{,}000}{37.974} = \$632.01$$

Your monthly payments will be not $500 but $632.01—again, to compensate the car dealer for not having immediate use of the total $24,000.

Special Types of Annuities. The annuity equations presented here are for ordinary annuities. An ordinary annuity is an annuity of fixed duration in which the first payment is made or received one period in the future. Several other types of annuities are used in personal finance. One is an *annuity due*, under which payments are made at the beginning of each time period (rather than at the end). Common examples of an annuity due are rental payments and life insurance premiums; landlords do not collect rent at the end of the month, nor do life insurers collect premiums at the end of the period of coverage.

Another type of special annuity is a perpetual annuity, or perpetuity, which provides periodic payments forever. Some corporations issue shares of stock that provide a fixed dividend and no maturity date. The dividends for such a stock issue are an example of a perpetual annuity. Finally, there are deferred annuities. A deferred annuity is an annuity that begins payments more than one period in the future. For example, you may purchase a retirement annuity during your working years. The retirement annuity does not begin to make payments to you until you retire.

Other Financial Planning Tools

A number of other tools are available to assist you in financial planning. Financial ("business") calculators have preprogrammed financial functions. Rather than using the time value of money equations or the interest rate tables, you need only supply the data, and the calculator automatically computes the present value, future value, or payment.

Another popular personal finance tool is a computer spreadsheet package. A spreadsheet is a grid of rows and columns that allows the user to format worksheets and to store and retrieve financial data. Thus, a spreadsheet can be designed to satisfy an individual user's specific needs. Standard spreadsheet packages (such as Lotus 1-2-3) have many "canned" functions that ease design and calculation. In the spreadsheet software that accompanies this text, you will find many useful spreadsheets that will help you prepare financial statements, plan a budget, and perform other financial planning tasks.

In addition to spreadsheet software, you can use financial planning software to perform other functions. Software packages are available that will allow you to pay bills by computer, track and categorize your expenses, complete your tax forms, track your investments, and prepare certain legal documents such as wills.

Many computer users today have access to the Internet, and more and more Internet sites are devoted to personal finance. Throughout this book, we offer examples of interesting financial sites for you to explore. In addition, CompuServe and America Online offer personal finance information for their subscribers.

Finally, many excellent how-to books and personal finance magazines offer helpful information on financial planning. You need only check your library or bookstore for a sampling.

SUMMARY

- Financial planning tools are instruments and techniques designed to assist in personal financial planning.

- Some important personal financial planning tools include personal financial statements, budgets, financial analysis, and time value of money analysis.

- Two important personal financial statements are the balance sheet and the income and expense statement.

- The personal balance sheet summarizes your assets, your liabilities, and your net worth on a specific date.

- Assets are things that you own that are of value. Assets consist of current assets, property, and investments.

- Liabilities are debts that you owe. Liabilities are dividend into current liabilities and long-term liabilities.

- Net worth is the difference between the value of your assets and your liabilities. A positive net worth exists if assets exceed liabilities; a negative net worth is present if liabilities exceed assets.

- The income and expense statement summarizes your income and expenses for a specified period.

- Income is money received. Expenses are cash outflows.

■ If your income exceeds expenses, you have a net gain; if your expenses exceed income, you have a net loss.

■ A budget is a forecast of planned income and expenditures for a future time period. The budget matches income and expenses for budget subperiods, such as months. If the income exceeds expenses, a surplus is forecast; if the expenses exceed income, a deficit is forecast.

■ The steps in the budgeting process include setting goals, gathering financial information, constructing the budget, analyzing the budget, implementing the budget, and reviewing and controlling performance.

■ After constructing personal financial statements, the financial position can be analyzed. Two important areas of analysis are savings and liquidity analysis, and debt and debt service analysis.

■ Liquidity analysis determines the level of current financial flexibility by comparing the level of current assets and current liabilities. Savings analysis indicates the level of disposable income saved rather than consumed.

■ Debt and debt service analysis examine the solvency position and the ability to repay borrowed funds.

■ When valuing cash flows in different time periods, the time value of money must be considered. A dollar received today is more valuable than a dollar received in the future because a dollar received today can earn interest immediately.

■ The present value of a future amount can be determined by discounting the future value back to present value. The future value of a present amount can be determined by compounding the amount for the specified period.

■ Annuities are streams of equal periodic payments. The present value and future value of annuities can be determined through the application of annuity equations.

■ A number of other tools are available to assist in personal financial planning, including financial calculators, computer spreadsheets, personal finance software, the Internet, and books and magazines.

KEY CONCEPTS AND TERMS

Annuity	Budget
Assets	Budget deficit
Balance sheet	Budget surplus

Compounding
Current assets
Current liabilities
Current market value
Debt service ratio
Debt-to-asset ratio
Discounting
Disposable income
Expenses
Financial ratio
Fixed expenses
Gross pay
Income
Income and expense statement
Installment loan
Investments
Liabilities

Liquidity
Liquidity ratio
Long-term liabilities
Net gain
Net loss
Net pay
Personal property
Property
Real property
Savings
Savings ratio
Short-term liabilities
Solvency
Solvency ratio
Time value of money
Variable expenses

QUESTIONS FOR REVIEW

1. Describe the three major sections of a personal balance sheet. What does it mean if your net worth is negative?

2. What is the current market value of an asset? Are assets listed at their original purchase price or current market value on the balance sheet?

3. Explain how a net gain or a net loss is determined on the income and expense statement.

4. How does an income and expense statement differ from a budget?

5. List and discuss the steps in the budgeting process.

6. What can you learn by analyzing your savings and liquidity position? Which financial ratios will assist with this analysis?

7. What can you learn by analyzing your debt and debt service position? Which financial ratios will assist with this analysis?

8. Why is a dollar received today more valuable than a dollar received one year from today?

9. Explain the difference between compounding and discounting.

10. Explain why the present value annuity equation is used to calculate installment loan payments.

PROBLEMS

1. Lindsey has current assets of $5,800 and current liabilities of $4,843. Lindsey owns property valued at $43,000, and she has no investments. Her long-term liabilities are $12,000. What is Lindsey's net worth?

2. Dave and Beth Franklin ended last year with a net loss of $3,432. Their variable expenses were $18,832, and their fixed expenses were $38,239. How much total income did the couple have last year?

3. Candace has disposable income of $2,000 per month. She will receive $80 in dividends in month 3 and again in month 6. Her fixed expenses are $800 per month. Candace believes that her variable expenses for the next six months will be $600, $800, $1,600, $1,800, $1,200, and $600, respectively.

   a. Calculate Candace's budget surplus or deficit for each of the next six months.

   b. Calculate Candace's cumulative budget position after six months.

4. Tameka constructed a personal balance sheet and an income and expense statement. Some of the values from these statements are provided here:

Total Assets	= $34,000	Monthly Gross Income	= $1,200
Net Gain	= $2,300	Annual Income	
Net Worth	= $16,000	After Tax	= $10,680
Current Liabilities	= $4,000	Monthly Long-Term	
Current Assets	= $10,000	Debt Payments	= $240

   Based on this information:

   a. What are Tameka's total liabilities? What are her long-term liabilities?

   b. What is Tameka's savings ratio?

   c. What is Tameka's debt service ratio?

   d. What is Tameka's liquidity ratio?

5. Kelvin deposited $5,000 in a bank account. What will the account balance equal one year from today if the bank pays:

   a. 12 percent interest, compounded annually?

   b. 12 percent interest, compounded semiannually? (6 percent per half-year, for 2 half-year periods)

   c. 12 percent interest, compounded quarterly? (3 percent per quarter, for 4 quarters)

   d. 12 percent interest, compounded monthly? (1 percent per month, for 12 months)

6. Sally would like to purchase a new car. The dealer is willing to accept $25,000 cash or equal monthly payments for four years (48 payments). If Sally agrees to make monthly payments, the car dealer will charge 9 percent interest, compounded monthly [.75 percent (.0075) per month]. Calculate Sally's monthly car payment if she agrees to the payment plan.

7. Bruce saves $2,000 each year for retirement. If his retirement savings can earn an 8 percent annual return, how much will Bruce have accumulated when he retires 30 years from now?

INTERNET EXERCISES

1. Go to the U.S. Census Bureau site at:

    http://www.census.gov/

    Click on "Household Economic Statistics," then on "Income," then on "Four-Person Median Family Income by State." Find out the median family income for your state. How does it compare with your family's income?

2. The Bank of America Student Union provides interactive worksheets to help college students create budgets for school. Visit the site at:

    http://www.bankamerica.com/tools/stud_budget.html/

    and see if you can fill out the budget worksheets.

3. Some sites provide financial calculators to help you with time value of money problems. For example, you can find out what your car payments (which are annuity payments) will be, given various prices, interest rates, and numbers of payments at the following sites:

    http://www.nia.com/autos/mcalculator1.cgi
    http://ussfcu.org/loancalc.htm

    You can choose from a list of loan calculators at:

    http://www.investorguide.com/Loans.htm#calculators

CASE APPLICATIONS

Case I

Sanchez and Maria Diaz have decided to construct some personal financial statements. They assembled the following information about their assets and liabilities:

Mortgage Balance Owed	$60,000	Stocks and Bonds	$85,000
Savings Account	$2,000	Value of Home	$180,000
Checking Account	$1,500	Value of Vehicles	$32,000

Retirement Accounts	$80,000	Short-Term Loan	$4,000
Credit Card Debt	$1,000	Car Loans	$8,000
Appliances/Furniture	$30,000	Certificate of Deposit	$10,000
Art Collection	$20,000	Clothing and Jewelry	$16,000
Rental Property Value	$80,000	Life Ins. Cash Value	$40,000

For the year just completed, the couple had the following income:

Gross Pay—Sanchez	$50,000	Savings Acct. Interest	$80
Gross Pay—Maria	$50,000	Checking Acct. Interest	$30
Stock Dividends	$1,000	Rental Income	$6,000
Bond Interest	$3,400		

For the year just completed, the couple had the following fixed expenses:

Mortgage Payments	$8,900	Property Taxes	$1,400
Car Loan Payments	$2,200	Auto Insurance	$1,400
Homeowners Insurance	$500	Income Taxes	$33,000
Social Security Taxes	$7,250	Life Insurance Prem.	$2,400
Other Fixed Expenses	$600		

For the year just completed, the couple had the following variable expenses:

Food	$4,000	Utilities	$1,500
Clothing	$4,200	Vacation	$1,400
Car (fuel, tires, etc.)	$1,900	Personal Care	$800
Entertainment	$1,000	Telephone	$600
Medical Care	$1,050	Other Variable Exp.	$750

1. Construct a personal balance sheet for Sanchez and Maria Diaz.

2. Construct a personal income and expense statement for Sanchez and Maria Diaz.

3. Calculate the following financial ratios for Sanchez and Maria Diaz:
   a. The savings ratio
   b. The liquidity ratio
   c. The solvency ratio

Case II

Monica Strauss is trying to make a difficult decision. She will graduate from college in one month and has been offered a job in another city. The job will pay $27,000 per year. The employer provides a generous employee benefit plan and will pay Monica's moving expenses. Currently, she is living at home with her parents and working part-time. Her boss at the part-time job has offered to make the job full-time after graduation with a $14,000 per year salary.

Monica would like to take the job in the other city, but she is concerned about making ends meet the first couple of months on the job.

She estimates she can rent an apartment for $500 a month, with a $100 damage deposit the first month. Renters insurance will cost $150, payable in the first month. She estimates she will have to spend $500 on new clothing in the first month, $300 in the second month, and $100 a month thereafter. She estimates she will spend $100 on food each month, $80 a month on utilities, and $50 a month for the phone bill. She believes her personal care expenses will be $50 a month. Vehicle expenses are expected to be $80 a month. Her auto insurance bill, $250, is due in the fourth month. Finally, she estimates she will spend $80 a month on entertainment (CDs, books, show tickets, movie rentals, and so on).

Monica believes her net pay will be around $1,500 a month. She has $1,000 in savings that can be used to help cover any deficits in the early months.

Can Monica afford to take the job? Based on the information provided, construct a budget for Monica for the next six months.

Case III

Dr. Sarah Allen is a psychologist. A number of time value of money applications have recently developed in her personal finances. Help Sarah perform these calculations:

1. Sarah deposited $2,000 in a savings account. Assuming the account will earn 6 percent interest per year, what will the account balance equal in 10 years?

2. Sarah has started a retirement savings program. At the end of each year, she contributes $2,500 to her retirement account. Assuming the account can earn an 8 percent return until she retires, what will the account balance equal at the end of 30 years?

3. Sarah is considering the purchase of a $120,000 home. She will pay $20,000 in cash and borrow the additional $100,000. Under terms of the mortgage, Sarah will repay the $100,000 through monthly payments over 30 years (360 months). The lender will charge 1 percent interest per month.

   a. What is Sarah's monthly mortgage payment?

   b. If Sarah makes all 360 mortgage payments, how much money will she pay to the lender over the life of the loan?

   c. How much interest will Sarah pay over the life of this loan?

4. Sarah was remembered in a deceased relative's will. Under the terms of the will, Sarah is to be paid $5,000 per year for the next ten years, with the first payment one year from today. Assuming an 8 percent interest rate, what is the present value of her inheritance?

5. Sarah would like to take an extended European vacation in five years. She estimates the vacation will cost $10,000. She would like to

save an equal amount each month to reach the $10,000 goal. Her bank is willing to pay 6 percent interest, compounded monthly (.5 percent or .005) on Sarah's savings account. How much must she deposit monthly for 60 months to reach her savings goal?

SUGGESTIONS FOR ADDITIONAL READING

Block, Stanley B. and Geoffrey A. Hirt. *Foundations of Financial Management.* 8th Edition Chicago, IL: Richard D. Irwin, 1997, Chapter 9.

Canner, Glenn B., Arthur B. Kennickell, and Charles A. Luckett. "Household Sector Borrowing and the Burden of Debt," *Federal Reserve Bulletin,* April 1995, pp. 323–338.

Consumer Expenditure Survey, 1992–1993. U.S. Department of Labor, Bureau of Labor Statistics, Bulletin 2462, September 1995.

Davis, Kristin. "Money Management Made Easy," *Kiplinger's Personal Finance Magazine,* January 1992, pp. 65–69.

Diamond, Michael A. *Financial Accounting.* Cincinnati, OH: South-Western Publishing Company, 1993, Chapters 2 and 3.

Dolan, Ken and Daria Dolan. *Straight Talk on Money.* New York: Simon and Schuster, 1993.

Morris, Kenneth M. and Alan M. Siegel. *Guide to Understanding Personal Finance.* New York, The Wall Street Journal, Lightbulb Press, 1992.

Personal Financial Planning Guide. Ernst & Young. New York: John Wiley & Sons, 1995.

Schall, Lawrence D. and Charles W. Haley. *Introduction to Financial Management.* New York: McGraw-Hill, 1991, Chapter 4.

Tyson, Eric. *Personal Finance for Dummies.* Foster City, Calif.: IDG Books Worldwide, 1995.

NOTES

1. Standard accounting textbooks provide an expanded discussion of the balance sheet and income and expense statement. See Michael A. Diamond, *Financial Accounting,* South-Western Publishing Company, 1993, Chapters 2 and 3, for example.

2. The average income before taxes for consumer units in 1993 was $34,868.

3. The annuity equations are derived in most introductory corporate finance textbooks. See Lawrence D. Schall and Charles W. Haley, *Introduction to Financial Management,* McGraw-Hill, 1991, Chapter 4, for example.

4. You can raise a value to a power using the y^x function on a standard calculator. For example, to evaluate the expression $(1 + .06)^2$, input 1.06 and then press the y^x key. Then input 2 for the exponent and press the "equals" key. The answer is 1.1236.

5. What's the best you could do? Hourly compounding? Compounding every minute? Every second? How about infinite (continuous) compounding! You may recall from your algebra class that the expression $[1 + (i/m)]^{mn}$ is very special. As m goes to infinity, the expression approaches e^{in}, where e is the base for natural

logarithms (2.718281). The expression for infinite, or "continuous," compounding is:

Present Value $\times$ e^{in} = Future Value

Going back to our original example, with a 12 percent interest rate and one year:

$1,000 $\times$ $e^{.12}$ = $1,127.50

With continuous compounding, the year-end balance ($1,127.50) and effective interest rate (12.75 percent) are highest.

APPENDIX 2.1

SOLVING TIME VALUE OF MONEY PROBLEMS

There are three standard methods of solving time value of money problems:

■ Using the time value of money equations

■ Using interest rate tables

■ Using a business calculator

This chapter described some uses of the equations and the tables. The equations are provided in Exhibit 2.10, and the tables appear in Appendix B at the end of this book.

Using the equations has two advantages over using the tables. First, because of space limitations, the tables usually display only the first four or five digits of the value derived from the equation. Thus, using the equations is more accurate. Second, also because of space limitations, most tables provide only the factors for "round" interest rates. Recently, an automobile sales finance company was offering 4.9 percent financing on new car purchases. Most sets of tables do not include factors using a 4.9 percent interest rate.

A third method of solving time value of money problems is by using a business calculator. Business calculators permit you to enter the interest rate (i), the number of years or the number of annuity payments (n), and other factors such as the present value (PV), future value (FV), or amount of the annuity payment (PMT)). Then the business calculator automatically solves for the unknown value. Let's solve three time value of money problems using each of these methods.

Example 1

Jack deposited $10,000 in a bank account that paid 12 percent annual interest. What will the account balance equal ten years later?

This question asks what a single amount deposited today will be worth ten years from today. Therefore, we are looking for the future value of a single amount.

Using the equation, we have:

$$\text{Future Value} = \text{Present Value} \times (1 + i)^n$$
$$= \$10,000 \times (1 + .12)^{10}$$
$$= \$10,000 \times (3.1058482)$$
$$= \$31,058.482$$

To use an interest rate table to solve this problem, refer to Appendix B and find the future value interest factor for ten periods and 12 percent interest. The factor is 3.1058. Multiplying this factor by the original investment (the present value), we have:

$$\text{Future Value} = \text{Present Value} \times \text{Present Value Interest Factor}$$
$$= \$10,000 \times (3.1058)$$
$$= \$31,058$$

Using a business calculator, you would input the following information:

Keystrokes	*Explanation*
$10,000 PV	$10,000 present value
12 %i	12 percent interest
10 N	10 years
CPT	Compute
FV	Future value

Future Value = $31,058.482

Example 2

Mary Beth deposited $2,000 per year for ten years in an account paying 12 percent interest. What will the account balance equal after ten years?

This question asks what a series of equal periodic payments will be worth in the future. Therefore, we are trying to determine the future value of an annuity.

Using the equation:

$$\text{Future Value} = \text{Annuity Payment} \times \frac{(1+i)^n - 1}{i}$$
$$= \$2,000 \times \frac{(1 + .12)^{10} - 1}{.12}$$
$$= \$2,000 \times 17.548735$$
$$= \$35,097.47$$

Using the table in Appendix B we find the future value interest factor for an annuity for ten periods and 12 percent. The factor is 17.5487.

$$\text{Future Value} = \text{Annuity Payment} \times \text{Future Value Interest Factor for an Annuity}$$

$$= \$2,000 \times 17.5487$$

$$= \$35,097.40$$

Finally, using a standard business calculator, you follow these steps:

Keystrokes	Explanation
$2,000 PMT	$2,000 annuity payment
12 %i	12 percent interest
10 N	10 payments
CPT	Compute
FV	Future value

Future Value = $35,097.47

Example 3

Rosalyn would like to purchase a new car. The cost of the car is $18,000. The car dealer is willing to accept equal monthly payments for three years and charge 1 percent interest per month. What will Rosalyn's monthly car payment equal?

This question involves the present value of an annuity. Since we already know the present value, our goal is to find the monthly payment. Using the equations:

$$\text{Annuity Payment} \times \frac{1 - \frac{1}{(1 + i)^n}}{i} = \text{Present Value}$$

$$\text{Annuity Payment} \times \frac{1 - \frac{1}{(1 + .01)^{36}}}{i} = \$18,000$$

$$\text{Annuity Payment} \times 30.107505 = \$18,000$$

$$\text{Annuity Payment} = \frac{\$18,000}{30.107505}$$

$$= \$597.86$$

If you are using interest rate tables to solve this problem, look for the present value interest factor for an annuity at 1 percent interest table and 36 periods in Appendix B. The factor is 30.1075.

$$\text{Annuity Payment} \times \text{Present Value Interest Factor for an Annuity} = \text{Present Value}$$

$$\text{Annuity Payment} = \frac{\text{Present Value}}{\text{Present Value Interest Factor for an Annuity}}$$

$$= \frac{\$18,000}{30.1075}$$

$$= \$597.86$$

Finally, using a standard business calculator:

Keystrokes	Explanation
$18,000 PV	$18,000 present value
1 %i	1 percent interest
36 N	36 payments
CPT	Compute
PMT	Payment

Payment = $597.86

As you can see, the methods yield essentially the same answers. As noted, however, the equation and business calculator methods provide more precise answers and can accommodate any interest rate. Tabular values are usually rounded to four or five decimal places.

Chapter **3**

Money Management and Saving

Learning Objectives

After studying this chapter, you should be able to:

- Explain the meaning of money management.

- Explain why individuals hold cash balances.

- Distinguish between savings and investment; between the money market and the capital market; and between money market instruments and capital market instruments.

- Explain what interest rates represent and the relationship between risk and the required rate of return.

- Explain how to calculate the rate of return on a savings or investment alternative.

- Describe the characteristics of deposit-type financial institutions.

- Explain the characteristics of checking accounts.

- Describe the characteristics of money market savings alternatives.

A penny saved is a penny earned.

—Benjamin Franklin

Money speaks sense in a language all nations understand.

—Apha Behn, The Rover

Heather Douglas graduated from college four years ago. She is single and works for a company that designs and installs computer systems. Heather has been living from paycheck to paycheck for the last four years, with the bulk of her income going to repay college loans, make car payments, and pay rent and other living expenses. Heather just paid off the last of her college loans, and she has four monthly payments remaining on her car loan.

Currently, Heather's only financial asset is a small checking account at her local bank. Heather uses the checking account to make her loan payments and to pay other bills. With her college loans paid off, and just a few payments remaining on her car loan, Heather looks forward to having "extra" money left over at the end of the month. Heather has begun to examine a number of savings alternatives.

In the previous chapter, you learned about assets and liabilities, income and expenses, and budgeting. In this chapter, we turn our attention to money management and savings. **Money management** refers to the effective utilization of cash and cash equivalents. Cash equivalents are financial assets that can be converted quickly to cash. Money management is necessary to make sure funds are available to pay for cash transactions and to make payments on short-term and long-term liabilities. If you spend less than you earn, a cash surplus may develop. You can use the cash surplus for a number of purposes. Although you may find it tempting to spend the surplus, you can instead save or invest it. We begin by describing the distinction between saving and investing, and the financial instruments and financial markets involved in each. We discuss investments in greater detail in Chapters 12 through 15.

money management The effective utilization of cash and cash equivalents.

Nature of Money Management

In talking about money management, it is important to understand the distinction between saving and investing. Some people use the terms interchangeably, and although there are similarities between the concepts, there are also important differences. *Essentially, saving emphasizes liquidity, safety of principal, and short-term goals; whereas investing involves a longer-term commitment of funds, less safety of principal, and longer-term goals.* Liquidity refers to how easily an asset can be converted into cash. Savings are highly liquid, whereas investments are less so, as we will see.

Both saving and investing may involve the use of **financial assets** which are intangible assets acquired today in the hope of some future return. The return may be in the form of current income, such as interest or dividends, or appreciation in the value of the financial asset. The difference between saving and investing is also reflected in the different financial assets employed in each. Savings takes the form of cash, cash

financial assets Intangible assets (such as stocks and bonds) acquired in the hope of some future return.

equivalents, and short-term interest-bearing debt instruments, such as U.S. Treasury bills and certificates of deposit (CDs). Short-term instruments are those of one year or less. These short-term debt instruments are created and traded in the **money market.** In accordance with its longer-term focus, investing involves purchasing longer-term debt instruments, common and preferred stock, and real estate. These assets are created and transferred in **capital markets.**

money market Financial market in which short-term financial instruments (with maturities of one year or less) are created and traded.

capital market Financial market in which long-term financial instruments (with maturities over one year) are created and transferred.

Investing in capital market securities generally offers the possibility of higher rates of return than those provided by money market instruments. Why, then, should you hold cash and cash equivalents? There are at least two compelling reasons: to pay ordinary expenses and to serve as an emergency fund with which you can cover unexpected expenses.

■ You need cash and cash equivalents to pay for ordinary expenses, such as fuel for your car, groceries, and utility bills. You would hardly wish to liquidate stocks or bonds to pay for these ordinary expenses.

■ In addition, you may need cash balances to meet unexpected expenses and emergencies. The uninsured portion of an unexpected operation is an example of an unanticipated expense; so is a major car repair. Consumer experts recommend establishing an emergency fund— a reserve held in cash and cash equivalents, that will finance living expenses for a time in case of emergency. An emergency may be the sudden loss of a job or a severe medical condition. As mentioned in Chapter 1, many consumer experts suggest maintaining an emergency fund equal to three to six months' living expenses. Insight 3.1 discusses some variables to consider in establishing an emergency fund.

Interest Rates and Rates of Return

interest rate The "price" of money; the rate required to compensate individuals or institutions for the use of their funds.

All commodities have a price, and money is no exception. The "price" of money is the **interest rate.** In other words, the interest rate is the rate that is required to compensate individuals or institutions for the use of their funds. On the one hand, you will earn interest when you save or invest because you are allowing others to use your funds—you are lending your money to the institutions providing the savings or investment vehicle. On the other hand, you will pay interest when you borrow money, as you will see in Chapters 4 and 5. Here, we look at two aspects of interest: the nominal interest rate and the required rate of return.

Nominal Interest Rate

Many theories abound regarding what is actually "priced" in an interest rate. According to a famous model proposed by economist Irving Fisher,

Insight   3.1   How Much Emergency Cash Is Enough?

Keep a cash reserve for emergencies to cover three to six months' expenses, goes the age-old rule of thumb. Some financial planners even recommend a six- to 12-month cushion. But do you really need to tie up half a year's wages in a low-yielding bank certificate of deposit or money-market account before you start saving for long-term goals? Probably not.

Until a year ago, Denise and Dave Duncan of Overland Park, Kan., kept as much as $70,000 in a bank money-market account yielding a paltry 2% to 3% a year. "We're just conservative, cash kind of people," says Denise. Indeed, they bought their home and cars outright and have a home-equity line of credit and credit cards on which they never carry a balance.

The Duncans had enough to cover 14 months of bills and expenses if they lost both their primary sources of income: Dave's salary as a store manager and rental income from a commercial building. Their financial planner, Kathleen Stepp, asked the Duncans what type of emergency would require immediate access to $70,000 in cash. They had no answer.

So Stepp put the money to work. The Duncans now keep $10,000 in a bank money-market account yielding 5% and another $10,000 in a short-term bond fund yielding 6.3%. They invested the rest in a mutual fund portfolio. "What's funny," says Denise, "is we're as comfortable with the $10,000 in cash as we were with the $70,000."

The New Rules

Some rainy-day money is a must. But how much you need depends on your age, health, job outlook—and your borrowing power in an emergency. It may be enough to be able to cover three to six months of expenses with a combination of cash and credit. With a paid-off house and no balance on their home-equity credit line, the Duncans have plenty of low-cost borrowing power. If necessary, they could also borrow against the money they now have in mutual funds.

"People are more conscious of their longer-term investment needs," says Vicki Schultz, a financial planner in Reno, Nev. "And they have easier access to their investments and to credit."

That doesn't mean everyone should plow all savings into the stock market, says Steven Camp, a financial planner and author. It means savers should strike a balance between a realistic assessment of rainy-day demands and the need to invest for the long term.

You may need a fat reserve when:
- Your income fluctuates because your work is seasonal, you own a business or you rely on commissions.
- Your job may be at risk.
- You are facing a long-term disability or illness.
- You expect to make a large cash outlay, such as payment for a parent's nursing-home care.

You can get by with less when:
- You can easily borrow against assets— for example, by using a home-equity line of credit.
- You have multiple sources of income. In a two-income household, for instance, it's unlikely that both spouses would lose their income at the same time.

Source: Reprinted with permission from the November 1995 issue of *Kiplinger's Personal Finance Magazine.* Copyright ©1995 The Kiplinger Washington Editors, Inc.

nominal interest rate The interest rate observed in the economy.

the **nominal interest rate**, the rate observed in the economy, is made up of two components, the real rate of interest and the rate of expected inflation:

$$\text{Nominal Interest Rate} = \text{Real Interest Rate} + \text{Expected Inflation}$$

real interest rate The interest rate necessary to compensate the lender for the use of funds, assuming no inflation.

The **real interest rate** is the interest rate necessary to compensate you for the use of your funds, assuming no inflation. The real rate is relatively stable over time and is around 2 to 3 percent. Expected inflation is the anticipated increase in price levels. Inflation is quite volatile, and the economy goes through periods of high and low actual and anticipated inflation.

Fisher's formula fits nicely with recent history. For example, you may remember that interest rates were very high in the early 1980s, coinciding with high actual and anticipated inflation. More recently, in the early 1990s, inflation and expected inflation were low, and nominal interest rates were also low.

monetary policy Policy utilized by the Federal Reserve to control the cost and supply of money.

The federal government acts to help stabilize interest rates and to promote economic growth through monetary policy. **Monetary policy** refers to the use of a number of tools by the Federal Reserve, the nation's central bank, in an effort to control the cost and supply of money. As you know, when the demand for a commodity (such as concert tickets for a "hot" group) is high, and the supply is low, the price increases. The price of money, the interest rate, is also sensitive to the supply and demand for money. Through monetary policy, the Federal Reserve can tighten or loosen the money supply, thereby influencing interest rates.

Consider This

The Federal Reserve Board maintains an Internet site at:

http://www.bog.frb.fed.us/

Required Rate of Return

required rate of return The minimum acceptable rate of return that a saver or investor is willing to accept for a given savings or investment alternative.

The **required rate of return** is the minimum acceptable rate of return that a saver or investor is willing to accept for a given savings or investment alternative. If you save or invest, a portion of your required rate of return is the real rate plus expected inflation. The real rate, in theory, compensates you for not having use of your money, whereas the expected inflation component compensates for any loss in the power of your money caused by inflation.

Another important aspect of the required rate of return is the degree of risk of the savings or investment alternative. Recall that risk is uncertainty about an outcome. The less certain the outcome, the greater the risk. With regard to rates of return, risk usually is measured in terms of the variability of the rate of return. Most savings alternatives have a fixed, guaranteed rate of return, whereas rates of return on investment alternatives often are variable.

We already mentioned that rates of return on savings alternatives are low compared to rates of return on investments. It is not surprising that the risk associated with savings vehicles is also low compared to the risk associated with investments. What makes some financial assets less risky than others? Four important factors are: liquidity, the time horizon, insurance, and the creditworthiness of the issuer.

■ *Liquidity, as noted, refers to how quickly the asset can be sold or converted to cash.* Assets that have greater liquidity are less risky than assets that are not liquid. For example, it is easier to withdraw funds from a savings account than it is to sell rental property that you purchased five years ago.

yield curve Relationship between rate of return and length of investment, as shown on a graph.

■ *The time horizon is also important.* It is less risky to commit your funds for a shorter period than for a longer period. This relationship is best demonstrated by the yield curve. The **yield curve** is a graph that shows the relationship between rates of return and the length of an investment. A "normal" yield curve is shown in Exhibit 3.1. Notice that a lower rate of return is earned on a shorter commitment of funds, and a higher return is earned if you are willing to commit your funds for a longer time. Perhaps you noticed a listing of rates of return on certificates of deposit (CDs) at your bank. A CD is an interest-bearing commitment of funds. You may also have noticed that the longer the period of the CD, the higher the rate of return provided. That is the usual relationship between rates of return and time horizons. You must be compensated for your willingness to commit funds for a longer time, and the compensation you receive is in the form of a higher rate of return.

Exhibit 3.1

The Yield Curve

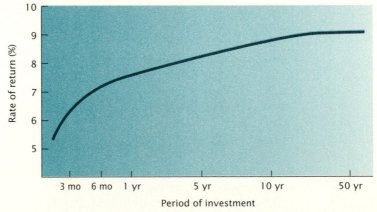

■ *Another factor that affects the riskiness of a financial asset is whether the asset is insured.* Many savings alternatives, including savings accounts at financial institutions and most CDs, are covered by federal deposit insurance. So if the financial institution fails, you do not lose the money in your savings account. Since most investment alternatives are not insured, they are more risky. Investors must be compensated for undertaking this higher level of risk, so the required rate of return is higher on uninsured savings alternatives.

■ *Finally, the creditworthiness of the issuer of the financial asset must be considered.* Using a federally-insured savings medium or lending money to the federal government through the purchase of U.S. savings bonds or Treasury bills is far less risky than lending money to a private company. The insured institution and the short-term financial assets issued by the federal government are very safe, in that the federal government has authority to raise revenues through taxes to fund repayment of its debt obligations. Hence you will earn a lower rate of return by lending money to the federal government than you will by lending money to a private company that could go broke and not repay the money you lent.

Calculating Earned Rates of Return

As a saver or an investor, you'll want to be able to determine the rate of return that you have earned. In the previous chapter, we examined the time value of money and how interest affects a sum of money saved or invested over long periods. We also discussed the importance of how frequently interest is compounded. Through more frequent compounding, a higher rate of return, called the effective rate, can be earned.

How are rates of return calculated on saving and investment alternatives? The rate of return that you earn depends on a number of variables: the original amount deposited or invested, the income received (such as interest or dividends), the maturity value or sales price of the asset, and the time period involved. The general formula for calculating a rate of return simply compares what you saved or invested initially with what you have at the end of the period of savings or investment. The specific formula depends on the situation. Let's consider some examples of rate of return calculations.

■ Suppose you purchase a one-year certificate of deposit for $1,000. At year end, after the interest earned has been credited, your new balance is $1,070. What rate of return have you earned? To calculate your rate of return, you must compare the interest earned with the original savings deposit. In other words, you committed $1,000 and earned $70 ($1,070 − $1,000) on this certificate of deposit over the course of the year. Thus you earned $70 on a commitment of $1,000. Your rate of return is:

$$\text{Rate of Return} = \frac{\text{Interest Earned}}{\text{Original Deposit}}$$

$$= \frac{\$70}{\$1,000}$$

$$= 7.00\%$$

■ Suppose you purchase a share of stock for $30 and sell it one year later for $33, after collecting a $1 dividend. What was your rate of return on this investment? Again, you must compare what you received with your original investment. In this case, you received income in the form of a $1 dividend and $3 ($33 − $30) in price appreciation by selling the stock for more than your original investment. Your rate of return is:

$$\text{Rate of Return} = \frac{\text{Price Appreciation} + \text{Income}}{\text{Purchase Price}}$$

$$= \frac{(\$33 - \$30) + \$1}{\$30}$$

$$= 13.33\%$$

■ Some investments involve price appreciation only. Suppose you purchase a piece of land for $30,000 and four years later you sell the land for $45,000. Obviously, your land has increased in value by 50 percent of the original purchase price over the four-year period. But what was your annual rate of return on this investment? Knowing the annual rate of return is important because it permits you to compare rates of return for investments of differing time periods on a consistent basis. Recall from Chapter 2 that the future value of a present amount is:

$$\text{Future Value} = \text{Present Value} \times (1 + i)^n$$

We can use this equation to find i, the interest rate. First, we substitute in the relevant values, then solve for i:

$$\$45,000 = \$30,000 \times (1 + i)^4$$

$$(1 + i)^4 = \frac{\$45,000}{\$30,000}$$

$$(1 + i)^4 = 1.5$$

$$i = 10.67\%$$

In other words, you would earn a 10.67 percent annual rate of return for four years if your investment increased in value from $30,000 to $45,000 over a four-year period.

The rate of return provided on savings, as well as investment, alternatives changes over time. Shop around before committing your funds in order to obtain the highest rate of return available for a given level of risk. Personal finance and business publications regularly print a summary of the best rates available. Insight 3.2 discusses the importance of the difference between the rate of return you earn as a saver or investor and the rate a financial institution charges you on loans as a borrower. Some additional rate of return formulas will be presented in Chapters 12 through 15, where we discuss investments.

Financial Institutions

As a saver, rather than keeping your cash at home, you can choose among an array of savings options offered by a number of financial institutions. Many of these institutions also offer checking accounts, an important vehicle in your money management program. Most saving is done through banks and other deposit-type financial institutions. Other institutions that will accept your savings and offer a return on your funds include insurance companies, brokerages, and the federal government.

Deposit-Type Financial Institutions

deposit-type financial institution A financial institution that accepts money from individuals who do not need the money for consumption or who wish to use the services of the institution to facilitate bill paying through checking accounts.

Deposit-type financial institutions accept money from individuals who do not need the money for immediate consumption or who wish to use the services of the financial institution to facilitate bill paying through checking accounts. We look next at the advantages and the types of deposit-type financial institutions.

Advantages of Deposit-Type Institutions. People use deposit-type institutions for several reasons—primarily for their safety, convenience, range of services, and return on savings.

A deposit-type financial institution is a safe place to deposit your money. Besides the obvious security measures, video cameras and vaults, for example, there is an "unseen" security measure: federal deposit insurance. Accounts at most deposit-type financial institutions are insured by the federal government up to $100,000. **Deposit insurance** is protection against financial loss for depositors provided by the federal government. This coverage is important because if the financial institution becomes insolvent, you will not lose the money you have on deposit. Since federal

deposit insurance Insurance provided by the federal government to protect depositors against the risk of financial loss associated with insolvency of the financial institution.

3.2 Why Is Your Banker Smiling?

Your friendly neighborhood banker just smiled as you renewed your one-year certificate of deposit. Why is your banker smiling? Because you just committed your funds for one year at a rate below the best rate available! The difference between what the bank will pay you on your savings deposits and the rate the bank requires on funds that it loans to borrowers is an important spread. It's easy for a bank to make money if it pays 5 or 6 percent interest on savings deposits, and loans the money out to borrowers at 9 percent interest.

So how do you get the best rates on savings deposits? Shop around and consider your alternatives. If you find a better rate, ask your present institution to match it. If your financial institution is unwilling to provide a better rate, consider moving your funds to another institution. Be sure to consider safety (deposit insurance, guarantees, and so on).

Where can you find the "best rates"? Many personal finance magazines and investment publications print tables displaying average rates and the best rates available. The following table is representative. Internet sites such as those mentioned in the text also give current rates.

Top Savings Deposit Yields*

Institution/Location	Telephone	Min. Deposit	Recent % Rate		Effect. % Yield
MONEY MARKET ACCOUNT					
Heritage Bank, Willmar, MN	(800) 344-7048	75000	5.65	(CM)	5.80
Stearns Cnty Natl, St. Cloud, MN	(800) 320-7262	75000	5.62	(CM)	5.77
Corus Bank, Chicago, IL	(800) 989-5101	10000	5.19	(CM)	5.32
SIX-MONTH CDs					
Sthrn Pacific Thrift, Los Angeles	(800) 428-5056	5000	5.80	(CD)	5.97
Safra Natl Bank, New York	(800) 223-2311	10000	5.64	(CD)	5.80
Pacific Crest, Agoura, CA	(800) 245-5626	1000	5.58	(CD)	5.75
ONE-YEAR CDs					
Sthrn Pacific Thrift, Los Angeles	(800) 428-5056	5000	6.00	(CD)	6.18
Midwest Svgs Bank, DeGraff, OH	(800) 686-2052	25000	5.97	(CD)	6.15
Calif Thrift, Santa Barb, CA	(800) 852-0587	5000	5.92	(CD)	6.10
2½-YEAR CDs					
Safra Natl Bank, New York	(800) 223-2311	10000	6.30	(CD)	6.50
Rep. Bk Ca. N, Beverly Hills	(310) 281-4271	5000	6.25	(CD)	6.45
MBNA America, Wilmingtn, DE	(800) 345-0397	5000	6.25	(CD)	6.44

Rates are the highest yields on six types of accounts offered by federally-insured banks and savings associations nationwide. Yields are based on the stated rate and compounding method in effect Friday and are subject to change. Phone to verify before investing or sending money.

(CC) Compounded continuously (CQ) Compounded quarterly (CA) Compounded annually
(CD) Compounded daily (CSA) Compounded semiannually (SI) Simple interest
(CM) Compounded monthly

deposit insurance is limited to $100,000 per depositor per bank, private insurance protection is also available to insure balances in excess of the amount.

A second reason that you may use a deposit-type financial institution is convenience. Most deposit institutions offer services at many of their branches, so you will not have to travel far to do your banking. Indeed, many banks have opened branches in grocery stores and other locations. The ability to access your savings quickly and easily is another convenience these institutions offer. You can write checks on demand deposit (checking) accounts and withdraw funds 24 hours a day through automated teller machines (ATMs).

Third, deposit-type financial institutions offer a wide range of services. In addition to accepting your savings and checking deposits, many deposit-type financial institutions offer other savings media, specialized checks (traveler's checks and cashier's checks, for example), brokerage services, trust and mortgage services, safe-deposit boxes, and other services. Some financial institutions are now offering banking and borrowing services online, as discussed in Insight 3.3.

Finally, deposit-type financial institutions will pay you interest on the funds you have deposited in savings and sometimes in checking accounts. As discussed earlier, the rate of return provided on money market instruments tends to be low, reflecting the short-term commitment of funds. Deposit-type financial institutions pool your deposits with the money deposited by others and make large blocks of funds available for loans and investment.

Types of Deposit-Type Institutions.

Types of Deposit-Type Institutions. If you would like to put your money in a deposit-type financial institution, you have a number of alternatives. These institutions include commercial banks, savings and loan associations, mutual savings banks, and credit unions.

commercial banks
Deposit-type financial institutions that offer individuals and businesses a complete range of financial services, including savings and checking accounts. Commercial banks are chartered by the federal government or the state.

■ **Commercial banks** are the largest deposit-type financial institutions. They offer individuals and businesses a complete range of financial services. At year-end 1993, there were 10,958 commercial banks in the United States, with assets of $3,706.2 billion.[1] In addition to savings and checking accounts, commercial banks offer other savings vehicles, loans, trust services, financial counseling, credit cards, automatic deposits and withdrawals, safe-deposit boxes, and other services.

Commercial banks are organized as corporations and may be chartered either by the federal government or by states. Commercial bank deposits are insured up to $100,000 per depositor, per bank, by the Federal Deposit Insurance Corporation (FDIC).

savings and loan associations Deposit-type financial institutions that offer a range of services similar to those offered by commercial banks. They may be organized as mutual or stock organizations and are chartered by the federal government or the state.

■ **Savings and loan associations** are another kind of deposit-type financial institution. Historically, savings and loan associations

Insight   3.3   Banking and Borrowing On-Line

These days, paying bills, transferring funds from one account to another, and applying for a credit card or mortgage are a few mouse clicks away. What you pay for virtual banking and borrowing isn't necessarily cheap, and you may not have a broad selection of services. But if you want to get your cyber feet wet, here is a sampling of the services available now or coming soon.

Banking. You now have more opportunities to bank on-line, thanks partly to the latest versions of two money-management programs—Intuit's *Quicken 5.0* and *Microsoft Money* for Windows 95. Both currently offer a menu of about 20 banks, including Chase Manhattan, Wells Fargo, Corestates (in Philadelphia) and Suntrust (in Atlanta). If your bank is in the lineup, you can pay bills electronically, invest in a certificate of deposit (often with a credit card), transfer funds between accounts, and get balances and account statements from your computer. *Quicken 5.0* retails for $39.95; *Microsoft Money* retails for $34.95—but some banks, such as Corestates and Chase, offer the software for free.

You can also sign up via *Prodigy,* the on-line service (jump to: *banking*), which offers a customized menu of institutions in your area offering on-line banking. Bank of America will soon offer on-line banking

on *America Online,* as well as via the software program *Managing Your Money* (about $30). Some banks on Prodigy let you apply for a new account on-line, too. With *Quicken* and *Microsoft Money,* you'll have to apply via a toll-free phone number or mail in an application.

The list of banks should jump dramatically now that Checkfree, known mostly for its bill-paying service, and Fiserv, a data-processing company for banks, have announced plans to offer home-banking software for more than 3,000 small banks, credit unions, and savings institutions. Some banks have already started offering the software.

To bank on-line you'll pay the going rate for a checking account, plus about $4 per month to view your statement, balance your checking account and transfer balances, or $10 to $15 a month to add bill-paying (plus a monthly fee if you're using an on-line service). Chase, Citibank and Corestates offer on-line banking and bill-paying for free (but there may be hidden costs).

Borrowing. You can shop for a mortgage using the HSH Associates data base (www.hsh.com) if you have *PC Mortgage Update* software. Downloads of the program from HSH's Web site are free; you'll pay a $10 fee for the data on disk (call 800-873-2837). From a list of 25 to 80 lenders in

your area, the program tells you what mortgages you qualify for and what you'll pay.

Most lenders who let you apply for mortgages on-line operate in only a few states or a limited regional area. However, Bank of America (*www.bankamerica.com*) accepts on-line applications from around the nation. Most national lenders still draw the line at prequalifying for a mortgage on-line. Norwest Mortgage (*www.norwest.com*), for example, lets you prequalify for a loan via the Internet by filling out an application and e-mailing it—and you'll receive a $350 credit applied to the closing costs. Countrywide (*www.countrywide.com*) will start on-line prequalifications beginning this spring.

Looking for a credit card? Try Ram Research (*www.ramresearch.com*), which lists the best no-fee, secured, and rebate cards on its Web site. About a dozen banks, including AFBA and Wachovia, let you download an application or receive information about their credit cards and then apply via their "800" number. On Credit Card Network (*www.creditnet.com*) you'll soon be able to transfer account balances from one credit card to another on-line.

emphasized mortgage lending. However, because of banking deregulation during the 1980s, savings and loan associations now offer a range of services similar to commercial banks. Savings and loan associations can be organized as mutual (depositor-owned) or stock organizations, and may be chartered by either states or the federal government. Many savings and loan associations failed during the 1980s. A number of factors led to the insolvencies, including bad loans, questionable investments, and the high rate of return demanded by savers and the low rate of return earned on the loan portfolio of the savings and loan association.

mutual savings banks
Deposit-type financial institutions similar to savings and loan associations. They are owned by their depositors and located primarily in Northeastern states.

■ **Mutual savings banks** are similar to savings and loan associations. Owned by their depositors, they are located primarily in Northeastern states. Although mutual savings banks traditionally have stressed mortgage lending, other consumer loans are also available. These institutions offer a variety of accounts to their depositors, including savings and interest-bearing checking accounts. Since mutual savings banks are owned by their depositors, a portion of profits earned are distributed to the depositors.

credit union Deposit-type financial institution owned by depositors who share a common bond, such as the same employer or the same occupation. They offer a number of services and are operated on a nonprofit basis for the benefit of the members.

■ A **credit union** is a depositor-owned, nonprofit financial institution whose members share a common bond, such as the same employer or the same occupation. In 1993, there were 12,317 credit unions operating in the United States, with assets of $277.2 billion.[2] Credit unions accept deposits from their members and offer consumer loans and other services. Since a credit union is run for the benefit of its members, the savings rates paid and borrowing rates charged tend to be quite favorable. Most credit union deposits are federally insured through the National Credit Union Insurance Fund. Some credit union deposits are backed by state insurance plans or through private insurance. Credit unions have expanded their operations to include credit cards, mortgage lending, and investment and retirement services.

Other Institutions That Offer Savings Options

A number of other institutions offer savings opportunities. You can lend money to the federal government through the purchase of Treasury Bills and a variety of government bonds, including U.S. savings bonds. Stock brokerages, investment companies, and insurance companies also offer savings alternatives. Regardless of the savings institution that you select, you should carefully match the services offered with your specific needs.

Checking Accounts

checking account, or demand deposit An account at a deposit-type financial institution that permits the holder to make withdrawals through negotiable instruments known as checks.

check A financial instrument written on a checking account that directs the financial institution to pay the party listed on the check a specified amount of money and to reduce the checking account balance by the same amount.

share draft account A checking account at a credit union.

regular checking accounts Noninterest-bearing checking accounts.

negotiable order of withdrawal (NOW) accounts Interest-bearing checking accounts.

An important facet of your money management strategy should be a checking account. A **checking account** is an account at a deposit-type financial institution that permits the account holder to make withdrawals through negotiable instruments known as checks. A **check** is a financial instrument written on a checking account that directs the financial institution to pay the party listed on the check a specified amount of money and to reduce the checking account balance by the same amount. Checking accounts are also known as **demand deposits** since the financial institution is directed to make payment to another party upon the demand of the holder of the checking account. A **share draft account** is a checking account at a credit union.

Some checking accounts pay interest on the account balance, and others do not. **Regular checking accounts** are noninterest-bearing accounts. Regular checking accounts normally do not charge fees, provided the depositor maintains a specified balance in the account. Deposit-type financial institutions also offer interest-bearing checking accounts called **negotiable order of withdrawal (NOW) accounts.** The depositor must satisfy a minimum deposit requirement imposed by the institution for interest to be credited, such as maintaining a balance of at least $1,000 at all times.

Traditionally, checking account deposits were made in person at the bank or through the mail. Withdrawals were made in person or by writing a check on the account. With the introduction of technology to banking, you can now perform many transactions electronically. Important technological innovations include automated teller machines (ATMs), debit cards, and electronic fund transfers (EFTs).

automated teller machines (ATMs) Computerized banking terminals that allow users to perform account transactions by inserting cards and entering personal identification numbers.

■ Many financial institutions offer **automated teller machines (ATMs).** ATMs are computerized banking terminals that allow you to perform account transactions 24 hours a day by inserting an ATM card and entering your personal identification number (PIN). In addition to making cash withdrawals, ATMs accept deposits, provide account balances, and permit you to transfer funds between your accounts. Since ATMs are often located at remote areas, special security concerns are associated with using them. Insight 3.4 provides some tips for ATM security.

debit card Specially coded card by which a user can automatically transfer funds from his or her account to another's account.

■ Another method of accessing the funds in your checking account is with a debit card. A **debit card** is a specially-coded plastic card that automatically transfers funds from your account to someone else's account. Some merchants, including supermarkets and gas stations, accept debit

Insight

3.4   ATM Security and You

ATMs are a fast and easy way to withdraw cash, check account balances, transfer funds and more. However, it is important that you make electronic banking security a priority. Here are some important steps you can take to make ATM security your business.

Keep Your ATM Card Secure

Treat your ATM card like cash. Always keep your card in a safe place. It's a good idea to store your card in a card sleeve. The sleeve protects the card's magnetic stripe and helps ensure that the card functions properly.

Keep your "secret code" a secret. Your ATM card will only work with your personal identification number or PIN. Memorize your code. Never write it on your card or store it with the card. Never tell your code to anyone. And never let someone else enter your code for you.

Do not give out any information over the telephone. No one needs to know your secret code.

Report a lost or stolen card at once. Even though your ATM card cannot be used without your secret code, promptly report a lost or stolen card. You will be issued another card at once.

Check your receipts against your monthly statement to guard against ATM fraud. You get a receipt every time you make an ATM transaction. Verify each transaction by checking the receipts against your monthly statements.

Security At Walk-Up ATMs

Always observe your surroundings before conducting an ATM transaction.
If you are driving to an ATM, park as close as possible to the terminal. Observe the entire area from the safety of your car before getting out. If you see anyone or anything suspicious, leave the area at once.
If an ATM is obstructed from view or poorly lit, go to another ATM. Report the problem to the financial institution that owns the ATM.

When possible, take a companion along when using an ATM—especially at night.

Minimize time spent at the ATM by having your card out and ready to use.
If the ATM is in use, give the person using the terminal the same privacy you expect. Allow them to move away from the ATM before you approach the terminal.

Stand between the ATM and anyone waiting to use the terminal so that others cannot see your secret code or transaction amount. Once you have completed your transaction, take your money, card and receipt and move away from the terminal.

If you see anyone or anything suspicious while conducting a transaction, cancel your transaction and leave.

If you are followed after making an ATM transaction, go immediately to a heavily-populated, well-lighted area and call the police.

Security At Drive-Up ATMs

Keep your engine running, the doors locked and the windows up at all times when waiting in line at the drive-up ATM.
When possible, leave enough room between cars to allow for a quick exit should it become necessary.
If an ATM is obstructed from view or poorly lit, go to another ATM. Report the problem to the financial institution.

Before rolling down the window to use the ATM, check the entire area for anything or anyone suspicious. If you see anyone or anything suspicious, drive away from the area at once.

Minimize time spent at the ATM by having your card out and ready to use. Once you have completed your transaction, take your money, card and receipt and drive away from the terminal.

If you see anyone or anything suspicious while conducting a transaction, cancel your transaction and leave. If you are followed after making an ATM transaction, go immediately to a heavily-populated, well-lighted area and call the police.

Source: Produced by Internet, Inc., Owner and Operator of the MOST Network.

card transfers as payment for goods or services. Debit cards look like credit cards (discussed in Chapter 4), but there are some important differences. Debit card transactions result in the automatic withdrawal of funds from your account, whereas credit card transactions do not—you pay for the purchase at a later date. In addition, credit cards are more readily accepted by retailers than are debit cards.

electronic fund transfer (EFT) An electronic debit (decrease) or credit (increase) in a checking account.

■ A third application of technology with respect to checking accounts is the **electronic fund transfer (EFT).** An electronic fund transfer is an electronic debit (decrease) or credit (increase) to your checking account. For example, you may authorize your employer to automatically deposit your monthly paycheck to your account or authorize your financial institution to automatically withdraw funds each month from your account to make your mortgage payment. Electronic fund transfers eliminate paperwork and are a convenient and secure method of transferring funds.

When deposits and withdrawals to your account are made, you should keep track of them in a checkbook ledger or register. You will receive these small record books with your supply of checks. Each month, your financial institution provides an account statement. The account statement is a summary of all transactions involving your account during the statement period, including deposits, withdrawals, checks cashed, and service charges. An example of a checking account statement appears in Exhibit 3.2. You should compare the statement to your checkbook ledger and reconcile your account statement each month. Reconciliation is the process of verifying the accuracy of the account statement. Any errors on the statement should be reported to your financial institution immediately.

overdraft A check written for more than the balance in the checking account.

overdraft protection An arrangement between the depositor and the financial institution through which the institution automatically covers the excess amount of the overdraft.

Checking accounts offer several advantages. Since the funds are payable on demand and checks are widely accepted, writing a check is a convenient method of payment. The canceled check serves as proof that you have made a payment. The financial institution may also provide overdraft protection. An **overdraft** is a check written for more than the balance in the checking account. **Overdraft protection** is an arrangement between the depositor and the financial institution through which the institution automatically covers the excess amount of the overdraft, within certain limits. This arrangement protects you from the unpleasant and potentially damaging situation in which your check "bounces."

There are, however, several disadvantages of checking accounts. As mentioned earlier, regular checking accounts do not pay interest. Even if your checking account does pay interest, the interest rate paid is typically lower than the rate paid on savings accounts. In addition, financial institutions assess a variety of fees and service charges on checking

Exhibit 3.2

Checking Account Statement

Michelle Robinson   Third National Bank
347 Maple Avenue   201 Main Street
Anytown, Anystate 00000   Anytown, Anystate 00000

Account Number 35-090873-20   Statement period: 3/1/97 to 3/31/97

SUMMARY FOR STATEMENT PERIOD

Account Type	Previous Balance	Withdrawals and Checks	Deposits	Ending Balance
Interest + Checking	$2,841.90	$1,653.72	$1,795.76	2,983.94

Summary of Account Transactions:

		Withdrawals/Checks	Deposits	Balance
3/1	Starting Bal.			$2,841.90
3/2	Check 744	15.00		2,826.90
3/6	ATM Withdrawal	50.00		2,776.90
3/7	Check 745	344.78		2,432.12
3/12	New Check Order	16.00		2,416.12
3/15	Payroll Check, ABC Co.		895.14	3,311.26
3/15	ATM Withdrawal	30.00		3,281.26
3/19	Check 746	87.19		3,194.07
3/21	Check 747	22.50		3,171.57
3/27	ATM Withdrawal	100.00		3,071.57
3/29	Check 749 *	59.37		3,012.20
3/31	Payroll Check, ABC Co.		895.14	3,907.34
3/31	Interest Earned		5.48	3,915.82
3/31	Service Charge	4.50		3,911.32
3/31	Auto W/D--Mortgage Pmt.	924.38		2,986.94
Totals for Period:		1,653.72	1,795.76	

* Denotes break in sequence.

accounts. For example, if your account balance drops below a specified level, a fee may be charged. What's more, if you write a check and do not have sufficient funds to cover the check, an insufficient fund check penalty may be assessed if you do not have overdraft protection.

Savings Media

Savings can take various forms, depending in part on the institution involved. The type of savings medium you select depends on a number of variables, including desired services, convenience, fees, liquidity, tax implications, and the rate of return provided. Your employer, for example, may provide the convenience of direct deposit of your paycheck to an account at the company credit union. If you do not believe that you will need your savings for the next few months, you may opt for a savings alternative that is more restrictive, but offers a higher rate of return, such as a certificate of deposit. Given the number of savings alternatives available, you can select a savings medium that best matches your financial needs. Savings alternatives include savings accounts, certificates of deposit, money market mutual funds, money market deposit accounts, U.S. Treasury bills (T-bills), and U.S. savings bonds.

Savings Accounts

savings account, passbook account, or time deposit An interest-bearing account at a deposit-type financial institution that permits deposits and withdrawals.

share accounts Savings accounts at credit unions.

The most commonly used savings medium is a savings account. A **savings account** is an interest-bearing account at a deposit-type financial institution that permits deposits and withdrawals. You may find a savings account to be the best place to keep emergency funds on deposit since the funds are liquid, usually covered by federal deposit insurance, and a higher rate of return is usually paid on savings accounts than on checking accounts. **Share accounts** are savings accounts at credit unions. Savings accounts are also called **passbook accounts,** because depositors often use a small booklet called a passbook to record account activity, or **time deposits,** because they are expected to remain on deposit with the financial institution for some period.

annual percentage yield (APY) The effective annual rate of return paid on an account.

Two important considerations regarding savings accounts are the interest rate credited and the account fees charged. Savings accounts are highly liquid and typically insured up to $100,000 per depositor per institution through federal deposit insurance. They are low-risk savings vehicles and earn a low rate of interest, typically 2 to 5 percent. The Truth in Savings Act requires savings institutions to disclose the **annual percentage yield (APY),** the effective annual rate of return, paid on the account. Financial institutions are required to use a standardized method of computing the APY, so you can compare the APY offered on savings accounts at different financial institutions directly.

Interest paid on your savings account can be calculated in a number of ways. Some institutions pay a flat rate on the entire account balance. Others pay interest on balances in excess of a minimum value, such as $500 or $1,000. Other institutions use a "tiered" interest rate schedule, crediting a low rate on balances up to a certain value, a higher rate on balances between that value and a second value, and a higher rate on amounts exceeding the second value. Exhibit 3.3 shows how interest is credited if your savings account uses tiered interest rates and how the APY offered by your financial institution is calculated.

You should be aware that your financial institutions may charge fees on your savings account. Some institutions have minimum account balance requirements. If your account balance drops below the minimum balance, you may be charged a fee or lose interest that otherwise would have been credited to the account. Depositors may also be charged fees for account transactions or if the number of account transactions exceeds a specified number during the month.

Most financial institutions will send you a monthly or quarterly account statement, similar to the checking account statement discussed in the previous section. The account statement details your deposits,

---

Exhibit 3.3

Tiered Interest Rates and APYs

Some financial institutions pay a flat rate of interest on savings accounts. Others use tiered interest rates, with a higher rate credited on larger account balances. For example, a financial institution may offer the following monthly interest rates and corresponding annual percentage yields (APYs) for savings:

Balances	Monthly Rate	Annual Percentage Yield (APY)
$0 to $1,000	0.2500%	3.0416%
$1,000 to $10,000	0.4167%	5.1162%
$10,000 and above	0.5000%	6.1678%

If you had $20,000 on deposit with the financial institution for the monthly period, your interest earnings would be:

$$(\$1,000 \times .2500\%) + (\$9,000 \times .4167\%) + (\$10,000 \times .5000\%) =$$

$$\$2.50 \quad + \quad \$37.50 \quad + \quad 50.00 \ = \$90.00$$

The annual percentage yield (APY) can be calculated by determining the rate of return earned on a $100 investment at each interest rate given the interest rate and the method of compounding. For example, $100 earning .25 percent monthly would grow to $103.04 in one year:

$$100 \times (1 + .0025)^{12} = \$103.0416$$

The gain in value, $3.0416, divided by the initial investment, $100, gives the annual percentage yield, 3.0416 percent. If $100 was invested at 0.5 percent monthly interest, the value would be $106.17 in one year:

$$100 \times (1 + .0050)^{12} = \$106.1678$$

The gain in value, $6.1678, divided by the initial investment, $100, gives the annual percentage yield, 6.1678 percent.

withdrawals, interest credits, and any fees the financial institution has assessed during the statement period.

Certificates of Deposit

certificate of deposit (CD) An interest-bearing savings instrument requiring the holder to commit funds for a specified period.

If you desire a higher rate of return and you are willing to commit your savings for a longer period, a certificate of deposit may be an appropriate savings vehicle. A **certificate of deposit (CD)** is an interest-bearing savings instrument requiring you to commit your funds for a specified period. At the end of the period, you will receive your initial deposit plus the interest earned on the CD. If you decide to redeem the CD before the originally agreed-on time, a penalty in the form of forfeited interest may be assessed. CDs are offered for a variety of time periods, ranging from 30 days to 10 or more years, and at denominations ranging from $100 to $100,000. CDs are offered by both deposit-type financial institutions and investment brokers. Although most CDs are insured by federal deposit insurance, it is a good idea to verify at the time of purchase that your CD is federally insured.

The rate of return earned on CDs is typically higher than the rate paid on savings accounts because you are committing your funds for a specified time period. Although most CDs offer fixed rates of return, some CDs with interest rates that fluctuate are also available. The rate of return financial institutions and brokers are willing to pay on CDs depends upon interest rates in general and the maturity of the CD selected.

A question you might ask when considering the purchase of a CD is, "How long should I commit my funds?" In other words, what maturity CD should I purchase? The question is important given that interest rates in the economy change over time. You do not want to lock yourself in to a long-term CD if interest rates increase, or purchase a short-term CD if interest rates fall. The yield curve shown in Exhibit 3.1 shows the usual relationship between time and the rate of return on CDs—longer-term CDs usually provide a higher rate of return than shorter-term CDs. Thus, many financial advisors recommend a technique called "laddering" CDs for those individuals who are willing to commit their funds for longer periods in order to earn a higher rate of return. Let's consider an example of laddering.

George and Ellen Newhart, both age 65, recently retired. They sold their home and received $180,000 in proceeds. They would like to use the $180,000 to earn interest to supplement their other sources of retirement income. They are considering certificates of deposit (CDs) and are aware that longer-term CDs usually provide a higher rate of return. The Newharts are concerned, however, about locking up their funds in long-term CDs.

The Newharts met with Rachel Turner, a financial planner. Rachel advised the Newharts to divide the $180,000 into six units of $30,000, and to purchase six CDs with durations of 6, 12, 18, 24, 30 and 36 months. When each CD matures, Rachel advises replacing it with a 36-month CD. By following Rachel's strategy, eventually, the Newharts will have six 36-month CDs, each earning the 36-month rate of interest with a CD maturing every six months.

Laddering CDs is the technique Rachel Turner suggested. This strategy permits the CD owner to earn the higher rate of return associated with longer-term CDs without sacrificing liquidity.

In order to attract CD purchasers, some financial institutions offer promotional CDs. The higher interest rate offered on the promotional CD may be available only to new customers of the financial institution.

Money Market Mutual Funds

money market mutual fund (MMMF) A pool of money collected from savers and used to purchase short-term, high-quality debt obligations of commercial banks, government entities, and corporations. MMMFs are offered by mutual fund investment companies and insurance companies.

A **money market mutual fund (MMMF)** is a pool of money collected from savers and used to purchase short-term, high-quality debt obligations of commercial banks, government entities, and corporations. The denominations of the debt obligations purchased by the fund may be much higher than you could afford to purchase. However, by pooling the savings of many individuals, the fund is able to purchase a variety of debt obligations and sell shares of the fund to individual savers. Money market mutual funds are offered by mutual fund investment companies and insurance companies rather than deposit-type financial institutions.

Money market mutual funds require a minimum deposit, often as little as $500 or $1,000. You are free to withdraw your funds at any time. You may write checks on the account, but some funds require the amount of the check to exceed a specified minimum. This requirement is meant to discourage use of the money market mutual fund as an everyday checking account. Interest is calculated daily, and the rate of return credited is higher than the rate paid on savings and checking accounts. Although savers enjoy the higher yields provided by money market mutual funds, there is a downside. These funds are not federally insured.

Money Market Deposit Accounts

money market deposit account (MMDA) A government-insured money market account offered through a deposit-type financial institution.

As a means of competing with money market mutual funds, deposit-type institutions offer money market deposit accounts. A **money market deposit account (MMDA)** is a government-insured money market account offered through a deposit-type financial institution. Money market deposit accounts usually require a minimum balance, such as $1,000 or $2,500. Depositors are permitted to write a specified number of checks and to make a limited number of funds transfers at no charge.

Fees are levied if additional transactions are made. Money market deposit accounts pay market-based rates of return. Often, tiered interest rates are used, with one rate credited to the required minimum balance, and a higher rate on the funds in excess of the required minimum.

U.S. Treasury Bills

U.S. Treasury bills (T-bills) Financial instruments that represent short-term loans to the federal government.

Another safe savings alternative is the purchase of U.S. government Treasury bills. **U.S. Treasury bills,** also known as **T-bills,** are short-term loans to the federal government, which borrows just as individuals do when they need funds for expenditures. U.S. Treasury bills are short-term debt instruments issued by the federal government. T-bills are considered money market instruments because they are sold with maturities of 1 year or less (13 weeks, 26 weeks, and 52 weeks). T-bills are issued on a discount basis, which means that the owner does not recieve periodic interest payments. Rather, when you purchase a T-bill, you pay less than the face amount, which is the value it will be worth at maturity.

You make a "return" on your purchase of a T-bill equal to the difference between the purchase price and the value at maturity, when the federal government must pay you the face amount of the T-bill. For example, suppose you paid $9,250 for a 1-year T-bill. At maturity 1 year later, you will be paid $10,000, the face amount. Thus, you will have earned $750 on an investment of $9,250. This represents a rate of return of 8.108 percent:

$$\text{Rate of Return} = \frac{\text{Interest Earned}}{\text{Original Deposit}}$$

$$= \frac{\$750}{\$9,250}$$

$$= 8.108\%$$

T-bills are sold in minimum denominations of $10,000 and are backed by the federal government. Many savers do not consider T-bills a viable savings alternative because of the high minimum investment required and the perceived difficulty in purchasing these instruments. However, if you have the necessary funds, you can purchase T-bills directly. Insight 3.5 presents a description of how to purchase T-bills directly from the federal government.

U.S. Savings Bonds

U.S. savings bonds Financial instruments representing long-term, tax-advantaged loans to the federal government made in exchange for a promised future payment.

Treasury bills represent short-term obligations of the federal government, but there are some longer-term alternatives. **U.S. savings bonds** are long-term, tax-advantaged loans to the federal government made in exchange for a promised future payment. U.S. savings bonds are often

Insight   3.5   Buying Directly From Uncle Sam

Under the Treasury Direct program, you can buy Treasury instruments from any of the Federal Reserve Bank offices around the country, or from the Bureau of Public Debt in Washington, D.C., or by mail. The interest is deposited directly into your checking or savings account. Here's how to get started:

1 Contact the closest Federal Reserve Bank (located in major cities; see map) or one of the 24 branches. Inquire about the Treasury Direct program and request that the appropriate forms be mailed to you.

   If you're unsure about a location, contact the Board of Governors of the Federal Reserve System, 20th and Constitution Ave. N.W., Washington, D.C. 20551 (202-452-3000).

2 Fill out and submit (either in person or by mail) a tender form. The form will require your name, address, social security number, and the number of the savings or checking account into which you want your interest deposited. If you'll be purchasing the Treasuries by mail, write "TENDER FOR TREASURY SECURITIES" in large letters on the envelope and enclose a check for the face value of the notes. You'll need a certified check if you're buying Treasury bills; personal checks are acceptable for notes and bonds.

3 The issues you're buying are new issues, IOUs hot off the presses from Uncle Sam. Every Monday, new 13- and 26-week T-bills are auctioned; every fourth Thursday, 52-week T-bills are auctioned. Two- and five-year Treasury notes are auctioned toward the end of each month, while three- and 10-year notes are auctioned once each quarter. Thirty-year Treasury bonds are on the block semiannually. You must send in your money (or submit it in person) prior to certain deadlines for each type of auction. For example, the auction for T-bills is held at noon on Monday. The Fed must receive your money by 1 a.m. Eastern time on that day for you to receive your purchase. Mail bids must be postmarked no later than the day before the auction. Any Federal Reserve Bank or branch can inform you of the deadlines.

4 After the sale, you will not receive the Treasury paper itself. For Treasury bills, the Fed returns a check to you for the yield determined at auction. Upon maturity, the full amount of the bill is deposited in the checking or savings account you indicated on the tender form. For example, you purchase a $10,000 six-month T-bill at a 4.875 percent discount to face value. A few days after the auction, the Fed sends you a check for $243.75. Six months later, the full $10,000 that you originally sent is deposited in your bank account. You will have earned an annualized yield of 5 percent on the $9,756.25 that stayed with the Treasury. For Treasury notes and bonds, you don't receive a discount (or yield) payment. Rather, interest is paid semiannually by direct deposit to a financial institution, and then plopped into your checking or savings account.

   For more information on the Treasury Direct program, write the Bureau of Public Debt, Department A, Room 429, 1300 C St. S.W., Washington, D.C. 20239-1000 (202-874-4000).

Source: *Your Money,* October/November 1994, p. 25. Reprinted with permission.

Minneapolis 612/340-2345
Cleveland 216/579-2000
San Francisco 415/974-2000
Chicago 312/322-5322
Boston 617/973-3000
New York 212/720-5000
Kansas City 816/882-2000
St. Louis 314/444-8444
Philadelphia 215/574-6000
Dallas 214/922-6000
Richmond 804/697-8500
Atlanta 404/521-8500

Consider This

The U.S. Treasury department provides information about U.S. savings bonds and Treasury bills at:

http://www.ustreas.gov/treasury/bureaus/pubdebt/

purchased through payroll deduction plans. Although savings bonds are longer-term in nature, they are usually considered savings alternatives.

Two popular savings alternatives are Series EE and Series HH savings bonds. Series EE savings bonds are issued on a discount basis by the federal government at a purchase price equal to half the value at maturity. Series EE bonds are issued in denominations ranging from $25 to $10,000 per bond. You are limited to the purchase of $15,000 in EE bonds per year ($30,000 maturity value). Rates of return on Series EE savings bonds are not guaranteed. Rather, Series EE bonds earn a market rate based on the yields of five-year Treasury notes. Series EE bond holders are paid 90 percent of the yield on five-year notes. Interest on Series EE bonds is credited monthly.[3]

Series EE bonds have several tax advantages. First, the interest earned on Series EE bonds is exempt from state and local taxes. Second, Series EE bond purchasers are not required to report interest on these instruments until the bonds are redeemed or they mature. Finally, there are tax advantages if the bonds are used to fund college education. Single persons who make less than $42,300 and married couples earning less than $63,450 will not be taxed on the accumulated interest if they sell EE

Exhibit 3.4

Savings Alternatives

Savings Instrument	Characteristics and Issuer
Savings account	Interest-bearing account at a deposit-type financial institution; permits holder to make deposits and withdrawals.
Certificate of deposit (CD)	Short-, medium-, or long-term instrument issued by deposit-type financial institution or brokerage. Provides a higher return than savings accounts; however, funds must be committed for a longer period. Interest may be forfeited if funds are withdrawn prior to maturity. May or may not be federally insured.
Money market mutual fund (MMMF)	Pool of funds collected from savers and used to purchase short-term, high-quality debt obligations. Savers purchase shares of the fund. Issued by insurers and mutual fund companies. Not insured by the federal government.
Money market deposit account (MMDA)	Similar to money market mutual fund, but offered by deposit-type financial institutions and insured by the federal government.
U.S. Treasury bills (T-bills)	Short-term debt issued by the U.S. government on a discount basis. Can be purchased directly from the government.
U.S. savings bonds	Short- to long-term tax-advantaged debt issued by the federal government. Series EE bonds issued on a discount basis at half the maturity value. Series HH bonds are fixed-maturity, interest-bearing bonds that may be purchased through the exchange of Series EE bonds.

bonds to defray the cost of college education. Note that Series EE bonds purchased for educational purposes must be registered in the name of a parent.

Series HH savings bonds are fixed-maturity, interest-bearing bonds that may be purchased through the exchange of Series EE (or their predecessor, Series E) bonds. Series HH bonds are purchased at face value and pay interest semiannually to the bondholder. For example, a $5,000 Series HH bond that pays a 6 percent interest will pay $300 ($5,000 × .06) to the bondholder each year through two semiannual installments of $150. Although interest income on Series HH bonds is exempt from state and local taxes, it must be included in your taxable income for federal income tax purposes.

A summary of saving alternatives, their characteristics and issuers, is provided in Exhibit 3.4.

SUMMARY

- Money management refers to the effective utilization of cash and cash equivalents.

- Individuals hold cash balances to meet ordinary expenses, to pay unexpected expenses, and as a fund to draw on in case of an emergency.

- Saving refers to putting money in interest-earning, short-term instruments, where the principal is safe in order to achieve a short-term goal. Investment means committing funds on a longer-term basis with less safety of principal in order to achieve long-term objectives.

- Saving involves the use of cash, cash equivalents, and money market instruments. Investment uses capital market securities, including stocks and bonds.

- An interest rate is simply the price of money. The interest rate depends on several factors, including the real rate of interest, expected inflation, and the degree of risk. The yield curve shows the relationship between rates of return and the duration of an investment.

- The rate of return on savings and investment represents the income generated and the appreciation in value of the savings or investment.

- There is a relationship between required rates of return and risk. Savers and investors must be compensated for bearing additional risk through higher required rates of return.

■ Consumers often use the services of deposit-type financial institutions as part of their money management program. These institutions offer safety, convenience, a range of services, and interest on savings deposits.

■ Deposit-type financial institutions include commercial banks, savings and loan associations, mutual savings banks, and credit unions.

■ Commercial banks offer a complete range of financial services to individuals and businesses.

■ Savings and loan associations are financial institutions that histori-cally emphasized mortgage lending. Because of deregulation, savings and loan associations now offer a range of services similar to those offered by commercial banks.

■ Mutual savings banks are depositor-owned institutions similar to sav-ings and loan associations, located primarily in Northeastern states.

■ Credit unions are depositor-owned institutions that accept deposits and offer consumer loans to members who share some type of common bond, such as working for the same employer.

■ Checking accounts are accounts at deposit institutions. Checking accounts accept deposits and permit withdrawals of funds through negotiable instruments called checks. Most checking accounts do not pay interest, but some do.

■ There are a number of sources of savings alternatives. Savers can save through deposit-type financial institutions, and instruments pro-vided by life insurers, brokers, investment companies, and the U.S. government.

■ Consumers have a number of savings alternatives available to them, including savings accounts, certificates of deposit, money market mutual funds, money market deposit accounts, U.S. Treasury bills, and U.S. savings bonds.

■ Savings accounts are interest-bearing time deposits at deposit-type financial institutions.

■ Certificates of deposit are financial instruments that provide a speci-fied return on funds committed for a specified period. Certificates of deposit are issued by the deposit-type institutions and securities bro-kerage firms.

■ Money market mutual funds are pools of funds collected from savers that are used to purchase short-term debt obligations. Savers can pur-chase shares of these funds. Money market mutual funds are products of investment companies and insurance companies.

■ Money market deposit accounts are money market mutual funds offered through financial institutions. Unlike money market mutual funds, money market deposit accounts are federally insured.

■ U.S. Treasury bills (T-bills) are short-term debt instruments issued by the federal government on a discount basis.

■ U.S. savings bonds are short- to long-term, tax-advantaged debt instruments issued by the federal government. Series EE bonds are issued on a discount basis at a price equal to half the maturity value. Series EE bonds are often purchased through payroll deduction plans. Series HH bonds are fixed-maturity, interest-bearing bonds that may be purchased through the exchange of Series EE bonds.

KEY CONCEPTS AND TERMS

Annual percentage yield (APY)
Automated teller machine (ATM)
Capital market
Certificate of deposit (CD)
Check
Checking account
Commercial bank
Credit union
Debit card
Demand deposit
Deposit insurance
Deposit-type financial institution
Electronic fund transfer (EFT)
Financial asset
Interest rate
Monetary policy
Money management
Money market
Money market deposit account (MMDA)

Money market mutual fund (MMMF)
Mutual savings bank
Negotiable order of withdrawal (NOW) account
Nominal rate of interest
Overdraft
Overdraft protection
Passbook account
Real interest rate
Regular checking account
Required rate of return
Savings account
Savings and loan association
Share account
Share draft account
Time deposit
U.S. savings bond
U.S. Treasury bill (T-bill)
Yield curve

QUESTIONS FOR REVIEW

1. What is money management? Why is money management important?

2. What is the difference between saving and investing?

3. What types of financial instruments and securities are used in saving and investing?

4. If higher rates of return are usually earned on capital market securities, what are the reasons for holding a portion of your assets in cash and cash equivalents?

5. What is the yield curve? Why is the rate of return on shorter-term savings alternatives usually lower than the rate of return on longer-term investment opportunities?

6. What does the rate of return on a savings or investment alternative represent? How are rates of return calculated?

7. What deposit-type financial institutions are available to savers? What advantages do these financial institutions offer savers?

8. Distinguish between savings accounts, regular checking accounts, and negotiable order of withdrawal (NOW) accounts.

9. What money market saving alternatives are available to savers?

10. What are the similarities and differences between money market mutual funds and money market deposit accounts?

PROBLEMS

1. Solve the following problems using Fisher's equation.
   a. If the real rate of interest is 2 percent and expected inflation is 5 percent, what is the nominal interest rate?
   b. If the nominal rate is 9 percent and the real rate of interest is 2 percent, what rate of inflation is expected?

2. Jack just deposited $10,000 in a savings account at the start of the month. The account pays 6 percent annual interest, compounded monthly (.50 percent per month).
   a. How much interest will Jack earn during the first month?
   b. What annual percentage yield (APY) is the financial institution in part (a.) paying on Jack's savings account?
   c. Jack's bank is considering changing the method by which savings account interest is calculated. Under the change, the bank would pay no interest on the first $1,000; 6 percent interest (.50 percent per month) on account balances between $1,000 and $5,000; and 9 percent interest (.75 percent monthly) on any balance in excess of $5,000. How much interest would Jack earn on his $10,000 deposit during the first month?

3. Tony is interested in calculating the rate of return that he earned on his savings. For each of the following, calculate Tony's rate of return:

   a. Tony's bank promised to pay 6 percent interest, compounded monthly, on Tony's savings account. What annual percentage yield (APY) is Tony earning on this account?

   b. Tony purchased a 1-year T-bill for $9,300. When the T-bill matured 1 year later, Tony was paid $10,000. What was Tony's rate of return on this T-bill?

4. Using the following list of rates of return for government debt securities of differing maturities, plot the yield curve as displayed in Exhibit 3.1.

Term	*Rate of Return*
3 months	5.2%
6 months	5.5%
1 year	6.0%
3 years	7.5%
5 years	8.0%
10 years	8.5%
20 years	8.7%
30 years	8.8%

INTERNET EXERCISES

1. Two Internet sources of up-to-date rates of return, as mentioned in the chapter, are BanxQuote at:

   http://www.banx.com/

   and Bank Rate Monitor Infobank at:

   http://www.bankrate.com/

   Go to one of these sites, and find tables that give current CD rates. Compare the rates of CDs of different maturities (three months, six months, one year, five years). Are the differences what you would expect based on the yield curve in Exhibit 3.1?

2. As noted in the chapter, some financial institutions are offering banking and borrowing services online. Links to banks and credit unions with home pages on the Internet are provided at Online Banking's site at:

   http://www.orcc.com/banking.htm/

   Find the homepages of several financial institutions in your area, and compare the services they offer.

CASE APPLICATIONS

Case I

Rhonda Nolan just inherited $15,000. Rhonda is a single parent with a son, age 3. She earns $30,000 per year working for a hotel reservation service. Her financial assets currently consist of a savings account with a balance of $500 and a checking account with a balance of $1,200. Rhonda receives $250 per month in child support payments. Rhonda's monthly expenses (rent, food, child care, entertainment, and so on) equal $1,400.

Rhonda is unsure of what to do with the money she inherited, and she has asked for your assistance. She is considering a number of alternatives:

- Spending the money on a new car
- Putting all the money in her checking account
- Putting the money in her savings account
- Investing the money in common stock

Which option makes the most sense for Rhonda given her income, family situation, and current level of savings?

Case II

Ken and Debra Wang, both age 35, have high-paying jobs. The couple owns their own home, and they do not have any children. Ken and Debra have arranged to have their paychecks deposited directly to their regular checking account and to have their monthly mortgage payment deducted automatically from their account. Neither Ken nor Debra is particularly interested in personal finance and money management—in fact, their checking account statements for the past six months are sitting unopened in a desk drawer in their home office. Today, another monthly statement arrived. Debra opened it and was surprised to see that the account balance had grown to more than $50,000. She was also surprised to see that her financial institution was levying a $5 service charge for the automatic withdrawal of the mortgage payment and that no interest is paid on the account.

What specific changes would you recommend for the Wang's money management program?

SUGGESTIONS FOR ADDITIONAL READING

Dolan, Ken and Daria Dolan. *Straight Talk on Money.* New York: Simon and Schuster, 1993, Chapter 3.

Morris, Kenneth M. and Alan M. Siegel. *The Wall Street Journal Guide to Understanding Personal Finance.* New York: Lightbulb Press, 1992, Chapter 1.

Personal Financial Planning Guide. Ernst & Young. New York: John Wiley & Sons, 1995.

Rose, Peter S. *The Financial System in the Economy.* Homewood, IL: Richard D. Irwin, Inc. for The American College, 1989.

Schall, Lawrence D. and Charles W. Haley. *Introduction to Financial Management.* New York: McGraw-Hill, 1991, Chapter 2.

Sloan, Leonard. *The New York Times Personal Finance Handbook.* New York: Times Books, 1995, Chapter 2.

Stern, Linda. "Series EE Strategies." *Newsweek,* May 22, 1995, p. 72.

"Understanding the Difference Between Saving and Investing," *At the Helm,* Scudder, Summer 1992.

NOTES

1. *Statistics on Banking,* Federal Deposit Insurance Corporation, 1993.

2. *Statistics on Banking,* Federal Deposit Insurance Corporation, 1995.

3. "Savings Bond Program Modified by Treasury," *Wall Street Journal,* May 1, 1997, p. C15.

Chapter 4

Credit and Financial Planning

Learning Objectives

After studying this chapter, you should be able to:

- Explain what consumer credit is, differentiating between consumer credit and consumer loans.

- Discuss the importance of consumer credit and its advantages and disadvantages.

- Explain how consumer credit is established, including the credit application, the credit investigation and credit report, and credit scoring.

- Determine how much you can afford to charge on credit cards.

- Understand important credit terms, including the credit limit, annual fee, calculation of finance charges, minimum payment, grace period, and cash advances.

- Explain the characteristics of credit cards, including bank credit cards, retail credit cards, and travel and entertainment cards.

- Determine what type of credit card is best for you, considering credit terms and other features.

- Discuss the forms of protection afforded credit card holders and applicants through legislative acts and private insurance.

The affluent society has become a credit society. Those who cannot get credit are second-class citizens. Those who try to limit their borrowing are sometimes viewed as economic subversives.

Time Magazine

I had plastic surgery last week. I cut up my credit cards.

—Henny Youngman

Tom Blake, age 35, is finally joining the ranks of credit card holders although much later than most people join. Tom dropped out of high school and has held a number of low-paying jobs. Four years ago, Tom ran a stop sign and hit another car. He did not have auto insurance at the time, nor enough money to pay the $3,600 judgment awarded against him. The judge ordered him to pay $100 per month until the judgment was satisfied. Tom repeatedly applied for credit cards, only to be turned down each time because of insufficient income and the unsatisfied judgment.

Earlier this year, however, things took a turn for the better. Tom made the last $100 payment that he owed on the judgment. He received a promotion and a nice raise at work. Tom applied for a credit card from Townsends, a local department store, and was surprised when the application was approved and the credit card issued. Tom uses his Townsends card each month to purchase a few items that he really needs, and then he pays the entire balance owed when the credit card statement arrives. Now Tom averages three credit card solicitations each month. A year ago, no one was willing to issue a credit card to Tom. Now it seems as if everyone would like him to carry their credit card.

In this chapter and the next, we shift our emphasis from saving money to spending money. Although people make many purchases with cash or checks, they make other purchases on credit or by taking out a loan. There are advantages to using credit and borrowing; however, consumers must be careful not to charge or borrow more than they can repay. Unfortunately, many consumers do not manage credit and debt successfully, leading to financial problems.

Perhaps the most familiar form of consumer credit and debt is using a credit card to charge a purchase. Credit cards are profitable products for banks, retail establishments, and other issuers. As Tom Blake is learning, not only is it easy to qualify for a credit card, but many credit card issuers are anxious to have you as a card holder. In this chapter, we examine the nature of consumer credit, how to establish credit, how to manage credit, different types of credit cards, how to select the best card for you, and safeguards for credit card holders and credit applicants.

What Is Consumer Credit?

consumer credit Credit extended to a purchaser in advance of the purchase.

Consumer credit is credit that is extended to the purchaser in advance of the purchase. Consumer credit differs from consumer loans. Once credit has been extended, the consumer can use the credit at his or her discretion. In addition, with most credit cards, the consumer decides the repayment schedule, as long as the required minimum payment is made.

consumer loan Loan involving specific agreed-upon terms and a scheduled repayment plan.

Consumer loans are more formal, requiring an application and an agreement on specific terms of the loan. Consumer loans are usually made for a specific purpose and have a repayment schedule. We will discuss consumer loans in Chapter 5.

The type of credit extended by most credit card issuers is called open account credit. **Open account credit** is credit extended to the card holder before purchases are made. The card holder is free to charge goods and services up to the limit of credit available on the card without preapproval of the purchase by the credit card issuer.

open account credit Credit extended to a credit card holder before any purchases are made.

You are probably already familiar with how open account credit works. You apply for a credit card from a retailer, bank, or other issuer. They review your application. If you are found acceptable, a certain amount of credit is assigned to your account and a credit card is issued. You are then able to make purchases and receive cash advances using the credit card, up to the available limit of credit. If you use the card to make a purchase or to receive a cash advance, the issuer sends you a monthly statement. You may pay the entire balance due, the minimum amount due, or any amount between these two values. If you carry a balance on the account, the credit card issuer charges interest on the outstanding balance. How to obtain a credit card and the terms of credit are discussed in greater detail later in this chapter.

You should not confuse credit cards with debit cards, which were discussed in the previous chapter. A debit card provides an immediate, direct transfer of funds from your bank account to the recipient's account. Credit cards involve the use of open account credit with repayment at some later date.

Using consumer credit as a means of payment is increasing in popularity. In 1990, 84 percent of sales were made by cash or check and only about 15 percent of sales were made on credit cards.[1] By 1994, sales paid for with cash or checks had declined to 80 percent of sales, whereas credit card sales had increased to 19 percent. It is projected that by 2005, sales by cash and check will drop to about 49 percent, and credit sales will account for around 42 percent of all sales. This information is summarized in Exhibit 4.1.

The two most popular credit cards are Visa and MasterCard. In 1995, there were 213.4 million Visa cards and 154.7 million MasterCards outstanding in the United States.[2] It is estimated that by the year 2000, there will be about 1.3 billion credit cards in circulation in the United States and that annual credit card sales will approach $1.4 trillion.[3]

More than 63 percent of families have at least one general-purpose credit card.[4] The median balance owed on general-purpose cards in 1992 was $1,000. Only 54 percent of families reported that they almost always paid off the credit balance each month, whereas 46 percent carried a balance from month to month.

Exhibit 4.1

Means of Payment for Goods and Services
U.S. transaction volume and percentage of market, in billions.

Payment System	1990		1994		2005*	
	Amount	% of Total	Amount	% of Total	Amount	% of Total
PAPER†	$2,509.44	84.4%	$2,889.40	79.8%	$3,306.19	48.6%
Personal Checks	1,822.05	61.3	2,077.93	57.4	2,118.48	31.1
Cash	579.32	19.5	664.40	18.4	948.01	13.9
CARDS§	442.71	14.9	686.00	19.0	2,824.86	41.5
Credit Cards	430.96	14.5	648.18	17.9	2,194.54	32.2
Debit Cards	11.74	0.4	36.89	1.0	592.97	8.7
ELECTRONIC	19.96	0.7	43.70	1.2	674.52	9.9
TOTAL	$2,972.10	100.0%	$3,619.10	100.0%	$6,805.57	100.0%

* Forecast.
† Includes personal checks, cash, money orders, traveler's checks, food stamps, and official checks.
§ Includes credit cards, debit cards, and prepaid cards.
Source: unknown.

Advantages of Consumer Credit

Using consumer credit has a number of advantages, including safety, convenience, flexibility, "float," and bonuses.

■ *Safety.* Credit cards are safe because when you carry credit cards you don't need to carry large amounts of cash. If your credit cards are lost or stolen, your liability is limited on a per-card basis. Furthermore, several forms of protection are available to credit card holders and credit applicants. This protection consists of legislative acts regulating the treatment of credit applicants and credit card holders, as well as private insurance designed to address the risks associated with credit. These topics are discussed in greater detail at the end of this chapter.

■ *Convenience.* The wide acceptability of credit cards makes using them convenient for card holders. When you use credit cards to make purchases, you don't need to withdraw funds from the bank, carry a checkbook, or apply for a loan each time you make a purchase.

■ *Flexibility.* Credit cards also offer financial flexibility. The card holder has a ready line of credit available without having to go through a loan approval process before each purchase. Although you must repay the entire balance due to avoid finance charges, you are required to pay only the minimum amount due, which is usually a small percentage of the total due. Credit cards provide flexibility if you are facing a short-term liquidity problem. Perhaps you are short of cash at the present time but will have funds available in one month, when the credit card statement is issued. Using a credit card provides the financial flexibility to overcome this short-term liquidity problem. As we shall see, however, the price of payment flexibility is a high interest rate on the unpaid balance.

float With respect to credit cards, the ability to use funds between the date of the purchase and the date payment is made.

■ *"Float."* Another advantage of using credit cards is **float**—the ability to use funds between the date of the purchase and the date that you make the payment. When you use cash for a purchase, the cash is gone—you no longer have the use of this money. But purchases charged after the close of the previous credit card statement will not appear until the next statement is sent to you. After you receive the statement, you normally have ten days to two weeks to make a payment and avoid finance charges. In reality, you are receiving an interest-free loan for the purchase price of the goods or services charged until you actually make the payment.

If you have funds on hand to pay for the item and use credit instead, you can actually earn interest on the funds before paying the credit card issuer. For example, suppose you charge an airline ticket that costs $300 rather than paying for the ticket in cash. While waiting for your credit card statement, you keep the $300 in an interest-bearing checking account at your bank. The $300 earns interest for you until you pay for the ticket when you receive the credit card statement.

■ *Bonuses.* Many credit card bonus offers are available. These bonuses take several forms, including cash rebates, credits toward the purchase of something, or some other type of service or privilege. Some cards (such as Discover) offer a cash rebate equal to a percentage of credit card purchases. Other cards offer a rebate in the form of credit against the purchase price of big-ticket items, such as automobiles and computers. Airline charge cards offer frequent flier miles for credit card purchases. Prestige cards (such as "gold" or "platinum" cards) offer travel accident insurance, collision coverage for rental cars, and other benefits. Some bonus benefits available through popular cards are discussed in Exhibit 4.2.

Disadvantages of Consumer Credit

Of course, using consumer credit also has some disadvantages, including the cost of consumer credit (fees and interest charges) and overutilization of credit cards.

Exhibit 4.2

Credit Card Bonus Offers

As an inducement to accept and use their credit card, many issuers offer bonuses. These bonuses come in a variety of forms, including cash rebates, credit toward gifts, frequent traveler credits, dollars off the purchase price of an auto, discounts on the purchase of financial services products and computers, and interest payment rebates. Here is a sampling of some of the deals available.

CREDIT CARD	PROGRAM	INTEREST RATE	ANNUAL FEE*	COMMENTS
Charles Schwab VISA 800 435-4000	One percent of purchases (one credit for each $100 charged) goes toward Schwab financial products.	11.9%V	None†	$20,000 charged annually only earns $200 toward a *Value Line* subscription.
Apple Citibank VISA/MasterCard 800 374-9999	Cardholders earn a 2.5% rebate on purchases up to $3,000 and 5% on purchases over $3,000 that can be applied toward Apple Computer products.	Prime plus 9.4%	$20	To earn the $500 maximum annual rebate, you'd have to charge $11,500.
Shell MasterCard 800 993-8111	Rebates 2% toward Shell merchandise and 1% toward gas to a total of $70. After $70, cardholders only receive 1% gas rebate.	Prime plus 11.4%	$20	To earn the first $70 in rebates, you'd have to spend $2,333.
American Express Membership Miles 800 297-6453	You earn one mile for every dollar charged. Cardholders can now also earn points toward hotel stays.	None	$25	Round-trip coach ticket (20,000 miles) requires $20,000 in charges.§
Nordstrom VISA 800 935-4210	Cardholders earn a 1 to 5% annual rebate that can be applied to Nordstrom purchases.	Prime plus 8.9%	$30	The full 5% rebate only applies to annual purchases over $5,000.
First Bank of South Dakota Worldperks VISA 800 360-2900	Each dollar charged earns one mile towards travel on Northwest Airlines.	Prime plus 9.75%	$55	Round-trip coach ticket (20,000 miles) requires $20,000 in charges.§
Merrill Lynch Omega VISA 800 854-7154	Offers a revolving line of credit based on value of investment securities held as collateral.	7.25%V	$65	For a $10,000 credit line, you must deposit securities worth $14,000.
Chase Manhattan CashBuilder VISA 800 AT-CHASE	Cardholders receive a 1% rebate on purchases and cash advances if monthly charges exceed $200; also, 10% rebate on monthly interest charges.	15.9%V	None	You must accumulate $500 in rebates or wait 3 years (which ever first) to receive any cash.
USAir/Nationsbank VISA 800 241-6295	Frequent Traveler Program grants one mile toward USAir travel for each dollar charged.	Prime plus 8.9%	$35	Round-trip coach ticket (20,000 miles) requires $20,000 in charges.§
American Express Optima 800/528-4800	Rewards program rebates points toward purchase of 80 different gifts for each dollar charged.	Prime plus 12.25% max	$15	You need to charge $150,000 to earn a free skiing trip to Colorado.
Fidelity Investor VISA/MasterCard 800 323-5353	A 1% rebate on purchases made up to $10,000 annually is held in a savings account paying 3.29% After $1,000, it can be transferred to Fidelity funds.	Prime plus 9.9%	None	If your monthly balance falls below $500, you're assessed a $2 fee fee; maximum annual rebate: $100.
First Chicago Mileage Plus VISA/MasterCard 800 368-4535	Grants one mile per each dollar charged, good toward travel on United Airlines; annual cap is 50,000 miles.	Prime plus 9.9%	$60	Round-trip coach ticket (20,000 miles) requires $20,000 in charges.§

* Some cards are free for the first year.   † If you don't charge a minimum of six times per year, the annual fee is $30.
§ By early 1995, the minimum mileage requirement for most domestic awards was 25,000 miles.
Source: *Your Money*, October/November 1994, p. 69. Reprinted with permission.

■ *Fees and Interest Charges.* Many credit card issuers charge an annual fee for the use of the card. Some card issuers also charge fees if you do not pay at least a minimum amount before a specified date or if you exceed the limit of credit available. Credit card issuers also charge interest on unpaid balances. The interest rate charged on most cards is very high, with the average interest rate around 18 percent on an annual basis. In addition, some credit card issuers consider current purchases when computing interest charges.

■ *Overutilization.* Using a credit card too often or charging more than you can afford to repay can also create financial problems. Some people simply do not know how to manage their use of credit. They charge large balances, pay only the minimum amount due, and continue to charge even more. The popular press often reports on these credit abusers. Stories about individuals who take cash advances on one card to pay the minimum balance due on another card have become commonplace. As we shall see, credit card borrowing is one of the most expensive types of borrowing available. Some warning signs of credit abuse are discussed in Exhibit 4.3.

Establishing Consumer Credit

Consumers begin the steps necessary to establish credit long before making a formal credit application. In deciding whether to award you credit, credit card issuers examine many factors, including your job, income, length of current residence, level of education, and current banking relationships. Credit card issuers are interested in whether you have an earned income, a stable work history, and good banking relationships since these variables indicate whether you have the ability to repay charged purchases.

Your first interaction with a credit card issuer was probably a credit card solicitation, an invitation for you to apply for a credit card. It is likely that you have received a number of letters or phone calls from credit card issuers asking you to apply for their cards. Credit card applications are a common sight on bulletin boards in college classrooms and dorms. Credit card issuers use direct mail and other media to distribute applications.

To answer a credit card solicitation, you complete a credit card application and return it to the credit issuer. A credit card application is a form requesting information that the credit issuer will use to assess your creditworthiness. A typical credit card application asks for your name, address, social security number, occupation, annual or monthly income,

Exhibit 4.3

Danger Signs of Credit Card Abuse

Are you headed for trouble with your credit cards? This quiz lists the danger signs of credit card abuse. If you answer true to six or more, you're headed for trouble. If you answer true to nine or more, you may have a serious problem with credit cards.

	True	False	
1.	☐	☐	You hide your monthly credit card statements, or the things you buy, so your family won't discover them.
2.	☐	☐	You spend more than 20 percent of your take-home pay on credit card payments.
3.	☐	☐	You're a juggler—you put off paying other bills so you can pay your credit cards on time.
4.	☐	☐	You've applied for a second credit card from a different bank that offers a higher credit limit.
5.	☐	☐	You usually pay only the minimum monthly payment.
6.	☐	☐	You charge more each month than you make in payments.
7.	☐	☐	You've used the cash advance on one credit card to make payments on other credit cards.
8.	☐	☐	You've seriously thought about getting a consolidation loan to pay off your credit cards.
9.	☐	☐	You really believe that someday you'll get the money to pay off all of your debts.
10.	☐	☐	You've received a phone call about your delinquent account.
11.	☐	☐	You pay your bills on time, but you continue using credit because you quickly run out of cash.
12.	☐	☐	You don't know how much you owe—within $50.
13.	☐	☐	The balance in your savings account is shrinking.
14.	☐	☐	You usually borrow from friends or relatives to make ends meet each month.
15.	☐	☐	Life would be difficult if you lost all of your credit cards.

Source: National Foundation for Consumer Credit. Reprinted with permission.

and employer, as well as information about the financial institution where you bank. The application may also ask about other sources of income and other credit cards that you have. A sample credit card application targeted at students is shown in Exhibit 4.4.

Exhibit 4.4

Sample Credit Card Application

The credit card application reproduced below is targeted at students. Because income is positively correlated with educational level, as a student, you are a prime credit card prospect.

A FEW QUESTIONS. NO WORRIES.

CHOOSE ONE: ____ | Visa | ____ | MC |

PLEASE TELL US ABOUT YOURSELF

Print Full Name: First, Middle Initial, Last		Social Security Number	Your Date of Birth (Month/Day/Year)	
Your Permanent Home Address	Apt. No.	City or Town	State	Zip
First and Last Name under which phone is listed with Directory Assistance		Your Permanent Area Code and Phone Number	Mother's Maiden Name	

PLEASE TELL US ABOUT YOUR SCHOOL

Full Name of College/University (Please Do Not Abbreviate)		Branch/Campus	Official School Zip	
Your Mailing Address at School (If different from above)	Apt. No.	City or Town	State	Zip
Your Area Code and Phone Number at School		First and Last Name under which school phone is listed with Directory Assistance		
Your Class: ❑ Fresh ❑ Junior ❑ Grad ❑ Other ❑ Soph ❑ Senior ❑ Faculty/Staff	Expected Graduation Date Mo/Yr	Permanent U.S. Resident? ❑ Yes ❑ No	Address to which you want card and billing statement mailed? ❑ Permanent ❑ School	

OTHER IMPORTANT INFORMATION

Money Market/Interest-Bearing Checking/NOW Account ❑ Yes ❑ No Bank Name	Annual Income* Source(s): ❑ Full-time job ❑ Summer job ❑ Savings $ _____ ❑ Part-time job ❑ Allowance ❑ Stipend
Checking Account ❑ Yes ❑ No Bank Name	*You do not have to include spouse's income, alimony, child support or separate maintenance payments paid if you are not relying on them to establish credit worthiness. Financial aid and tuition are not applicable as sources of income.
Savings Account CDs/Treasury Bills ❑ Yes ❑ No Bank Name	Name of Employer (Present, Future or Previous Summer) Employer Area Code and Phone Number

VERIFICATION OF SCHOOL ENROLLMENT

Please include a legible copy of one of the following: ❑ The front and back of your VALIDATED Student I.D. for current semester.
❑ PAID tuition bill for current semester.

Your application cannot be processed without the information and will be substantially delayed if you omit any information requested. (Be sure the copy shows your name, the date and your current enrollment status. Photocopy both sides if necessary.)

PLEASE SIGN HERE

I certify that I meet and agree to all Citibank credit terms and conditions. Please allow 30 days to process this application.

X _____

Applicant's Signature   Date

Source: Citibank. Reprinted with permission.

Suppose you complete the application and return it to the credit issuer. What happens then? Once the completed application has been received, the credit card issuer will perform a credit investigation. A **credit investigation** is a thorough review and examination of the credit applicant. Typically, as part of the investigation, the credit card company will verify the data you supplied on the application. It will also perform additional analysis, such as checking credit references.

As part of the credit investigation, the credit card issuer will probably also request a copy of your credit report. A **credit report** is a detailed record of an individual's credit history that provides some of the same information requested in the application as well as additional data. Credit reports also include a record of unsatisfied judgments, bankruptcy filings, former addresses, other outstanding credit cards, and current status of other outstanding credit cards (for example, whether you pay on time and if a balance is owed that is past due).

Organizations known as credit bureaus prepare credit reports. A **credit bureau** collects credit-related data about individuals who have been granted credit and makes the data available to interested parties. There are three national credit bureaus: Experian (formerly called TRW), Equifax, and Trans-Union. Credit card issuers obtain detailed credit reports from these credit bureaus.

As a consumer, you should periodically check your credit report to verify that it is accurate. A sample credit report is provided in Exhibit 4.5.

In deciding whether to approve your application and in determining how much credit to grant if the application is approved, credit card issuers use a technique called credit scoring. **Credit scoring** is a system in which point values are assigned to responses to a number of questions on the credit application. The credit decision is based upon the applicant's total score. For example, a bank that issues credit cards may assign point values to responses relating to a number of variables, such as annual income, form of housing (renting versus owning), outstanding loans, employment, bank accounts, length of current residence, other credit cards, and credit history. An applicant might receive 20 points for an annual income over $75,000 a year, 15 points for an annual income between $50,000 and $75,000, 10 points for an income between $25,000 and $50,000, and 5 points for an income less than $25,000. Point values are assigned to the other variables in a similar fashion. Applicants who have a total score above the required number of points are approved for credit, and the credit card is issued. Some credit issuers have developed detailed models that attempt to predict which applicants will be the best credit risks.

If your credit card application is rejected, you should contact the credit issuer to determine why they denied your application. Some typical reasons that credit card applications are rejected include insufficient

credit investigation A thorough review of data supplied by a credit applicant.

credit report A detailed record of an individual's credit history.

credit bureau An organization that collects credit-related data about individuals and makes the data available to interested parties.

credit scoring A system in which point values are assigned to responses to questions on the credit application; the results are used in deciding whether to approve an application and how much credit to grant.

Consider This

Equifax has an Internet site at:

http://www.equifax.com/

Exhibit 4.5

How to Read Your Credit Report

The decision to grant or deny you credit may hinge on your credit report. Although a credit report provides a wealth of information about you, you may not be able to tell what that information is unless you know the "code." An annotated sample credit report from Equifax is shown here.

I.D. Section

Your name, current address and other identifying information reported by your creditors.

Credit History Section

List of both open and closed accounts.

Collection Accounts

Accounts that your creditors turned over to a collection agency.

Courthouse Records

Public record items obtained from local, state and federal courts.

Additional Information

Primarily consists of former addresses and employments reported by your creditors.

Inquiry Section

List of businesses that have received your credit report in the last 24 months.

Please address all future correspondence to the address shown on the right.

CREDIT REPORTING OFFICE
BUSINESS ADDRESS
CITY, STATE 00000
PHONE NUMBER

The Name and Address of the office you should contact if you have any questions or disagreement with your credit report

JOHN DOE
123 HOME ADDRESS
CITY, STATE 00000

DATE 03/04/94
SOCIAL SECURITY NUMBER 123-45-6789
DATE OF BIRTH 04/19/57
SPOUSE JANE

CREDIT HISTORY

Company Name	Account Number	Whose Acct.	Date Opened	Months Re-viewed	Date of Last Activity	High Credit	Terms	Balance	Past Due	Status	Date Reported
SEARS	11251514	J	05/86	66	12/93	3500		0		R1	02/94
AMOUNT IN H/C COLUMN IS CREDIT LIMIT											
CITIBANK	2953900000100473	I	11/86	48	11/93	9388	48M	0		I1	12/93
DINERS	355411251511	A	06/87	24	10/92	500		0		01	12/93
CLOSED ACCOUNT											
CHASE	54229778	I	05/85	48	01/94	5000	340	3000	680	R3	02/94

>>> PRIOR PAYING HISTORY - 30(03) 60(04) 90+(01) 08/92-R2, 02/92-R3, 10/91-R4 <<<

>>> COLLECTION REPORTED 06/90; ASSIGNED 09/89 TO PRO COLL (800) 555-1234
CLIENT-ABC HOSPITAL; AMOUNT-$978; STAT UNPAID 06/90; BALANCE-$978 06/90
DATE OF LAST ACTIVITY 09/89; INDIVIDUAL; ACCOUNT NUMBER 787652JC

>>>>>>>>>>>>>>>>>>> COLLECTION AGENCY TELEPHONE NUMBER(S) <<<<<<<<<<<<<<<<<<<<
PRO COLL (800) 555-1234

********************COURTHOUSE RECORDS**********************

>>> LIEN FILED 03/92; FULTON CTY; CASE NUMBER-32114; AMOUNT-$26667; CLASS-CITY/
COUNTY; RELEASED 07/92; VERIFIED 09/93

>>> BANKRUPTCY FILED 12/89; NORTHERN DIST CT; CASE NUMBER-673HC12; LIABILITIES-
$15787; PERSONAL; INDIVIDUAL; DISCHARGED; ASSETS-$780

>>> JUDGMENT FILED 07/91; FULTON CTY; CASE NUMBER-898872; DEFENDANT-JOHN DOE
AMOUNT-$8984; PLANTIFF-ABC REAL ESTATE; SATISFIED 03/92; VERIFIED 05/93

********************ADDITIONAL INFORMATION**********************
FORMER ADDRESS 456 JUPITER RD, ATLANTA, GA 30245

FORMER ADDRESS P.O. BOX 2138, SAVANNAH, GA 31406

LAST REPORTED EMPLOYMENT - ENGINEER, SPACE PATROL

****************COMPANIES THAT REQUESTED YOUR CREDIT HISTORY*************

03/04/94	EQUIFAX	02/12/94	MACYS
12/16/93	PRM VISA	08/01/93	AM CITIBANK
06/11/93	NATIONS BANK	04/29/93	GE CAPITAL
02/17/93	JC PENNEY	02/12/93	AR SEARS

STATUS
Type of Account
O = Open (entire balance due each month)
R = Revolving (payment amount variable)
I = Installment (fixed number of payments)
Timeliness of Payment
0 - Approved not used; too new to rate
1 = Paid as agreed
2 = 30+ days past due
3 = 60+ days past due
4 = 90+ days past due
5 = 120+ days past due or collection account
7 = Making regular payments under wage earner plan or similar arrangement
8 = Repossession
9 = Charged off to bad debt

WHOSE ACCOUNT: Indicates who is responsible for the account and the type of participation you have with the account.
J = Joint
I = Individual
U = Undesignated
A = Authorized user
T = Terminated
M = Maker
C = Co-Maker/Co-Signer
B = On behalf of another person
S = Shared

THE FOLLOWING INQUIRIES ARE NOT REPORTED TO BUSINESSES:
PRM—This type of inquiry means that only your name and address were given to a credit grantor so they could offer you an application for credit. (PRM inquiries remain for six months.)
AM or AR—These inquiries indicate a periodic review of your credit history by one of your creditors. (AM and AR inquiries remain for six months.)
EQUIFAX, ACIS or UPDATE—These inquiries indicate Equifax's activity in response to your contact with us for either a copy of your credit report or a request for research.
PRM, AM, AR, EQUIFAX, ACIS and UPDATE inquiries do not show on credit reports that businesses receive, only on copies provided to you.
Source: Equifax. Reprinted with permission.

income, unsatisfied financial judgments, and lack of an established history of paying bills. You can establish such a record by making mortgage or rental payments and paying utility bills. You may also consider taking out a small loan from your financial institution and repaying it or obtaining a credit card from a local retailer, as Tom Blake did in the chapter introduction. Credit cards issued by retailers are often easier to obtain than credit cards issued by banks. If your credit card application was denied because of previous credit and borrowing problems, you may have to consider a collateralized (secured) credit card, discussed later in this chapter.

Managing Credit

Once you have qualified for credit, it is important that you use it in an appropriate way. Credit management refers to using credit effectively. To be a good credit manager, you need to know how much credit you can afford to use, understand credit terms, and be able to interpret credit card statements.

How Much Credit Can You Afford?

There are several measures of the amount of credit that you can afford to use. One commonsense rule of thumb is that you should never charge more than you can afford to repay. Although credit cards are easy to use, remember that if you do not repay the entire balance when due, interest is charged.

debt payments to income ratio The ratio of monthly debt payments, excluding mortgage debt, to monthly take-home pay.

Another measure of the amount of credit that you can afford is the debt payments to income ratio. The **debt payments to income ratio** is the ratio of monthly debt payments, excluding mortgage debt, to take-home pay:

$$\text{Debt Payments to Income Ratio} = \frac{\text{Monthly Credit Payments}}{\text{Monthly Take-Home Pay}}$$

This ratio simply determines what percentage of your monthly take-home pay is used to repay debts, including credit card payments, student loan payments, auto loans, and other personal loans. So if your take-home pay is $2,000 a month and your only monthly credit payment is $200 for credit card debt, your debt payments to income ratio is 10 percent.

Consider This

Financenter provides credit card information and calculations to help you figure out how much you can borrow, what your payments will be, and the like. Check out Financenter's site at:

http://www.financenter.com/

You should not view your credit card debt in isolation. Rather, you should consider all credit payments that you are required to make. If you do not have other obligations, you are able to manage a higher level of credit card debt. If you already have other sources of debt, you will not be

Insight   4.1   Credit Companies Catch Card Users Early

Nicole Walters, 20-year-old junior at the University of Texas, carries two Visa cards, two Mastercards, two department store credit cards—and two part-time jobs to dig herself out of debt.

"I was buying things here and there and all of a sudden, $4,000 later, those little things added up," Walters said. She recalls buying a $600 car stereo, some clothes and gas for her car, but nothing else major.

Just a few hours on the university campus here turned up nearly a dozen students with similar tales of woe: a 19-year-old freshman with five cards said he owed $2,200, a 22-year-old senior acknowledged running up $8,000 on eight cards and a 26-year-old senior described $9,000 in bills on eight cards.

The spending sprees weren't for school-related essentials, but for personal items and luxuries. For the card holders who graduate with thousands of dollars in student loans, too, managing the debt may amount to a crash course in personal finance.

Credit counselors in college towns across the country say students with large card debts are increasingly common.

"Five years ago, we weren't seeing anybody still in college with as much debt as we are seeing now," said Candace Acevedo of the San Francisco office of the Consumer Credit Counseling Service, a nonprofit group providing financial education and debt advice.

Five percent of the clients in Acevedo's debt management program are students with at least $5,000 in credit card debt, she said. And the group's other offices in big university cities such as Austin, Raleigh, N.C., and Columbia, Mo., report similar figures.

Although some students reach out to credit counseling agencies for help when their card bills become overwhelming, many resort to the most reliable creditors of all: Mom and Dad.

Thus, parents paying for books, tuition and housing may also wind up paying their son's or daughter's Visa and American Express bills. If they don't pick it up before, parents may be tempted to pay off card debt at college graduation so their children can embark on their working lives without a burden.

"I think it's the parents who really take the brunt of this," said Irene Leech, a credit counselor and assistant professor of consumer studies at Virginia Tech in Backsburg, Va. "Parents want their child to have the best,

able to carry as large a credit card balance. Personal finance experts suggest that the debt payments to income ratio should never exceed 20 percent, with 15 percent a more manageable level. If too large a percentage of your take-home pay is required to service outstanding debts, including credit card debt, you need to take corrective action, such as not making additional charges or attempting to repay the outstanding balance.

College students are not immune from overspending on credit cards. Card issuers hope to build a loyal customer base by extending credit to students who will have higher earned income after graduation. More and more students, however, are having difficulty in managing credit card debt. Insight 4.1 discusses the credit card problems faced by some college students.

so they do all they can to help their children deal with these debts."

For a student, a credit card is as readily available as a class syllabus. Card applications are found in bookstores, campus publications and student mailboxes. To attract students, card issuers offer free concerts, plane tickets, T-shirts, even candy.

According to Roper College Track, a research division of Roper Starch Worldwide, more than half of the 5.1 million full-time undergraduate students at four-year universities in the United States now have at least one major credit card.

In 1994, Americans used more than 350 million major credit cards—Visa, Discover, Mastercard and American Express—to purchase more than half a trillion dollars of goods and services. With that much plastic money coursing through the system, why are issuers bothering with relatively poor college students?

They want to build loyal customers at an early age. A study several years ago by *Marketing Week* magazine showed that 75 percent of college students keep their first card for 15 years, and 60 percent keep that card for life.

In addition, college students are not entirely without money. Roper says the average student has an annual income of $4,000.

But if a student owes $2,000 on a credit card, repaying the debt can take years, especially when interest rates rise. The recent increase in rates caught Kevin LeBlanc by surprise. LeBlanc, a senior at the University of Texas, has two major credit cards with $500 credit lines, both of which are at their limit.

"I just got a letter that said, 'We are changing your interest rate from 14.9 percent to 18.9 percent' and you can't do anything about it," he said.

Before the rate increase, LeBlanc said, his minimum pay-

ment "used to pay off a little bit of the balance." Now, he said, "all it does is pay my interest."

Overall delinquency rates on credit cards have been declining since 1989, when nearly 5 percent of card holders were behind in their payments. Last year, the delinquent portion fell to about 3 percent.

Although no statistics are available on late card payments by students, counselors suggest the group may be having more trouble than other borrowers. "I think it's a much bigger problem than is being recognized," said Allen Clary, a credit counselor in Raleigh, who figures that the average student in his program has $10,000 in card debt.

Credit Terms

credit terms The conditions under which credit is extended.

Credit terms are simply the conditions under which credit is extended to the card holder. The conditions specify such things as how much can be borrowed, annual fees, the interest rate charged, how finance charges are computed, minimum required payments, transaction fees, and cash advance provisions. Exhibit 4.6 displays typical credit card terms.

credit limit The maximum amount of credit provided.

Credit Limit. The **credit limit** is the maximum amount of credit that the issuer provides. This limit applies to the total outstanding balance. Thus, if you have a credit limit of $5,000, you can purchase a single item for $5,000 on credit if your current balance is zero. If you have an outstanding balance of $1,500, only $3,500 of additional credit is available. When

Exhibit 4.6

Sample Credit Terms Disclosure

Credit card issuers are required to disclose credit terms when issuing a credit card. The terms disclosed here are for a Gold MasterCard. Notice the "teaser" interest rate for the first six months, with a higher, variable rate thereafter. This card has no annual fee and uses the average daily balance method (excluding new purchases) to determine finance charges. A variety of fees are disclosed in the first two sections. Notice the fee for cash advances is 2 percent of the advance, subject to a $25 maximum. Although the actual credit terms vary from card to card, the format for disclosure is standard.

Transaction fee for purchases	The transaction fee for the purchase of wire transfers, money orders, bets, lottery tickets, and casino gaming chips is 2% of each such purchase; $2 minimum, $25 maximum.
Transaction fee for cash advances and fees for late payment or exceeding the credit limit	Transaction fee for bank and ATM cash advances: 2% of each cash advance; $2 minimum, $25 maximum. Transaction fee for Premium Access Checks* and Preferred Access Checks cash advances: 1% of each cash advance; $2 minimum, $10 maximum. Late-payment fee: $15; Over-the-credit-limit fee: $15.
Annual fees	NO ANNUAL FEE
Method of computing the balance for purchases	Average Daily Balance (including new purchases).
Grace period for repayment of balances for purchases	At least 25 days from statement closing date.
Variable rate information	The APR may vary. The APR is based upon the highest U.S. Prime Rate, as published in *The Wall Street Journal*, plus two margins. The first margin is 8.8 percentage points. The second margin is either 0 percentage points or 2.0 percentage points based upon your payment history. The current indexed APR is 16.55%.
Annual percentage rate (APR)	8.9% through your first 6 Statement Closing Dates, commencing on the month after your account is opened. Thereafter, the APR (applies to both new and outstanding cash advance balances) will be 16.55%, which may vary.

APR for cash advances will be 8.9% through your first six statement closing dates commencing on the month after your account is opened and may vary thereafter (applies to both new and outstanding cash advance balances); current indexed APR is 16.55%.

you repay the $1,500 balance, the entire credit limit, $5,000, will once again be available. Some retailers check to see if there is enough credit available before they will permit you to charge a purchase. Card issuers may charge a fee if you exceed your credit limit.

Your credit history, your income, and other factors determine your initial credit limit. Credit card issuers periodically increase the credit limit to keep pace with inflation and to recognize a card holder's demonstrated ability to manage credit purchases. You may be able to increase your credit limit by simply asking the card issuer to raise it.

annual fee With respect to credit cards, the yearly fee a card holder pays for having the use of the card. Not all credit cards require an annual fee.

Annual Fee. The **annual fee** is a yearly fee the card holder pays for having use of the credit card. Some credit cards charge no annual fee, whereas others charge $20, $25, or more for the right to carry and use the credit card. Consumers should consider annual fees when selecting which credit card to accept. Although credit cards that charge a fee may offer some added benefits, obviously the annual fee increases the cost of carrying the credit card.

In some cases, the annual fee may be "negotiable." Some credit card issuers will waive the fee or make other arrangements (for example, rebate the fee or offer a credit against the next monthly balance equal to the amount of the fee) in order to keep a valued card holder who is considering dropping the card.

Grace Period. Another important credit term is the length of the grace period. The **grace period** is the time (typically 25 to 30 days) from the statement closing date during which the card holder can pay the outstanding balance in full and not be assessed any finance charges. The grace period provides the "float" advantage discussed earlier in this chapter. Some credit card issuers have reduced or eliminated the grace period in an effort to increase revenues by collecting finance charges.

grace period The period, starting at the statement closing date, during which the card holder can pay the outstanding balance and not be assessed any finance charges.

Minimum Payment. The **minimum payment** is the lowest amount of the outstanding balance that the card holder is permitted to pay for the account to remain current. A **current account** is one in which the card holder is not behind in his or her payments. For example, an open account credit card may require the card holder to make a minimum payment of at least 5 percent of the outstanding balance plus any past due amount. Paying only the minimum amount, however, can be very costly. Exhibit 4.7 shows how many months it will take to repay specified levels of credit card debt for a given monthly payment at two different interest rates. Notice that for some debt levels, the debt is never retired because the payment is not large enough to cover the monthly interest charge on the debt.

minimum payment The lowest amount the card holder is permitted to pay for the account to remain current.

current account An account on which the card holder is not behind in his or her payments.

A **past due amount** is a required payment that the card holder did not make in time. Some credit card issuers charge a **late fee** if the card holder fails to pay at least the minimum amount by the date the payment is due. As we mentioned, making only the minimum payment is advantageous in terms of flexibility, but when you make the minimum payment rather than repaying the full amount, you must pay interest on the unpaid balance.

past due amount A payment not made in time.

late fee A fee assessed for late payment.

Finance Charges. **Finance charges** are interest charges levied on unpaid balances. Some credit cards use a fixed interest rate to determine interest charges. Others use a variable interest rate that changes over time. Often the variable rate is tied to some observable market rate, such as the prime rate. The **prime rate** is the interest rate banks charge their most creditworthy customers. For example, the credit card issuer might charge

finance charges Interest charges levied on unpaid debt.

prime rate The interest rate banks charge their most creditworthy customers.

Exhibit 4.7

How Long Does It Take to Pay Off Credit Card Debt?

Suppose that you have an outstanding balance on your credit card equal to the amount in the column on the left. The columns on the right show how many months it will take to repay the amount owed for a given monthly payment and a specified interest rate. The interest rates, stated as annual rates, were converted to monthly rates to determine the period of repayment. For example, if you owe $1,000 on a card that charges 18 percent annual interest (1.5 percent monthly), it will take you 24 months to repay the debt.

Amount Owed	$50 per month		$100 per month		$200 per month	
	18%	21%	18%	21%	18%	21%
$1,000	24 mos.	25 mos.	11 mos.	12 mos.	6 mos.	6 mos.
$2,500	94 mos.	120 mos.	32 mos.	34 mos.	14 mos.	15 mos.
$5,000	Never	Never	94 mos.	120 mos.	32 mos.	34 mos.
$7,500	Never	Never	Never	Never	56 mos.	62 mos.
$10,000	Never	Never	Never	Never	94 mos.	120 mos.

The calculations assume no additional charges are made on the credit card. "Never" indicates that the monthly payment is not large enough to ever repay the amount owed. For example, a $50 payment on a $5,000 balance with 18 percent annual interest (1.5 percent monthly) will not cover the interest charge for the first month. Rather than a declining balance, the amount owed would actually increase each month! The number of months is rounded up to the next full month.

teaser rate A low interest rate offered by a credit card issuer so as to attract new card holders.

annual percentage rate (APR) The actual rate of interest charged on an outstanding balance.

"the prime rate plus 6.9 percent." If the prime rate is 10 percent, the rate applied will be 16.9 percent. Some credit card issuers offer "teaser" rates. A **teaser rate** is a low interest rate offered by a credit card issuer as an inducement for you to become a card holder. Teaser rates are usually good for only a specified time period or apply only to the balance on another card that you transfer to the new card.

Credit issuers are required to disclose the annual percentage interest rate they charge on outstanding balances. The **annual percentage rate (APR)** is the actual rate of interest charged on the outstanding balance. Some card holders will pay no interest since they repay the amount due each month. Others will pay large amounts of interest because they carry a large balance and pay only the minimum due. Although the actual interest expense will vary according to the card holder's balance, the interest rate will be the same—the APR.

This annual percentage rate, when converted to a monthly interest rate, is the rate applied to the balance to determine monthly finance charges. For example, a credit card issuer may apply an 18 percent APR to the outstanding balance. Since statements are mailed monthly, the equivalent monthly rate is 1.5 percent. Although 1.5 or 1.75 percent per month may sound harmless, these rates, when converted back to annual percentage rates, are 18 and 21 percent, respectively. The effective interest rate is even higher if the card holder carries a balance from month to month and interest is paid on interest. Interest rates charged on credit card balances are usually very high, typically around 18 percent. Many credit card issuers charge a higher interest rate on cash advances.

If you are able to repay the entire outstanding balance, you can avoid interest charges. If you pay less than the entire outstanding balance, you will be assessed finance charges. Credit card issuers are required to disclose how finance charges are calculated. Several methods may be used to calculate finance charges, including the previous balance method, the adjusted balance method, the average daily balance method (including or excluding new purchases), and the two-cycle balance method (including or excluding new purchases).

previous balance method A method of calculating finance charges in which finance charges are levied on the outstanding balance at the end of the previous period.

■ Under the **previous balance method,** the outstanding balance at the end of the previous period is the balance on which finance charges are levied. Assume your ending balance from the previous statement was $1,000 and the monthly interest rate is 1.50 percent. The finance charge would be $15.00 ($1,000 × .015). This technique ignores any payments made on the outstanding balance during the period, so it is advantageous for the credit card issuer since interest is charged on the entire previous balance.

adjusted balance method A method of calculating finance charges in which finance charges are levied on the outstanding balance less any payments made during the period.

■ Under the **adjusted balance method,** finance charges are calculated on the outstanding balance less any payments that you make during the period. Returning to our previous example, assume that you make a payment of $400 on the tenth day of the statement period. Your adjusted balance at the end of the period would be $600 ($1,000 − $400), and finance charges would be levied on this amount. The credit card issuer would charge you $9 in interest ($600 × .015) for the period. Since this method considers the reduction in the outstanding balance because of your payment, it is advantageous for the card holder.

average daily balance method A method of calculating finance charges in which the average outstanding daily balance is calculated and used as the basis for finance charges.

■ The most commonly used method of calculating finance charges is the average daily balance method. Under the **average daily balance method,** the average outstanding daily balance is calculated, and finance charges are based on this amount. New charges made during the period may or may not be considered in calculating the average daily balance. Continuing with our previous example, we assumed that the original balance was $1,000 and that $400 was paid on the tenth day of the 30-day statement period. Further assume that $200 in additional charges were made on the 20th day of the period. Exhibit 4.8 shows calculation of finance charges using the average daily balance method, including and excluding new charges.

two-cycle balance method A method of calculating finance charges in which finance charges are based on the sum of average daily balances for the present and previous billing periods.

■ The final method of calculating finance charges is the **two-cycle balance method.** Under the two-cycle balance method, finance charges are

Exhibit 4.8

Finance Charges Using the Average Daily Balance Method

The average daily balance method bases finance charges on the average balance outstanding during the statement period, including or excluding new purchases. In our example, we assume the starting balance was $1,000. On the 10th day of the 30-day period, a $400 payment was received. On the 20th day, an additional $200 was charged. The average daily balance including and excluding new purchases is calculated as follows:

Including New Purchases				
Days		Balance		Weighted Balance
10	×	$1,000	=	$10,000
10	×	600	=	6,000
10	×	800	=	8,000
30				$24,000

Excluding New Purchases				
Days		Balance		Weighted Balance
10	×	$1,000	=	$10,000
20	×	600	=	12,000
30				$22,000

Average Daily Balance $= \dfrac{\$24,000}{30} = \$800$

Average Daily Balance $= \dfrac{\$22,000}{30} = \$733.33$

Once the average daily balance is calculated, finance charges are levied upon the balance. Assuming a 1.5 percent monthly interest rate, the finance charges, respectively, are:

$$\$800 \times .015 = \$12 \qquad\qquad \$733.33 \times .015 = \$11$$

In this example, the card holder would pay $12 in finance charges if new purchases are considered, and $11 if new purchases are not considered.

based on the sum of average daily balances for the present and previous billing period. Obviously, this practice results in higher interest charges for consumers unless the entire balance is repaid each month. As with the average daily balance method, the two-cycle method can be calculated including or excluding new purchases.

Returning to the previous example, assume that the average daily balance for the previous 30-day period was $1,000 and that no new purchases were made during the period. The average daily balance for the present period, as shown in Exhibit 4.8, is $800 considering new purchases, and $733.33 not considering new purchases. Under two-cycle billing, the average daily balance for the previous and current period are summed to determine the base upon which finance charges are assessed. Considering new purchases, the total balance is $1,800 ($1,000 + $800), and the finance charge is $27 ($1,800 × .015). Not considering new purchases, the total balance is $1,733.33 ($1,000 + $733.33), and the finance charge is $26 ($1,733.33 × .015). Again, notice that the finance charge is higher because the interest rate is applied to a higher base value.

As you can see, the method of calculating finance charges makes an important difference if you carry a balance on your card.

Cash Advances. In addition to using the credit card to pay for goods and services, many credit cards permit the card holder to take cash advances. A **cash advance** is simply a cash loan to the card holder through the credit card. The ability to obtain cash quickly through this provision can be helpful in case of emergency. However, using credit card cash advances is expensive for two reasons. First, there is usually a fee levied if you take a cash advance. The fee may be a flat dollar amount or a percentage of the cash advance. Second, interest begins to be charged immediately on cash advances.

cash advance With respect to credit cards, a cash loan made to a credit card holder through use of the credit card.

Credit Card Statement

Credit card holders are sent credit card statements periodically, typically once a month. A **credit card statement** is a summary of the credit card account activity during the previous time period. The statement shows new charges and cash advances, payments made by the card holder during the previous period, finance charges levied, the outstanding balance, the amount of credit available, and the minimum payment due. Many of these values depend on the credit terms of the account. An annotated credit card statement is provided in Exhibit 4.9. Credit card holders should review the statement each month to verify that the charges are correct.

credit card statement A summary of credit card account activity during the previous billing period.

Types of Credit Cards

Credit cards may look the same, but there are some major differences in the various types of cards. These differences involve where the card is accepted, payment terms, account conditions, and special benefits. The major types of credit cards are bank cards, retail credit cards, and travel and entertainment cards.

Bank Cards

Bank cards are open account credit cards issued by banks, other financial institutions, and some nonfinancial institutions that allow the card holder to charge the purchase of goods and services wherever the card is accepted and to receive cash advances. Visa, MasterCard, and Discover are the most popular and most widely accepted bank cards. Although financial institutions are the most frequent bank card issuers, some

bank card Open account credit card, issued by banks, other financial institutions, and some nonfinancial institutions that allows the card holder to charge goods and services wherever the card is accepted and also to receive cash advances.

Exhibit 4.9

Understanding Credit Card Statements

Knowing how to read your statement can help you to monitor spending, reduce interest payments, catch errors, and more.

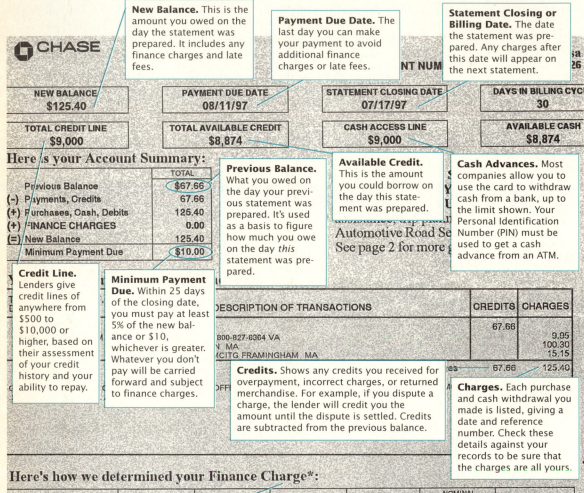

New Balance. This is the amount you owed on the day the statement was prepared. It includes any finance charges and late fees.

Payment Due Date. The last day you can make your payment to avoid additional finance charges or late fees.

Statement Closing or Billing Date. The date the statement was prepared. Any charges after this date will appear on the next statement.

NEW BALANCE	PAYMENT DUE DATE	STATEMENT CLOSING DATE	DAYS IN BILLING CYCLE
$125.40	08/11/97	07/17/97	30

TOTAL CREDIT LINE	TOTAL AVAILABLE CREDIT	CASH ACCESS LINE	AVAILABLE CASH
$9,000	$8,874	$9,000	$8,874

Here's your Account Summary:

	TOTAL
Previous Balance	$67.66
(-) Payments, Credits	67.66
(+) Purchases, Cash, Debits	125.40
(+) FINANCE CHARGES	0.00
(=) New Balance	125.40
Minimum Payment Due	$10.00

Previous Balance. What you owed on the day your previous statement was prepared. It's used as a basis to figure how much you owe on the day *this* statement was prepared.

Available Credit. This is the amount you could borrow on the day this statement was prepared.

Cash Advances. Most companies allow you to use the card to withdraw cash from a bank, up to the limit shown. Your Personal Identification Number (PIN) must be used to get a cash advance from an ATM.

Credit Line. Lenders give credit lines of anywhere from $500 to $10,000 or higher, based on their assessment of your credit history and your ability to repay.

Minimum Payment Due. Within 25 days of the closing date, you must pay at least 5% of the new balance or $10, whichever is greater. Whatever you don't pay will be carried forward and subject to finance charges.

DESCRIPTION OF TRANSACTIONS	CREDITS	CHARGES
	67.66	
800-827-6364 VA		9.95
N MA		100.30
CITG FRAMINGHAM MA		15.15
	67.66	125.40

Credits. Shows any credits you received for overpayment, incorrect charges, or returned merchandise. For example, if you dispute a charge, the lender will credit you the amount until the dispute is settled. Credits are subtracted from the previous balance.

Charges. Each purchase and cash withdrawal you made is listed, giving a date and reference number. Check these details against your records to be sure that the charges are all yours.

Here's how we determined your Finance Charge*:

	MONTHLY PERIODIC RATE	AVERAGE DAILY BALANCE	PERIODIC / MIN. FINANCE CHARGE	TOTAL FINANCE CHARGE	NOMINAL ANNUAL PERCENTAGE RATE	ANNUAL PERCENTAGE RATE
Purchases	V 1.491%	$0.00	$0.00	$0.00	17.90%	0.00%
Cash	V 1.670%	$0.00	$0.00	$0.00	20.05%	0.00%

* Please see reverse side for balance computation method and other important information.

Finance Charge. This is the interest charged on the amount you owe. Two cards with the same finance charge won't necessarily cost you the same interest, even if you owe the same amount. That's because what you pay depends on how the company figures the balance on which they charge you interest.

nonfinancial organizations (such as General Electric, AT&T, and General Motors) also issue bank cards.

Banks and other organizations issue credit cards because they are profitable products. Many bank cards require card holders to pay an annual fee, and levy high interest rates on outstanding unpaid balances. In addition, the issuer pays the retailer less than the full value of the charged goods or services. Finally, the issuer collects penalties for failure to pay the minimum amount on time and fees for certain card services, such as issuing cash advances.

There are a number of specialized bank credit cards—cards that are designed for some special purpose. These cards include prestige cards, affinity cards, and collateralized (secured) cards.

prestige card Bank card that provides high credit limits and various other benefits to the card holder.

Prestige Cards. **Prestige cards** are bank cards that provide a high limit of credit and a variety of other benefits to the card holder. Examples of prestige cards include Visa Platinum and MasterCard Gold. Prestige cards are issued to higher-income individuals. Some prestige cards require an annual fee, whereas others do not. Besides the high credit limit, prestige cards commonly provide travel accident insurance, collision coverage on rental cars when the card is used to charge the rental, and other benefits. Although banks issue many prestige cards, travel and entertainment cards (discussed shortly) are also examples of prestige cards.

affinity card Bank card issued to individuals who have some common bond. Educational, religious, civic, and other groups sponsor affinity cards and in return receive some percentage of the profits from the card.

Affinity Cards. **Affinity cards** are bank credit cards issued to individuals who have some common bond or tie. Educational, religious, civic, sports, and charitable organizations sponsor affinity cards. In return for their sponsorship, a portion of the amount charged is donated to the organization. For example, a university alumni association may offer a credit card to all the graduates of the institution, with one-half of 1 percent of the amount charged donated to the university's general scholarship fund. Obviously, affinity cards are less profitable for issuing banks, and the issuer may attempt to recoup some of the loss through annual fees and higher interest rates. Since cash contributions to many of the organizations sponsoring affinity cards are tax deductible for the donor, it may be better to make separate donations to the organization and select a credit card that offers better credit terms.

collateralized, or secured, credit card Credit card that requires the card holder to maintain a specified dollar deposit with the issuer as a condition for the issuance and use of the card.

Collateralized (Secured) Cards. Whereas prestige cards cater to individuals with excellent credit histories and high incomes, **collateralized (secured) credit cards** are targeted at those individuals at the other end of the credit spectrum. A collateralized credit card is a type of credit card that requires the card holder to maintain a specified dollar deposit with the issuer as a condition for the issuance and use of the card. The deposit serves as security for the issuer if the card holder is unable to repay the

balance owed. Banks issue collateralized cards to individuals who have never been granted credit or who have failed to manage credit successfully in the past and are seeking to rebuild their credit worthiness. Once a collateralized card holder demonstrates that he or she can manage the use of credit, the issuer may waive the required deposit, or the card holder may be able to obtain a credit card from another issuer that does not require a deposit. Collateralized credit cards have the same physical appearance as other bank cards.

Retail Credit Cards

retail credit card Credit card issued by a retail establishment that can be used to purchase goods and services from that establishment.

A **retail credit card** is a credit card issued by a retail establishment that can be used to charge purchases of goods and services from that particular retailer. For example, retailers Sears, Penney's, Mobil, and Texaco issue charge cards that can be used to purchase goods and services at any of their retail establishments. Local retailers with single stores may also issue their own charge cards. Retail credit cards, like bank cards, permit the card holder to use open account credit. The card holder may repay the entire balance at the time of the statement, the minimum amount due, or any amount between these two values. Like bank cards, if you do not repay the entire balance due, you will be assessed finance charges.

Retail credit cards are often easier to obtain than bank credit cards. However, their acceptance is limited to the issuer's retail establishments. Individuals who have been denied bank credit cards because they do not have a credit history, as was the case for Tom Blake in the chapter introduction, may be able to obtain a retail credit card. By demonstrating the ability to manage a retail credit card, you may be able to obtain a bank card.

Travel and Entertainment Cards

travel and entertainment card Credit card that can be used to charge travel- and entertainment-related expenses, such as airline tickets, hotel rooms, and meals at restaurants.

Travel and entertainment cards are credit cards that can be used to charge travel- and entertainment-related expenses, including such things as airline tickets, hotel rooms, and meals at restaurants. Many retailers also accept travel and entertainment cards. Some common travel and entertainment cards include Diners Club, Carte Blanche, and American Express. (American Express also offers the Optima card, a traditional bank card, complete with open account credit.) Although similar to bank cards, travel and entertainment cards require you to pay the entire balance in full each time you receive an account statement. These cards are aimed at more affluent clientele and require the payment of an annual fee. There may also be an initiation fee the first year as a card holder.

Bank cards and travel and entertainment cards command the greatest share of the credit card market because more sellers accept them. Retail credit cards are limited in acceptability. Exhibit 4.10 provides worldwide data for the five largest credit cards: Visa, MasterCard, American Express, Discover, and Diner's Club.

Exhibit 4.10

Who's Who in the Credit Card Market
A breakdown of the worldwide market, based on 1995 data.

Card	Card holders (millions)	Point of Sale Volume (billions)	Market Share	Profile
VISA	86	$588	51%	Bank-run association uses cobranding; moving into debit, home banking; seeking exclusivity with banks; now signing up law firms, hospitals, gyms; has bylaw forbidding Visa-member banks to issue American Express
MASTERCARD	74	354	31	Bank-run association; playing catch-up to Visa; similar target customers and merchants but fewer rules for member banks; hasn't taken position on American Express
AMERICAN EXPRESS	22	158	14	Trying to move beyond personal charge card to wide variety of co-branded consumer and business credit cards; appealing to banks to overturn Visa bylaw and offer Amex products
DISCOVER	31	39	6	Dean Witter & Co. unit; fast growth as newcomer; uses simple, cash-back rebate concept and cards that target different market segments; U.S.-focused; challenging Visa bylaw with American Express
DINER'S CLUB	1	25	2	Citicorp subsidiary; charge cards only; strong overseas, primarily for business and travel customers; focused on airlines, restaurants and hotels; rewards program earns points for airlines and hotels

Source: *Who's Who in the Credit-Card Market*, 6/6/96. Reprinted by permission of *The Wall Street Journal*, ©1996 Dow Jones & Company, Inc. All Rights Reserved Worldwide.

Selecting the Best Card

Which credit card is best for you? You can determine the answer to this question only after examining your present financial position, credit history, spending patterns, preferences, credit card terms, and other variables. For example, if you normally do not pay the entire balance each month, look for a card with the lowest interest rate. If you always repay the entire balance before finance charges are levied, consider the card with the lowest annual fee. If you have been denied credit because you do not have an established credit history or because you have failed to manage credit effectively in the past, a collateralized credit card may be the answer.

Consider This

A tremendous amount of information on bank cards, including what banks are offering the most favorable rates, can be found at the RAM Research Group site at:

http://www.ramresearch.com/

Where can you get information on the best credit card deals? Several financial publications print listings of cards that have the lowest interest rates and the lowest annual fees. A sample listing appears in Exhibit 4.11.

The bonuses discussed earlier may also be of interest. If you enjoy traveling, an airline charge card that earns frequent flier miles with each charged purchase may be the card for you. Some brand-loyal vehicle purchasers ("I'd never drive anything but a Chevy") may find credit cards that offer rebates toward the purchase of vehicles enticing.

Whichever credit card you select, make sure that you read and understand the credit terms before accepting the card. Some credit cards have additional fees and terms that are unfavorable to consumers (for example, the two-cycle balance method used to calculate finance charges discussed earlier). Unfortunately, many consumers learn the hard way about unfavorable credit card terms.

Competition among credit card issuers has led many card holders to consider switching credit cards. Credit card surfing refers to transferring your balance to a new card that offers more favorable terms than the credit card you currently hold. Suppose you answer a solicitation for a card that does not require an annual fee for the first year and that offers

---

Exhibit 4.11

The Best Credit Card Deals

Some financial publications print a listing of the best credit card deals available, considering fees and interest rates. For card holders who carry a balance, the interest rate charged is the key concern. For card holders who pay the balance due each month, the annual fee becomes the key concern. Here is a sample listing from *Money* magazine.

FOR PEOPLE WHO CARRY A BALANCE				FOR PEOPLE WHO PAY IN FULL EACH MONTH			
Card Type National Average	Rate	Fee[2]	Telephone	Card Type National Average	Rate	Fee[2]	Telephone
STANDARD/18%				STANDARD			
Pulaski B&T (Ark.)	8.75%	$35	800-980-2265	USAA Fed. Svgs. (Texas)	12.78%	$0	800-922-9092
Wachovia Bank (Del.)	9.00	88	800-842-3262	Horizon B&T (Texas)	12.90	0	800-571-3462
Metropol. Natl. (Ark.)	9.96	25	800-883-2511	Cole Taylor Bank (Ill.)	14.90	0	800-727-2265
Federal Savings (Ark.)	10.20	33	800-374-5600	AFBA Industrial (Colo.)	15.00	0	800-776-2265
GOLD/17.02%				GOLD			
Pulaski B&T[1] (Ark.)	8.75	50	800-980-2265	USAA Fed. Svgs. (Texas)	12.78%	$0	800-922-9092
Wachovia Bank (Del.)	9.00	98	800-842-3262	Amalgam Bank[1] (Ill.)	13.50	0	800-365-6464
Federal Savings (Ark.)	10.20	48	800-374-5600	Union Planters[1] (Tenn.)	13.50	0	800-628-8946

Notes: Rates are as of April 25. All cards are variable rate. Selection is based on rates and annual fees.
[1]Mastercard only, all others are Mastercard/Visa. [2]Annual.
Source: *Bank Rate Monitor*™, www.bankrate.com. Reprinted with permission.

a low initial interest rate of 8.9 percent for the first year. During the year, you carry a large balance on the card. At the end of the year, you receive a notice stating that the annual fee for the second year is $25 and the interest rate will increase to 21 percent. What can you do?

One solution is to transfer your balance to another credit card that offers more favorable terms. Although transferring to a new credit card may offer some advantages, there could also be some hidden dangers. Insight 4.2 discusses some credit card surfing traps to avoid.

Consumer Credit Protection

Your rights as a credit card holder and credit applicant are protected through a number of important legislative acts. Private insurance coverages are also available to you as a credit card holder.

Legal Protection

Federal legislation was enacted to address a number of important concerns relating to credit. Federal legislative acts protecting the interests of credit card holders and credit card applicants are summarized in Exhibit 4.12. Some of the major issues addressed by these laws include discrimination in the awarding of credit, incomplete or unclear disclosure of credit terms, unfair billing and collection practices, correction of credit report errors, and credit card fraud.

Discrimination. As a credit card applicant, you are protected against discrimination in the awarding of credit by the Equal Credit Opportunity Act. This act prohibits discrimination on a number of grounds and requires that credit applicants be informed of the credit issuer's decision within 30 days of receiving the credit application. The original act prohibited discrimination based on gender and marital status. It was amended to also prohibit discrimination based on age, race, national origin, religion, and whether the applicant receives public assistance (welfare) benefits.

The act also addresses special credit problems that some women face. It requires creditors to report information on joint accounts to credit bureaus in both a husband's and a wife's name if both spouses use the account and are liable for account obligations. Prior to this change, creditors could report information in one name, usually the husband's. This practice created problems for a woman who wanted to obtain credit after divorce or the death of her husband because the credit history was only in the former husband's name.

Exhibit 4.12

Federal Legislative Acts Protecting Credit Card Holders and Credit Card Applicants

Act	Date	Important Provisions
TRUTH IN LENDING ACT	1969, amended in 1971 and 1982	Requires lenders to disclose credit terms (fees, interest rate charged [APR], loan conditions, etc.) before extending credit. Prohibits lenders from issuing cards that have not been requested. Limits a card holder's liability for lost or stolen credit cards to $50 per card.
FAIR CREDIT REPORTING ACT	1971, amended in 1994	Gives consumers the right to review their credit files and to have errors in the files corrected. Consumers also have the right to know of any credit reporting service that provided a report that led to the denial of credit or increased borrowing costs.
EQUAL CREDIT OPPORTUNITY ACT	1975, amended in 1977	Prohibits discrimination in the granting of credit based on gender, marital status, age, race, or national origin. Creditors must report information to credit bureaus in the names of both spouses if a husband and wife have a joint account and each is liable for payments due. Alimony and child support must be regarded as income.
FAIR CREDIT BILLING ACT	1975	Regulates billing practices of creditors and sets forth procedures for correction of errors in credit card statements. Permits consumers to withhold payment for charges if goods purchased are defective.
FAIR DEBT COLLECTION PRACTICES ACT	1977	Protects consumers from unreasonable attempts by debt collectors to collect past due balances. Since creditors may enlist a collection service or "sell" debts to a collection agency, debtors must be notified in writing of the amount owed and to whom it is owed.
FAIR CREDIT AND CHARGE CARD DISCLOSURE ACT	1988	Requires direct mail solicitations and credit card applications to disclose important information (APR, annual fees, grace period, and other financial terms).

Disclosure of Credit Terms. You are protected against incomplete and unclear disclosure of credit terms by the Truth in Lending Act (also known as the Consumer Credit Protection Act). This act requires lenders to disclose specific credit terms in a consistent manner. Important information that must be disclosed includes fees, the annual percentage interest rate charged, how finance charges are computed, and other credit terms. Because of this act, you can make a more informed decision about credit since you can compare relevant information that has been prepared in a consistent fashion.

Credit card issuers who use direct mail solicitations are also required to disclose credit terms in a consistent manner under the Fair Credit and

Charge Card Disclosure Act. This act also requires credit card issuers to notify you before your account is renewed.

Billing and Collection Practices. What do you do if you find an error in your credit card statement? You are protected against unfair billing practices by the Fair Credit Billing Act. This act regulates billing practices and sets forth procedures for correcting errors in your credit card statement. If there is a billing error, you are required to notify the credit issuer within 60 days of receiving the statement. The credit issuer is required to resolve the dispute within 90 days. The act also permits you to withhold payment for certain charges if the goods purchased were defective.

You are also protected against unreasonable collection practices by creditors if your account is past due. Often creditors contract with collection agencies or "sell" overdue debts to bill collectors. Under the Fair Debt Collection Practices Act, you must be notified in writing of the amount owed and to whom the debt is owed. Certain practices by debt collectors, such as repeated contacts, contacts at unreasonable hours, misrepresentation, and threats are forbidden under the act.

Correction of Credit Report Errors. Suppose your application for credit is denied, and you believe that credit should have been granted. What recourse do you have? Under the Fair Credit Reporting Act, you have the right to review your credit file, to have errors in the credit file corrected, and to be given the name and address of any credit reporting service that provided reports that led to denial of credit. If there is a dispute between you and the credit bureau over the accuracy of information in your file, the credit bureau must reexamine the disputed information. You have the right to have a statement of your own (100 words or less) inserted in the file explaining disputed information.

Credit Card Fraud. Several legislative acts, including those listed in Exhibit 4.12, contain provisions designed to reduce credit card fraud. For example, credit card issuers must disclose credit card terms and are prohibited from sending out credit cards that have not been requested. Credit card fraud, however, remains a billion-dollar-a-year problem. Insight 4.3 discusses some simple things that you can do as a credit card holder to reduce your chance of being a victim of credit card fraud (see page 136).

Insurance Protection

Insurance protection is available to protect you if your credit cards are lost or stolen. Insurance protection is also available to repay the outstanding balance in certain situations.

Insight   4.2   Surfing Traps That Wipe Out Your Savings

It doesn't take an act of great skill to catch a low-rate credit card offer: Your mailbox is probably overflowing with them. But when the rate is about to spike and your balance is still high, you're a candidate for credit card "surfing"—transferring your balance to a new card with another low-rate offer.

Surfing can save balance carriers a lot of money by keeping their interest rate in the 6%-to-9% range, rather than the 12%-to-20% range that it jumps to after the introductory period is over. If you're carrying, say, a $5,000 balance at 18.2% (the average credit card rate nationwide), lowering the rate to 5.9% will save you $615 a year.

But it can take a bit of fancy footwork to hop onto the low-rate wave from another issuer without wiping out. A tantalizing offer could contain fees or conditions that cancel your savings.

"What the bold print says may have little to do with the actual deal," warns Ruth Sussswein, executive director of Bankcard Holders of America. "Most important is the rate: what it is, what it applies to, how long it lasts, where it's going."

That means poring over the fine print or working the phones to avoid these surfing traps:

A Too-High Rate

Among the major national low-rate players are AFBA Industrial Bank (800-776-2265), Oak Brook (800-536-3000) and Wachovia (800-842-3262). Their standard offers—generally the prime rate (recently 8.5%) for a year, followed by a rate in the teens—are available to anyone with a steady salary and a decent credit record; a higher income will usually entitle you to a higher credit limit.

Those offers are good, but you can do better. If you meet additional criteria—including a clean-to-spotless credit record and a history of spending a lot and carrying a balance—you should get even lower-rate deals in the mail. These offers go as low as 4.9% or 5.9% for six to 12 months. If your mailbox is bare and you think you qualify for a lower-than-prime rate, Chase Manhattan (800-282-4273), First USA (800-347-7887) or Wachovia will mail you an application.

The Cash Trap

Many teaser-rate offers are for transferred balances and new purchases only, while cash advances are charged a much higher rate. American Express's Optima card, for example, recently offered a 7.9% teaser rate on purchases—but charged 21.65% on cash advances.

Slow Balance Transfers

Bell Atlantic's new cash-back Visa card offers a 7.9% annual percentage rate for six months. But according to the application's fine print, transferring a balance to this card will take "up to an average of eight weeks,"

---

credit card insurance
Insurance designed to provide coverage against unauthorized use of a credit card if the card is lost or stolen.

Lost or Stolen Card. If your credit cards are lost or stolen, you should report this information to the credit card issuer immediately. Your liability if someone else uses your credit is limited to $50 per card under the Truth in Lending Act. Some credit card issuers offer credit card insurance. **Credit card insurance** is designed to provide coverage against unauthorized use of your credit card if the card is lost or stolen. Standard homeowners and renters insurance policies provide similar coverage. These policies commonly provide up to $500 in coverage for unauthorized use of credit cards. Since this coverage is provided by homeowners during which time you are still responsible for payments to your old card. Worse, that's two fewer months to enjoy the introductory rate.

The "Ticking Clock" Offer

Some mail solicitations, such as the one for Advanta Visa Gold, tout a teaser rate that expires on a set date—in a recent offer, September 1—so the longer you wait, the less attractive the deal becomes. Look for an offer with a fixed rate for a set period that begins when you open your account. Wachovia First Year Prime, for example, offers the prime rate for 12 months, starting when you get the card.

Disappearing Grace Periods

Certain issuers, such as AFBA Industrial and AT&T Universal, treat balance transfers like cash advances—and start charging interest as soon as the transfer is completed. Oak Brook charges interest immediately on transferred balances—and tacks on a 4% surcharge as well. Wachovia gives you a 25-day grace period before charging interest on transferred balances.

Two-Cycle Billing

With two-cycle billing—used by among others, First USA Visa—you must pay off your balance for at least two consecutive months to avoid interest charges. If you pay off your balance in March but not in April, then the grace period you earned in March will be retroactively taken away and you will be charged interest for both months. If you're a credit card surfer, that may not affect you until you want to pay off the balance in full and start using the card for "convenience"—that is, pay off the balance in full each month to avoid interest charges. Any backsliding will be costly.

Hidden Fees

Penalties have been increasing for more than a year. The average late-payment fee was recently $12.81, while the average over-limit fee was $13.02. Wachovia charges a whopping $18 if you exceed your credit limit or don't mail your check in time—the equivalent of a month's prime-rate interest on a $2,500 balance.

If you don't keep your account "in good standing," AT&T Universal will increase the rate on the entire balance by up to 13.9 percentage points. That judgment, says an AT&T spokeswoman, is made on a case-by-case basis. Miss two payments on your new Citibank card and you could see your 5.9% teaser rate jump to prime plus 12.9 percentage points.

If you don't want to sort through the fine print, you can always try telling your current card issuer that you're about to take your business elsewhere. The issuer might lower your rate rather than lose your monthly interest payments, says Robert McKinley, president of RAM Research, a card-tracking firm. And don't worry that surfing may hurt your credit record. "We've done an informal survey of the low-rate issuers to see if people will be penalized," says BHA's Susswein. "The issuers know what you're doing, and it's not showing up on anyone's scoring."

and renters insurance, and your liability is limited, credit card insurance may not be a wise purchase.

credit life insurance
Insurance designed to pay the card holder's credit card debt when the card holder dies.

Repayment of Outstanding Balance. Several other forms of insurance are available to you as a credit card holder. Each of these coverages is designed to repay the outstanding balance if you are unable to do so. **Credit life insurance** is designed to repay your credit card debt if you die. Some credit life insurance policies also provide coverage if you are unable to make payments because of disability. Credit disability insurance can also

Insight

4.3   Eight Ways to Sidestep Credit Card Fraud

1 Never tell anyone your credit card number over the phone unless *you* called *them*.

2 Be careful how you dispose of credit card carbons and receipts—anything that displays our card number. Trash cans are gold mines for thieves, so outsmart them by tearing paperwork into small pieces, says Ken McEldowney, executive director of Consumer Action. If possible, use only your home trash cans, which are less accessible to strangers. And don't leave credit card statements or applications lying around where others can see them.

3 A merchant may ask to see a credit card as personal identification when you pay with a check. Hand it over, but don't let them jot down your card number. It's unnecessary and, in some states, illegal.

4 Keep a list of all your card numbers and the issuers' 800 numbers so you can cancel them easily if your wallet is stolen. Some cards offer a fraud protection service for $20 to $30 a year—you notify them about one card loss and they make calls to all your other credit card companies. "They're not worth it," says McEldowney. "Why pay $30 a year to have someone make calls you could easily make yourself?"

5 Consider signing up for credit cards that have your photo printed on them—they may cut down on fraud.

6 When charging, don't give the merchant your address and telephone number. They aren't required for credit card purchases, and a crafty thief could use the information to get a new card reissued.

7 If you have been a victim of fraud, ask the three big credit bureaus to place a "fraud alert" on your credit file. They will then double-check with you any time a credit card application comes in with your name on it. Call Equifax Inc. (800-685-1111), Trans Union (800-680-7289) and Experion (800-301-7195).

8 Finally, the simplest way to limit your exposure to credit card fraud is also the most obvious: Carry fewer cards, and use them less frequently.

Source: unknown.

be written as a separate insurance coverage. These coverages tend to be expensive when you consider the premium, the coverage provided, and the probability of death or disability. Similar coverage can be provided more economically through regular life insurance and disability income coverage. Some insurers also offer credit unemployment insurance, which is designed to make credit card payments if you are unable to because of unemployment.

SUMMARY

■ Consumer credit is credit extended to the purchaser in advance of the purchase. Consumer loans are more formal, requiring an application and agreement between the parties upon the specific terms of the loan.

■ Consumer credit has a number of advantages, including safety, convenience, flexibility, "float" (grace period), and bonuses.

■ There are some disadvantages to consumer credit, including the cost of consumer credit (interest and fees) and overutilization.

■ To be awarded credit, a credit card applicant must complete and submit a credit card application. The credit card applicant must provide relevant information to the card issuer, including address, banking relationship, employer, income, and other credit accounts.

■ Once submitted, the bank or other issuer examines the application and assesses the applicant's creditworthiness.

■ As part of the credit investigation, the applicant's credit report is requested. A credit report is a detailed record of an individual's credit history and other pertinent information.

■ Credit terms are the conditions under which credit is extended to card holders.

■ The credit limit is the maximum amount that the card holder can charge.

■ The annual fee is an expense the card holder must pay to use the credit card. Not all credit card issuers charge an annual fee.

■ The minimum payment is the lowest amount of the outstanding debt that you can pay to have your account remain current.

■ Finance charges are interest charges levied on unpaid credit card debts. A number of methods are used to compute finance charges, including the previous balance method, the average daily balance method, the adjusted balance method, and the two-cycle balance method.

■ Cash advances are cash loans to the card holder through the credit card. There may be a cash advance fee, and interest begins to be charged immediately on cash advances.

■ Types of credit cards include bank cards, retail cards, and travel and entertainment cards.

- Retail credit cards are issued by retail establishments and may be used only to charge the purchase of goods and services purchased from the retailer issuing the card.

- Bank cards are open account credit cards issued by financial institutions and other entities. Bank cards permit the card holder to charge goods and services wherever the card is accepted.

- Travel and entertainment cards can be used to charge travel- and entertainment-related expenses. Unlike bank cards, the entire balance must be paid upon receiving the monthly statement.

- There are a number of specialized bank credit cards, including prestige cards, affinity cards, and collateralized (secured) cards.

- Prestige cards are credit cards that provide a high limit of credit and added benefits to the card holder. They are issued to individuals who have a higher income and a strong credit record.

- Affinity cards are credit cards issued to individuals with a common bond. A portion of the charged purchases is given to the group sponsoring the card.

- Collateralized (secured) credit cards are issued to individuals who are attempting to establish credit or who have failed to manage credit successfully in the past. These cards require the card holder to maintain an interest-bearing deposit with the issuer as collateral for the line of credit.

- You should select a credit card based upon the credit terms offered and your spending patterns. Other factors, such as rebate offers, may also be considered.

- Consumers are protected through a number of legislative acts, including Truth in Lending, Equal Credit Opportunity, Fair Credit Reporting, Fair Credit Billing, Fair Debt Collection Practices, and Fair Credit and Charge Card Disclosure.

- Consumers are also protected through limited liability for lost and stolen cards, credit card insurance, and credit life insurance.

KEY CONCEPTS AND TERMS

Adjusted balance method
Affinity card
Annual fee
Annual percentage rate (APR)
Average daily balance method

Bank card
Cash advance
Collateralized (secured) credit card
Consumer credit

Consumer loan

Credit bureau

Credit card insurance

Credit card statement

Credit investigation

Credit life insurance

Credit limit

Credit report

Credit scoring

Credit terms

Current account

Debt payments to income ratio

Finance charges

Float

Grace period

Late fee

Minimum payment

Open account credit

Past due amount

Prestige card

Previous balance method

Prime rate

Retail credit card

Teaser rate

Travel and entertainment card

Two-cycle balance method

QUESTIONS FOR REVIEW

1. What are the differences between consumer credit and consumer borrowing?

2. What are the advantages and disadvantages of using consumer credit?

3. What criteria do card issuers use when determining whether to grant credit to an applicant?

4. What measures can you use to determine how much credit card debt you can reasonably handle?

5. Name two differences between the treatment of regular charges and cash advances on credit cards.

6. What are the methods that credit card issuers use to determine interest charges? Which method is best for credit card holders? Which method is worst for them?

7. Is it better for a credit card holder to have a higher annual fee and a lower interest rate, or no annual fee and a higher interest rate? Explain.

8. What are the differences between retail credit cards and bank credit cards? How do bank credit cards differ from travel and entertainment cards?

9. Some bank credit cards are targeted at certain groups of individuals. What are the target markets for prestige cards, affinity cards, and collateralized (secured) credit cards?

10. What is required of creditors under the Truth in Lending Act?

PROBLEMS

1. Joachim and Emily Zietz have monthly take-home pay of $4,000. Their monthly credit card payments (their only credit payments) are $320.

   a. What is their debt payments to income ratio?

   b. Joachim and Emily believe that their credit card payments should never exceed 12 percent of their monthly take-home pay. Assuming their monthly take-home pay remains constant at $4,000, what is their maximum monthly credit card payment?

2. Sharon needed cash quickly. She decided to take a cash advance for $2,000 on her bank credit card. Under the terms of her card, the fee for cash advance is 2.5 percent of the advance or $25, whichever is greater. Her credit card charges 18 percent interest (1.5 percent monthly) on regular charges and 21 percent interest (1.75 percent monthly) on cash advances. Interest begins to be charged immediately on cash advances.

   a. What fee must Sharon pay for this cash advance?

   b. Assume that the cash advance balance remains constant at $2,000. What is Sharon's monthly interest expense on the cash advance?

3. Cindy has a Visa card issued by Second National Bank. Cindy's balance at the start of the previous period was $2,000. On the 15th day of the previous 30-day period, Second National received a $1,200 check from Cindy. On the 20th day of the period, Cindy charged a $2,400 purchase. Second National charges 18 percent annual interest, 1.50 percent interest monthly.

   a. How much interest did Second National charge Cindy for the previous statement period, assuming Second National uses the average daily balance method, excluding new purchases?

   b. How much interest did Second National charge Cindy for the previous statement period, assuming Second National uses the average daily balance method, including new purchases?

4. Brad has a $6,000 credit limit on this Continental Savings Bank (CSB) Visa card. The card requires a $25 annual fee and uses the previous balance method to calculate finance charges. Brad is a little "overextended" at the present time and is carrying a $3,000 balance from month to month. CSB charges 21 percent interest (1.75 percent per month) on the outstanding balance.

   Brad just received a credit card offer from Bank of Sommerville (BOS). The BOS MasterCard has no annual fee and a 12 percent interest rate (1.0 percent per month) for the first year. Brad can transfer the $3,000 balance from his Visa card at no charge. The BOS MasterCard also uses the previous balance method to calculate finance charges.

How much will Brad save in interest and fees during the coming year by switching to the Bank of Sommerville MasterCard? Assume the outstanding debt remains constant at $3,000 from month to month.

INTERNET EXERCISES

1. Internet sites that provide up-to-date interest rates on credit cards include BanxQuote, Bank Rate Monitor Infobank, and RAM Research Group at:

   http://www.banx.com/

   http://www.bankrate.com/

   http://www.ramresearch.com/

   Visit one or all of these sites, and check out the differences among various rates.

2. As mentioned, Financenter provides calculators to help you with various calculations. Go to the Financenter site at:

   http://www.financenter.com/

   Click on "Credit Cards." At the credit card page, you should see this question: "How important is the interest rate?" Click on the question, and then select one of the other questions that will appear (such as "What will it take to pay off my balance?"). Select the calculator, and work through the calculations.

CASE APPLICATIONS

Case I

Rosalie Chavez has a retail charge card from Swenson's, a large department store. A portion of Rosalie's credit card statement is provided:

Account Activity, June 20–July 20

Date:

June 30	Women's Wear	234.60
July 10	Payment **THANK YOU**	−250.00
July 15	Beauty Salon	60.00
July 15	Nursery/Greenhouse	44.75

Previous Balance	New Charges	Finance Charges	Payment Received	New Balance	Minimum Payment
$420.00	$339.35		$250.00		

Other information: The monthly period runs from the 20th of the previous month through the 20th of the current month. The interest rate charged is 1.5 percent per month (18.0 percent annually). The minimum payment is 10 percent of the new balance, rounded up to the nearest dollar.

1. If Swenson's uses the previous balance method, what finance charge would appear on the statement? What would the ending balance equal? What minimum payment would be required?

2. If Swenson's uses the average daily balance method, including her purchases, what finance charge would appear on the statement? What would the ending balance equal? What minimum payment would be required?

3. If Swenson's uses the adjusted balance method, what finance charge would appear on the statement? What would the ending balance equal? What minimum payment would be required?

Case II

Donna Philips just graduated from college. She has never had a credit card. Today, she received two credit card applications in the mail, each offering a preapproved credit limit of $2,500. The first application was for a Second National Bank Visa card. Second National charges a $20 annual fee and a low interest rate of 9 percent for the first year and 18 percent thereafter. Second National uses the average daily balance method, excluding new purchases, to calculate finance charges. The second application was for a CountryBank MasterCard. Under the credit terms, there is no annual fee, with a guaranteed interest rate of 18 percent. CountryBank uses the two-cycle balance method, including new purchases, to calculate finance charges.

1. Which of these two cards would be more beneficial for Donna if she plans to use the card infrequently and to pay off the entire balance as soon as the monthly statement arrives? Justify your answer.

2. Which of these two cards would be more beneficial for Donna if she intends to use the card frequently and to carry a high balance from month to month? Justify your answer.

Case III

For each of the following scenarios, discuss how a specific type of credit card could be employed:

1. Wentworth Furniture just opened their fourth retail outlet. Paul Wentworth, owner, is looking for additional profit opportunities. When asked about credit purchases, he replied, "I'm tired of accept-

ing Visa and MasterCard. I'm making the banks that issue those cards a lot of money on goods purchased at my stores." How can Paul "get a piece of the action" on credit sales?

2. Caroline started a support/advocacy group called Citizens for the Victims of Violent Crime (CVVC). The group has some excellent programs and support services; however, they need additional funding. Caroline wonders if there is any way the group can raise money by offering a credit card to CVVC members and friends.

3. Brad has a horrible credit history. Three years ago, he declared personal bankruptcy. He is trying to rebuild credit, but with the bankruptcy in his credit file, he has not been able to find any willing credit card issuers.

SUGGESTIONS FOR ADDITIONAL READING

Choosing and Using Credit Cards. Federal Trade Commission, 1993.

Dolan, Ken and Daria Dolan. *Straight Talk on Money.* New York: Simon & Schuster, 1993, Chapter 2.

Personal Financial Planning Guide. Ernst & Young. New York: John Wiley & Sons, 1995, pp. 28–30, 240–241, 263.

Knecht, G. Bruce. "MasterCard, Visa Report Big Gains in First Quarter." *The Wall Street Journal,* May 31, 1995, pp. A2, A8.

Morris, Kenneth M. and Alan M. Siegel. *The Wall Street Journal Guide to Understanding Personal Finance.* New York: Lightbulb Press, 1992, pp. 38–49.

Sloane, Leonard. *The New York Times Personal Finance Handbook.* New York: Times Books, 1995, Chapter 4.

Tyson, Eric. *Personal Finance for Dummies.* Foster City, Calif.: IDG Books Worldwide, 1995, Chapter 5.

NOTES

1. These statistics were taken from "Visa's Dominance Seems a Debit-Credit Liability," *The Wall Street Journal,* June 6, 1996, pp. B1, B10.

2. G. Bruce Knecht, "MasterCard, Visa Report Big Gains in First Quarter," *The Wall Street Journal,* May 31, 1995, pp. A2, A8.

3. *Statistical Abstract of the United States,* 1995, Table 812.

4. Figures quoted in this paragraph were taken from the *Statistical Abstract of the United States,* 1995, Table 811. General-purpose credit cards include MasterCard, Visa, Optima, and Discover.

Chapter 5

Borrowing and Debt Management

Learning Objectives

After studying this chapter, you should be able to:

- Discuss the nature of consumer borrowing and differentiate between consumer credit and consumer borrowing.

- Explain the uses of consumer borrowing and its advantages and disadvantages.

- Explain the types of consumer loans.

- Identify the sources of consumer loans.

- Explain the process of obtaining a consumer loan, including the loan application, evaluation of the loan application, and the loan decision.

- Discuss the management of consumer debt, including the amount of money a consumer can borrow and the provisions of the loan agreement.

- Explain the remedies available to people overburdened by debt, including credit counseling and bankruptcy.

> *Neither a borrower nor a lender be;*
> *For loan oft loses both itself and friend,*
> *And borrowing dulls the edge of husbandry.*
>
> —William Shakespeare, *Hamlet*
>
> *A bank is a place that will lend you money if*
> *you can prove that you don't need it.*
>
> —Bob Hope, as quoted in *Life in the Crystal Palace*

Money was always "tight" for Tom and Nancy Andrews before they got married two years ago. Tom earns $20,000 per year working for a printing company, and Nancy makes $25,000 per year as an elementary school teacher. When they married, they thought their "tight money" days had ended. Surely by combining their incomes and eliminating one set of housing and utility expenses, they would achieve financial prosperity. Tom and Nancy spent most of their accumulated savings on their wedding. After they married, they moved into a nice apartment. They purchased a new car, stereo system, furniture, and computer, all made possible by borrowing the money. At the same time, Tom and Nancy continued to use their credit cards liberally.

Now they are in trouble. Between consumer loans and using their credit cards, they owe more than $20,000! What went wrong? Simply put, the couple spent too much money and did not properly manage their consumer debt. Borrowing money is often necessary, and managing the debt is a critical aspect of personal financial planning.

This chapter is our second on spending money. In the previous chapter, we discussed using credit to pay for purchases. In this chapter, we examine a second method of funding purchases: consumer borrowing. We describe the differences between consumer credit and consumer borrowing, discuss the advantages and disadvantages of consumer loans. We also explain the various types of consumer loans, discuss the sources of consumer loans, examine the management of consumer debt, including the amount consumers can reasonably borrow, and discuss the consequences of not managing consumer debt effectively.

What is Consumer Borrowing?

Suppose that you want to purchase a new car and the cost of the model that you like is $18,000. Unfortunately, you have only $2,000 in your savings account. You do have a credit card, but your credit limit is only $3,000. How can you get the money to purchase the new car? The answer may be through a consumer loan.

Although the use of credit and consumer borrowing are similar in that both entail debt, there are some important differences. Recall that credit is granted up to an approved amount before the credit is used. The grantor of credit does not have to approve your use of credit each time you want to use it. In addition, credit card payments are flexible. You are required to pay only a specified minimum amount, or you may repay the entire outstanding balance.

consumer borrowing
Obtaining funds from a lender under specific loan provisions.

In contrast, **consumer borrowing** refers to obtaining funds from a lender under specific loan provisions. The funds obtained through consumer borrowing are called consumer loans. These loans are usually made for a specified purpose and must be repaid according to a specified schedule. This chapter discusses consumer loans made for purposes other than the purchase of a home, such as borrowing to finance the purchase of a new car or furniture, to finance an education, or to start up a business. Loans for the purchase of homes, called mortgage loans, are discussed in Chapter 7. Consumer loans are necessary because few people can pay cash for big-ticket items, such as cars or appliances, so they must borrow the money to make the purchase.

Consumer loans offer several advantages. Without them, many of us could not afford expensive goods and services. Of course, you can wait to purchase a car until you have saved enough money, but borrowing permits you to enjoy the use of the car while you pay for it. The ability to borrow also provides financial flexibility since payments can be stretched over a longer period, if necessary. For example, you can repay four years of college loans over ten years after you graduate. Finally, you can borrow to cover unexpected expenses and emergencies, such as uninsured medical bills or unexpected car repairs.

interest A charge levied by a lender to compensate the lender for loss of the use of the loaned funds.

There are, however, some disadvantages of consumer borrowing. For one thing, you must pay interest on the loan. **Interest,** as we discussed in Chapter 3, is a charge levied by lenders to compensate them for not having the use of the funds they lend. If you have a weak credit history, you may be charged a higher interest rate than you otherwise would be charged, and thus pay more in interest. In addition, some loans require pledging the asset purchased or other assets as security for the loan. Should you fail to repay the amount owed, the lender will have a legal right to your property. Finally, if you overuse consumer credit and consumer borrowing, as the Andrews did in the chapter introduction, you may be unable to repay your debts. Inability to repay borrowed funds can have serious financial consequences, including bankruptcy.

When does it make sense to borrow? What sources of loans are the best? What lenders should be avoided? Insight 5.1, on pages 148 and 149, provides some tips on "borrowing like an expert."

Types of Consumer Loans

There are many types of consumer loans, and they can be classified in several ways. The purpose of the loan, the creditworthiness of the borrower, and the economic conditions present at the time the money is borrowed determine the type of consumer loan that is used. Exhibit 5.1 displays the types of consumer loans.

single-payment loan A loan requiring the borrower to pay the entire loan principal at the maturity of the loan.

■ *Single-payment versus installment loans.* One differentiating characteristic of consumer loans is the number of payments the borrower is required to make to repay the loan. **Single-payment loans** require the borrower to pay the entire loan principal at the maturity of the loan.

Exhibit 5.1

Types of Consumer Loans

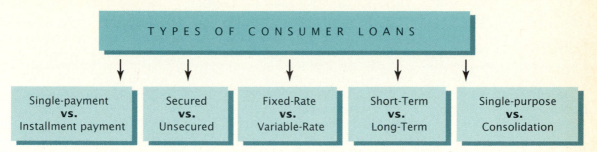

		TYPES OF CONSUMER LOANS		
Single-payment **vs.** Installment payment	Secured **vs.** Unsecured	Fixed-Rate **vs.** Variable-Rate	Short-Term **vs.** Long-Term	Single-purpose **vs.** Consolidation

Note that the categories of characteristics are not mutually exclusive. For example, your car loan may require installment payments for three years, be secured by using the car as collateral, have a fixed rate, and be for a single purpose.

Installment loans, as mentioned in Chapter 2, require the borrower to make a series of scheduled payments to repay the loan. Car loans are an excellent example of installment payment loans, with monthly payments usually required for three to five years.

■ *Secured versus unsecured loans.* A second differentiating characteristic of consumer loans is whether or not the lender requires collateral for the loan. **Collateral** consists of items of value that are pledged to secure the loan. Should the debtor default on a secured loan, the lender has legal recourse to the property pledged as collateral. A **secured loan** is a loan that requires the pledge of collateral. Loans for big-ticket items, such as a new car, usually require that the asset purchased serve as collateral for the loan. Collateral may also be required on loans for smaller amounts to protect the lender from losing money if the borrower does not have a strong credit history. **Unsecured loans** are loans that do not require collateral. Such loans normally involve smaller dollar amounts or are made to borrowers who have excellent credit records.

■ *Fixed-rate versus variable-rate loans.* A third distinctive characteristic of a consumer loan is the interest rate. As we noted, interest is a charge levied by the lender in exchange for not having use of the funds. For example, a lender could purchase a four-year certificate of deposit and earn interest rather than lending the money to you so that you can purchase a new car. Thus, the lender must be compensated for not having use of the funds. The interest rate, the amount of money borrowed, the length of the loan, and the method used to calculate interest charges determine the amount of interest to be paid on the loan.

Consumer loans can have either a fixed interest rate or a variable interest rate. With a **fixed-rate loan,** the interest rate agreed to when

collateral Items of value pledged to secure a loan.

secured loan A loan that requires the pledge of collateral.

unsecured loan A loan that does not require the pledge of collateral.

fixed-rate loan A loan with an interest rate that remains constant over the life of the loan.

Insight   5.1   How to Borrow Like an Expert

The one really vexing thing about borrowing money is that, once you borrow it, it only *seems* to be yours. Yes, you can spend or invest it. You can even lend it to somebody else. But one day, even though it's gone, you will have pay it back—with interest. So the primary rule of borrowing couldn't be simpler: As Little as Possible, at the Lowest Possible Rate.

Before suggesting how and where to borrow, here are three lenders to avoid:

Pawn shops. The $300 ring you pawn for $100 and redeem a month later for $110 has just cost you 10% interest—more than 120% a year.

"Tax-refund loans." Millions of Americans will pay tax preparers anywhere from 2.5% to 12% to get their refunds three or four weeks early this year. In actual dollars, they're only tossing away $30 or $60 or $90. But the annual interest rate that represents ranges from 30% to 140% or more.

Credit cards. Do you know how many people have a few dollars in a savings account earning 5%—which is maybe only 3.5% after taxes—at the same time as they carry a credit-card balance on which they're paying 15% or 18% or 22%? *Pay off your credit cards.* There are much cheaper ways to borrow.

But there are only a few things worth borrowing for. So what *does* it make sense to borrow for?

An education. Students: If you're really needy, the "financial-aid package" your college offers may include a 5% fixed-rate, government-subsidized "Perkins" loan. Grab it. Or you may be offered a floating-rate (currently 8 1/4%) "Stafford" loan that accrues no interest until you graduate. Also good. *Any* student can get the kind of Stafford loan that *does* begin accruing interest right away, and that's still a lot better than a regular personal loan.

Parents: Ask your bank about the Federal PLUS Loan program. If you own a home worth significantly more than its mortgage, take out a home-equity loan. The rate should be low, and it is tax-deductible.

Avoid "search firms" that charge a fee. They provide no more help than should be available for free from your school's financial-aid office, your local bank and via the Internet.

A used car. I know, I know. But is it really worth borrowing an extra $10,000 for that new-car smell? It's your choice, but I buy my cars for cash. Not having to pay 10% or 11% on a

the money is borrowed is constant for the life of the loan. Fixed-rate loans are favorable to borrowers when interest rates rise after the money is borrowed because the interest rate on the loan remains at the lower level. For example, suppose you take out a loan at 10 percent interest to purchase a car, and then the interest rate for similar loans rises to 12 percent. Your interest rate remains at 10 percent if the rate is fixed. However, if you borrow money with a fixed rate of 10 percent and the interest rate for similar loans later drops to 8 percent, you must continue to pay the higher fixed rate. With a **variable-rate loan,** the interest rate changes over time, reflecting current market interest rates. Thus your interest rate could increase or decrease from the initial interest rate charged when you borrowed the money.

variable-rate loan A loan on which the interest rate changes over time to reflect current market rates.

car loan is as good as *earning* 10% or 11% tax-free and risk-free—a sensational return these days. If you must borrow for a car, try to borrow as little as possible for as short a term as possible—and, of course, at the lowest possible rate.

Your bank or credit union generally will give you a better rate than your auto dealer (unless it's a "come-on" rate—"1.9% financing or $500 cash back"—in which case, it's usually smarter to take the cash). You'll do better still by dipping into your home-equity line, if you have one, because then not only will the rate be low but also the interest will be tax-deductible. Just be sure you have the discipline to handle a home-equity loan well. If you keep borrowing against it and not replenishing it with the payments you would have made on a car loan, you'll just fall deeper into debt with each new car.

Steer clear of: leasing (a way, essentially, to borrow the *whole* price of the car); "prepayment penalties" (a form of extra interest); loans calculated with the "rule of 78s" (which hurts if you prepay); and the "credit life insurance" that many lenders are eager to sell you (a good deal only if you're not well).

A home. Unlike a fancy car, let alone a restaurant meal or a vacation, it *does* make sense to borrow to buy a home. For one thing, homes often appreciate.

A business. Any number of multimillionaires financed the start-up of their business by maxing out their credit cards and building a prototype in their garage. It's a great story when it works—and nothing I say could (or should) stop you if you have that kind of fire in your belly. It's like being *possessed*. But ordinarily, starting a business is very risky, so you should try to persuade your backers to provide "nonrecourse" loans, where your own funds are not at stake. Your only prayer of persuading them to do this: Give them a share in your business.

An emergency. Well, an emergency is an emergency. One route: Many 401(k) retirement plans allow borrowing—ask your personnel department. (But try to repay quickly to get the money working for your retirement again!) If you have cash-value life insurance, you may be able to borrow against it. (The case for paying *that* money back is less compelling.)

Then there are friends and relatives. For their sake as well as yours, you might consider having them guarantee a small bank loan rather than lend directly to you. Of course, that way you'll have to pay it back—with interest. But you're also less likely to lose a friend. Indeed, if you do pay it back in a timely way, you'll enhance your credit rating.

Source: Excerpted from Andrew Tobias, "How to Borrow Like an Expert," *Parade Magazine,* 3/17/96, p. 24. Reprinted with permission from *Parade* ©1996.

■ *Short-term versus long-term loans.* Loans can also be distinguished by their duration—the period over which the money is borrowed—also referred to as the **loan maturity.** Although the labels are somewhat arbitrary, **short-term loans** generally are considered to have a duration of one year or less. **Long-term loans** have a duration of more than one year. Some authors further divide long-term loans, into intermediate-term loans (loans of one to five years) and long-term loans (loans for more than five years). Almost all consumer loans, including auto loans, are for five years or less.

■ *Single-purpose versus consolidation loans.* Most consumer loans are made for a specific purpose. The most common purpose is the purchase

loan maturity The duration of a loan; the period over which the money is borrowed.

short-term loan Generally, a loan with a duration of one year or less.

long-term loan Generally, a loan with a duration of more than one year.

of a new car or truck. People also use consumer loans to purchase other costly durable goods, such as furniture and appliances. Student loans and loans to fund the startup of a business are other examples of loans made for a specific purpose. Another type of loan is more general. Some credit card users and borrowers do not successfully manage their use of credit and consumer borrowing. They borrow too much, become overextended, and have difficulty repaying the amount borrowed and the interest charges. Borrowers who find themselves in this position sometimes use a consolidation loan. A **consolidation loan** is a loan taken out from a single source that is used to repay other outstanding debt obligations. In essence, the borrower exchanges multiple payments with several creditors for a single payment to a single creditor. Although consolidation loans are expensive, the interest rate charged may be less than the rate charged on some of the outstanding loans, and the borrower may avoid certain fees, such as late payment fees, through a consolidation loan. Furthermore, the issuer of the consolidation loan may be more willing to cooperate with the debtor in establishing a payment plan suited to the debtor's financial constraints.

consolidation loan A loan taken out from a single source and used to repay other outstanding debts.

Sources of Consumer Loans

Suppose you want to borrow money to purchase a new car. Where can you get a loan? Consumers can borrow from a number of sources. The most important sources of consumer loans include deposit-type financial institutions, consumer finance companies, sales finance companies, life insurance policy loans, real estate equity loans, friends and family, and pawnshops.

Deposit-Type Financial Institutions

Deposit-type financial institutions include commercial banks, savings and loan associations, mutual savings banks, and credit unions. Such institutions have a ready source of loanable funds: money that has been deposited by savers. Regulators require these institutions to hold a portion of the deposits accepted on hand, but surplus funds can be used to make loans. Commercial banks are the leaders in consumer lending, followed by credit unions, and other savings institutions.

Commercial Banks. Commercial banks are the most numerous and widespread deposit-type financial institution. At year-end 1994, outstanding consumer installment loans from commercial banks totaled $434 trillion.[1] Commercial banks offer secured and unsecured loans for a variety of purposes, including personal loans, auto loans, home improvement loans, and student loans. Interest rates on commercial bank loans are favorable to borrowers because commercial banks have a ready source of funds (deposits), and commercial banks are selective in granting loans. Although you are not required to be a depositor of the commercial bank where you apply for a loan, some preference is given to regular customers of the bank, especially when the supply of loanable funds is tight.

Credit Unions. Credit unions are deposit-type institutions that serve members who have a common bond, such as working for the same employer. Credit unions offer some of the best credit terms available to their members. Credit unions can offer favorable loan terms for three reasons. First, as a deposit-type financial institution, the credit union has deposits on hand from which loans can be made. Second, many credit unions are nonprofit, cooperative entities. Finally, credit unions are characterized by low expenses.

Credit unions concentrate their lending efforts on consumer loans and offer competitive interest rates. At year-end 1994, outstanding consumer installment loans from credit unions totaled $121.7 trillion. Credit unions offer a variety of types of loans, including secured and unsecured loans and single-payment and installment payment loans. Credit unions commonly extend personal loans, auto loans, and home improvement loans. Most credit unions also provide the borrower with "free" credit life insurance, which is designed to repay the outstanding debt should the borrower die.

Savings and Loan Associations and Mutual Savings Banks. Savings and loan associations and mutual savings banks are other important sources of consumer loans. Although savings and loan associations are found throughout the United States, mutual savings banks are located primarily in the Northeastern states. At year-end 1994, consumer installment loans from these institutions totaled $38.8 trillion. Savings and loan associations and mutual savings banks have historically concentrated their lending efforts on home mortgages, but recently they have become more active in other consumer lending markets. Today, they offer secured and unsecured installment loans for autos, appliances, and furniture, as well as home improvement and educational loans. Lending rates may be lower at these institutions than at commercial banks.

Consumer Finance Companies

consumer finance company A lending business that does not accept deposits and offers small secured and unsecured loans to qualified individuals on an installment basis.

A number of institutions that do not accept deposits also make consumer loans. **Consumer finance companies** are lending businesses that do not accept deposits and offer small secured and unsecured loans to qualified individuals on an installment basis. The maximum loan amount is typically $2,000 to $5,000, with installment periods of five

usury rate The maximum interest rate that lenders are permitted to charge under state law.

years or less. The interest rates charged by consumer finance companies are higher than those charged by deposit-type financial institutions. Indeed, the interest rate charged may equal the **usury rate,** which is the maximum interest rate that lenders are permitted to charge by state law.

Higher interest rates are charged because consumer finance companies do not accept savings deposits from which loans can be offered. Thus consumer finance companies must raise their own capital. In addition, the loans made by consumer finance companies tend to be riskier and the default rate higher compared to loans from deposit-type financial institutions. Loans from consumer finance companies may be used for debt consolidation, to finance trips, and for the purchase of assets (for example, cars and furniture). Some consumer finance companies are locally owned and operated, whereas others are well-known national organizations, such as Household Finance Company and Beneficial Finance.

Sales Finance Companies

sales finance company An organization that assists consumers with the purchase of high-priced assets by purchasing loans from the seller.

Another borrowing alternative is a sales finance company. A **sales finance company** is an organization that assists consumers with the purchase of high-priced assets by buying loans from the sellers. For example, a furniture dealer may extend an installment loan if you purchase a living room set from the dealer. Instead of waiting to receive the installment payments from you, the furniture dealer may sell the loan to a sales finance company. The furniture dealer receives cash when the loan is sold, and the borrower makes installment payments to the sales finance company. Sales finance companies are similar to consumer finance companies in some ways, but there are some important differences. Obviously, the average loan size is larger with sales finance companies. In addition, the borrower deals directly with a consumer finance company when the loan is extended. With sales finance companies, the initial lender sets the terms of the loan, and then the sales finance company purchases the loan from the initial lender.

The manufacturers of some big-ticket assets own the sales finance company that handles loans for purchases. For example, General Motors owns General Motors Acceptance Corporation (GMAC), and Ford owns Ford Motor Credit Corporation. When a consumer wants to purchase a General Motors vehicle, the dealer may arrange financing for the transaction with GMAC. Sales finance companies owned by manufacturers can serve as a profit center for the manufacturer through the collection of finance charges on the loans. In addition, sales finance companies can serve as marketing tools by offering favorable interest rates to purchasers of the manufacturer's products.

Life Insurance Policy Loans

Life insurance, which we will discuss in greater detail in Chapter 9, is another source of consumer loans. Some life insurance policies require premiums that exceed what is needed to pay current expected death claims. As a by-product of the premium payment method, such life insurance policies develop a savings reserve over time called the cash value. **Cash value life insurance** provides a savings element in addition to life insurance protection. Policyowners can borrow the cash value through a life insurance policy loan. A **life insurance policy loan** is a loan against the cash value of a life insurance policy. Although it may appear that you are borrowing your own money when you borrow from your life insurance policy, technically, the cash value belongs to the insurer. Thus, interest is charged on life insurance policy loans.

Before the 1980s, life insurance policy loans carried low, fixed, interest rates (for example, 5 percent). The high interest rates during the late 1970s and early 1980s led many life insurance policyowners to borrow the cash value at the low fixed interest rate or invest the borrowed funds elsewhere at higher rates. Today, many life insurance policy loans carry higher fixed loan rates and variable loan rates tied to market interest rates. Life insurance policy loans are a readily available source of funds, with no loan qualification necessary. All that is required is a cash value to borrow against. Life insurance policy loans need not be repaid. If the insured dies while a policy loan is outstanding, the life insurance company will reduce the life insurance proceeds payable to the beneficiary by the amount owed on the policy loan.

Real Estate Equity Loans

Just as you can borrow against the savings in a cash value life insurance policy, you can also borrow against another asset you may own: real estate. Such loans are called real estate equity loans. A property owner's equity position in real estate is the amount by which the owner's interest exceeds the amount owed on the property. Thus a homeowner who owes $80,000 on a home valued at $140,000 has an equity position of $60,000 in the home.

One way of tapping the equity in your home is through a second mortgage. A **second mortgage** is a loan against the equity in a home that is subordinate (secondary) to the first mortgage on the property in case of default. The first mortgage is the original loan that was made when the home was purchased. Second mortgages are of shorter duration than first mortgages and are commonly used when a portion of the first mortgage has been retired or when the home has appreciated in value. Second mortgages are installment loans, often with a large payment called a balloon payment at the end of the loan period. Since a second mortgage is riskier than a first mortgage because the claim of the first mortgage lender takes precedence over the claim of the second lender, the interest rate charged on a second mortgage is usually higher than the interest rate on the first mortgage. Common uses of second mortgages are to fund remodeling the home, college education, and business startup costs.

cash value life insurance A form of life insurance that provides a savings element in addition to life insurance protection.

life insurance policy loan A loan against the cash value of a life insurance policy.

second mortgage A loan against the equity in a home that is subordinate (secondary) to the first mortgage on the property in case of default.

home equity loan A line of credit issued against the equity in a home.

A second, more flexible, method of borrowing against the equity in a home is through a home equity loan. A **home equity loan** is a line of credit with either a fixed or variable interest rate issued against the equity in a home. A line of credit is similar to a preapproved credit limit on a credit card. The line of credit typically extends for 10 or 15 years, and you can borrow up to the approved limit when you need the money. A home equity loan is repaid through flexible monthly payments. One of the major advantages of home equity loans is the favorable tax treatment afforded the interest paid on them. Before the 1980s, interest on many forms of consumer borrowing was a tax deductible expense. Tax law changes in the 1980s eliminated interest deductibility for most types of consumer debt. However, the interest paid on home equity loans remains a tax deductible expense. Thus homeowners who itemize their deductions can reduce their taxable income by the amount of interest paid on a home equity loan.

Obviously, the borrower must have an equity position in real estate to obtain a home equity loan. Lenders typically limit the amount that can be borrowed through a home equity loan to 70 or 80 percent of the home-owner's equity in the property. This practice helps assure repayment should the home decline in value. Obtaining a home equity loan requires an appraisal and closing costs, just as when purchasing a home. Some mortgage lenders now offer two-in-one loans, combining a first mortgage and a home-equity credit line in the same loan. Such loans avoid duplication of certain expenses and encourage the homeowner to borrow from the same mortgage lender. As with other types of consumer loans, you should carefully review the terms of the loan before borrowing money.

Friends and Family

Friends and family members are another source of loans. Indeed, if you need funds, friends and family may appear to be a great resource—a loan from someone you know at favorable terms. Loans of this type are at times successful, but they have an obvious downside. Instead of dealing with an otherwise disinterested party, such as a bank or finance company, you are dealing with someone you know. Should the loan go sour, you risk losing a friend or creating discord in your family. Recently, a candidate for public office was criticized for lending money to his brother-in-law who invested the funds in a movie some perceived to be objectionable. One political pundit suggested the incident raised serious questions about the candidate's judgment—not for investing in the movie, but rather for lending money to a family member! If you do borrow money from a friend or family member, put the terms of the agreement in writing and make sure each party clearly understands the terms of the loan.

cosigner One who signs a loan agreement along with the borrower and promises to repay the outstanding loan obligation if the bor-rower defaults.

As an alternative to obtaining a loan from a friend or family member, you can ask that person to cosign a loan agreement from another lender. A **cosigner** signs the loan agreement and promises to repay the outstanding obligations of the borrower if the borrower defaults. For example, a lender may be unwilling to extend a loan to you. However, if another person who is in a stronger financial position is willing to cosign the loan, the lender may grant the loan. Under this relationship, you receive the loan from a lender, with a friend or relative helping to secure the loan. A cosigner should be wary, however, because he or she has the same legal responsibilities to the lender as the borrower has in case of default.

Pawnshops

pawnshop A business that extends single-payment loans for short periods at high interest rates, with the amount of the loan based on a percentage of the value of property that is pledged as collateral for the loan.

Pawnshops also provide consumer loans. **Pawnshops** are businesses that extend single-payment loans for short periods at high interest rates, with the amount of the loan based on the value of property that is pledged as collateral for the loan. Pawnshop loans are typically made for 25 to 35 percent of the value of the item pledged, and the interest rate charged on the loan may be more than three or four times the rate offered by banks and other savings institutions. If the borrower is unable to repay the loan plus interest and other fees when the loan matures (typically after one to six months), the pawnbroker has the legal right to sell the property and retain the proceeds. Although pawnshops have the advantage of making cash available quickly, they have several disadvantages. Borrowers must pay high interest rates on the funds borrowed and risk losing the property pledged as collateral if they are unable to repay the loan. In addition, the loan amount is less than half the value of the property securing the loan.

Exhibit 5.2 provides a summary of these sources of consumer loans, the types of loans they provide, and their advantages and limitations.

Obtaining a Consumer Loan

You may decide to purchase an asset, start a business, or go back to college. If you do not have the required financial resources on hand, you will have to try to obtain a consumer loan. As noted in the previous section, there are many sources of consumer loans. How do you go about obtaining a consumer loan? The steps involved in obtaining a consumer loan are portrayed in Exhibit 5.3.

The first step is to determine if you are going to purchase the asset, remodel your home, take a vacation, start a business, or enroll in college —that is, spend the money now. You may decide to postpone spending until a later date or not to spend the money at all. In the case of a car, you may need to decide whether to purchase or lease, a decision examined in Insight 5.2.

Exhibit 5.2

Consumer Loans

Lenders	Types of Loans	Advantages	Limitations
Commercial Banks	Home improvement, Education, Personal, Auto, Mobile home	Widely available locations and funds, Better rates for bank, customers	Higher rates than some other sources Requires good credit rating
Savings & Loans	Home improvement, Education, *Personal, Auto, *Mobile home *(in some states only)	Loans often cost less than at commercial banks.	Requires good credit rating
Savings Banks	Home improvement, Personal	Some loans cost less than at commercial banks; More personal service	Exist only in some states, Requires good credit rating
Credit Unions	Home improvement, Education, Personal, Auto, Mobile home	Easy to arrange for members in good standing, Lowest rates, Better service	Membership required in organization or group
Consumer Finance Companies	Auto, Personal	Easy to arrange, Good credit rating not required	High rates Cosigner often required
Sales Finance Companies	Auto, Appliance (major), Boat, Mobile home	Convenience, Good terms during special promotions	High rates. Since loan is secured, defaulting can mean loss of item and payments already made.
Insurance Companies	General purpose	Easy to arrange, Low rates, Can borrow up to 95% of policy's surrender value, No obligation to repay	Outstanding loan and accumulated interest reduce payment to survivors, Policy ownership is required.
Real Estate Equity Loans	Home improvement, Education, Business startup, Personal	Easy to arrange, Competitive rates but higher on second mortgage than first; Interest on home equity loans is tax deductible.	Must have equity in a home to use
Friends and Family	General purpose	Readily available, Favorable terms	May strain family relationship or friendship
Pawnshops	General purpose	Quick approval	High interest rate. Loan for less than value of pledged asset; Loss of pledged asset if unable to repay loan

Source: Rows 1–7 based on Kenneth M. Morris and Alan M. Siegel, *Wall Street Journal Guide to Understanding Personal Finance* (New York: Lightbulb Press, 1992), p. 35.

Exhibit 5.3

The Process of Obtaining a Consumer Loan

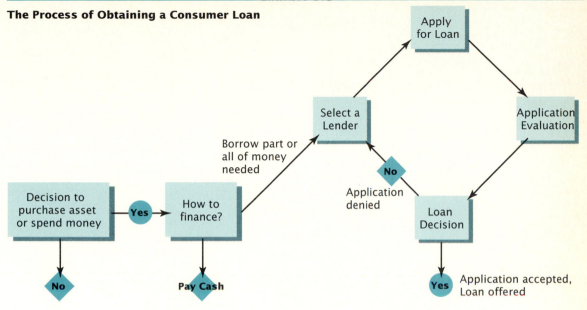

If you decide to make the expenditure, you can either pay cash for the entire amount or borrow part or all the money needed. If you decide to borrow the money, you must first select a lender.

The selection of a lender involves several factors. Some sources of loans can immediately be eliminated. For example, you need an equity position in real estate or a cash value in a life insurance policy to borrow from these sources. There may not be any mutual savings banks in your area, you may not be a member of a credit union, or a certain lender may be unwilling to offer a loan for your intended purpose.

Selecting a lender involves some "leg work." Logic dictates that you should start with the lender that makes the type of loan that you desire and that provides the most favorable terms (for example, lowest interest rate, desired loan duration). Phone calls and visits to lending institutions can provide the general information you will need. You should also consider more than one lender in the desired category. For example, if you determine that a commercial bank is your best source of funds, you should contact several commercial banks to compare loan terms. Lending institutions sometimes offer special loan deals for qualified applicants during specified time periods.

Just because you decide that one source of consumer loans is best for you does not guarantee that the lender will concur with your conclusion. The lender must determine if it should loan you the money. As a first

 **5.2   Buy or Lease Your Car?**

The Auto Loan

Should you borrow the money to buy the car?

If you don't have the cash on hand to buy a new car outright—and many people don't—you might consider an auto loan to spread the payments over time. A bank or other lender will give you the money to buy the car, and you repay the loan, with interest, over a period of 3–5 years. The new car is your collateral; if you can't make your payments, the lender can repossess it.

Should You Borrow or Buy?

If you have enough money to buy the car, should you take the loan anyway? That depends. If you pay cash, you'll lose the investment interest on the amount you spend. That could be substantial if interest rates are high, or your investment is paying a good return.

But the interest you'll pay on the loan will drive up the real cost of the car. For example, if you take a 3-year loan at 8% to buy a $15,000 car, the actual cost would be about $17,000. The same loan paid back over 5 years would increase the cost to over $18,000.

Special Deals from Dealers

To promote sales, car companies periodically offer very low financing terms, sometimes as low as 2% or 3%. Provided there are no strings attached—read the agreement carefully—these loans can be very good deals. (*Zero percent financing* means you can buy the car on time without paying any interest, but check carefully for other charges.)

Loan Features

- You own the car.
- You can pay off the loan at any time.
- You can put as many miles on the car as you want.
- You are responsible for maintenance, but can get the car serviced wherever you like and keep whatever records you like.
- You arrange for insurance. Usually the rates drop as the car gets older.
- If the car is stolen or totalled, you settle with the insurance company.
- You can sell the car or trade it in whenever you want if you pay off the loan.
- Conventional wisdom says major repair costs don't occur within the first 3 years—but you may be saddled with expenses if you keep the car longer.

The Auto Lease

Should you borrow the car instead of the money?

Leasing is an increasingly popular way to use credit to get a car. When you lease, you never really own the car, but make monthly payments for the period of the lease—usually 3–5 years. When the lease is up, you can return the car, buy it back from the dealer for the price specified in the lease agreement, or sometimes extend the lease a month at a time.

To get the lease, you must file a credit application to establish your credit-worthiness, just as though it were a loan.

The Appeal of Leasing

Leasing's greatest appeals are upscaling—you can afford to lease a more expensive car—and exceptionally low initial costs: you pay only a leasing fee and one month's installment as security (which you get back at the end). And there's no up front sales tax—you pay a small amount of tax with each payment.

The kicker, of course, is the added cost of the car if you decide to buy it back when the lease ends. *For example, if you lease a $17,000 car for 3 years, with payments of $300 a month, you'll pay $10,800 for the lease period. But if the buy-back price is $12,000, your total cost to buy the car will then be $22,800.*

Closed vs. Open-end Leases

If you get a *closed-end lease*, the lease period and monthly payments are fixed. So is the price of the car, if you want to buy it when the lease ends. In an *open-end lease*, the lease period is variable, and the price to purchase the car varies with the market value and the car's condition.

Lease Features

- Leasing company owns the car.

- You must pay the full lease amount—even if you want to turn in the car before the lease is up. (*However, if you trade your leased car in for a new one with the same dealer, you may be able to negotiate.*)

- There are mileage limits—usually 45,000 for 3 years and 60,000 for 4 years. If you exceed the limits, you pay a mileage charge, usually 10–15¢ each additional mile.

- You are responsible for maintenance. Dealers may have special plans or may provide some services free as part of the lease. You may be required to use an authorized dealer for service, and you must keep careful records to show required service was done.

- You arrange for insurance, though the dealer may help. However, you must insure the full value of the new car throughout the lease, so the insurance may cost more.

- If the leasing company does not agree to an insurance settlement for a loss, you may have to pay the difference.

- You're stuck with the car—or at least the car payments—until the lease ends.

- You turn in the car at the end of 3 or 4 years. Repairs after that become the dealer's—or the next owner's—problem.

The Wiggly Bottom Line

Deciding whether to pay cash, borrow, or lease is not simple: money, convenience, and lifestyle are all considerations.

The chart at the left gives you a rough estimate of the cost factors. You can plug in your own numbers. (*Assuming the car is held for 4 years, the cost of a car for one year is the final cost divided by 4.*)

Source: Reprinted with permission of Simon & Schuster from *The Wall Street Journal Guide To Understanding Personal Finance* by Kenneth M. Morris and Alan M. Siegel. Copyright ©1992 by Lightbulb Press, Inc..

Loan

	$_____	Down payment
+	$_____	Sales tax
+	$_____	Monthly payment ($___ × 48)
=	$_____	Cost
−	$_____	Resale value
−	$_____	Interest earned on untouched investment
=	$_____	FINAL COST

Lease

	$_____	Leasing fee
+	$_____	Prepayment
+	$_____	Monthly payment including tax ($___ × 48)
=	$_____	Cost
−	$_____	Interest earned on untouched investment
=	$_____	FINAL COST

Cash

	$_____	Purchase Price
+	$_____	Sales tax
+	$_____	Loss of investment interest (purchase price $___ × ___% interest × 4)
=	$_____	Cost
−	$_____	Resale value
=	$_____	FINAL COST

step, the lender will provide a loan application form, as displayed in Exhibit 5.4, for you to complete.

Much of the information required on a credit card application is also required on a consumer loan application. You must provide your name, address, employer, salary, and other outstanding obligations. Unlike a credit card application, most consumer loan applications require you to list the specific purpose of the loan (for example, auto purchase, home improvement, loan consolidation, education, furniture purchase). For some loans, property that you list may serve as collateral for the loan.

Besides the loan application, the potential lender may require submission of a "personal statement." A personal statement is a summary of your assets, liabilities, income, expenses, and other personal financial information, similar to the financial statements we constructed in Chapter 2. Most lenders will also obtain a copy of your credit report and check credit references that you provide.

As with obtaining credit, you actually begin the loan qualification process long before you apply for a loan. Lenders consider many factors when evaluating your application for a loan. These factors generally fall into five categories, which have been dubbed the **five Cs of consumer borrowing:** character, capital, capacity, collateral, and conditions.

five Cs of consumer borrowing Five factors that lenders consider in evaluating loan applications. The five Cs are character, capital, capacity, collateral, and conditions.

1. *Character* refers to the integrity of the prospective borrower. In considering the character of the prospective borrower, the lender seeks answers to a number of questions. Does he or she honor outstanding loan obligations by making required payments on time? Has the borrower declared bankruptcy? Are there outstanding legal judgments against the borrower that have not been satisfied? Are there liens against any of the borrower's property? A **lien** is legal protection for a creditor since it entitles the creditor to have the debtor's property sold to satisfy the outstanding debt.

lien A claim on property as security for a debt.

2. *Capital* refers to the net worth position of the applicant. Recall from Chapter 2 that net worth is the difference between your assets and your liabilities. Obviously, prospective borrowers that have a stronger net worth position are better risks for lenders. Should the borrower's current stream of income be interrupted, net worth provides a cushion of funds that can be drawn upon to continue to make payments on the debt.

3. *Capacity* refers to the ability of the borrower to repay borrowed amounts based upon current income and expenses. Capital, discussed above, considers the wealth of the borrower—the surplus of assets over liabilities that has been accumulated over time. Capacity is a "flow" measure. It considers your monthly income in relation to your monthly expenses. Obviously, the higher the net cash flow, the difference between income and expenses, the greater your capacity to repay a loan.

Exhibit 5.4

Typical Financial Institution Loan Application

☐ Individual or ☐ Joint ☐ Secured or ☐ Unsecured

UNION PLANTERS BANK

Credit Application
(Closed end, unsecured/secured)

PERSONAL NOTES ABOUT YOURSELF

Name	Your Birthday
Current Address	Home Phone No.

City   State   Zip   How long at this address? Yrs. _____ Mos.

If you have lived at current address less than 5 years, please list your previous address.

Employer	Your Social Security No.
Employer's Address	Phone Number
Employed Since	Position	Monthly Salary (Gross)
Previous Employer		Years There

Alimony, child support or separate maintenance income need not be revealed if you do not choose to have it considered as a basis for repaying this obligation. You may want to list other income.

Other Income $ _____ per _____   Source

YOUR REFERENCES

Checking account is with (Acct. No.)	Savings account is with (Acct. No.)
Name of nearest relative not living with you	Relationship
Address	Phone number

Mortgage Holder/Landlord name and address

Mortgage/Rental Mo. Pmt.	Current Balance	Value of Home

Name of Other References	Balance	Mo. Pmt.

Have you ever filed bankruptcy or had any judgements filed against you? ☐ Yes ☑ No

FOR SECURED CREDIT (complete only if applying for secured credit)

Automobile	Year	Make/Model	List or Cost	Down Payment	Amount to Finance
☐ New ☐ Used					

Other Security (fully describe)

Application completed by ☐ Applicant ☐ Bank. By signing below, you certify that all above information is true and complete and you authorize Union Planters National Bank to request and obtain all credit information necessary to process your application.

Applicant Signature _____ Date _____

NOTES ABOUT JOINT APPLICANT (Complete only if applying for joint credit)

Name	Your Birthday
Current Address	Home Phone No.

City   State   Zip   How long at this address? Yrs. _____ Mos.

If you have lived at current address less than 5 years, please list your previous address.

Employer	Your Social Security No.
Employer's Address	Phone Number
Employed Since	Position	Monthly Salary (Gross)
Previous Employer		Years There

Alimony, child support or separate maintenance income need not be revealed if you do not choose to have it considered as a basis for repaying this obligation. You may want to list other income.

Other Income $ _____ per _____   Source

JOINT APPLICANT REFERENCES (Complete only if applying for joint credit)

Checking account is with (Acct. No.)	Savings account is with (Acct. No.)
Name of nearest relative not living with you	Relationship
Address	Phone number

Mortgage Holder/Landlord name and address

Mortgage/Rental Mo. Pmt.	Current Balance	Value of Home

Name of Other References	Balance	Mo. Pmt.

Have you ever filed bankruptcy or had any judgements filed against you? ☐ Yes ☐ No

Joint Applicant Signature (if applicable) _____ Date _____

YOUR LOAN REQUEST

Amount	Months Desired

Purpose

☐ Home Purchase
☐ Home Refinance
☐ Home Improvement

Notes
If this loan is for Home Purchase, Home Re-Finance or Home Improvement, the HMDA Addendum to Application is required at time of application.

☐ Automobile
☐ Personal
☐ Home Equity Line
☐ Other _____ (Check primary loan purpose)

FOR BANK USE

Branch

Interviewer   Date

Terms

Remarks

055-0176-02 REV 7/93

4. *Collateral* consists of items of value that may be pledged to secure the loan. Should the debtor default on a loan secured by collateral, the lender has a legal right to the property pledged as security. Some loans require the asset purchased through the loan to be pledged as collateral. Some loans use other property owned by the borrower to secure the loan.

5. *Conditions* refer to general economic conditions and conditions that are particular to the loan applicant. Lenders, for example, may be wary of extending loans during a recession for fear that the borrower may be laid-off from work. The same lenders may be more willing to extend credit during a period of economic expansion when lenders have greater confidence. Conditions relating to the individual applicant are also considered. The borrower may be a seasonal worker at the beginning or end of the busy season, or he or she may be employed in a cyclical industry. Lenders will incorporate this information when evaluating the prospective borrower's creditworthiness.

The decision to grant a loan may not simply be a yes-or-no decision. The lender may be unwilling to extend credit under the terms reserved for the best credit risks. However, the lender may be willing to extend the loan if the loan terms are adjusted to reflect the higher degree of risk. Recall that the interest rate reserved for the best, most creditworthy borrowers is called the prime rate. Applicants who are in a weaker financial condition may be required to pay the prime rate plus two or three additional percentage points to compensate for this increased risk. Borrowers in a weaker financial position may also be required to pledge collateral to secure the loan or have someone cosign for them.

Just because your loan application is denied by one lender does not mean that a second lender will also deny the application. However, the second lender may be willing to lend you the money only at terms that are less favorable than the first lender would have offered had you qualified. If you are willing to agree to less favorable terms, you will probably be able to obtain a loan. Some auto loan companies, for example, specialize in purchasing the loans of car dealers that have extended credit to purchasers who have already defaulted on other loans or filed for personal bankruptcy. In seeking a loan, always start with the lender that offers the best terms for the type of loan desired, and consider other sources only if the lender denies your application.

Managing Debt

Most individuals will borrow money at one time or another. It is important that you manage your consumer debt effectively. Knowing how much you can and should borrow, and understanding loan provisions, including how finance charges are assessed, are the keys to effective consumer debt management.

Amount of Debt

A popular adage for borrowers is "never borrow more than you can afford to repay." Although this standard sounds reasonable, how can you determine how much you can borrow? Two standards are commonly used to assess the amount of consumer debt: the level of disposable personal income versus required debt payments, and the level of net worth in relation to the amount owed.

Ratio of Debt Payments to Disposable Income. The first measure, the ratio of debt payments to disposable income, measures your ability to make your nonmortgage debt payments from current disposable income. Debt payments include both repayment of loan principal and interest. So if your monthly debt payments, excluding mortgage payments, are $300, and your monthly take-home pay is $2,000, your ratio is 15 percent. According to the National Foundation for Consumer Credit, the ratio of monthly payments for personal debts, excluding mortgage payments, to your take-home pay should not exceed 20 percent. For "average" American households, this ratio has hovered around the 10 percent figure over the last 25 years.[2]

This ratio is a "flow" measure since it matches cash inflows, your take-home pay, with cash outflows, the amount needed to make payments on the debt. A low ratio of debt payments to disposable income (less than 10 percent) indicates that you can borrow more. With a ratio of 10 to 20 percent, the borrower may feel pressured to make required payments. Ratios exceeding 20 percent indicate that too much has been borrowed, based on the disposable income available to repay the debt. Financial distress may soon follow.

Ratio of Debt to Net Worth. The second measure of your use of debt is the ratio of debt to net worth, excluding mortgage debt and the value of the home from this calculation. This ratio is a "stock" measure since it relates the level of debt owed to accumulated net worth. Recall that net worth equals the difference between assets and liabilities. Thus if you have total assets, excluding your home, of $80,000 and total debts, excluding your mortgage, of $20,000, your ratio of debt to net worth would be:

$$\text{Ratio of Debt to Net Worth} = \frac{\$20,000}{\$80,000 - \$20,000} = 33.33\%$$

A ratio of 100% or more indicates that no additional debt should be undertaken until existing debt is retired or net worth increases. Obviously, the lower the ratio, the greater the ability to safely service additional debt.

At year-end 1994, the ratio of household assets to total debt (consumer debt plus mortgage debt) was about six to one, whereas the ratio of financial assets to total debt was a little under four to one. Although the average net worth of consumers increased from 1989 to 1994, the ratio of debt to net worth also increased, indicating greater use of debt by consumers.[3]

Loan Provisions

loan principal The amount of a loan on which interest is paid.

Consumer debt has a language all its own. It is important to "speak the language" before you apply for a consumer loan. The **loan principal** is simply the amount of money that you borrow and on which you pay interest. The loan maturity, as explained earlier, is the duration of the loan. Thus, if you borrow $3,000 and agree to repay the money you borrowed in three years, the loan principal is $3,000, and the loan maturity is three years. If you repay $1,000 of the loan one year later, the loan principal is now $2,000, and the loan maturity is now two years.

Finance charges, as noted in Chapter 4, are the interest payments you must make to compensate the lender for the use of the funds. Finance charges are determined by the maturity of the loan, the principal, the interest rate charged, and the method of calculating finance charges.

There are three common methods of determining finance (interest) charges on consumer loans: the simple interest method, the discount method, and the add-on method.

simple interest method A method of determining interest charges under which interest is charged on the outstanding loan balance.

1. Under the **simple interest method,** interest is charged only on the amount that you actually owe at any point in time. Thus if you borrow $3,000 at 10 percent interest for one year, the interest charged under the simple interest method would be:

$$\$3,000 \times .10 = \$300$$

At maturity, you would pay $3,300, consisting of $3,000 in loan principal plus $300 in interest.

You may also be charged simple interest on an installment loan. As with a single-payment, simple interest loan, you only pay interest on the outstanding balance at any point in time under a simple interest installment loan. Simple interest installment loans require equal periodic payments. Although the installment payments are equal amounts, the portion of each payment that is repayment of principal increases with each payment, whereas the portion of each payment that represents interest decreases. Exhibit 5.5 illustrates the mechanics of principal and interest payments with a simple interest, installment loan.

discount method A method of determining interest charges under which interest is calculated based on the loan principal and then deducted from the principal; the borrower receives the remainder but repays the original principal amount.

2. A second method of calculating finance charges is the discount method. Under the **discount method,** finance charges are calculated

Exhibit 5.5

Simple Interest on Installment Loans

Assume that you borrowed $3,000 at 10 percent interest, to be repaid through 12 monthly payments. As you may recall from Chapter 2, the loan payment can be determined by using the formulas, interest rate tables, or a financial calculator:

$3,000 PV   ($3,000 is the present value)

.8333 %i   ([10%/12] interest per month)

12 n   (there are 12 payments)

CPT PMT   (compute the payment) = $263.75

or through the present value annuity formula:

$$A \times \frac{1 - 1/(1 + .008333)^{12}}{.008333} = \$3,000$$

Over the life of the loan, you will pay a total of $3,164.97 (12 × $263.75), of which $164.97 is interest. Although the payments are level, each payment can be divided into two components—interest and repayment of principal. Since you are charged only interest on the outstanding loan balance, the portion of each payment that is interest declines over the life of the loan, while the principal portion increases:

Month	Outstanding Balance	Monthly Payment	Principal	Interest	Ending Balance
1	$3,000.00	$263.75	$238.75	$25.00	$2,761.25
2	2,761.25	263.75	240.74	23.01	2,520.52
3	2,520.52	263.75	242.74	21.00	2,277.77
4	2,277.77	263.75	244.77	18.98	2,033.01
5	2,033.01	263.75	246.81	16.94	1,786.20
6	1,786.20	263.75	248.86	14.88	1,537.34
7	1,537.34	263.75	250.94	12.81	1,286.40
8	1,286.40	263.75	253.03	10.72	1,033.37
9	1,033.37	263.75	255.14	8.61	778.24
10	778.24	263.75	257.26	6.49	520.97
11	520.97	263.75	259.41	4.34	261.57
12	261.57	263.75	261.57	2.18	0.00
Total		$3,164.97	$3,000.00	$164.97	

Note that the interest portion of each payment is simply .8333 percent multiplied by the outstanding loan balance. Numbers appearing in the table have been rounded to the nearest cent.

based upon the loan principal, and then are deducted from the principal, with the borrower receiving the net amount. Thus in the previous example, the borrower would receive only $2,700 and would be required to repay $3,000 at maturity. Although using the simple interest method and discount method result in equal interest payments ($300 in either case), there is a major difference. With simple interest, the borrower paid $300 of interest in exchange for the use of $3,000 for one year. Using the discount method, the borrower paid $300 of interest in exchange for having the use of $2,700 for one year. The annual percentage rates (APRs) of the two loans are 10 and 11.11 percent, respectively.[4]

3.   A third method of calculating finance charges is the add-on method. Under the **add-on method,** finance charges are calculated based on the original loan principal. Then the finance charges are added back to the principal, and installment payments are based upon the sum of these two values. Once again, using the $3,000, 10 percent interest loan, with monthly installment payments for one year, the monthly payment would be:

add-on method A method of determining interest charges under which interest is calculated based on the loan principal and added to the principal; installment payments are based on the sum of these values.

$$\frac{(\$3,000 + \$300)}{12 \text{ Payments}} = \$275$$

Notice that this monthly payment ($275) exceeds the monthly payment determined under the simple interest method ($263.75), as shown in Exhibit 5.5. What accounts for this difference? The difference in monthly payments is explained by the fact that under the simple interest method, you only pay interest on the amount of principal outstanding at any time. Thus as you repay the loan, less interest is charged. Under the add-on method, interest is paid on the original (full) loan principal for the entire year. Obviously, the add-on method is an expensive form of borrowing. Some retail stores, finance companies, and deposit-type institutions use this method to calculate finance charges.

The interest rate charged varies with economic conditions, the duration of the loan, the type of loan, and the creditworthiness of the borrower. Several financial publications print current representative loan rates, as illustrated in Exhibit 5.6.

Although the timing of loan payments is detailed in the loan agreement, you may have the funds necessary to repay the loan early. If you pay off the balance due before the loan matures, you may be able to reduce your finance charges since the money is not borrowed for as long. The loan agreement specifies whether the consumer can repay the loan before maturity. If you have been making regular payments when due, the lender may prefer to continue to receive the periodic principal payments plus interest. The loan agreement may specify a prepayment penalty if the loan is repaid early. A **prepayment penalty** is an additional charge made by the lender in order to recoup some of the interest lost when the loan was repaid early.

prepayment penalty An additional charge made by a lender to recoup some of the interest lost when a consumer repays a loan early.

Rule of 78s A widely used method of determining how much interest should be charged on an installment loan if the loan is repaid early; the rule favors lenders.

The prepayment penalty may be in the form of an additional month's interest or may be determined through application of a technique called the "Rule of 78s." The **Rule of 78s** is a widely used method of determining how much interest should be charged on an installment loan if the loan is repaid early. The Rule of 78s favors lenders by assessing larger interest charges than interest charges based on simple interest

Exhibit 5.6

Representative Loan Rates
Lowest Auto Loan Rates*

City	Institution	Phone	Rate (%)	Monthly Payment
New York	Bank of New York	800/942-1784	8.40	$319.81
Los Angeles	Sanwa Bank	213/896-7778	7.75	315.84
Chicago	St. Paul Federal Bank	312/622-5000	8.00	317.37
San Francisco	Sumitomo Bank	415/445-8000	7.75	315.84
Philadelphia	Firstrust	215/722-4000	7.99	317.31
Detroit	Standard Federal Bank	313/643-9600	7.50	314.33
Boston	Citizens Bank of Mass.	800/222-4322	8.00	317.37
Houston	First Heights Bank	800/456-8940	8.00	317.37
Dallas	First Madison Bank	800/345-0587	8.25	318.90
Washington	Columbia First Bank	703/247-5664	7.25	312.81
Miami	Executive National Bank	305/274-8382	6.90	310.70
Atlanta	Metrobank	404/255-8550	7.25	312.81
Cleveland	Huntington National Bank	216/344-6610	7.99	317.31
St. Louis	Roosevelt Bank	314/576-4500	7.50	314.33
Seattle	First Interstate Bank	206/292-3401	7.75	315.84

AVERAGE LOAN RATES			MORTGAGE RATES		
	1 Year Ago	This Issue		1 Year Ago	This Issue
Home-equity line	7.13%	7.95%	30-year fixed	6.98%	8.39%
Personal loans	15.54%	15.44%	15-year fixed	6.49%	7.91%
Auto loans	8.20%	8.55%	ARM	4.25%	5.47%

* Lowest rate from among the largest banks and thrifts in each of the 15 largest markets. Fixed rates are based on $13,000 borrowed for 48 months by walk-in customers. Rates may vary by branch.
Data are from Bank Rate Monitor, P.O Box 088888, North Palm Beach, FL 33408-8888; 800/327-7717. Figures as of 8/17/94
Source: *Your Money* (October/November 1994), p. 14. Reprinted with permission.

or add-on interest. The rule is also called the sum of the years digits method because it takes its name from the sum of the digits in the months of a one-year loan (1 + 2 + 3 + ... + 11 + 12 = 78).

An example will show how the Rule of 78s is applied. Again, assume that you borrow $3,000, at 10 percent add-on interest, to be repaid through 12 monthly payments. Under the add-on method, as we saw earlier, the monthly payment is $275, consisting of $250 of principal plus $25 in interest. Further assume that your loan agreement includes a prepayment penalty to be assessed according to the Rule of 78s. If you decided to pay off the loan early, your interest is recalculated under the

Rule of 78s. Rather than paying one–twelfth of the interest each month, this method assumes that you pay 12/78 of the interest the first month, 11/78 the second month, and so on, for a 12-month loan. Exhibit 5.7 shows how much you would be required to pay to retire the loan after eight months. Notice how this technique moves most of the interest to the early payments of the loan, permitting the lender to earn more interest while the borrower retires less principal with each payment.

Alternatively, a borrower may not have the funds necessary to repay the loan when it comes due. Single-payment loans are especially susceptible to this problem since consumers are required to repay the entire amount borrowed, with interest, through a single lump sum payment when the loan matures. Depending upon the specific provisions of the loan, the lender has several options available. For example, the lender may offer a loan extension. A **loan extension** increases the duration of the loan, providing the borrower additional time to repay the loan. Alternatively, the lender may seek a legal remedy against the borrower. Another option is a loan rollover. A **loan rollover** is a loan taken out to repay the first loan. Financial institutions that offer rollovers usually require that at least part of the original loan principal and interest be repaid by the borrower.

Installment loans are also susceptible to default by the borrower. To protect their interests, many lenders include an acceleration clause in installment loan contracts. An **acceleration clause** specifies that if the borrower misses a scheduled installment payment, the entire debt automatically becomes payable at that time. Some lenders charge late fees or other penalties instead of demanding payment in full when an installment payment is missed even though the loan agreement may include an acceleration clause.

Some installment loan agreements are structured to include a balloon payment. A **balloon payment** is a single, large payment at the end of the series of smaller installment payments. Under the Truth in Lending Act, any payment that is more than twice the value of the regular installment payment must be specifically disclosed as a balloon payment. Balloon payments are favorable to lenders since a larger amount of the loan principal remains outstanding for a longer period. Balloon payments may produce an undue hardship for borrowers in that higher finance charges must be paid since a greater portion of the loan remains outstanding longer and a payment in excess of the normal amount is required to retire the loan.

loan extension An agreement increasing the duration of a loan, thereby providing the borrower with additional time to repay the loan.

loan rollover A loan taken out to repay another loan.

acceleration clause A clause in a loan agreement that specifies that if the borrower misses a scheduled installment payment, the entire debt automatically becomes payable at that time.

balloon payment A single large payment at the end of a series of smaller installment payments.

Credit Counseling and Personal Bankruptcy

People who fail to manage credit and consumer borrowing wisely face severe consequences. If you are not able to make your scheduled pay-

Exhibit 5.7

The Rule of 78s

Assume that you borrow $3,000 for one year at 10 percent add-on interest. The total interest would be $300. Your monthly payment would be $275, of which $25 would be interest. How much would you have to pay to retire the loan after eight months if the loan included a prepayment penalty according to the Rule of 78s?

To determine how much of each installment payment is interest according to the Rule of 78s, sum the digits or use this shortcut formula:

Sum of the digits $= \dfrac{N}{2} * (N + 1)$, where N is number of months

For a 12-month loan, the sum is: $\dfrac{12}{2} \times (12 + 1) = 78$

Thus (12/78) of the $300 in interest is paid in the first month, (11/78) is paid in the second month, and so on. Knowing the interest ratios from the Rule of 78s and the amount of interest payable, you can recalculate principal and interest:

Month	Payment Assuming Add-On Interest	Interest According to the Rule of 78s	Principal According to the Rule of 78s
1	$275.00	$46.15	$228.85
2	275.00	42.31	232.69
3	275.00	38.46	236.54
4	275.00	34.62	240.38
5	275.00	30.77	244.23
6	275.00	26.92	248.08
7	275.00	23.08	251.92
8	275.00	19.23	255.77
9	275.00	15.38	259.62
10	275.00	11.54	263.46
11	275.00	7.69	267.31
12	275.00	3.85	271.15
	$3,300.00	$300.00	$3,000.00

Suppose that after making eight payments, you decide to retire the loan. The lender is not entitled to interest on the four remaining payments:

$15.38 + 11.54 + 7.69 + 3.85 = \$38.46$ or $(10/78) \times \$300 = \$38.46$

To determine how much you must pay to retire the loan immediately after the eighth payment, the interest remaining at that time is deducted from the total owed:

Total to be repaid ($3,000 + 300)	$3,300.00
Less total repaid with eight payments (8 * 275)	2,200.00
	1,100.00
Less interest "refunded" to borrower	38.46
Total needed to retire loan	1,061.54

Notice that the total paid after eight months ($2,200) plus the amount needed to retire the loan ($1,061.54) equals $3,261.54. Although the loan was retired in two-thirds of the time, you paid more than 87 percent of the originally scheduled interest.

ments, you may receive calls and letters from creditors. The creditors may also seek the assistance of a collection agency or "sell" your account to the collection agency, which in turn will attempt to collect from you. Assets that you pledged to secure loans may be repossessed by the lender. Legal proceedings may be filed against you, and in some jurisdictions, your pay may be garnished. A **garnishment** is a legal attachment to your earnings, directing your employer to withhold a portion of your earnings to be used to satisfy outstanding debt.

What can you do if you find yourself overburdened by debt? One alternative is to enlist the services of a credit counseling organization.

garnishment Legal attachment of a debtor's earnings, directing the debtor's employer to withhold a portion of the debtor's earnings to be used to satisfy the outstanding debt.

 **5.3   Six Ways to Repay Your Debts**

After engineer Charles King, 37, of Spring, Texas was laid off from his job four years ago, borrowing became his way of making ends meet. In no time, he was awash in debt. "I'd take a cash advance from a lower-rate credit card to pay off another," he says. "My total payments became so high that I was falling behind on my house payments." When creditors began hounding him at home, King knew he needed help.

Even if creditors aren't hounding you yet, your debt could be on the verge of choking your finances. Take this test: If your total monthly payments on personal, short-term debts—including car loans, and bank, department store and gas cards, but excluding your mortgage—exceed 20% of your take-home pay, you may be in over your head, says the National Foundation for Consumer Credit.

And you wouldn't be alone. After decreasing in the early 1990s, consumer borrowing is on the upswing. Installment-

debt payments as a portion of disposable income now average 7%, according to economist Susan Sterne, compared with just below 6% three years ago.

If you're swamped by debt, here are six moves you can make to get your head above water:

Resolve to pay till it hurts.

First, add up your debts, totaling the combined required monthly payments for each account. Next, review your budget and determine the maximum you can afford to spend on debt payments. A good goal would be to commit at least 25% of your net income to paying down debt. Then resolve to stifle your charging habits. "If you're in substantial debt trouble," says Peg Downey, a financial planner in Silver Spring, MD, "figure that you'll have to limit discretionary spending for at least a couple of years." Ouch.

Establish priorities.

Devise a strategy to eliminate first those short-term debts with

the highest interest charges— usually balances on department store cards whose interest rates hover around 21%. Say, for example, you have outstanding balances on six credit cards totaling $6,000. If you pay only the minimum monthly payment without regard to the varying interest charges on each card, you would need more than 21 years (258 months) to clear the debt and you'd pay $7,667 in interest alone. By paying only $10 more each month and making high-rate cards a priority, you can wipe out that load in 3 1/2 years (43 months) and get nicked for a more bearable $2,183 in interest.

Get in touch with your creditors.

If you can't meet your minimum payments, explain your total debt picture to creditors and tell them the amount you can pay each one now. While banks and card issuers will not forgive loans, you may be able to negotiate some short-term

Consider This

You can visit the Consumer Credit Counseling Service online at:

http://cccsedu.org/

Another nonprofit credit counseling agency is American Consumer Credit Counseling, Inc., at:

http://www.consumer-credit.com/

Should that fail, you may have to consider personal bankruptcy. Insight 5.3 provides additional advice about what you should do if you cannot pay your debts.

Credit Counseling Organizations

Credit counseling organizations attempt to assist debtors by providing advice on debt management and by helping negotiate repayment terms with creditors on the debtor's behalf. The repayment terms may include

relief—such as waived late fees and penalties or even a reduced interest rate.

Refinance.

You can also lower your interest rate in a number of other ways: Refinance your mortgage; shift your high-rate credit-card balances to a low-rate card; use a low-rate home-equity loan to pay off expensive debt; or as a last resort borrow from your 401(k) plan.

"Paying off one loan with another is a good tool only if you're disciplined and have changed your spending habits," says Mary Stephenson, head of the financial counseling service at the University of Maryland's cooperative extension. Otherwise, you may simply run up more debts.

Also, avoid consolidation loans, available at many banks and finance companies. Interest rates on these products tend to be higher—as high as 40%—than those on credit cards.

Get dependable help.

The Consumer Credit Counseling Service (CCCS) offers free or low-cost financial help at more than 1,100 offices nationwide (800-388-2227). The CCCS and similar groups negotiate directly with all your creditors to devise a debt-repayment plan that satisfies everyone. Then, instead of paying each creditor each month, you pay only CCCS and they distribute the money.

Charles King turned to the Houston office of CCCS two years ago when the balances on his five credit cards were approaching $20,000. Now, employed once again and two years into a five-year repayment plan, King sends CCCS a monthly check for $460. And he now buys everything with cash. "I still get those offers for new credit cards," says King, "but now I throw them in the trash."

For CCCS offices that charge for this service (about two-thirds of them do), it costs an average of $9 a month, but their help can pay off many times over. Card issuers are more likely to agree to favorable repayment terms with CCCS than with you because of the group's long-standing relationship with the credit industry. Those easier terms can save you plenty.

Avoid bad advice.

That includes so-called credit doctors and repair clinics that offer to clean up your credit report. At best, these outfits take your money ($250 to $1,000) to do what you can do for yourself: Get copies of your credit reports from the three credit reporting agencies, Experion, Equifax and Trans Union, and challenge inaccurate entries. At worst, credit repair clinics take your money and do nothing. Quite simply, credit reports can't be "cleaned up." Even if you ultimately eliminate your debt, late- or missed-payment histories will remain on your record for as many as seven years. You are, however, entitled to add a 100-word statement to your credit reports indicating why you ran into trouble. Otherwise, only paying your debts in a timely manner can improve your credit report and get you back afloat financially.

Source: Excerpted from Ellen Stark, "Swamped by Debt? Here Are Six Ways to Get Out," Reprinted from the September 1995 issue of *Money*, by special permission; copyright 1995 Time Inc.

waiver of certain fees, such as finance charges and late fees, and extension of the time period over which the debt may be repaid.

Consumer Credit Counseling Service (CCCS) is the largest and best-known credit counseling organization. Since the 1950s, CCCS offices throughout the United States have assisted consumers who have become overextended. About one third of the consumers who use the services of CCCS set up debt consolidation plans, and of this group, about one half finish debt repayment.[5] The CCCS charges low fees or no fees to consumers for their assistance. Although there are other credit and debt assistance programs, you should be wary of organizations that promise to "fix" your credit in exchange for a fee.

Bankruptcy

Should credit counseling fail, at some point, the debtor may attempt to obtain relief from creditors through filing a personal bankruptcy petition. **Personal bankruptcy** is an official declaration that an individual is unable to repay amounts owed. If the court approves the bankruptcy petition, the assets and earnings of the debtor will be administered in the creditors' best interests, and certain financial obligations may be discharged. Bankruptcy petitions must be filed in U.S. federal court. The debtor must pay a filing fee and have legal representation.

There are several forms of bankruptcy. The two most popular forms are Chapter 13 and Chapter 7, named after the actual sections of the U.S. Bankruptcy Code in which the provisions of each appear. **Chapter 13 bankruptcy** is a legal remedy through which the debts of the individual are restructured according to a repayment plan. Chapter 13 is designed for debtors who have a regular earnings stream and when there is a reasonable chance that the debtor may be able to repay his or her obligations if given time and protection from creditors. Chapter 13 bankruptcy is also known as the Wage Earner Plan and the Regular Income Plan.

Under Chapter 13, the debtor prepares a list of financial obligations and a plan for repayment of part or all of these obligations over the next three to five years. The court and a majority of creditors must approve the plan. If it is approved, the debtor makes regular payments to the court or a court-appointed trustee, who in turn makes payments to the creditors. During this period of structured payments, interest and late payment fees are waived. The debtor is prevented from taking on additional debt without the permission of the trustee. Should the debtor make the scheduled payments, any remaining obligations are discharged. Note that the debtor retains the use of his or her assets, and no assets are liquidated. The upper limit for total debt under Chapter 13 bankruptcy was increased from $450,000 to $1 million under the Bankruptcy Reform Act of 1994. The $1 million limit includes up to $750,000 in secured debt and $250,000 in unsecured debt.

personal bankruptcy
A legal declaration that an individual is unable to repay amounts owed.

Chapter 13 bankruptcy A legal remedy through which the debts of an individual are restructured according to a repayment plan.

Consider This

LawLinks provides detailed information about personal bankruptcy at:

http://www.lawlinks.com/

Go to the "Consumer Center" and then the "Law Library."

Chapter 7 bankruptcy
A legal remedy through which a debtor's assets are immediately liquidated and the debtor is relieved of further obligations to his or her creditors.

The majority of individuals filing for bankruptcy protection elect the more drastic declaration, Chapter 7 (or "straight bankruptcy"). **Chapter 7 bankruptcy** is a legal remedy through which a debtor's assets are immediately liquidated, and the debtor is relieved of further obligations to his or her creditors. A declaration of Chapter 7 is granted when a debtor is so overburdened by debt that there is a low probability that the debtor will ever be able to recover. Under Chapter 7, the debtor is permitted to retain minimal assets such as work-related tools and basic household furnishings, but the remainder of assets is liquidated, and the proceeds distributed to creditors. Declaring bankruptcy relieves only certain obligations, including credit card debt, medical bills, auto loans, utility bills, and rent. It does not cancel other debts, such as child support, alimony, student loans, income taxes, and court-ordered damages.

The Bankruptcy Reform Act of 1994 addressed some important bankruptcy issues.[6] In the past, divorced spouses were subject to creditor claims for debts incurred during marriage that were supposed to be the other spouse's responsibility as part of the divorce settlement. The act should prevent divorced spouses from being held responsible for debts the other spouse agreed to pay. The act also targeted fraud and recently incurred debt. Henceforth bankruptcy will not forgive debts incurred for luxury items and cash advances taken within 60 days of filing for bankruptcy protection.

Obviously, there are some benefits for the debtor who declares bankruptcy. Certain debts are either forgiven or restructured, and the debtor is permitted to retain certain assets. Debt restructuring provides more time to repay the amount owed and reduces or eliminates interest penalties and late fees. Through bankruptcy, those who have not managed debt and credit successfully in the past have the opportunity to wipe the slate clean and start over again.

However, bankruptcy also has some serious negative consequences. Real dollar costs are associated with bankruptcy—attorney fees and filing fees. Second, as mentioned earlier, not all of your debts can be discharged through bankruptcy. For example, income taxes owed, student loans, loans for luxury items, and cash advances taken just prior to filing for bankruptcy are not discharged. Third, if you declare bankruptcy, your personal finances become a matter of public record. Fourth, you cannot apply for Chapter 7 bankruptcy again for six years after your debts are discharged. Finally, and most importantly, landlords, lenders, and employers view a prior declaration of bankruptcy unfavorably. It may be difficult to obtain housing, credit, short-term loans, long-terms loans, and employment if there is a declaration of bankruptcy in your credit history. Credit reporting agencies can keep a bankruptcy on your record for ten years.

SUMMARY

- Consumer borrowing refers to obtaining funds from a lender under specific loan provisions. Such loans are made for a specified purpose and must be repaid according to a specified schedule.

- Consumers borrow for a number of reasons, including to purchase expensive assets, to finance education or business startup, and for other reasons.

- Consumer borrowing has a number of advantages, including enabling the borrower to purchase expensive items, earlier enjoyment of these items, financial flexibility, and assistance should unexpected expenses or emergencies arise.

- Consumer borrowing has a number of disadvantages, including finance charges, loss of pledged assets if the borrower defaults, and serious consequences, including bankruptcy, if consumer debt is not well managed.

- Single payment consumer loans are repaid through one payment at maturity, whereas installment loans involve a series of payments.

- Secured loans require the borrower to pledge assets as collateral, whereas unsecured loans do not require posting collateral.

- Fixed-rate loans have a constant interest rate until the loan matures. With a variable-rate loan, the interest rate fluctuates over the life of the loan.

- Short-term loans are loans with a duration of one year or less. Long-term loans are loans for more than one year.

- Most consumer loans are for a specified, single, purpose. Consolidation loans are used to repay other outstanding loan obligations.

- Consumer loans are available from a number of sources, including deposit-type financial institutions, consumer finance companies, sales finance companies, life insurance policy loans, real estate equity loans, friends and family, and pawnshops.

- Banks, savings and loan associations, and credit unions offer a variety of types of consumer loans. These institutions have a ready source of loanable funds—deposits.

- Consumer finance companies offer small secured and unsecured loans on an installment basis at high rates of interest.

- Sales finance companies assist consumers with the purchase of high-priced assets by purchasing the debt of the seller. The largest sales finance companies are owned by the product manufacturers.

■ Cash value life insurance policies develop a savings reserve. Policy-owners can borrow the cash value through a life insurance policy loan.

■ Loans can also be taken against the equity in real estate. A second mortgage is a fixed-period installment loan that is subordinate to the first mortgage. A home equity loan is a line of credit issued against the equity in a home. Interest on home equity loans is tax deductible.

■ Family and friends may offer another source of consumer loans. Such loans, however, risk the loss of a friend or family discord should the borrower default.

■ Pawnshops extend single-payment loans at high rates for short periods, with the loan amount based on a percentage of the value of property pledged as collateral.

■ To obtain a consumer loan, the prospective borrower must complete a loan application. The application is evaluated by the lender, and a decision is made on whether the loan will be granted.

■ In evaluating the application, lenders consider the five Cs of consumer borrowing: character, capital, capacity, collateral, and conditions.

■ To determine how much you can borrow, debt payments should be compared to disposable income, and the amount borrowed should be compared to net worth.

■ The loan principal is the amount of money that you owe. The maturity of a loan is the loan's duration.

■ Finance charges are interest payments that must be made to compensate the lender for not having use of the funds. The simple interest method, discount method, and add-on method are used to determine finance charges.

■ If you repay a loan early, a prepayment penalty may be assessed. The Rule of 78s is sometimes used to determine the prepayment penalty.

■ If you are unable to a make a scheduled loan payment, the lender may offer an extension, roll the loan over, or seek a legal remedy. If an installment loan contains an acceleration clause, the entire loan balance becomes immediately due if a payment is missed.

■ Some installment loans include a balloon payment A balloon payment is a single, large payment at the end of the loan.

■ Borrowers experiencing financial distress may enlist the services of a credit counseling organization. These organizations provide advice and attempt to negotiate more favorable terms with creditors on behalf of the borrower.

■ Should credit counseling fail, the borrower may file for personal bankruptcy. If the bankruptcy petition is approved, the assets and earnings of the debtor will be administered in the best interests of the creditors.

■ Chapter 13 bankruptcy is elected if the debtor has a regular income and may be able to repay obligations if given time and protection from creditors.

■ Chapter 7 bankruptcy is granted if the debtor is so overburdened with debt that there is a low probability the debtor will recover. The debtor is permitted to keep certain assets, with the remainder liquidated and the proceeds distributed to creditors.

KEY CONCEPTS AND TERMS

Acceleration clause	Loan extension
Add-on method	Loan maturity
Balloon payment	Loan principal
Cash value life insurance	Loan rollover
Chapter 7 bankruptcy	Long-term loan
Chapter 13 bankruptcy	Pawnshop
Collateral	Personal bankruptcy
Consolidation loan	Prepayment penalty
Consumer borrowing	Rule of 78s
Consumer finance company	Sales finance company
Cosigner	Second mortgage
Discount method	Secured loan
Five Cs of consumer borrowing	Short-term loan
Fixed-rate loan	Simple interest method
Garnishment	Single-payment loan
Home equity loan	Unsecured loan
Interest	Usury rate
Lien	Variable-rate loan
Life insurance policy loan	

QUESTIONS FOR REVIEW

1. How are consumer credit and consumer borrowing similar? How do they differ?

2. What are some common uses of consumer borrowing? What are the advantages and disadvantages of consumer borrowing?

3. What is the difference between a single-payment loan and an install-ment payment loan? Explain how a loan may be secured by collateral.

4. How does a fixed-rate loan differ from a variable-rate loan? Which type of loan is better if interest rates decrease during the life of the loan?

5. What are the deposit-type financial institutions that offer consumer loans? Where do these institutions get funds to loan to consumers?

6. How does a consumer finance company differ from a sales finance company?

7. What information is usually required on a loan application? What are the five Cs of consumer credit, and why is each C important to lenders?

8. What are the methods of calculating finance charges? Which method is most advantageous to the borrower? Why?

9. Why do some loan agreements include a prepayment penalty? How is a prepayment penalty assessed according to the Rule of 78s?

10. What are the differences between Chapter 7 and Chapter 13 bank-ruptcy?

PROBLEMS

1. Donna would like to purchase some new furniture. Furniture Liq-uidators, "the home of low, Low, LOW furniture prices" is offering a sofa/sleeper pit set for the low, Low, LOW price of $1,200. The credit terms are simple interest with the low, Low, LOW interest rate of 1.75 percent per month and 12 monthly payments.
   a. What will Donna's monthly payment equal?
   b. How much interest will Donna pay over the life of this loan?

2. Carl would like to borrow some money to purchase a new car. Carl's current nonmortgage consumer debt payments are $250 per month. Carl's take-home pay is $2,400 per month. What is the maximum monthly car payment that Carl can afford such that his monthly nonmortgage debt payments (including the car payment) will not exceed 20 percent of take-home pay?

3. Stan borrowed $1,000 at 12 percent interest for one year. The lender uses the discount method to calculate finance charges.

    a. How much money will Stan be given at the time the loan is made?

    b. What is the actual interest rate on this loan?

4. Elizabeth borrowed $3,000 at 12 percent add-on interest, to be repaid through 12 monthly payments. The loan agreement included a pre-payment penalty, using the Rule of 78s. Five months later, Elizabeth received a promotion at work and a significant raise in pay. She decided to repay the remaining loan balance at that time. How much will Elizabeth have to pay at that time to retire the loan?

INTERNET EXERCISES

1. Internet sources for credit card rates given in Chapter 4 also give rates for consumer loans, such as car loans, home equity loans, and unsecured loans. Find the best rates in your area at:

    http://www.banx.com/

    or

    http://www.bankrate.com/

2. The Consumer Credit Counseling Service site mentioned in the text provides worksheets for consumers. Go to:

    http://cccsedu.org/

    and work through some of the worksheets.

3. Visit the Better Business Bureau at:

    http://www.bbb.org/

    and find out how to submit consumer complaints online.

CASE APPLICATIONS

Case I

Casey Adams is owner and operator of Shear Delight, a unisex hair styling salon. Like many entrepreneurs, Casey invested her life savings in the business and took out a loan for the balance necessary to open the salon. Business has been less than expected, and Casey is struggling to make ends meet. Another problem has recently surfaced—Casey has been having sharp abdominal pain. She consulted a physician who recommended a surgical procedure that will cost $4,000. Health insurance was a "luxury" that Casey thought she could do without. Since the hospital does not consider Casey's condition acute, they are unwilling to perform the operation unless Casey can provide evidence that she can pay for the procedure. Casey will have to borrow the money. Explain the advantages and disadvantages of each of the following alternatives as a source of funds for Casey:

1. Getting a personal loan from her bank

2. Borrowing the money from her ex-husband

3. Pawning the equipment from the salon

4. Obtaining a loan from a consumer finance company

Case II

Gerald Crenshaw is considering borrowing some money to finance the purchase of new furniture for his home. The furniture will cost $3,000. Gerald is considering several sources of loans, and each is offering different terms.

1. A consumer finance company is willing to loan Gerald $3,000 for one year using simple interest and charging a rate of 15 percent interest. How much will Gerald have to pay to retire the loan after one year?

2. The furniture retailer is willing to assist Gerald in obtaining financing through the furniture retailer's sales finance company. The sales finance company is willing to loan Gerald the money for one year using the discount method and charging 12 percent interest.

   a. Assuming Gerald must pay $3,000 at the maturity of the loan, how much money will Gerald receive at the time the loan is granted?

   b. What is the annual percentage rate (APR) of this loan?

3. Gerald visited a commercial bank to see what type of loan he could obtain. The commercial bank is willing to loan Gerald $3,000 under the following terms: monthly payments for one year and 9 percent add-on interest. What will Gerald's monthly payment equal under this alternative?

4. Gerald is a member of a credit union. The credit union is willing to provide a 9 percent interest, one-year loan to be repaid through four quarterly payments. The credit union uses the simple interest method to compute the quarterly payments. How much will Gerald be required to pay at the end of each quarter?

Case III

Walt owns a home valued at $140,000. Walt still owes about $80,000 on the property. Walt would like to help fund the cost of his daughter Josey's college education; however, Walt has no liquid savings available. A friend suggested that Walt should borrow against the equity in his home for this purpose.

1. Explain two ways in which Walt can use the existing equity in his home to assist with Josey's college expenses.

2. Suppose that Walt borrows $20,000 through a five-year home equity loan. The financial institution charges 10 percent interest annually, with the full amount due five years later.

   a. What is Walt's annual interest payment?

   b. Walt itemizes deductions when computing his federal income tax liability. Walt's taxable income, not considering the home equity loan, was $30,000 the first year. What impact will the home equity loan have upon Walt's taxable income?

Case IV

Mark and Tina Rogers have some serious debt problems. Both Mark and Tina are employed. Mark earns $18,000 per year, and Tina earns $22,000 per year. The couple has amassed $40,000 in debt through credit cards and consumer loans. Creditors and bill collectors have repeatedly contacted the couple. They are two payments behind on most loans and have been able to pay only the minimum amount due on their credit cards while charging more each month. The couple is wondering how they can ever recover from the "debt hell" in which they find themselves.

1. How could Consumer Credit Counseling Service help Mark and Tina?

2. Mark said, "I think the simple answer to our problems is to declare bankruptcy. We'll just write-off the $40,000 and start over again. No sweat. That's what bankruptcy is for." Which form of bankruptcy is Mark considering? Is there another type of bankruptcy that may be better suited in this situation?

SUGGESTIONS FOR ADDITIONAL READING

Canner, Glenn B., Arthur B. Kennickell, and Charles Luckett. "Household Sector Borrowing and the Burden of Debt." *Federal Reserve Bulletin,* April 1995, pp. 323 338.

Davis, Kristin. "Now You Won't Get Stuck If Your Ex Goes Bankrupt." *Kiplinger's Personal Finance Magazine,* December 1994, p. 34.

Dolan, Ken and Daria Dolan. *Straight Talk on Money.* New York: Simon & Schuster, 1993.

Morris, Kenneth M. and Alan M. Siegel. *The Wall Street Journal Guide to Understanding Personal Finance.* New York: Lightbulb Press, 1992.

Personal Financial Planning Guide. Ernst & Young. New York: John Wiley & Sons, 1995.

Sloane, Leonard. *The New York Times Personal Finance Handbook*. New York: Times Books, 1995, Chapter 4.

Tyson, Eric. *Personal Finance for Dummies*. Foster City, Calif.: IDG Books Worldwide, 1995.

NOTES

1. The figures for installment credit from commercial banks, savings institutions, and credit unions presented in this section were taken from Table 1.55, "Consumer Installment Credit," *Federal Reserve Bulletin*, April 1995, p. A39.

2. Figures presented in this paragraph are from Glenn B. Canner, Arthur B. Kennickell, and Charles Luckett, "Household Sector Borrowing and the Burden of Debt," *Federal Reserve Bulletin*, April 1995, pp. 324 and 325.

3. A simple example demonstrates how these seemingly contradictory events could occur at the same time. For example, assume that in 1989, an individual had total assets of $100,000 and total debts of $20,000. Thus the person's net worth was $80,000, and the ratio of debt to net worth is .25. In 1994, the individual's total assets were $120,000, and total liabilities were $30,000. Thus the person's net worth was $90,000, and the ratio of debt to net worth is .333. So even though the level of net worth increased ($80,000 to $90,000), the ratio of debt to net worth also increased.

4. The APR under the discount method is simply:

$$\frac{\$300}{\$2,700} = 11.11\%$$

5. *Kiplinger's Personal Finance Magazine*, "Credit Counseling Services: Debtors Find Relief." Date unknown.

6. The implications of the Bankruptcy Reform Act of 1994 were discussed in Kristin Davis, "Now You Won't Get Stuck If Your Ex Goes Bankrupt," *Kiplinger's Personal Finance Magazine*, December 1994, p. 34.

Chapter **6**

Tax Planning

Learning Objectives

After studying this chapter, you should be able to:

- Explain the meaning of gross income, adjusted gross income, and taxable income.

- Explain the difference between the standard deduction and itemized deductions.

- Identify the tax deductions that are typically itemized.

- Show how a tax credit differs from a tax deduction.

- Explain how the federal income tax is calculated.

- Prepare your own tax return by using Form 1040EZ.

- Explain how capital gains and losses are treated for tax purposes.

- Describe several tax planning strategies for reducing federal income taxes.

I'm proud to be paying taxes in the United States. The only thing is, I could be just as proud for half the money.

—Arthur Godfrey

The income tax has made more liars out of American people than golf has.

—Will Rogers

This chapter deals with taxes, primarily the federal income tax. It is one of the most important chapters in the entire text. Why is it so important? The biggest expenditure you will make in your lifetime will be the money you pay in taxes. The money you spend on a home, new car, vacations, and so on will dwarf the money you spend on taxes. *An average income worker can easily spend 40 percent or more of his or her annual income on taxes in all forms.* This is not an exaggeration. For example, assume that you earn $30,000 and are purchasing a home. You are in the 28 percent federal income tax bracket. You may be paying a state income tax of 4 percent or more on your income, a state and local sales tax of 6 percent or more, and a social security tax of 7.65 percent on covered earnings. You may also pay a property tax on your home that absorbs 3 percent or more of your income. Finally, you pay hidden taxes that you never see. The list is endless—gasoline taxes, telephone taxes, cigarette and liquor taxes, tire taxes, excise taxes, personal property taxes, license fees, real estate transfer tax, and dozens of additional taxes.

What's more, taxation does not end when you die. A taxable estate in excess of $600,000 must pay a federal estate tax on behalf of the deceased; the federal estate tax on taxable estates exceeding $3 million is now 55 percent. Unless you do some tax planning, you will be in tax bondage to the government for a large percentage of your working career. *Indeed, according to the Tax Foundation, in 1996, May 7 was tax freedom day. This means that in 1996, the average American worked 128 days to pay all federal, state, and local taxes based on the assumption that every dollar earned from the beginning of the year goes toward the paying of taxes.*[1] In view of these dismal statistics, it is not surprising that many middle-income taxpayers find the present tax system to be oppressive. Obviously, tax planning is a necessity.

This chapter discusses the role of tax planning in an overall financial plan. The thrust of the chapter is devoted to the federal income tax, which is one of the most important taxes in the United States. We will discuss the federal estate tax in Chapter 17.

This chapter discusses five important areas. In the first part of the chapter, we explain how the federal income tax is calculated, which requires an understanding of gross income, adjusted gross income, taxable income, deductions, and tax credits. In the second part, we discuss the different types of income tax forms that taxpayers use to pay their taxes. In the third part, we examine the tax treatment of capital gains and losses. In the fourth part, we discuss the major taxes paid at the state and local level. The chapter concludes with an important discussion of several legal tax strategies that you can use to reduce federal income taxes.

Understanding the Federal Income Tax

Consider This

For information and publications about income taxes, as well as tax forms and filing instructions, visit the IRS's "Digital Daily" at:

http://www.irs.ustreas.gov/prod/cover.html

The federal income tax law is horribly complex and consists of thousands of pages of detailed regulations. It is beyond the scope of this text to discuss the tax code in great detail. However, you should understand certain tax fundamentals and know how your income tax is calculated.[2] For ease of understanding, we will discuss the federal income tax under the following categories:

- Filing status

- Gross income

- Adjustments to income

- Taxable income

- Tax computation

- Tax credits

- Other taxes

- Tax payments

Filing Status

All persons with gross incomes over a certain amount must file a federal income tax return. The filing requirements apply even if you do not owe any tax. The obligation to file a tax return depends on your filing status and the amount of your gross income. Your **filing status** is a category that identifies you based on your marital and family situation; it is an important factor in determining whether you are required to file, the amount of the standard deduction (discussed later), and whether you can take other deductions and credits. There are five types of filing statuses:

filing status A category that identifies a taxpayer based on marital and family situation. The categories are single, married filing jointly, married filing separately, head of household, and qualifying widow(er) with dependent child.

- *Single.* A single taxpayer is unmarried, divorced, or legally separated.

- *Married filing jointly.* This category applies when you are married, and both you and your spouse file a joint return; the joint return shows your combined income and combined allowable deductions.

- *Married filing separately.* This category applies to married taxpayers who file separate tax returns. This method is used when you want to be responsible for only one return, or the tax payable is less than that payable under a joint return.

- *Head of household.* This category refers to someone who is unmarried or is considered unmarried on the last day of the year. In addition, you must have paid more than half the cost of keeping up a home for yourself and a qualifying person (such as a dependent child) for more than half the year.

■ *Qualifying widow(er) with dependent child.* This category refers to the filing status of a taxpayer with a dependent child whose spouse dies within two years of the current tax year. This filing status allows you to use joint-return rates and the highest standard deduction amount (if you do not itemize your deductions).

Exhibit 6.1 shows the filing requirements and filing status for most taxpayers for 1995.

Exhibit 6.1

Filing Requirements for Most Taxpayers (1995)

Read across to find your filing status and age at the end of 1995. You must file a return if your **gross income** was at least the amount shown in the last column.

Marital Status	Filing Status	Age	Gross Income*
Single (including divorced and legally separated)	Single	Under 65 65 or older	$6,400 7,350
	Head of household	Under 65 65 or older	$8,250 9,200
Married with a child and living apart from your spouse during the last 6 months of 1995	Head of household	Under 65 65 or older	$8,250 9,200
Married and living with your spouse at end of 1995 (or on the date your spouse died)	Married, joint return	Under 65 (both spouses) 65 or older (one spouse) 65 or older (both spouses)	$11,550 12,300 13,050
	Married, separate separate return	Any age	$2,500
Married, not living with your spouse at end of 1995 (or on the date your spouse died)	Married, joint or separate return	Any age	$2,500
Widowed before 1995 and not remarried in 1995	Single	Under 65 65 or older	$6,400 7,350
	Head of household	Under 65 65 or older	$8,250 9,200
	Qualifying widow(er) with dependent child	Under 65 65 or older	$9,050 9,800

*__Gross income__ means all income you received in the form of money, goods, property, and services that is not exempt from tax, including any gain on the sale of your home (even if you may exclude or postpone part or all of the gain).
Source: Internal Revenue Service.

Gross Income

Before we proceed, you may find it helpful to refer to Exhibit 6.2 as you study this section. Exhibit 6.2 outlines the structure of Form 1040, which is widely used by taxpayers who itemize their deductions.

Gross income is the starting point for determining the total amount of income tax due. **Gross income** is all income you receive from money, goods, property, and services that is not exempt from taxation. Unless the item is specifically excluded in the Internal Revenue Service (IRS) code, you must include it in gross income. Thus, gross income includes wages and salaries, commissions and fees, profits from a business, interest, dividends, rents, capital gains, royalties, tips, prizes, gambling winnings, pension income, and similar items. For most workers, wages and salaries are the largest component of gross income.

Certain items are excluded from gross income, including gifts and inheritances, life insurance death benefits, workers compensation benefits, tax exempt interest on securities issued by states and municipalities, and certain other items (see Exhibit 6.3).

Example: During the current tax year, Michelle received $40,000 in salary as a marketing analyst, $350 in interest and dividends in a stock brokerage account, $50,000 as beneficiary of her mother's life insurance policy, and $500,000 as her share of her deceased mother's estate. The

gross income All income received from money, goods, property, and services that is not exempt from taxation.

Exhibit 6.2

Understanding the Federal Income Tax (Form 1040)

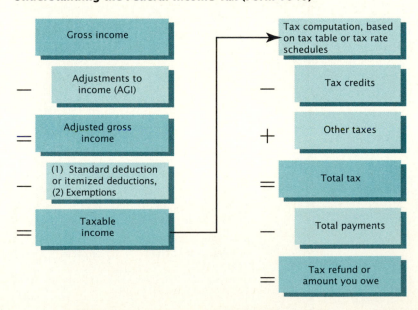

salary, dividends, and interest must be included in Michelle's gross income. However, the IRS Code excludes life insurance proceeds and inheritances from gross income.

Adjustments to Income

adjusted gross income
Gross income less certain deductions.

After gross income is determined, it is reduced by certain deductions to arrive at adjusted gross income. **Adjusted gross income** is gross income less certain deductions. The following deductions can reduce gross income:

■ Individual retirement account (IRA) contributions

■ Allowable moving expenses

Exhibit 6.3

Examples of Gross Income

GROSS INCOME

Wages, salaries, commissions, bonuses, tips

Taxable interest, dividends

Taxable refund of state and local income taxes

Alimony received

Business income

Capital gains

IRA distributions (taxable amount)

Pensions and annuities (taxable amount)

Rental real estate, royalties, partnerships, S corporations, trusts

Farm income

Unemployment compensation

Social security benefits (taxable amount)

Prizes and awards, gambling winnings

EXCLUDED FROM GROSS INCOME

Gifts and inheritances

Life insurance proceeds

Tax exempt interest from state or municipal bonds

Child support payments

Workers compensation benefits

Benefits from medical expense health insurance plans

Employer contributions into a qualified retirement plan

Certain qualified scholarships

Social security benefits (for taxpayers with incomes under certain amounts)

- One half the self-employment tax

- Self-employed health insurance deduction

- Keogh retirement plan and simplified employee pension (SEP) contributions

- Penalty for early withdrawal of savings

- Alimony paid

Adjusted gross income is an important calculation since it is the base for calculating certain itemized deductions, such as medical expenses and miscellaneous deductions.

Taxable Income

taxable income The actual amount of income subject to taxation for a given year.

The next step is to determine your taxable income. **Taxable income** is the actual amount of income that is subject to taxation for a given year. Taxable income is calculated by subtracting the standard deduction (or itemized deductions) and all exemptions from adjusted gross income.

standard deduction A specific amount deducted from adjusted gross income by taxpayers who do not itemize their deductions.

itemized deductions Deductions from adjusted gross income for various types of personal expenses that are listed on Schedule A in Form 1040.

1. *Standard deduction.* The **standard deduction** is a specific amount that taxpayers who do not itemize their deductions may deduct from adjusted gross income. **Itemized deductions** are deductions for various types of personal expenses that are listed on Schedule A in Form 1040. You should use the standard deduction if it exceeds the total of your itemized deductions. Most taxpayers filing individual returns take the standard deduction.

The amount of the standard deduction depends on your filing status and age. Taxpayers age 65 or older and the blind receive a higher standard deduction. The standard deduction amount is increased each year for increases in the cost of living. For 1995, the standard deduction amounts for most taxpayers under age 65 are as follows:

Single	$3,900
Married filing joint return	$6,550
Married filing separate returns	$3,275
Head of household	$5,750
Qualifying widow(er)	$6,550

2. *Itemized Deductions.* You should itemize your deductions if they exceed the standard deduction. Itemizing such deductions can often substantially reduce taxable income. As stated earlier, itemized deductions are listed on Schedule A in Form 1040 (see Exhibit 6.4).

The most common types of itemized deductions are the following:

Exhibit 6.4

SCHEDULES A&B	Schedule A—Itemized Deductions	OMB No. 1545-0074

SCHEDULES A&B
(Form 1040)

Department of the Treasury
Internal Revenue Service   (O)

Schedule A—Itemized Deductions

(Schedule B is on back)

► **Attach to Form 1040.** ► **See Instructions for Schedules A and B (Form 1040).**

OMB No. 1545-0074

1995

Attachment
Sequence No. **07**

Name(s) shown on Form 1040 — Your social security number

Medical and Dental Expenses

Caution: *Do not include expenses reimbursed or paid by others.*

1 Medical and dental expenses (see page A-1) . . . . | 1
2 Enter amount from Form 1040, line 32. | 2 |
3 Multiply line 2 above by 7.5% (.075) . . . . . . | 3
4 Subtract line 3 from line 1. If line 3 is more than line 1, enter -0- . . . . . . | 4

Taxes You Paid

(See page A-1.)

5 State and local income taxes . . . . | 5
6 Real estate taxes (see page A-2) . . . . | 6
7 Personal property taxes . . . . | 7
8 Other taxes. List type and amount ►................. | 8
....
9 Add lines 5 through 8 . . . . | 9

Interest You Paid

(See page A-2.)

Note:
Personal interest is not deductible.

10 Home mortgage interest and points reported to you on Form 1098 | 10
11 Home mortgage interest not reported to you on Form 1098. If paid to the person from whom you bought the home, see page A-3 and show that person's name, identifying no., and address ►
....
....
.... | 11
12 Points not reported to you on Form 1098. See page A-3 for special rules . . . . | 12
13 Investment interest. If required, attach Form 4952. (See page A-3.) . . . . | 13
14 Add lines 10 through 13 . . . . | 14

Gifts to Charity

If you made a gift and got a benefit for it, see page A-3.

15 Gifts by cash or check. If you made any gift of $250 or more, see page A-3 . . . . | 15
16 Other than by cash or check. If any gift of $250 or more, see page A-3. If over $500, you **MUST** attach Form 8283 | 16
17 Carryover from prior year | 17
18 Add lines 15 through 17 . . . . | 18

Casualty and Theft Losses

19 Casualty or theft loss(es). Attach Form 4684. (See page A-4.) . . . . | 19

Job Expenses and Most Other Miscellaneous Deductions

(See page A-5 for expenses to deduct here.)

20 Unreimbursed employee expenses—job travel, union dues, job education, etc. If required, you **MUST** attach Form 2106 or 2106-EZ. (See page A-5.) ►...............
....
.... | 20
21 Tax preparation fees . . . . | 21
22 Other expenses—investment, safe deposit box, etc. List type and amount ►............................ | 22
23 Add lines 20 through 22 . . . . | 23
24 Enter amount from Form 1040, line 32. | 24 |
25 Multiply line 24 above by 2% (.02) . . . . . . | 25
26 Subtract line 25 from line 23. If line 25 is more than line 23, enter -0- . . . . | 26

Other Miscellaneous Deductions

27 Other—from list on page A-5. List type and amount ►..........................
.... | 27

Total Itemized Deductions

28 Is Form 1040, line 32, over $114,700 (over $57,350 if married filing separately)?
NO. Your deduction is not limited. Add the amounts in the far right column for lines 4 through 27. Also, enter on Form 1040, line 34, the **larger** of this amount or your standard deduction.
YES. Your deduction may be limited. See page A-5 for the amount to enter. | ► | 28

For Paperwork Reduction Act Notice, see Form 1040 instructions.   Cat. No. 11330X   **Schedule A (Form 1040) 1995**

■ *Medical and dental expenses.* Only those expenses exceeding 7.5 percent of adjusted gross income are deductible.

■ *Taxes.* Deductible taxes include state and local income taxes, real estate taxes, and personal property taxes.

■ *Interest.* Deductible interest includes mortgage interest, investment interest up to the amount of investment income received, and interest on home equity loans of $100,000 or less. Certain other limits on mortgage interest apply. However, personal loan interest is not deductible, including credit card interest, finance charges on installment purchases and consumer loans, and life insurance loans.

■ *Charitable contributions.* Gifts of money or property to charity are deductible subject to certain limits based on adjusted gross income. If you make a contribution of $250 or more, you must have written acknowledgment of the contribution from the charity before you file your tax return. A canceled check is no longer sufficient. In addition, if the payment is more than $75 and is partly a contribution for goods and services received, the statement must say that you can deduct only the value of the payment that exceeds the value of the goods or services received. For example, if you contribute $200 at a fund-raising dinner, and the dinner is valued at $50, only $150 is deductible.

■ *Casualty and theft losses.* Property losses from hurricanes, tornadoes, earthquakes, storms, accidents, and similar events, as well as the theft of property, are deductible subject to severe limitations. The loss must be reduced by any payments from insurance or other sources; the loss must be further reduced by $100 and 10 percent of adjusted gross income. Only the amount exceeding those requirements is deductible.

■ *Job expenses and other miscellaneous expenses.* Unreimbursed job expenses and other miscellaneous expenses are deductible only to the extent they exceed 2 percent of adjusted gross income. Examples include job travel, uniforms, union dues, required education courses, investment expenses, and safe deposit box fees.

Itemized deductions can often substantially reduce taxable income. However, the current tax code has reduced the value of itemized deductions for upper-income taxpayers. *Under current law, itemized deductions are reduced for taxpayers who have adjusted gross incomes exceeding a certain level.* For 1995, itemized deductions are reduced by 3 percent of the amount of adjusted gross income in excess of $114,700 ($57,350 if married filing separately). This reduction cannot exceed 80 percent of the itemized deductions affected by the limit. These amounts are annually adjusted for increases in the cost of living. The reduction applies to all itemized deductions except medical expenses, investment interest, casualty and theft losses, or gambling losses. The effect of the reduction is to increase the marginal tax rate (discussed later) for upper-income taxpayers.

exemption An amount subtracted from adjusted gross income to determine taxable income.

personal exemption An amount each individual taxpayer may deduct from adjusted gross income.

dependency exemption An amount an individual taxpayer may deduct from adjusted gross income for each eligible dependent.

3. *Personal exemptions and dependency exemptions.* **Exemptions** are additional amounts that are subtracted from adjusted gross income to determine taxable income. For 1995, each exemption is $2,500, which is increased annually for increases in the cost of living. Each taxpayer is entitled to a **personal exemption;** a married couple filing jointly is entitled to two personal exemptions. The total amount of the exemptions is subtracted from adjusted gross income in determining taxable income.

In addition, you may be providing financial support to dependents, such as a child, parent, or grandparent. A **dependency exemption** is an additional exemption for each eligible dependent. The dependency tests for taking a dependency exemption are complex and strict. Five dependency tests must be satisfied for each dependent claimed as an exemption. Discussion of these tests, however, is beyond the scope of the text. In addition, if you claim an exemption for a dependent, that dependent cannot claim a personal exemption on his or her own tax return.

There is a phaseout of personal exemptions when your adjusted gross income exceeds a certain amount for your filing status. *Personal exemptions are reduced or eliminated completely for taxpayers who have adjusted gross incomes (AGIs) exceeding certain amounts.* For 1995, the threshold amounts are $86,025 for married taxpayers filing separately, $114,700 for single taxpayers, $143,350 for heads of households, and $172,050 for married taxpayers filing jointly and for qualifying widows(ers). The dollar amount of your personal exemptions is reduced 2 percent for each $2,500, or each part of $2,500 ($1,250 if married filing separately), that exceeds the AGI thresholds. Once again, the effect of the phaseout provision is to increase the marginal tax rate for upper-income taxpayers.

Finally, you are required to obtain a social security number for any dependent you claim as an exemption. You must list the dependent's social security number on the tax form.

The following examples show how adjusted gross income, deductions, and exemptions interact to determine taxable income:

Example 1. In 1995, Scott, age 23, has an adjusted gross income of $20,000. He takes the standard deduction of $3,900 and has one personal exemption of $2,500. Scott's taxable income is $13,600.

Example 2. Pedro and Rosa, both age 38, are married and have two dependent children. In 1995, they have an adjusted gross income of

$45,000 and allowable itemized deductions of $8,000. They claim four exemptions. The couple's taxable income is $27,000.

Tax Computation

tax table A table that shows the amount of tax owed for taxable incomes up to $100,000.

After taxable income is determined, you must compute the amount of the tax. The income tax is based on taxable income. The Internal Revenue Service has prepared a tax table and tax rate schedules to determine the amount of tax payable. The **tax table** is a table that shows the amount of tax owed for taxable incomes up to $100,000. Exhibit 6.5 is an excerpt from the 1995 tax table for taxpayers with taxable incomes between $29,000 and $30,000.

tax rate schedules Schedules for determining taxes based on filing status and income; tax rate schedules must be used by taxpayers with taxable incomes of $100,000 or more.

The **tax rate schedules** are based on the taxpayers' filing status and require a separate calculation to determine the amount of tax due. Tax-

---

Exhibit 6.5

Example of Tax Table (1995)

If line 37 (taxable income) is—		And you are—			
At least	But less than	Single	Married filing jointly	Married filing separately	Head of a household
		Your tax is—			
29,000					
29,000	29,050	5,092	4,354	5,592	4,354
29,050	29,100	5,106	4,361	5,606	4,361
29,100	29,150	5,120	4,369	5,620	4,369
29,150	29,200	5,134	4,376	5,634	4,376
29,200	29,250	5,148	4,384	5,648	4,384
29,250	29,300	5,162	4,391	5,662	4,391
29,300	29,350	5,176	4,399	5,676	4,399
29,350	29,400	5,190	4,406	5,690	4,406
29,400	29,450	5,204	4,414	5,704	4,414
29,450	29,500	5,218	4,421	5,718	4,421
29,500	29,550	5,232	4,429	5,732	4,429
29,550	29,600	5,246	4,436	5,746	4,436
29,600	29,650	5,260	4,444	5,760	4,444
29,650	29,700	5,274	4,451	5,774	4,451
29,700	29,750	5,288	4,459	5,788	4,459
29,750	29,800	5,302	4,466	5,802	4,466
29,800	29,850	5,316	4,474	5,816	4,474
29,850	29,900	5,330	4,481	5,830	4,481
29,900	29,950	5,344	4,489	5,844	4,489
29,950	30,000	5,358	4,496	5,858	4,496

Source: Internal Revenue Service.

payers who have taxable incomes of $100,000 or more must use the tax rate schedules (see Exhibit 6.6).

progressive income tax
An income tax system in which the effective tax rate increases as taxable income increases.

marginal tax rate The tax rate that applies to the last dollar of income.

The tax table and tax rate schedules are based on a progressive income tax. A **progressive income tax** means that the effective tax rate increases as taxable income increases. The tax rate that applies to each taxable income bracket is referred to as a marginal tax rate. The **marginal tax rate,** which should not be confused with the average tax rate, is the tax rate that applies to the last dollar of income. In contrast, the **average tax rate** is the total tax paid divided by taxable income. For example, if Megan is single and has a taxable income of $25,000, her federal

Exhibit 6.6

Tax Rate Schedules (1995)

If the amount on Form 1040, line 37, is over—	but not over—	Enter on Form 1040 line 38		of the amount over—
Single				
$ 0	$23,350	_____	15%	$0
23,350	56,550	$3,502.50	+ 28%	23,350
56,550	117,950	12,798.50	+ 31%	56,550
117,950	256,500	31,852.50	+ 36%	117,950
256,500	——	81,710.50	+ 39.6%	256,500
Married filing jointly or Qualifying widow(er)				
$ 0	$39,000	_____	15%	$0
39,000	94,250	$5,850.00	+ 28%	39,000
94,250	143,600	21,320.00	+ 31%	94,250
143,600	256,500	36,618.50	+ 36%	143,600
256,500	——	77,262.50	+ 39.6%	256,500
Married filing separately				
$ 0	$19,500	_____	15%	$0
19,500	47,125	$2,925.00	+ 28%	19,500
47,125	71,800	10,660.00	+ 31%	47,125
71,800	128,250	18,309.25	+ 36%	71,800
128,250	——	38,631.25	+ 39.6%	128,250
Head of household				
$ 0	$31,250	_____	15%	$0
31,250	80,750	$4,687.50	+ 28%	31,250
80,750	130,800	18,547.50	+ 31%	80,750
130,800	256,500	34,063.00	+ 36%	130,800
256,500	——	79,315.00	+ 39.6%	256,500

Source: Internal Revenue Service.

average tax rate The total tax paid divided by taxable income.

income tax would be $3,972 based on the 1995 tax table. However, if Megan's taxable income increases to $26,000, the total tax would be $4,252, or an additional $280. Megan's marginal tax rate is 28 percent ($280/$1,000). In contrast, her average tax rate is only 16.4 percent ($4,252/$26,000).

At the time of this writing, the tax code provides for marginal tax rates of 15 percent, 28 percent, 31 percent, 36 percent, and 39.6 percent. The latter two rates apply to taxpayers whose taxable incomes exceed certain amounts and are due largely to the reduction in itemized deductions and phaseout of exemptions for upper-income taxpayers.

In summary, the marginal tax rate for each tax bracket increases as taxable income increases. The higher marginal tax rate applies only to the additional taxable income in the higher tax bracket and not to your total income.

Marginal tax rates are important since they have a significant impact on work incentives and taxpayer behavior. High marginal tax rates discourage working and often lead to tax evasion and the nonreporting of income. In addition, for purposes of tax planning and tax-reduction strategies (discussed later), the marginal tax rate is more important than the average tax rate.

After taxable income is determined, the amount of tax payable is determined by referring to the tax table or tax schedule. As we noted earlier, taxpayers with taxable incomes of $100,000 or more must use the tax rate schedules.

Example. Jennifer, age 35, is an account executive for a national stock brokerage firm. She is single and has taxable income of $100,000 in 1995. Based on the tax rate schedule, her 1995 income tax is $26,268.

Tax Credits

After you calculate the income tax due, you may be able to reduce the tax by various tax credits. You can use tax credits whether you take the standard deduction or itemize your deductions.

tax credit A credit that reduces dollar for dollar the actual income tax due.

You should not confuse a tax credit with a tax deduction. A **tax credit** is a credit that reduces dollar for dollar the actual income tax due. A tax credit is more valuable than a tax deduction. For example, a tax credit of $100 for a taxpayer who is in the 28 percent tax bracket would reduce the income tax due by $100. In contrast, a tax deduction of $100 would reduce the income tax due by only $28.

A number of tax credits are available to certain taxpayers. They include the following:

■ Credit for child and dependent care expenses

■ Credit for elderly and disabled

■ Foreign tax credit (for income taxes paid to a foreign country)

■ Other credits (such as a low-income housing credit)

Example. Kirsten, age 31, works full time and has a dependent child, age 1. Assume that Kirsten qualifies for a tax credit of $500 for child-care expenses. If her income tax liability is $3,000 before the credit is considered, the tax credit would reduce the actual tax to $2,500.

earned income credit
A tax credit available to certain low-income persons who work.

The **earned income credit** is another valuable tax credit that may be available to certain low-income persons who work. The credit can be taken even if there is no tax liability. Thus, low-income taxpayers receive a refund even if they do not pay any income tax. The purposes of the credit are to encourage individuals to work and to offset the negative impact of the social security payroll tax on low-income persons who work.

The earned income credit is available to workers with one or more qualifying children and to workers who do not have a qualifying child. The amount of the tax credit is based on earned income. A special worksheet must be filled out to determine the amount of earned income. In general, earned income includes taxable earned income (such as wages, salaries, and tips) and nontaxable earned income (such as meals furnished by an employer and voluntary contributions into a Section 401(k) plan). You must also include any self-employment income. The amount of the tax credit increases as earned income increases up to a certain level and then gradually declines from that level and eventually disappears. For 1995, you could receive a credit if your total taxable and nontaxable earned income was less than $9,230, and you did not have a qualifying child; you could earn up to $24,396 if you had one qualifying child, and up to $26,673 if you had two or more qualifying children. The maximum credit was $314 if you did not have a qualifying child, $2,094 if you had one qualifying child, and $3,110 if you had two or more qualifying children.

Other Taxes

Some taxpayers owe additional taxes that they must also report on Form 1040. These taxes include the following:

■ Self-employment tax (social security payroll tax on self-employed income)

■ Alternative minimum tax

■ Recapture of taxes (such as disposing of property on which you received a low-income housing credit)

■ Social security and Medicare tax on tips not reported to the employer

■ Tax on distribution from qualified retirement plans, including Individual Retirement Accounts (IRAs), such as receiving a premature IRA distribution before age 59 1/2.

■ Advance earned income credit payments (for earned income credits paid in advance)

■ Household employment taxes (payroll taxes for household employees)

The preceding items are self-explanatory, but a brief discussion of the alternative minimum tax is needed at this point. A small fraction of taxpayers are subject to the **alternative minimum tax (AMT),** which is a separate and parallel system for taxing upper-income taxpayers who have large itemized deductions or substantial amounts of tax-sheltered income. Tax rates of 26 percent and 28 percent are applied to a tax base known as alternative minimum taxable income. However, the deduction rules are different, so the tax rate is applied to a larger base of income. The taxpayer must pay the AMT if it is higher than the regular tax. The purpose of the AMT is to force upper-income taxpayers who itemize deductions to pay at least a minimum amount of income tax. The rules for calculating the AMT are complex and beyond the scope of the text.

After the additional taxes, if any, are added in, you arrive at the total tax. The total tax is offset by tax payments already made.

alternative minimum tax (AMT) A system for taxing upper-income taxpayers who have large itemized deductions or substantial amounts of tax-sheltered income.

Tax Payments

Tax payments made before the return is filed reduce or eliminate the total tax. Basic methods for paying taxes are payroll deductions and estimated tax payments.

Payroll Deduction. Most taxpayers pay their taxes throughout the year by payroll deduction. The actual amount of tax withheld depends on the W-4 form filed with your employer, which indicates your filing status and the number of exemptions claimed. Almost all taxpayers receive a tax refund because they have overpaid their taxes. *Many taxpayers deliberately have more money withheld from their wages than is necessary because of the tax refund they will receive. This is poor financial planning since, in effect, you are making an interest-free loan to the federal government.* A better approach is to have the correct amount withheld and have the equivalent amount of tax payments automatically deducted from your wages and deposited in a savings account or other investment plan. You would receive the investment earnings rather than the federal government.

Estimated Tax Payments. Many taxpayers receive income that is not subject to automatic withholding, including interest, dividends, royalties, rents, gains from the sales of assets, prizes, and other sources of income. If you expect to owe $500 or more, you must pay (1) at least 90 percent of the actual tax that will be reported on your current tax return or (2) 100 percent of the tax reported on your previous year's return. However, if your adjusted gross income for the previous year exceeded $150,000, you must pay 110 percent of the prior year's tax. If you have any income subject to an estimated tax payment, you must make the payment by the due date, which is April 15, June 15, September 15, and January 15 of the next year. Interest and penalties are imposed if you fail to meet these requirements and substantially underpay your taxes before the filing date.

Finally, total tax payments are subtracted from the total tax. If you have overpaid your taxes, you will receive a tax refund. If you have underpaid, you must pay the additional tax.

Which Form to File?

Understanding the federal income tax also requires knowledge of the correct form to file, filing deadlines, record keeping requirements, the possibility of an audit by the IRS, and the various groups that provide tax advice and prepare tax returns.

Types of Forms

Form 1040EZ A simple one-page tax form for taxpayers with taxable incomes under $50,000 who do not itemize deductions or claim dependents.

Three principal tax forms are used currently: (1) Form 1040EZ, (2) Form 1040A, and (3) Form 1040. **Form 1040EZ** is a simple one-page form for taxpayers with taxable incomes under $50,000 who do not itemize deductions or claim dependents. You can use Form 1040EZ if you meet the following requirements:

- Your filing status is single or married filing jointly, and you do not claim any dependents.

- You (and your spouse if married) are under age 65 and not blind.

- Your taxable income is less than $50,000.

- You have income only from wages, salaries, tips, taxable scholarship or fellowship grants, unemployment compensation, and taxable interest income of $400 or less.

- You did not receive any advance earned income credit payments.

- If you are a nonresident alien anytime during the year, your filing status must be married filing jointly.

- If you are married filing jointly, and either you or your spouse worked for more than one employer, the total wages of that person did not exceed $61,200 (1995).

Form 1040A A tax form designed for taxpayers with less than $50,000 in taxable income who do not itemize deductions but do claim exemptions for qualified dependents.

If you do not meet all the preceding requirements, you cannot use Form 1040EZ. Instead, you must use Form 1040A or Form 1040. **Form 1040A** is designed for taxpayers with less than $50,000 in taxable income who do not itemize deductions but do claim exemptions for qualified dependents. You can use Form 1040A if you meet the following requirements:

■ Your income comes *only* from wages, salaries, tips, IRA distributions, pensions and annuities, taxable social security and Railroad Retirement benefits, taxable scholarship and fellowship grants, interest, dividends, and unemployment compensation.

■ Your taxable income is less than $50,000, and you do not itemize deductions.

■ Your only adjustment to income is the deduction for an IRA contributions.

■ Your only taxes are the amount shown in the tax table, household employment taxes, the alternative minimum tax, and any advance earned income credits.

■ Your only tax credits are the credit for child and dependent care expenses, credit for the elderly or disabled, and the earned income credit.

Form 1040 A complex tax form for reporting all types of income, deductions, and tax credits; it must be used by taxpayers who have taxable incomes of $50,000 or more or who wish to itemize their deductions.

If you do not meet all the preceding requirements or wish to itemize deductions, you cannot use Form 1040A. Instead, you must use Form 1040. **Form 1040** is a complex form for reporting all types of income, deductions, and tax credits. You must use Form 1040 if you have taxable income of $50,000 or more or wish to itemize your deductions. You must also use it if you have any adjustments to income, capital gains or losses, business profits or losses, estimated tax payments, a sale of a principal residence, and numerous additional situations that are too complex to discuss here.

In the following section, we briefly examine how the different tax forms are used. You should understand how the forms are used in order to file your own tax return.

Illustration of Form 1040EZ. Assume that Karen, age 22, is a single college student who works part time in a fast-food restaurant. Her parents do not claim her as an exemption on their return. She takes the standard deduction and claims one personal exemption. The following items apply to Karen for 1995:

Total wages in 1995	$6,700
Taxable interest	50

Standard deduction	3,900
Personal exemption	2,500
Federal income tax withheld	150
Earned income credit	188

Karen has an adjusted gross income of $6,750. After taking the standard deduction and claiming one exemption, her taxable income is $350. Based on the 1995 tax table, the tax is $54. However, she has already paid $150 in taxes because of federal withholding. In addition, Karen is eligible for an earned income credit because she worked and earned less than $9,230 in 1995. Although the worksheet calculations are not shown, Karen is eligible for an earned income credit of $188. Thus, her total payments are $338. After subtracting the tax of $54, she is entitled to a tax refund of $284 (see Exhibit 6.7).

Exhibit 6.7

Illustration of Form 1040EZ

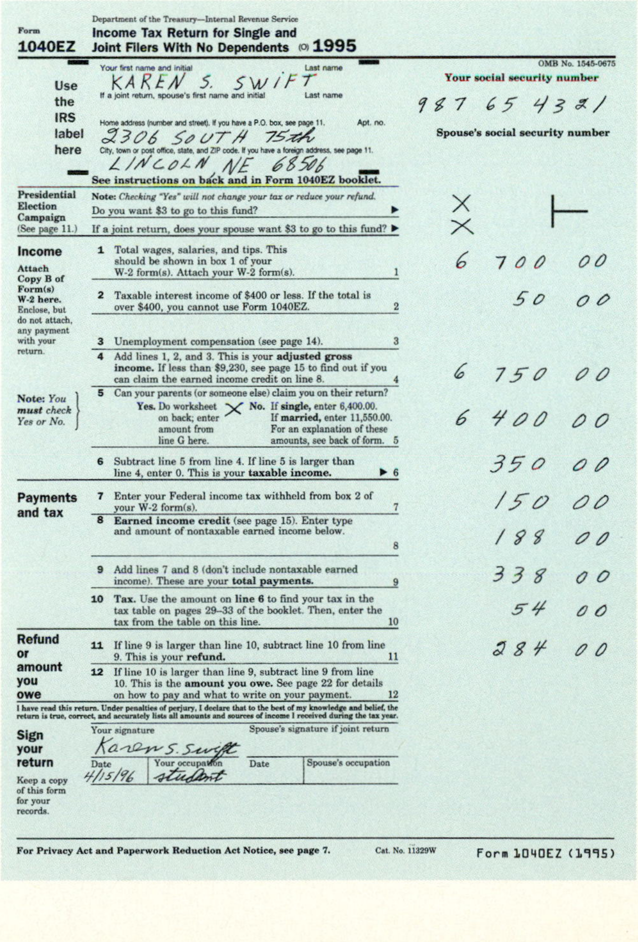

Form 1040EZ — Department of the Treasury—Internal Revenue Service — Income Tax Return for Single and Joint Filers With No Dependents (0) 1995

OMB No. 1545-0675

Use the IRS label here

Your first name and initial / Last name: KAREN S. SWIFT

If a joint return, spouse's first name and initial / Last name

Home address (number and street). If you have a P.O. box, see page 11. Apt. no.: 2306 SOUTH 75th

City, town or post office, state, and ZIP code. If you have a foreign address, see page 11.: LINCOLN, NE 68506

See instructions on back and in Form 1040EZ booklet.

Your social security number: 987 65 4321

Spouse's social security number

Presidential Election Campaign (See page 11.) — Note: *Checking "Yes" will not change your tax or reduce your refund.* Do you want $3 to go to this fund? If a joint return, does your spouse want $3 to go to this fund?

Income Attach Copy B of Form(s) W-2 here. Enclose, but do not attach, any payment with your return.	1 Total wages, salaries, and tips. This should be shown in box 1 of your W-2 form(s). Attach your W-2 form(s).	6,700 00
	2 Taxable interest income of $400 or less. If the total is over $400, you cannot use Form 1040EZ.	50 00
	3 Unemployment compensation (see page 14).	
	4 Add lines 1, 2, and 3. This is your **adjusted gross income.** If less than $9,230, see page 15 to find out if you can claim the earned income credit on line 8.	6,750 00
Note: *You must check Yes or No.*	5 Can your parents (or someone else) claim you on their return? **Yes.** Do worksheet on back; enter amount from line G here. X **No.** If **single,** enter 6,400.00. If **married,** enter 11,550.00. For an explanation of these amounts, see back of form.	6,400 00
	6 Subtract line 5 from line 4. If line 5 is larger than line 4, enter 0. This is your **taxable income.**	350 00
Payments and tax	7 Enter your Federal income tax withheld from box 2 of your W-2 form(s).	150 00
	8 **Earned income credit** (see page 15). Enter type and amount of nontaxable earned income below.	188 00
	9 Add lines 7 and 8 (don't include nontaxable earned income). These are your **total payments.**	338 00
	10 **Tax.** Use the amount on **line 6** to find your tax in the tax table on pages 29–33 of the booklet. Then, enter the tax from the table on this line.	54 00
Refund or amount you owe	11 If line 9 is larger than line 10, subtract line 10 from line 9. This is your **refund.**	284 00
	12 If line 10 is larger than line 9, subtract line 9 from line 10. This is the **amount you owe.** See page 22 for details on how to pay and what to write on your payment.	

I have read this return. Under penalties of perjury, I declare that to the best of my knowledge and belief, the return is true, correct, and accurately lists all amounts and sources of income I received during the tax year.

Sign your return — Keep a copy of this form for your records.

Your signature: Karen S. Swift — Date: 4/15/96 — Your occupation: student

Spouse's signature if joint return — Date — Spouse's occupation

For Privacy Act and Paperwork Reduction Act Notice, see page 7. Cat. No. 11329W Form 1040EZ (1995)

Illustration of Form 1040. Scott and Lorri, both age 32, are married and have two dependent children, ages 2 and 5. Scott is an underwriter for a large life insurer. Lorri is a registered nurse who works part time. They file a joint return and itemize their deductions. The following items apply to them for 1995:

Gross Income

Scott's wages	$27,000
Lorri's wages	12,000
Taxable interest	350
Dividend income	650

Adjustments to Income

IRA contribution—Scott	2,000
IRA contribution—Lorri	2,000

Itemized Deductions

State income tax paid	1,700
Property tax on home	2,100
Home mortgage interest	2,700
Charitable contributions	500

Tax Payments and Exemptions

Federal income taxes withheld	3,000
Four exemptions	10,000

Scott and Lorri had a gross income of $40,000 in 1995. Because of the IRA contributions, they have adjustments to income of $4,000, and adjusted gross income is $36,000. Itemized deductions are $7,000 (state income tax, property tax on home, home mortgage interest, and charitable contributions). After subtracting the itemized deductions and four exemptions from adjusted gross income, taxable income is $19,000. Based on the 1995 tax table, the tax is $2,854. They are not eligible for any tax credits, and they do not have other taxes to pay. Since they have already paid $3,000 in taxes because of federal withholding, they are entitled to a tax refund of $146 (see Exhibit 6.8).

Filing Deadline

After the appropriate tax form is filled out, the form must be filed with the IRS. For calendar-year taxpayers, April 15 is the deadline date for filing the tax return. When the due date falls on a weekend or legal holiday, the deadline is the next business day. The return must be postmarked no later than midnight of April 15. Tax accountants suggest that you send the return by certified mail with a return receipt to document the time of mailing. If you cannot meet the deadline because you need additional time to file, you can obtain a four-month extension by filing

Exhibit 6.8

Form 1040

Form **1040** Department of the Treasury—Internal Revenue Service
U.S. Individual Income Tax Return **1995** (99) IRS Use Only—Do not write or staple in this space.

For the year Jan. 1–Dec. 31, 1995, or other tax year beginning , 1995, ending , 19 | OMB No. 1545-0074

Label (See instructions on page 11.) Use the IRS label. Otherwise, please print or type.

Your first name and initial: Scott J. | Last name: Smith | Your social security number: 123 45 6789
If a joint return, spouse's first name and initial: Lorri P. | Last name: Smith | Spouse's social security number: 321 54 9876
Home address (number and street). If you have a P.O. box, see page 11.: 2306 South 45th | Apt. no.
City, town or post office, state, and ZIP code. If you have a foreign address, see page 11.: Perchville, NE 68506

For Privacy Act and Paperwork Reduction Act Notice, see page 7.

Presidential Election Campaign (See page 11.)
Do you want $3 to go to this fund? — No: X
If a joint return, does your spouse want $3 to go to this fund? — Note: Checking "Yes" will not change your tax or reduce your refund.

Filing Status (See page 11.) Check only one box.
1 Single
2 X Married filing joint return (even if only one had income)
3 Married filing separate return. Enter spouse's social security no. above and full name here. ▶
4 Head of household (with qualifying person). (See page 12.) If the qualifying person is a child but not your dependent, enter this child's name here. ▶
5 Qualifying widow(er) with dependent child (year spouse died ▶ 19). (See page 12.)

Exemptions (See page 12.)
6a Yourself. If your parent (or someone else) can claim you as a dependent on his or her tax return, do not check box 6a. But be sure to check the box on line 33b on page 2
b Spouse
No. of boxes checked on 6a and 6b
c Dependents:

(1) First name / Last name	(2) Dependent's social security number. If born in 1995, see page 13.	(3) Dependent's relationship to you	(4) No. of months lived in your home in 1995
Lynn R. Smith	301 00 1234	Daughter	12
Todd B. Smith	301 01 1235	Son	12

No. of your children on 6c who:
• lived with you
• didn't live with you due to divorce or separation (see page 14)
Dependents on 6c not entered above
If more than six dependents, see page 13.

d If your child didn't live with you but is claimed as your dependent under a pre-1985 agreement, check here ▶
e Total number of exemptions claimed: 4

Income
Attach Copy B of your Forms W-2, W-2G, and 1099-R here.
If you did not get a W-2, see page 14.
Enclose, but do not attach, your payment and payment voucher. See page 33.

7 Wages, salaries, tips, etc. Attach Form(s) W-2 ... 7 | 39,000 00
8a Taxable interest income (see page 15). Attach Schedule B if over $400 ... 8a | 350 00
b Tax-exempt interest (see page 15). DON'T include on line 8a | 8b
9 Dividend income. Attach Schedule B if over $400 ... 9 | 650 00
10 Taxable refunds, credits, or offsets of state and local income taxes (see page 15) ... 10
11 Alimony received ... 11
12 Business income or (loss). Attach Schedule C or C-EZ ... 12
13 Capital gain or (loss). If required, attach Schedule D (see page 16) ... 13
14 Other gains or (losses). Attach Form 4797 ... 14
15a Total IRA distributions | 15a | b Taxable amount (see page 16) | 15b
16a Total pensions and annuities | 16a | b Taxable amount (see page 16) | 16b
17 Rental real estate, royalties, partnerships, S corporations, trusts, etc. Attach Schedule E | 17
18 Farm income or (loss). Attach Schedule F | 18
19 Unemployment compensation (see page 17) | 19
20a Social security benefits | 20a | b Taxable amount (see page 18) | 20b
21 Other income. List type and amount—see page 18 | 21
22 Add the amounts in the far right column for lines 7 through 21. This is your total income ▶ | 22 | 40,000 00

Adjustments to Income
23a Your IRA deduction (see page 19) | 23a | 2,000 00
b Spouse's IRA deduction (see page 19) | 23b | 2,000 00
24 Moving expenses. Attach Form 3903 or 3903-F | 24
25 One-half of self-employment tax | 25
26 Self-employed health insurance deduction (see page 21) | 26
27 Keogh & self-employed SEP plans. If SEP, check ▶ | 27
28 Penalty on early withdrawal of savings | 28
29 Alimony paid. Recipient's SSN ▶ | 29
30 Add lines 23a through 29. These are your total adjustments ... ▶ | 30 | 4,000 00

Adjusted Gross Income
31 Subtract line 30 from line 22. This is your adjusted gross income. If less than $26,673 and a child lived with you (less than $9,230 if a child didn't live with you), see "Earned Income Credit" on page 27 ▶ | 31 | 36,000 00

Form **1040** (1995)

Form 1040 (1995) — Page **2**

Tax Computation (See page 23.)
32 Amount from line 31 (adjusted gross income) | 32 | 36,000 00
33a Check if: ☐ You were 65 or older, ☐ Blind; ☐ Spouse was 65 or older, ☐ Blind. Add the number of boxes checked above and enter the total here ... ▶ 33a
b If your parent (or someone else) can claim you as a dependent, check here ... ▶ 33b ☐
c If you are married filing separately and your spouse itemizes deductions or you are a dual-status alien, see page 23 and check here ... ▶ 33c ☐
34 Enter the larger of your:
Itemized deductions from Schedule A, line 28, OR
Standard deduction shown below for your filing status. But if you checked any box on line 33a or b, go to page 23 to find your standard deduction. If you checked box 33c, your standard deduction is zero.
• Single—$3,900 • Married filing jointly or Qualifying widow(er)—$6,550
• Head of household—$5,750 • Married filing separately—$3,275
| 34 | 7,000 00
35 Subtract line 34 from line 32 | 35 | 29,000 00
36 If line 32 is $86,025 or less, multiply $2,500 by the total number of exemptions claimed on line 6e. If line 32 is over $86,025, see the worksheet on page 23 for the amount to enter | 36 | 10,000 00
37 Taxable income. Subtract line 36 from line 35. If line 36 is more than line 35, enter -0- | 37 | 19,000 00
38 Tax. Check if from a ☒ Tax Table, b ☐ Tax Rate Schedules, c ☐ Capital Gain Tax Worksheet, or d ☐ Form 8615 (see page 24). Amount from Form(s) 8814 ▶ | 38 | 2,854 00
39 Additional taxes. Check if from a ☐ Form 4970 b ☐ Form 4972 | 39
40 Add lines 38 and 39 | 40 | 2,854 00

If you want the IRS to figure your tax, see page 35.

Credits (See page 24.)
41 Credit for child and dependent care expenses. Attach Form 2441 | 41
42 Credit for the elderly or the disabled. Attach Schedule R | 42
43 Foreign tax credit. Attach Form 1116 | 43
44 Other credits (see page 25). Check if from a ☐ Form 3800 b ☐ Form 8396 c ☐ Form 8801 d ☐ Form (specify) | 44
45 Add lines 41 through 44 | 45
46 Subtract line 45 from line 40. If line 45 is more than line 40, enter -0- ... ▶ | 46 | 2,854 00

Other Taxes (See page 25.)
47 Self-employment tax. Attach Schedule SE | 47
48 Alternative minimum tax. Attach Form 6251 | 48
49 Recapture taxes. Check if from a ☐ Form 4255 b ☐ Form 8611 c ☐ Form 8828 | 49
50 Social security and Medicare tax on tip income not reported to employer. Attach Form 4137 | 50
51 Tax on qualified retirement plans, including IRAs. If required, attach Form 5329 | 51
52 Advance earned income credit payments from Form W-2 | 52
53 Household employment taxes. Attach Schedule H | 53
54 Add lines 46 through 53. This is your total tax ... ▶ | 54 | 2,854 00

Payments
Attach Forms W-2, W-2G, and 1099-R on the front.
55 Federal income tax withheld. If any is from Form(s) 1099, check ▶ ☐ | 55 | 3,000 00
56 1995 estimated tax payments and amount applied from 1994 return | 56
57 Earned income credit. Attach Schedule EIC if you have a qualifying child. Nontaxable earned income: amount ▶ and type ▶ | 57
58 Amount paid with Form 4868 (extension request) | 58
59 Excess social security and RRTA tax withheld (see page 32) | 59
60 Other payments. Check if from a ☐ Form 2439 b ☐ Form 4136 | 60
61 Add lines 55 through 60. These are your total payments ... ▶ | 61 | 3,000 00

Refund or Amount You Owe
62 If line 61 is more than line 54, subtract line 54 from line 61. This is the amount you OVERPAID | 62 | 146 00
63 Amount of line 62 you want REFUNDED TO YOU ... ▶ | 63 | 146 00
64 Amount of line 62 you want APPLIED TO YOUR 1996 ESTIMATED TAX ▶ | 64
65 If line 54 is more than line 61, subtract line 61 from line 54. This is the AMOUNT YOU OWE. For details on how to pay and use Form 1040-V, Payment Voucher, see page 33 ▶ | 65
66 Estimated tax penalty (see page 33). Also include on line 65 | 66

Sign Here
Keep a copy of this return for your records.
Under penalties of perjury, I declare that I have examined this return and accompanying schedules and statements, and to the best of my knowledge and belief, they are true, correct, and complete. Declaration of preparer (other than taxpayer) is based on all information of which preparer has any knowledge.
Your signature: Scott J. Smith | Date: 4-4-96 | Your occupation: Underwriter
Spouse's signature. If a joint return, BOTH must sign.: Lorri P. Smith | Date: 4-4-96 | Spouse's occupation: Nurse

Paid Preparer's Use Only
Preparer's signature | Date | Check if self-employed ☐ | Preparer's social security no.
Firm's name (or yours if self-employed) and address ▶ | EIN | ZIP code

an appropriate form. *However, an extension of time to file is not an extension of time to pay.* You must make an accurate assessment of the amount of tax owed and pay the amount due by the deadline date. If you cannot pay the full amount due, you will be charged interest on the unpaid amount. In addition, you may also be charged a **failure-to-pay penalty** for paying the tax late unless you have reasonable cause for not paying the tax when due. The failure-to-pay penalty is 1/2 of 1 percent of your unpaid taxes for each month, or part of the month, after the due date that the tax is not paid. However, the penalty cannot be more than 25 percent of the unpaid tax. The interest and penalties are assessed from the original due date of the return.

The penalties are even more severe if you do not file a tax return by the due date (including extensions) and you owe taxes. In addition to interest and a failure-to-pay penalty, you may have to pay a **failure-to-file penalty.** The penalty is usually 5 percent for each month or part of a month that a return is late, but not more than 25 percent of the tax. The penalty will not apply if you can show that you failed to file on time because of reasonable cause and not because of willful neglect.

Record Keeping

You must substantiate itemized deductions and exemptions if your tax return is audited by the IRS. Thus, proper record keeping is extremely important. The tax code does not require any special form of record keeping. However, you should keep all receipts, canceled checks or other proof of payment, bank statements, credit card statements, and other documentation to substantiate any deductions or tax credits that you claim.

You should keep records that support an income or expense item until the period of limitations for the tax return runs out. The **period of limitations** is a limited period after which no legal action can be taken against you. This period is usually three years from the date you file the return, or two years from the date you pay the tax, whichever is later. However, the period of limitations is six years if you do not report income that should have been reported, and the unreported income is more than 25 percent of the income shown on the return. If you file a false or fraudulent return with intent to evade the tax, action generally can be brought against you anytime.

Some records should be kept for more than three years. For example, you should keep property records, such as the purchase or sale of a home, as long as they are needed to calculate the cost basis of the original or replacement property. Tax accountants recommend that real estate records should be kept for seven years after you sell the property. Finally, you should keep tax returns for at least six years and indefinitely if possible.

---

failure-to-pay penalty
Penalty for failing to pay income taxes when they are due.

failure-to-file penalty
Penalty for failing to file a tax return by the due date.

period of limitations A limited period after which no legal action can be taken against a taxpayer with respect to a given tax return; usually three years from the date the return is filed or two years from the date the tax is paid, whichever is later.

Consider This

At the Nolo Press Self-Help Law Center at:

http://www.nolo.com/

choose "Reference Library" and then "Money and Consumer Matters" to find legal information about income taxes and tax audits.

Surviving an IRS Audit

The IRS audits less than 1 percent of tax returns each year. However, the value of good records becomes readily apparent if you are part of that group (see Insight 6.1). An **audit** is an IRS examination of the tax return and records that substantiate the various deductions, tax credits, and income items reported on the tax return. Your return may be audited because the IRS thinks you owe more tax; indeed, most taxpayers who are audited end up paying additional taxes.

audit An examination by the Internal Revenue Service of a tax return and the records that substantiate the various deductions, tax credits, and income items reported on the tax return.

The IRS uses a complex computer program to select most of the tax returns that it audits. The program allows for certain taxpayer norms with respect to items reported on the return. Taxpayer returns containing items that exceed the norms are flagged for a possible audit. For example, total itemized deductions exceeding a certain amount for your level of income may trigger an audit, or high charitable contributions for your income level may also result in an audit. The formula for determining such norms is kept secret.

Types of IRS Audits. There are different types of IRS audits. The simplest is the **correspondence audit** by which you are audited by mail and asked to send specific records to substantiate the items under review. An **office audit** is conducted in an IRS office, and you are told what records to bring with you to substantiate your tax return. A **field audit** is done at your home or office or at your tax professional's office if he or she is qualified to practice before the IRS. In a field audit, the entire tax return is open to review, including all supporting documentation.

correspondence audit An audit conducted by mail.

office audit An audit conducted in an office of the Internal Revenue Service.

field audit An audit conducted in the taxpayer's home or office or the tax professional's office if that person is qualified to practice before the Internal Revenue Service.

In addition, you may receive a letter from the IRS stating that you owe additional taxes. For example, you may get a letter stating that you did not report a certain amount of taxable interest or report a common stock dividend. These automated adjustments are not audits but notices from the IRS that you owe more tax or you have a mistake in your tax return. You have 60 days to appeal if you disagree. Do not ignore the letter. However, if the letter is in error, respond promptly by providing the correct information. Never send original records, only copies. *The IRS makes thousands of mistakes in trying to match correctly the millions of tax items it receives each year.* As a result, thousands of IRS letters to taxpayers demanding additional taxes are in error.

Appealing an IRS Decision. Many tax experts believe you should never appear personally before an IRS auditor if your return is audited but instead have a professional, such as a tax accountant, represent you. The reason is that many taxpayers voluntarily provide too much information, which then opens up the tax return for additional scrutiny and possibly higher taxes.

However, if the IRS auditor says you owe additional taxes and you disagree, you have the right to appeal. You appeal first to the auditor's super-

6.1   Three Ways to Deal with an IRS Audit: Organize, Organize, Organize

The Rev. Kenneth Paris has always been more concerned with saving souls than saving receipts for income taxes.

Since an audit by the Internal Revenue Service, though, he documents nearly everything.

Paris, who once filed receipts by throwing them into a can, now logs expenses on a computer and in a file cabinet. In an audit, the IRS determines whether taxpayers properly reported their income and deductions.

"After that experience, if you are going to McDonald's, you will get some kind of receipt if you are going to claim it," he said.

About 1 million Americans are about to go through the same audit experience with the IRS.

For those who go unprepared, it will be like walking into a

threshing machine, said Lee Wagers, a Lexington tax attorney and certified public accountant.

Wagers said there are three keys to dealing with an audit: organization, organization, organization.

Won't Go out of Way

"You have to push back or you tend to be a casualty instead of a survivor," Wagers said. "They won't trample your rights, but they won't look for unreported deductions either."

The audit ordeal for Paris began two years ago when the IRS questioned several of his tax returns. The dispute concerned money Paris had received from his church, Quinn Chapel AME Church in Lexington, reimbursing him for robes, books, office expenses, mileage and travel.

Paris was flabbergasted. After all, he had hired an Indiana

firm that specialized in preparing returns for ministers.

When Paris initially could not produce all the receipts and statements to prove he had been properly compensated, the IRS assessed him about $13,000 in back taxes, he said. His preparer said the IRS was right.

"I knew what the IRS was saying was not correct," Paris said.

He also made a big mistake, he said. Initially, he met with the IRS alone instead of having a tax adviser attend in his place.

Going it alone can cause problems. Not only can an audit be intimidating, but taxpayers will volunteer unnecessary information and rashly answer questions that should be carefully considered.

Hired an Attorney

"Auditors frequently ask taxpayers for copies of additional

visor and then to the IRS Appeals Office if there still is a disagreement. Most disagreements are settled at this level, often by a compromise between the IRS and taxpayer. Finally, if you still disagree, you can go to court, which is expensive and slow. Depending on the amount of tax in dispute, the case can be litigated in the U.S. Tax Court (essentially, a small-claims court for amounts under $10,000), your U.S. District Court, or U.S. Court of Federal Claims. Your chances of winning in the tax court are about 50 percent. Your last appeal is to the U.S. Supreme Court.

In addition to the amount of income and itemized deductions, the chance of an audit is increased depending on the state where you live. Western states have much higher audit rates than the rest of the country (see Insight 6.2).

returns or for information not related to the areas listed on the audit notice," writes Frederick Daily, author of "Stand Up to the IRS."

Paris hired an attorney to appeal his audit.

To build his case, they meticulously gathered old hotel receipts, bank statements, canceled checks, mileage logs, documents from the church treasurer and even old brochures from seminars he attended.

In fact, the receipts collected for one year showed expenses far exceeded what he had been reimbursed.

The IRS decided Paris owed nothing.

But the audit, he said, "was the most intimidating experience in my life."

Audit notices usually are sent up to 18 months after a return is filed. Generally, after that time a taxpayer is not audited, according to Daily.

With more than 100,000 pages of tax regulations, rulings, manuals and publications, even the IRS has difficulty understanding everything.

"Americans have the dubious honor of having the most complex income tax laws in the world," Daily writes.

80% of Audits Won

Auditors have a stunning record of success.

"The IRS wins 80 percent of all audits, mostly because taxpayers can't properly verify the information on their tax returns," Daily writes.

"IRS auditors say that the biggest reason for this is poor record keeping, not taxpayer dishonesty."

That's why it's important to keep old bank statements, canceled checks and receipts to prove what is claimed on a return. Keep a record of every expense for improving a house to calculate what the gain or loss is when it is sold.

"Anyone who is not ready with the proper documents for an audit should call and ask to postpone, Wagers said. The government will often allow people about a month to organize their finances.

Make sure to get very familiar with the tax return being audited. Remember: Don't provide information not related to the items and year under audit.

Other keys are to be polite, on time, responsive and honest in any dealings with the IRS. Lying could launch a five-year career, stamping license plates in jail.

"If the taxpayer has an attitude the IRS will respond in kind, and they will use the full arsenal," Wagers said.

The main thing the government is interested in is getting money, not sending people to jail, according to tax attorneys.

Source: Kevin Osborne, *"Three Ways to Deal With An IRS Audit: Organize, Organize, Organize,"* 8/22/94. Reprinted with permission of Associated Press.

Tax Preparation Help

Because of the complexity of the tax code, millions of taxpayers seek help in filling out their tax returns. However, you are still responsible for a correct tax return even though someone else prepares the return. The following groups provide tax advice and prepare tax returns:

■ *Internal Revenue Service.* The IRS has a toll-free 800 number that you can call to have tax questions answered. However, expect a busy signal when you call and be patient in trying to reach a representative. IRS representatives sometimes give erroneous answers to tax questions. If you rely on such information, you are still responsible for paying the correct

Insight   6.2   Hate Audits? Stay Out of Montana

This year, the IRS will audit less than 1 percent of the nation's 115 million individual taxpayers after they file their returns. Those are good odds if you're worried about facing an auditor. But there's a catch. "Your chances of an IRS audit rise or fall depending on where you live and how much money you earn," says Marvin Michelman, director of IRS practice and procedure at Deloitte & Touche LLP in New York City.

The accompanying table shows the IRS's audit rates according to the agency's domestic district offices. Located in 63 different cities, these house the IRS's audit army. (Seven states have more than one office.) The audit rates posted are for individuals who earn $25,000 to $49,999, $50,000 to $99,999, and $100,000 or more.

As the table shows, the IRS is more likely to audit those who live in the western United States than those east of the Mississippi. Furthermore, the probability of being called in by the IRS increases as your income rises, no matter where you live. By far,

the worst audit area for high-income individuals is Montana, where the IRS audits a whopping 9.31 percent of the well-off. In contrast, just 1.27 percent of high-income individuals in Chicago can expect to be audited.

Why do some offices audit more taxpayers than others? "Basically it's because some districts have more auditors," says Michelman. "Also, in more urban areas, agents have to deal with corporations, whereas in rural areas they're dealing with a taxpayer population composed mostly of individuals."

Wherever you live, if the IRS sends you the dreaded audit notice, don't be bullied; you have rights. For instance, you can request a postponement and a second appointment if you need more time to prepare for the audit. Consider having a so-called enrolled agent, an individual certified to represent taxpayers before the IRS. Certified public accountants are automatically entitled to this privilege, too. Next, assign power of attorney to that person. That way, he or she can repre-

sent you at the audit, so you don't have to worry about making costly blunders.

If your auditor disallows deductions based on an interpretation of the law and you don't agree with the final audit bill, "your tax pro can haggle the amount down for you," says Shelly Jacobson, an enrolled agent in New York City. "Just because they give you a bill doesn't mean it's etched in stone." Auditors would much rather settle rapidly, given their huge workload.

Roughly 10 percent of audits leave tax bills unchanged or result in a refund. If you get stuck with a bill and can't pay up, your auditor can help you get an installment plan. But you'll be paying an effective annual rate of 15 percent, after interest charges and late penalties. "If you can get cheaper money elsewhere, then do so," says Jacobson.

Source: Elizabeth MacDonald, "Hate Audits? Stay Out of Montana," *Worth*, Vol. 4, No. 3, April 1995, p. 106. Reprinted with permission of *Worth*.

tax. However, you will not be charged any penalty. The IRS will also figure your tax and certain tax credits if your taxable income is less than $100,000 and you do not itemize deductions. Finally, if you have a personal computer, you can file your return electronically by using Form 1040PC, which you can obtain from a paid tax preparer.

■ *Commercial tax firms.* The yellow pages of your telephone directory lists dozens of tax preparation firms. These firms range from a one-person, part-time operation during the tax-filing season to national

1993 Audit Rates by IRS District and Income Class

Location	$25–$49,999 %	Rank	$50–$99,999 %	Rank	$100,000+ %	Rank
Aberdeen, SD	0.50	25	0.89	17	2.61	37
Albany, NY*	0.28	54	0.47	52	2.24	45
Albuquerque, NM	0.43	33	0.70	26	2.87	30
Anchorage, AK	1.44	2	0.93	13	3.58	15
Atlanta, GA	0.48	28	0.50	44	2.33	42
Augusta, ME	0.49	26	0.53	40	4.85	5
Austin, TX*	0.40	39	0.55	37	3.47	17
Baltimore, MD	0.23	59	0.32	61	1.39	58
Birmingham, AL	0.59	18	0.72	24	3.40	21
Boise, ID	0.97	6	1.32	7	4.58	6
Boston, MA	0.21	61	0.34	59	1.37	59
Brooklyn, NY*	0.31	49	0.50	48	1.80	56
Buffalo, NY*	0.48	29	0.61	31	1.88	55
Burlington, VT	0.62	17	1.06	10	3.46	18
Cheyenne, WY	0.71	13	1.09	9	5.27	2
Chicago, IL*	0.28	55	0.37	58	1.27	62
Cincinnati, OH*	0.29	53	0.41	55	2.81	31
Cleveland, OH*	0.28	56	0.46	53	2.75	33
Columbia, SC	0.47	30	0.55	38	1.99	53
Dallas, TX*	0.38	42	0.63	30	3.03	25
Denver, CO	0.66	15	0.70	27	3.69	14
Des Moines, IA	0.33	47	0.53	39	2.05	51
Detroit, MI	0.29	52	0.49	50	1.99	52
Fargo, ND	0.50	24	0.79	20	4.95	3
Fort Lauderdale, FL*	0.48	27	0.82	19	2.55	39
Greensboro, NC	0.24	58	0.37	57	2.10	48
Hartford, CT	0.39	41	0.60	32	2.63	36
Helena, MT	0.66	16	1.50	4	9.31	1
Honolulu, HI	0.33	48	0.50	47	2.49	40
Houston, TX*	0.59	19	0.59	33	2.27	43
Indianapolis, IN	0.34	45	0.50	46	3.30	23
Jackson, MS	0.80	7	0.73	23	3.78	12
Jacksonville, FL	0.42	35	0.77	21	3.99	10
Laguna Niguel, CA*	1.05	4	1.33	6	3.40	22
Las Vegas, NV	1.69	1	2.00	3	3.78	13
Little Rock, AR	0.53	22	0.67	29	2.80	32
Los Angeles, CA*	1.03	5	1.48	5	3.01	26
Louisville, KY	0.40	40	0.52	42	3.00	28*
Manhattan, NY*	0.42	38	0.92	15	0.44	63
Milwaukee, WI	0.15	63	0.29	62	1.44	57
Nashville, TN	0.42	37	0.57	35	2.19	47
Newark, NJ	0.30	51	0.20	63	1.34	60
New Orleans, LA	0.71	12	2.08	2	4.11	9
Oklahoma City, OK	0.73	10	1.00	11	4.94	4
Omaha, NE	0.43	34	0.52	41	2.08	50
Parkersburg, WV	0.38	43	0.69	28	2.36	41
Philadelphia, PA*	0.19	62	0.33	60	1.98	54
Phoenix, AZ	0.68	14	0.92	14	4.14	8
Pittsburgh, PA*	0.27	57	0.50	45	2.57	38
Portland, OR	0.71	11	1.11	8	3.00	27
Portsmouth, NH	0.22	60	0.56	36	2.98	29
Providence, RI	0.73	8	0.99	12	3.26	24
Richmond, VA	0.34	46	0.40	56	1.30	61
Sacramento, CA*	0.73	9	0.75	22	2.72	34
Salt Lake City, UT	0.55	21	0.71	25	3.43	20
San Francisco, CA*	1.25	3	2.15	1	4.15	7
San Jose, CA*	0.56	20	0.90	16	2.68	35
Seattle, WA	0.50	23	0.83	18	3.44	19
Springfield, IL*	0.42	36	0.44	54	2.23	46
St. Louis, MO	0.43	32	0.48	51	2.26	44
St. Paul, MN	0.36	44	0.50	49	2.08	49
Wichita, KS	0.30	50	0.51	43	3.52	16
Wilmington, DE	0.46	31	0.57	34	3.91	11

*More than one IRS office in this state.

firms like H&R Block with thousands of offices throughout the United States. The quality of the tax services provided varies from excellent to marginal, depending on the training and knowledge of the preparer. Remember, however, you are still responsible for any errors on your tax return.

■ *Certified public accountants (CPAs).* CPAs who specialize in tax accounting provide solid but expensive advice. Fees for preparing a tax return can range from at least $300 for an uncomplicated return to several thousands of dollars for complex returns. Some CPAs are aggressive and advise clients to take questionable deductions. Others are nothing more than "order takers" who only fill out the various forms and provide little or no tax advice. Although expensive, CPAs can represent you in a tax audit by the IRS and probably do a much better job in defending the tax return than you can.

■ *Tax attorneys.* Tax attorneys typically provide tax advice rather than tax preparation. Such attorneys are familiar with details of the current tax code, latest tax rulings, private letter opinions by the IRS, and relevant court decisions; they can also represent you in court or before the IRS. Tax attorneys are expensive. In a complex and extended court case, fees can exceed several thousands of dollars.

■ *Enrolled agents.* Enrolled agents are tax preparers who are accredited by the IRS and must meet continuing education requirements. Enrolled agents can fill out your tax return, provide tax advice, and represent you before the IRS in a tax audit. Fees charged are substantially less than the fees charged by CPAs.

■ *Computer software programs.* If you have a personal computer and your return is not complex, you can save hundreds of dollars in tax preparation fees by using a software program to calculate your taxes. Leading software programs include TurboTax, Tax Cut, and Personal Tax Edge.

Capital Gains and Losses

capital asset Property a person owns and uses for personal purposes, pleasure, or investment.

An understanding of capital gains and losses is extremely important in tax planning. Capital gains and losses are due solely to the sale or exchange of capital assets. With certain exceptions, **capital assets** are property you own and use for personal purposes, pleasure, or investment. Examples include stocks and bonds; personal residence; personal automobiles; household furnishings; collectibles, such as coins, stamps, jewelry, gold, or art; and land held for investment. You realize a **capital gain** when the property is sold or exchanged for an amount that exceeds your adjusted cost basis in the property (your cost increased or decreased by certain allowable transactions). The rules of determining your cost basis are complex and depend on the type of property acquired, especially common stocks (see Insight 6.3).

capital gain A gain realized when a capital asset is sold or exchanged for an amount that exceeds the seller's adjusted cost basis in the property.

Example. Tanya purchased 100 shares of common stock at $39 a share and paid a brokers' commission of $100. Her cost basis is $4,000. The stock is sold two years later at $102 a share less a commission of $200. Tanya has a long-term capital gain of $6,000.

Capital gains and losses are divided into two categories: short-term and long-term. Short-term capital gains (or loss) result from the sale or exchange of assets held for one year or less. Long-term capital gains (or loss) result from the sale or exchange of assets held for more than one year. This distinction is important since long-term gains are taxed at a lower rate. Long-term capital gains (at the time of this writing) are taxed

Insight

6.3 Everything You Need to Tot Up a Capital Gain

To compute a gain or loss when you sell, take the proceeds of the sale and subtract your basis—or cost of acquiring the shares. Sounds simple. But the tax code can make it tricky, depending on how you obtained the stock. Follow these rules.

Source: Reprinted from the January issue of *Money* by special permission. copyright 1995, Time Inc.

If You Got Stock by:	Your Basis Is:
Buying it directly	The price you paid for the shares, plus any fees or commissions you paid to buy them. (Fees or commissions on the sale do not add to your basis, but can be subtracted from the proceeds—thus also reducing your gain.)
Buying it through a dividend-reinvestment plan (DRIP)	The full market value of the stock on the date the dividend was paid, plus any fees or commissions, even if—as is often true—the DRIP lets you buy shares at a discount.
Receiving it as a gift	The donor's original basis, plus any gift tax the donor has to pay. Exception: If you later sell the stock for a loss, your basis is the lesser of the donor's basis or the stock's fair market value on the date the gift was given.
Inheriting it	The market value of the shares on the date you inherited them. Often this is the same as the donor's date of death, but in some cases the executor may choose an "alternate valuation date." (To check, ask the executor or review the estate tax return.) Note: Even if you sell the stock within a year, any profit is considered a long-term rather than a short-term capital gain because the stock was inherited.
Receiving it after a stock split	The same, for your total stake, as it was before the split. To find out your new per-share basis, take the original basis of your holding and divide it by the number of shares you own after the split.
Obtaining it as part of a stock dividend	Essentially, whatever the company tells you it is. Explanation: Sometimes a company issues a dividend in the form of stock, or spins off part of its business and gives shareholders stock in the new firm. You usually won't owe any tax on this so-called stock distribution, even if it came as a dividend. But the per-share basis of your holding will be reduced by a percentage that the company will calculate and report to you.
Exercising a stock option	The price you paid for the shares (plus fees or commissions), even though it is lower than the market value at the time of purchase. However, you must retain the shares for at least a year after buying them, and for two years after receiving the option, or else any profit from their sale will be taxed as ordinary income rather than capital gains.

at a maximum rate of 28 percent even if you have ordinary income taxed at a higher rate.

In determining the amount of tax, short-term transactions and long-term transactions are calculated separately. Short-term capital gains are netted against short-term capital losses, which results in a net short-term capital gain (or loss). Likewise, long-term capital gains are netted against long-term capital losses, which results in a net long-term capital gain (or loss). The two resulting figures are then combined to determine if you have a **net capital gain (or loss)** for the current tax year. The net capital gain (or loss) is subject to a number of rules for purposes of determining the amount of tax. We discuss only three of them here.

net capital gain (or loss)
The difference between capital gains and capital losses for a particular period.

1. If your net long-term gain exceeds your net short-term loss, the net capital gain is considered long-term and is taxed at a maximum rate of 28 percent.

   Example. Luis has a short-term gain of $1,000 and a short-term loss of $2,500. He also has a long-term gain of $12,000 and a long-term loss of $3,000. He has a net capital gain of $7,500, which is subject to a maximum rate of 28 percent.

2. If your net short-term gain exceeds your net long-term loss, the difference is considered a short-term gain, which is taxed at the taxpayer's ordinary income tax rate.

   Example. Nicole has a short-term gain of $5,000 and a long-term loss of $2,000. The net capital gain of $3,000 is considered a short-term gain that is added to Nicole's ordinary income and taxed at that rate.

3. If your net short-term loss exceeds your net long-term gain, the net loss can be used to reduce your ordinary income up to the maximum of $3,000. Any loss not used during the current tax year can be carried over to a future tax year.

   Example. Kimberly has a short-term loss of $5,000 and a long-term gain of $2,000. The net capital loss of $3,000 can be used to reduce Kimberly's ordinary income by $3,000.

State and Local Taxes

In addition to the federal income tax, effective tax planning requires an understanding of other types of taxes. Most states have a state income tax as a major source of revenue. Some local communities also have an income tax or wage tax. The marginal tax rates vary widely among the various jurisdictions. In 1994, a married couple filing jointly would pay a flat tax of 2.8 percent on a broad base of income in Pennsylvania; the same couple would pay a top rate of 9.5 percent on income over $20,000 in the District of Columbia, and a top rate of 11 percent on income over $61,000 in Montana.

In addition, nearly all states have a state sales tax, and many cities have a local sales tax as well. There is considerable variation in sales tax rates among the states. In 1994, the highest combined state and local sales tax ranged from 4 percent in Hawaii to 12 percent in Alabama.

At the local level, many cities rely heavily on property taxes as the major source of revenue, especially to fund schools. Homeowners in many cities are revolting because of the heavy financial burden of the property tax on their homes. Depending on the state, you can easily spend 3 percent or more of your adjusted gross income on property taxes on your home. However, many cities will reduce the property tax for people age 65 and older, veterans, disabled persons, and low-income families.

Strategies for Reducing Federal Income Taxes

A number of legal tax strategies can be used to reduce the federal income tax. Before we proceed, however, you should be aware of the distinction between *tax avoidance* and *tax evasion.* Tax avoidance refers to legal methods that can be used to reduce taxes. Tax evasion refers to illegal acts to escape taxation, such as not reporting income, overstating deductions, or failing to file a tax return.

Certain legal strategies can reduce the federal income tax. You do not have to be wealthy to use these strategies, which include the following:

- Take maximum advantage of tax-deferred retirement plans.
- Establish a flexible spending account.
- Roll over a lump sum retirement distribution into an IRA.
- Eliminate nondeductible interest with a home equity loan.
- Invest in tax-exempt bonds or mutual funds.
- Sell securities for a tax loss.
- Accelerate deductions or defer income.
- Sell a home without income tax consequences.
- Shift investment income to the children.
- Make a charitable contribution with appreciated assets.

Take Maximum Advantage of Tax-Deferred Retirement Plans

tax-deferred retirement plan Retirement plan that receives favorable income tax treatment.

Your number-one tax strategy for reducing income taxes is to take maximum advantage of tax-deferred retirement plans. **Tax-deferred retirement plans** are retirement plans that receive favorable income tax treatment. These plans include employer-sponsored private pension plans, Section 401(k) plans, profit sharing and thrift plans, Keogh plans for the self-employed, simplified employee pensions (SEPs), and the individual retirement account (IRA). We discuss the characteristics of these plans in Chapter 16. You should try to make the maximum contribution each year into such plans because of the enormous income tax advantages they provide. The tax advantages include the following:

■ Investment income on plan contributions accumulates free of taxation until the funds are actually withdrawn. As a result of tax-deferred compounding, a substantial fund can be accumulated over a long period (see Exhibit 6.9).

■ Many employer-sponsored retirement plans permit employees to contribute with before-tax dollars. Thus, you receive investment income on the taxes that would have been paid.

■ Employer contributions to qualified tax-deferred retirement plans are not currently taxable to participating employees.

Establish a Flexible Spending Account

flexible spending account Account established by an employer for an employee into which a certain amount of the employee's annual salary is paid, to be used for medical and dental bills or dependent care; contributions into the account are not included as taxable income.

Many employers have established flexible spending accounts for their employees. A **flexible spending account** allows you to exclude a certain amount of annual income from your salary, which is then used to pay medical and dental bills or dependent care expenses. Since contributions into a flexible spending account are not included in your salary,

Exhibit 6.9

Significant Value of Tax-Deferred Compounding
This chart serves as an illustration and assumes $2,000 invested every year, earning 10 percent annual interest and a 31 percent marginal tax rate. Note: Actual performance will depend upon the investments selected, and the market conditions.

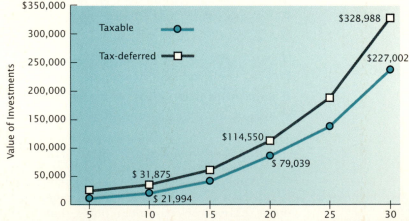

Source: *The Charles Schwab Guide to Retirement Planning*, Charles Schwab & Co., Inc., 1995, p. 6. Reprinted with permission.

you pay less income tax. Employees typically have medical and dental bills that are not covered under a health insurance plan, such as the annual deductible, coinsurance payments, and other expenses excluded under the plan. Other employees incur sizable child-care expenses each year. With a flexible spending account, you pay the expenses and are then reimbursed out of your account. However, your contributions into the flexible spending account are with pretax dollars, which provide valuable tax savings (see Exhibit 6.10).

A word of caution is in order. Amounts in a flexible spending account that are not spent by the end of the year are forfeited to the employer. Thus, in determining the amount to be deducted from your pay, you should be conservative and not overstate the amount needed.

Roll Over a Lump Sum Retirement Distribution into an IRA

If you quit your job or are laid off or fired, you may be entitled to a lump sum distribution from your employer's retirement or Section 401(k) plan. If the distribution is paid directly to you, the employer must withhold 20 percent for federal income taxes. Further, with certain exceptions, if you are under age 59 1/2, you must pay a stiff 10 percent tax penalty in addition to the regular tax. However, if you roll over the entire distribution into an IRA within 60 days of the distribution, including the amount of tax withheld, the tax on the entire distribution can be deferred. (You take credit for the tax withheld when you file your tax return.) However, in order to roll over the entire distribution, you may

---

Exhibit 6.10

Paying Expenses with Pretax Dollars

Compare two wage earners, each earning $75,000 a year, and claiming tax deductions of $15,000. Both have medical expenses of $2,100, and both file a joint return. The first wage earner covers the expenses under a flexible spending account; the second one does not.

	Wage Earner Using Flexible Spending	Wage Earner Paying Expenses
Salary	$75,000	$75,000
Flexible spending	–2,100	
Reportable income	72,900	75,000
Tax deductions	15,000	15,000
Taxable income	57,900	60,000
Tax	**11,792**	**12,380**

The wage earner using flexible spending account **saves $588** in taxes.

Source: Reprinted with permission of Simon & Schuster, Inc. from *The Wall Street Journal Guide to Personal Finance* by Kenneth M. Morris and Alan M. Siegel. Copyright ©1992 by Lightbulb Press, Inc.

have to borrow the amount withheld for taxes, which can be a problem if you are unemployed.

A better solution is to ask your employer to transfer the entire distribution directly into the IRA (or another eligible retirement plan that accepts rollovers). Since you did not receive the distribution, no tax is withheld, and the 10 percent tax penalty does not apply. The entire amount is transferred tax-free from the employer's plan into the IRA.

Eliminate Nondeductible Interest with a Home Equity Loan

Another effective tax strategy is to eliminate nondeductible interest by obtaining a home equity loan. We noted earlier that personal interest and finance charges on car loans, consumer installment debts, and credit card debt are not deductible. However, if you have equity in a home, you can obtain a home equity loan and pay off the consumer loans. The interest on home equity loans of $100,000 or less is currently income tax deductible. *As a result, you will be converting nondeductible interest into deductible interest.* The tax savings are often substantial. For example, if you are in the 28 percent income tax bracket and have a credit card with an annual percentage rate (APR) of 18 percent, none of the interest paid is deductible. However, assume that you obtain a home equity loan at 10 percent and pay off the credit card balance. The net cost of the loan after taxes is only 7.2 percent. If you itemize deductions and have $1,000 of interest on a home equity loan, your tax bill is reduced by $280.

Although home equity interest is deductible, remember you are pledging your home as collateral for a home equity loan. If you fail to make the required payments, the lender may foreclose, and you could lose your home. Thus, you should be certain to make the monthly payments on time. If you were to lose your job and could not make the monthly payments, you should contact the lender immediately so that alternatives to foreclosure might be considered.

Invest in Tax-Exempt Bonds or Mutual Funds

Taxpayers who are in the 28 percent or higher tax bracket can reduce taxes by investing in tax-exempt municipal bonds or mutual funds that invest in tax-exempt bonds. Interest on municipal bonds is free from federal taxation and, in some cases, from state and local income taxes as well. Tax-exempt municipal bonds or mutual funds often provide higher after-tax returns than taxable investments. To determine if you should purchase a tax-exempt security, you must first calculate the tax-equivalent yield. For example, if you are in the 36 percent federal tax bracket, a municipal bond yielding 7 percent is the equivalent of a taxable investment yielding 10.94 percent. The tax-equivalent yield is even higher if the interest is exempt from state and local taxes as well (see Exhibit 6.11). All other factors being equal, you should purchase the tax-exempt security if it has a higher tax-equivalent yield than a comparable taxable investment.

Sell Securities for a Tax Loss

Selling securities for a tax loss to offset capital gains is another effective tax strategy. You may have realized capital gains from the sale of securities. You may also have securities in your portfolio that show paper losses. You should consider **tax loss switching**—that is, you sell the securities for a capital loss and reinvest the proceeds in other securities that are not substantially identical. Alternatively, after 31 days, the securities originally sold could be repurchased to maintain your original position. This later rule must be followed to avoid a wash sale in which the loss would not be deductible. A **wash sale** occurs when you sell a security at a loss and then purchase securities that are substantially identical to the security sold within a 61-day period, starting 30 days before the sale date and ending 30 days after the sale date.

tax loss switching Practice of selling securities at a capital loss and reinvesting the proceeds in other securities that are not substantially identical.

wash sale Transaction in which securities are sold at a loss and substantially identical securities are bought within a certain time period.

Example. Maria has realized capital gains of $1,000. Assume that she owns IBM stock, which has a paper loss of $1,000. She could sell the IBM stock for a tax loss and then reinvest the proceeds in another computer stock, such as Compaq Computer. Alternatively, she could wait 31 days and repurchase the IBM stock to maintain her original position. In both cases, the capital loss is deductible.

Selling securities for a tax loss can still be advantageous even if you have no capital gains to offset. *You can use capital losses to offset ordinary income up to a maximum of $3,000.* Any unused capital losses can be carried forward to the next tax year. However, if you intend to repurchase the securities, make certain you observe the wash sale rule discussed earlier.

Accelerate Deductions or Defer Income

If you expect your tax bracket to be the same or lower next year, it may be advantageous to accelerate deductions to the current tax year. For example, in December of the current tax year, you could prepay the property tax on your home and state and local income taxes. You could also prepay charitable contributions to a church or charity. Likewise, you may be able to consolidate unreimbursed job expenses into one tax year (such as uniforms, union dues, work tools, and subscriptions) so that they exceed 2 percent of adjusted gross income (current threshold for deductibility). If you lack funds to prepay expenses but have equity in your home, you could get a short-term home equity loan. The tax savings typically will exceed the mortgage interest paid, which is also deductible.

Exhibit 6.11

The Value of Tax-Free Yields

Munis can make the most sense for people whose tax-equivalent yield on a tax-free bond or bond fund would be greater than the yield from a similar taxable alternative. Here are two equations to determine whether tax-exempt yields are right for you:

1) For tax-equivalent yields:

$$\frac{\text{tax-free yield}}{(1 - \text{tax rate})} = \text{tax-equivalent yield}$$

2) For combined effective federal/state tax rates (if you are considering buying bonds or funds with bonds issued in your home state):

$$\text{state rate} \times (1 - \text{federal}) = \text{effective state rate}$$

$$\text{effective state rate} + \text{federal rate} = \text{combined effective federal/state tax rate}$$

Tax free yield (%)	Tax-equivalent yield if free from federal taxes* (%)	Tax-equivalent yield if free from state, federal, and local (if applicable) taxes in the following states* (%)											
		AZ	CA	CT	FL	MA	MD	MI	MN	NJ	NY	OH	PA
2.00	3.13	3.31	3.51	3.27	3.13	3.55	3.40	3.27	3.42	3.35	3.55	3.38	3.39
3.00	4.69	4.97	5.27	4.91	4.69	5.33	5.10	4.90	5.12	5.02	5.33	5.07	5.08
4.00	6.25	6.62	7.02	6.54	6.25	7.10	6.79	6.54	6.83	6.69	7.11	6.76	6.78
5.00	7.81	8.28	8.78	8.18	7.81	8.88	8.49	8.17	8.54	8.36	8.88	8.45	8.47
6.00	9.38	9.93	10.53	9.82	9.38	10.65	10.19	9.81	10.25	10.04	10.66	10.14	10.16
7.00	10.94	11.59	12.29	11.45	10.94	12.43	11.89	11.44	11.95	11.71	12.44	11.82	11.86

* Based on the 1995 federal tax rate of 36%: all yields are hypothetical. There is no assurance that the funds will attain any particular yields. Actual share prices (except on money market portfolios), yields, and returns will vary with market conditions; in bond portfolios, you may have a gain or loss when you sell your shares. A portion of income may be subject to the federal alternative minimum tax, or, in some cases, state and local taxes. Based on the following combined effective 1995 federal, state and if noted, local tax rate: AZ-39.58%; CA-43.04%; CT-38.88%; MA-43.68%; MD-41.12% (includes county tax); MI-38.82%; MN-41.44%; NJ-40.21%; NY-43.71% (includes New York City rate); OH-40.80%; PA-40.97% (includes Philadelphia).

Source: Dian Vujovich, "Choosing Munis That Are Right for You," *Fidelity Focus*, Summer 1995, p. 13. Reprinted with permission.

Likewise, if you expect to be in the same or lower tax bracket, it may be advantageous to defer income to the following year. Taxpayers who have some control over their incomes can use this strategy. For example, you may be able to defer receiving a cash bonus until next year, or a professional may delay billing clients so that he or she receives the amounts owed next year. Finally, some investors receive interest currently from money market funds. Part or all of the money market fund assets could be transferred into a short-term certificate of deposit that matures next year, or into a short-term Treasury bill that does not pay interest until the following year. The result is that taxable income is deferred to the following year.

Sell a Home without Income Tax Consequences

On average, homeowners live in their homes five to seven years and then move. You may have a sizable capital gain when you sell your home. If you have a loss on the sale, you cannot deduct it.

You can defer payment of the tax on any gain if you meet the following requirements:

■ You buy or build a new home within two years either before or after the sale.

■ The purchase price of the new home is at least as much as the adjusted sales price of the old home. (Adjusted sales price generally is the sale price of the old home less selling expenses less any fixing-up expenses.)

■ Both the old and new homes are your principal residence.

You are not required to use the money you receive from the sale of your old home to buy the new home. You can use less cash than you receive by increasing the amount of your mortgage on the new home and still postpone tax on the gain. However, the purchase price of the new home must be at least equal to the adjusted sales price of the old home.

Homeowners age 55 or older can receive a special one-time tax break when the home is sold. Older homeowners can exclude any gain from the sale of your home up to a maximum of $125,000 ($62,500 if married and filing separately). You must meet certain requirements to exclude the gain from taxation:

■ You are age 55 or older on the date of sale.

■ During the five-year period ending on the date of sale, you have owned your main home for at least three years, and you have lived in your main home for at least three years.

Shift Investment Income to the Children

Children typically are in a lower tax bracket than the parents. Under present law, you can shift a limited amount of investment income to the children, which trims your income tax. For example, a savings account can be opened in the name of the child. For 1995, the first $650 of investment income is not taxable to the child. The next $650 is taxed at the child's rate. However, investment income in excess of $1,300 is taxed to the child but at the parents' rate. Children age 14 or older pay taxes based on their own rates.

Make a Charitable Contribution with Appreciated Assets

Another effective tax strategy is to make a charitable contribution with long-term assets that have substantially appreciated. For example, assume that the common stock you purchased several years ago for $1,000 is now worth $5,000. If you are in the 28 percent federal tax bracket and sell the stock outright, you must pay a capital gains tax of 28 percent on the $4,000 profit, or $1,120. The charity would receive only $3,880, and your tax deduction would be limited to that amount. However, if you donated the stock outright to the charity, your tax deduction would be $5,000. Since the charity is a nonprofit organization, it could sell the stock without paying any capital gains tax.

SUMMARY

- Filing status is a category that identifies you based on your marital and family situation. There are five types of filing status: single, married filing jointly, married filing separately, head of household, and qualifying widow(er) with dependent child.

- Gross income is all income you receive from money, goods, property, and services that is not exempt from taxation.

- Adjusted gross income is gross income less certain deductions, such as IRA contributions and allowable moving expenses.

- Taxable income is the actual amount of income that is subject to taxation for a given year. It is calculated by subtracting the standard deduction (or itemized deductions) and all exemptions from adjusted gross income.

- The standard deduction is a specific amount that is deducted from adjusted gross income by taxpayers who do not itemize their deductions. The amount of the standard deduction is based on your filing status.

- Itemized deductions are deductions for various types of personal expenses that are listed on Schedule A in Form 1040.

- Exemptions are additional amounts that are subtracted from adjusted gross income to determine taxable income. Each taxpayer receives one personal exemption. A married couple filing jointly receives two personal exemptions. A dependency exemption is an additional exemption for each eligible dependent. The exemption amounts are annually adjusted for increases in the cost of living.

- The income tax is based on taxable income. The tax table shows the amount of tax for taxable incomes up to $100,000. Tax rate schedules are based on the taxpayer's filing status and require a separate calculation to determine the amount of tax. Taxpayers who have taxable incomes of $100,000 or more must use the tax rate schedules.

■ A progressive income tax means the effective tax rate increases as taxable income increases.

■ The marginal tax rate is the tax rate that applies to the last dollar of income.

■ A tax credit reduces dollar for dollar the actual income tax due. A tax credit is more valuable than a tax deduction since the dollar amount of the tax credit reduces taxes. Examples of tax credits include the credit for child and dependent care expenses, credit for the elderly and disabled, and the earned income credit.

■ Some taxpayers owe additional taxes that they must report on Form 1040, such as the self-employment tax and alternative minimum tax.

■ The alternative minimum tax (AMT) is a separate and parallel system for taxing upper-income taxpayers who have large itemized deductions or substantial amounts of tax-sheltered income. The taxpayer must pay the AMT if it is higher than the regular tax.

■ Taxpayers may be required to make estimated tax payments under certain conditions. If you expect to owe $500 or more, you must pay at least 90 percent of the actual tax that will be reported on your current tax return or 100 percent of the tax reported on your previous year's return.

■ Form 1040EZ is a simple one-page form for taxpayers with taxable incomes less than $50,000 who do not itemize deductions or claim dependents, and who receive limited amounts of taxable interest income.

■ Form 1040 is designed for taxpayers who cannot use Form 1040A. Taxpayers who have taxable incomes of $50,000 or more or who wish to itemize deductions must use this form.

■ Failure to file a tax return by the filing date or underpaying the required amount of tax can result in interest and penalties.

■ An audit is an IRS examination of the tax return and records that substantiate the items shown on the return. The audit can be a correspondence audit, office audit, or field audit. An IRS audit can be appealed if there is a disagreement.

■ Help in preparing the tax return can be obtained from the Internal Revenue Service, commercial tax firms, certified public accountants (CPAs), tax attorneys, and enrolled agents. Computer software programs can also be used to file the tax return.

■ Short-term capital gains (or losses) result from the sale or exchange of assets held for one year or less. Long-term capital gains (or losses) result from the sale or exchange of assets held more than one year. Long-term capital gains are taxed at a maximum rate of 28 percent.

■ The state income tax and state sales tax are the most important taxes at the state level. The property tax is a controversial tax that is important at the local level.

■ Certain strategies can be used to reduce the federal income tax: take maximum advantage of tax-deferred retirement plans; establish a flexible spending account; roll over a lump sum retirement distribution into an IRA; eliminate nondeductible interest with a home equity loan; invest in tax-exempt bonds or mutual funds; sell securities for a tax loss; accelerate deductions or defer income; sell a home without tax consequences; shift investment income to the children; make a charitable contribution with appreciated assets.

KEY CONCEPTS AND TERMS

Adjusted gross income
Alternative minimum tax (AMT)
Audit
Average tax rate
Capital asset
Capital gain
Correspondence audit
Dependency exemption
Earned income credit
Exemption
Failure-to-file penalty
Failure-to-pay penalty
Field audit
Filing status
Flexible spending account
Form 1040
Form 1040A

Form 1040EZ
Gross income
Itemized deductions
Marginal tax rate
Net capital gain (or loss)
Office audit
Period of limitations
Personal exemption
Progressive income tax
Standard deduction
Taxable income
Tax credit
Tax-deferred retirement plan
Tax loss switching
Tax rate schedules
Tax table
Wash sale

QUESTIONS FOR REVIEW

1. Explain the meaning of filing status, and identify the five types of filing status.

2. Explain the meaning of gross income, adjusted gross income, and taxable income. Give an example of each.

3. How does the standard deduction differ from itemized deductions? Identify the major deductions that are typically itemized.

4. Explain the meaning of a personal exemption and dependency exemption.

5. Describe how taxable income is calculated.

6. Explain the meaning of a tax credit, and show how a tax credit differs from a tax deduction. Give an example of a tax credit.

7. Briefly explain the major differences between Form 1040EZ, Form 1040A, and Form 1040.

8. Identify the major types of IRS audits.

9. Explain how capital gains and losses are calculated for tax purposes.

10. Describe several strategies that can be used to reduce the federal income tax.

PROBLEMS

1. Jennifer, age 22, recently graduated from college. She is single and has no dependents. During the past year, she received the following:

Wages from a part-time job	$9,500
Christmas gift from parents	100
Proceeds of student loan	3,000
Interest on savings account	35
Dividends on common stock	25
Gambling winnings at a local casino	500
Proceeds from the sale of used textbooks at the college bookstore	110
Amount received from Jennifer's auto insurer to repair her car when she was involved in an accident with another motorist	4,800
Benefits paid by a student health insurance plan for a surgical operation	1,200

Assume that the standard deduction that applies to Jennifer is $3,900, and that the personal exemption is $2,500.

a. What is the amount of Jennifer's gross income? Show your calculations.

b. What is the amount of Jennifer's taxable income? Show your calculations.

2. In determining the amount of income tax owed, a married couple with one dependent child has the following items:

Charitable contributions	$300
State income tax paid	2,100
Property tax on home	2,000
Mortgage interest	3,500
Credit card interest	600
Interest on car loan from a bank	2,400
Medical expenses in excess of 2.5 percent of adjusted gross income	1,200
Job expenses in excess of 2 percent of adjusted gross income	300
Three exemptions at $2,500 each	7,500
Standard deduction for a married couple filing a joint return	6,550

Based on this information, should the couple take the standard deduction or itemize their deductions on Schedule A of Form 1040? Show your calculations. In your answer, identify the items that are deductible on Schedule A of Form 1040.

3. Christian, age 62, is a retired physician who is in the 36 percent federal income tax bracket. He would like to invest $10,000 in high-quality bonds to obtain additional income. He has narrowed his choice to two bonds. One bond is a tax-free municipal bond with a current yield of 5 1/2 percent. The other bond is a taxable bond with a current yield of 7 1/2 percent. Assuming both bonds are of equal value and duration, which of the two bonds should Christian purchase? Show your calculations.

4. On January 5, 1995, Carter purchased 100 shares of Computer Company for a total cost of $1,000. All shares of Computer Company were later sold on January 5, 1997; total net proceeds were $2,500. On February 1, 1997, Carter purchased 100 shares of Generic Drug, a new experimental drug company, for a total cost of $3,000. Because of a poor earnings report, Carter sold all shares of Generic Drug on November 20, 1997; net proceeds were $2,000. On December 29, 1997, Carter bought back the 100 shares of Generic Drug at a total cost of $1,900.

   a. Calculate the amount of capital gains (or losses) that Carter must report on his tax return.

   b. Did Carter violate the "wash sale" rule in any of the aforementioned transactions? Explain your answer.

INTERNET EXERCISES

1 . Go to the IRS's "Digital Daily" at:

http://www.irs.ustreas.gov/prod/cover.html

Explore to learn what's available. For example, choose "Tax Info for You" and then "Tax Trails" to answer yes-or-no questions that will give you information about your deductions, credits, and more.

2. Some states make their tax forms available online. Go to:

http://www.taxweb.com/taxforms.html

and find out if tax forms from your state are available for electronic transfer.

CASE APPLICATIONS

Case I

Lisa, age 29, is single and lives alone. In 1995, Lisa earned $35,000 as a computer programmer for a global corporation. She also received $400 in taxable interest on a savings account at a local bank. Since Lisa did not itemize her deductions, she used Form 1040EZ to file her tax return. She took the standard deduction ($3,900 in 1995) and claimed one personal exemption ($2,500 in 1995) for a total amount of $6,400. During the year, federal withholding totaled $5,300. Lisa is not eligible for the earned income credit. Based on the preceding information, answer the following questions:

1. What is the amount of adjusted gross income? Show your calculations.

2. What is the amount of taxable income? Show your calculations.

3. What is the amount of federal income tax? (Use Form 1040EZ and Exhibit 6.5 in the text.)

4. Will Lisa receive a refund, or does she owe additional taxes? Show your calculations.

Case II

Richard and Wendy, both age 32, are married and have a dependent son, age 1. In 1995, Richard earned $21,000 as an orderly in a nursing home. Wendy earned $28,000 as a copy editor for a publishing firm. The couple received $250 in taxable interest and $100 in common stock dividends. In 1995, they paid mortgage interest of $6,500, property taxes of $2,800, and state income taxes of $2,200. They also contributed $500 to their local church. Federal withholding totaled $4,300. In 1995, the couple filed a joint return. Since they wished to itemize their deductions, they had to use Form 1040. They claimed three exemptions ($2,500 each for 1995). They did not owe any other taxes and were not eligible for any tax credits. Based on the preceding information, answer the following questions:

1. What is the amount of gross income? Show your calculations.

2. What is the amount of adjusted gross income? Show your calculations.

3. What is the amount of taxable income? Show your calculations.

4. What is the amount of tax? (Use Form 1040 and Exhibit 6.5 in the text.)

5. Will the couple receive a refund, or do they owe additional taxes? Show your calculations.

Case III

Pedro and Maria are married and have two dependent children, ages 6 and 10. Both work and are in the 31 percent federal income tax bracket. Pedro's employer has a retirement plan that allows the employees to contribute 6 percent of their before-tax salary into the plan. At the present time, Pedro is contributing only 4 percent of his salary into the plan. The couple finances most consumer purchases with a credit card that has an annual percentage rate (APR) of 18 percent. However, they are currently financing the purchase of a new car with a bank loan of 9.5 percent. Bank interest and credit card charges totaled $3,000 during the current tax year. Several years ago the couple purchased a home that is currently valued at $100,00. The current mortgage balance of $60,000. They also have a savings account in the amount of $20,000 at a local bank, which is currently yielding 4 percent. They file a joint tax return and use Form 1040. The couple would like to reduce the amount of income taxes that they pay. Assume that you are a financial planner. Based on the preceding information, answer the following questions:

1. With specific reference to the bank and credit card interest, explain one tax strategy that Pedro and Maria might consider to reduce their income tax.

2. Identify two additional tax strategies for reducing income taxes that might be appropriate for Pedro and Maria.

SUGGESTIONS FOR ADDITIONAL READING

Davis, Kristin. "Don't Miss These Tax Savers." *Kiplinger's Personal Finance Magazine,* Vol. 49, No. 12 (December 1995), pp. 40–42.

____. "21 Ways to Cut Your Own Taxes." *Kiplinger's Personal Finance Magazine,* Vol. 50, No. 2 (February 1996), pp. 32–38.

MacDonald, Elizabeth. "Breakdown at the IRS." *Smart Money,* Vol. 4, No. 2 (March 1995), pp. 64–72.

MacDonald, Elizabeth, and Teresa Tritch. "Stop Paying Up to 50% in Taxes." *Money,* Vol. 24, No. 1 (January 1995), pp. 80–85.

Your Federal Income Tax for Individuals, 1996 Tax Guide, Publication 17, Department of the Treasury, Internal Revenue Service.

"Your Taxes: A Special Report." *Smart Money,* Vol. IV, No. III (March 1995).

NOTES

1. Tax Foundation, "Tax Freedom Day Climbs Another Notch: May 7," *Tax Features,* Vol. 40, No. 4 (April 1996), p. 1.

2. This chapter is based largely on *Your Federal Income Tax for Individuals, Tax Guide 1995,* Publication 17, Department of the Treasury, Internal Revenue Service. To maintain technical accuracy, certain parts of this document were reprinted in their entirety.

Chapter 7

Housing

Learning Objectives

After studying this chapter, you should be able to:

- Explain the advantages and disadvantages of renting an apartment or home and those of buying a home.

- Describe the characteristics of the various types of housing, including rental property, homes, condominiums, cooperatives, manufactured housing, and mobile homes.

- Explain the home-buying process, including selecting where to live, determining how much the prospective buyer can afford to spend on housing, and financing the purchase of the property.

- Describe the characteristics of mortgages, including types of mortgages, mortgage duration, mortgage interest rates, and, mortgage payments.

- Discuss refinancing and borrowing against the value of a home.

- Explain the tax advantages associated with the purchase of residential real estate.

For a man's house is his castle.

—Sir Edward Coke

Buy land. They ain't making it anymore.

—Will Rogers

Tom and Frances Sullivan were married a little over two years ago. Currently, they are renting an apartment, but they would rather purchase a home. When she wrote last month's rent check, Frances did some quick calculations. The numbers surprised her—since they have been married, the couple has paid more than $10,000 in rent! Although the $10,000 could have been put toward the purchase of a home, the couple never had that much money available at one point in time. Rather, they have been paying rent out of their monthly income. Tom and Frances are trying to save enough money for the down payment on a home. In the meantime, they are trying to familiarize themselves with the steps involved in purchasing a home. They look forward to the day when their monthly housing expenditures will go toward ownership of the property.

Owning a home is part of the American Dream. The purchase of a home is probably the largest financial commitment that you will ever make. In addition to providing for a basic need, shelter, you can regard a home as a long-term, tax-advantaged investment. Just as financial securities increase or decrease in value, real estate values also fluctuate over time. In this chapter, we examine the housing decision. We consider the advantages and disadvantages of renting and owning housing, alternative types of housing, the home-buying process, types of mortgages and mortgage terms, refinancing and borrowing against the value of a home, the tax advantages of owning a home, and related topics.

The Rent versus Buy Decision

When considering housing, you will probably make not one but many different decisions. The first is whether to rent a house or apartment or buy a home. The rent versus buy decision is based on many variables, two of the most important of which are lifestyle preferences and financial considerations.

Some rent versus buy decisions are based on lifestyle preferences. Older persons, for example, may prefer not to be responsible for maintenance of property. Persons moving to a new community often prefer to rent for a time until they know the community better and can make a more informed decision about where to purchase or build a home. Persons desiring more room and the ability to make whatever changes to the property they wish may choose to purchase a house.

But at the heart of many rent versus buy decisions is simple economics. Home purchasers are required to make a **down payment** —a portion of the purchase price paid at the time of purchase. Thereafter, they make monthly mortgage payments, usually for 15 or 30 years. Renters are not required to make a large down payment, but must make rental payments to the property owner, usually on a monthly basis, for as long as they live

down payment A portion of the purchase price paid at the time of purchase.

equity The difference between what property is worth and what is owed on the property.

in the rental property. Property owners build **equity** through their mortgage payments. Equity is the difference between what the property is worth and the amount that is owed on the property. In addition, home buyers reap a number of tax benefits associated with the purchase of the property. Renting does not build equity in the property or provide tax advantages to the renter. Many home buyers, as Tom and Frances Sullivan hope to be, start as renters while accumulating enough funds to make the down payment on a home.

Exhibit 7.1 provides an example comparing the costs of renting an apartment versus purchasing a home. If you rent an apartment, the dollar cost of renting includes the actual rent payments that you make and the cost of renters insurance. If you purchase a home, you incur some direct expenses, you forego some income, and you receive some tax benefits. The direct costs of owning a home include mortgage payments, property taxes, homeowners insurance (which costs more than renters insurance because you are insuring a home), and maintenance expenses. The income that you forego is money that you could have

Exhibit 7.1

The Cost of Renting versus Buying

This example compares the annual cost of renting an apartment for $750 per month versus making the mortgage payments on a $144,000 home, assuming a 30-year mortgage at 9 percent interest with a $24,000 down payment ($120,000 borrowed).

Rental Costs		
Annual rental payments (12 × $750)	$9,000	
Renter's insurance	250	
Total		$9,250

Buying Costs and Benefits		
Mortgage payments (12 × $966)	$11,592	
Property taxes	2,400	
Homeowners insurance	500	
Maintenance	1,000	
After-tax cost of interest foregone on down payment ($24,000 × .05)	1,200	
Reduction of loan balance	− 764	
Tax savings from interest and property tax deductions ($10,828 + 2,400) × .28	−3,704	
Estimated home value appreciation	−3,600	
Total		$8,624

Note: The example assumes mortgage interest and property taxes are fully deductible, the down payment was $24,000, the purchaser's marginal tax rate is 28 percent, and the home will appreciate in value by 2.5 percent per year. The interest paid is simply the difference between the total mortgage payments ($11,592) and principal repaid ($764) during the first year of the mortgage.

earned from investing the down payment elsewhere. Since this investment income would have been taxed, the proper value to consider is the after-tax value of the investment income. The reduction in the loan balance through principal repayment and appreciation are obvious benefits of ownership. Owning a home also provides some tax savings since mortgage interest and property taxes are tax deductible expenses.[1]

In short-term financial comparisons of renting versus buying, renting often appears to be the better alternative. However, in longer-term comparisons, buying has definite advantages. The rent versus buy decision, however, is not a simple matter of dollars and cents. Both renting and buying offer several advantages and disadvantages. We examine some of them in the following sections.

Advantages and Disadvantages of Renting

Renting an apartment or a house has several advantages. As a renter, you do not commit large amounts of financial capital to housing. You make no large down payment although you will probably be required to make a security deposit or damage deposit (for example, you may have to pay the first and last month's rent when you move in). Thus, if you have surplus funds, you can invest them elsewhere. Furthermore, because you do not own the property, you are not responsible for repairs and maintenance or property taxes. Renting is less risky than owning because if you do not like the rental property, you can simply move elsewhere when the lease expires without penalty. In some areas, rents are controlled, which means that if you choose to renew your lease when it expires, your rent can be raised only a certain amount. Finally, some leases include utilities, protecting renters from increases in energy rates during the term of the lease.

Of course, there are also disadvantages in renting. If there are no rent controls where you live, there are no limits on how much your rent can be raised when you renew your lease. In particular, rents may go up where there is strong demand for rental property and a limited supply of rental units. As mentioned earlier, rental payments do not build equity, and renting provides no tax benefits to the renter. In addition, as a renter, you are generally very limited in what changes you can make to the rental property. Even if the owner would allow it, you would probably not want to invest in expensive changes that would stay with the property when you moved. Finally, rental units often offer less living space than what is available through the purchase of a home.

Advantages and Disadvantages of Buying

Buying a home has several advantages. A portion of each mortgage payment goes toward reducing the outstanding debt and building equity in

Consider This

You can search for an apartment via the Internet. For example, RentNet, at:

http://www.rent.net/

lists apartment units for rent in hundreds of cities. For legal information about tenants (as well as homeowners), see the Nolo Press Self-Help Law Center at:

http://www.nolo.com/

Choose "Reference Library" and then "Homeowner/Landlord/ Tenant."

the property. The home may also appreciate in value, building additional equity on a tax-deferred basis for the owner. Indeed, numerous tax advantages are associated with the purchase of a home. One of the most important tax advantage is that a portion of each mortgage payment represents tax deductible interest. The tax advantages of buying a home are discussed further at the end of this chapter. In addition, as a property owner, you can borrow against the built-up equity in your property. Your mortgage payments will not be subject to increase at the whim of a landlord, and you are free to change the property to suit your tastes. You can rent the property or a portion of the property to generate rental income. Finally, you often get more living space for less money by purchasing real estate than by renting.

There are also disadvantages associated with the purchase of real estate, however. Of course, the purchase of real estate requires a greater financial commitment. In addition to the monthly mortgage payments, you must make a down payment, typically 5 to 20 percent of the price of the property. You are responsible for all repairs and maintenance of your property, and you will have to pay property taxes, utilities, and insurance on the structure. You also face the risk that real estate in the area may depreciate in value, and it may be hard to sell your property. If you own the home for a short time, selling expenses may offset any equity that you have built up in the home if you decide to move.

Types of Housing

A number of housing alternatives are available to you. They include renting a house or apartment; or buying a single or multiple-family dwelling, condominium, cooperative, manufactured home, or mobile home.

■ Many people rent apartments and houses rather than purchasing housing. About 36 percent of all Americans rent rather than own their own home.[2] The advantages and disadvantages of renting were discussed in the previous section. Many younger individuals rent because they have not accumulated enough savings to purchase a home. Additionally, there may be uncertainties involving their jobs and their family situation. Renting also relieves you of a number of responsibilities, including maintenance of the property and property taxes.

Several types of rental property are available, including efficiency and studio apartments, single- and multiple-bedroom apartments, and homes. When you rent property, you are required to sign a lease. A **lease** is a formal rental agreement between you, the lessee, and the property

lease A formal rental agreement between a lessee, the person who is leasing property, and a lessor, the owner of the property.

owner, the lessor. The lease specifies such things as the time period during which you may use the property, the monthly rent payment, amount of any security deposit, whether you can sublet the property to someone else, and any restrictions, such as the number of persons who can occupy the premises and whether pets are permitted. Although you do not own the structure, you should consider renters insurance to insure your personal property from damage or theft. Renters insurance also provides personal liability coverage.

multiple-family dwelling
A structure designed to accommodate more than one family.

■ Single- and multiple-family dwellings are the principal forms of home ownership. A **multiple-family dwelling** is a structure designed to accommodate more than one family. Examples of multiple-family dwellings include duplexes and three- or four-family homes. Owners of multiple-family dwellings usually live in one of the living spaces and rent the other space(s). Some owners use the rental payments generated by the other living spaces to provide income to pay the mortgage payment. The homeowner owns the structure and any accompanying land. The homeowner is responsible for property taxes, maintenance and repair of the structure, insurance, and mortgage payments. We discuss the steps involved in the home-buying process in the next section.

condominium Individual ownership of a unit in a multiunit structure (such as an apartment building) or on land owned in common (such as a townhouse complex).

■ A third housing alternative is the purchase of a condominium (condo) unit. A **condominium** is a type of ownership through which units in a multiunit structure are individually owned and common elements are jointly owned. Common elements include such things as stairways, hallways, land, walls, and in some cases, recreational facilities, such as tennis courts, pools, fitness centers, and clubhouses. Condominium unit owners are usually free to sell their units to whomever they choose without the approval of other condominium owners. Unit owners are responsible for property taxes based on the value of their unit, insurance, and mortgage payments. They are usually assessed monthly fees to cover the cost of maintaining the property and to pay property taxes on the common elements.

cooperative A multiunit structure that is owned by a corporation and operated for the benefit of the shareholders who live in the units.

■ A fourth housing alternative is a cooperative. A **cooperative** is a multiunit structure that is owned by a corporation and operated for the benefit of the shareholders who live in the units. The corporation holds title to the units and leases them to the shareholders. Each unit owner has a proportional interest in all common elements and pays monthly fees to compensate managers, pay for maintenance and upkeep of the structure, contribute to repayment of the cooperative's debt, and pay property taxes. Each shareholder's proportional amount of interest and property taxes is a tax deductible expense for the shareholder.

mobile home Transportable dwelling constructed without a permanent foundation.

■ Mobile homes present another housing alternative. **Mobile homes** are transportable dwellings that are constructed without a permanent foundation. Mobile homes are usually considered personal property rather than real property, but some states have enacted laws classifying mobile homes that are permanently anchored to land to be real property. The distinction between personal property and real property is important from a tax perspective. Mobile home owners usually are not required to pay real estate taxes; however, they are subject to licensing fees. Rental fees are also required if the mobile home owner leases a spot in a mobile home park. Mobile homes present an affordable housing alternative for those who wish to own their living accommodations and desire mobility or for those who cannot afford other housing alternatives. You should remember, however, that mobile homes often depreciate in value, whereas other forms of housing often appreciate in value.

manufactured housing Housing constructed away from the location where the house will be used.

■ The final category of housing we will consider is manufactured housing. **Manufactured housing** consists of all housing that is constructed away from the location where the house will be used by the homeowner. An example of manufactured housing is a prefabricated home. Such homes are mass-produced by home builders, shipped in pieces, and assembled when they reach the homeowner. Such housing is less expensive than customized housing since the builder produces many similar units.

The Home-Buying Process

Once you have made the decision to buy and have decided what type of property you want to purchase, many more decisions lie ahead. The home-buying process includes a number of steps, as illustrated in Exhibit 7.2: selecting where to live, determining how much you can afford to spend on housing, searching for property you would like to purchase, negotiating the terms of sale, arranging financing, and closing on the property. Next, we look briefly at each of these steps.

Selecting Where to Live

A popular real estate adage says: "The three most important things about real estate are location, location, and location." The adage has some validity. Where you buy or build a home is an important consideration. Your personal preferences, economics, and other factors influence the location decision. For example, you may desire to be close to shopping areas, your church, and medical facilities, whereas others would rather live away from urban areas. For families with children, the quality of the

Exhibit 7.2

Steps in Buying a Home

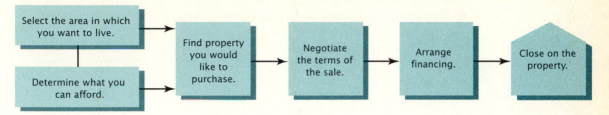

Select the area in which you want to live.

Determine what you can afford.

Find property you would like to purchase.

Negotiate the terms of the sale.

Arrange financing.

Close on the property.

local school system may be an important consideration. You should also consider commuting time to work.

Affordability is another issue. Comparable homes in two different areas may have significantly different prices. Higher home prices and property tax differences may force you to purchase property in one area rather than another. You should also consider the resale value of the home when selecting where to live. Check to see how comparable homes in the area have been selling (number of sales and sales prices).

Determining What You Can Afford

Another key question is "how much house" you can afford to purchase. By far the greatest number of home buyers finance the purchase by making a down payment and borrowing the balance in the form of a mortgage. A **mortgage** is a written loan agreement in which the real estate purchased is used to secure the loan. The home buyer repays the mortgage loan by making periodic payments (usually monthly) to the lender over the life of the mortgage, which, as mentioned, is usually 15 or 30 years. If you are unable to make the mortgage payments, you risk foreclosure and the loss of your property.

One concern, then, is how much down payment you can afford. Typically, the down payment is 10 or 20 percent of the purchase price, although as little as 5 percent may be required. Thus if you purchase a $150,000 house, you will likely need at least $15,000 (10 percent of the purchase price) just for the down payment of the home.

Another concern is how large a mortgage loan a lender will be willing to give you. Lenders use many different measures to make this determination. One rule of thumb is that you can afford to purchase a home that costs up to two and one-half times your annual income.

Insight 7.1 describes another measure, the "28 percent rule." Americans, on average, spend about 28 percent of their income on housing (mortgage, property taxes, and insurance). Even if you satisfy the 28 percent rule, you may be turned down for a mortgage loan if you have other

mortgage A written loan agreement for the purchase of real estate through which the real estate purchased is used to secure the loan and the purchaser agrees to repay the loan by making periodic payments (usually monthly) over the life of the mortgage.

debts. You can use a worksheet like the one displayed in Insight 7.1 to estimate what amount you will be able to borrow when you apply for a mortgage loan. The spreadsheet package included with this text also includes a worksheet for determining how much you can afford to

---

Insight   7.1   How Much Can You Borrow?

Lenders use lots of different ratios to determine how much of a mortgage you can afford. One common method is to take your monthly gross income—including any alimony or dividends—and multiply it by 28 percent (e.g., $5,200 × .28 = $1,456.00). That figure represents the maximum monthly mortgage payment the bank will likely allow.

A more comprehensive approach to figuring out what you can reasonably afford, one that takes into account your existing monthly debts, would be to follow the worksheet shown here. It's been adapted from one used by HSH Associates, a Butler, N.J., mortgage tracking firm.

This figure is the maximum amount a lender will probably allow you to pay each month. Now, take that number back to your bank or real-estate office and have someone there determine—through its mortgage pre-qualification tables—the total amount of the mortgage for which you can qualify. That figure will vary, obviously, on the kind of mortgage you get and the length of its term. For example, someone whose monthly payment was $1,456 and who was applying for a 30-year fixed mortgage at 8 percent would qualify for a loan that totaled about $204,000.

Source: *Smart Money,* April 1993, p. 108. Reprinted with permission.

Step One
Monthly recurring debt:
(Include only debt that will take more than 10 months to pay off.)

Auto loan(s)	_____
Student loan	_____
Furniture loan	_____
Credit card	_____
Credit card	_____
Credit card	_____
Bank loan	_____
Alimony	_____
Child support	_____
Other	_____
TOTAL	_____

Step Two
Multiple monthly gross income by .36 _____

Step Three
Subtract total monthly debt payments −_____

Subtract monthly tax and home insurance payments −_____

(Ask a real-estate agent or loan officer at a local bank for average tax and insurance payments in the neighborhoods you are interested in.)

TOTAL _____

borrow for a home purchase. Obviously, the amount that you can borrow will be determined by your ability to repay the loan. Lenders consider your savings, investments, and current income when deciding how much you can borrow.

In addition to the mortgage payment, other expenses are associated with the purchase of a home. Two important expenses are property taxes and homeowners insurance. If you finance your home through a mortgage—and most people do—you will probably be required to prepay these expenses, especially in the early years of the mortgage. Mortgage lenders often require the borrower to pay an additional amount for insurance and property taxes as part of each monthly payment. The lender pools these excess payments, and pays property insurance premiums and property taxes as they come due.

Local government units (such as cities and counties) use property taxes on real estate to finance a variety of services, including schools. Real estate property taxes are based on the market value or assessed value of your property. For example, the property tax rate might be 3 percent of 50 percent of the assessed value of the property. Thus, the annual property tax on a $200,000 home would be $3,000 a year (.03 × .50 × $200,000). Property tax rates are not uniform from community to community, but generally range from .5 to 3 percent of a home's market value.

Homeowners insurance provides coverage against damage to the dwelling, other structures such as detached garages and tool sheds, and personal property; as well as coverage for loss of use, personal liability, and medical payments to others. If the home is damaged or destroyed, the property securing the loan is reduced in value. That is why mortgage lenders require the purchase of insurance on the property. Chapter 11 will provide additional information about homeowners insurance.

Searching for Property to Purchase

If you know where you want to live and know what you can afford, you are ready to start searching for property to purchase. There are several avenues that you can use to learn what properties are available for purchase. Many realtors publish a listing of available properties in the area, and some realtors have television shows showing available properties. In addition, most local newspapers print a listing of new and existing homes that are for sale. You may also notice a "For Sale" sign in the front yard of a home indicating that the property is available for purchase.

There are a variety of ways that you can contact the owner of the property that is for sale. If the housing is new construction, you can deal directly with the builder or the builder's representative. Most purchasers enlist the services of a real estate agent. A **real estate agent** is a representative of the seller who assists the prospective purchaser by helping to locate suitable housing in the area and showing the property. Since real

real estate agent
A representative of sellers of real estate who assists prospective purchasers by helping them to locate suitable property.

Insight   7.2   Ten Ways to Buy a Home with Bad Credit

Thousands of prospective home buyers think they can't buy a home just because they have bad credit or they declared bankruptcy a few years ago. But every day, people with bad credit and even a bankruptcy in their backgrounds buy homes. Here's how:

(1) Correct Mistakes on Your Credit Report.

Before starting your home buying search, get a copy of your credit report and have any mistakes corrected by the credit bureau. If you were rejected for credit within the last 30 days, the bureau must give you a free copy of your credit report. Otherwise, it will cost between $5 and $10. The major nationwide credit-reporting companies are Experion, Trans Union and CBI. They are listed in the yellow pages under credit-reporting agencies.

If you dispute any item on your credit report, report the error in writing to the credit bureau. It has 30 days to contact the firm, such as a department store, to verify the entry. If no reply is received within 30 days, the disputed item must be removed from your credit report, but you will have to follow up to be sure this is done.

(2) Buy a Home with an Existing Assumable Mortgage.

If you have bad credit, the easiest way to buy a home is to assume an existing mortgage such as a VA or FHA home loan. No qualifying is necessary. Only a $45 fee is required.

If the home seller insists on being released of further liability on the old loan, then a loan application with a credit check is required. But most FHA and VA lenders are not as tough on assumptions as when originating new loans. In addition, to assumable FHA and VA loans, millions of ARMs (adjustable-rate mortgages) are assumable. However, ARM lenders usually require a loan application and credit check.

(3) Buy a Home with Seller Financing.

Many home sellers, especially retirees, will carry back a first or second mortgage for buyers. Most sellers do not check the buyer's credit because they realize the property, not the borrower's credit or income, is the security for the loan.

(4) Obtain an "Easy Qualifier" Loan.

Many banks and S&Ls offer "easy qualifier" mortgages when the home buyer makes a cash down payment of at least 20 percent or 25 percent. These loans are so safe for lenders that they usually eagerly rush the applications through even if the buyer has credit blemishes.

---

buyer's agent A representative of prospective purchasers who assists them in locating suitable property and negotiating the terms of the purchase.

estate agents represent the seller, you may enlist the services of a buyer's agent. A **buyer's agent** is a representative of the prospective purchaser who assists home buyers in locating suitable property and in negotiating the terms of the purchase of real estate. Because real estate agents and buyer's agents are compensated through fees and commissions, you may wish to deal directly with the seller to avoid these costs. Some homes are sold without the services of an intermediary. Such properties are offered on a "for sale by owner" (FSBO) basis. In purchasing such properties, you or your representative deals directly with the seller.

Before you purchase a home, you should do your homework on the property. Some things you should consider include the age of the heating and cooling system and monthly utility bills, property taxes, age and

(5) Obtain a Co-signer.

If your credit report isn't good, but you earn good income, all the lender may need to approve your loan is a co-signer with good credit. Your parents would be ideal. However, most lenders require the co-signer to take title to the property along with the owner-occupant.

(6) Obtain an Equity-share Co-owner.

Should you be unable to find a co-signer, another alternative is to obtain a co-owner who will invest all or part of the down payment and share part of the probable appreciation in the home's market value.

Parents often will share in home ownership with their adult offspring. Internal Revenue Code 280A requires all equity-sharing co-owners to hold title to the property if they want to claim any tax benefits, such as for part of the mortgage-interest and property-tax deductions. Incidentally, the non-resident equity-sharing co-owner who rents his share of the house to the resident co-owner is entitled to depreciate his portion of the house.

(7) Equity-share with the Home Seller.

If you can't find an equity-share investor, ask the seller to share with you by retaining a partial ownership interest in the home. If you obtain a new mortgage, the seller will co-sign and strengthen your loan application. The equity-share contract should provide a buy-out clause and a termination date, such as five or 10 years, when the home will be sold or refinanced to buy out the non-resident co-owner.

(8) Lease with an Option to Buy.

There are many lease-option benefits for buyers such as (a) full or partial rent credit toward the down payment; (b) ability to try out the home before buying; (c) time to clear up credit problems; (d) purchase price lock-in at today's market value; (e) option money payment is usually less than a down payment; and (f) rent is usually cheaper than mortgage payments.

(9) Get the Seller to Guarantee the Loan.

If the home seller is highly motivated to sell and the home has been for sale a long time, the seller may be willing to guarantee the mortgage, such as by depositing part of the cash received from the sale with the lender. The seller should insist on a second mortgage on the house as security in case the first-mortgage lender has to enforce the loan guarantee.

(10) Pledge Other Assets or Have Your Relatives Do So.

If you own other real estate, or if relatives are willing to pledge their property, then the lender can receive a "blanket mortgage" on both the house being purchased and the real estate already owned. However, be sure the blanket mortgage contains a release clause, so the additional property can be removed from the mortgage when the loan balance drops.

Source: Robert Bruss, "Ten Ways to Buy a Home With Bad Credit," 7/7/90, ©Tribune Media Services, Inc. All Rights Reserved. Reprinted with permission.

quality of the roof, whether the plumbing works, the integrity of the home's foundation, and so on. You may enlist a home inspection service to perform many of these tasks when you find property that you are serious about purchasing.

Negotiating the Terms of Sale

Although you may or may not enlist the services of a buyer's agent, there is another party who should be part of your team when you purchase a home: a lawyer. Given the complexities of real estate contracts and real estate law, and the magnitude of the purchase involved, competent legal representation is important. Your lawyer should review all offers, counteroffers, and the purchase contract. Your lawyer should also be present to represent you when you close on the home.

When you find property that you want to buy, the negotiation process begins. Home sellers generally set asking prices higher than the amount they are willing to accept for the property. For example, someone hoping to sell a home for $150,000 may set an asking price of $160,000 or $165,000. If you are serious about purchasing the property, you can make a formal purchase offer to the seller. Your offer specifies a price you are willing to pay, plus a listing of any conditions that the seller must meet (for example, repair of the roof, inclusion of the kitchen appliances, a termite inspection, certification of the heating and cooling system, and so on).

earnest money A good-faith deposit demonstrating the intent of a prospective buyer to purchase a particular home.

Your offer may also include **earnest money,** which is a good-faith deposit demonstrating your intent to purchase the home. The offer usually states that if a deal is struck, the earnest money will count toward the purchase of the home. If you balk after an agreement has been reached, you risk forfeiting this deposit.

Once you have made an offer, the seller is free to accept the offer that you have made or to present a counteroffer. Perhaps you offered $145,000 plus a set of conditions. The seller may counteroffer at $155,000 with some changes in the conditions listed. Through offers, counteroffers, and negotiations, you may finally reach an agreement.

purchase contract A contract reflecting the details of an agreement between a buyer and a seller.

If the buyer and seller can agree on the terms, a purchase contract is signed by the buyer and the seller. The **purchase contract** reflects the details of the agreement, including the agreed-upon price, the date of

Exhibit 7.3

Sample Interest Rates and Points for Various Types of Mortgages

Loan Type	Range Rate/points	Last Week Rate/points
30Y-Fixed (FHA-VA)	6.5/2.75p-7.375/0p	6.5/2.25p-7.5/0p
30Y-Fixed (Conv.)	6.625/2.75p-7.25/0p	6.625/2p-7.25/0p
30Y-Fixed (JUMBO)	6.875/3p-7.75/0p	7/2.125p-8/0p
15Y-Fixed (FHA-VA)	6/2.25p-7/0p	6.5/0p-7/0p
15Y-Fixed (Conv.)	6/2.625p-6.875/0p	6.25/1.25p-6.75/0p
15Y-Fixed (JUMBO)	6.375/2.25p-7.375/1p	6.625/1.75p-7.5/0p
1-YR FHA-ARM	5.5/0p-6/.625p	5/3p-6.375/0p
1-YR ARM (Conv.)	4.75/1.125p-6.125p	4.875/1.25p-6/0p
1-YR ARM (JUMBO)	4.75/1.126p-6.125/1p	5/1.5p-6/0p

Notes: FHA-VA ARM rate has a 1 percent annual cap, and 5 percent life cap, and a 2 percent margin. Conventional ARM rates may have 2 percent annual and 6 percent life caps, and typically have margins of 2.75. JUMBO loans exceed $202,300, the loan limit for major secondary mortgage lenders.
Memphis area mortgage lenders. Lenders show their best rate with no more than 3 points. One point is one percent of the loan amount charged as a front end fee at closing.
Source: ©1997, *The Commercial Appeal*, Memphis, TN. Reprinted with permission.

**mortgage contingency
clause** A clause in a purchase contract specifying
that the agreement is void
unless the buyer is able to
arrange financing for the
purchase.

sale, conditions that must be satisfied, and a mortgage contingency
clause. The **mortgage contingency clause** specifies that the agreement
is void unless the buyer is able to arrange financing for the purchase.

Arranging Financing

While you are negotiating with the seller (or while your representative is
negotiating), it is a good idea to begin the process necessary to qualify
for a mortgage. You begin the process by contacting mortgage lenders,
primarily commercial banks, savings and loan associations, and mortgage companies. These institutions lend large amounts of money to
home buyers for long periods. Thus it is important for mortgage lenders
to carefully screen mortgage applicants before extending a loan. After
you contact a lender, the lender will require you to complete a mortgage
application, and a credit report is ordered. A sample uniform residential
mortgage application is provided in Appendix 7.1 at the end of this chapter. Even if your credit history is unfavorable, you may still be able to
purchase a home. Insight 7.2 provides some suggestions for home buyers
who have bad credit.

Exhibit 7.4

Sample Estimated Closing Costs
One mortgage lender's rough estimate of closing costs for various mortgage
amounts. Some costs (e.g. the loan origination fee) increase with the size of the
loan, while others (e.g. the credit report, surveyor's fee) are fixed.

Mortgage Amount	Estimated Closing Costs	Estimated Prepays
$30,000	$900	$450
$40,000	$1200	$600
$50,000	$1500	$750
$60,000	$1800	$900
$70,000	$2100	$1050
$80,000	$2400	$1200
$90,000	$2700	$1350
$100,000	$3000	$1500
$110,000	$3300	$1650
$120,000	$3600	$1800
$130,000	$3900	$1950
$140,000	$4200	$2100
$150,000	$4500	$2250
$160,000	$4800	$2400
$170,000	$5100	$2550
$180,000	$5400	$2700
$190,000	$5700	$2850
$200,000	$6000	$3000

Source: *Home Buyer's Guide*, Union Planters Bank, Memphis, TN. Reprinted with permission.

Referring to the mortgage application at the end of the chapter, note that the first section of the application describes the type of mortgage and the terms (time period, interest rate, and so on) of the mortgage. Section two provides information about the property and how the property will be used by the buyer. Sections three and four provide background information about the borrower, including name, address, marital status, employer, and other information. Sections five and six are similar to the personal income statement and balance sheet discussed in Chapter 2. The lender is concerned with the borrower's ability to make mortgage payments and how much of the borrower's income will be available for mortgage payments. The lender is also concerned with the borrower's net worth, as determined in section six, assets and liabilities. If the borrower's income stream is interrupted for any reason, the borrower can draw upon surplus assets to continue to make mortgage payments. The final sections provide details of the transaction, declarations by the borrower, a statement of acknowledgment of the terms and agreement to them that the borrower signs, and information for government-monitoring purposes.

Returning to the first section of the application, the type and terms of the mortgage are important considerations. Committing yourself to a mortgage loan at unfavorable terms can have serious negative financial consequences, given the amount of money involved and the long-term financial commitment.

A critical concern is the interest rate charged on the loan. So where do home buyers get information about mortgage interest rates? Financial publications and local newspapers often print representative mortgage rates (see Exhibit 7.3). Prospective borrowers should "shop" their mortgage, contacting a number of area mortgage lenders and inquiring about available rates. As little as half an interest point may cost you thousands of dollars of interest over the life of your mortgage. We discuss mortgage interest rates in greater detail later in this chapter.

Closing on the Property

closing A meeting at which all arrangements of the sale, including any payments due, are made final and title is transferred to the new owner.

title Evidence of ownership of a property.

Having agreed upon the terms with the seller and having obtained a commitment from a mortgage lender, you are ready to consummate the sale, an event that takes place at the closing. The **closing** is a meeting at which all arrangements of the sale, including any payments that are due, are made final and title is transferred to the new owner. **Title** is evidence of ownership of the property. At the closing, the buyer, the seller, and/or their legal representatives, the lender, and sometimes intermediaries (agents and brokers) gather to complete the deal.

To paraphrase the advice given to many home buyers with respect to the closing, "Bring your checkbook and come prepared to sign your name many times." As you might suspect, a number of important issues must be addressed before title passes to you. Most of these issues involve

loan origination fee A fee charged by the mortgage lender for making the loan.

appraisal fee A fee charged by an appraiser who sets a value on the property.

title insurance Insurance coverage that guarantees clear and unencumbered title to the property.

escrow account A savings reserve account established to hold funds designated to cover the cost of certain prepaid items, such as insurance and real estate taxes, when they come due.

closing statement A statement summarizing all the costs (fees and pre-payments) the buyer is to pay at closing.

costs. Closing costs include the loan origination fee, the appraisal fee, the cost of the credit report, title insurance, filing fees, legal fees,[3] and the cost of surveys and inspections. The **loan origination fee** is a fee charged by the mortgage lender for making the loan. This fee is a percentage of the amount of the loan. The **appraisal fee** is a fee charged by an appraiser to set a value on the property. **Title insurance** is insurance coverage that guarantees clear and unencumbered title to the property. Title problems can arise for a number of reasons, including forged deeds, falsified records, and errors in copying or filing forms.

The buyer may also be required to fund a number of prepaid items at the time of closing. Typical prepayments are required for homeowners insurance and certain real estate taxes. An **escrow account** is normally established for these prepayments. An escrow account is a reserve account established to hold funds designated to pay future expenses. For example, at the time of purchase, you may prepay the property taxes for the first year. These funds are placed in the escrow account until the property taxes are actually due. The escrow account provides security to the lender since it guarantees that physical damage insurance and property taxes will be paid when due.

A **closing statement** summarizes all the costs (fees and prepayments) that you will pay at closing. One lender's estimate of closing costs and prepayments based on the size of the loan is provided in Exhibit 7.4.

Types of Mortgages

As mentioned, the features of your mortgage are of critical concern when you buy a home. This section considers mortgages in some detail. A number of different types of mortgages are available. Three of the most popular are conventional mortgages, VA mortgages, and FHA mortgages.

conventional mortgage A mortgage under which the lender assumes the risk of loss.

loan-to-value ratio The ratio of a mortgage loan amount to the value of the property.

Conventional Mortgages. A **conventional mortgage** is a mortgage under which the lender assumes the risk of loss—meaning that the lender stands to lose if you are unable to make your scheduled mortgage payments. Since the lender is at risk with respect to repayment of the borrowed funds, a low loan-to-value ratio is required unless additional security is provided by the borrower. The **loan-to-value ratio** is the ratio of the mortgage loan amount to the value of the property. The ratio declines with the size of the down payment. Your lender may require a down payment of 20 percent (corresponding to a loan-to-value ratio of 80 percent) without additional security. The rate of default is lower when a higher down payment is required.

private mortgage insurance (PMI) Insurance that protects a portion of the loan, typically 20 to 25 percent, against default by the borrower.

The lender may be willing to accept a lower down payment if the borrower purchases private mortgage insurance. **Private mortgage insurance (PMI)** protects a portion of the loan, typically 20 to 25 percent, against default by the borrower. The borrower is charged a fee for PMI at closing and an additional fee each month to cover the cost of the coverage. As the borrower repays the loan through monthly mortgage payments, the borrower's equity in the home increases. Once the loan is repaid to a specified level, the PMI may be dropped.

VA Mortgages. A second alternative, if you qualify, is a loan guaranteed by the U.S. Department of Veteran's Affairs. This department was formerly called the Veteran's Administration, hence the name "VA loan." A **VA-guaranteed loan** is a loan available to qualified armed services veterans that is backed up to a specified amount by the Department of Veteran's Affairs. If the veteran defaults on the mortgage loan, and the home is sold for less than the outstanding indebtedness, the Department of Veteran's Affairs will pay the difference, up to the amount of the guarantee. Note that the Department of Veteran's Affairs does not make the loan—it simply guarantees repayment up to a specified amount. The veteran must have satisfied minimum service requirements to be eligible for a VA-guaranteed loan. In addition to members of the armed forces, National Guard/Reservists are also eligible if they have served for six years. The unmarried surviving spouse of a previously eligible individual may also obtain a VA-guaranteed loan.

VA-guaranteed loan A loan available to qualified armed services veterans that is backed up to a specified amount by the U.S. Department of Veteran's Affairs.

FHA-insured loan A mortgage loan that is guaranteed by the U.S. Federal Housing Administration.

FHA Mortgages. A third popular mortgage alternative is a loan insured by the Federal Housing Administration (FHA). An **FHA-insured loan** is a mortgage that is guaranteed by the FHA. FHA mortgages have a high loan to value ratio when issued. Recall that a high loan-to-value ratio indicates that you are borrowing a high percentage of the value of the home. If the borrower defaults, the FHA will cover the loss to the lender, up to a specified maximum. The borrower and the property must meet FHA requirements in order to obtain the FHA guarantee. The loan amount that is insured cannot be greater than 97 percent of the first $25,000 of appraised value, plus 95 percent up to $125,000, and 90 percent thereafter. The purchase price of the home cannot exceed a specified value based on median home prices in the area. The borrower pays for the FHA insurance at the closing and through monthly payments. As with VA-guaranteed loans, the FHA does not make the loan; rather, it guarantees repayment of the loan up to a specified level.

Duration of the Mortgage

Currently, 15- and 30-year mortgages are popular. When interest rates are high, many home buyers select 30-year mortgages. Low interest rates during the early and mid-1990s led to an increase in the number of 15-

Consider This

Current mortgage rates are widely available online. For example, see HSH Associates' Current Mortgage Rates at:

http://hsh.com/ hshhome.html

or Today's Mortgage Rates by State at:

http://www.microsurf.com/

or Bank Rate Monitor Infobank at:

http://www.bankrate.com/

year mortgages. By paying a lower interest rate and borrowing the money for a shorter period, dollars that would have gone toward interest when interest rates were higher are used to reduce the principal. Shorter-term mortgages provide substantial interest savings, as discussed in Insight 7.3.

Some mortgage lenders are willing to alter the payment schedule of the mortgage, issuing bimonthly or biweekly mortgages. A bimonthly mortgage requires two payments per month, rather than one. Since loan principal is reduced earlier, less interest is paid. Other lenders issue biweekly mortgages, meaning that the borrower will pay a total of 26 payments a year, rather than the 24 that would be paid under the bimonthly mortgage. For borrowers who wish to pay a little more each month but who don't want to be contractually obligated to do so, most lenders will voluntarily accept additional funds, reducing the duration of the mortgage. These extra payments, even as little as $50 per month, can result in substantial interest savings over the life of the mortgage. Insight 7.4 and Exhibit 7.5 discuss and illustrate the value of these additional payments.

Exhibit 7.5

How to Pay off Your Mortgage Quicker and Save Money
This table shows how you can reduce the duration of your mortgage by paying a little extra each month. A $150,000, 9.5 percent 30-year mortgage can be repaid in 25 years if you pay an extra $50 per month, 23.2 years if you pay an extra $75 per month, and 21.8 years if you pay an extra $100 per month.

Loan Amount	Duration of loan if you make monthly payment of		
	Extra $50	Extra $75	Extra $100
$30,000	16.3 years	13.9 years	11.9 years
$40,000	18.1	15.6	13.8
$50,000	19.5	17.0	15.1
$60,000	20.6	18.1	16.3
$70,000	21.4	19.0	17.3
$80,000	22.1	19.9	18.1
$90,000	22.7	20.5	18.8
$100,000	23.2	21.1	19.5
$110,000	23.6	21.6	20.0
$120,000	24.0	22.1	20.5
$130,000	24.4	22.5	21.0
$140,000	24.7	22.9	21.4
$150,000	25.0	23.2	21.8
$160,000	25.2	23.5	22.1
$170,000	25.4	23.8	22.4
$180,000	25.5	24.0	22.6
$190,000	25.6	24.2	22.9
$200,000	25.8	24.5	23.1

Source: *Home Buyer's Guide*, Union Planters Bank, Memphis, TN. Reprinted with permission..

Insight

7.3 Low Interest Rates Make 15-Year Mortgage Popular

When Patricia Fox realized that lower interest rates would allow her to pay off the mortgage on her three-bedroom ranch house in Brookhaven, N.Y., in 15 years instead of 30 with only a $100 increase in her payments, she leaped at the opportunity.

Confounding the expectations of some economists, an increasing number of people like Ms. Fox are taking advantage of low interest rates and refinancing their houses not to cut their payments but to pay off their debts faster. They want to build equity and cut their anticipated interest costs, often by tens of thousands of dollars.

"People are using this windfall as a device for saving," said Robert Van Order, the chief economist for the Federal Home Loan Mortgage Association, known as Freddie Mac, a government-created mortgage financing company that is one of the main sources of credit for American home buyers.

"In normal times, 15-year mortgages tend to be about 15 percent of our purchases. Lately, they've been about a third."

While the value of houses is not normally counted as part of a household's savings, housing purchases have traditionally been a way for Americans to accumulate wealth. Indeed, houses are often a family's most valuable asset and one the government subsidizes through tax deductions for mortgages.

When housing prices soared in the 1980s, most consumers took the biggest, longest mortgages they could get, with the lowest monthly payments, and counted on rising prices to effectively increase the value of the house.

Now, with prices steady and income growth having stalled, the psychology has changed. Economists say many people are looking more than ever to build equity fast, in effect saving money in their houses.

"It's almost like a forced savings plan," said George H. Felker, the vice president and sales manager for residential

lending at the Apple Bank for Savings in New York. "It's an excellent tool for people who are maybe not savers. At the end of the 15 years, they'll have all the equity in their home."

A third of those who are refinancing 30-year mortgages are switching to new 15-year mortgages, according to Freddie Mac. In places, the portion is even higher: At the Greater New York Savings Bank, 61 percent of the fixed-rate refinancings this year have gone to 15-year mortgages, said Russell G. Matthews, the executive vice president and chief lending officer.

Sanford R. Goodkin, a San Diego real estate consultant, said many people think of their houses as savings accounts.

"The biggest effect of shorter-term refinancing is that it saves tons of interest," he said. "Before, people were taking a lot of money and stuffing it into the piggy bank every month, and a lot of it was falling on the floor. But now almost all of it's getting into the slot."

---

prepayment penalty A charge paid by a buyer who repays a mortgage early to compensate the lender for lost interest income.

Since early repayment creates a loss of interest income for the lender, some mortgages include a prepayment penalty. A **prepayment penalty** is a charge paid by the buyer to compensate the lender for lost interest income.

Mortgage Interest Rates

The interest rate charged by the lender is a critical concern for the home purchaser. Home purchasers have two options: fixed-rate mortgages and adjustable-rate mortgages (ARMs).

The fact that these funds are being used to reduce mortgage debt, rather than being spent on refrigerators or cars or apparel, may come as good news to those concerned that America is a country of spenders, not savers.

But since it is coming at a time when economic growth remains sluggish, the move to pay off debt is bad news for retailers and others who have expected that reduced mortgage payments would translate into higher retail sales and faster economic growth.

The wave of refinancings started a couple of years ago, as interest rates dropped sharply. Last year, about 3.6 million people refinanced mortgages totaling about $429 billion, and almost as many are expected to refinance this year, according to David Lereah, the chief economist for the Mortgage Bankers Association of America, an industry group in Washington.

Source: Jeanne S. Pinder, "Owners Refinancing Homes To Cut Debt, Not Payments," August 9, 1993. Copyright ©1993 by The New York Times Company. Reprinted with permission.

A Tale of Two Mortgages

Refinancing can lower monthly payments or reduce costs over the term of the loan. Here are two examples.

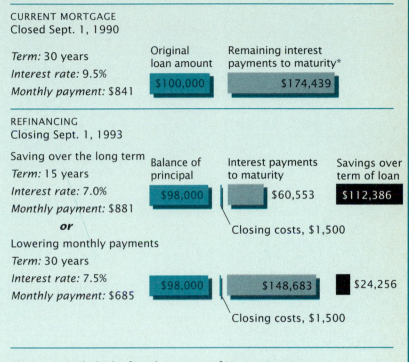

CURRENT MORTGAGE
Closed Sept. 1, 1990

Term: 30 years
Interest rate: 9.5%
Monthly payment: $841

Original loan amount $100,000

Remaining interest payments to maturity* $174,439

REFINANCING
Closing Sept. 1, 1993

Saving over the long term
Term: 15 years
Interest rate: 7.0%
Monthly payment: $881

Balance of principal $98,000

Interest payments to maturity $60,553

Savings over term of loan $112,386

Closing costs, $1,500

or

Lowering monthly payments
Term: 30 years
Interest rate: 7.5%
Monthly payment: $685

Balance of principal $98,000

Interest payments to maturity $148,683

$24,256

Closing costs, $1,500

*Does not include the first three years of interest payments.
Source: The Greater New York Savings Bank

---

fixed-rate mortgage A mortgage in which the interest rate does not change over the life of the loan.

Fixed-Rate Mortgages. A **fixed-rate mortgage** is a mortgage in which the interest rate does not change over the life of the loan. There are obvious advantages and disadvantages to fixed-rate mortgages. One advantage is that should interest rates increase after the purchase of the home, the fixed-rate borrower is locked in at a lower interest rate. Another advantage is that the mortgage payment will be the same each month, which makes planning housing expenditures easier. On the negative side, if interest rates fall, you are locked in at the higher rate. In addition, lenders charge higher fixed rates on mortgage loans than the rates charged on shorter-term loans to hedge against interest rate uncertainty

Insight 7.4   If You've Got Money to Squirrel Away, Sometimes There's No Place Like Home

Investment experts say you shouldn't pay off your mortgage early. Yet I'm doing just that, and so are lots of folks I know.

Are we all fools? I don't think so.

By adding just $50 or $100 to your mortgage check every month, you can save thousands of dollars in interest over the life of your mortgage and pay off your loan far more quickly.

Many financial experts, however, argue that homeowners would be better off funneling any spare cash into the stock and bond markets. That way, say the experts, you'll earn a higher investment return, ensure easy access to your money and you'll continue to have plenty of tax-deductible mortgage interest.

This argument has some merit. But I don't think it has nearly as much merit as the experts think. Clearly, you shouldn't scramble to pay down your mortgage, while neglecting other goals like college and retirement savings. But I think adding a few dollars to your monthly mortgage check can make a lot of financial sense.

Consider, for instance, the question of investment returns. When I make additional mortgage payments, I effectively earn 7.7% a year, which is the interest rate on my 30-year fixed-rate mortgage. How much better would I fare if I put this money into the market instead of my house?

Let's say I bought a balanced portfolio that's split equally between stocks and bonds. History suggests that the stocks would return some 10% a year. Meanwhile, today's buyer can purchase a 30-year Treasury bond and lock in an interest rate of around 7%. Thus, a balanced portfolio might deliver 8.5% a year.

That's better than the 7.7% in annual interest costs I save by paying off my mortgage. But it's not that much better, especially when you consider that I'm sacrificing a sure thing for a far more iffy proposition. I'll definitely save 7.7% by paying off my mortgage. But there's no guarantee that I'll make 8.5% by buying a balanced portfolio, especially after this year's heady stock and bond market gains.

Next, let's turn to the issue of financial flexibility. If you need cash immediately, you can't sell your house. But on any day that the market is open, you can unload your stocks and bonds.

A big advantage? It sure won't seem that way if you have to sell your securities during a brutal stock and bond

over the life of the mortgage. Borrowers commonly prefer fixed-rate mortgages when interest rates are low so that they can lock-in a lower rate for the duration of the mortgage.

Adjustable-Rate Mortgages. When interest rates are high, adjustable-rate mortgages are more popular. An **adjustable-rate mortgage (ARM)** is a mortgage in which the interest rate that is charged fluctuates over time. The interest rate charged is pegged to some readily observable market interest rate, such as the one-year Treasury bill rate, which is used as an index. As interest rates fluctuate, the mortgage payment is adjusted to

adjustable-rate mortgage (ARM) A mortgage in which the interest rate fluctuates over time.

bear market. Under those circumstances, you would be far better off tapping your home's value through a home-equity line of credit.

Finally, there's the question of your mortgage-interest deduction. If you pay off your mortgage more quickly, you will save thousands of dollars in interest, which means you'll also lose thousands of dollars in tax deductions.

That might seem like a drawback, until you consider the alternative. If you invest your spare cash rather than pay down your mortgage, you may have more tax-deductible interest to report on your tax return, but you will also have greater investment earnings to pay tax on. After all, your stocks and bonds are likely to kick off a fair amount in dividends, interest income and capital gains.

Thus, the tax argument doesn't hold water--unless you plan to invest through a tax-deferred account like a variable annuity or an individual retire-ment account. But if you do that, you'll sacrifice financial flexibility, because the money typically can't be withdrawn before age 59$^{1}/_{2}$ without paying a 10% tax penalty. In addition, there could be other with-drawal costs, like the back-end sales charges on some mutual funds and the surrender penal-ties levied by many variable annuities.

Making extra mortgage pay-ments every month does more than just save you money. Jonathan Pond, a financial planner and author in Water-town, Mass., says that once you've paid off your mortgage, you'll eliminate a major monthly expense, which makes it easier to retire.

But Mr. Pond has a more ambitious goal. "I want to pay off the mortgage by the time my kids go to college," he says. "That'll free up enough money each month to pay a big chunk of the tuition bill." Moreover, if you pay down your mortgage instead of accumulating invest-ments in a regular taxable account, you'll probably improve your family's chances of getting student financial-aid.

Making extra mortgage pay-ments also has the virtue of simplicity. You don't have to spend hours at the library or with an investment adviser, trying to figure out which stocks, bonds and mutual funds to buy. All you have to do is fill in a bigger number when you write your monthly mortgage check.

But what if your broker or financial planner still insists that paying down your mort-gage is a dumb idea? "Maybe they have a different agenda," Mr. Pond suggests. "Every dollar you put toward your mortgage is one dollar less they have to manage."

reflect these changes. Adjustable-rate mortgages are popular, as noted, when interest rates are high because many borrowers do not wish to lock-in at the high prevailing rate. Home buyers often choose an ARM with the expectation that interest rates will fall in the future. ARMs are also popular with individuals who do not plan to own the home for a long time since they can take advantage of the low initial rates that some lenders offer.

There are several advantages of adjustable-rate mortgages. If interest rates fall, the monthly mortgage payment will also fall. In addition, many lenders offer teaser rates and rate caps with these mortgages. A

teaser rate A low interest rate charged for an initial period, offered to entice a borrower to accept a mortgage.

rate cap A limitation on the amount by which an adjustable-rate mortgage can increase.

points Fees paid to the lender when a borrower closes a loan.

teaser rate is a low interest rate charged for an initial period that is offered to attract borrowers. A **rate cap** is a limit on the amount by which the interest rate can increase. There are two types of rate caps. Annual rate caps limit the amount by which the interest rate can increase from year to year. Lifetime rate caps limit the amount by which the interest rate can increase over the life of the loan. On the negative side, mortgage payments fluctuate under an adjustable-rate mortgage, making it more difficult to plan housing expenditures. And, of course, if interest rates increase, your mortgage payments will also increase.

Points. The interest rate charged by the mortgage lender depends in part on whether the borrower is willing to pay "points." **Points** are fees that the borrower pays the lender at closing. One point is equal to 1 percent of the value of the mortgage loan, so one point on a $100,000 loan is $1,000. Home buyers can pay some points at the time the loan is extended in exchange for a more favorable interest rate. For example, a lender may be willing to lend money for the purchase of the home at 9.75 percent interest with no points or at 9.25 percent interest if the borrower will pay two points. As we shall see later in this chapter, there are some significant tax advantages for borrowers who are willing to pay points. Of course, paying points creates an additional up-front expenditure.

Your Mortgage Payments

Mortgage payments include an amount to repay principal and an amount to pay interest. Three variables determine the size of your mortgage payment: the amount borrowed, the period for which the funds are borrowed, and the interest rate charged by the lender. Mortgage payments are calculated using the present value annuity formula introduced in Chapter 2. You can also use interest rate tables and financial calculators to determine the mortgage payment. Monthly mortgage payments for selected loan amounts, interest rates, and time periods, as well as an example mortgage payment calculation, are provided in Exhibit 7.6.

For example, assume that you buy a home for $150,000, with a 20 percent down payment. Your down payment will be $30,000, and the mortgage loan will be $120,000. If you borrow the money through a 30-year mortgage at 12 percent annual interest (1 percent monthly), your monthly mortgage payment (principal and interest) will be $1,234.34. Thus, you are scheduled to make 360 payments (monthly payments for 30 years) of $1,234.34 to repay the loan. Note that over the life of the mortgage, you are scheduled to pay a total of $444,362.40 (360 × $1,234.34). Of this amount, only $120,000 is repayment of principal. The balance is interest!

Mortgage payments may include the amount necessary to pay for property taxes and for insurance on the home. In that case, your mort-

Exhibit 7.6

Monthly Mortgage Payments for Selected Loan Principal Amounts by Interest Rate and Term of Loan

Annual Interest Rate	Amount Borrowed and Term of the Loan					
	$80,000		$120,000		$160,000	
	15-year	30-year	15-year	30-year	15-year	30-year
6%	675.09	479.64	1,012.63	719.46	1,350.17	959.28
9	811.41	643.70	1,217.12	965.55	1,622.83	1,287.40
12	960.13	822.89	1,440.20	1,234.34	1,920.27	1,645.78
15	1,119.67	1,011.56	1,679.50	1,517.33	2,239.34	2,023.11
18	1,288.34	1,205.67	1,932.51	1,808.50	2,576.67	2,411.34

Monthly mortgage payments are determined by converting the annual interest rate to a monthly rate, changing the number of years to months, and using the present value annuity formula.

For example, assume that the amount of the loan is $120,000 and that this amount is borrowed for 30 years (360 months) at 12 percent annual interest (one percent per month). Substituting these values into the present value annuity formula, we have:

$$A \times \frac{1 - \dfrac{1}{(1 + .01)^{360}}}{.01} = \$120,000$$

$$A = \$1,234.34$$

The monthly payment can also be found by using the interest rate tables, as demonstrated in Chapter 2 and by using a calculator that offers financial functions.

PITI Principal, interest, taxes, and insurance—the four components of a mortgage payment.

gage payment consists of four components: principal, interest, taxes, and insurance—**PITI** for short. The lender will accumulate the tax and insurance portion of your payments in an escrow account, as discussed earlier in this chapter.

Other Types of Mortgages and Mortgage Provisions

assumable mortgage A mortgage passed on to a purchaser of property from the seller of the property.

There are several other mortgage-related terms with which you should be familiar. Some mortgages are assumable. An **assumable mortgage** is one that can be passed on to a new purchaser of the property. The purchaser makes a down payment equal to the seller's equity position and agrees to be liable for the remaining payments required under the existing mortgage. This arrangement avoids closing costs and may preserve a favorable interest rate on the original mortgage loan.

wraparound mortgage A new mortgage that incorporates the existing mortgage.

Another mortgage arrangement is a **wraparound mortgage.** A seller may offer to sell you property upon which there is an existing, assumable mortgage at favorable terms. Since a portion of the original debt has been repaid and the property may have appreciated in value, you may need to borrow more than the existing mortgage to purchase the property. A wraparound mortgage assumes the existing mortgage, so you can continue to pay off that portion of the loan at favorable terms. The lender will charge you current market rates on the additional funds that you borrow in excess of the existing mortgage.

Some mortgages are set up so that the loan principal is not fully repaid over the life of the loan. The monthly payments on such mortgages are lower than if the entire amount were repaid, but a balloon payment is required at the end of the loan period to make up for the difference. A **balloon payment** is a large final mortgage payment designed to repay the remaining loan balance.

balloon payment A large final mortgage payment designed to repay the remaining loan balance.

Finally, some mortgages involve a buy-down. A **buy-down** is a financing arrangement through which a builder or seller pays points up front to lower the interest rate and the payments required by the buyer. Buy-downs are often used by builders to stimulate sales by offering a lower interest rate to prospective buyers.

buy-down A financing arrangement through which a builder or seller pays points to lower the interest rate and the payments of the buyer.

Refinancing and Borrowing Against Your Property

If you think that once the mortgage payment is calculated that your only other financial concern is making the monthly mortgage payment, you are mistaken. There may be times when it is advantageous to refinance your home. In addition, you may borrow against the equity that you have built up in the property.

Refinancing

What happens, if, after you have purchased a home, more favorable financial terms become available? For example, assume that you thought interest rates would go higher after you purchased your home, so you opted for a fixed-rate mortgage. Since then, however, interest rates for comparable mortgage loans have dropped three percentage points. You may decide to refinance the mortgage. **Refinancing** refers to replacing the present mortgage loan with a new loan at more favorable terms. Unfortunately, many of the closing costs discussed earlier are incurred again when the loan is refinanced, although some of the fees may be waived or reduced through negotiation if you refinance either through the same lender or not long after negotiating the original mortgage. Many of the same decisions you made when the original mortgage was taken out must be made again when you refinance. For example, should

refinancing Replacing an existing mortgage loan with a new loan at more favorable terms.

you take out a fixed-rate loan or a variable-rate loan, should you go with a 15- or 30-year mortgage, and should you pay points?

Borrowing Against Your Property

home equity loan A loan secured by the value of a principal residence.

home equity line of credit A home equity loan in which the homeowner is approved for the loan and then is allowed to borrow on an as-needed basis.

After a homeowner has built some equity in the property, through the down payment, mortgage payments, and price appreciation, he or she may consider a home equity loan. A **home equity loan** is a loan secured by the value of a principal residence. A **home equity line of credit** permits the homeowner to be approved for the loan and then borrow on an as-needed basis. Homeowners can usually borrow up to 80 percent of the home's current value less any outstanding mortgages. For example, suppose that you still owe $50,000 on a home with an appraised value of $150,000. You would be able to borrow up to $80,000 through a home equity loan or home equity line of credit (80 percent of the $100,000 equity position in the home). Competition for home equity loans has increased among financial institutions, and many lenders are willing to extend loans for more than 80 percent of the homeowner's equity position.

Although home equity loans have tax advantages (discussed in greater detail in the next section) and are relatively easy to obtain, there are some disadvantages to consider. A number of fees and expenses, in addition to interest payments, are associated with home equity loans.

Tax Advantages of Residential Real Estate

To foster the construction and purchase of homes, the federal government offers a number of tax advantages to purchasers of residential real estate. First, the home appreciates in value on a tax-deferred basis. That is, the homeowner is not taxed on the appreciation in a home until the home is sold. Second, the homeowner is not taxed on the gain from the sale of a home, provided the homeowner purchases another home that costs at least as much as the previous home within two years of the sale date. Third, homeowners 55 years of age and older are entitled to a one-time $125,000 capital gains exclusion on residential real estate gains. To qualify, the homeowner must have lived in the home for three of the previous five years.

There are also tax benefits associated with interest paid when the home is purchased and interest paid throughout the life of the mortgage. The tax law permits you to deduct interest on money borrowed to purchase, build, or substantially improve a principal or second residence, up to a limit of $1 million in indebtedness. For taxpayers who itemize their deductions, mortgage interest is a valuable tax deduction. Most mortgage lenders calculate the interest and principal paid for the borrower for tax purposes and forward this information to the borrower.

In the early years of a mortgage, most of each mortgage payment goes to cover interest, and very little principal is repaid. Exhibit 7.7 shows the breakdown of principal and interest for selected years of a 30-year mortgage. The interest that you pay each year, shown in the far-right column, is the tax deductible portion of the mortgage payment.

In addition to interest paid over the life of the mortgage, points paid at the origination of the mortgage loan are also tax deductible. The allure of points is the immediate deductibility up-front, and a lower interest rate, hence lower monthly payments, over the life of the loan. Points paid when a mortgage loan is refinanced are not deductible at the origination of the loan; rather, they are deductible over the life of the refinanced loan.

Another tax advantage associated with residential real estate is available through home equity loans and home equity lines of credit. What is the tax advantage associated with this type of borrowing? The Tax Reform Act of 1986 eliminated the tax deductibility of interest paid on most other types of consumer loans. Interest paid on home equity loans and money borrowed through home equity lines of credit, however,

---

Exhibit 7.7

Annual Principal and Interest Payments

Although your mortgage payment may be the same from month to month, the portion of each payment that goes to repay principal increases and the interest portion decreases each month. Recall that interest is only charged on the amount owed. As the debt is repaid, less interest is charged.

The monthly payment for a $120,000, 30-year mortgage loan at 9 percent interest (0.75 percent per month) is $965.55. Thus each year of the mortgage you will pay a total of $11,586.60 ($965.55 × 12). But how much of that annual expenditure is principal repayment and how much is interest? The break-down for selected years of the mortgage is provided here. As you can see, the tax-deductible interest paid decreases each year.

Year of Mortgage	Total Paid— Principal and Interest	Principal Paid	Interest Paid
1	$11,586.60	$819.48	$10,767.12
5	$11,586.60	$1,173.53	$10,413.07
10	$11,586.60	$1,837.36	$9.749.24
15	$11,586.60	$2,876.72	$8,709.88
20	$11,586.60	$4,504.03	$7,082.57
25	$11,586.60	$7,051.87	$4,534.73

remains a tax deductible expense. Consumers are not restricted with respect to how the borrowed funds are used; however, interest is deductible only on loans of $100,000 or less.

SUMMARY

■ The advantages of renting include no commitment of capital, freedom from responsibility for maintenance and repairs, mobility, and in some cases, limitations upon the ability of the property owner to raise rents.

■ The disadvantages of renting include increased rents, no equity in the property, limitations on the ability to alter the property, and limited living space.

■ The advantages of owning a home include mortgage payments that build equity in the property, appreciation potential, tax advantages, the ability to add betterments and customize the property, the ability to rent the property, and greater living space.

■ The disadvantages of owning a home include greater capital commitment, possible decline in the value of the home, possible difficulty in selling the home, responsibility for repairs and maintenance, and payment of taxes and utilities.

■ A number of housing alternatives are available, including renting an apartment or home, and buying a single or multiple-family dwelling, condominium, cooperative, mobile home, or manufactured home.

■ Single-family homes account for most housing units. Multiple-family dwellings have living spaces designed to accommodate more than one family.

■ A condominium is a form of ownership through which units in a multiunit structure are individually owned and common elements are owned with the other unit owners.

■ A cooperative is a multiunit structure owned by a corporation and operated for the benefit of shareholders who live in the units.

■ Mobile homes are transportable dwellings that are constructed without a permanent foundation.

■ Manufactured housing consists of all housing that is constructed away from the location where the house will be used by the homeowner.

■ Steps in the home-buying process include selecting where to live, determining how much you can afford to spend on housing, searching for desirable property, negotiating the terms of sale, arranging financing, and closing on the property.

■ The decision where to live is based upon personal preferences, economics, and other factors.

■ In determining how much you can afford to spend on a house, the home buyer should consider his or her gross monthly income and net worth position. The buyer will be required to make a down payment and monthly mortgage payments over the life of the mortgage.

■ The magnitude of the mortgage payment depends upon the amount borrowed, the term of the loan, and the interest rate charged.

■ The prospective purchaser can deal directly with a builder, a real estate agent, a buyer's agent, or the owner of an existing property.

■ After finding the "right" home, the negotiation process begins. You should have the home inspected, and you should review prices for comparable homes in the area. The buyer and seller exchange offers and counteroffers, and purchase terms are made final in a purchase contract.

■ The purchase contract includes a mortgage contingency clause, requiring the buyer to obtain qualified financing as a condition of sale.

■ The closing is the culminating event with respect to the purchase of a home. At the closing, all arrangements of the sale are finalized and title is transferred to the new owner.

■ A number of fees and prepaid items must be paid at the closing. An escrow account is established to hold the prepaid funds until the payments are due.

■ The homeowner should purchase homeowners insurance to provide physical damage coverage for the home, coverage on personal property, and personal liability insurance. The homeowner should also purchase title insurance to guarantee clear title to the property.

■ There are several different types of mortgages. The most popular types of mortgages are conventional mortgages, VA-guaranteed mortgages, and FHA-insured loans.

■ Under a conventional mortgage, the lender assumes the risk of loss. A lower loan-to-value ratio is required unless the borrower purchases private mortgage insurance.

■ VA-guaranteed mortgages and FHA-insured loans provide a government guarantee up to a specified amount of the loan.

■ The borrower may choose a fixed-rate mortgage under which the payment is constant from month to month, or an adjustable-rate mortgage (ARM) under which payments fluctuate with changes in interest rates.

■ In exchange for a lower mortgage interest rate, the borrower may agree to pay points. Points are fees paid to the lender when you close the loan. One point equals one percent of the loan amount.

■ The homeowner may choose to refinance the loan at a later date if there is a financial justification to do so.

■ After equity is built up in the home, a home equity loan or home equity line of credit may be established.

■ Home buyers must also consider property taxes that are based on the value of the property.

■ Several tax advantages are associated with the purchase of residential real estate: (1) The home appreciates on a tax-deferred basis. (2) The homeowner is not taxed on a gain from the sale of a home provided a home of equal or greater value is purchased within two years of the sale of the old home. (3) Homeowners age 55 and older are permitted a one-time capital gains exclusion of $125,000 on residential real estate gains. (4) Interest on money borrowed to purchase, build, or improve a first or second residence, up to $1 million in indebtedness, is tax deductible. (5) Points paid at the origination of a loan are deductible at that time. Points paid when a loan is refinanced are deductible over the life of the refinanced loan. (6) Interest paid on home equity loans and lines of credit is tax deductible.

KEY CONCEPTS AND TERMS

Adjustable-rate mortgage (ARM)
Appraisal fee
Assumable mortgage
Balloon payment
Buy-down
Buyer's agent
Closing
Closing statement
Condominium
Conventional mortgage
Cooperative
Down payment
Earnest money

Equity
Escrow account
FHA-insured loan
Fixed-rate mortgage
Home equity line of credit
Home equity loan
Lease
Loan origination fee
Loan-to-value ratio
Manufactured housing
Mobile home
Mortgage
Mortgage contingency clause

Multiple-family dwelling
PITI (principal, interest, taxes,
  and insurance)
Points
Prepayment penalty
Private mortgage insurance (PMI)
Purchase contract
Rate cap

Real estate agent
Refinancing
Teaser rate
Title
Title insurance
VA-guaranteed loan
Wraparound mortgage

QUESTIONS FOR REVIEW

1. What are the advantages and disadvantages of renting an apartment? What are the advantages and disadvantages of owning a home?

2. What are the characteristics of these housing alternatives: cooperatives, condominiums, manufactured housing, and mobile homes?

3. Discuss the steps involved in the home-buying process.

4. What information is provided to a mortgage lender in a completed residential loan application?

5. What expenses are normally included in closing costs?

6. What is the relationship between the level of interest rates and the level of monthly mortgage payments? What is the relationship between the duration of a mortgage and the level of monthly mortgage payments?

7. How do VA-guaranteed loans and FHA-insured loans differ from conventional mortgage loans?

8. What are the advantages and disadvantages of fixed-rate mortgages and adjustable-rate mortgages?

9. When does it make sense for a homeowner to consider refinancing a mortgage loan?

10. What are the principal tax advantages that are associated with the purchase of residential real estate? Why are home equity loans so popular?

PROBLEMS

1. Tom and Frances Sullivan paid $525 per month the first year they rented their apartment. They were also required to pay a $200 damage deposit when they signed the lease. The second year, their rent was increased to $550 per month. Over the first two years, how much has the couple paid out-of-pocket to live in the apartment (rental payments plus damage deposit)?

2. Angela Marbury is considering the purchase of two different homes. Calculate Angela's down payment and the amount of the mortgage loan for each property.

   a. The first home costs $140,000. The seller requires a 10 percent down payment.

   b. The second home costs $125,000. The seller requires a 15 percent down payment.

3. Philip Chu decided to purchase a home valued at $200,000.

   a. If the loan-to-value ratio of Philip's mortgage loan is 80 percent, how much money did Philip borrow to purchase the property?

   b. Based on your answer, how much interest would Philip pay at the origination of the loan if he agreed to pay two points in exchange for a lower fixed interest rate?

4. Calculate the monthly mortgage payments for each of the following mortgage loans. Compare your answers with the monthly payments listed in Exhibit 7.5.

   a. The mortgage loan is for $80,000. The borrower will make monthly payments for 15 years and pay 12 percent annual interest, compounded monthly (1 percent per month).

   b. The mortgage loan is for $120,000. The borrower will make monthly payments for 30 years and pay 9 percent annual interest, compounded monthly (0.75 percent per month).

5. Sheldon Jones owes $50,000 on a home valued at $180,000. He would like to take out a home equity loan. A mortgage lender is willing to extend a loan for up to 80 percent of Sheldon's equity position in the property. What is the most that the lender will lend Sheldon?

INTERNET EXERCISES

1. There are many online sources for mortgage calculators that will help you figure out such things as what your monthly payments will be for a loan of a certain size at a particular interest rate, how large a mortgage loan you can qualify for, and whether to refinance. Visit some of the following sites, find their calculators, and work through some calculations:

Home Buyer's Fair	http://www.homefair.com
FinanCenter	http://www.financenter.com/
HSH Associates Current Mortgage Rates	http://hsh.com/hshhome.html
The Mortgage Mart	http://mortgagemart.com/
The Mortgage Calculator	http://alfredo.wustl.edu/mort.html

2. Many government publications for consumers can be ordered or accessed directly at the Consumer Information Center at:

   http://www.pueblo.gsa.gov/

   Go to the site, choose "Housing," and see what publications are available. If possible, print one or two publications of interest and bring them to class.

CASE APPLICATIONS

Case I

Margaret Kane is a buyer's agent. Recently, she has received a number of calls seeking her assistance with finding a place to live. For each of the following, describe the housing alternative that makes the most sense:

1. Keith and Velda Young recently retired. Both are 65 years old. They no longer wish to be responsible for mowing lawns and shoveling snow off sidewalks. At the same time, they want to be able to customize their living accommodations to fit their own tastes—they would rather own than rent, and money is not a problem.

2. Mike and Beth Collins are "yuppies." Each has a good job earning in excess of $60,000 per year. They have been renting the past four years. They have no children. The couple believes they are paying too much in taxes, and they are tired of renting.

3. Manny Scherich just graduated from college. He took a job in Margaret's city and will be moving there next month. Manny has no savings and extensive credit card debt and student loans.

Case II

Bob and Geraldine Tyler are first-time home buyers. They have found a neighborhood that they like, and have visited several homes that are for sale in the neighborhood. The Tylers decided to begin to look into financing the home and visited Mary Beth Reid, a mortgage lender at Community Savings and Loan. A number of questions have arisen with respect to the type of mortgage and mortgage terms that would be best for Bob and Geraldine. Treat each question independently.

1. Bob was honorably discharged from the United States Air Force after 12 years of service. Does this have any bearing upon the types of mortgages available to Bob and Geraldine?

2. Bob and Geraldine are expecting "extra income" this year. They are willing to pay more up-front at the time of the closing in exchange for some immediate tax relief and a lower fixed interest rate over the life of the loan. Explain a loan provision that will be of interest to Bob and Geraldine.

3. Mortgage interest rates have reached a 30-year high. Bob and Geraldine are confident that interest rates will decrease in the near future. They do not wish to be locked-in at a high interest rate.

4. The owner of one of the homes for sale was just transferred by his employer to another city. The home was purchased three years ago when interest rates were more favorable. The seller is motivated to sell, and Bob and Geraldine are wondering if it might be possible to avoid some expense involved in the purchase transaction and to continue the old mortgage at the favorable terms.

Case III

Stephanie Coleman purchased a home 20 years ago. She financed the home through a loan from a savings and loan association. She has ten years remaining on her mortgage, and the outstanding mortgage balance is $25,000. The market value of the home is $142,000.

1. What is Stephanic's equity position in her property?

2. Stephanie's mortgage lender is willing to lend her up to 75 percent of her equity position in the home. What is the most that the lender will lend Stephanie through a home equity loan?

3. Stephanie is considering remodeling the kitchen and finishing the basement. She visited her savings and loan, and inquired about bor-

rowing the money to finance the project. She was given two alternatives: a regular bank loan at 8 percent interest or a home equity loan at 9 percent interest. Why might the 9 percent interest loan be more favorable for Stephanie than the loan with the lower interest rate?

4. Assume that Stephanie takes out a home equity loan and that during the first year she pays $2,000 in interest. Further assume that her taxable income before considering the interest on the home equity loan is $11,500. How much will Stephanie save on taxes as a result of the home equity loan? Assume that the $2,000 is fully deductible and that Stephanie pays taxes at a rate of 28 percent.

SUGGESTIONS FOR ADDITIONAL READING

Bloch, H. I. Sonny and Grace Lichtenstein. *Inside Real Estate—The Complete Guide to Buying and Selling your House, Co-op, or Condominium.* New York: Grove and Weidenfeld, 1987.

Dunnan, Nancy. *Dun & Bradstreet's Guide to $Your Investments$.* New York: HarperCollins Publishers, Inc., 1994.

Ficek, Edmund F., Thomas P. Henderson, and Ross H. Johnson. *Real Estate Principles and Practices,* 6th ed. New York: MacMillan Publishing Company, 1994.

Galaty, Fillmore W., Willington H. Allaway, and Robert C. Kyle. *Modern Real Estate Practice,* 13th ed. Chicago: Dearborn Financial Publishing, 1994.

Morris, Kenneth M. and Alan M. Siegel. *The Wall Street Journal Guide to Understanding Personal Finance.* New York: Lightbulb Press, 1992.

Vila, Bob with Carl Oglesby. *Bob Vila's Guide to Buying your Dream House.* Boston: Little, Brown and Company, 1990.

NOTES

1. The value of the tax savings attributable to mortgage interest may be overstated in this illustration. Taxpayers are always entitled to at least the standard deduction. The temptation may be to consider only the mortgage interest in excess of the standard deduction. However, with mortgage interest, more taxpayers are able to itemize their deductions. Hence additional deductions (for example, certain medical expenditures and charitable contributions) also become deductible expenses.

2. *The Wall Street Journal Guide to Understanding Personal Finance,* by Kenneth M. Morris and Alan M. Siegel. New York: Lightbulb Press, 1992, page 53.

3. It bears repeating: When purchasing real estate, it is advisable to have legal representation. Your lawyer can review the contract and advise you with respect to the contractual provisions. Given the magnitude of the purchase, qualified legal counsel is important.

APPENDIX 7.1

Sample Uniform Residential Mortgage Application

Uniform Residential Loan Application

This application is designed to be completed by the applicant(s) with the lender's assistance. Applicants should complete this form as "Borrower" or "Co-Borrower", as applicable. Co-Borrower information must also be provided (and the appropriate box checked) when ☐ the income or assets of a person other than the "Borrower" (including the Borrower's spouse) will be used as a basis for loan qualification or ☐ the income or assets of the Borrower's spouse will not be used as a basis for loan qualification, but his or her liabilities must be considered because the Borrower resides in a community property state, the security property is located in a community property state, or the Borrower is relying on other property located in a community property state as a basis for repayment of the loan.

I.   TYPE OF MORTGAGE AND TERMS OF LOAN

Mortgage Applied for:	☐ V.A. ☐ FHA	☐ Conventional ☐ FmHA	☐ Other:	Agency Case Number		Lender Case Number
Amount $	Interest Rate %	No. of Months	Amortization Type:	☐ Fixed Rate ☐ GPM	☐ Other (explain): ☐ ARM (type):	

II.   PROPERTY INFORMATION AND PURPOSE OF LOAN

Subject Property Address (street, city, state, ZIP)	No. of Units
Legal Description of Subject Property (attach description if necessary)	Year Built

Purpose of Loan	☐ Purchase ☐ Construction ☐ Other (explain): ☐ Refinance ☐ Construction-Permanent	Property will be: ☐ Primary Residence ☐ Secondary Residence ☐ Investment

Complete this line if construction or construction-permanent loan.

Year Lot Acquired	Original Cost $	Amount Existing Liens	(a) Present Value of Lot $	(b) Cost of Improvements $	Total (a + b)

Complete this line if this is a refinance loan.

Year Acquired	Original Cost $	Amount Existing Liens	Purpose of Refinance	Describe Improvements ☐ made ☐ to be made Cost: $

Title will be held in what Name(s)	Manner in which Title will be held	Estate will be held in: ☐ Fee Simple ☐ Leasehold (show expiration date)
Source of Down Payment, Settlement Charges and/or Subordinate Financing (explain)		

III.   BORROWER INFORMATION

Borrower	Co-Borrower
Borrower's Name (include Jr. or Sr. if applicable)	Co-Borrower's Name (include Jr. or Sr. if applicable)

Social Security Number	Home Phone (incl. area code)	Age	Yrs. School	Social Security Number	Home Phone (incl. area code)	Age	Yrs. School
☐ Married ☐ Separated ☐ Unmarried (include single, divorced, widowed)	Dependents (not listed by Co-Borrower) no. ages			☐ Married ☐ Separated ☐ Unmarried (include single, divorced, widowed)	Dependents (not listed by Borrower) no. ages		
Present Address (street, city, state, ZIP) ☐ Own ☐ Rent ___ No. Yrs.				Present Address (street, city, state, ZIP) ☐ Own ☐ Rent ___ No. Yrs.			

If residing at present address for less than two years, complete the following:

Former Address (street, city, state, ZIP) ☐ Own ☐ Rent ___ No. Yrs.	Former Address (street, city, state, ZIP) ☐ Own ☐ Rent ___ No. Yrs.
Former Address (street, city, state, ZIP) ☐ Own ☐ Rent ___ No. Yrs.	Former Address (street, city, state, ZIP) ☐ Own ☐ Rent ___ No. Yrs.

IV.   EMPLOYMENT INFORMATION

Borrower		Co-Borrower	
Name & Address of Employer ☐ Self Employed	Yrs. on this job	Name & Address of Employer ☐ Self Employed	Yrs. on this job
	Yrs. employed in this line of work/profession		Yrs. employed in this line of work/profession
Position/Title/Type of Business	Business Phone (incl. area code)	Position/Title/Type of Business	Business Phone (incl. area code)

If employed in current position for less than two years or if currently employed in more than one position, complete the following:

Name & Address of Employer ☐ Self Employed	Dates (from - to)	Name & Address of Employer ☐ Self Employed	Dates (from - to)
	Monthly Income $		Monthly Income $
Position/Title/Type of Business	Business Phone (incl. area code)	Position/Title/Type of Business	Business Phone (incl. area code)
Name & Address of Employer ☐ Self Employed	Dates (from - to)	Name & Address of Employer ☐ Self Employed	Dates (from - to)
	Monthly Income $		Monthly Income $
Position/Title/Type of Business	Business Phone (incl. area code)	Position/Title/Type of Business	Business Phone (incl. area code)

Freddie Mac Form 65 10/92   Fannie Mae Form 1003 10/92

VMP -21 (9210)   Page 1 of 4   ♻ Printed on Recycled Paper

VMP MORTGAGE FORMS • (313)293-8100 • (800)521-7291

Mortgage Application *(continued)*

V. MONTHLY INCOME AND COMBINED HOUSING EXPENSE INFORMATION

Gross Monthly Income	Borrower	Co-Borrower	Total	Combined Monthly Housing Expense	Present	Proposed
Base Empl. Income*	$	$	$	Rent	$	▓▓▓▓▓▓
Overtime				First Mortgage (P&I)		$
Bonuses				Other Financing (P&I)		
Commissions				Hazard Insurance		
Dividends/Interest				Real Estate Taxes		
Net Rental Income				Mortgage Insurance		
Other (before completing, see the notice in "describe other income," below)				Homeowner Assn. Dues		
				Other:		
Total	$	$	$	**Total**	$	$

* Self Employed Borrower(s) may be required to provide additional documentation such as tax returns and financial statements.

B/C	Describe Other Income *Notice:* Alimony, child support, or separate maintenance income need not be revealed if the Borrower (B) or Co-Borrower (C) does not choose to have it considered for repaying this loan.	Monthly Amount
		$

VI. ASSETS AND LIABILITIES

This Statement and any applicable supporting schedules may be completed jointly by both married and unmarried Co-Borrowers if their assets and liabilities are sufficiently joined so that the Statement can be meaningfully and fairly presented on a combined basis; otherwise separate Statements and Schedules are required. If the Co-Borrower section was completed about a spouse, this Statement and supporting schedules must be completed about that spouse also.

Completed ☐ Jointly ☐ Not Jointly

ASSETS Description	Cash or Market Value	Liabilities and Pledged Assets. List the creditor's name, address and account number for all outstanding debts, including automobile loans, revolving charge accounts, real estate loans, alimony, child support, stock pledges, etc. Use continuation sheet, if necessary. Indicate by (*) those liabilities which will be satisfied upon sale of real estate owned or upon refinancing of the subject property.		
Cash deposit toward purchase held by:	$	**LIABILITIES**	Monthly Pmt. & Mos. Left to Pay	Unpaid Balance
		Name and address of Company	$ Pmt./Mos.	$
List checking and savings accounts below				
Name and address of Bank, S&L, or Credit Union				
		Acct. no.		
		Name and address of Company	$ Pmt./Mos.	$
Acct. no.	$			
Name and address of Bank, S&L, or Credit Union				
		Acct. no.		
		Name and address of Company	$ Pmt./Mos.	$
Acct. no.	$			
Name and address of Bank, S&L, or Credit Union				
		Acct. no.		
		Name and address of Company	$ Pmt./Mos.	$
Acct. no.	$			
Name and address of Bank, S&L, or Credit Union				
		Acct. no.		
		Name and address of Company	$ Pmt./Mos.	$
Acct. no.	$			
Stocks & Bonds (Company name/number & description)	$			
		Acct. no.		
		Name and address of Company	$ Pmt./Mos.	$
Life insurance net cash value	$			
Face amount: $				
Subtotal Liquid Assets	$			
Real estate owned (enter market value from schedule of real estate owned)	$	Acct. no.		
Vested interest in retirement fund	$	Name and address of Company	$ Pmt./Mos.	$
Net worth of business(es) owned (attach financial statement)	$			
Automobiles owned (make and year)	$			
		Acct. no.		
		Alimony/Child Support/Separate Maintenance Payments Owed to:	$	▓▓▓▓▓
Other Assets (itemize)	$	Job Related Expense (child care, union dues, etc.)	$	
		Total Monthly Payments	$	
Total Assets a.	$	**Net Worth** (a minus b) ➤	$	**Total Liabilities b.** $

**Mortgage
Application**
(continued)

VI. ASSETS AND LIABILITIES (cont.)

Schedule of Real Estate Owned (If additional properties are owned, use continuation sheet.)

Property Address (enter S if sold, PS if pending sale or R if rental being held for income)	Type of Property	Present Market Value	Amount of Mortgages & Liens	Gross Rental Income	Mortgage Payments	Insurance, Maintenance, Taxes & Misc.	Net Rental Income
		$	$	$	$	$	$
Totals		$	$	$	$	$	$

List any additional names under which credit has previously been received and indicate appropriate creditor name(s) and account number(s):

Alternate Name	Creditor Name	Account Number

VII. DETAILS OF TRANSACTION

a. Purchase price	$
b. Alterations, improvements, repairs	
c. Land (if acquired separately)	
d. Refinance (incl. debts to be paid off)	
e. Estimated prepaid items	
f. Estimated closing costs	
g. PMI, MIP, Funding Fee	
h. Discount (if Borrower will pay)	
i. **Total Costs (add items a through h)**	
j. Subordinate financing	
k. Borrower's closing costs paid by Seller	
l. Other Credits (explain)	
m. Loan amount (exclude PMI, MIP, Funding Fee financed)	
n. PMI, MIP, Funding Fee financed	
o. Loan amount (add m & n)	
p. Cash from/to Borrower (subtract j, k, l & o from i)	

VIII. DECLARATIONS

If you answer "Yes" to any questions a through i, please use continuation sheet for explanation.

Borrower Yes No / Co-Borrower Yes No

a. Are there any outstanding judgments against you?

b. Have you been declared bankrupt within the past 7 years?

c. Have you had property foreclosed upon or given title or deed in lieu thereof in the last 7 years?

d. Are you a party to a lawsuit?

e. Have you directly or indirectly been obligated on any loan which resulted in foreclosure, transfer of title in lieu of foreclosure, or judgment? (This would include such loans as home mortgage loans, SBA loans, home improvement loans, educational loans, manufactured (mobile) home loans, any mortgage, financial obligation, bond, or loan guarantee. If "Yes," provide details, including date, name and address of Lender, FHA or V.A. case number, if any, and reasons for the action.)

f. Are you presently delinquent or in default on any Federal debt or any other loan, mortgage, financial obligation, bond, or loan guarantee? If "Yes," give details as described in the preceding question.

g. Are you obligated to pay alimony, child support, or separate maintenance?

h. Is any part of the down payment borrowed?

i. Are you a co-maker or endorser on a note?

j. Are you a U.S. citizen?

k. Are you a permanent resident alien?

l. **Do you intend to occupy the property as your primary residence?** If "Yes," complete question m below.

m. Have you had an ownership interest in a property in the last three years?

(1) What type of property did you own—principal residence (PR), second home (SH), or investment property (IP)?

(2) How did you hold title to the home—solely by yourself (S), jointly with your spouse (SP), or jointly with another person (O)?

IX. ACKNOWLEDGMENT AND AGREEMENT

The undersigned specifically acknowledge(s) and agree(s) that: (1) the loan requested by this application will be secured by a first mortgage or deed of trust on the property described herein; (2) the property will not be used for any illegal or prohibited purpose or use; (3) all statements made in this application are made for the purpose of obtaining the loan indicated herein; (4) occupation of the property will be as indicated above; (5) verification or reverification of any information contained in the application may be made at any time by the Lender, its agents, successors and assigns, either directly or through a credit reporting agency, from any source named in this application, and the original copy of this application will be retained by the Lender, even if the loan is not approved; (6) the Lender, its agents, successors and assigns will rely on the information contained in the application and I/we have a continuing obligation to amend and/or supplement the information provided in this application if any of the material facts which I/we have represented herein should change prior to closing; (7) in the event my/our payments on the loan indicated in this application become delinquent, the Lender, its agents, successors and assigns, may, in addition to all their other rights and remedies, report my/our name(s) and account information to a credit reporting agency; (8) ownership of the loan may be transferred to successor or assign of the Lender without notice to me and/or the administration of the loan account may be transferred to an agent, successor or assign of the Lender with prior notice to me; (9) the Lender, its agents, successors and assigns make no representations or warranties, express or implied, to the Borrower(s) regarding the property, the condition of the property, or the value of the property.

Certification: I/We certify that the information provided in this application is true and correct as of the date set forth opposite my/our signature(s) on this application and acknowledge my/our understanding that any intentional or negligent misrepresentation(s) of the information contained in this application may result in civil liability or criminal penalties including, but not limited to, fine or imprisonment or both under the provisions of Title 18, United States Code, Section 1001, et seq. and liability for monetary damages to the Lender, its agents, successors and assigns, insurers and any other person who may suffer any loss due to reliance upon any misrepresentation which I/we have made on this application.

Borrower's Signature	Date	Co-Borrower's Signature	Date
X		X	

X. INFORMATION FOR GOVERNMENT MONITORING PURPOSES

The following information is requested by the Federal Government for certain types of loans related to a dwelling, in order to monitor the Lender's compliance with equal credit opportunity, fair housing and home mortgage disclosure laws. You are not required to furnish this information, but are encouraged to do so. The law provides that a Lender may neither discriminate on the basis of this information, nor on whether you choose to furnish it. However, if you choose not to furnish it, under Federal regulations this Lender is required to note race and sex on the basis of visual observation or surname. If you do not wish to furnish the above information, please check the box below. (Lender must review the above material to assure that the disclosures satisfy all requirements to which the Lender is subject under applicable state law for the particular type of loan applied for.)

BORROWER
☐ I do not wish to furnish this information

Race/National Origin:
☐ American Indian or Alaskan Native   ☐ Asian or Pacific Islander   ☐ White, not of Hispanic Origin
☐ Black, not of Hispanic origin   ☐ Hispanic
☐ Other (specify) _____

Sex: ☐ Female   ☐ Male

CO-BORROWER
☐ I do not wish to furnish this information

Race/National Origin:
☐ American Indian or Alaskan Native   ☐ Asian or Pacific Islander   ☐ White, not of Hispanic Origin
☐ Black, not of Hispanic origin   ☐ Hispanic
☐ Other (specify) _____

Sex: ☐ Female   ☐ Male

To be Completed by Interviewer

This application was taken by:
☐ face-to-face interview
☐ by mail
☐ by telephone

Interviewer's Name (print or type)	Name and Address of Interviewer's Employer
Interviewer's Signature ___ Date	
Interviewer's Phone Number (incl. area code)	

Part Two

Protection Against Financial Insecurity

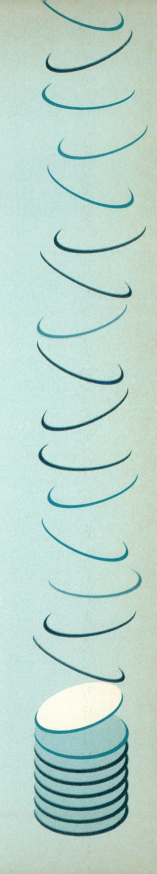

Chapter  **8**

Introduction to Risk Management and Insurance

Learning Objectives

After studying this chapter, you should be able to:

- Explain the meaning of risk.

- Identify the major pure risks associated with great financial insecurity, including personal risks, property risks, and liability risks.

- Define personal risk management.

- Describe the steps in the personal risk management process.

- Explain the major methods for handling risk, including avoidance, loss control, retention, noninsurance transfers, and insurance.

- Define insurance and explain the basic characteristics of insurance.

- Identify the major types of private insurance sold today.

- Explain the difference between stock and mutual insurers.

 There are worse things in life than death. Have you ever spent an evening with an insurance salesman?

—Woody Allen

Insurance: An ingenious modern game of chance in which the player is permitted to enjoy the comfortable conviction that he is beating the man who keeps the table.

—Ambrose Bierce

Jennifer and Mark graduated from a large midwestern university, married, and moved to Dallas, Texas. Like many married couples, they wanted to save money for a down payment on a home. Shortly after they moved into an apartment, a burglar broke into the apartment and stole a new television set, stereo, camera, jewelry, silverware, and cash hidden in a jewelry box. The loss totaled $7,200. The couple had no insurance. As a result, their goal of accumulating a down payment for a home received a serious setback. What went wrong? The couple made the mistake of paying inadequate attention to risk and insurance in their financial plan.

It is clear that we live in a risky world. Numerous events can threaten our financial security, such as the death of a family head in a car accident, destruction of a home and personal property in a hurricane or earthquake, and sickness and catastrophic medical bills. Insurance can provide protection against such losses. Insurance, however, is only one of several personal risk management techniques that deal with risk.

This chapter discusses the fundamentals of personal risk management and insurance. Topics discussed include the meaning of risk, identification of the major risks that can result in great financial insecurity, steps in the development of a sound personal risk management program, and the major methods for handling risk. The chapter concludes with a discussion of insurance as a major technique for handling risk.

Importance of Risk in a Financial Plan

A sound financial plan requires an analysis of major risks that can threaten your financial security. If you fail to plan for these risks, you may not attain your financial goals.

Meaning of Risk

risk Uncertainty of loss.

There is no single definition of risk. Economists, behavioral scientists, risk theorists, and actuaries have their own concept of risk. However, risk traditionally has been defined in terms of uncertainty. Based on this concept, **risk** is defined as uncertainty of loss. For example, the risk of lung cancer for smokers is present because uncertainty is present. The risk of being killed in a car accident is present because uncertainty is present. And the risk that your wallet or purse may be stolen is present because uncertainty is present.

pure risk Risk present in a situation in which the only possibilities are loss and no loss.

Risk can be classified as either pure or speculative. **Pure risk** is a situation in which there are only the possibilities of loss or no loss. The only possible outcomes are adverse (loss) and neutral (no loss). You ordinarily do not profit if a loss occurs. Examples of pure risks include premature death of a family head, car accidents, sickness or injury, unemployment, and destruction of a home and personal property in a tornado.

speculative risk Risk present in a situation in which either profit or loss is possible.

Speculative risk is a situation in which either profit or loss is possible. For example, if you buy 100 shares of common stock, you would profit if the stock price increases, but you would lose if the price declines. Other examples of speculative risk include betting on a horse race, investing in real estate, and going into business for yourself. In these situations, both profit and loss are possible.

The distinction between pure and speculative risk is important because, with certain exceptions, speculative risks are not insurable. Other techniques for treating such risks must be used.

Major Types of Pure Risk

Major pure risks associated with great financial insecurity include personal risks, property risks, and liability risks. If you fail to plan properly for these risks in your financial plan, the financial consequences of a major loss can be catastrophic.

personal risk Risk that directly affects an individual.

Personal Risks. **Personal risks** directly affect an individual and include the following:

1. *Risk of premature death.* Premature death is the death of a household head with unfulfilled financial obligations. These obligations can include dependents to support, children to educate, or a mortgage to be repaid. If the surviving family members lack additional sources of income or have insufficient financial assets to replace the lost income, financial hardship can result.

human life value The present value of the family's share of the deceased breadwinner's future earnings.

Four costs can result from the premature death of a household head. First, the **human life value** of the family head is lost forever. The human life value is the present value of the family's share of the breadwinner's future earnings. This loss can be substantial; the actual or potential human life value of most college graduates can exceed $500,000. Second, additional expenses may be incurred because of burial costs, uninsured medical bills, probate costs, and estate taxes on large estates. Third, the family's replacement income from all sources may be inadequate just in terms of its basic needs. Finally, certain noneconomic costs are incurred, such as the emotional grief of the surviving spouse and the loss of a role model for the children.

2. *Risk of insufficient income during retirement.* The major risk associated with old age is insufficient income during retirement. When older workers retire, they lose their normal work earnings. Unless they have accumulated sufficient financial assets from which to draw, or have access to

8.1   How Are the Aged 65 and Older Doing Financially?

The risk of insufficient income during retirement should receive high priority in financial planning. How are the aged 65 and over doing financially? In answering this question, it is a mistake to assume that all aged are wealthy; it is equally wrong to assume that all aged are poor. *The aged are an economically diverse group, and the incomes they receive are far from uniform.* In 1993, about 42 percent of the households with a household head age 65 and over had total incomes under $15,000. This amount is relatively low and may be insufficient for those with substantial additional expenses, such as high uninsured medical bills, the cost of long-term care in a nursing home, or high property taxes. At the other extreme, 11 percent of the aged households had total incomes of $50,000 or more. The median total income for all aged households in 1993 was only $17,751.

In addition, many aged persons live in poverty. In 1993, 12.2 percent of all persons aged 65 and older had incomes below the poverty line. People living in poverty typically are not financially secure.

Source: Data cited are based on U.S. Bureau of the Census, Current Population Reports, P60-180, *Income, Poverty, and Valuation of Non-cash Benefits: 1993* (Washington, D.C.: U.S. Government Printing Office, 1995), Table 2, p. 5, and Table C, p. xvi.

other sources of retirement income, such as social security or a private pension, they may be faced with financial insecurity during retirement. As a practical matter, many older retired workers are financially insecure because of insufficient income (see Insight 8.1).

3. *Risk of poor health.* The risk of poor health includes both catastrophic medical bills and the loss of earned income. The cost of major surgery has increased substantially in recent years. For example, a coronary bypass operation can easily cost $75,000, and recovery and rehabilitation from a near-fatal auto accident can cost $150,000 or more. The inability to pay catastrophic medical bills is a major cause of personal bankruptcy.

The loss of earned income is another major cause of financial insecurity if the disability is prolonged and severe. In cases of long-term disability, work earnings are lost, medical bills are incurred, employee benefits may be lost or reduced, and savings are often depleted.

Most workers seldom think about the financial consequences of long-term disability and that the disability can occur without warning. The probability of becoming disabled before age 65 is much higher than is commonly believed, especially at the younger ages. Exhibit 8.1 shows the

Exhibit 8.1

Probability of at Least One Person Becoming Disabled for 90 Days or More before Age 65

Age	Number of Persons 1	2	3	4	5	6
25	54%	79%	90%	95%	98%	99%
30	52	77	89	95	98	99
35	50	75	88	94	97	99
40	48	73	86	93	96	98
45	44	69	83	90	95	97
50	39	63	78	87	92	95
55	32	54	69	79	86	90
60	9	18	25	32	39	44

Based on 1985 Commissioners Disability Table

Source: Edward E. Graves, ed., *McGill's Life Insurance* (Bryn Mawr, Pa.: The American College, 1994), Table 7-2, p. 141. Used with permission from *McGill's Life Insurance*. Copyright © 1994 by The American College.

probability of becoming totally disabled for at least 90 days before age 65. The table is based on joint probabilities and is applicable to families or business firms with up to six persons. *Exhibit 8.1 shows that a person age 25 has a 54 percent chance of becoming totally disabled for at least 90 days before age 65.* In view of the high probability of becoming disabled before age 65, you should not ignore this important risk in your financial plan.

4. *Risk of unemployment.* Unemployment is another major threat to financial security. Regardless of the cause, unemployment can cause financial insecurity in at least three ways. First, the worker loses his or her earned income. Unless there is adequate replacement income or past savings on which to draw, the unemployed worker will be financially insecure. Second, because of economic conditions, the worker may be able to work only part time. The reduced income may be insufficient in terms of the worker's needs. Finally, if the duration of unemployment extends over a long period, past savings may be exhausted.

Property Risks. People who own property are exposed to the risk of having their property damaged or destroyed from numerous causes. A home and personal property can be damaged or destroyed because of a fire, hurricane, earthquake, or other causes. Two types of loss can result from the destruction or theft of property—a direct loss and an indirect, or consequential, loss. A **direct loss** is a financial loss that results from the physical damage, destruction, or theft of the property. Examples of a direct loss include the destruction of your personal property in a fire and the theft of your automobile.

direct loss A financial loss that results from the physical damage, destruction, or theft of property.

indirect loss A financial loss that results indirectly from the occurrence of a direct loss from physical damage or theft.

An **indirect loss** is a financial loss that results indirectly from the occurrence of a direct physical damage or theft loss. Extra expenses resulting from a direct physical damage loss are an example of an indirect or consequential loss. For example, if a fire damages your home or apartment, you may be forced to move to a furnished apartment during the period of rebuilding; moving expenses are incurred, and monthly rent must be paid. These extra expenses are the consequence of a direct physical damage loss and can be substantial.

Liability Risks. Liability risks are another type of pure risk that most people face. Under our legal system, you can be held legally liable if you injure someone or damage someone's property. A court of law may order you to pay substantial damages to the person you have injured or whose property you have damaged.

Liability risks are extremely important in financial planning. *First, there is no maximum upper limit on the amount of loss.* You can be sued for any amount. In contrast, if you own property, any loss has a maximum limit. For example, if your automobile has a market value of $10,000, the maximum physical damage loss is $10,000. If you are negligent, however, and cause an accident that results in serious bodily injury or death to another motorist, you can be sued for any amount—$50,000, $500,000, or $1 million or more—by the person you have injured.

Second, a lien can be placed on your income and financial assets to satisfy a legal judgment. For example, assume that you injure someone, and a court of law orders you to pay damages to the injured party. If you cannot pay the judgment, your income and financial assets can be attached to satisfy the judgment. If you declare bankruptcy to avoid payment of the judgment, your credit rating will be impaired.

Finally, legal defense costs can be enormous. If you have no liability insurance, the cost of hiring an attorney to defend you can be staggering. If the suit goes to trial, attorney fees and other legal expenses can be substantial.

In summary, major pure risks associated with financial insecurity include premature death of a family head, insufficient income during retirement, poor health, unemployment, damage or destruction of a home and personal property, and liability lawsuits. Let us next consider how personal risk management can be used to deal with these risks.

Personal Risk Management

Risk management is widely used by corporations and government organizations to manage the pure risks to which they are exposed. Consumers can use the same principles in a personal risk management program.

Meaning of Personal Risk Management

personal risk management The identification and evaluation of pure risks faced by an individual or family and the selection of the most appropriate techniques for treating such risks.

Personal risk management refers to the identification and evaluation of pure risks faced by an individual or family, and to the selection of the most appropriate technique for treating such risks. Personal risk management is a broader concept than insurance management and considers other methods for handling risk in addition to insurance.

Steps in Personal Risk Management

There are four steps in the development of a sound personal risk management program: (1) identify potential losses, (2) evaluate potential losses, (3) select the appropriate technique for handling losses, and (4) review the program periodically (see Exhibit 8.2).

Identify Potential Losses. The first step is to identify all potential losses that can cause serious financial problems. Based on our earlier discussion, catastrophic financial losses can result from the following:

1. Personal risks

   ■ Loss of earned income to the family because of premature death of the family head
   ■ Insufficient income and financial assets during retirement
   ■ Catastrophic medical bills and the loss of earnings during an extended period of disability
   ■ Loss of earned income from unemployment

Exhibit 8.2

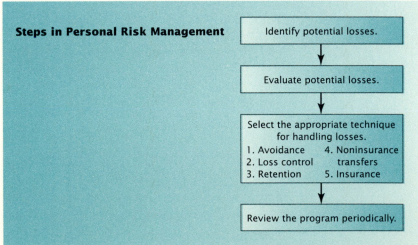

2. Property risks

   ■ Direct physical damage to a home and personal property because of fire, lightning, windstorm, flood, earthquake, or other causes
   ■ Indirect losses resulting from a direct physical damage loss, including extra expenses, moving to another apartment or home during the period of reconstruction, loss of rents, and loss of use of the building or property
   ■ Theft of valuable personal property, including money and securities, jewelry and furs, paintings and fine art, cameras, coin and stamp collections, and antiques
   ■ Direct physical damage losses to automobiles, motorcycles, and other vehicles from a collision and other-than-collision losses
   ■ Theft of automobiles, motorcycles, or other vehicles

3. Liability risks

   ■ Legal liability arising out of personal acts that cause bodily injury or property damage to others
   ■ Legal liability arising out of libel, slander, defamation of character, and similar exposures
   ■ Legal liability arising out of the negligent operation of a car, motorcycle, boat, or recreational vehicle
   ■ Legal liability arising out of business or professional activities
   ■ Payment of attorney fees and legal defense costs

Evaluate Potential Losses. The second step is to evaluate the impact of a potential loss on your financial position. This involves an estimate of the frequency and severity of a potential loss so that the most appropriate technique, or combination of techniques, can be used to deal with the risk. For example, the chance that your home will be totally destroyed by a fire, tornado, or hurricane is relatively small, but the severity of such a loss would be catastrophic. These losses should be insured because of their catastrophic potential. However, if loss frequency is high, but loss severity is low, such losses should not be insured (such as minor scratches and dents to your car). Other techniques such as retention (discussed later) are more appropriate for handling small losses. For example, minor physical damage losses to your car can be retained by purchasing collision insurance with a deductible.

Select the Appropriate Technique for Handling Losses. The third step is to select the most appropriate technique for handling each potential loss. The major methods for handling potential losses are avoidance, loss control, retention, noninsurance transfers, and insurance.

avoidance A method for handling potential losses by avoiding certain situations in which losses might occur.

1. **Avoidance. Avoidance** is one method for handling a potential loss. For example, you can avoid being mugged in a high-crime-rate area by staying out of the area, and you can avoid the loss from the sale of a home in a depressed real estate market by renting instead of buying.

loss control Certain activities that reduce both the frequency and the severity of loss.

2. **Loss control. Loss control** consists of certain activities that reduce both the frequency and severity of loss. Thus, loss control has two major objectives: loss prevention and loss reduction. For example, auto accidents can be reduced by driving within the speed limit, taking a safe driving course, and driving defensively. Car thefts can be prevented by locking the car, removing the keys from the ignition, and installing antitheft devices.

The second objective of loss control is to reduce the severity of a loss. For example, wearing a helmet reduces the severity of a head injury in a motorcycle accident. Wearing a seat belt or installing an air bag reduces the severity of an injury in an auto accident.

retention A method for handling potential losses by retaining part or all of a loss if it should occur.

3. **Retention. Retention** is another major method for handling a potential loss. Retention means that you retain part or all of the loss if it should occur. Risk retention can be either active or passive. Active risk retention means you are consciously aware of the risk and deliberately plan to retain part or all of it. For example, you can retain small collision losses to your car by buying a collision insurance policy with a deductible. Likewise, you can retain part of a loss to your home or to personal property by buying a homeowners policy with a deductible.

Risk can also be retained passively because of ignorance, indifference, or laziness. This can be dangerous if the retained risk can result in a catastrophic loss. For example, many workers are not insured against the risk of long-term disability; however, the adverse financial consequences from a long-term permanent disability generally are more severe than premature death. Thus, workers who are not insured against this risk are using risk retention in a most dangerous and inappropriate manner.

noninsurance transfers Methods other than insurance by which a pure risk and its potential financial consequences are transferred to another party other than an insurance company.

4. **Noninsurance transfers. Noninsurance transfers** refer to methods other than insurance by which a pure risk and its potential financial consequences are transferred to another party other than an insurance company. For example, assume that you invest in real estate and own an apartment house. The risk of damage to the property can be transferred to the tenant by requiring a damage deposit and by inserting a provision in the lease holding the tenant responsible for damages. Likewise, the risk of a defective television set can be transferred to the retailer by purchasing an extended-warranty contract making the retailer responsible for labor and repairs after the warranty expires. As a practical matter, many consumer experts do not recommend purchase of an extended warranty contract (see Insight 8.2).

Insight 8.2   Wise Up—Why Stores Push Extended Warranties That You Don't Need

Next time you buy a stereo, a television or a refrigerator, chances are you'll get a sales pitch for an extended warranty. "You've spent enough money," the salesperson may say. "For just a small additional investment, you can protect yourself from ever having to pay for repairs." If you buy that line--and the warranty--you'll pay anywhere from 10% to 50% of the appliance's price for a one- to three-year contract that you will probably never need. No more than 10% to 20% of extended-warranty buyers ever use them, say industry experts.

Extended warranties are supposed to take over where the manufacturer's warranty leaves off. In practice, however, most home appliances and electronic products that need repair will break down almost immediately--while the original warranty is still in effect-- or many years later, after the extended warranty has lapsed. Explains James J. Hodl of the trade publication *Appliance Service News:* "The products that are being sold today are the most reliable they have ever been. If you don't have a problem within the first three to six months, chances are you won't have one for another 12 years."

Because extended warranties are almost pure profit for the stores, salespeople can sometimes charge whatever they think the customer will pay. And salespeople have strong incentives to push them: commissions and, in some cases, quotas on how many warranties they must sell.

Our advice: Skip the extended warranty, and put the money in reserve instead. Chances are you'll never need to touch that money, and it can compound away happily ever after.

Source: Reprinted from the September 1995 issue of *Money* by special permission; copyright 1995, Time Inc.

5. **Insurance. Insurance** is an extremely important method for handling major risks. In a personal risk management program, most people rely heavily on insurance as the major method for dealing with risk. We discuss the basic characteristics of insurance later in the chapter.

Review the Program Periodically. The final step is to review the program periodically. At least every two or three years, you should determine if all major risks are adequately covered. You should also reevaluate your program at every major milestone in your life, such as a divorce, birth of a child, purchase of a home, or change of jobs.

Insurance and Personal Risk Management

As we stated earlier, most people rely heavily on insurance as the major method of handling risk. As an informed consumer, you should have a clear understanding of how insurance works.

Basic Characteristics of Insurance

insurance The pooling of fortuitous losses by the transfer of pure risk to the insurer, who agrees to indemnify the insured for a covered loss.

We define **insurance** as the pooling of fortuitous losses by the transfer of pure risk to the insurer who agrees to indemnify the insured for a covered loss. This definition is useful for capturing the essential elements of insurance. Based on our definition, insurance has several distinct characteristics, including pooling of losses, payment of fortuitous losses, risk transfer, and indemnification.

Pooling of Losses. Pooling, or the sharing of losses, is the heart of insurance. **Pooling** is the spreading of losses incurred by the few over the entire group so that, in the process, average loss is substituted for actual loss. For example, assume that 1,000 farmers in southeastern Nebraska agree that if any farmer's home is damaged or destroyed by a fire, the other members of the group will indemnify or pay the actual costs of the unlucky farmer who has a loss. Assume also that each home is valued at $100,000, and that, on average, one home burns each year. In the absence of insurance, the maximum loss to each farmer is $100,000 if the home is totally destroyed in a fire. However, by pooling the loss, it can be spread over the entire group. Thus, if one farmer has a total loss, the maximum amount that each farmer would have to pay is only $100 ($100,000/1,000). In effect, the pooling technique results in the substitution of a certain average loss of $100 for an uncertain loss of $100,000.

pooling The spreading of losses incurred by the few over the entire group so that, in the process, average loss is substituted for actual loss.

Payment of Fortuitous Losses. A second characteristic of private insurance is the payment of fortuitous losses. A **fortuitous loss** is one that is unforeseen and unexpected and occurs as a result of chance. For example, if you slip on an icy sidewalk and break a leg, the loss would be fortuitous.

fortuitous loss A loss that is unforeseen and unexpected and occurs as a result of chance.

Risk Transfer. Risk transfer is another essential element of insurance. **Risk transfer** means that a pure risk is transferred to the insurer who typically is in a stronger financial position to pay the loss than the insured. For example, if you buy an auto insurance policy, the risk of a liability lawsuit arising out of the negligent operation of your car is transferred to the insurer.

risk transfer A process in which a pure risk is transferred to the insurer, who typically is in a stronger financial position to pay the loss than the insured

Indemnification. A final characteristic of insurance is indemnification for losses. **Indemnification** means that the insured is restored to his or her approximate financial position prior to the occurrence of the loss. For example, if your car is damaged in an auto accident, a collision insurance policy will pay for the property damage (less the deductible) and restore you to your previous position.

indemnification A process by which an insured person who has suffered a loss is restored to his or her approximate financial position prior to the occurrence of the loss

Characteristics of an Insurable Risk

Not all pure risks are insurable. From the viewpoint of a private insurer, certain requirements must be met before a pure risk is insured. These requirements include a large number of exposure units, an accidental and unintentional loss, a determinable and measurable loss, a noncatastrophic loss, and an economically feasible premium.

The first requirement of an insurable risk is the existence of large number of exposure units. Ideally, there should be a large number of roughly similar, but not necessarily identical, exposure units. For example, a large group of frame dwellings in a city can be grouped together to provide property insurance on the dwellings. The purpose of this requirement is to enable the insurer to predict loss based on the **law of large numbers.** *As the number of exposure units increases, the actual results will more closely approach the expected results.* As a result, an actuary can predict losses for the group with some precision, and premiums can be calculated more accurately.

law of large numbers A principle stating that the larger the number of exposure units, the more closely will the actual results approach the expected results.

The second requirement is that the loss should be accidental and unintentional. Ideally, the loss should be fortuitous and outside the insured's control. The law of large numbers is based on the random occurrence of events. An intentional loss is not random since the insured knows when the loss will occur.

The third requirement is that the loss should be determinable and measurable. The purpose is to enable the insurer to determine if the loss is covered under the policy and the correct amount to pay for a covered loss.

The fourth requirement is that the loss should not be catastrophic. This means that a large percentage of insureds should not incur losses at the same time. Pooling is the essence of insurance. If most or all insureds in a certain class simultaneously incur a loss, then the pooling technique discussed earlier breaks down. Premiums would have to be increased to prohibitive levels, and the insurance technique would no longer be a viable arrangement by which losses of the few are spread over the entire group.

Although insurers wish to avoid all catastrophic losses, in the real world, this is impossible because of hurricanes, tornadoes, earthquakes, riots, and other causes (see Exhibit 8.3). Insurers deal with a catastrophic loss by dispersing their coverage over a wide geographic area, which reduces the possibility of a catastrophic loss from a single event. In addition, insurers purchase reinsurance from a reinsurer to cover a catastrophic loss. **Reinsurance** is the shifting of part or all of the insurance originally written by one insurer to another insurer. The reinsurer is responsible for paying part of the covered losses up to certain limits. As a result, the insurer writing the business initially is not forced into bankruptcy because of a catastrophic loss.

reinsurance Shifting of part or all of the insurance originally written by one insurer to another insurer. The reinsurer pays part of a covered loss up to certain limits.

Exhibit 8.3

The 10 Most Costly Insured Catastrophies

Month/Year	Catastrophe	Estimated Insured Loss
Aug. 1992	Hurricane Andrew: wind, flooding, tornadoes	$16,500,000,000
Jan. 1994	Northridge earthquake	9,000,000,000
Sept. 1989	Hurricane Hugo: wind, flooding, tornadoes	4,200,000,000
Oct. 1991	Oakland, Calif. fire	1,700,000,000
March 1993	Blizzard of 1993	1,750,000,000
Sept. 1992	Hurricane Iniki	1,600,000,000
Oct. 1989	Loma Prieta, Calif. earthquake	960,000,000
Oct.–Nov. 1993	California brush fires	950,000,000
Dec. 1983	Wind, snow, freezing, 41 states	880,000,000
April–May 1992	Los Angeles Riots	775,000,000

Source: *The Fact Book 1995, Property/Casualty Insurance Facts* (New York: Insurance Information Institute, 1995), p. 83.

Consider This

Information about auto, home, and life insurance can be found on the Insurance News Network at:

http://www.insure.com/

life insurance Insurance that pays death benefits to designated beneficiaries when the insured dies.

health insurance Insurance that pays medical expenses if the insured becomes sick or injured.

disability income insurance Insurance that provides periodic income payments when the insured is unable to work because of sickness or injury.

cafeteria plan A group benefit plan in which an employer provides a variety of benefits, including insurance benefits, and employees select those benefits that best meet their financial needs.

The final requirement of insurable risks is that the premium should be financially feasible. This means that the insured should be able to afford to pay the premium; if the premium is too high, the coverage cannot be sold.

Types of Insurance

From the viewpoint of the insurance consumer, private insurance can be classified into two major categories: life and health insurance and property and liability insurance.

Life and Health Insurance. **Life insurance** pays death benefits to designated beneficiaries when the insured dies. The death benefits are designed to pay burial expenses, uninsured medical bills, and other expenses as a result of death. The death benefits can also be arranged to provide periodic income payments to the deceased's dependents. **Health insurance** pays benefits if the insured becomes sick or injured. **Disability income insurance** provides periodic income payments when the insured is unable to work because of sickness or injury.

Life and health insurance is also available through group insurance plans. A substantial amount of life and health insurance in force today consists of group insurance plans sponsored by employers. Many employers offer **cafeteria plans** that permit employees to select those benefits that best meet their financial needs. Cafeteria plans typically permit employees to select among the following:

- Group life insurance plans
- Group medical expense plans
- Health maintenance organizations (HMOs)
- Preferred provider organizations (PPOs)
- Group dental insurance plans
- Short-term and long-term disability income plans

We will discuss the characteristics of group insurance plans in Chapters 9 and 10.

property insurance Insurance that pays for losses to the insured person's home, auto, boat, or other personal property because of fire, windstorm, vandalism, theft, or other causes.

liability insurance Insurance that pays for losses arising out of the negligence of an individual that results in bodily injury or property damage to others.

Property and Liability Insurance. **Property insurance** pays for losses to your home, auto, boat, and other personal property because of fire, windstorm, vandalism, theft, or other causes. **Liability insurance** pays for losses arising out of the negligence of an individual, which results in bodily injury or property damage to others; liability insurance typically pays the damages awarded by a court up to the policy limits and also pays attorney fees and other legal defense costs.

Exhibit 8.4 illustrates the major lines of property and liability insurance sold currently. Fire insurance and allied lines cover the loss of real estate and personal property because of fire, lightning, windstorm, and other causes. Marine insurance covers loss to goods in transit. Casualty insurance is a broad field of insurance and covers everything not covered by fire, marine, and life insurance. Automobile insurance is an important example of a casualty line. In addition, multiple-line insurance combines both property and casualty coverages into one contract; a homeowners policy is an important example of multiple-line insurance. Finally, fidelity bonds provide protection against loss caused by dishonest employees, whereas surety bonds provide monetary compensation in the event the bonded party fails to perform certain acts.

Exhibit 8.4

Property and Liability Insurance

1. Fire insurance and allied lines
2. Marine insurance
   - Ocean marine
   - Inland marine
3. Casualty insurance
   - Automobile insurance
   - General liability insurance
   - Burglary and theft insurance
   - Workers compensation
   - Glass insurance
   - Boiler and machinery insurance
   - Nuclear insurance
   - Crop–hail insurance
   - Health insurance
   - Other miscellaneous lines
4. Multiple-line insurance (e.g. homeowners policy)
5. Fidelity and surety bonds

It is beyond the scope of the text to discuss all property and liability insurance lines in detail. Instead, we will focus primarily on automobile insurance, homeowners insurance, and personal liability insurance. These coverages are extremely important in financial planning since they provide substantial protection against major property and liability risks that can result in great financial insecurity. Auto, homeowners, and personal liability insurance will be discussed in greater detail in Chapter 11.

Government Insurance. In addition to private insurance, certain federal and state government insurance programs are extremely important in financial planning. One of the most important is the **Old-Age, Survivors, Disability, and Health Insurance (OASDHI)** program, commonly known as social security. Social security provides retirement benefits, survivor benefits, disability income benefits, and Medicare benefits to eligible beneficiaries and family members. We will discuss the characteristics of social security in greater detail in Chapter 16.

Unemployment insurance is an important government insurance program that provides some protection against the risk of unemployment. **Unemployment insurance programs** are state programs that provide weekly cash benefits to eligible workers who experience short-term involuntary unemployment.

In addition, all states have workers compensation laws that require covered employers to provide certain benefits to workers who have a job-related accident or disease. **Workers compensation insurance** pays the medical bills and disability income benefits for workers who have a job-related accident or disease; it also pays death benefits to the dependents of an employee whose death is job related.

Finally, the Federal Deposit Insurance Corporation (FDIC) provides insurance on checking and savings accounts in commercial banks and saving and loan associations; **federal flood insurance** provides flood insurance at subsidized rates to property owners who reside in flood zones; and **federal crop insurance** provides crop insurance for unavoidable crop losses, including those resulting from hail, wind, excessive rain, disease, and other causes.

Types of Private Insurers

Some 1,736 life insurers are doing business in the United States. They include such financial giants as New York Life, Teachers Insurance and Annuity Association, and Northwestern Mutual Life. More than 3,300 property and liability insurers are also operating in the United States. Many of them are large, well-known insurers such as State Farm, Allstate, and Farmers Insurance Group.

Old-Age, Survivors, Disability, and Health Insurance (OASDHI) An insurance program of the U.S. government, commonly known as social security, that provides retirement benefits, survivor benefits, disability income benefits, and Medicare benefits to eligible beneficiaries and family members.

unemployment insurance Insurance provided by the states that pays weekly cash benefits to eligible workers who experience short-term involuntary unemployment.

workers compensation insurance Insurance that pays medical bills and disability income benefits for workers who have job-related accidents or disease.

federal flood insurance Flood insurance provided at subsidized rates to property owners who reside in flood zones.

federal crop insurance Insurance against unavoidable crop losses, including those resulting from hail, wind, excessive rain, and disease.

stock insurer A private insurance corporation owned by stockholders who participate in the profits and losses of the corporation.

mutual insurer A private insurance corporation owned by the policy owners; there are no stockholders.

Most private insurers can be classified as either a stock or mutual insurer. A **stock insurer** is a corporation owned by stockholders who participate in the profits and losses of the insurer. Stock insurers predominate in the property and liability insurance industry, especially in the commercial lines market.

A **mutual insurer** is a corporation owned by the policyowners; there are no stockholders. Mutual insurers predominate in the life insurance industry. For example, if you buy a life insurance policy from a mutual insurer, you are part owner of the company. As a policyowner, you have the right to elect the board of directors. However, since relatively few policyowners bother to vote, the board of directors has effective management control of the company. In addition, mutual insurers typically pay dividends or give a rate reduction in advance, which reduces the cost of the insurance protection to consumers. Dividends are especially important in life insurance since they have a powerful impact on the cost of life insurance.

Agents and Brokers

agent With regard to insurance, someone who represents the insurer and has the legal authority to act on the insurer's behalf.

As an informed consumer, you should also understand the difference between an agent and a broker. An **agent** is someone who represents the insurer and has the legal authority to act on the insurer's behalf. If you buy insurance, you will probably buy it from an agent. However, there is an important difference between a property and liability insurance agent and a life insurance agent. A property and liability insurance agent typically has the power to bind the insurer immediately with respect to certain types of coverage. In contrast, a life insurance agent normally does not have the authority to bind the insurer but must first submit the application to the insurer for approval.

broker With regard to insurance, someone who legally represents the insured.

independent agent With regard to insurance, a businessperson who represents several insurers.

exclusive agent With regard to insurance, an agent who represents only one insurer or a group of insurers under common ownership.

direct response insurer An insurer that sells directly to the public; the insurer does not employ agents but sells through the mails or mass media.

In contrast to an agent who represents the insurer, a **broker** is someone who legally represents the insured. Brokers are extremely important in commercial property and liability insurance. Large brokerage firms have knowledge of highly specialized insurance markets and control the accounts of large corporate insurance buyers. However, unless you are operating a business, you probably will buy insurance from an agent and not from a broker.

Some agents are independent. An **independent agent** is a businessperson who represents several insurers. The independent agent has authority to write business on behalf of these insurers. In contrast, the agent may be an exclusive agent. An **exclusive agent** is an agent who represents only one insurer or group of insurers under common ownership. For example, an agent for State Farm is an exclusive agent.

Finally, some insurers sell directly to the public and do not employ agents. These insurers are called **direct response insurers** since they sell through the mails or other mass media, such as radio, television, and newspapers. Applicants for insurance typically have access to a toll free telephone number to request an application for insurance. Examples of direct response insurers include Government Employees Insurance Company, AMICA Mutual Insurance, and Teachers Insurance and Annuity Association. Since marketing costs are reduced, the cost to the insurance consumer often is dramatically reduced.

In summary, private and government insurance plans are extremely important in financial planning. In this chapter, we have only touched on the fundamentals of private insurance. You should also understand the different types of insurance policies and amounts of insurance to buy, how to select an insurer and agent, how to compare policies issued by different insurers, how to file a claim and what to do if your claim is denied, and common errors to avoid in buying insurance. We will cover these important topics in Chapters 9 through 11.

SUMMARY

- There is no single definition of risk. Risk traditionally has been defined as uncertainty of loss.

- Pure risk is a situation in which the only possibilities are loss and no loss.

- Speculative risk is a situation in which either profit or loss is possible.

- The following types of pure risk can threaten an individual's financial security: personal risks, property risks, and liability risks.

- Personal risks directly affect an individual. Major personal risks include risk of premature death, risk of insufficient income during retirement, risk of poor health, and risk of unemployment.

- Property risks affect people who own property. If property is damaged or lost, two principal types of loss may result: direct loss to property, and indirect, or consequential, loss. A direct loss is a financial loss that results from the physical damage, destruction, or theft of the property. An indirect, or consequential, loss is a financial loss that results indirectly from the occurrence of a direct physical damage or theft loss. Examples of indirect losses are extra expenses, loss of use of the property, and loss of rents.

- Liability risks are extremely important in financial planning because there is no maximum upper limit on the amount of loss; a lien can be placed on your income and assets to satisfy a legal judgment; and substantial legal defense costs and attorney fees may also be incurred.

■ Personal risk management refers to the identification and evaluation of pure risks faced by an individual and family, and to the most appropriate technique, or combination of techniques, for treating such risks.

■ There are four steps in the development of a personal risk management program: identify potential losses, evaluate potential losses, select the appropriate technique for handling losses, and review the program periodically.

■ There are five major techniques for handling potential losses: avoidance, loss control, retention, noninsurance transfers, and insurance.

■ Insurance can be defined as the pooling of fortuitous losses by the transfer of pure risk to the insurer, who agrees to indemnify the insured for a covered loss.

■ A typical insurance plan has four characteristics: pooling of losses, payment of fortuitous losses, risk transfer, and indemnification. Pooling means that losses of the few are spread over the group, and average loss is substituted for actual loss. Fortuitous losses are unforeseen and unexpected and occur as a result of chance. Risk transfer means that a pure risk is transferred to the insurer. Indemnification means that the insured is restored to his or her approximate financial position prior to the occurrence of the loss.

■ From the viewpoint of the insurer, ideally, an insurable risk should meet the following requirements: There should be a large number of exposure units. The loss should be accidental and unintentional. The loss should be determinable and measurable. The loss should not be catastrophic. The premium should be feasible.

■ Private insurance can be divided into life and health insurance, and property and liability insurance. In the development of a sound financial plan, important insurance contracts include life insurance, health insurance, auto insurance, homeowners insurance, and personal liability insurance.

■ Certain government insurance programs are important in financial planning, including the OASDHI program, unemployment insurance, and workers compensation.

■ A stock insurer is a corporation owned by stockholders who participate in the profits and losses of the insurer. A mutual insurer is a corporation owned by the policyowners; there are no stockholders.

■ An agent is someone who legally represents the insurer and has the authority to act on the insurer's behalf. A broker legally is someone who represents the insured.

■ An independent agent is a businessperson who represents several insurers. An exclusive agent represents only one insurer or group of insurers under common ownership. Some insurers do not employ agents and use the direct response system of selling.

KEY CONCEPTS AND TERMS

Agent	Loss control
Avoidance	Mutual insurer
Broker	Noninsurance transfers
Cafeteria plan	Old-Age, Survivors, Disability, and
Direct loss	Health Insurance (OASDHI)
Direct response insurer	Personal risk management
Disability income insurance	Personal risks
Exclusive agent	Pooling
Federal crop insurance	Property insurance
Fortuitous loss	Pure risk
Health Insurance	Reinsurance
Human life value	Retention
Indemnification	Risk
Independent agent	Risk transfer
Indirect loss	Speculative risk
Insurance	Stock insurer
Law of large numbers	Unemployment insurance
Liability insurance	Workers compensation insurance
Life insurance	

QUESTIONS FOR REVIEW

1. Explain briefly the meaning of *risk*.

2. Explain the difference between pure and speculative risk. Why is this distinction important?

3. Identify the major types of pure risk that are associated great financial insecurity.

4. Property risks involve the possibility of a direct physical damage loss to covered property and an indirect, or consequential, loss. Explain the meaning of *direct physical damage loss* and *indirect, or consequential, loss.*

5. Why is the recognition of liability risks so important in the development of a sound financial plan?

6. Define personal risk management, and explain the four steps in a personal risk management program.

7. Briefly describe the five major methods for handling potential losses. Give an example of each method.

8. Explain the basic characteristics of insurance and the requirements of an insurable risk.

9. Identify the major types of private insurance programs that are important in financial planning.

10. What is the legal distinction between a stock and mutual insurer?

INTERNET EXERCISES

1. Find the Insurance News Network's home page at:

    http://www.insure.com/

    Go to "States" and look up insurance statistics for your state.

2. The Insurance Information Institute (III) is a nonprofit communications organization sponsored by the property and casualty insurance industry. III has an Internet service at:

    http://www.iii.org/

    Choose the "Consumer" page, and browse the articles available—for example, "How to File an Insurance Claim."

CASE APPLICATIONS

Case I

Jennifer is a college junior who is majoring in business administration. She resides in a college dorm and has a roommate, Karen. Jennifer has a part-time job to help pay her miscellaneous expenses, but her parents are paying her tuition. Both parents must work to pay her tuition. In addition to an extensive wardrobe, books and supplies for her courses, and personal items, Jennifer owns an expensive stereo, a television set, and a trumpet that she plays as a member of the college band. She also owns a late model sports car that she drives to and from her part-time job and to the beach and mountains where she loves to surf and ski. Jennifer and Karen frequently visit a local college bar on Friday evening where they drink and relax after a hard week of study and work. Jennifer sometimes drinks excessively, but she will not allow Karen to drive her back to the dorm.

1. Describe briefly the four steps in the personal risk management process.

2. Identify the major pure risks or loss exposures to which Jennifer is exposed with respect to each of the following:
   a. Personal risks
   b. Property risks
   c. Liability risks

3. With respect to each of the pure risks or loss exposures mentioned, identify an appropriate personal risk management technique that could be used to treat the exposure.

Case II

Chris and Karen Swift are married and own a three-bedroom home in a large midwestern city. Their son, Kenneth, is attending college away from home and lives in a fraternity house. Their daughter, Kelly, is a senior in high school. Chris is an accountant who works for a local accounting firm. Although he works long hours, he is usually home at night. Karen is an analyst for a large public relations firm and is often away from home several days at a time. Kelly earns extra cash by babysitting on a regular basis.

Their home contains typical household furniture, personal property, a computer that Chris uses to prepare business tax returns on weekends, and a laptop computer that Karen uses while traveling. Karen's prized possessions include an expensive sterling silver collection and jewelry inherited from her grandmother. The Swifts also own three cars. Kenneth drives a 1988 Ford while away at school; Chris drives a 1993 Pontiac that is used for both personal and business use; and Karen drives a 1997 Toyota and a rental car when she is traveling. Although the Swifts have owned their home for several years, they are considering moving because of the recent increase in violent crime in their neighborhood.

1. Describe briefly the four steps in the personal risk management process.

2. Identify the major pure risks or loss exposures to which Chris and Karen are exposed with respect to each of the following:
   a. Personal risks
   b. Property risks
   c. Liability risks

3. With respect to each of the pure risks or loss exposures mentioned, identify an appropriate personal risk management technique that could be used to treat the exposure.

Case III

Tyrone is a college senior who is majoring in journalism. He owns a high-mileage 1984 Ford that has a current market value of $900. The current replacement value of his clothes, television set, stereo, furniture, and other personal property in a rented apartment total $5,000. He wears disposable contact lenses, which cost $200 for a six-months supply. He also has a waterbed in his rented apartment that has leaked water in the past. Tyrone is an avid runner who runs five miles daily in a nearby public park that has the reputation of being extremely dangerous because of drug dealers, numerous assaults and muggings, and drive-by shootings. Tyrone's parents both work to help him pay his tuition.

For each of the following loss exposures, identify an appropriate risk management technique that Tyrone might use to deal with the exposure. Explain your answer.

1. Physical damage to the 1984 Ford because of a collision with another motorist

2. Liability lawsuit against Tyrone arising out of the negligent operation of his car

3. Total loss of clothes, television, stereo, furniture, and personal property because of a grease fire in the kitchen of his rented apartment

4. Disappearance of one contact lens

5. Waterbed leak that causes property damage to the apartment

6. Physical assault on Tyrone by gang members who are dealing drugs in the park where he runs

7. Loss of tuition from Tyrone's father who is killed by a drunk driver in an auto accident

SUGGESTIONS FOR ADDITIONAL READING

Hallman, G. Victor and Karen L. Hallman. *Personal Insurance: Life, Health, and Retirement.* Malvern, Pa.: American Institute for CPCU, 1994.

Hamilton, Karen L. and Donald S. Malecki. *Personal Insurance: Property and Liability.* Malvern, Pa.: American Institute for CPCU, 1994.

Rejda, George E., Constance M. Luthardt, Cheryl L. Ferguson, and Donald R. Oakes. *Personal Insurance,* 3rd ed. Malvern, PA.: Insurance Institute of America, 1997.

Rejda, George E. *Principles of Risk Management and Insurance,* 6th ed. Reading, MA.: Addison Wesley Longman, 1998.

___. *Social Insurance and Economic Security,* 5th ed. Englewood Cliffs, N.J.: Prentice-Hall, 1994.

Wood, Glenn L. et al. *Personal Risk Management and Insurance,* 4th ed., Volumes I and II. Malvern, Pa.: American Institute for Property and Liability Underwriters, 1989.

Chapter 9

Life Insurance

Learning Objectives

After studying this chapter, you should be able to:

- Explain the financial impact of premature death on the different types of families.

- Explain the needs approach for determining the amount of life insurance to own.

- Describe the major characteristics of term life insurance.

- Explain the basic types of whole life insurance, including ordinary life, limited-payment life, and modified life insurance.

- Describe the major characteristics of variable life, universal life, and variable universal life insurance.

- Explain the incontestable clause, grace period, and policy loan provisions in a life insurance policy.

- Identify the dividend options, nonforfeiture options, and settlement options in life insurance policies.

- Explain the important rules that consumers should follow when purchasing life insurance.

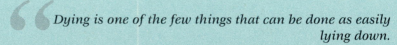

Dying is one of the few things that can be done as easily lying down.

—Woody Allen

We are but tenants and shortly the great Landlord will give us notice that our lease has expired.

—Joseph Jefferson

In financial planning, the risk of premature death must be given a high priority. If a family head dies prematurely, the surviving family members can experience considerable financial insecurity. For example, Louise, who earns $28,000 a year, is the sole support of her disabled husband and two small children. At the age of 35, she has saved only $10,000. If she has only $40,000 of life insurance and dies suddenly at age 35, can her family survive on the $50,000 left to them? Although social security survivor benefits may be available, there are other financial factors to consider, such as a college education for the children and financial support for the disabled spouse. Clearly, $50,000 will not go far. Her premature death will create financial insecurity for the surviving family members. However, she can use life insurance to restore the lost earnings.

This chapter discusses the problem of premature death and how life insurance can alleviate the financial consequences of premature death. Topics discussed include the meaning of premature death, the need for life insurance based on family type, the amount of life insurance to own, the major types of life insurance sold currently, and important life insurance contractual provisions. The chapter concludes with a discussion of the steps to follow in developing a sound life insurance program.

Premature Death

premature death The death of a family head with outstanding unfulfilled financial obligations, such as dependents to support, children to educate, or a mortgage or other installment debts to pay off.

Premature death is the death of a family head with outstanding unfulfilled financial obligations, such as dependents to support, children to educate, or a mortgage to pay off. Premature death can cause serious financial problems for the surviving family members because their share of the deceased breadwinner's earnings is lost forever. Surviving family members will be exposed to great financial insecurity if replacement income from other sources or accumulated financial assets available to the family are inadequate.

The problem of premature death has declined over time because of breakthroughs in medical science, improvements in health due to economic growth and higher real incomes, and improvements in public health and sanitation. In 1995, life expectancy at birth was 79.2 years for females and 72.3 years for males.[1] Although life expectancy has increased over time, millions of Americans die annually from the three major causes of death: heart disease, cancer, and stroke.

Who Needs Life Insurance?

The need for life insurance varies enormously depending on the type of family. Premature death has a greater financial impact on certain types of families than on others.[2]

Consider This

Information on life insurance is available at many sites on the World Wide Web. For example, see LifeNet, at:

http://www.lifenet.com/

and InsWeb at:

http://www.insweb.com/

Single People

The number of single people has increased in recent years. Younger adults are postponing marriage, often beyond age 30, and many young and middle-aged adults are single because of divorce.

Premature death of a single person who has no dependents to support or outstanding financial obligations is not likely to create a financial problem for others. Other than needing a modest amount of life insurance for burial purposes and uninsured medical bills, this group does not need large amounts of life insurance.

Single-Parent Families

The number of single-parent families with children under age 18 has increased sharply in recent years because of the large number of children born outside marriage, divorce, legal separation, and death. Premature death of a family head in a single-parent family can cause great financial insecurity for the surviving children. *The need for large amounts of life insurance on the family head is great.* However, many single-parent families are living in poverty, and their ability to purchase large amounts of life insurance is limited. In 1992, 47 percent of female-headed families with children and no husband present were poor, compared to 9 percent of the families with a male present.[3] These families are simply too poor to purchase large amounts of life insurance.

Two-Income Earners

Families in which both spouses work have largely replaced the traditional family in which only one spouse works. The number of women in the labor force with children has increased dramatically over time, especially for married women with children. *In two-income families with children, the death of one income earner can cause considerable financial insecurity for the surviving family members since both incomes are normally needed to maintain the family's standard of living.* The need for life insurance is great since life insurance can replace the lost earnings, and the family can maintain its previous standard of living.

Traditional Families

Traditional families are families in which only one parent is in the labor force, and the other parent stays at home to take care of dependent children. *Premature death can cause great financial insecurity in families with children in which only one parent works outside the home. The need for life insurance on family heads in this group is great.* If the working spouse dies with an insufficient amount of life insurance, the family may have to adjust its standard of living downward.

Blended Families

A blended family is one in which a divorced spouse with children remarries, and the new spouse also has children. *Premature death of a working spouse in a blended family can cause great financial insecurity. The need for life insurance on both family heads within this group is great.* Both spouses may be in the labor force at the time of remarriage, and the death of one spouse may result in a reduction in the family's standard of living since the family's share of that income is lost.

Sandwiched Families

A sandwiched family is one in which a son or daughter with children is also supporting one or both parents. Thus, the son or daughter is "sandwiched" between the younger and older generation. *Premature death of a working spouse in a sandwiched family can cause considerable financial insecurity to the surviving family members, and the need for life insurance is great.* Premature death can result in the loss of financial support to both the surviving children and the aged parent(s). These families need to be protected by life insurance to replace the loss of income to the surviving family members.

How Much Life Insurance Do You Need?

If you need life insurance, the next step is to determine the correct amount of insurance to own. Most families own an insufficient amount of life insurance. In 1995, the average amount of life insurance in force per household in the United States was only $124,100, representing about 27 months of total disposable income per household.[4] The correct amount of life insurance to own, however, is an individual matter since family needs and goals vary widely.

needs approach An approach to determining how much life insurance to purchase in which the financial needs that must be met after the family head dies are determined and, after considering other sources of income and financial assets, converted into specific amounts of life insurance.

The Needs Approach

The needs approach is widely used to determine the amount of life insurance to own. Under the **needs approach,** the financial needs that must be met after the family head dies is determined. The amount of existing life insurance and financial assets is then subtracted from the total amount needed to determine the amount of new life insurance, if any, to purchase. The most important family needs are listed below.

estate clearance fund
Fund to provide immediate cash following a person's death for burial expenses; uninsured medical bills; installment debts; estate administration expenses; and estate, inheritance, and income taxes.

Estate Clearance Fund. An **estate clearance fund** or cleanup fund is immediately needed when the family head dies. Immediate cash is needed for burial expenses; uninsured medical bills; installment debts; estate administration expenses; and estate, inheritance, and income taxes.

readjustment period A one- or two-year period following the breadwinner's death.

Income During the Readjustment Period. The **readjustment period** is a one- or two-year period following the breadwinner's death. During this period, the family should receive approximately the same amount of income received while the family head was alive. The purpose of the readjustment period is to give the family time to adjust its living standard to a different level.

dependency period A period following the breadwinner's death that follows the readjustment period and lasts until the youngest child reaches age 18.

Income During the Dependency Period. The **dependency period** follows the readjustment period; it is the period until the youngest child reaches age 18. The family should receive income during this period so that the surviving spouse can remain at home, if necessary, to care for the children. The income needed during the dependency period is substantially reduced if the surviving spouse is already in the labor force and plans to continue working.

Life Income to the Surviving Spouse. Another important need is to provide life income to the surviving spouse, especially if he or she is older and has been out of the labor force for many years. There are two income periods to consider: (1) income during the blackout period, and (2) income to supplement social security benefits after the blackout period. The **blackout period** refers to the period from the time that social security survivor benefits terminate to the time they are resumed. Social security benefits to a surviving spouse terminate when the youngest child reaches age 16 and start again at age 60.

blackout period The period from the time that social security survivor benefits to a surviving spouse terminate, when the youngest child reaches age 16, to the time they are resumed, when the surviving spouse reaches age 60.

If a surviving spouse has a career and is already in the labor force, the need for life income is greatly reduced or eliminated. However, this is not true of an older spouse under age 60 who has been out of the labor force for years, and for whom social security survivor benefits have temporarily terminated. The need for income during the blackout period is especially important for this group.

Special Needs. Families should also consider certain special needs, including a mortgage redemption fund, an educational fund, and an emergency fund.

1. *Mortgage redemption fund.* It is often desirable to provide the family with a mortgage-free home. The amount of monthly income needed by surviving family members is greatly reduced when monthly mortgage payments or rent payments are not required.

2. *Educational fund.* The family head may also wish to provide an educational fund for the children. If the children plan to attend a private college or university, the cost will be considerably higher than at a public institution.

3. *Emergency fund.* A family should also have an emergency fund. An unexpected event may occur that requires large amounts of cash, such as major dental work, home repairs, or a new car.

Retirement Needs. Since the family head may survive to retirement, a family should consider the need for adequate retirement income. Most retired workers are eligible for social security retirement benefits and may also be eligible for retirement benefits from an employer. If retirement income from these sources is inadequate, you can obtain additional income from cash-value life insurance, individual investments, a retirement annuity, or an individual retirement account (IRA). We will discuss these retirement products in Chapter 16.

An Illustration of the Needs Approach

Exhibit 9.1 contains a worksheet that you can use to determine the amount of life insurance you need. The first part of the worksheet shows the amount needed to meet your various cash needs, income needs, and special needs. The second part analyzes your present financial assets for meeting these needs. The final part determines the amount of additional life insurance needed by subtracting total assets from total needs. For example, Jennifer and Scott Smith are married and have a son, age 1. Jennifer, age 33, earns $40,000 annually as a marketing analyst for a large oil company. Scott, age 35, earns $30,000 as an elementary school teacher. Jennifer would like her family to be financially secure if she dies prematurely.

Cash Needs. Jennifer estimates that her family will need at least $10,000 for funeral expenses. Although she is currently insured under a group health insurance plan, certain services are excluded, and she must pay an annual deductible and coinsurance charges. Thus, she estimates that the family will need $3,000 for uninsured medical expenses. She is also making monthly payments on a new car loan and credit card debts. Installment debts currently total $12,000. In addition, she estimates that the cost of probating her will and attorney fees will be $3,000. Jennifer's estate will have no current federal estate tax liability because all of her property is left to her husband under the unlimited marital deduction (discussed in Chapter 17).

Exhibit 9.1

How Much Life Insurance Do You Need?

What you will need	Jennifer Smith		Your needs	
Cash needs				
Funeral costs	$ 10,000		$ _____	
Uninsured medical bills	3,000			
Installment debts	12,000		_____	
Probate costs	3,000		_____	
Federal estate taxes	0		_____	
State inheritance taxes	0		_____	
Total estate clearance fund		$ 28,000		$ _____
Income needs				
Readjustment period	14,400		_____	
Dependency period	108,000		_____	
Blackout period	0		_____	
Retirement income	0		_____	
Total income needs		$ 122,400		$ _____
Special needs				
Mortgage redemption fund	110,000		_____	
Emergency fund	25,000		_____	
College education fund	100,000		_____	
Total special needs		$ 235,000		$ _____
Total needs		$ 385,400		$ _____

What you have today	Jennifer Smith		Your assets	
Checking account and savings	$ 10,000		$ _____	
Mutual funds and securities	25,000		_____	
IRAs and Keogh plan	4,200		_____	
Section 401(k) plan and				
employer savings plan	4,500		_____	
Private pension death benefit	10,000		_____	
Current life insurance	50,000		_____	
Other financial assets	0		_____	
Total assets		$ 103,700		$ _____
Additional life insurance needed				
Total needs		$ 385,400		$ _____
Less total assets		103,700		_____
Additional life insurance needed		$ 281,700		$ _____

Income Needs. Jennifer also wants to provide monthly income to her family during the readjustment and dependency periods until her son reaches age 18. Jennifer and Scott's net take-home pay is approximately $4,000 each month. She believes that her family can maintain its present standard of living if it receives 75 percent of that amount, or $3,000 monthly. Thus, she wants the family to receive $3,000 monthly for 17 years during the readjustment and dependency periods.

Consider This

You can also request information about social security benefits from Social Security Online at:

http://www.ssa.gov/

The family's need for $3,000 monthly is reduced if there are other sources of income. Scott's net take-home pay is about $1,800 monthly. In addition, Scott and his son are eligible for social security survivor benefits. Scott's benefits are payable until the son reaches age 16, whereas his son's benefits are payable until age 18. However, in this example, we assume that only the son will receive social security survivor benefits. Because Scott's earnings substantially exceed the maximum annual limit allowed under the social security earnings test ($8,640 for beneficiaries under age 65 in 1997), he will lose all of his social security survivor benefits. However, his son will continue to receive benefits until age 18. The Social Security Administration has prepared a simplified form that will give you an accurate estimate of the social security survivor benefits payable if you should die. (Call 800-772-1213 for a form to determine your estimated benefits.) Jennifer's son will receive an estimated $600 each month from social security until age 18. Thus, the family would receive a total of $2,400 monthly from Scott's take-home pay and the son's social security benefit. Because their income goal is $3,000 monthly, there is a monthly shortfall of $600. Jennifer's family needs an additional $14,400 to provide monthly income of $600 during the 2-year readjustment period, and another $108,000 to provide monthly income for an additional 15 years during the dependency period. Thus, the family needs a total of $122,400 to meet the monthly goal of $3,000 during the readjustment and dependency periods.

If Jennifer considers the time value of money, it will take less than $122,400 of life insurance to accomplish the desired income goal. Likewise, if she takes inflation into account, she must increase the amount of life insurance just to maintain the real purchasing power of the benefits. However, she can ignore both present value and future inflation if she assumes that one offsets the other. *Thus, in our example, we assume that the life insurance proceeds are invested at an interest rate equal to the rate of inflation.* Such an assumption builds into the program an automatic hedge against inflation that preserves the real purchasing power of the death benefit. In addition, the calculations are simplified, and the use of present value tables and assumptions concerning future inflation rates are unnecessary.

In addition, Scott is currently in the labor force and plans to continue working if Jennifer should die. Thus, there is no need to provide additional income during the blackout period.

A final need to consider is retirement income. Scott will receive social security retirement benefits and a lifetime pension from the school district's retirement plan. He also has an individual retirement account (IRA) that will provide additional retirement income. Jennifer believes that Scott's total retirement income will be sufficient to meet his needs, so he does not need additional retirement income.

In summary, after considering Scott's take-home pay and social security survivor benefits, Jennifer determines that she will need an additional $122,400 to meet the income goal of $3,000 monthly during the readjustment and dependency periods. Additional income during the blackout period is not needed.

Special Needs. Jennifer would like the mortgage paid off if she should die; the current mortgage balance is $110,000. She also wants to establish an emergency fund of $25,000 for the family and an educational fund of $100,000 for her son. Thus, her special needs total $235,000.

Determining the Amount of New Life Insurance Needed. After determining total family needs, the next step is to add up all financial assets that can be used to satisfy these needs. Jennifer has a checking account and personal savings in the amount of $10,000. She owns several mutual funds and individual stocks with a current market value of $25,000. She has an individual retirement account with a current balance of $4,200, and $4,500 in a Section 401(k) plan sponsored by her employer; a lump-sum pension benefit of $10,000 is also payable when she dies. She is insured for $40,000 under her employer's group life insurance plan, and she has an individual policy in the amount of $10,000. Total financial assets available upon her death are $103,700.

Total family needs are $385,400, but her current financial assets are only $103,700. Thus, Jennifer needs an additional $281,700 of life insurance to protect her family.

Which Type of Life Insurance Should You Buy?

After determining the amount of life insurance to own, the next step is to consider the type of life insurance to buy. Currently, two types of life insurance are widely sold: term insurance and whole life insurance. Numerous variations and combinations of both types are also available.

Term Insurance

term insurance Life insurance providing protection for a temporary period, such as 1, 5, 10, or 20 years or up to age 65.

Term insurance has several characteristics. First, it provides protection for a temporary period, such as 1, 5, 10, or 20 years, or up to age 65. Unless the insured renews the policy, the protection expires at the end of the period.

renewable A term insurance policy that can be renewed for additional periods without evidence of insurability.

Most term insurance policies are also **renewable,** which means you can renew the policy for additional periods without evidence of insurability. The premium is increased at each renewal and is based on the insured's attained age. The purpose of the renewal provision is to protect the insurability of the insured. However, because premiums increase with age, insureds in good health tend to drop their insurance, whereas those in poor health continue to renew, despite the premium increase. To minimize this problem, many insurers limit the age beyond which renewal is not allowed, such as age 70.

convertible A term insurance policy that can be exchanged for a cash value policy without evidence of insurability.

Most term insurance policies are also **convertible,** which means you can exchange the term policy for a cash value policy without evidence of insurability. A policyowner who later decides that he or she needs permanent protection can exercise the conversion right.

Finally, term insurance policies usually have no cash value or savings component. Thus, term insurance cannot be used as a savings vehicle to save for retirement or other purposes.

Types of Term Insurance. Numerous term insurance policies are dicussed below:

yearly renewable term insurance Term life insurance that is issued for a one-year period and can be renewed for successive one-year periods to some stated age without evidence of insurability.

■ **Yearly renewable term insurance** is issued for a one-year period and can be renewed for successive one-year periods to some stated age without evidence of insurability. Premiums increase at each renewal date. Insureds may convert most policies to a permanent policy.

■ Term insurance can also be issued for 5, 10, 15, or 20 years, or for longer periods. The premiums paid during the term period are level, but they increase when the policy is renewed.

term to age 65 policy Term life insurance that provides protection to age 65, at which time the policy expires.

■ A **term to age 65 policy** provides protection to age 65, when the policy expires. The insured may convert the policy to permanent insurance, but he or she must exercise the conversion right before age 65.

decreasing term insurance Term life insurance for which the face amount gradually declines.

■ With **decreasing term insurance,** the face amount gradually declines, but the premium is level throughout the period. Some policies are fully paid for a few years before the coverage expires. For example, a 20-year decreasing term policy may require premium payments for only 17 years.

reentry term Term life insurance for which renewal premiums are based on lower rates if the insured periodically demonstrates evidence of insurability.

■ With **reentry term,** the renewal premiums are based on lower rates if the insured periodically demonstrates evidence of insurability. To remain on the low-rate schedule, the insured must periodically show that he or she is in good health and is still insurable. If the insured is unable to provide satisfactory evidence of insurability, the insurer will substantially increase the premiums.

Exhibit 9.2

Best Buys in Term Life Insurance, $500,000 (January 1997)

Age	10 Year Level Premium	15 Year Level Premium	20 Year Level Premium
35	$280	$320	$420
40	$375	$440	$565
45	$585	$700	$900
50	$910	$1,115	$1,370
55	$1,345	$1,675	$1,800
60	$2,185	$2,709	$3,560
65	$3,779	$4,437	$6,235
70	$6,470	$9,330	$11,304

Note: The premiums shown are guaranteed annual premiums for males, no tobacco, and are based on a market survey of 445 policies offered by 140 insurers as of December 31, 1996.

Source: Quotesmith Corporation.

When to Use Term Insurance. Term insurance is appropriate in three situations. First, if the amount of income you have available for life insurance is limited and you need substantial amounts of life insurance, you can effectively use term insurance. Because of a reduction in death rates and keen price competition, term insurance rates have declined sharply in recent years. You can purchase substantial amounts of life insurance for a modest annual outlay (see Exhibit 9.2).

Term insurance is also appropriate if the need for protection is temporary. For example, you can use term insurance to provide income during the readjustment and dependency periods. You can use decreasing term to pay off the mortgage if the family head dies prematurely.

Finally, you can use term insurance to guarantee future insurability. If you need large amounts of permanent insurance but cannot afford the premiums, you can purchase a term insurance policy, which you can convert later into a permanent policy without evidence of insurability.

Whole Life Insurance

whole life insurance Life insurance that provides lifetime protection and accumulates cash values; a stated amount is paid to a designated beneficiary when the insured dies, regardless of when the death occurs.

Whole life insurance provides lifetime protection. A stated amount is paid to a designated beneficiary when the insured dies, regardless of when the death occurs. Several types of whole life insurance are sold currently. Some policies are traditional policies that have been widely sold in the past, whereas newer variations of whole life insurance are constantly evolving. Traditional whole life insurance policies that merit some discussion include ordinary life insurance, limited-payment life insurance, modified life insurance, "special" whole life policies, and second-to-die life insurance.

ordinary life insurance
Whole life insurance that provides lifetime protection to age 100 with level premiums; also called continuous premium whole life and straight life.

Ordinary Life Insurance. **Ordinary life insurance** (also called continuous premium whole life and straight life) is a level-premium policy that provides lifetime protection to age 100. The premiums paid during the early years are higher than is necessary to pay current death claims, whereas those paid in the later years are inadequate for paying death claims. The excess premiums paid during the early years are accumulated at compound interest and are then used to supplement the inadequate premiums paid during the later years of the policy. Because state law regulates the method of accumulating the fund, it is referred to as a **legal reserve,** technically, a liability item that must be offset by sufficient assets; otherwise, regulatory authorities may declare the insurer to be insolvent.

legal reserve Liability item on a life insurer's balance sheet representing the excess premiums paid under the level-premium method during the early years.

Exhibit 9.3 shows the concept of the legal reserve under an ordinary life policy. As the death rate increases with age, the legal reserve or saving component steadily increases, and the pure insurance portion of the policy declines. As a result, the insurer can provide lifetime protection.

cash value amount paid to a policyowner who surrenders the policy for its cash surrender value.

An ordinary life policy also accumulates **cash surrender values,** which is the amount paid to a policyowner who surrenders the policy. As we noted earlier, under a system of level premiums, the policyowner overpays for the insurance protection during the early years, which results in a legal reserve and the accumulation of cash values. A policy-

Exhibit 9.3

**Proportion of Protection and Savings Elements
$1,000 Ordinary Life Contract, Issued to a Male Age 30;
1980 C.S.O. Table, 5 Percent Interest**

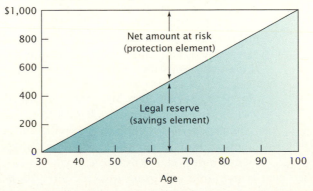

Source: *Life Insurance 12th Edition* by Black/Skipper, © 1987. Reprinted by permission of Prentice-Hall, Inc., Upper Saddle River, NJ.

owner who no longer wants the insurance can surrender the policy for its cash surrender value.

When to Use Ordinary Life Insurance. There are two situations where ordinary life insurance is appropriate: (1) when you need lifetime protection, and (2) when you desire to accumulate savings.

Ordinary life insurance is appropriate whenever you need lifetime protection. This means the need for life insurance will continue beyond age 65 or 70. For example, a policyowner still needs an estate clearance fund; there may be a sizable federal estate tax problem if the estate is large, and the insured needs large amounts of life insurance for estate liquidity and taxes; or a divorce settlement may require the purchase and maintenance of a life insurance policy on a divorced spouse, regardless of age. Because an ordinary life policy provides lifetime protection, these objectives are attainable even though the insured dies at an advanced age.

You can also use ordinary life insurance when you desire additional savings. Some insureds wish to meet their protection and savings needs by an ordinary life policy. As we noted, ordinary life insurance accumulates a cash surrender value that you can obtain by surrendering the policy or by borrowing the cash value.

Some insureds purchase ordinary life insurance as an investment because of the accumulation of cash value. However, most insureds do not know the yearly rate of return they are earning on the cash value buildup. Appendix E in the text provides a simplified method for determining the yearly rate of return on a cash value policy.

Another limitation is that some people are still underinsured after they purchase the policy. Because of the savings feature, some people may voluntarily purchase, or a life insurance agent may persuade them to purchase, an ordinary life insurance policy when term insurance would be a better choice. For example, assume that Tamara, age 35, is a single parent with one dependent to support. She estimates that she can afford to spend only $400 annually on life insurance. Based on the rates of one insurer, this premium would buy about $64,000 of ordinary life insurance. The same premium would buy more than $500,000 of yearly renewable term insurance from many insurers.

limited-payment life insurance Whole life insurance for which premiums are paid for a specified period, after which time the policy is paid up. The insured has permanent protection.

Limited-Payment Life Insurance. **Limited-payment life insurance** is a whole life policy in which premiums are paid for a specified period, after which time the policy is paid up. The insured has permanent protection, and the premiums are level, but the insured pays them only for a certain period. For example, if you buy a 20-year limited-payment policy, you would pay premiums for only 20 years; after that time, the policy would be completely paid up.

You should use a limited-payment policy with caution. Because of high premiums, the amount of permanent life insurance that you can purchase is substantially lower than if you were to purchase an ordinary life policy. As a result, consumers with modest incomes may find it extremely difficult to insure their lives adequately with a limited-payment policy.

modified life insurance
Whole life insurance for which premiums are lower for the first three to five years and higher thereafter.

Modified Life Insurance. Modified life insurance is a form of whole life insurance in which premiums are lower for the first three to five years and are higher thereafter. The initial premium is slightly higher than for term insurance, but considerably lower than an ordinary life policy issued at the same age.

Modified life insurance is appropriate for consumers who need permanent life insurance but cannot presently afford the higher premiums for an ordinary life policy. Modified life insurance is particularly attractive to insureds who expect that their incomes will increase and that higher premiums will not be financially burdensome.

"special" whole life insurance Whole life insurance with a reduced rate that requires purchase of a minimum amount of insurance or is sold only to preferred risks.

"Special" Whole Life Insurance. "Special" whole life insurance is a generic name for a whole life policy with a reduced rate that requires purchase of a minimum amount of insurance or is sold only to preferred risks. For example, an insurer may require the purchase of a minimum amount of life insurance, such as $100,000, $200,000, or even higher amounts. The rate per $1,000 of insurance declines as the amount of insurance increases.

preferred risk A person whose health history, weight, occupation, and habits are more favorable in terms of mortality risk than the average.

Many insurers also sell policies at reduced rates to individuals known as **preferred risks** whose mortality experience is expected to be lower than average. The insurance is carefully underwritten and sold only to individuals whose health history, weight, occupation, and habits indicate more favorable mortality than the average. The insurer may also require the purchase of minimum amounts of insurance, such as $100,000. If an individual qualifies for a preferred rate, substantial savings are possible. For example, most insurers offer substantially lower rates to nonsmokers.

second-to-die life insurance Life insurance (usually whole life) that insures two or more lives and pays the death benefit upon the death of the second or last insured.

Second-to-Die Life Insurance. Second-to-die life insurance (also called survivorship life) is a form of life insurance that insures two or more lives and pays the death benefit upon the death of the second or last insured. The insurance is usually whole life insurance. Since the death proceeds are paid only upon the death of the second or last insured, the premiums are substantially lower than if two individual policies were issued.

Second-to-die life insurance is widely used in estate planning. Under present law, the deceased's entire estate can be left to a surviving spouse free of any federal estate tax. However, when the second spouse dies, a sizable federal estate tax may have to be paid. A second-to-die policy would provide the cash to pay the estate tax.

Variations of Whole Life Insurance

Insurers have developed a wide variety of whole life contracts that combine insurance protection with an investment element. These newer variations of whole life insurance include variable life insurance, universal life insurance, and variable universal life insurance.

Variable Life Insurance

variable life insurance
Life insurance in which the death benefit and the cash surrender value vary according to the investment results of a separate account maintained by the insurer.

Variable life insurance is a policy in which the death benefit and cash surrender value vary according to the investment results of a separate account maintained by the insurer. The amount of life insurance and cash surrender value may increase or decrease depending on the investment results of the separate account.

Although there are different policy designs, variable life insurance policies have certain common characteristics. *First, a variable life policy is a permanent whole life contract with a fixed premium.* The premium is level and guaranteed not to increase.

Second, the entire reserve is held in a separate account and invested in equities or other investments. The policyowner generally has the option of investing the cash value in a variety of investments, such as a common stock fund, bond fund, balanced fund, money market fund, or other fund. If the investment experience is favorable, the face amount of insurance is increased. If the investment experience is poor, the amount of insurance could be reduced, but it can never be less than the initial death benefit payable under the policy.

Finally, the cash surrender value is not guaranteed, and there is no minimum guaranteed cash value. The actual cash value depends on the investment experience. Thus, although the insurer bears the risk of excessive mortality and expenses, the policyowner retains the entire investment risk.

Universal Life Insurance

universal life insurance
Flexible-premium life insurance that can provide lifetime protection under a contract that unbundles the protection and savings elements.

Universal life insurance is a flexible premium policy that provides lifetime protection under a contract that unbundles the protection and saving elements. The policyowner pays a premium from which the cost of the insurance protection and expense charges are deducted with the balance credited to the cash value account at a stated rate of interest.

Basic Characteristics. Universal life insurance has certain characteristics that distinguish it from traditional whole life insurance policies, including the following:

■ *A distinct characteristic of universal life insurance is the separation or unbundling of three components: protection, saving, and expense.* The insurer issues an annual statement to the policyowner that shows the premiums paid, death benefit, cash surrender value, mortality charge, expense charge, and interest credited to the cash value account.

■ *The policy guarantees a minimum interest rate and provides for a higher current market rate.* The cash value account is credited with a contractually guaranteed minimum interest rate, such as 4 or 4 1/2 percent. However, the cash value earns a much higher rate of return based on the current interest rate declared by the company, such as 5 or 6 percent. The current interest rate is not guaranteed but changes periodically depending on market conditions and company experience.

■ *Two forms of universal life insurance are available (see Exhibit 9.4).* Option A pays a level death benefit during the early policy years. Option B provides for an increasing death benefit; the death benefit is equal to a specified amount of insurance plus the accumulated cash value. Option B is more expensive because a higher death benefit is paid.

■ *Universal life insurance provides considerable flexibility.* You can increase or decrease premiums, and you can change the frequency of payments. You can also increase or decrease the death benefit (evidence of insurability is required to increase the face amount of insurance). Subject to company limitations, you can add to the cash value at any time. In addition, you can make partial cash withdrawals and add insureds if the policy so permits.

■ *Universal life insurance enjoys the same favorable federal income-tax advantages as traditional whole life policies.* Interest credited to the cash value is not taxable to the policyowner in the year credited, and the death benefit paid to a named beneficiary is normally received income-tax free.

Exhibit 9.5 provides an illustration of a universal life policy issued to a nonsmoking male age 25. The level amount of insurance is $100,000, the annual premium is $497, the guaranteed interest rate is 4 percent, and the current interest rate is 6 1/2 percent. Although not shown, mortality and expense charges for the first year total $174. After these charges are deducted, the remainder of the premium ($323) goes into the cash value account and is credited with interest at 6 1/2 percent. At the end of the first year, the cash value account is $344 based on the current interest rate. However, if the policyowner surrenders the policy at the end of the first year, the cash surrender value is zero because of the surrender charge. The surrender charge reflects the loading for expenses under the policy. In this case, a declining surrender charge applies if the policy is terminated within 19 years of the issue date. *Thus, you can lose a substantial amount of money if you surrender the policy during the early years.*

Limitations of Universal Life Insurance. Universal life insurance has several important limitations. *First, the advertised rates of return are mislead-*

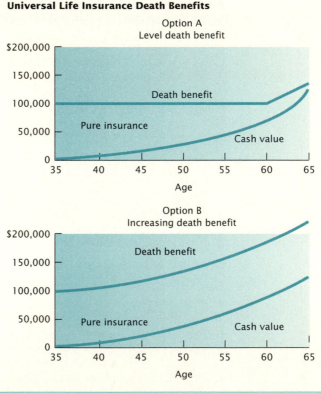

Exhibit 9.4

Universal Life Insurance Death Benefits

Option A
Level death benefit

Option B
Increasing death benefit

Source: *Life Insurance 12th Edition* by Black/Skipper, © 1987. Reprinted by permission of Prentice-Hall, Inc., Upper Saddle River, NJ.

Exhibit 9.5

$100,000 Universal Life Policy, Male Age 25, Nonsmoker, 6 1/2 Percent Assumed Interest

| | | | End of Year | | | | | |
| | | Guaranteed* | | | Assumed† | | | |
Year	Annual Premium	Death Benefit	Cash Value	Surrender Value	Death Benefit	Cash Value	Surrender Value	Age
1	$497.00	$100,000	$291	$0	$100,000	$344	$0	26
2	497.00	100,000	595	0	100,000	723	21	27
3	497.00	100,000	912	210	100,000	1,122	420	28
4	497.00	100,000	1,242	540	100,000	1,546	844	29
5	497.00	100,000	1,585	930	100,000	1,999	1,344	30
6	497.00	100,000	1,943	1,335	100,000	2,481	1,873	31
7	497.00	100,000	2,315	1,753	100,000	2,995	2,433	32
8	497.00	100,000	2,703	2,188	100,000	3,531	3,016	33
9	497.00	100,000	3,095	2,627	100,000	4,103	3,635	34
10	497.00	100,000	3,504	3,083	100,000	4,712	4,291	35
11	497.00	100,000	3,942	3,568	100,000	5,387	5,013	36
12	497.00	100,000	4,387	4,059	100,000	6,095	5,767	37
13	497.00	100,000	4,839	4,558	100,000	6,849	6,568	38
14	497.00	100,000	5,298	5,064	100,000	7,642	7,408	39
15	497.00	100,000	5,765	5,578	100,000	8,508	8,321	40
16	497.00	100,000	6,241	6,101	100,000	9,423	9,283	41
17	497.00	100,000	6,714	6,620	100,000	10,389	10,295	42
18	497.00	100,000	7,195	7,148	100,000	11,411	11,364	43
19	497.00	100,000	7,675	7,675	100,000	12,493	12,493	44
20	497.00	100,000	8,153	8,153	100,000	13,672	13,672	45
40	497.00	100,000	9,944	9,944	100,000	60,197	60,197	65

* The guaranteed values are based on a 4 percent guaranteed interest rate.
† The assumed values are based on an assumed interest rate of 6 1/2 percent and are not guaranteed.

ing. The rates advertised are gross rates, not net rates. The advertised rates are the rates credited to the cash value account after the cost of the insurance protection and expense charges are deducted. After these deductions, the effective yearly returns are substantially lower and often negative during the early years. For example, an earlier study by the National Insurance Consumer Organization of four universal life policies for a 40-year-old nonsmoking male, based on a $250,000 death benefit and $2,500 annual premium, showed the following:[5]

Company	Quoted Interest Rate on Saving Portion	Net Rate of Return		
		5 years	10 years	20 years
Jefferson Standard	10.75%	−19.1%	5.0%	9.0%
Life of Virginia	10.25	8.9	9.4	9.9
Massachusetts Mutual	9.70	−11.7	2.9	7.5
USAA	10.25	6.8	8.6	9.8

As you can see, the advertised rates of return overstate the net rate of return on the saving component because the gross rates do not reflect charges for sales commissions and expenses.

Another limitation is that sales illustrations showing projected cash values can be misleading. Earlier sales illustrations by many insurers showed sizable cash values at some future date based on high interest rates. The sales illustrations also showed that premium payments would vanish after a short period, such as 10 years. However, interest rates have declined sharply in recent years, and the cash value projections based on higher interest rates are now invalid.

Variable Universal Life Insurance

variable universal life insurance Life insurance similar to universal life, with two major exceptions: (1) the policyowner has a variety of options for investment of the cash value, and (2) there is no minimum guaranteed interest rate.

Variable universal life insurance is similar to a universal life policy with two major exceptions: (1) the policyowner has a variety of options for investment of the cash values, and (2) there is no minimum guaranteed interest rate.

The policyowner can invest the cash values in a variety of investments, such as an aggressive stock fund, bond fund, balanced fund, international fund, and money market fund. The policyowner can invest the funds depending on his or her investment goals and tolerance for risk.

There is also no minimum guaranteed interest rate, and the cash value is not guaranteed. Thus, the investment risk falls entirely on the policyowner. There is wide variation in the investment returns, depending on how the policyowner invests the funds.

Group Life Insurance

Group life insurance is another important form of life insurance that merits some discussion. In 1995, group life insurance amounted to 38 percent of the total life insurance in force in the United States.[6]

group life insurance Life insurance that provides coverage to members of a group under a single master contract.

Group life insurance provides life insurance to members of a group under a single master contract; physical examinations are not required, and members receive certificates of insurance as evidence of insurance protection. Most groups today are eligible for group life insurance, including employer employee groups, labor unions, members of trade associations and professional associations, fraternities and sororities, and other groups.

Group life insurance is an important employee benefit. Employers typically provide group term life insurance on the lives of employees equal to one or two times salary. Most group plans also allow a modest amount of life insurance to be written on the employee's spouse and dependent children. Most group insurance in force today is term insurance, which remains in force as long as the employee is part of the group. If the employee quits or is terminated, he or she has the right to convert the group term insurance to an individual cash value policy within 31 days without evidence of insurability. Group term insurance has the major advantage of providing low-cost protection to employees that can effectively supplement individual life insurance policies. However, group term has two major disadvantages. The insurance is temporary and terminates when the individual is no longer part of the group. It is also expensive for an older worker to convert to a permanent policy when he or she retires.

Life Insurance Contractual Provisions

State laws require certain contractual provisions to appear in life insurance policies; other contractual provisions are optional. You should be aware of the important contractual provisions that can have a financial impact on you as an insured, policyowner, or beneficiary.

Incontestable Clause

incontestable clause
Clause in a life insurance contract stating that the insurer cannot contest the policy after it has been in force two years during the insured's lifetime.

The **incontestable clause** states that the insurer cannot contest the policy after it has been in force two years during the insured's lifetime. Once the policy has been in force for two years, the insurer cannot contest a death claim on the basis of a material misrepresentation, concealment, or fraud when the policy was first issued. The insurer has two years in which to contest any technical or legal irregularities in the contract. For example, Mark, age 23, applies for a life insurance policy and conceals the fact that he has high blood pressure. If he dies within the two-year period, the insurer could contest the claim. After the two-year period expires, the insurer must pay the claim.

Suicide Clause

Most policies contain a suicide clause to protect the insurer against the individual who purchases life insurance with the intention of committing suicide. The **suicide clause** states that if the insured commits suicide within two years after the policy is issued, the face amount of insurance will not be paid. There is only a refund of the premiums. If the suicide occurs after the period expires, the insurer pays the death benefit just like any other claim.

Grace Period

The **grace period** is a provision that allows the policyowner 31 days to pay an overdue premium. Universal life policies usually have a longer grace period, such as 61 days. The insurance remains in force during the grace period. If the insured dies within the grace period, the insurer deducts the overdue premium from the death benefit.

Policy Loan Provision

Cash value life insurance policies contain a **policy loan provision** that allows the policyowner to borrow the cash value. The interest rate is stated in the policy, and the loan typically bears interest at 5, 6, or 8 percent. Insurers can also issue policies with a flexible loan interest rate based on a market index such as Moody's Composite Yield.

Many life insurance policies pay dividends. However, many insurers will reduce the dividend based on the amount of cash value borrowed. *This has the effect of indirectly increasing the effective interest rate on the policy loan.* For example, one insurer would have paid a dividend of about $314 on a $10,000 policy issued to a male age 30 with no outstanding loans. However, since the insured borrowed $5,300, the dividend was reduced to $107, a reduction of almost two thirds.[7] In addition, under a universal life policy, the current interest rate credited to the cash value borrowed is typically reduced, which again increases the effective interest rate on the loan. You must pay interest annually, or it is added to the outstanding loan. If the loan is not repaid by the time of death, the insurer reduces the death benefit by the amount of indebtedness.

The **automatic premium loan provision** can be added to most cash value policies. An overdue premium is automatically borrowed from the cash value after the grace period expires provided the policy has a loan value sufficient to pay the premium. The purpose of the provision is to prevent the policy from lapsing because of nonpayment of premiums.

Beneficiary Designation

beneficiary The party named in a life insurance policy to receive the death benefits.

The **beneficiary** is the party named in the policy to receive the death benefits. Two types of beneficiary designations are extremely important in financial planning: primary and contingent. A **primary beneficiary** is the person entitled to the death benefits when the insured dies. A **contingent beneficiary** is the person entitled to the death benefits if the primary beneficiary dies before the insured. In most families, one spouse will name the other as primary beneficiary and name the children as contingent beneficiaries.

primary beneficiary The beneficiary entitled to death benefits when the insured dies.

contingent beneficiary The beneficiary entitled to death benefits if the primary beneficiery dies before the insured.

There is a legal problem in naming minor children as contingent beneficiaries because they lack the legal capacity to receive the death benefits directly. Insurers typically require a guardian to receive the benefits on the minor's behalf. If a court of law appoints a guardian, the insurer may delay payment of the death benefits. One solution is to have a guardian named in the will.

Dividend Options

participating policy A policy that pays dividends.

Many life insurance policies sell participating policies. A **participating policy** is one that pays dividends to the policyholder. A **dividend** is a refund of part of the gross premium if the insurer has favorable operating experience regarding mortality, investment earnings, and expenses. Because dividends are determined by the insurer's actual operating experience, they cannot be guaranteed. If the policy pays dividends, the policyowner has a choice of **dividend options.** Policyowners can take the dividends in several ways:

dividend A refund of part of the gross life insurance premium; payment of the dividend depends on the insurer's operating performance.

dividend options Ways in which life insurance dividends can be taken; they include cash, reduction of premiums, accumulation of cash at interest, paid-up additions, and in some companies, term insurance.

- The policyowner can receive the dividend as cash after the policy has been in force for a stated period, usually one or two years.

- The insured can use the dividend to reduce the next premium coming due; this option is appropriate whenever premium payments become financially burdensome.

- The insurer can retain the dividend and accumulate it at interest; generally, the insured can withdraw the accumulated dividends at any time.

- The insured can use the dividend to purchase a reduced amount of paid-up whole life insurance; for example, a dividend of $20 would purchase about $50 of paid-up whole life insurance for a female, age 20.

- Finally, some insurers have a fifth option by which the dividend is used to purchase term insurance.

Nonforfeiture Options

When an individual purchases a cash value policy, the policyowner has paid more than is actuarially necessary for the insurance protection. Thus, the policyowner should get something back if the policy is surrendered. The payment to a withdrawing policyowner is known as a **nonforfeiture value,** or cash surrender value.

nonforfeiture value The cash surrender value of a cash-value life insurance policy.

All states have nonforfeiture laws that require insurers to provide at least a minimum nonforfeiture value to policyowners who surrender their policies. There are three nonforfeiture or cash surrender options:

■ The insured can surrender the policy for its *cash value,* at which time all benefits under the policy cease. A policy normally does not build any cash value until the end of the second or third year though some policies have a small cash value at the end of the first year. The cash values are small during the early years but can be substantial over a long period. The cash surrender option is appropriate if the policyowner no longer needs the insurance protection, such as an individual who retires and has no dependents to support.

■ The insured can use the cash value to purchase a *reduced paid-up policy.* This option is appropriate if life insurance is still needed, but the policyowner does not wish to pay premiums. For example, assume that Tyrone has a $10,000 ordinary life insurance policy that he purchased at age 21. He is now age 65 and wants to retire, but he does not want to pay premiums after retirement. He can use the cash value to purchase a reduced paid-up policy of about $8,300.

■ The insured can also use the cash value to extend the full face amount of insurance into the future as *extended term insurance* for a limited period. In effect, the cash value is used to purchase a paid-up term insurance policy equal to the original face amount (less any indebtedness) for a limited period. For example, in our earlier illustration, if Tyrone stopped paying premiums at age 65, the cash value would be sufficient to keep the policy in force for another 15 years and 272 days. If he is still alive after that time, the policy is no longer in force.

All cash value policies contain a table of nonforfeiture values that indicates the benefits under the three options at various ages. Exhibit 9.6 illustrates the nonforfeiture values for an ordinary life policy issued at age 21.

Settlement Options

Most life insurance death benefits are paid in a lump-sum cash payment to a stated beneficiary or beneficiaries. When a lump-sum death benefit

Exhibit 9.6

Nonforfeiture Options (Dollar Amount for Each $1,000 of Ordinary Life Insurance Issued at Age 21)

End of Policy Year	Cash or Loan Value	Paid-Up Insurance	Extended Term Insurance Years	Extended Term Insurance Days
1	$0.00	$0	0	0
2	0.00	0	0	0
3	4.79	15	1	315
4	16.21	48	6	161
5	27.91	81	11	15
6	39.91	113	14	275
7	52.20	145	17	158
8	64.78	176	19	157
9	77.66	206	20	342
10	90.84	236	22	29
11	104.33	265	22	351
12	118.13	294	23	231
13	132.25	322	24	54
14	146.69	350	24	191
15	161.43	377	24	290
16	176.47	403	24	356
17	191.79	429	25	28
18	207.38	454	25	42
19	223.22	478	25	36
20	239.29	502	25	13
Age 60	563.42	806	17	26
Age 65	608.49	833	15	272

settlement options The ways in which death benefits are payable other than in a lump sum; also called optional methods of settlement. They include the interest option, the fixed-period option, the fixed-amount option, and the life income option.

interest option A settlement option in which the policy proceeds are retained by the insurer and interest is periodically paid to the beneficiary.

is paid, the insurer has no further obligation under the policy. However, life insurance policies also contain several alternative settlement options. **Settlement options** (also called optional methods of settlement) refer to the various ways that death benefits are payable other than in a lump sum. The policyowner may elect the settlement options prior to the insured's death, or the beneficiary may be granted the right. The most common settlement options are the fixed-period option, the fixed-amount option, and life income options.

The **interest option** pays interest periodically to the beneficiary, and the insurer retains the policy proceeds. The beneficiary may be given withdrawal rights, by which part or all of the proceeds can be withdrawn at a later date. The interest option is appropriate to use if the funds will not be needed until later. For example, educational

fixed-period option A settlement option in which the beneficiary receives the policy proceeds over some fixed period, such as 10, 20, or 30 years; also called the installment-time option.

fixed-amount option A settlement option in which the beneficiary received a fixed amount periodically; also called the installment-amount option.

life income option A settlement option in which the policy proceeds are paid during the lifetime of the beneficiary.

funds could be retained at interest until the children are ready for college.

The **fixed-period option** (or installment-time option) pays the policy proceeds to a beneficiary over some fixed period, such as 10, 20, or 30 years. If the primary beneficiary dies before receiving all payments, the remaining payments will be paid to a contingent beneficiary or to the primary beneficiary's estate. The fixed-period option is appropriate when income is needed for a definite period, such as income during the readjustment and dependency periods.

The **fixed-amount option** (or installment-amount option) pays a fixed amount periodically to the beneficiary. For example, assume that the death benefit is $50,000, the credited interest rate is 4 percent, and the desired monthly payment is $3,000. In this case, the beneficiary would receive $3,000 monthly for 18 months, with the first payment due immediately. The fixed-amount option is appropriate for providing income during the readjustment and dependency periods. It can also be used to provide income to a surviving spouse from the time that social security survivor benefits terminate when the youngest child reaches age 16 to the time the benefits are resumed at age 60.

The death benefits can also be paid to a designated beneficiary under a life income option. There are various types of **life income options** Under a life income option with no refund feature, installment payments are paid only while the beneficiary is alive, and cease on the beneficiary's death. Under the life income with period certain option, a life income is paid to the beneficiary with a certain number of guaranteed payments, such as 10 or 20 years. If the primary beneficiary dies before receiving the guaranteed number of payments, the remaining payments are paid to a contingent beneficiary.

Other Life Insurance Benefits

Certain benefits can be added to a life insurance policy. These benefits include the waiver-of-premium provision, guaranteed purchase option, double indemnity rider, cost-of-living rider, and accelerated death benefits rider.

Waiver-of-Premium Provision

waiver-of-premium provision Provision by which, if the insured becomes totally disabled from injury or disease before some stated age, all premiums coming due during the period of disability are waived.

Under the **waiver-of-premium provision,** if the insured becomes totally disabled from injury or disease before some stated age, such as age 60 or 65, all premiums coming due during the period of disability are waived. The insured must also be continuously disabled for six months (four months in some policies). In addition, the insured must meet the definition of disability stated in the policy. There is a retroactive refund of premiums paid by the insured during the first six months of disability if all premiums are being waived under the policy. Some newer policies, however, do not provide for a retroactive refund.

Guaranteed Purchase Option

guaranteed purchase option An option permitting the insured to purchase additional amounts of life insurance without evidence of insurability.

The **guaranteed purchase option** permits the insured to purchase additional amounts of life insurance without evidence of insurability. This option allows additional amounts of life insurance to be purchased at standard rates even though the insured is substandard in health or is uninsurable.

The typical option permits the insured to purchase additional amounts of life insurance without evidence of insurability when he or she attains ages 25, 28, 31, 34, 37, and 40. Some insurers permit an option to be exercised beyond age 40 up to age 65.

Double Indemnity Rider

double indemnity rider Provision doubling the face amount of life insurance if death occurs as a result of an accident.

A **double indemnity rider** doubles the face amount of life insurance if death occurs as a result of an accident. In some policies, the face amount is tripled. The cost of the rider is small. For example, one insurer charges $69 annually when the rider is added to a $100,000 policy issued to a male age 35. Thus, if the insured dies as a result of an accident, his beneficiary would be paid a total of $200,000.

Consumer experts generally do not recommend the purchase of the double indemnity rider. There are two major objections to the rider. First, the economic value of a human life is not doubled or tripled if death occurs from an accident. Second, most persons will die from disease and not from accidents; industry statistics show that accidents account for only 6 percent of the deaths in the United States.[8]

Cost-of-Living Rider

cost-of-living rider Provision allowing the policy owner to purchase one-year term insurance equal to the percentage change in the consumer price index without evidence of insurability.

Under the **cost-of-living rider,** the policyowner is allowed to purchase one-year term insurance equal to the percentage change in the consumer price index without evidence of insurability. The purpose is to maintain the real purchasing power of the death benefit. The amount of term insurance changes each year and reflects the cumulative change in the consumer price index from the issue date of the policy.

Accelerated Death Benefits Rider

accelerated death benefits rider Provision allowing insured persons who are terminally ill or have certain catastrophic diseases to collect part or all of their life insurance before they die, primarily to pay for the care they require.

terminal illness rider Provision allowing insured persons with life expectancy of six months to one year to receive part or all of the face amount of their insurance.

catastrophic illness rider Provision allowing insured persons who have certain catastrophic diseases to collect part or all of the policy's face amount.

long-term care rider Provision allowing insured persons who require long-term care to collect part of their life insurance.

Many insurers now make available a living benefits rider that can be added to a life insurance policy. An **accelerated death benefits rider** allows insureds who are terminally ill or have certain catastrophic diseases to collect part or all of their life insurance before they die, primarily to pay for the care they require. Benefits may also be payable if the insured is receiving care in a nursing home.

There are three major types of living benefits. The **terminal illness rider** allows insureds with a life expectancy of six months or one year to receive part or all the face amount of insurance. Any lump sums advanced are discounted for interest to reflect the time value of money. The **catastrophic illness rider** allows insureds who have certain catastrophic diseases—such as AIDS, life-threatening cancer, coronary artery disease, and similar types of catastrophic diseases—to collect part or all of the policy face amount. Finally, the **long-term care rider** allows insureds who require long-term care to collect part of their life insurance; the rider may cover care in a skilled nursing facility, intermediate care facility, or custodial care facility. Some riders also cover certain types of home care.

Developing A Sound Life Insurance Program

Developing a sound life insurance program involves seven steps, which are illustrated in Exhibit 9.7 and discussed below.

Determine If You Need Life Insurance

The first step is to determine if you need life insurance. If you are married or single with one or more dependents to support, you need a substantial amount of life insurance. *However, if you are single and no one presently depends on you for financial support, you do not need life insurance, other than a modest amount for burial purposes and other limited expenses.* The arguments for buying life insurance when you are young and insurable are not compelling. Even if your situation should change and you need life insurance in the future, *more than nine of ten applicants for life insurance are accepted at standard rates.* Thus, it is a waste of money to buy life insurance when it is not needed.

You may also need life insurance if you have a temporary need, such as paying off the mortgage on your home. In addition, if you have accumulated substantial assets, you may need large amounts of life insurance to provide estate liquidity and to pay federal estate taxes.

Exhibit 9.7

Determine if you need life insurance.

Estimate the amount of life insurance you need.

Decide on the best type of life insurance for you.

Decide whether you want a policy that pays dividends.

Shop around for a low cost policy.

Consider the financial strength of the insurer.

Deal with a competent agent.

Estimate the Amount of Life Insurance You Need

Persons with dependents often need surprisingly large amounts of life insurance. In determining the amount you need, you must consider your family's present and future financial needs, potential survivor benefits from social security, and the financial assets you currently own. In addition, as your needs change, you should periodically reevaluate the amount of life insurance you need. An increase or reduction in income, marriage, divorce, birth of a new child, or inflation can dramatically change the amount of life insurance you need.

Decide on the Best Type of Life Insurance for You

The next step is to select the best type of life insurance policy for you. *The best policy is one that best meets your financial needs.* If the amount of money you can spend on life insurance is limited, or if you have a temporary need, consider term insurance. If you need lifetime protection, consider ordinary life insurance or universal life insurance. If you believe that you cannot save money without being forced to do so, consider ordinary life insurance or universal life insurance as a savings vehicle. However, remember that the annual rates of return on cash value policies can vary enormously.

Avoid purchasing a policy that you cannot afford. A large percentage of new life insurance policies sold lapse for nonpayment of premiums during the first two years. The lapse rate for policies in force for less than two years was 17 percent in 1995.[9] *If you drop the policy after a few months or years, you will lose a substantial sum of money. Be sure you can afford the premium.*

Decide Whether You Want a Policy That Pays Dividends

In recent decades, participating life insurance policies that pay dividends generally have been better buys than nonparticipating policies because of high interest rates that permitted insurers to raise their dividends. However, interest rates have declined sharply from their peak in the early 1980s, and many insurers have substantially reduced their dividends because of declining excess interest earnings. Thus, if you believe that interest rates will remain high, you should consider a participating policy because excess interest has a powerful impact on dividends. If you believe that interest rates will fall and will remain at lower levels in the future, consider a nonparticipating policy. Policies that do not pay dividends generally require a lower initial premium outlay.

Shop Around for a Low-Cost Policy

Another important suggestion is to shop carefully for a low-cost policy. There is enormous variation in the cost of life insurance. You should not purchase a life insurance policy from the first agent who approaches you. *Instead, you should compare the interest-adjusted cost (discussed later) of similar policies from several insurers before you buy.* Otherwise, you may be overpaying for the insurance protection. If you make a mistake and purchase a high-cost policy, this mistake can cost you thousands of dollars over your lifetime.

The cost of life insurance is determined by four major factors: (1) annual premiums, (2) cash value, (3) dividends, and (4) the time value of money. Two cost methods that reflect some or all of the preceding factors are the traditional net cost method and interest-adjusted cost method.

traditional net cost method Traditional method of determining the cost of a life insurance policy to an insured; the total dividends received and cash value at the end of a period are subtracted from the total premiums paid during that period.

Traditional Net Cost Method. Historically, insurers used the **traditional net cost method** in their sales illustrations to illustrate the cost of life insurance. Under this method, the annual premiums for some time period (usually 10 or 20 years) are added together. Total dividends received during the period and the cash value at the end of the period are then subtracted from the total premiums to determine the net cost of

Exhibit 9.8

Traditional Net Cost Method

Total premiums for 20 years	$2642
Subtract dividends for 20 years	−599
Net premiums for 20 years	$2043
Subtract the cash value at the end of 20 years	−2294
Insurance cost for 20 years	−$251
Net cost per year (−$251 ÷ 20)	−$12.55
Net cost per $1000 per year (−$12.55 ÷ 10)	−$1.26

insurance. For example, assume that the annual premium for a $10,000 ordinary life policy for a female age 20 is $132.10. The policy pays an estimated $599 in dividends over a 20-year period, and the cash surrender value at the end of the twentieth year is $2294. The net cost at the end of 20 years is a minus $251, or a net cost per year of minus $12.55 (−$1.26 per $1,000). These steps are summarized in Exhibit 9.8.

The traditional net cost method does not accurately measure the cost of insurance and is misleading. *The most glaring defect is that the time value of money is ignored.* Interest that could be earned on the premiums by investing them elsewhere is ignored. Because this method is deceptive, some states prohibit insurers from using it in their sales illustrations.

Interest-Adjusted Method. The interest-adjusted method developed by the National Association of Insurance Commissioners is a more accurate measure of life insurance costs. Under this method, the time value of money is taken into consideration by applying an interest factor to the premiums and dividends.

surrender cost index
Method of measuring the cost of an insurance policy to an insured if the policy is surrendered at the end of some specified time period. The time value of money is taken into account.

net payment cost index
Method of measuring the cost of an insurance policy to an insured if death occurs at the end of some specified time period. The time value of money is taken into account.

There are two principal types of interest-adjusted cost indexes—the **surrender cost index** and the net payment cost index. The surrender cost index measures the cost of life insurance based on the assumption that the policy will be surrendered for its cash surrender value at some future date, such as the end of 10 or 20 years. It is the appropriate index to use if cash surrender values are of primary importance to you.

The **net payment cost index** measures the cost of life insurance if death occurs at the end of some time period, such as the end of 10 or 20 years. It is based on the assumption that the policy is not surrendered for its cash value. It is the appropriate index to use if you intend to continue paying premiums and do not surrender the policy.

There are enormous cost variations among insurers based on the interest-adjusted cost indexes. For example, one survey of 40 participat-

 **9.1   Term-Insurance Quotes: Online vs. By Mail**

Here are the results of our online shopping for the lowest annual premiums on $200,000, 15-year term policies for healthy, nonsmoking, 45-year-old women and men.

QUOTE SERVICE/WEB ADDRESS	INSTANT QUOTE?	BEST RATES FOR WOMEN AND MEN	PREMIUM
Insurance Quote Services	No	W: Old Republic Life Insurance Co.	$246
(http://www.lquote.com)		M: CNA Insurance Cos.	$309
800-972-1104			
MasterQuote	No	W: First Penn-Pacific LIfe Insurance Co.	$280
(http://www.masterquote.com)		M: First Penn-Pacific Life	$350
800-337-5433			
QuickQuote	Yes	W: Old Republic Life	$306
(http://www.quickquote.com)		M: Lincoln Benefit LIfe Co.	$381
800-867-2404			
Quotesmith	Yes	W: First Penn-Pacific Life/	$280
(http://www.quotesmith.com)		Lincoln Benefit LIfe	
800-431-1147		M: First Penn-Pacific Life/	$350
		Lincoln Benefit Life	
TermQuote	No	W: First Penn-Pacific LIfe	$280
(http://www.rcinet.com/ termquote)		M: First Penn-Pacific LIfe	$350
800-444-8376			

Source: Reprinted with permission from the October 1996 issue of *Kiplinger's Personal Finance Magazine*. Copyright © 1996 The Kiplinger Washington Editors, Inc.

ing whole life policies issued in the amount of $250,000 to males age 35 showed a wide variation in annual cost. Based on the surrender cost index, the annual cost at the end of 20 years ranged from a high of $2.69 per $1,000 for Woodmen of the World and the Knights of Columbus to a low of a minus $1.84 for Central Life Assurance.[10]

Because of the substantial cost variation, you should compare the interest-adjusted costs of several policies before you buy. *Remember the lower the index number, the less costly is the policy.* Insurers must give you interest-adjusted cost data in their sales illustrations. In addition, your state insurance department may publish a shoppers' guide on life insurance that provides interest-adjusted cost data. Finally, you can easily

Insight   9.2   Should You Replace a Life Insurance Policy?

If you already own a life insurance policy, a health insurance policy, or an annuity contract, you should be careful if you consider replacing it. Although the relative financial strength of the original company and the replacing company is an important factor in your decision, you should consider other factors as well. Some of those additional factors are described briefly in the following paragraphs.

If you consider replacing life or health insurance, your state of health and other items affecting your eligibility should be reviewed. You may not qualify for new insurance, or you may qualify only at high rates.

You should determine the cost of getting out of the original policy. Many policies contain substantial surrender charges.

You should determine the cost of getting into the replacement policy. Many policies involve substantial front-end expenses.

You should determine whether the cost of continuing the original policy is reasonable. If the cost is reasonable, there may be little if any reason to replace it. (A procedure for making such a determination is described in the June 1982 issue of *The Insurance Forum*.)

You should consider the tax implications of a replacement. In some situations, the termination of a life insurance policy or an annuity contract may trigger an income tax liability. You may be able to defer the tax, but you should consult your tax adviser.

You should consider the incontestability clause. For example, if a life insurance policy is more than two years old, the company usually is barred from alleging that the policy is void because of false statements you made in the application. Thus the original policy may not be contestable, while the replacement policy may be contestable for two years.

You should also be aware of the suicide clause. Suicide usually is excluded during the first two years of a life insurance policy. Thus the original policy may currently cover suicide, while the replacement policy may not cover suicide for two years.

If someone recommends replacement, you should try to determine the amount of compensation the person making the recommendation will receive if you follow the advice. Some who recommend replacement are motivated by a genuine desire to help you reduce your expenses or avoid the problems that may arise if your original company gets into financial trouble. However, in the current environment of public concern about the financial strength of insurance companies, some persons may descend on the policyowners of a troubled company like sharks who detect blood in the water. The fact that a person receives a commission does not necessarily mean he or she is giving bad advice, but you should be on guard.

Source: Joseph M. Belth, ed., "The Replacement Problem." *The Insurance Forum*, Vol. 24, No. 7 (September 1997), pp. 263–64. Reprinted with permission.

obtain cost data by calling certain price-quoting services for information on low-cost policies. Cost data are also available on the Internet (see Insight 9.1).

low-load life insurance
Life insurance sold directly to the public through telephone representatives or fee-only financial planners.

When you are shopping for a low cost policy, you should also consider **low load life insurance.** A small number of life insurers sell insurance directly to the public by using telephone representatives or fee-only financial planners. The major advantage is that marketing expenses account for only 10 to 25 percent of the first year's premium rather than 90 to 125 percent on policies sold by agents. Two major low-load insurers that sell policies by phone are Ameritas (800-552-3553) and USAA (800-531-8000).

Finally, if you are thinking about replacing your present life insurance policy with a new one, you should not base your decision solely on cost. Other factors should also be considered (see Insight 9.2).

Consider the Financial Strength of the Insurer

Besides cost, you should consider the financial strength of the insurer. Some life insurers become insolvent and have gone out of business. Although all states have state guaranty funds that pay the claims of insolvent life insurers, there are limits on the amounts guaranteed. Death claims are paid promptly, but you may have to wait years before you can borrow or withdraw your cash value. Thus, it is important to buy life insurance only from insurers that are financially sound.

A number of rating organizations periodically grade and rate life insurers on their financial strength. The ratings by the A.M. Best Company are widely used by life insurance agents to illustrate the insurer's financial strength (see Exhibit 9.9). However, other rating agencies, such as Standard & Poor's, Moodys, Duff and Phelps, and Weiss Research, also rate the various insurers.

Consider This

Best's ratings are available on the Internet at:

http://www.ambest.com/

There are wide variations in the grades given by the different rating agencies. A is the third-highest grade from Best, whereas for Standard & Poor's, A is the sixth-highest grade. A is only the second-highest grade from Weiss. Thus, you should be careful and conservative when you are evaluating the financial strength of an insurer. Joseph Belth, a nationally known consumer expert in life insurance, recommends that an insurer should receive a high rating from at least three of five rating agencies before you purchase a policy from them.[11]

Deal with a Competent Agent

You should also deal with a competent agent when you buy life insurance. Selling life insurance is a tough job, and only a small number of new life insurance agents are successful. The industry turnover rate is high; the four-year retention rate is only 17 percent.

Most new agents receive only minimal training before they are licensed to sell life insurance. New agents also are often placed under intense pressure to sell life insurance. Even mature agents are expected

Exhibit 9.9

Guide to Best's Ratings

Secure Ratings

A++, A+	Superior
A, A-	Excellent
B++, B+	Very Good

Vulnerable Ratings

B, B-	Adequate
C++, C+	Fair
C, C-	Marginal
D	Very Marginal
E	Under State Supervision
F	In Liquidation

Note: Best's also uses a number of special "not assigned" categories when a rating is not assigned to an insurer.
Source: A.M. Best Company, Inc.

to sell a certain amount of insurance. As a result, some agents have engaged in deceptive sales practices by misrepresenting the insurance to clients or by recommending policies that maximize commissions rather than meeting the client's needs.

To reduce the possibility of receiving bad advice or being sold the wrong policy, consider the professional qualifications of the agent. An agent who is a Chartered Life Underwriter (CLU), Chartered Financial Consultant (ChFC), or Certified Financial Planner (CFP) should be technically competent to give proper advice. More important, agents who hold the preceding professional designations are expected to abide by a code of ethics that places their clients' interests ahead of their own.

SUMMARY

■ Premature death means a family head dies with outstanding unfulfilled financial obligations, such as dependents to support, children to educate, or a mortgage to pay off.

■ The financial impact of premature death on the family varies by the type of family. Premature death can cause great financial insecurity if a family head dies in a single-parent family, in a family with two income earners with children, or in a traditional, blended, or sandwiched family. In contrast, if a single person without dependents dies, financial problems for others are unlikely.

■ The needs approach can be used to determine the amount of life insurance to own. After considering other sources of income and financial assets, the various family needs are converted into specific amounts of life insurance. The most important family needs are an estate clearance fund, income during the readjustment period, income during the dependency period, life income to the surviving spouse, special needs (mortgage redemption fund, education fund, emergency fund), and retirement needs.

■ Term insurance provides temporary protection and is renewable and convertible without evidence of insurability. Term insurance is appropriate when income is limited or temporary needs must be fulfilled. However, because term insurance premiums increase with age, term insurance is inappropriate for lifetime protection.

■ Ordinary life insurance is a form of whole life insurance that provides lifetime protection to age 100. The premiums are level and payable for life. The policy develops a savings component called the cash surrender value, which results from the overpayment of premiums during the early years. An ordinary life policy is appropriate when lifetime protection or additional savings are desired.

■ There are other types of traditional whole life policies. A limited-payment policy is a whole life policy in which premiums are paid for a specified period, after which time the policy is paid up. A modified life policy is a policy in which premiums are lower for the first three to five years and are higher thereafter.

■ Variable life insurance is a policy in which the death benefit and cash surrender value vary according to the investment results of a separate account maintained by the insurer. The entire reserve is held in a separate account and is invested in stocks or other investments. The cash surrender value is not guaranteed.

■ Universal life insurance is a flexible premium policy that provides lifetime protection under a contract that separates the protection and saving components. Universal life has the following features: unbundling of protection, savings, and expense components; guaranteed minimum interest rate and current market interest rate; two forms of universal life insurance; considerable flexibility; cash withdrawals permitted; and favorable income-tax treatment.

■ Variable universal life insurance is similar to universal life insurance with two major exceptions. First, the cash values can be invested in a wide variety of investments. Second, there is no minimum guaranteed interest rate, and the investment risk falls entirely on the policyowner.

■ The incontestable clause states the insurer cannot contest the policy after it has been in force two years during the insured's lifetime.

■ The suicide clause states that if the insured commits suicide within two years after the policy is issued, the face amount is not paid. There is only a refund of the premiums.

■ The grace period allows the policyowner a period of 31 days to pay an overdue premium. Universal life policies usually have a longer period, such as 61 days. The insurance remains in force during the grace period.

■ A primary beneficiary is the party entitled to receive the policy proceeds upon the insured's death. A contingent beneficiary is entitled to the proceeds if the primary beneficiary dies before the insured or dies before receiving the guaranteed number of payments under an installment settlement option.

■ A participating policy is a policy that pays dividends. Dividends can be taken in several ways: as cash, reduction of premiums, accumulation at interest, paid-up additions, or term insurance (with some insurers).

■ There are three nonforfeiture options or cash surrender options: cash, reduction of paid-up insurance, and extended term insurance.

■ Settlement options are the various ways that the policy proceeds can be paid other than in a lump-sum cash payment. The most common settlement options are: interest option, fixed-period option, fixed-amount option, and life income options.

■ Additional benefits that can be added to a life insurance policy include the waiver-of-premium provision, guaranteed purchase option, double indemnity rider, cost-of-living rider, and accelerated death benefits rider.

■ Certain steps should be followed in the development of a sound life insurance program: (1) Determine if you need life insurance. (2) Estimate the amount of life insurance you need. (3) Decide on the best type of life insurance for you. (4) Decide whether you want a policy that pays dividends. (5) Shop around for the lowest-cost policy. (6) Consider the financial strength of the insurer. (7) Deal with a competent agent.

KEY CONCEPTS AND TERMS

Accelerated death benefits rider	Nonforfeiture value (cash surrender value)
Automatic premium loan provision	Nonparticipating policy
Beneficiary	Ordinary life insurance
Blackout period	Participating policy
Cash surrender value	Policy loan provision
Convertible	Premature death
Cost-of-living rider	Readjustment period
Decreasing term insurance	Reentry term
Dependency period	Renewable
Dividend	Second-to-die life insurance
Dividend options	Settlement options
Double indemnity rider	"Special" whole life insurance
Estate clearance fund	Suicide clause
Grace period	Surrender cost index
Group life insurance	Term insurance
Guaranteed purchase option	Term to age 65 policy
Incontestable clause	Traditional net cost method
Legal reserve	Universal life insurance
Limited-payment life insurance	Variable life insurance
Low-load life insurance	Variable universal life insurance
Modified life insurance	Waiver-of-premium provision
Needs approach	Whole life insurance
Net payment cost index	Yearly renewable term insurance

QUESTIONS FOR REVIEW

1. Explain the meaning of premature death. Identify the types of families that may experience great financial insecurity because of premature death.

2. Identify the various cash needs and income needs that should be considered under the needs approach.

3. Describe the major characteristics of term insurance. Why is term insurance inappropriate for lifetime protection?

4. Explain the major characteristics of an ordinary life insurance policy.

5. Describe the major characteristics and limitations of a universal life insurance policy.

6. How does variable universal life insurance differ from universal life insurance?

7. Briefly explain the following life insurance contractual provisions:

   a. Incontestable clause

   b. Suicide clause

   c. Grace period

   d. Policy loan provision

   e. Beneficiary designation

8. Explain the following life insurance contractual provisions:

   a. Dividend options

   b. Nonforfeiture options (cash surrender options)

   c. Settlement options

9. Describe the following benefits that can be added to a life insurance policy:

   a. Waiver-of-premium provision

   b. Guaranteed purchase option

   c. Double indemnity rider

   d. Cost-of-living rider

   e. Accelerated death benefits rider

10. List the important rules that consumers should follow when life insurance is purchased.

PROBLEMS

1. Kim, age 22, is a single parent who is the sole support of her son, age 3. She has the following cash and income needs:

   a. $1,500 monthly to her son for 15 years following her death

   b. $6,000 for funeral expenses

   c. $100,000 educational fund for her son

   Estimated social security survivor benefits to her son are $800 monthly. Kim does not own any life insurance at the present time. How much life insurance should she purchase to accomplish her goals? (Assume that the life insurance proceeds can be invested at a rate of return equal to the rate of inflation.)

2. John, age 25, purchased a five-year term life insurance policy in the amount of $200,000 from Friendly Insurer. The policy has a double

indemnity rider attached to it. The monthly premium is $20. John committed suicide 30 months after the policy was issued. What is the amount, if any, that Friendly Insurer must pay when proof of death is received?

3. James, age 32, purchased a $500,000 universal life insurance policy from Mutual Insurer. When answering the health questions, James told the agent that he had not visited a doctor within the last five years. James had, however, seen a doctor two months earlier. At that time, the doctor told James he had a serious heart disease. James did not reveal this information to the agent when he applied for life insurance. James died three years after the policy was issued. Only then did the insurer learn about James's heart ailment. Explain the extent of Mutual Insurer's obligation, if any, with respect to payment of the death claim.

INTERNET EXERCISES

1. Each state has an insurance regulatory agency. Go to the Internet site of the National Association of Insurance Commissioners (NAIC) at:

   http://www.naic.org/

   Choose "Consumer and Regulatory Information" and then "Insurance Regulators." See if your state's regulatory agency is listed.

CASE APPLICATIONS

Case I

Shannon, age 35, is director of public relations at a local community college. She earns $40,000 annually. After attending a public lecture on death and dying, she decides to purchase additional life insurance so that her son, age 3, will not be financially insecure if she should die prematurely. Shannon does not know how much life insurance to purchase. She has the following financial goals:

Pay funeral expenses	$10,000
Pay off credit card debts and car loan	15,000
Pay off the mortgage on her home	110,000
Establish an educational fund for her son	100,000
Pay her sister who will be legal guardian for her son for 15 years	15,000

Shannon has $15,000 in a savings account at a local bank. She also owns an individual life insurance policy in the amount of $25,000 and is insured for $40,000 under the college's group life insurance plan. She participates in the college's retirement plan, and her retirement account has a current balance of $18,000. Estimated social security survivor benefits to her son are $7,000 annually. Based on the needs approach, how much additional life insurance, if any, should she purchase to attain her financial goals? (Assume that the rate of return earned on the policy proceeds is equal to the rate of inflation.)

Case II

Scott, age 28, and Brenda, age 25, are married and have a daughter, age 3. Scott has the following cash and income needs:

Cash needs

Estate clearance	$20,000
Mortgage redemption	90,000
Emergency fund	20,000
Education fund	50,000

Income needs

Readjustment period	$2,000 monthly
Dependency period	2,000 monthly
Blackout period	1,000 monthly

Brenda is now working outside the home. Her monthly net take-home pay is $1,500 after taxes and other deductions. She plans to continue working if Scott should die. Assuming that she can invest the life insurance proceeds at a rate of interest equal to the rate of inflation, answer the following questions:

1. How much additional life insurance, if any, is needed to meet Scott's cash needs if his present life insurance and financial assets total $100,000?

2. Ignoring the availability of social security survivor benefits, how much additional life insurance, if any, is needed to provide the desired amount of income during the readjustment and dependency periods?

3. How much additional life insurance, if any, is needed if social security survivor benefits of $500 monthly are paid to the child until age 18?

4. How much additional life insurance, if any, is needed to provide the desired amount of income during the blackout period if Brenda does not work outside the home?

Case III

Richard, age 32, is married and has one child, age 1. He needs additional life insurance to protect his family. He is considering purchasing one of the following policies:

Five-year renewable and convertible term
Decreasing term insurance
Ordinary life insurance
Universal life insurance
Variable universal life insurance

1. Which of these five policies will best meet Richard's financial objectives? Treat each objective separately.

   a. He can afford to spend only $250 on life insurance each year and would like to buy the policy with lowest annual premium outlay.

   b. He wants to invest the premiums in stocks, bonds, and other investments.

   c. He wants to save money for a down payment on a house.

   d. He wants to have the mortgage on his home paid off if he should die.

   e. He wants to accumulate a retirement fund to supplement social security retirement benefits.

2. Assume you are a financial planner. Recommend a specific life insurance policy or rider that will accomplish each of the following objectives. Treat each objective separately.

   a. Payment of federal estate taxes by a married couple when a surviving spouse dies.

   b. Funds to pay the cost of long-term care in a nursing facility.

   c. Protection against inflation to preserve the real purchasing power of the insurance protection.

   d. A policy that allows the insured to increase, reduce, or suspend premium payments.

   e. A policy that increases the face amount of insurance if the investment results are favorable.

SUGGESTIONS FOR ADDITIONAL READING

Belth, Joseph M. *Life Insurance: A Consumer's Handbook,* 2nd ed. Bloomington: Indiana University Press, 1985.

Black, Kenneth, Jr. and Harold D. Skipper, Jr. *Life Insurance,* 12th ed. Englewood Cliffs, N.J.: Prentice Hall, 1994.

Davis, Kristin. "Making Life Insurance Easier to Swallow," *Kiplinger's Personal Finance Magazine,* Vol. 47, No. 8 (August 1993), pp. 42–48.

Graves, Edward E., ed. *McGill's Life Insurance.* Bryn Mawr, Pa.: The American College, 1994.

Holson, Laura M. and Liz Comte Reisman. "Lessons in Life," *Smart Money,* Vol. III, No. XII (December 1994), pp. 130–139.

Longo, Tracey. "There Is No Free Insurance," *Kiplinger's Personal Finance Magazine,* Vol. 49, No. 10 (October 1995), pp. 97–101.

Rejda, George E. *Principles of Risk Management and Insurance,* 6th ed. Reading, MA.: Addison Wesley Longman, 1998. Chapters 15–19.

"When It's Time to Buy Life Insurance, How Much Coverage Do You Need?" *Consumer Reports,* Vol. 58 (July 1993), pp. 431–450. See also "Life Insurance, Part 2: Choosing a Universal Life Policy," *Consumer Reports,* Vol. 58 (August 1993), pp. 525–539.

NOTES

1. *The 1996 Annual Report of the Board of Trustees of the Federal Old-Age and Survivors Insurance and Disability Insurance Trust Funds* (Washington, D.C.: U.S. Government Printing Office, 1996), p. 61.

2. George E. Rejda, *Social Insurance and Economic Security,* 5th ed. (Englewood Cliffs, N.J.: Prentice-Hall, Inc., 1994), pp. 52-55.

3. U.S. Congress, House, Committee on Ways and Means, *Overview of Entitlement Programs, 1994 Green Book,* Background Material and Data on Programs Within the Jurisdiction of the Committee on Ways and Means (Washington, D.C.: U.S. Government Printing Office, 1994), p. 1159.

4. *1996 Life Insurance Fact Book Update* (Washington, D.C.: American Council of Life Insurance, 1996), p. 15.

5. Karen Slater, "Return on Universal Life Insurance Can Be a Lot Less Than Expected," *Wall Street Journal,* February 11, 1986.

6. *1996 Life Insurance Fact Book,* p. 17.

7. *Life Insurance: How to Buy the Right Policy from the Right Company at the Right Price* (Mount Vernon, N.Y. : Consumers Union, 1988), p. 69.

8. *1996 Life Insurance Fact Book Update,* p. 116.

9. *1996 Life Insurance Fact Book Update,* p. 67.

10. Andrew D. Gold, "Whole Life Policy Survey," *Best's Review, Life/Health* (April 1994), p. 38.

11. Joseph M. Belth, ed., "Financial Strength Ratings of Life-Health Insurance Companies," *The Insurance Forum ,* Vol. 20, No. 9-10 (September–October 1993), p. 165.

Chapter 10

Health Insurance

Learning Objectives

After studying this chapter, you should be able to:

- Explain the problem of health care in the United States.

- Describe the basic medical expense coverages.

- Explain the important characteristics of major medical insurance.

- Describe the major characteristics of individual disability income insurance.

- Identify the basic characteristics of long-term care insurance.

- Describe the following types of managed care plans: health maintenance organizations (HMOs) and preferred provider organizations (PPOs).

- Describe the basic characteristics of the Medicare and Medicaid programs.

- Explain the important rules that consumers should follow when purchasing health insurance.

Health nuts are going to feel stupid, lying in hospitals dying of nothing.

—Redd Foxx

They had me on the operating table all day. They looked into my stomach, my gall bladder, they examined everything inside of me. Know what they decided? I need glasses.

—Joe E. Lewis

Tim, age 32, is a self-employed carpenter who was diagnosed as having a brain tumor that required immediate surgery. The surgeon's fee, hospital expenses, and related bills totaled $102,000. He had no health insurance. In addition, he was off work for more than one year and did not have an individual or group disability income policy to restore his lost earnings. In short, Tim was exposed to serious financial insecurity because of his unexpected surgery. He eventually was forced to declare bankruptcy.

As Tim's experience demonstrates, health insurance should be given high priority in a personal insurance program. If you are seriously ill or injured, you face two major financial problems: payment of your medical bills and loss of earned income. A serious illness can result in catastrophic medical bills. Without proper protection, you may have to pay thousands of dollars out of your own pocket. In addition, an extended disability can result in the loss of thousands of dollars of earned income.

This chapter discusses the major individual and group health insurance coverages that insure the risk of poor health. These coverages include basic medical expense insurance, major medical insurance, dental insurance, disability income insurance, long-term care insurance, and managed care plans, such as health maintenance organizations (HMOs). The chapter also discusses certain government insurance programs, including Medicare and Medicaid, and concludes with a discussion of important rules to follow when purchasing health insurance.

The Problem of Health Care in the United States

Although the United States provides the highest-quality health care in the world and the health of Americans has improved remarkably, there is considerable dissatisfaction with the present health-care delivery system. The present system has four major problems:[1]

- Soaring health-care expenditures

- Inadequate access to medical care

- Uneven quality of medical care

- Waste and inefficiency

Soaring Health-Care Expenditures

Health-care expenditures in the United States have soared in recent years. The United States spends more on health care than any other nation in the world. *In 1995, national health expenditures totaled $989 billion, or 13.6 percent of the gross domestic product (see Exhibit 10.1). If pre-*

Exhibit 10.1

National Health Insurance Expenditures as a Percent of Gross Domestic Product

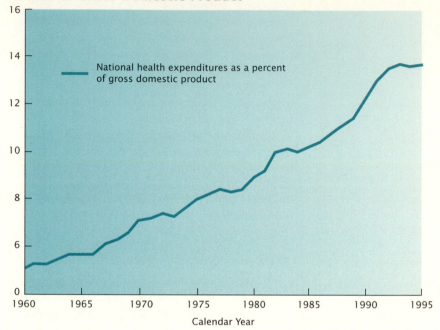

Source: Katharine R. Levit et al, "National Health Expenditures, 1995," *Health Care Financing Review,* 18 (Fall 1996): 176.

sent trends continue, by the year 2000, projected national health expenditures will total some $1.5 trillion, or about 16 percent of the gross domestic product (see Exhibit 10.1).[2]

Several factors help explain the rise in health-care expenditures. They include population growth that increases the demand for medical care, general price inflation, newer and more expensive medical technology, aging of the population, cost shifting by Medicare and Medicaid to private health insurers, and state-mandated health insurance benefits. The growth in private health insurance has also contributed to the problem because health insurance removes a financial barrier to care and increases the demand for medical care. Finally, the tax subsidy of health insurance has also contributed to the problem. Health insurance premiums paid by employers are income-tax deductible and not presently taxable to the employees. As a result, the tax subsidy has encouraged the growth of expensive group health insurance plans that employers and employees are more likely to use.

Inadequate Access to Medical Care

Certain groups have inadequate access to medical care. *First, millions of Americans have no health insurance.* In 1995, 40.3 million Americans, or

17.4 percent of the nonelderly population, had no private or public health insurance.[3] People likely to be uninsured include single adults under age 25, employees working for smaller firms that cannot afford to provide health insurance, African Americans and Hispanics, some unemployed persons, and poor families not covered by government health insurance programs.

Uneven Quality of Medical Care

In addition, the quality of medical care is uneven and varies widely depending on physician specialty and geographic location. For example, one study showed that residents in New Haven, Connecticut, are twice as likely to undergo coronary artery bypass surgery as residents in Boston, Massachusetts.[4] The increase in medical malpractice suits is another indication that some physicians provide low-quality care.

Waste and Inefficiency

The present system also has considerable waste and inefficiency. There is excessive paperwork by both health-care providers and insurers; claim forms are not uniform; some medical care that physicians provide is considered inappropriate; there is duplication of expensive technology in many areas; the practice of defensive medicine by physicians results in unnecessary tests and procedures; and fraud and abuse by health-care providers are widespread.

As you can see, the health-care problem in the United States is complex. To deal with the risk of poor health, most individuals and families are insured under private health insurance plans. In the following section, we discuss the major types of private health insurance coverages sold today.

Types of Private Health Insurance Coverages

Private health insurers sell both individual and group coverages that reimburse insureds for covered medical expenses. Because most people today are insured under some type of group medical expense plan, our discussion will center primarily on group health insurance coverages. Although individual medical expense plans are still being sold, they are relatively unimportant in terms of the total volume of business. Group health insurance premiums currently account for more than 90 percent of all health insurance premiums paid.

Insurers sell numerous individual and group health insurance plans. The most important coverages include the following:

■ Basic medical expense coverages

■ Major medical insurance

■ Dental insurance

■ Disability income insurance

■ Long-term care insurance

Basic Medical Expense Coverages

Many individual and group medical expense plans provide only basic protection. Basic plans cover routine medical expenses and generally are not designed to cover a catastrophic loss. Basic plans typically include coverage for hospital expenses, surgical expenses, physicians' visits, and certain other expenses.

hospital expense insurance Insurance that pays for medical expenses the insured incurs while in a hospital.

Hospital Expense Insurance. Hospital expense insurance pays for medical expenses incurred while in a hospital. A typical hospital policy provides benefits for (1) daily room-and-board charges and (2) miscellaneous services and supplies provided during the hospital confinement.

indemnity plan An approach by which hospital expense insurance pays for hospital room-and-board charges; actual room-and-board charges are paid up to some maximum daily limit.

There are two basic approaches for paying room-and-board charges. Under an **indemnity plan,** actual room-and-board charges are paid up to some maximum daily limit, such as up to $400 daily for 120 days. Under a plan that provides **service benefits,** the full cost of a semiprivate room is paid up to a maximum number of days.

service benefits An approach by which hospital expense insurance pays for hospital room-and-board charges; the full cost of a semiprivate room is paid up to a maximum number of days.

Hospital expense plans also cover miscellaneous hospital charges, such as x-rays, drugs, laboratory fees, and other ancillary charges. Depending on the plan, part or all of the miscellaneous expenses are paid up to some maximum limit.

surgical expense insurance Insurance that pays physicians' fees for surgery.

Surgical Expense Insurance. Medical expense plans typically include benefits for surgery. **Surgical expense insurance** pays physicians' fees for surgical operations. Several methods are used to compensate surgeons. Under the older *schedule approach,* the various surgical operations are listed in a schedule, and a maximum dollar amount is paid for each procedure, such as $400 for an appendectomy and $2,000 for a valve replacement in the heart. A variation of the schedule approach is a *relative-value schedule,* in which units or points are attached to each operation based on the degree of difficulty. A conversion factor is then used to convert the relative value of the operation into a dollar amount that is paid to the physician. One advantage of a relative-value schedule is that it can be adapted to differences in the cost of living and in surgeons' fees in different geographic areas.

usual, reasonable, and customary charges An approach by which medical expense plans reimburse physicians; reimbursement is based on the physician's usual fee as long as the fee is considered reasonable and customary.

Most newer medical expense plans reimburse physicians based on their **usual, reasonable, and customary charges.** Under this approach, a physician is reimbursed his or her usual fee as long as it is considered reasonable and customary. Many insurers consider a fee to be reasonable and customary if it does not exceed the 90th percentile for a similar medical procedure performed by other physicians in the same area. The insured must pay that part of the fee that exceeds the upper limit. However, insurers differ in how they calculate usual and customary fees. As a result, some insureds may have to pay substantial amounts out-of-pocket because insurers consider provider fees and charges to be excessive.

physicians' visits insurance Insurance that pays a benefit for nonsurgical care by an attending physician other than a surgeon.

Physicians' Visits Insurance. **Physicians' visits insurance** pays a benefit for *nonsurgical care* by an attending physician other than a surgeon. The coverage usually applies to physician visits while the patient is in the hospital, but some plans cover office and home visits as well. The amount paid can be a fixed amount, or it can be based on the physician's reasonable and customary charges.

Other Benefits. In addition to the previous benefits, newer basic medical expense plans provide a wide variety of additional benefits. Many plans cover *outpatient surgery,* by which surgery is performed in the hospital or physician's office, and the patient recovers at home. Many plans also cover *preadmission testing,* by which diagnostic tests are given to a patient prior to admission into a hospital. In addition, some hospital patients who have not recovered completely may still require medical care before they are discharged. Many plans provide *extended care facility benefits,* in which hospital patients receive care at an extended-care facility, such as a skilled nursing facility or convalescent nursing home. Finally, some of these plans cover *home health visits,* such as care provided by a registered nurse or physical, occupational, or speech therapist.

Major Medical Insurance

major medical insurance An insurance plan that pays a large proportion of the covered expenses of a catastrophic illness or injury.

Consumers often desire broader and more comprehensive protection than that provided by the basic medical expenses coverages. **Major medical insurance** is a plan that pays a large proportion of the covered expenses of a catastrophic illness or injury. Both individual and group major medical plans are sold today, but most people are insured under a group plan.

Basic Characteristics. Major medical insurance plans have several generic characteristics.

■ *Broad coverage.* There is broad coverage of all reasonable and necessary medical expenses and other related expenses from a covered illness or injury. Eligible medical expenses include hospital room-and-board charges, miscellaneous hospital services and supplies, treatment by licensed physicians, prescription drugs, artificial limbs and eyes, durable medical equipment, and numerous other expenses.

■ *High limits.* Major medical plans are commonly written with limits of $250,000, $500,000, $1 million, or even higher amounts. A few plans have no maximum limit. In most plans, the maximum amount paid is a life-time limit. High limits are necessary to meet the crushing financial burden of a major catastrophic illness or injury.

■ *Deductible.* A deductible must be satisfied before benefits are paid. The deductible is designed to eliminate small claims so that catastrophic expenses can be paid. Although major medical plans use different deductibles, a calendar-year deductible is widely used. Under a **calendar-year deductible,** the deductible has to be met only once during the calendar year. All covered medical expenses incurred during the calendar year can be applied toward the deductible. Once the deductible is met, no additional deductible has to be satisfied during the calendar year.

calendar-year deductible
Amount payable by an insured during a calendar year before a group or individual health insurance policy begins to pay for medical expenses.

■ *Coinsurance.* Major medical plans contain a coinsurance provision. The **coinsurance** provision requires the insured to pay a certain percentage of the eligible medical expenses in excess of the deductible. The purposes are to reduce premiums and prevent overutilization of policy benefits by requiring the insured to pay part of the cost. A typical plan requires the insured to pay 20 or 25 percent of covered expenses in excess of the deductible. For example, Jennifer has a $1 million major medical policy with a $500 calendar-year deductible and a coinsurance percentage of 80 percent. If she incurs covered medical expenses of $10,500, the insurer will pay $8,000, and she will pay $2,000 (plus the deductible). This settlement is summarized as follows:

coinsurance A provision in a health insurance policy that requires the insured to pay a certain percentage of the eligible medical expenses in excess of the deductible.

Covered expenses	$10,500
Less the deductible	− 500
Remaining expenses	10,000
80 percent paid by the insurer	8,000
20 percent paid by the insured	2,000

The coinsurance provision is usually modified by a stop-loss limit, which places a dollar limit on the maximum amount that the insured must pay. Under a **stop-loss limit,** once out-of-pocket expenses exceed a certain amount, such as $2,000, all remaining covered medical expenses are paid in full. The purpose is to reduce the financial burden of a catastrophic loss. Referring to our earlier example, assume that Jennifer is severely injured in an auto accident and incurs covered medical expenses of $100,500, and that the stop-loss limit is $2,000. In the absence of such a provision, she would have to pay $20,000 out of pocket (plus the

stop-loss limit A provision in a health insurance policy by which, once the insured's out-of-pocket expenses exceed a certain amount, all remaining covered medical expenses are paid in full.

deductible), which would be a heavy financial burden and defeat the purpose of major medical insurance. However, because of the stop-loss limit, she would pay only $2,000 out of pocket (plus the deductible).

■ *Exclusions.* major medical plans contain certain exclusions. Common exclusions include elective cosmetic surgery, routine physical examinations, dental care except as a result of an accident, eye glasses and hearing aids, expenses covered by a workers compensation law, services furnished by governmental agencies unless the patient has an obligation to pay, and experimental surgery.

internal limit The maximum amount an insurer will pay for certain covered services.

In addition to the preceding exclusions, major medical plans contain certain internal limits to control cost. An **internal limit** is the maximum amount an insurer will pay for certain covered services. For example, there may be a limit on the maximum daily amount paid for a semiprivate room. There may also be limits on the amounts paid for alcoholism and drug addiction. For example, inpatient treatment in an alcohol or drug rehabilitation program may be limited to 30 days each year. Finally, the plan may not pay for any expense in excess of reasonable and customary charges.

comprehensive major medical insurance A combination of basic health plan benefits and major medical insurance in one policy.

Comprehensive Major Medical Insurance. Comprehensive major medical insurance is a combination of basic plan benefits and major medical insurance in one policy. This type of plan is widely used today and is designed for insureds who want both basic benefits and major medical protection in a single policy. Comprehensive major medical insurance is typically characterized by a calendar-year deductible, such as $200 or $250 per year, high maximum limits of $250,000 to $1 million, and coinsurance. In addition, in many plans, the deductible and coinsurance provisions are not applied to certain medical expenses. For example, in one plan, the deductible does not apply to hospital expenses. The first $3,000 of covered hospital expenses are paid in full, and a coinsurance rate of 80 percent is applied to the remaining hospital expenses.

Important Contractual Provisions. Major medical insurance contains several important contractual provisions that can have a significant financial impact on the insured.

preexisting condition A medical condition diagnosed or treated during the six months prior to the effective date of coverage of a group health insurance plan.

■ *Preexisting conditions.* Major medical insurance plans and other health insurance plans usually contain a preexisting conditions clause that excludes coverage for a medical condition for a limited period after entry into the plan. The new Health Insurance Portability and Accountability Act of 1996 places limitations on the right of employers and insurers to exclude or limit coverage for a preexisting condition under group plans. A **preexisting condition** is defined as a medical condition diagnosed or treated during the previous six months prior to the effective date of coverage. Under the new law, group health insurance plans cannot impose a waiting period for a preexisting condition for more than 12 months (18 months for late enrollees). Once the 12-month period expires, no new preexisting conditions period can ever be imposed on workers who maintain continuous coverage (without a gap of 63 days) even if they should change jobs or group health insurance plans. The new law also requires employers and health insurers to give credit for previous coverage under a group plan. For example, a worker previously covered under a group plan for nine months when he or she changes jobs would face a maximum additional exclusion of only three months for a preexisting condition. In addition, a preexisting conditions limitation cannot be applied to pregnancy, newly born children, or adopted children.

■ *Coordination of benefits.* Group insurance plans typically contain a **coordination-of-benefits provision,** which specifies the order of payment when an individual is covered under two group health insurance plans. The purpose is to prevent overinsurance and duplication of benefits if a person is covered by more than one plan.

coordination-of-benefits provision A provision in a group health insurance plan that specifies the order of payment when an individual is covered under two group health insurance plans.

Most states have adopted part or all of the coordination-of-benefit provisions developed by the National Association of Insurance Commissioners (NAIC). *The rules are complex and beyond the scope of the text to discuss in detail. Only the major provisions are discussed here. Under these rules, the plan covering an active employee usually pays first; the other plan pays second.* For example, Karen and Richard Swift both work, and each is insured as a dependent under the other's group health insurance plan. If Karen incurs covered medical expenses, her policy pays first. She then submits her unreimbursed expenses (such as the deductible and coinsurance payments) to Richard's insurer for payment. No more than 100 percent of the eligible medical expenses are paid under both plans.

With respect to dependent children, the plan of the parent whose birthday occurs first during the year pays first; the other plan pays second. For example, if Karen's birthday is in January and Richard's birthday is in July, Karen's plan would pay first if her daughter is hospitalized. Richard's plan would be secondary.

■ *Continuation of group health insurance.* Employees often quit their jobs, are laid off, or are fired. Employees who lose their jobs, or whose dependents are no longer eligible for coverage under an employer's plan, can keep their group insurance for up to 18 months. Under the Consolidated Omnibus Budget Reconciliation Act of 1985 (also known as COBRA), group health insurance plans in companies with 20 or more employees must allow terminated employees and their dependents to continue their group health insurance protection for up to 18 months. However, the former employee must pay 102 percent of the group rate. In addition, under the COBRA law, if the employee dies or is divorced, the employee's family has the right to continue the group coverage for up to three years.

Dental Insurance

Dental insurance is an important coverage that is sold on both an individual and a group basis. Most people, however, are covered under group plans. There are two basic types of plans. Under a **comprehensive dental insurance** plan, most dental services are covered, including oral examinations, x-rays, cleaning, fillings, extractions, orthodontia, and dentures. Under this approach, dentists are reimbursed on the basis of their reasonable and customary charges subject to any limitations on benefits stated in the plan.

comprehensive dental insurance An insurance plan that covers most dental services.

Under a **schedule approach,** the various dental services are listed in a schedule, and a specific dollar amount is paid for each service. If the dentist charges more than the specified amount, the patient must pay the difference.

schedule approach An insurance plan in which specific dollar amounts are paid for each dental service.

Insurers use a number of techniques to control costs. The patient must pay an annual deductible, such as $25 or $50, and meet a coinsurance requirement, such as 20 percent. To encourage regular visits to the dentist, many plans do not impose any coinsurance requirements for one or two routine dental examinations. In addition, insurers use maximum limits on benefits to control costs, such as $2,000 during the calendar year. Exclusions are also used, including cosmetic dental work, lost dentures, and benefits provided under a workers compensation law. Finally, many insurers use a **predetermination-of-benefits provision.** Under this provision, if the cost of treatment exceeds a certain amount, such as $200, the dentist submits a plan of treatment to the insurer. The insurer then specifies the services that are covered and the amount the plan will play.

predetermination of benefits provision A provision, widely used in dental insurance policies, under which the provider submits a plan of treatment to the insurer when the cost of treatment exceeds a certain amount.

Disability Income Insurance

Disability income insurance provides periodic income payments when the insured is unable to work because of sickness or injury. As a result, disabled workers can maintain their financial security during a period of disability.

disability income insurance Insurance that provides periodic income payments to the insured when he or she is unable to work because of sickness or injury.

Many workers seldom think about the financial consequences of a severe disability. However, the probability of becoming disabled before age 65 is much higher than is commonly believed, especially at the younger ages. As we noted in Chapter 8, *the probability that a person age 25 will become totally disabled for at least 90 days prior to age 65 is 54 percent.* Some workers may become totally and permanently disabled prior to retirement. In such cases, there is the loss of earned income, medical bills are being incurred, employee benefits may be lost, savings are depleted, and someone must care for the disabled person. Clearly, disability income insurance should be a high-priority item in the development of a sound health insurance plan.

Disability income insurance is available from a number of sources, including the following:

- Individual disability income insurance
- Group disability income insurance
- Social security disability income benefits
- Workers compensation insurance

Individual Disability Income Insurance

An individual policy pays monthly income benefits to an insured who becomes totally disabled from a sickness or accident. The amount of disability income insurance you can buy is related to your earnings. To prevent overinsurance, most insurers generally limit the amount of disability income to no more than 60 to 80 percent of your gross earnings.

Meaning of Total Disability. The most important policy provision in a disability income policy is the meaning of total disability. Most policies require the worker to be totally disabled to receive benefits.

The definition of total disability varies among insurers. The most liberal definition defines total disability in terms of your own occupation. **Total disability** *is the complete inability of the insured to perform each and every duty of his or her own occupation.* An example would be a surgeon whose hand is blown off in a hunting accident. The surgeon could no longer perform surgery and would be totally disabled under this definition.

The second definition is more restrictive. *In this case, total disability is the complete inability to perform the duties of any occupation for which the insured is reasonably fitted by education, training, and experience.* Thus, if the surgeon who lost a hand in a hunting accident could get a job as a professor in a medical school or as a research scientist, he or she would not be considered disabled because these occupations are consistent with the surgeon's training and experience.

The third definition is the most restrictive and is commonly used for hazardous occupations where a disability is likely to occur. *Total disability is defined as the inability to perform the duties of any gainful occupa-*

total disability As defined by insurers, (1) the complete inability of the insured to perform each and every duty of his or her own occupation; or (2) the complete inability of the insured to perform the duties of any occupation for which he or she is reasonably fitted by education, training, and experience; or (3) the inability of the insured to perform the duties of any gainful occupation. Many insurers use a combined definition whereby the first definition applies for an initial period, after which the second definition applies.

tion. Strict application of this definition would make the disability income policy worthless because the insured could sell pencils and apples even if requiring the assistance of a wheelchair. The courts have wisely intervened and generally have interpreted this definition to mean that the person is totally disabled if he or she cannot work in any gainful occupation reasonably fitted by education, training, and experience.

Many insurers now combine the first two definitions. *For the initial period of disability—typically, one to five years—total disability is defined in terms of the insured's own occupation. After the initial period of disability expires, the second definition is applied.* For example, Dr. Myron Pudwill is a dentist who can no longer practice because of arthritis in his hands. For the first two years, he would be considered totally disabled. However, after two years, if he could work as a dental supply representative or even as a professor in a dental school, he would no longer be considered disabled because he is reasonably fitted for these occupations by his education and training.

Finally, the policy may contain a definition of *presumptive disability.* It is presumed a total disability exists if the insured suffers the total and irrecoverable loss of the sight of both eyes, or the total loss or use of both hands, both feet, or one hand and one foot.

Residual Disability Benefit. Many disability income plans also contain a residual disability benefit or make it available as an optional benefit. A **residual disability benefit** pays a pro rata disability income benefit to an insured who returns to work but has a reduction in earnings. Most plans require an earnings reduction of at least 20 or 25 percent before a partial benefit is paid.

residual disability benefit A pro rata disability income benefit paid to an insured who returns to work but has a reduction in earnings.

The major advantage of a residual disability benefit is the payment of a partial benefit to the insured who returns to work but has reduced earnings. For example, Michelle is a dental supply salesperson who earns an average of $4,000 monthly. She is seriously injured in an auto accident. When she returns to work, her earnings are only $3,000 monthly, or a reduction of 25 percent. If she has a disability income policy that pays a monthly benefit of $2,000, she would receive a monthly residual benefit of $500, and her total income would be $3500.

Elimination Period. Most individual policies are written with an **elimination period,** a waiting period during which time benefits are not paid. Insurers typically offer a range of elimination periods, such as 30, 60, 90, 180, or 365 days. Most insurers have stopped offering elimination periods that are shorter than 14 days, and elimination periods of 30 or more days are now the rule.

elimination period A waiting period during which benefits are not paid.

To make disability income insurance more affordable, some insurers sell policies with initially lower rates that gradually increase with age. This approach is similar to term life insurance rates that increase as the insured gets older.

Insight

10.1 Buying Individual Disability Coverage Is Best Policy

Sales of disability insurance policies to individuals have been increasing at a double-digit rate for the past several years. Not only are the self-employed buying policies, but many people covered by an employer's plan are supplementing it.

"Although it is more expensive, individual disability insurance is the only way to make sure you will have dis-ability insurance throughout your working life," says Ms. Virginia Applegarth, a Boston financial planner. She learned the value of disability insur-ance when a serious back injury left her bedridden for five years. Her recommenda-tion: Get as much disability insurance as you can while you can get it.

But before you start shop-ping, take note. The policies can be difficult to understand, and they are expensive--costing 2% to 3% of your annual income or more.

Moreover, not everyone can get disability insurance. *If you work part time, have just set up a new business, have a heart condition or are a construction worker, you may find such poli-cies are prohibitively expensive, if available at all.*

Expensive, If You Can Get It

Typical yearly cost of a noncancelable, annually renewable individual disability policy for a 40-year-old who earns $60,000 a year and wants to be able to replace 60% of lost income to age 65. Premiums include "own-occupation" coverage, which pays benefits if the insured is unable to engage in his or her own occupation.

Profession	Benefits Start After			Partial Disability	Cost-of-Living Adjustment
	90 Days	180 Days	One Year		
Executive	$1,092	$973	$862	Add $172–$231	Add $252
Computer programmer	1,281	1,141	1,010	Add $205–$272	Add $321
Carpenter*	1,429	1,265	1,129	NA	Add $399
Part-time editor†	NA	NA	NA	NA	NA

* Can buy coverage for only five years and then only for $2,400 a month.
† No coverage generally available for people working fewer than 26–30 hours a week.
NA = No coverage available

Source: Adapted from Lynn Asinof, "Buying Individual Disability Coverage Is Best Policy," April 20, 1993. Reprinted by permission of *The Wall Street Journal*, © 1993 Dow Jones & Company, Inc. All Rights Reserved Worldwide.

High-quality disability income policies are expensive and can cost as much as 2 to 3 percent of your annual earnings. However, increasing the elimination period from 30 to 90 days can substantially reduce the pre-miums. For example, in one plan, a male accountant who purchases a monthly benefit of $4,250 to age 65 would pay $4,036 annually for a policy with a 30-day elimination period. However, if he elects a 90-day elimination period, the annual premium would be about $1,888, or 53 percent less. The majority of employers have sick leave or short-term disability plans that would provide some income during the longer elimination period. One disadvantage, however, is that a group disability income plan normally cannot be converted into an individual policy if the worker is no longer employed. Thus, group insurance is not a satisfactory substitute for a high-quality disability income policy (see Insight 10.1).

Benefit Period. The benefit period is the length of time that disability benefits are payable after the elimination period is met. The insured has a choice of benefit periods, such as 2, 5, or 10 years, or up to age 65.

Most disabilities are short-term. About 98 percent of all disability claimants recover within the first year of disability.[5] However, this does not mean that a one-year benefit period is adequate. The longer the disability lasts, the less likely the disabled person will recover. For example, a person who became disabled at age 22 and remains disabled for one year has a 32 percent chance of remaining disabled for at least five more years.[6] Thus, because of uncertainty concerning the duration of disability, you should elect a longer benefit period—ideally, one that pays benefits to age 65.

Renewability Provisions. The renewability provisions refer to the length of time an individual disability income policy can remain in force. Two important renewal provisions are (1) guaranteed renewable and (2) noncancelable.

Most policies sold currently are guaranteed renewable. A **guaranteed renewable policy** is one that cannot be canceled, and the insurer guarantees to renew the policy to some stated age, such as age 65. However, the insurer has the right to increase the premiums for the underwriting class in which the insured is placed.

A **noncancellable policy** is one that cannot be cancelled, and the insurer agrees to renew the policy to some stated age. In addition, the premiums are guaranteed and cannot be increased. Because premiums cannot be increased, a noncancellable policy costs substantially more than a guaranteed renewable policy.

Waiver of Premium. A **waiver-of-premium** provision is built into the policy, which states that if the insured is totally disabled for 90 days, future premiums will be waived as long as the insured remains disabled. In addition, there is a refund of the premiums paid during the initial 90-day period. If the insured recovers from the disability, premium payments must be resumed.

Optional Benefits. Several optional benefits can be added to a disability income policy. They include the following:

guaranteed renewable policy A policy that cannot be canceled and is renewable to some stated age; the insurer has the right to increase the premiums for the underwriting class.

noncancellable policy A policy that cannot be cancelled and is renewable to some stated age; the insurer cannot increase the premiums as stated in the policy.

waiver of premium A provision in a disability income policy stating that if the insured is totally disabled for 90 days, future premiums will be waived as long as the insured remains disabled.

■ *Cost-of-living rider.* Under this option, the disability benefits are periodically increased for inflation based on the Consumer Price Index. The option is expensive and can increase the basic premium by 25 to 50 percent.

■ *Option to purchase additional insurance.* Your income may increase, and you may need additional disability benefits. Under this option, the insured has the right to purchase additional disability income insurance at specified times in the future with no evidence of insurability.

■ *Return of premium.* This rider refunds a specified percentage of the premium less any claims paid. For example, in one plan, after 10 years, 80 percent of the premium less claims paid is refunded to the insured. This rider is controversial and has little to recommend it. Disability income insurance is designed to provide income protection and should not be viewed as cash-value life insurance. The rider is expensive and can increase premiums by 30 to 100 percent.

Group Disability Income Insurance

Disabled workers may also be eligible for disability income benefits under a group plan. Group disability income plans pay weekly or monthly cash payments to employees who become disabled from accidents or sickness. There are two basic types of plans: short-term plans and long-term plans.

Short-Term Plans. Many employers provide short-term disability benefits to their employees, which pay benefits for short periods ranging from 13 weeks to 2 years. The majority of short-term plans today pay benefits for a maximum period of 26 weeks. In addition, short-term plans usually have a brief elimination period of one to seven days for sickness, whereas accidents are covered from the first day of disability. The elimination period reduces nuisance claims, holds down cost, and discourages malingering and excessive absenteeism.

Most short-term plans cover only *nonoccupational disability,* which means that sickness and accidents must occur off the job. Disability is usually defined in terms of your own occupation. You are totally disabled if you are unable to perform all the duties of your own occupation.

The amount of the disability income benefit is usually a specified percentage of weekly earnings, such as 50 to 70 percent. There is also a maximum limit on the weekly benefit paid regardless of earnings. For example, the plan may pay a weekly benefit of 70 percent of earnings up to $280. Thus, if Megan's weekly earnings are $400, she could collect a maximum weekly benefit of $280.

Short-term plans have few exclusions. As we noted, a disability that occurs on the job is not covered because occupational disability is covered under a workers compensation law (discussed later). Moreover, except for very small groups, preexisting conditions are immediately covered. Most plans also cover alcoholism, drug addiction, and nervous and mental disorders.

Long-Term Plans. Many employers also provide long-term plans that pay benefits for longer periods, typically ranging from two years to age 65. However, for workers who become disabled beyond age 65, the benefits are paid for a limited duration. For example, based on the plan of one insurer, a worker disabled at age 60 would be paid benefits to age 65. A worker disabled at age 66, however, would be paid benefits for only 21 months.

In contrast to short-term plans, long-term plans cover both occupational and nonoccupational disability. *A dual definition of disability is commonly used to determine if the worker is disabled. For the first two years, you are considered disabled if you are unable to perform all the duties of your occupation. After two years, you are still considered disabled if you are unable to work in any occupation for which you are reasonably fitted by training, education, and experience.*

The monthly benefits are substantially higher than those offered under short-term plans. Maximum monthly benefits are usually limited to 50 to 66 2/3 percent of your normal earnings. Many larger plans pay maximum monthly benefits of $4,000, $5,000, or more. An elimination period of three to six months is required before the benefits are paid.

The long-term benefit is reduced if the disabled worker is also receiving social security disability benefits or workers compensation benefits. The purpose of the reduction is to prevent overinsurance and malingering.

Some plans also have a *cost-of-living adjustment* by which the benefits paid are periodically adjusted for increases in the cost of living. The plan may also provide a *pension accrual benefit* by which the insurer makes a pension contribution so that the disabled worker's pension benefit remains intact.

Social Security Disability Income Benefits

Disabled workers may also be eligible for disability income benefits under the social security program. The eligibility requirements are strict. There are three major eligibility requirements.

First, you must satisfy the work requirements. You need a certain number of credits (also called quarters of coverage) to qualify for benefits. For 1997, you earn one credit for each $670 of earnings in covered employment. You can earn a maximum of four credits annually. Exhibit 10.2 shows the number of required credits for workers age 31 and older. At least 20 of the credits must be earned during the past ten years immediately before you became disabled.

Special rules, however, apply to younger workers who can qualify with fewer credits. If you are disabled before age 24, you must have earned six credits in the three-year period ending when your disability starts. For ages 24 through 30, you must have worked half the time between age 21 and the time you become disabled. For example, if you are disabled at age 27, you would need credit for only three years of work out of the past six years.

Second, you must meet a five-month waiting period. Benefits are payable after a waiting period of five full calendar months, which eliminates a large number of short-term disabilities.

Third, you must satisfy the definition of disability. The social security disability program uses a strict definition of disability. *You must have a physical or mental condition that prevents you from doing any substantial gainful work in the national economy and that is expected to last (or has lasted) at least 12 months or is expected to result in death.* If you cannot work at your own occupation but can engage in other substantial gainful work, the disability claim will not be allowed.

Exhibit 10.3 shows the approximate monthly disability benefits for workers who became disabled in 1995. Benefits can also be paid to unmar-

---

Exhibit 10.2

Number of Work Credits Needed to Qualify for Social Security Disability Benefits

Born After 1929, Become Disabled at Age	Credits You Need
31 through 42	20
44	22
46	24
48	26
50	28
52	30
54	32
56	34
58	36
60	38
62 or older	40

Note: In 1997, workers received one credit for each $670 of earnings in covered employment. A maximum of four credits can be earned each year.

Source: Social Security Administration.

Exhibit 10.3

Examples of Monthly Social Security Disability Benefits

Approximate Monthly Benefits If You Become Disabled In 1995 And Had Steady Earnings

Your Age	Your Family	Your Earnings In 1994				
		$20,000	$30,000	$40,000	$50,000	$60,000 or More*
25	You	$771	$1,033	$1,174	$1,297	$1,409
	You, your spouse, and child[†]	1,156	1,549	1,762	1,946	2,113
35	You	768	1,028	1,171	1,293	1,383
	You, your spouse, and child[†]	1,152	1,542	1,757	1,940	2,075
45	You	767	1,027	1,170	1,271	1,329
	You, your spouse, and child[†]	1,151	1,541	1,756	1,906	1,993
55	You	767	1,027	1,143	1,211	1,251
	You, your spouse, and child[†]	1,150	1,540	1,715	1,817	1,876
64	You	764	1,017	1,117	1,171	1,203
	You, your spouse, and child[†]	1,147	1,526	1,675	1,757	1,805

*Use this column if you earn more than the maximum social security earnings base.
[†]Equals the maximum family benefit.

Note: The accuracy of these estimates depends on the pattern of your actual past earnings. Your benefit probably will be higher because these estimates are shown in today's dollars.

Source: Social Security Administration.

ried dependent children until age 18 and to a spouse of a disabled worker until the youngest child reaches age 16. Social security disability benefits, however, are difficult to get. More than half the initial claims for disability benefits are denied because the claimants cannot meet the harsh eligibility requirements or satisfy the definition of disability. Thus, because of the uncertainty in qualifying for benefits, you should not rely on social security disability benefits as your major source of protection. You also need a high-quality individual disability income policy.

Workers Compensation Insurance

workers compensation laws State laws that require covered employers to provide workers compensation benefits to employees who have job-related accidents or diseases.

All states have **workers compensation laws** that require covered employers to provide workers compensation benefits to employees who have a job-related accident or disease. Under a workers compensation law, the employer is held *absolutely liable* for the occupational injury or disease suffered by the workers, regardless of who is at fault. Disabled workers are paid for their injuries according to a schedule of benefits established by law. They are not required to sue their employers to receive benefits.

Eligibility Requirements. The worker who has a job-related accident or disease must meet two major eligibility requirements. First, he or she must work in an occupation covered by workers compensation. Today, a workers compensation law covers most occupations. Second, the worker must have a job-related accident or disease. *This means the injury or disease must arise out of and in the course of employment.* If the disability is not job related, it would not be covered.

Types of Benefits. Workers compensation laws provide four major benefits:

- Unlimited medical care

- Disability income benefits

- Death benefits

- Rehabilitation services

Medical care is covered in full in virtually all states. The disabled worker is usually not required to pay a deductible or meet a coinsurance requirement.

Weekly disability income benefits are paid after the disabled worker meets a short waiting period that typically ranges from three to seven days. The weekly benefit is based on a percentage of the disabled worker's average weekly wage, typically 66 2/3 percent, and the degree of disability. Most states have minimum and maximum dollar limits on weekly benefits. For example, a worker in Nebraska may break a leg and be totally disabled for three months. After a one-week waiting period, he or she would receive a maximum weekly benefit of $427 during the period of disability.

Death benefits are also paid if the worker dies as a result of a job-related accident or disease. A burial allowance is paid up to some maximum limit. Weekly income benefits are also payable to eligible surviving dependents, such as a surviving spouse and dependent children.

Finally, all states provide rehabilitation services to help injured workers return to work. Workers undergoing rehabilitation are compensated for room and board, travel, books, and equipment. Some states also pay training allowances.

Exhibit 10.4 contains a convenient worksheet that will help you determine if you have adequate disability income insurance. If you are covered under a group plan you can contact your employee benefits office to get an estimate of the disability benefits paid by your company. By contacting the Social Security Administration (phone 800-772-1213) and asking for a *Request for Earnings and Benefit Estimate Statement,* you can obtain an estimate of your social security disability benefits. After filling out the form, you will receive an estimate of your retirement, survivor, and disability benefits.

Exhibit 10.4

How Much Disability Income Insurance Do You Need?

1. Estimated monthly expenses

Mortgage/rent _____

Utilities _____

Miscellaneous home expenses _____

Loan payments _____

Food _____

Clothing _____

Insurance payments/expenses _____

Medical and dental expenses _____

Miscellaneous (vacation, entertainment, etc.) _____

Education _____

Transportation _____

Total _____

3. Existing benefits

Social security/workers compensation _____

Other government insurance _____

Group disability income insurance _____

Individual disability income insurance _____

Total _____

4. The amount of disability insurance you need

If the total from 3 is greater than the total from 2, you probably have adequate coverage. But if the total from 3 is less than the total in 2, subtract total 3 from total 2. This is the amount of additional monthly coverage you need.

2. Estimated monthly income

If you are single:

Current monthly take-home pay _____

Subtract investment income _____

Total _____

If you are married*

Current monthly take-home pay _____

Subtract investment income _____

Subtract spouse's pay _____

Total _____

5. How many months can you afford to live without your salary?

Amount from savings accounts that you would feel comfortable spending

_____   =   The number of months you can get by without long-term disability coverage

Total expenses—short-term disability benefits provided by your employer

*This worksheet should be completed for each spouse.

Source: G. E. Rejda, *Principles of Risk Management & Insurance* 5/E (table 20.2, p. 426). © 1995 HarperCollins College Publishers. Reprinted by permission of Addison Wesley Longman, Inc.

Long-Term Care Insurance

long-term care insurance
Insurance that pays a daily or monthly benefit for medical or custodial care received in a nursing facility or hospital or at home.

Long-term care insurance is another coverage that is rapidly growing in popularity. **Long-term care insurance** pays a daily or monthly benefit for medical or custodial care received in a nursing facility, hospital, or at home.

Chance of Entering a Nursing Home

Many older Americans will spend some time in a nursing home. One study projects that 43 percent of the people who attained age 65 in 1990 will enter a nursing home sometime during their lifetime. Among all persons who live to age 65, about 1 in 3 will spend three months or more in a nursing home; about 1 in 4 will spend one year or more in a nursing home; and about 1 in 11 will spend five years or more in a nursing home. Stated differently, two of three people who attained age 65 in 1990 will either never enter a nursing home or reside there for less than three months.[7]

The cost of long-term care in a nursing home is staggering. Many long-term facilities charge $40,000 or more annually (see Exhibit 10.5). The Medicare program does not cover long-term care. In addition, most elderly are not initially eligible for long-term care under the Medicaid program, a welfare program that imposes strict eligibility requirements and a stringent means test. As a result, many older Americans have purchased long-term care policies to meet the crushing financial burden of an extended stay in a nursing facility.

Basic Characteristics

More than 130 insurers sell long-term care policies. Newer policies sold today generally have certain generic characteristics.

Type of Care Provided. The policies typically cover skilled nursing care, intermediate nursing care, and custodial care. *Skilled nursing care* is medical care provided by skilled medical personnel 24 hours a day under the supervision of a physician, such as care provided by a registered nurse or physical therapist. *Intermediate nursing care* is medical care for a stable condition that requires daily but not continuous 24-hour nursing supervision. The care is ordered by a physician and is supervised by registered nurses. It is less specialized than skilled nursing care and often involves more personal care. *Custodial care* is care that helps the patient with daily living activities, such as bathing, eating, dressing, and using the toilet.

Many policies also cover home health care. Some plans cover only skilled nursing care provided in the home by registered nurses; licensed

---

Exhibit 10.5

How Much Does Long-Term Care Cost?

This graph assumes an average of $100 per day in nursing home costs and an average of $240 per week in home care costs. You can see the enormous expenses a person requiring either form of long-term care could incur in five years.

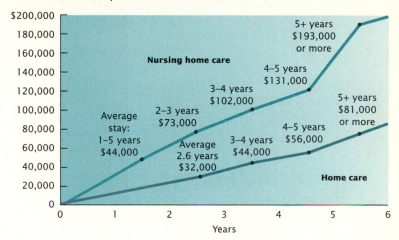

Home care: The Long Term Care Group estimates based on 1982-1984 National Long Term Care Survey, Channelling Demonstration results, 1977 Current Medicare Survey.

Nursing home care: The Long Term Care Group estimates based on 1985 National Home Survey and Work Completed at the Brookings Institution.

practical nurses; and physical, occupational, or speech therapists. Other policies are broader and also cover the services of home health aides who provide patients with personal or custodial care. However, few policies pay for someone to come into your home and cook meals or run errands.

Aggregate Benefits. Purchasers are given a choice of benefits, such as a daily benefit of $60, $80, or $100, which may be payable for a maximum period of two, three, or four years, or a lifetime. Other plans have a choice of lifetime maximum benefits, such as $120 daily and a $250,000 lifetime limit.

Elimination Period. An elimination period is a waiting period during which time benefits are not paid. Elimination periods can range from zero to 365 days. Common elimination periods are 30, 60, 100, or 180 days. A longer elimination period can substantially reduce premiums.

Eligibility for Benefits. All policies have a "gatekeeper provision," which determines if the insured is eligible to receive benefits. One common gatekeeper provision requires the insured to be unable to perform a certain number of *activities of daily living* (commonly called ADLs). Examples include bathing, dressing, eating, getting into and out of bed, and using the toilet. Benefits are paid if the insured cannot perform a certain number of ADLs listed in the policy, such as two of five, without help from another person.

Inflation Protection. Protection against inflation is usually made available as an optional benefit. Assuming an inflation rate of 5 percent annually, a daily charge of $86 will increase to $228 in 20 years. Protection against inflation is especially important if the policy is purchased at a younger age.

Two methods are used to provide protection against inflation. One method allows the insured to purchase additional amounts of insurance in the future without evidence of insurability. For example, one insurer allows the insured to exercise four options, one every five years, to increase his or her coverage 20 percent each time an option is exercised.

A second method provides for an automatic benefit increase by which the daily benefit is increased by a fixed percentage, such as 5 percent for the next 10 or 20 years. The dollar amount of the annual increase will depend on whether the inflation adjustment is based on simple or compound interest. A daily benefit of $80 will increase to $160 in 20 years based on 5 percent simple interest; however, if the benefit is compounded, it will increase to $212. However, adding an automatic benefit increase to the policy is expensive and could double the amount of the annual premium in some cases.

Guaranteed Renewable. Most policies are guaranteed renewable. Once issued, the policy cannot be canceled. However, rates can be increased for classes of insureds.

Premiums. Coverage is expensive. For example, one insurer charges $740 annually for a policy sold to a person age 60 with a $100 daily benefit, a four-year maximum limit per confinement, and a seven-day elimination period. That same policy sold to a person at age 79 would cost $5,190 annually.

Managed Care Plans

managed care A generic term describing medical expense plans that provide necessary medical care to covered persons in a cost-effective manner.

In order to hold down health-care costs, employers and insurers have designed new types of managed care plans for employees and their families. **Managed care** is a generic term for medical expense plans that provide necessary medical care to covered persons in a cost-effective manner. Under such plans, the employees' choice of physicians and hospitals may be limited to certain health-care providers; utilization review is done at all levels; preventive care and healthy lifestyles are emphasized; the quality of the care is monitored; and health-care providers share in the financial results through various risk-sharing techniques.

There are several types of managed care plans. The most important include the following:

- Health maintenance organizations (HMOs)
- Preferred provider organizations (PPOs)
- Exclusive provider organizations (EPOs)
- Point-of-service (POS) plans

Health Maintenance Organizations (HMOs)

health maintenance organization (HMO) An organized system of health care that provides comprehensive services to its members for a fixed pre-paid fee.

A **health maintenance organization (HMO)** is an organized system of health care that provides comprehensive services to its members for a fixed prepaid fee. Nearly one in four workers in employer-sponsored health plans was enrolled in an HMO in 1995.

Basic Characteristics. HMOs have a number of basic characteristics.

1. *The HMO has the responsibility for organizing and delivering comprehensive health services to its members.* The HMO owns or leases medical facilities, enters into agreements with hospitals and physicians to provide medical services, hires ancillary personnel, and has general managerial control over the various services provided.

2. *A HMO provides broad comprehensive health services to the members.* Most services are covered in full, with few maximum limits on individual services. However, many HMOs now limit the amount paid for the treatment of alcoholism and drug addiction. Covered services typically include the full cost of hospital care, surgeons' and physicians' fees, maternity care, laboratory and x-ray services, outpatient services, special-duty nursing, and numerous other services. Office visits to HMO physicians are also covered, either in full or at a nominal charge for each visit.

3. *Selection of a physician is usually limited to those affiliated with the HMO.* However, some newer types of HMOs allow insureds to select any physician at higher out-of-pocket costs. In addition, because HMOs operate in a limited geographic area, there may be limited coverage for treatment received outside the area; however, they typically provide for emergency medical treatment received outside their geographic area.

4. *HMO members pay a fixed prepaid fee (usually paid monthly) for the medical services provided.* High deductibles and coinsurance requirements are usually not emphasized. However, many HMOs now require

copayments for certain diseases, such as alcoholism and drug addiction. There may also be a nominal fee for certain services, such as $10 for an office visit or $10 for a prescription drug.

5. *There is heavy emphasis on controlling costs.* Many HMO physicians are paid a salary, which holds down costs since the provider has no financial incentive to provide unnecessary services. HMOs also enter into contracts with specialists and providers to provide certain services at negotiated fees. Access to expensive specialists is controlled by a gatekeeper physician, a primary care physician who determines if medical care from a specialist is necessary. Finally, HMOs emphasize preventive care and healthy lifestyles, which also hold down costs.

Types of HMOs. There are several types of HMOs. Under a *staff model,* physicians are employees of the HMO and are paid a salary and possibly an incentive bonus to hold down costs.

Under a *group model,* physicians are employees of another group that has a contract with the HMO to provide medical services to its members. The HMO pays the group of physicians a monthly or annual capitation fee for each member, which is a fixed amount for each member regardless of the number of services provided . In return, the group agrees to provide all covered services to the members during the year. The group model typically has a closed panel of physicians that requires members to select physicians affiliated with the HMO.

Under a *network model,* the HMO contracts with two or more independent group practices to provide medical services to covered members. The HMO pays a fixed monthly fee for each member. The group decides how the fees are distributed among the individual physicians.

A final type of HMO is an *individual practice association plan (IPA).* An IPA is an open panel of physicians who work out of their own offices and treat patients on a fee-for-service basis. However, the individual physicians agree to treat HMO members at reduced fees. Physicians may be paid a capitation fee for each member or may be paid a reduced fee. For example, physicians may be paid only 90 percent of their usual fee for an office visit. In addition, to encourage cost containment, most IPAs have risk-sharing agreements with the participating physicians. Payments may be reduced if the plan experience is poor. A bonus is paid if the plan experience is better than expected.

HMOs have the major advantages of providing broad comprehensive medical care to the members; they stress loss prevention and healthy lifestyles; and members do not have to fill out claim forms.

preferred provider organization (PPO) A plan that contracts with health-care providers to provide medical services to members at reduced fees.

Preferred Provider Organizations (PPOs)

A **preferred provider organization (PPO)** is a plan that contracts with health-care providers to offer medical services to the members at reduced fees. The employer, insurer, or other group negotiates contracts with physicians, hospitals, and other providers of care to offer certain medical services to the plan members at discounted fees. To encourage patients to use PPO providers, deductibles and copayments are reduced. In addition, the patient may be charged a lower fee for certain routine treatments or offered increased benefits such as preventive health-care services.

PPOs should not be confused with HMOs. There are two important differences.[8] First, PPO providers typically do not give medical care on a prepaid basis, but are paid on a fee-for-service basis. However, as stated earlier, the fees charged are below the provider's regular fee. Second, unlike an HMO, patients are not required to use a preferred provider but have freedom of choice every time they need care. However, the patients have a financial incentive to use a preferred provider because the deductible and copayment charges are reduced.

PPOs have the major advantage of controlling health-care costs because provider fees are negotiated at a discount. PPOs also help physicians build up their practice. Patients benefit as well because they pay less for their medical care.

Exclusive Provider Organizations (EPOs)

exclusive provider organization (EPO) A plan that does not cover medical care received outside a network of preferred providers.

An **exclusive provider organization (EPO)** is a plan that does not cover medical care received outside a network of preferred providers. If patients receive medical care outside the network, they must pay the entire cost themselves. The preferred providers who are in the network are reimbursed on a fee-for-service basis based on a schedule of negotiated fees.

Point-of-Service (POS) Plans

point-of-service (POS) plan A hybrid managed care plan that combines the characteristics of HMOs and PPOs; members pay little or nothing out of pocket for care by providers in the network but pay substantially higher deductibles and copayments for care by providers outside the network.

A **point-of-service (POS) plan** is a newer form of managed care that is rapidly growing in importance. A point-of service plan is also known as an open-ended HMO or hybrid plan that combines the characteristics of HMOs and PPOs.

The POS plan establishes a network of preferred providers. If patients see providers who are in the network, they pay little or nothing out of pocket, which is similar to an HMO. However, if the patients receive care from providers outside the network, the care is covered, but the patients must pay substantially higher deductibles and copayments. For example, a patient who sees a physician outside the network may be required to pay a $500 annual deductible and a coinsurance charge of 30 percent. If the patient sees a participating physician within the network, there is no additional charge.

The POS plan has the major advantage of preserving freedom of choice for plan members; it also eliminates the fear that plan members will not be able to see a physician or specialist of their choice. The major disadvantage is the substantially higher cost that a member must pay to see a provider outside the network.

In summary, managed care plans include HMOs, PPOs, EPOs, and POS plans. These plans have considerable potential for holding down health-care costs because of the emphasis on cost containment (see Exhibit 10.6). However, critics of managed care argue that emphasis on cost containment may reduce the quality of care these plans provide. It is argued that some gatekeeper physicians are slow in referring sick patients to specialists for treatment because of the additional cost; also, certain diagnostic tests may not be performed; and in some HMOs, members may have to wait a long time to get an appointment.

Providers of Private Health Insurance Coverages

Private individual and group health insurance coverages are available from a number of sources. Major sources include commercial insurers, Blue Cross and Blue Shield plans, and self-insured plans by employers.

Exhibit 10.6

Reported Annual HMO Premium Rate Changes (straight averages), 1991 to 1995.

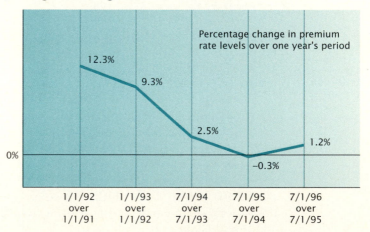

Source: "HMO Rates: Watch Them Rise," *On Managed Care,* Vol. 2, No. 1 (January 1997), Fig. 1, p. 1. Reprinted with permission of Aspen Law *&* Business Publishers.

Commercial Insurers

Commercial life and health insurers sell both individual and group plans. In addition, some property and liability insurers sell private health insurance plans. However, as we noted, most individuals and families who are insured by commercial insurers are covered under group plans. The medical expense coverages sold by commercial insurers are highly concentrated. About 30 insurers write more than half the business. Commercial insurers also sponsor various types of managed care plans, especially health maintenance organizations (HMOs) and preferred provider organizations (PPOs).

Blue Cross and Blue Shield Plans

Blue Cross and Blue Shield plans are medical expense plans that cover hospital expenses, physician services, major medical expenses, and other services. In early 1997, 49 joint plans were in existence that wrote both Blue Cross and Blue Shield coverages. Six separate Blue Cross plans and four separate Blue Shield plans were also in existence. In most states, Blue Cross and Blue Shield plans are organized as nonprofit corporations and receive favorable tax treatment.

Blue Cross plans cover hospital expenses and other related expenses. The plans typically provide service benefits rather than cash benefits to the insured. Most plans cover the full cost of a semiprivate room, and payment is made directly to the hospital rather than to the insured. Blue Shield plans cover physicians' and surgeons' services and related medical expenses.

Blue Cross and Blue Shield plans sell individual, family, and group coverages. Most subscribers are covered by group plans. Blue Cross and Blue Shield group plans typically provide *basic medical expense coverages,* including hospital daily room-and-board benefits, physicians' and surgeons' fees, diagnostic testing, outpatient services, and numerous other expenses. In addition, most plans provide *major medical insurance* to cover a catastrophic illness or accident. Major medical protection typically has a front-end deductible and coinsurance of 80 to 20 percent. Maximum lifetime benefits are $1 million or higher.

Finally, like commercial insurers, Blue Cross and Blue Shield plans sponsor a number of managed care plans, including HMOs and PPOs.

Self-Insured Plans by Employers

self-insured plan A health insurance plan by which the employer pays part or all of the cost of providing health insurance benefits to employees, also known as self-funding.

Many employers self-insure part or all of the health insurance benefits provided to the employees. **Self-insurance** (also called self-funding) means that the employer pays part or all of the cost of providing health insurance benefits to the employees.

Self-insured plans are usually established with stop-loss insurance and a third-party administration (TPA) contract. Stop-loss insurance means that a commercial insurer will pay claims that exceed a certain dollar limit up to some maximum dollar amount. A TPA contract is an arrangement by which an insurer or other independent organization is paid a fee for performing the administrative functions of the plan, such as enrollments, claim payments, and record keeping.

Employers use self-insurance for several reasons. First, health insurance costs can be reduced or held down because of savings in commissions, state premium taxes, and the insurer's profit. Second, cash flow can be improved; the employer retains part or all of the funds needed to pay claims and earns interest until the claims are paid. Finally, self-insured plans are often exempt from state laws that require health insurance plans to provide certain mandated benefits.

Consider This

The Blue Cross and Blue Shield Association has an Internet site at:

http://www.bluecares.com/

In summary, private health insurance is available from commercial insurers, Blue Cross and Blue Shield plans, and self-insured plans by employers. Because of the rapid rise in health-care costs over time, providers have a keen interest in controlling costs. In addition to managed care plans, employers and insurers have introduced a wide variety of techniques for controlling health-care costs (see Insight 10.2).

Government Health-Care Programs

Although most workers and their families are covered by private health insurance plans, two government health-care programs are also worthy of discussion: Medicare and Medicaid.

Medicare

Medicare A federal program that covers the medical expenses of the elderly age 65 and older and certain people with disabilities under age 65.

The **Medicare** program is a federal program that covers the medical expenses of the elderly age 65 and older and certain disabled people under age 65.

Medicare is divided into two separate programs: (1) Hospital Insurance (Part A) and (2) Supplementary Medical Insurance (Part B). Hospital Insurance provides inpatient hospital care, care in a skilled nursing facility, home health-care visits, and hospice benefits. Inpatient hospital care is provided up to 90 days. For the first 60 days, all covered hospital charges are paid in full except for an initial inpatient deductible ($760 in 1997). For the next 30 days, the patient must pay a daily coinsurance charge ($190 in 1997).

In addition, care in a skilled nursing facility is covered up to 100 days. The first 20 days of covered services are paid in full. For the next 80 days, the patient must pay a daily coinsurance charge ($95 in 1997).

Insight

10.2   How Can Health-Care Costs Be Controlled?

Employers and insurers have introduced a wide variety of techniques and approaches for controlling health-care costs, including the following:

■ *Managed care*. Managed care is a generic term for a medical expense plan that attempts to provide necessary medical care in a cost-effective manner. HMOs and PPOs are examples of managed care plans.

■ *Preadmission testing*. Various tests are given as an outpatient before a patient is admitted into a hospital, which eliminates one or two days of room-and-board charges.

■ *Hospital certification.* Before a patient enters a hospital for surgery, approval by the insurer is required. The intent is to reduce unnecessary hospitalization and length of stay.

■ *Second opinion.* Many plans pay for a second opinion by another physician to determine if surgery is necessary.

■ *Outpatient surgery.* Surgery is performed as an outpatient, and the patient recovers at home. Thus, hospital costs are reduced.

■ *Ambulatory surgical centers.* Minor surgery is performed in a walk-in center or the physician's office rather than in a hospital.

■ *Home health care.* A patient may be discharged early from a hospital to recover at home. Various services are provided in the home, such as nursing services or speech therapy.

■ *Nursing home care.* Most plans pay for care in a less costly nursing home or extended care facility if the patient is disabled from an accident or sickness.

■ *Claim audits.* Hospitals often make billing mistakes. Independent auditing firms are used to verify hospital charges. Substantial savings have been realized.

■ *Fee negotiation.* Some physicians and hospitals may overcharge their patients. Insurers have staff personnel to deal directly with physicians and hospitals to ensure that charges are fair.

■ *Hospice coverage.* Many plans cover hospice care where the cost of treating terminally ill patients is lower than traditional forms of treatment.

■ *Prospective payment system (PPS)*. Under this system, the amounts paid to hospitals and other providers are negotiated in advance. If actual charges are less than the negotiated charge, the provider can retain the profit. If actual costs exceed the negotiated charge, the provider must absorb the extra cost. Thus, there is a strong financial incentive to keep costs down.

■ *Wellness programs.* Many firms have wellness programs that hold down medical costs by promoting a healthy lifestyle.

■ *Employee assistance programs.* Many firms have treatment and counseling programs for employees who are addicted to drugs or alcohol or have other problems.

■ *Case management (utilization review).* Expensive hospital cases are monitored by a case manager who may be a registered nurse. The case manager works closely with the patient's physician to determine if less costly alternatives are available. For example, the family of a premature baby received special home training. As a result, the baby left the intensive care unit four months earlier than had been expected, with a savings in medical costs of $135,000.

Source: *Social Insurance and Economic Security*, 5/E by Rejda, George E., © 1994. Adapted by permission of Prentice-Hall, Inc., Upper Saddle River, NJ.

Hospital Insurance covers an unlimited number of home health-care visits by health-care professionals. It also provides hospice benefits for terminally ill beneficiaries. A hospice program provides inpatient, out-patient, and home health-care services to terminally ill beneficiaries, such as cancer patients; it does not provide curative treatment.

Supplementary Medical Insurance (Part B) is a voluntary program that covers physician's fees, outpatient hospital services, home health visits if the patient is not covered under Part A, and other related med-ical services. Part B pays 80 percent of the approved charges for covered medical services after the beneficiary pays a calendar-year deductible of $100. Part B beneficiaries must pay a monthly premium for the coverage provided ($43.80 in 1997).

The Medicare program is extremely important in retirement plan-ning. It provides considerable protection against the risk of poor health during retirement. We discuss the Medicare program in greater detail in Chapter 16.

Medicaid

Medicaid A joint state fed-eral welfare program that covers the medical expenses of low-income persons who satisfy a strin-gent means test.

The **Medicaid** program is a joint state–federal welfare program that covers the medical expenses of low-income persons who can satisfy a stringent means test. A means test (also called a needs test) requires that Medicaid applicants show that their income and assets are below certain levels in order to qualify for benefits. A large number of low-income groups are covered, including the aged, blind, disabled, families with dependent children, and certain pregnant women and children.

Medicaid provides certain basic medical services, including inpatient and outpatient hospital services, physicians' services, prenatal care, lab-oratory and x-ray services, and long-term care in nursing homes.

Consider This

Information on Medicare and Medicaid is available from the U.S. Health Care Financing Administration at:

http://www.hcfa.gov/

Shopping for Health Insurance

Because of the high cost of medical care, individual and group health insurance plans are expensive. You should not waste money by buying health insurance coverages that do not provide meaningful financial protection. When purchasing health insurance, you should follow cer-tain rules (illustrated in Exhibit 10.7). They include the following:

■ Insure for the catastrophic loss.

■ Consider group health insurance first.

■ Use preferred providers whenever possible.

■ Don't ignore disability income insurance.

Exhibit 10.7

Guidelines for Health Insurance Shoppers

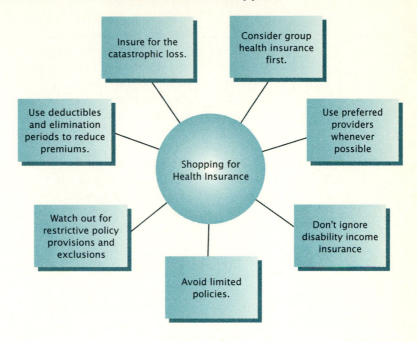

- Avoid limited policies.
- Watch out for restrictive policy provisions and exclusions.
- Use deductibles and elimination periods to reduce premiums.

Insure for the Catastrophic Loss

The most important rule is to purchase health insurance that provides protection against a catastrophic loss that can destroy you financially. The cost of a serious illness or injury can be ruinous. Open heart surgery can cost more than $75,000; a kidney or heart transplant can cost more than $100,000; and the cost of a crippling automobile accident requiring several major operations, plastic surgery, and rehabilitation can cost more than $200,000. Unless you have adequate health insurance or financial assets to meet these expenditures, you will be financially insecure. The inability to pay for catastrophic medical bills is a major cause of personal bankruptcy. *Thus, you should purchase a high-quality individual major medical policy or be covered under a group major medical plan.* To limit out-of-pocket expenses, make certain the major medical policy has a stop-loss limit that requires the insurer to pay 100 percent of all covered expenses in excess of the stop-loss limit.

Consider Group Health Insurance First

In dealing with the risk of poor health, you should first consider whether group health insurance is available. You may be eligible to participate in a group health insurance plan sponsored by your employer.

Group health insurance is preferable to individual coverage for several reasons. First, employers frequently make available a number of group health insurance plans to their employees, ranging from traditional group indemnity plans to managed care plans, such as HMOs and PPOs. The various group indemnity plans have different deductible amounts, coinsurance requirements, and stop-loss limits. Managed care plans typically have no deductible or coinsurance requirements, or the amounts paid by the insured may be low. Depending on your financial circumstances and need for protection, you can choose the plan that best meets your needs and ability to pay.

Second, group health insurance is typically broader in coverage than individual protection with fewer exclusions and restrictions. Further, some employers do not use a preexisting condition clause to deny benefits to new employees who have preexisting physical or mental conditions as long as they apply for the insurance during their eligibility period—usually a one-month period during which they can apply for the insurance with no evidence of insurability.

Third, employers often pay a large part of the monthly premiums, which makes the plan financially attractive to the employees and their families. Some employers pay the entire cost.

In addition, there are substantial tax advantages to employees under present law. The employer's contributions do not result in taxable income to the employee, and the employee's contributions can often be made with *before-tax dollars*. Employees should not ignore these tax advantages in a group health insurance plan.

Use Preferred Providers Whenever Possible

Another important suggestion is to use preferred providers whenever possible. As we noted earlier, employers and insurers frequently establish networks of preferred providers who agree to provide medical services to the employees at discounted fees. Preferred providers include physicians, dentists, hospitals, pharmaceutical firms, and other health-care providers. If you use a preferred provider, your out-of-pocket cost will be substantially less because of a lower deductible amount and reduced coinsurance requirement. For example, a group health insurance plan may have a calendar year deductible of $250. If you use a preferred provider, the deductible may be reduced to $200. In addition, major medical plans typically require insureds to meet a coinsurance requirement of 20 or 25 percent. If you use a preferred provider, the coinsurance requirement may be reduced to 15 or 20 percent. Finally, the preferred provider usually absorbs that portion of the fee or charge that exceeds the amount allowed by the insurer. Thus, if a physician's actual fee is $800 but the insurer allows only $700, the physician absorbs the disallowed portion of $100.

Don't Ignore Disability Income Insurance

You should not ignore the importance of disability income insurance in your health insurance program. A substantial amount of earned income is lost each year because of sickness and injury, which is not replaced by disability income and sick leave benefits. Data show clearly that many workers are paying insufficient attention to the risk of disability in their personal insurance programs. In 1992, the income lost from temporary nonoccupational disabilities of six months or less, as well as the income lost during the first six months of a long-term disability, totaled about $74 billion. However, individual and group benefits to workers in private employment, sick leave for government employees, and social security benefits for the sixth month of disability totaled about $35 billion. *Insurance and sick leave benefits replaced only 47 percent of the income lost.*[9] The proportion of income replaced during a long-term disability would be even less. Thus, it is clear that most workers are underinsured for both short-term and long-term disability.

You should consider purchasing an individual guaranteed renewable or noncancellable disability income policy that will pay at least two thirds of your earnings up to age 65 with an elimination period of 30 to 90 days. Even if you are covered under a group short-term or long-term disability income plan, you should still consider an individual policy. If you lose your job, group disability income benefits generally cannot be converted into an individual policy.

Avoid Limited Policies

limited policy A health insurance policy that covers only certain specified diseases or accidents, pays limited benefits, or places serious restrictions on the right to receive benefits. Examples include hospital indemnity policies, cancer policies, and accident-only policies.

A **limited policy** is one that covers only certain specified diseases or accidents, pays limited benefits, or places serious restrictions on the right to receive them. A *hospital indemnity policy* is one example of a limited policy. It pays a fixed daily or monthly benefit if you are confined to a hospital. For example, the plan may pay $3,000 monthly ($100 daily) for up to five years if you are hospitalized, no health questions are asked, and the first month's premium is only $1. It sounds like a good deal, but the policy is limited. Most people will never collect benefits for an extended period. The average hospital stay for people under age 65 is fewer than seven days. Even if you are confined for only seven days, the benefit paid would only be $700. During that time, you may have incurred several thousands of dollars of medical expenses, but only a small amount would be paid by the hospital indemnity benefit. In addition, the policy covers you only in the hospital. If you recover at home, no payment is made. Finally, the application contains a preexisting conditions clause that excludes a preexisting condition for one or two years after you purchase the policy.

A *cancer policy* is another example of a limited policy. If you are insured under a high-quality individual or group major medical policy, you do not need a cancer policy. Many consumer experts recommend that a cancer policy should not be purchased. They argue that it is illogical to insure yourself more heavily against only one disease.

Finally, you should avoid *accident-only policies* because they are limited in coverage and benefits. The list of these policies is endless and includes accident insurance offered by sponsors of credit cards, travel accident policies to cover you while on vacation, and airline accident policies sold over the counter or from vending machines in airports.

Watch Out for Restrictive Policy Provisions and Exclusions

If you are shopping for an individual policy, you should be aware of any restrictions on coverage that might apply. Two common restrictions are a *preexisting conditions clause* and an *exclusionary rider*. You should not purchase an individual policy with a preexisting conditions clause longer than one year. If possible, you should also avoid purchasing an individual policy in which an exclusionary rider appears. If you have been treated for a certain disease, such as cancer or heart disease, the insurer may add a rider to the policy that excludes the condition.

Finally, as a last resort, if you are uninsurable and cannot obtain either individual or group coverage, you may be eligible for coverage from a state high-risk pool for the uninsurable (see Insight 10.3).

Use Deductibles and Elimination Periods to Reduce Premiums

High-quality individual and group health insurance coverages are expensive. A comprehensive major medical policy that covers the entire family can easily cost more than $4,000 annually. You can reduce premiums by purchasing the policy with a substantial deductible. If you can afford it, an annual deductible of $500 or $1,000 will substantially reduce your premiums. Likewise, you can substantially reduce premiums for a disability income policy by buying the policy with a 90-day elimination period.

SUMMARY

■ The present health-care delivery system in the United States has four major problems: soaring health-care expenditures, inadequate access to medical care, uneven quality of medical care, and waste and inefficiency.

Insight

10.3   The Last Resort: State High Risk Pools for the Uninsurable

At least 27 states have special high-risk pools that provide health insurance to people who are medically uninsurable. Applicants must show they have been refused health insurance elsewhere before they are accepted. Two eligibility requirements are commonly imposed. First, the applicant must be a resident of the state. Second, the applicant must provide proof of one or more of the following: (1) be rejected by at least one insurer, (2) be presently insured under a plan with a higher premium than the pool premium, (3) be presently insured with a restrictive rider or rated policy, or (4) be offered a policy with a restrictive waiver or rider.

Maximum lifetime benefits typically range from $250,000 to $1 million. A $500 calendar-year deductible and 80 to 20 percent coinsurance are common. The plans typically have an annual stop-loss limit that caps the out-of-pocket expenses, such as $2,000 per person and $3,000 for the family. The insurance is expensive, with maximum rates generally ranging from 125 to 400 percent of individual standard rates. For example, in 1992, the quarterly premium in Connecticut for a female age 60 was $2,166 with a $1,250 annual deductible. Despite high premiums, the pools have incurred substantial underwriting losses. Health insurers doing business in the state are assessed their pro rata share of excess losses. In many states, the insurers can deduct all or part of the assessments from the state premium taxes paid. General revenue appropriations and taxes on tobacco and cigarettes are also used to fund excess losses in some states.

The major advantage of these pools is that they provide health insurance coverage to the medically uninsurable. The pools, however, are not a viable solution to the national problems of health insurance affordability and accessibility.

The pools have incurred substantial underwriting deficits; the assessment method of funding such deficits is defective since the true cost is hidden and is shifted indirectly to taxpayers through premium tax offsets or to policyowners through higher premiums; only a small fraction of the medically uninsurable have obtained insurance through the pools; high premiums make the insurance unaffordable to many applicants; the use of a preexisting-condition clause initially denies benefits to those most in need; and enrollment limits and waiting lists in some states defeat the basic purpose of the plans.

Source: Adapted with permission from George E. Rejda, Michael J. McNamara, and Gerald P. Hanner, "State High-Risk Pools for the Uninsurable: A Critical Analysis," *Journal of the American Society of CLU & ChFC,* Vol. XLVII, No. 5 (September 1993): 61–73. Copyright © 1993 by the American Society of CLU and ChFC, 270 Bryn Mawr Avenue, Bryn Mawr, PA 19010.

■ Individual and group health insurance coverages generally fall into the following categories: basic medical expense insurance, major medical insurance, dental insurance, disability income insurance, and long-term care insurance.

■ Basic medical expense insurance includes coverage for hospital expenses, surgical expenses, physicians' visits, and certain other expenses.

■ Major medical insurance is designed to cover the expenses of a catastrophic illness or injury. A typical major medical plan has certain basic characteristics: broad coverage, high maximum limits, an annual deductible, coinsurance requirements, internal limits, and certain exclusions.

■ Comprehensive major medical insurance is a combination of basic plan benefits and major medical insurance in one policy.

■ Important contractual provisions that frequently appear in group health insurance plans include a preexisting conditions provision, a coordination-of-benefits provision, and a provision that allows terminated employees to continue their group health insurance under the COBRA law for a limited period.

■ Under a comprehensive dental insurance plan, most dental services are covered. Dentists are reimbursed on the basis of their customary charges subject to any limitations on benefits stated in the plan. Under a schedule approach, the various dental services are listed in a schedule, and a specific dollar amount is paid for each service.

■ An individual disability income policy pays periodic income benefits when the insured is unable to work because of sickness or injury. The benefits are paid after an elimination period is satisfied. The insured generally has a choice of the length of the benefit period. After 90 days, all premiums are waived if the insured is totally disabled.

■ The definition of disability is stated in a disability income policy. In an individual policy, for the first two years, total disability is typically defined as the inability to perform all duties of the insured's own occupation. After that time, total disability is defined as the inability to perform the duties of any occupation for which the insured is reasonably fitted by training, education, and experience.

■ Some disability income plans contain a residual disability benefit by which a pro rata disability benefit is paid if the insured returns to work, but earnings are reduced.

■ A short-term group disability income plan typically pays benefits ranging from 13 weeks to 2 years. This plan covers only nonoccupational disabilities that occur off the job. Disability is usually defined in terms of your own occupation.

■ A group long-term disability income plan pays benefits for longer periods, typically ranging from two years to age 65. You must satisfy an elimination period of 90 days or 6 months. This plan covers both occupational and nonoccupational disabilities. Group plans commonly use a dual definition of disability to determine if the worker is totally disabled.

■ Social security disability benefits are payable if the disabled worker meets certain strict eligibility requirements. Depending on age, the disabled worker must earn a certain number of credits in covered employment; a full five-month waiting period must be satisfied; and the definition of disability must be met. You must have a physical or mental condition that prevents you from doing any substantial gainful work and that is expected to last (or has lasted) at least 12 months or is expected to result in death.

■ Workers compensation benefits may be payable if a covered worker has a job-related injury or disease. Workers compensation has four major benefits: weekly disability income benefits, payment of all medical expenses, death benefits to eligible survivors, and rehabilitation services.

■ Long-term care insurance pays a daily or monthly benefit for medical or custodial care received in a nursing facility, hospital, or at home.

■ Managed care is a generic term for medical expense plans that provide necessary medical care in a cost-effective manner. Major types of managed care plans are health maintenance organizations (HMOs), preferred provider organizations (PPOs), exclusive provider organizations (EPOs), and point-of-service (POS) plans.

■ An HMO is an organized system of health care that provides comprehensive medical services to its members for a fixed prepaid fee. These policies usually restrict the choice of a physician to those affiliated with the HMO. There is great emphasis on cost containment.

■ A PPO is a plan that contracts with health-care providers to provide medical services to the members at reduced fees. Members are not required to use a preferred provider, but deductibles and copayment charges are reduced if one is used.

■ An EPO is a plan that does not cover medical care received outside the network of preferred providers.

■ A POS plan is an open-ended HMO that allows members to use providers outside the network. However, if care is received from providers outside the network, the care is covered, but the member must pay a substantial deductible and meet a coinsurance requirement. If care is received from a network provider, little or no additional charges are imposed.

■ Private individual and group health insurance coverages are available from commercial insurers, Blue Cross and Blue Shield plans, and self-insured plans by employers.

■ Medicare is a federal health insurance program that covers the medical expenses of the elderly age 65 and older and certain disabled people under age 65.

■ Medicaid is a state and federal program that covers the medical expenses of low-income persons who can satisfy a stringent means test.

■ Certain rules should be followed when health insurance is purchased: (1) Insure for the catastrophic loss. (2) Consider group health insurance first. (3) Use preferred providers whenever possible. (4) Don't ignore disability income insurance. (5) Avoid limited policies. (6) Watch out for restrictive policy provisions and exclusions. (7) Use deductibles and elimination periods to reduce premiums.

KEY CONCEPTS AND TERMS

Calendar-year deductible
Coinsurance
Comprehensive dental insurance
Comprehensive major medical
  insurance
Coordination-of-benefits provision
Disability income insurance
Elimination period
Exclusive provider organization
  (EPO)
Guaranteed renewable policy
Health maintenance organization
  (HMO)
Hospital expense insurance
Indemnity plan
Internal limit
Limited policy
Long-term care insurance
Major medical insurance
Managed care
Medicaid

Medicare
Noncancelable policy
Physicians' visits insurance
Point-of-service (POS) plan
Predetermination-of-benefits
  provision
Preexisting condition
Preferred provider organization
  (PPO)
Residual disability benefit
Schedule approach
Self-insured plans
Service benefits
Stop-loss limit
Surgical expense insurance
Total disability
Usual, reasonable, and customary
  charges
Waiver of premium
Workers compensation laws

QUESTIONS FOR REVIEW

1. Explain the problem of health care in the United States.

2. Describe the benefits typically payable under a hospital expense and surgical expense policy.

3. Explain the basic characteristics of a major medical insurance policy. Why are deductibles and coinsurance used in major medical insurance?

4. Describe the major characteristics of an individual disability income policy.

5. Explain the various definitions of total disability that are found in individual disability income policies.

6. What are the basic characteristics of group short-term and long-term disability income plans?

7. Explain the eligibility requirements for receiving (a) social security disability benefits and (b) workers compensation benefits.

8. Identify the major characteristics of long-term care insurance.

9. Define the meaning of managed care. Explain the major characteristics of the following types of managed care plans: health maintenance organizations (HMOs), preferred provider organizations (PPOs), exclusive provider organizations (EPOs), and point-of-service (POS) plans.

10. Why do numerous firms self-insure or self-fund their group health insurance benefits?

11. Explain the major characteristics of the Medicare and Medicaid programs.

12. List the important rules that consumers should follow when purchasing health insurance.

PROBLEMS
---

1. Megan has a major medical policy with a lifetime limit of $1 million. The policy has a $500 calendar-year deductible and a coinsurance requirement of 20 percent. She was seriously injured in an auto accident, and her medical bills totaled $100,500. She also lost $10,000 of work earnings because she was undergoing rehabilitation and could not work. What is the amount that Megan's insurer will pay under the policy? Show your calculations. Would your answer be different if Megan's policy contained a stop-loss limit of $3,000? Explain.

2. Jeff, age 28, currently earns $3,000 monthly. He has a guaranteed renewable disability income policy that pays $2,000 monthly to age 65 if he should become totally disabled. The policy has a 90-day elimination period. The policy also pays residual disability benefits.

   a. If Jeff is seriously injured in a skiing accident and is unable to work for nine months, how much, if any, will he collect under the policy?

    b. If Jeff returns to work but can earn only $2,100 monthly, how much, if any, will he collect under the policy?

    c. Following the accident, could Jeff's insurer cancel the policy or increase his premiums?

3. Managed care plans have increased rapidly in recent years, and new forms of managed care are constantly appearing. Two types of managed care plans are a group model HMO and a preferred provider organization (PPO). Compare each of these plans with respect to the following:

    a. Freedom to select an individual physician of one's choice

    b. Use of deductibles and coinsurance (percentage participation clause)

INTERNET EXERCISES

1. Insurance and Risk Management Central provides information about a number of insurance-related topics. Visit the site at:

    http://www.irmcentral.com/

    Go to the "Shopping for Personal Insurance" page to access information on health and disability insurance.

2. One good jumping-off place to explore the many health-related sites on the Internet is HealthSeek, which brings together hundreds of links. You can find it at:

    http://www.healthseek.com/

CASE APPLICATIONS

Case I

Mark and Jennifer are married and have two daughters. Both Mark and Jennifer work. The entire family is insured under a group major medical plan provided by Mark's employer. The plan has a calendar-year deductible of $300, a stop-loss limit of $2,000, and a coinsurance requirement of 20 percent. Jennifer recently had an appendectomy operation and incurred the following medical expenses:

Outpatient diagnostic tests	$ 700
Hospital expenses	18,000
Surgeon's fee	1,500
Prescription drugs outside the hospital	100

In addition, Jennifer could not work for four weeks and lost $2,000 in earnings.

1. Based on the preceding information, how much of the loss will be paid by the insurance company? Show your calculations.

2. If Mark's plan did not have a stop-loss limit, how much would the insurance company pay? Show your calculations.

3. Assume that Jennifer is insured under her employer's group health insurance plan. Mark and his two daughters are also covered as dependents under Jennifer's plan. If Mark is injured in an auto accident, which plan would pay first? Explain your answer.

4. Mark was recently laid off work during a business recession. How can Mark keep his group health insurance in force?

Case II

Lorri, age 28, is a registered nurse who earns $3,000 monthly in a hospital. She is seriously injured in an automobile accident in which she is at fault and is expected to be off work for at least one year. She has a guaranteed renewable disability-income policy that pays $1,800 monthly up to age 65 for accidents and sickness after a 90-day elimination period. A residual disability benefit is included in the policy. Lorri's policy contains the following provisions:

Total disability means: (a) your inability during the first 24 months to perform substantially all of the important duties of your occupation; and you are not working at any gainful occupation; (b) After the first 24 months that benefits are payable, it means your inability to engage in any gainful occupation.

Gainful occupation means: Any occupation or employment for wage or profit which is reasonably consistent with your education, training, and experience.

a. If Lorri is off work for one year, indicate the extent, if any, of the insurer's obligation to pay disability benefits.

b. Assume that Lorri is disabled for one year, recovers, and returns to work on a part-time basis. If she earns $1500 monthly, indicate the extent, if any, of the insurer's obligation to pay her disability benefits.

c. Assume that after two years, Lorri is unable to return to work as a full-time hospital nurse. A drug manufacturer offers her a job as a lab technician, which she accepts. Indicate the extent, if any, of the insurer's obligation to pay her disability benefits.

d. Following the accident, could Lorri's insurer cancel her policy or increase her premiums? Explain your answer.

Case III

Nancy Olson is president of a consulting firm that has 20 employees. The only employee benefit is a paid two-week vacation for employees with one or more years of service. Profits have increased substantially, and Nancy would like to provide some health insurance benefits to the employees. She is aware of group health insurance but knows nothing about managed care plans. Assume that you are a financial planner. Based on the preceding facts, answer the following questions:

1. Explain to Nancy the meaning of managed care, and show how managed care plans differ from traditional group health insurance plans.

2. Explain to Nancy the advantages of a preferred provider organization (PPO) plan for her employees.

3. Nancy is concerned that freedom to select a specialist would be restricted if a health maintenance organization (HMO) were installed. What type of managed care plan would overcome this objection? Explain your answer.

4. After careful consideration, Nancy decided to offer both a comprehensive major medical plan and a group model HMO to the employees. Compare these two plans with respect to the following:

   a. Use of deductibles and coinsurance

   b. Immediate access to a specialist of your choice

SUGGESTIONS FOR ADDITIONAL READING

Beam, Burton T., Jr. and John J. McFadden. *Employee Benefits,* 4th ed. Chicago: Dearborn Financial Publishing, 1996, Chapters 8 11, 13.

Rejda, George E. *Principles of Risk Management and Insurance,* 6th ed. Reading, MA.: Addison Wesley Longman, 1998, Chapters 20, 21, 23.

—. *Social Insurance and Economic Security,* 5th ed. Englewood Cliffs, N.J.: Prentice-Hall, 1994, Chapter 8.

NOTES

1. This section is based on George E. Rejda, *Social Insurance and Economic Security,* 5th ed. (Englewood Cliffs, N.J.: Prentice Hall, 1994), pp. 191–205.

2. Catherine R. Levit, et al., "National Health Expenditures, 1995," *Health Care Financing Review,* 18 (Fall 1996), pp. 175–77; and Salley T. Burner and Daniel R. Waldo, *Health Care Financing Review,* 16 (Summer 1995), p. 221.

3. Employee Benefit Research Institute, *Sources of Health Insurance and Characteristics of the Uninsured, Analysis of the March 1996 Current Population Survey,* EBRI Issue Brief Number 179 (November 1996), p. 1.

4. Rejda, *Social Insurance and Economic Security,* 5th ed., p. 204.

5. Jeff Sadler, *Disability Income, The Sale, The Product, The Market,* 2nd ed. (Cincinnati, Ohio: National Underwriter, 1995), p. 157.

6. Edward E. Graves, ed., *McGill's Life Insurance* (Bryn Mawr, PA: The American College, 1994), p. 143.

7. *A Shopper's Guide to Long-Term Care Insurance* (Kansas City, MO, National Association of Insurance Commissioners, 1993), pp. 5–6.

8. Burton T. Beam, Jr. and John J. McFadden, *Employee Benefits,* 4th ed. (Chicago: Dearnborn Financial Publishing, Inc., 1996), pp. 263, 270.

9. U.S. Bureau of the Census, *Statistical Abstract of the United States: 1995* (115th edition). Washington, DC, 1995, Table 608, p. 386.

Chapter **11**

Property and Liability Insurance

Learning Objectives

After studying this chapter, you should be able to:

- Identify the major types of policies to insure homeowners, condominium owners, and renters.

- Describe the major property coverages that appear in Section I of the Homeowners 3 policy.

- Describe the personal liability insurance coverages that appear in Section II of the homeowners policy.

- Explain the basic characteristics of the personal umbrella policy.

- Describe the major coverages that appear in the Personal Auto Policy (PAP).

- Explain the different approaches taken by society to compensate injured auto accident victims.

- Identify the important rules that consumers should follow when purchasing homeowners insurance and auto insurance.

*There's no place like home,
after the other places close.*

—English proverb

*A careful driver is one who honks
his horn when he goes through
a red light.*

—Henry Morgan

Consumers spend billions of dollars each year on homes, cars, boats, furniture, clothes, and other types of property. The property can be damaged or destroyed from numerous causes, including fire, hurricanes, tornadoes, earthquakes, and floods. In addition, you can suffer an enormous financial loss if you should injure someone and are held legally liable for the payment of damages to the injured party.

This chapter discusses the important property and liability coverages that you should consider in your personal risk management program.[1] Topics discussed include homeowners insurance, auto insurance, approaches used by society to indemnify injured auto accident victims, and the personal umbrella policy. In addition, the chapter discusses certain rules to follow when shopping for a homeowners policy and auto insurance.

Overview of Homeowners Policies

In the following section, we examine the homeowners forms drafted by the Insurance Services Office (ISO). The ISO forms are widely used throughout the United States. Some insurers, such as State Farm and Allstate, have developed their own homeowners forms that differ somewhat from the ISO forms. The differences, however, are relatively minor.

The most important homeowners forms used currently include the following:

- HO-2 (broad form)
- HO-3 (special form)
- HO-4 (contents broad form)
- HO-6 (unit owners form)
- HO-8 (modified coverage form)

Each homeowners form is divided into two major sections. Section I covers the home, other structures, and personal property. Section II provides personal liability insurance and also covers the medical expenses of others who may be injured on the premises or by an insured.

Homeowners 2 (Broad Form)

Homeowners 2 A type of homeowners insurance that provides coverage on a named-perils basis on the dwelling, other structures, and personal property; personal liability is also covered.

peril The cause of loss.

Homeowners 2 is a named-perils policy that insures the dwelling, other structures, and personal property against loss from certain listed perils. A **peril** is defined as the cause of loss. Covered perils include fire, lightning, windstorm, hail, explosion, and numerous others. Additional living expenses are also covered in the event a covered loss makes the dwelling uninhabitable. In addition, Section II provides coverage for personal liability insurance and medical payments to others.

Exhibit 11.1

Comparison of ISO Homeowners Coverages

Coverage	HO-2 (broad form)	HO-3 (special form)
Section I Coverages		
A. Dwelling	Minimum varies by company.	Minimum varies by company.
B. Other structures	10% of A	10% of A
C. Personal property	50% of A	50% of A
D. Loss of use	20% of A	20% of A
Covered perils	Fire or lightning Windstorm or hail Explosion Riot or civil commotion Aircraft Vehicles Smoke Vandalism or malicious mischief Theft Falling objects Weight of ice, snow, or sleet Accidental discharge or overflow of water or steam Sudden and accidental tearing apart, cracking, burning, or bulging of a steam, hot water, air conditioning, or automatic fire protective sprinkler system, or from within a household appliance Freezing of a plumbing, heating, air conditioning, or automatic fire sprinkler system, or of a household appliance Sudden and accidental damage from artificially generated electrical current Volcanic eruption	Dwelling and other structures are covered against risk of direct loss to property; all losses are covered except those losses specifically excluded. Personal property is covered for the same perils as HO-2.
Section II Coverages		
E. Personal liability	$100,000	$100,000
F. Medical payments to others	$1,000 per person	$1,000 per person

Homeowners 3 (Special Form)

Homeowners 3 A type of homeowners insurance that covers the dwelling and other structures on an "all-risks" basis against the risk of direct loss.

"all-risks" basis An insurance coverage that promises to cover all losses except those losses specifically excluded.

Homeowners 3 insures the dwelling and other structures against the risk of direct loss to property. In effect, the dwelling and other structures are insured on an **"all-risks" basis.** *This means that all direct physical losses to the dwelling and other structures are covered, except certain losses specifically excluded.* In addition, losses to the dwelling and other structures are paid on the basis of full replacement cost with no deduction for depreciation if certain conditions are met (discussed later). Personal property is covered for the same *broad form perils* listed in HO-2. Finally, Section II provides coverage for personal liability insurance and medical payments to others.

HO-3 is a popular and widely used form that is discussed in greater detail later in the chapter.

HO-4 (contents broad form)	HO-6 (unit-owners form)	HO-8 (modified coverage form)
Section I Coverages		
Not applicable Not applicable Minimum varies by company. 20% of C	$1,000 minimum on the unit Included in coverage A Minimum varies by company. 40% of C	Minimum varies by company. 10% of A 50% of A 10% of A

Same perils as HO-2 for
personal property
	Same perils as HO-2 for personal property	Fire or lightning
		Windstorm or hail
		  Explosion
		  Riot or civil commotion
		  Aircraft
		  Vehicles
		  Smoke
		  Vandalism or malicious mischief
		  Theft (applies only to loss on the
		        residence premises or in a bank or
		        public warehouse up to a
		        maximum of $1,000)
		Volcanic eruption

Section II Coverages		
$100,000	$100,000	$100,000
$1,000 per person	$1,000 per person	$1,000 per person

Homeowners 4 (Contents Broad Form)

Homeowners 4 A type of homeowners insurance for tenants that covers the tenant's personal property against loss or damage and provides personal liability insurance.

Homeowners 4 is designed for tenants who rent apartments, houses, or rooms. **Homeowners 4** covers the tenant's personal property against loss or damage and also provides personal liability insurance. Personal property is covered for the same named perils listed in Homeowners 2.

Homeowners 6 (Unit Owners Form)

Homeowners 6 A type of homeowners insurance for the owners of condominium units; it provides coverage for personal property for the same named perils as Homeowners 2 and provides coverage for personal liability.

Homeowners 6 is designed for the owners of condominium units. As explained in Chapter 7, a condominium is a form of ownership in which individuals own their separate housing units; however, common areas such as hallways, tennis courts, swimming pools, and the outside grounds are owned by the condominium owners' association. The condominium association carries insurance on the building and other property owned in common by the owners of the different units. Homeowners 6 covers the personal property of the insured for the same named perils listed in Homeowners 2. The policy also provides coverage for personal liability insurance and medical payments to others.

Homeowners 8 (Modified Coverage Form)

Homeowners 8 A type of homeowners insurance designed for older homes; the dwelling and other structures are indemnified on the basis of repair cost using common construction materials and methods; personal liability is also covered.

Homeowners 8 is a modified coverage form for older homes that covers loss to the dwelling and other structures based on the amount required to repair or replace using common construction material and methods. In some states, actual cash value is used as the basis of settlement. Thus, payment for loss to the dwelling and other structures is not based on replacement cost. The policy also provides coverage for personal liability insurance and medical payments to others.

Exhibit 11.1 compares the various homeowners forms, basic coverages, and insured perils.

Analysis of Homeowners 3 Policy (Special Form)

This section discusses the major provisions in the Homeowners 3 policy (special form). As you study this section, you may find it helpful to refer to the HO-3 policy in Appendix C of the text.

Persons Insured

The HO-3 policy covers the *named insured and spouse* if he or she is a resident of the same household. The named insured refers to the person(s) stated in the policy. The policy also covers *family members* who reside in the named insured's household. Children attending college who are temporarily away from home are also insured under their parent's policy; however, other relatives must reside in the same household to be covered. Finally, the policy covers *others persons under age 21 in the care of an insured* if they reside in the named insured's household, such as a foreign exchange student, a foster child, or a ward of the court.

Section I Coverages

The major coverages that appear in Section I of the Homeowners 3 policy are as follows:

- Coverage A: Dwelling
- Coverage B: Other structures

■ Coverage C: Personal property

■ Coverage D: Loss of use

■ Additional coverages

Coverage A: Dwelling. Coverage A insures the dwelling located on the residence premises and any structure attached to the dwelling. Thus, the home and an attached garage or carport are insured under this section.

Coverage B: Other Structures. Coverage B insures other structures on the residence premises that are separated from the dwelling by clear space, such as a detached garage, tool shed, or horse stable. Structures connected to the dwelling only by a fence or utility line are also considered to be other structures.

Coverage C: Personal Property. Personal property owned or used by an insured is covered anywhere in the world. Coverage also applies to borrowed property. In addition, the insurance can be extended to cover the personal property of a guest or resident employee while the property is in any residence occupied by an insured.

Special limits of liability.   Certain types of personal property have maximum dollar limits on the amount paid for any one loss. The special limits of liability are as follows:

■ $200 on money, bank notes, bullion, gold, silver, platinum, coins, and metals

■ $1,000 on securities, valuable papers, manuscripts, personal records, passports, tickets, and stamps

■ $1,000 on boats, trailers, and equipment

■ $1,000 on other trailers not used with boats

■ $2,500 on business property on the residence premises

■ $250 on business property away from the residence premises

■ $1,000 for adaptable electronic equipment designed to run off a car's electrical system, such as a cellular mobile telephone, fax machine, or lap-top computer (the limit applies whether the equipment is in or out of the motor vehicle)

   In addition, certain limits apply to the theft peril, including the following:

■ $1,000 for the theft of jewelry, watches, furs, and precious and semi-precious stones

- $2,000 for the theft of firearms

- $2,500 for the theft of silverware, goldware, and pewterware

The preceding limits are self-explanatory, but certain points should be noted. The $200 limit on money includes coin collections. If you own a valuable coin collection, it should be scheduled and specifically insured. A **schedule** is a list of covered property with specific amounts of insurance. A valuable stamp collection should also be specifically insured because of the $1,000 limit on stamps. In addition, boats have limited coverage under the homeowners policy. A boat with a value in excess of $1,000 should be specifically insured. Finally, the theft of jewelry and furs is limited to a maximum of $1,000 for any one loss. Expensive jewelry and furs and other types of valuable personal property should be specifically insured. This can be done by adding a rider or endorsement to the policy.

schedule In relation to homeowners insurance policies, a list of covered property with specific amounts of insurance designated.

Property not covered.   Coverage C excludes certain types of personal property. They include the following:

- Articles separately described and specifically insured

- Animals, birds, and fish

- Motor vehicles and motorized land conveyances (including automobiles and motorcycles and their equipment while in or on the vehicle, such as stereo tapes and discs)

- Aircraft and parts (except model or hobby aircraft)

- Property of roomers, boarders, and other tenants (except personal property of persons related to the insured)

- Personal property in a regularly rented apartment on the residence premises (coverage is limited to $2,500)

- Property rented to others or held for rental off the residence premises

- Business records

Coverage D: Loss of Use. Coverage D provides loss-of-use protection when the dwelling cannot be used because of a covered loss. If a covered loss makes the residence premises unfit to live in, the policy pays the additional living expense if the insured must temporarily reside elsewhere temporarily. **Additional living expense** is the increase in living expenses required to maintain the household's normal standard of living. For example, if a fire damages your home and you rent a furnished apartment for three months at $800 monthly, the additional increase in living expenses of $2,400 would be covered.

additional living expense In relation to homeowners insurance policies, the increase in living expenses required to maintain the household's normal standard of living when the insured dwelling cannot be used.

Additional Coverages. The HO-3 policy provides several additional coverages. These coverages include debris removal; cost of reasonable repairs to protect the property after a loss; damage to trees, shrubs, plants, and lawns from certain perils; coverage on property moved to another location for 30 days because of danger from an insured peril; unauthorized use of credit cards ($500 maximum); and certain other coverages.

Deductible. A deductible of $250 applies to each covered loss. To reduce premiums, higher deductibles such as $500 or $1,000 are available. The deductible does not apply to a fire department service charge or to losses involving credit cards, ATM cards, forgery, or counterfeit money.

Section I Perils Insured Against

The HO-3 policy describes the insured perils that apply both to the dwelling and other structures and to personal property.

Dwelling and Other Structures. The dwelling and other structures are insured against "risk of direct loss to property." *This means that all direct physical losses are covered except those losses specifically excluded.* If the loss to the dwelling or other structure is not excluded, it is covered under the policy.

Personal Property. Personal property (Coverage C) is covered on a *named-perils* basis. The policy pays for direct physical loss to personal property only from the following named perils:

- Fire or lightning
- Windstorm or hail
- Explosion
- Riot or civil commotion
- Aircraft
- Vehicles
- Smoke
- Vandalism or malicious mischief
- Theft
- Falling objects
- Weight of ice, snow, or sleet

■ Accidental discharge or overflow of water or steam from a plumbing, heating, air conditioning, or automatic fire protective sprinkler system, or from a household appliance

■ Sudden and accidental tearing apart, cracking, burning, or bulging of a steam, hot water, air conditioning, or automatic fire protective sprinkler system, or appliance for heating water

■ Freezing of a plumbing, heating, air conditioning, or automatic fire protective sprinkler system, or household appliance

■ Sudden and accidental damage from an artificially generated electrical current

■ Volcanic eruption

Additional Exclusions

The HO-3 contains a number of the general exclusions that apply to both the dwelling and other structures and to personal property. It is beyond the scope of the text to discuss these exclusions in detail. Two exclusions, however, merit some discussion: (1) earth movement and (2) water damage.

Earth Movement. Property damage from earth movement is specifically excluded. This includes damage from an earthquake, shock waves from a volcanic eruption, landslide, mudflow, or earth sinking. Thus, the homeowners policy clearly excludes earthquake damage to the home, other structures, and personal property.

Water Damage. The policy also excludes certain water damage losses. This includes damage from floods, surface water, or waves; water that backs up through sewers or drains; and water below the surface of the ground that seeps through a building, foundation, sidewalk, driveway, swimming pool, or other structure.

Duties After a Loss

The homeowners policy imposes certain duties on the insured if a property loss occurs. First, if a loss occurs, you must give immediate notice to the insurer or agent. If you delay in reporting the loss without good reason, you could jeopardize your right to recover. Second, you must protect the property from further damage and make reasonable and necessary repairs to protect the property. Third, you must prepare an inventory that describes the damaged property and the amount of loss. An inventory of your property before a loss occurs is highly advisable. A videocamera can be effectively used to inventory the property before a loss occurs. In addition, you may be required to show the damaged property to the insurer as often as is reasonably required and submit to questions under oath. Finally, you must file a proof of loss within 60 days after the insurer's request.

Loss Settlement

The homeowners policy has an important loss-settlement provision that specifies how losses are paid. Covered losses to *personal property* are paid on the basis of actual cash value at the time of loss but not to exceed the amount necessary to repair or replace the property. **Actual cash value** is defined as replacement cost less depreciation. Replacement cost is the current cost of restoring the damaged property with new material of like kind and quality. Depreciation is a deduction for physical wear and tear, age of the property, and economic obsolescence.

actual cash value Value of property at the time of its damage or loss, determined by subtracting depreciation of the item from its replacement cost.

For example, assume that Megan has a favorite couch that burns in a fire. Assume that she bought the couch five years ago, that the couch is 50 percent depreciated, and that a similar couch today would cost $1,000. Under the actual cash value rule and ignoring the deductible, Megan will collect $500 for the loss of her couch because replacement cost is $1,000, and depreciation is 50 percent, or $500. This can be summarized as follows:

$$\text{Replacement Cost} = \$1,000$$
$$\text{Depreciation} = \$500 \text{ (couch is 50 percent depreciated)}$$
$$\text{Actual Cash Value} = \text{Replacement Cost} - \text{Depreciation}$$
$$\$500 = \$1,000 - \$500$$

Payment of loss based on actual cash value can result in a substantial loss to the insured since few people budget for depreciation. However, an endorsement can be added to the policy that covers personal property on the basis of full replacement cost with no deduction for depreciation. This important endorsement will be discussed later in the chapter.

replacement cost In regard to homeowners insurance policies, the amount necessary to repair or replace the dwelling with material of like kind and quality at current prices.

Covered losses to the *dwelling and other structures* are paid on the basis of *replacement cost* with no deduction for depreciation. Replacement-cost insurance on the dwelling is one of the most important features of a homeowners policy. If the insurance carried is equal to at least 80 percent of the replacement cost of the damaged building at the time of loss, full replacement cost is paid with no deduction for depreciation up to the policy limit. **Replacement cost** is the amount necessary to repair or replace the dwelling with material of like kind and quality at current prices. For example, assume that a home has a current replacement value of $100,000 and is insured for $80,000. If the home is damaged by a tornado, and damages are $20,000, the full $20,000 is paid with no deduction for depreciation. However, if the home is totally destroyed, the maximum amount paid is the face amount of the policy—in this case, $80,000.

A different set of rules applies if the amount of insurance is less than 80 percent of the replacement cost at the time of loss. Stated simply, if the insurance carried is less than 80 percent of the replacement cost, the insured receives the larger of the following two amounts:

1. Actual cash value of that part of the building damaged

2. $\dfrac{\text{Amount of Insurance Carried}}{80\% \times \text{Replacement Cost}} \times \text{Loss}$

For example, assume that a dwelling has a replacement cost of $100,000 but is insured for only $60,000. The roof of the house is 10 years old and has a useful life of 20 years, or is 50 percent depreciated. Assume that the roof is severely damaged by a tornado, and that the replacement cost of a new roof is $20,000. Ignoring the deductible, the insured receives the larger of

1. Actual cash value $= \$20,000 - \$10,000$
$= \$10,000$

or

2. $\dfrac{\$60,000}{\$80\% \times \$100,000} \times \$20,000 = \$15,000$

The insured receives $15,000 for the loss. The entire loss would have been paid if the insured had carried a minimum of $80,000 of insurance.

Many insurers now offer a **guaranteed replacement-cost endorsement** by which the insured agrees to insure the home to 100 percent of its replacement cost rather than 80 percent. *In the event of a total loss, the insurer agrees to replace the home exactly as it was before the loss even though the replacement cost exceeds the amount of insurance stated in the policy.* Coverage is typically restricted to homes that are less than 25 years old, and homes that are of unique or unusual construction are ineligible.

guaranteed replacement-cost endorsement An endorsement to a home-owners insurance policy by which the insured agrees to insure a home to 100 per-cent of its replacement cost. Replacement cost is paid even if the loss exceeds the amount of insurance.

Section II Coverages

Section II in the homeowners policy provides personal liability insurance to the named insured and family members for legal liability out of their personal acts. The insurer will provide you with a legal defense and pay those sums that you are legally obligated to pay up to the policy limit. The following coverages are provided:

■ Coverage E: Personal liability, $100,000 per occurrence

■ Coverage F: Medical payments to others, $1,000 per person

Higher limits are available by paying a small additional premium.

personal liability insurance Insurance that protects the insured against a claim or suit for damages arising from bodily injury or property damage caused by the insured's negligence.

Coverage E: Personal Liability. **Personal liability insurance** protects the insured against a claim or suit for damages because of bodily injury or property damage caused by the insured's negligence. This means if you are legally liable for damages, the insurer will pay up to the policy limit the amount that you are legally obligated to pay.

In addition, the insurer will provide a legal defense and defend you even if the suit is groundless, false, or fraudulent. The legal defense costs are paid in addition to the policy limit. The insurer has the right to investigate and settle the claim or suit either by defending you in a court of law or by settling out of court. As a practical matter, most personal liability suits are settled out of court. However, the insurer's obligation to defend you ends when the amount paid for damages from the occurrence equals the policy limit.

Coverage F: Medical Payments to Others. This coverage is a mini-accident policy that is part of the homeowners policy. Unlike personal liability insurance, medical payments to others is not based on negligence and legal liability. **Medical payments to others** pays the reasonable medical expenses of someone who is accidentally injured on an insured location, or by the activities of an insured, resident employee, or animal owned by or in the care of an insured.

medical payments to others In regard to homeowners insurance, coverage that pays the reasonable medical expenses of someone who is accidentally injured on an insured location or by the activities of an insured, a resident employee, or an animal owned by or in the care of an insured.

Section II Exclusions. Section II contains numerous exclusions. The most important include the following:

■ *Business activities.* Liability arising out of business activities is excluded, such as operating a beauty shop in the home.

■ *Professional liability.* Legal liability arising out of professional services is excluded. Thus, physicians, lawyers, dentists, and accountants are not covered for professional activities.

■ *Motor vehicles.* Legal liability arising out of cars, trucks, motorcycles, and similar motorized vehicles is excluded. The exclusion does not apply to motor vehicles used to maintain the premises (for example, a garden tractor) or to a golf cart used while golfing.

■ *Larger watercraft.* Legal liability arising out of the operation of smaller boats is covered, but certain larger watercraft are excluded. This would include a boat owned by the insured with an inboard-outdrive engine exceeding 50 horsepower and a boat with one or more outboard engines exceeding 25 horsepower.

■ *Property in the care of an insured.* Personal liability insurance does not apply to property rented to, occupied or used by, or in the care of an insured. Thus, if you damage the carpet in a rented apartment, coverage does not apply.

■ *Other exclusions.* Other exclusions include liability arising out of the transmission of a communicable disease; sexual molestation; corporal punishment; physical and mental abuse; use, sale, or manufacture of illegal drugs; and the operation of a home day-care business. In addition, medical payments to others does not apply to the named insured or any family members.

Endorsements to the Homeowners Policy

Depending on your needs, an appropriate endorsement can be added to the homeowners policy to broaden the coverage. Important endorsements include the inflation-guard endorsement, earthquake endorsement, personal property replacement-cost endorsement, and scheduled personal property endorsement.

Inflation-Guard Endorsement

Many homeowners are underinsured because of inflation. If you do not carry insurance at least equal to 80 percent of the replacement cost at the time of loss, you will be penalized because full replacement cost will not be paid.

inflation-guard endorsement An endorsement to a homeowners insurance policy that increases the amount of insurance on the dwelling, other structures, and personal property by a specified annual percentage.

To deal with inflation, you should add an **inflation-guard endorsement** to your policy. The endorsement increases the amount of insurance on the dwelling, other structures, and personal property by a specified annual percentage. The annual increase is prorated over the policy year. For example, if the specified inflation rate is 4 percent, a home originally insured for $100,000 would be insured for $102,000 at the end of six months.

Earthquake Coverage

earthquake endorsement An endorsement to a homeowners insurance policy to cover earthquakes, landslides, volcanic eruption, and earth movement.

We noted earlier that the homeowners policy excludes damage from earthquakes. An **earthquake endorsement** can be added that covers earthquakes, landslides, volcanic eruption, and earth movement. A deductible is applied to each loss.

Although earthquakes can cause a catastrophic loss, most homeowners in earthquake zones do not have coverage. For example, the majority of homeowners in California are not insured for earthquakes. The major reasons for the lack of coverage are cost, a 10 percent deductible, the mis-

Insight

11.1 You Should Consider the Big Gap Between Replacement Cost and Actual Cash Value

If you own personal property, you should consider the big gap between replacement cost and actual cash value. You stand to pay a large amount out of pocket because of depreciation if the loss payment is based on actual cash value. The following table, based on the depreciation schedule of a large property and liability insurer, shows that the insured would receive $7,790 (less the deductible) based on *replacement cost* compared with only $3,967 based on *actual cash value*. Actual cash value is replacement cost less depreciation.

Item	Age	Replacement Cost	Depreciation	Actual Cash Value
Television set	5 years	$900	$450	$450
Sofa	4 years	1,500	600	900
Draperies	2 years	2,000	400	1,600
Five women's dresses	4 years	500	400	100
Three men's shoes	2 years	200	133	67
Three end tables	15 years	1,200	900	300
Refrigerator	10 years	800	560	240
Area rug	New	200	0	200
Cosmetics	6 months	200	180	20
Kitchen dishes	4 years	250	200	50
Thirty cans of food	New	40	0	40
Totals		$7,790	$3,823	$3,967

Note: The above hypothetical losses show the effect of depreciation, which is based on age and condition of the property; the older the item, the greater is the amount of depreciation.

taken belief that earthquakes will not occur, and the belief that federal disaster relief will be available.

Personal Property Replacement-Cost Endorsement

personal property replacement-cost endorsement An endorsement to a homeowners insurance policy that provides replacement cost coverage on personal property, carpets, domestic appliances, and outdoor equipment with no deduction for depreciation.

Losses to personal property are paid on the basis of actual cash value, which includes a deduction for depreciation. However, a **personal property replacement-cost endorsement** can be added that provides replacement-cost coverage on personal property, carpets, domestic appliances, and outdoor equipment. There is no deduction for depreciation.

You should consider adding the replacement-cost endorsement for personal property to your homeowners policy. Because of depreciation, the amount paid for a loss under an actual cash value policy is substantially less than that payable under a replacement-cost policy. Most insureds generally are unaware of the big gap between replacement cost and actual cash value (see Insight 11.1).

Scheduled Personal Property Endorsement

scheduled personal property endorsement
An endorsement to a homeowners insurance policy that provides coverage for items specifically listed, such as jewelry, furs, and paintings.

You may own valuable personal property and desire broader protection than that provided by the homeowners policy. The **scheduled personal property endorsement** can be added to the homeowners policy to provide broader coverage. The coverage can be added as an endorsement to the homeowners policy, or it can be written separately. When written separately, it is known as a personal articles floater. Nine optional classes of property can be insured, including jewelry, furs, cameras, musical instruments, silverware, golfer's equipment, fine arts, stamps, and coin collections. Each individual item must be described and insured for a specific amount. The property is insured on an "all-risks" basis. All direct physical losses are covered except those losses specifically excluded.

Other Property and Liability Insurance Coverages

Additional property and liability insurance coverages merit a brief discussion. They include federal flood insurance and the personal umbrella policy.

Federal Flood Insurance

federal flood insurance
A government insurance program that provides flood insurance at subsidized rates to property owners in flood zones.

Federal flood insurance is a government insurance program that provides flood insurance at subsidized rates to property owners in flood zones. Flood insurance is now available in all states, the District of Columbia, Puerto Rico, and the Virgin Islands.

Under the program, private insurers sell federal flood insurance policies under their own names, collect the premiums, retain a specified percentage for operating expenses and commission, and invest the remainder. The insurers service the policies and pay all claims. If the insurer's losses exceed premiums and investment income, they are reimbursed for the difference.

Under the regular flood insurance program, the maximum amount of insurance on a single-family home is limited to $250,000 and $100,000 on the contents. If a flood loss occurs, a $500 deductible must be satisfied, which applies separately to both the building and contents. Higher deductibles are available with a saving in premiums.

Exhibit 11.2

Typical Underlying Coverage Amounts Required to Qualify for a Personal Umbrella Policy

Automobile liability insurance	$250,000/$500,000/$50,000 or $500,000 single limit
Comprehensive personal liability insurance (separate contract or homeowners policy)	$100,000
Large watercraft	$300,000 or higher
Employers liability insurance (where required or permitted by law)	$100,000

Personal Umbrella Policy

personal umbrella policy Insurance policy designed to provide protection against a catastrophic law-suit or judgment; coverage generally ranges from $1 million to $10 million.

Personal liability claims occasionally reach catastrophic levels and exceed the liability limits of the basic contracts. After these basic limits are exhausted, you may be required to pay thousands of dollars from your personal assets. The **personal umbrella policy** is designed to provide protection against a catastrophic lawsuit or judgment. Most insurers write this coverage in amounts ranging from $1 million to $10 million. Coverage is broad and covers the catastrophic liability exposures associated with the home, boats, automobiles, sports, and recreational vehicles.

Although personal umbrella policies are not standard contracts, they contain several common characteristics. *First, the personal umbrella policy is excess insurance over any basic underlying insurance that may apply.* The umbrella policy pays only after the basic limits of the underlying contracts are exhausted. The insured must carry certain minimum amounts of liability insurance on the underlying contracts (see Exhibit 11.2).

Second, the personal umbrella policy provides broad coverage of personal liability loss exposures. The policy covers legal liability arising out of both personal injury and property damage. Personal injury includes bodily injury, shock, mental anguish, false arrest and imprisonment, libel, slander, and defamation of character. Property damage is defined as physical injury to tangible property and includes the loss of use of the damaged property.

self-insured retention A provision in a personal umbrella policy whereby, when a loss is covered by the umbrella policy but not by any underlying insurance policy, the insured must retain, or pay, a certain amount of the loss.

Third, a **self-insured retention** *must be satisfied if the loss is covered by the umbrella policy but not by any underlying insurance.* The self-insured retention is at least $250 per occurrence, but it can be higher. Examples of claims not covered by any underlying contract but insured under the umbrella policy include libel, slander, defamation of character, and a wide variety of additional claims (see Insight 11.2).

Insight 11.2 The Perils an Umbrella Policy Can Protect Against

Auto accidents cause most of the personal injuries that result in huge monetary settlements paid by umbrella liability insurance. But there are plenty of other calamities that can put your assets at serious risk. Consider these recent real-life cases:

- You know the game: One person kneels behind another and a third pushes the "victim" over. In a case settled last year, three 10-year-olds were the players. One child broke his arm and the other two were sued. The case cost the kneeling boy $100,000 and the one who did the pushing $195,000.

- A 40-year-old window washer broke his heel in a fall after a downspout he was holding onto broke away from the house on which he was working. Although the worker was found partially responsi-ble, the fall cost the home-owner $1.2 million.

- A 22-year-old suffered per-manent eye damage when he was struck by a golf ball. He sued, claiming that the golfer who hit the ball had failed to look out for other players. The errant shot cost the golfer $160,000.

- A professional dancer suf-fered permanent knee damage—and an end to her career—when she was knocked down on a begin-ner's ski slope. She offered to settle for the $300,000 cov-ered by the defendant's insurance, but was rebuffed. The case went to trial, where it cost the defendant $2.2 million.

- A woman suffered severe cuts when her leg was hit by the propeller of a boat she was attempting to board. She sued, claiming that the boat began to move before she was safely aboard. The injury cost the boat owner $175,000.

- At an end-of-school swim party, a 16-year-old dove and hit his head on the bottom of the pool. He became a quad-riplegic, and the case resulted in a $1.5-million set-tlement against the home-owner.

- A 5-year-old suffered brain damage when a dinner bell at his grandfather's home fell and struck him in the head. A lawsuit against the grandfather led to a $500,000 settlement.

Source: Reprinted with permission from the July 1995 issue of *Kiplinger's Personal Finance Magazine.* Copyright © 1995 The Kiplinger Washington Editors, Inc.

Finally, the personal umbrella policy is reasonable in cost. For most families, protection can be obtained by an annual premium of less than $250 for a $1 million policy. Payment of a relatively modest premium should provide you with greater peace of mind because you are covered for a catastrophic lawsuit arising out of personal acts.

Shopping for a Homeowners Policy

As an informed consumer, you should understand how the cost of a homeowners policy is determined. You should also understand the rules to follow when a homeowners policy is purchased.

Cost of Homeowners Insurance

Premiums for a homeowners policy are based on several important rating factors.

■ First, *construction* of the home is extremely important. The more fire resistant the home is, the lower is the rate. Thus, brick homes are less expensive to insure than frame homes.

■ *Location* is another important rating factor. Insureds who live in territories with high losses from fires, natural disasters, or crime must pay higher rates. In addition, accessibility of the home to the fire department is important. Rural areas generally have higher rates than urban areas.

■ *Construction costs* have a significant impact on rates. The higher it costs the insurer to repair or rebuild your home, the higher the premium is likely to be.

■ *Age of the home* also affects the rates charged. Older homes have higher rates because they are more susceptible to damage from fire and storms. Further, old wiring and outdated building code standards can make older homes more costly to insure.

Exhibit 11.3

Tips for Buying a Homeowners Policy

■ Finally, the *type of policy* and *deductible amount* are also important rating factors. HO-3 is more expensive than HO-2 because broader coverage is provided. Likewise, the higher the deductible amount, the lower is the premium.

Suggestions for Buying a Homeowners Policy

As a careful insurance consumer, you should remember certain suggestions when a homeowners policy is purchased (see Exhibit 11.3).

Carry Adequate Insurance.   The first suggestion is to carry adequate amounts of property insurance on both your home and personal property. This is particularly important if a room is added or home improvements are made since the value of the home may be substantially increased. The home must be insured for at least 80 percent of its replacement cost to avoid a penalty if a loss occurs. *However, you should seriously consider insuring your home to 100 percent of replacement cost.* Few homeowners can afford an additional 20 percent payment out of pocket if a total loss occurs. By adding the guaranteed replacement cost endorsement to the policy, full replacement cost is paid even if the actual cost exceeds the policy limit.

Exhibit 11.4

Homeowners 3 Premiums for Phoenix, Arizona

		Annual Premium	
Rank	Name	Masonry	Frame
	Five Lowest-Cost Policies		
1.	Unisun Insurance Co.	$328	$328
2.	United Services Automobile Assn.	335	372
3.	Hartford Insurance Co. of the Midwest	363	386
4.	Federated Mutual Insurance Co.	373	393
5.	Bankers Standard Insurance Co.	379	399
	Five Highest-Cost Policies		
44.	American Economy Insurance Co.	$650	$656
45.	Grain Dealers Mutual Insurance Co.	684	684
46.	American Spirit Insurance Co.	769	769
47.	Sentry Ins. A Mutual Co.	781	805
48.	Metropolitan Prop. & Cas. Insurance Co.	789	789

Note: Premiums are annual premiums based on the rates in effect 10/1/95. The hypothetical house is a one-story, single-family dwelling with 2,200 square feet. The insurance limits are $115,000 on the dwelling, $57,500 on the contents, $11,500 for additional living expenses, $100,000 personal liability coverage, $2,000 medical payments coverage, and a flat $250 deductible.

Source: Arizona Department of Insurance.

Add Necessary Endorsements. Certain endorsements may be necessary depending on your needs, local property conditions, or high values for certain types of personal property. To deal with inflation, you should add an *inflation-guard endorsement* to your homeowners policy if your insurer does not include it. An *earthquake endorsement* is desirable if you live in an earthquake zone. The *personal property replacement-cost endorsement* is also desirable because you are indemnified on the basis of replacement cost with no deduction for depreciation; the replacement-cost endorsement provides for a more adequate loss payment if your personal property is damaged or stolen. In addition, if you own valuable property, such as jewelry, furs, fine art, or a valuable coin or stamp collection, you should add the *scheduled personal property* endorsement to your policy. Each item is listed and specifically insured for a certain amount.

Consider This

You can get state-by-state information (including rates) on both homeowners and auto insurance from the Insurance News Network at: http://www.insure.com/

Shop Around for a Homeowners Policy. Another important suggestion is to shop around for a homeowners policy. Since there is considerable price variation among insurers, you can reduce your homeowners premium by shopping around. Consequently, it pays to get a price quote from several insurers before you buy a homeowners policy. Some states publish shoppers' guides to assist consumers who purchase homeowners policies. These guides indicate wide variation in premiums charged by insurers. For example, Exhibit 11.4 shows the five lowest- and five highest-cost policies in Phoenix, Arizona, as a result of a survey of 48 insurers by the Arizona Department of Insurance. *The cost difference between the lowest- and highest-cost policy is about 141 percent.* It pays to shop around.

Consider a Higher Deductible. Another suggestion for reducing premiums is to purchase the policy with a higher deductible. The standard homeowners deductible is $250. *However, a higher deductible can substantially reduce your premiums.* You can usually get a discount of 10 percent with a $500 deductible and a 20 to 30 percent discount with a $1,000 deductible. For example, Tom Beam has a $1,000 deductible in his homeowners policy instead of the standard $250, which saves him $180 annually. In other words, Tom saves $180 each year but loses only $750 in coverage. That additional $750 is very expensive coverage.

Take Advantage of Discounts. When you shop for a homeowners policy, you should inquire whether you are eligible for any discounts or credits, which can further reduce your premiums. Insurers offer a wide variety of discounts based on numerous factors, including age of the home, fire and smoke alarms, sprinkler system, deadbolt locks, and fire extinguishers.

Don't Ignore Natural Disaster Perils. The homeowners policy covers hurricanes, tornadoes, windstorm, and fire losses. However, earthquakes and floods are specifically excluded. Although federal flood insurance is available, and an earthquake endorsement can be added to the homeowners policy, most property owners are not insured against these two perils. If you reside in a flood or earthquake zone, you should seriously consider covering such perils in your personal risk management program.

Purchase a Personal Umbrella Policy to Complete Your Program. An unendorsed homeowners policy provides only $100,000 of personal liability insurance, which is insufficient in the event of a catastrophic liability loss. As we noted earlier, a personal umbrella policy provides an additional $1 million to $10 million of liability insurance after the underlying coverage is exhausted. A personal umbrella policy also covers liability arising out of personal injury, including coverage for libel, slander, and defamation of character. The homeowners policy does not cover this exposure without an endorsement. Finally, in addition to coverage on your home and personal activities, the personal umbrella policy provides excess liability insurance on your cars, boats, and recreational vehicles.

Automobile Insurance and the Personal Auto Policy

Automobile insurance is one of the most important coverages that should be emphasized in a personal risk management program. Legal liability arising out of the negligent operation of an automobile can reach catastrophic levels. Medical expenses, pain and suffering, the unexpected death of a family member, and the damage or theft of an expensive automobile can have a traumatic financial impact on the individual or family.

In this section, we examine the major provisions of the **personal auto policy (PAP).** The PAP is drafted by the Insurance Services Office (ISO) and is widely used throughout the United States. The following section is based on the current (1994) edition of the PAP. As you study this section, you may find it helpful to refer to the PAP that appears in Appendix D in the text.

The PAP is designed to cover legal liability arising out of the ownership or operation of a covered automobile. The PAP can also be used to insure physical damage losses to the vehicle. The major coverages include the following:

- Part A: Liability coverage

- Part B: Medical payments coverage

personal auto policy (PAP) Automobile insurance policy drafted by the Insurance Services Office and widely used throughout the United States; major coverages are liability coverage, medical payments coverage, uninsured motorists coverage, and coverage for damage to your auto.

- Part C: Uninsured motorists coverage

- Part D: Coverage for damage to your auto

Part A: Liability Coverage

liability coverage (Part A) That part of a personal auto policy that protects a covered person against a suit or claim involving bodily injury or property damages arising out of negligent operation of an automobile.

single limit With respect to liability coverage in a personal auto policy, a provision by which the total amount of insurance applies to the entire accident without a separate limit for each person and without a distinction between bodily injury and property damage liability.

split limits With respect to liability coverage in a personal auto policy, a provision by which the amounts of insurance for bodily injury and property damage liability are stated separately.

covered auto As defined in the personal auto policy, (1) any vehicle shown in the declarations, (2) a vehicle acquired by the insured during the policy period, (3) a trailer owned by the insured, or (4) a temporary substitute auto.

Liability coverage (Part A) is the most important part of the PAP. It protects a covered person against a suit or claim arising out of the negligent operation of an automobile. In the insuring agreement, the insurer agrees to pay any damages for bodily injury or property damage for which an insured is legally responsible because of an auto accident.

Liability coverage generally is written as a **single limit** that applies to both bodily injury and property damage liability. This means that total amount of insurance applies to the entire accident without a separate limit for each person. For example, a single limit of $500,000 would apply to both bodily injury and property damage liability. However, the PAP policy can also be written with split limits. **Split limits** mean the amounts of insurance for bodily injury liability and property damage liability are stated separately. For example, split limits of $250,000/$500,000/$100,000 mean you have bodily injury liability coverage of $250,000 for each person and $500,000 for each accident. You also have $100,000 of property damage liability coverage.

In addition to the payment for damages for which you are legally liable, the insurer agrees to defend you and pays all legal defense costs. The defense costs are paid in addition to the policy limits.

Your Covered Auto. An extremely important definition with respect to liability coverage is the definition of your **covered auto.** Four classes of vehicles are considered to be covered autos:

First, any vehicle listed in the declaration is a covered auto. The declarations page is the first page in the auto policy that provides relevant information about a covered auto, such as the named insured, coverages provided, and amount of insurance.

Second, a newly acquired private passenger auto, pickup, or van is also a covered auto if the vehicle is acquired by the named insured during the policy period. If the newly acquired vehicle is an additional vehicle, you are automatically insured from the date of acquisition provided you notify the insurer within 30 days after you become the owner and ask the insurer to insure it. For example, if you own one car and purchase a second car, you are automatically covered when you drive away from the lot. An additional premium must be paid for the newly acquired vehicle.

If the new vehicle you acquire *replaces* one shown in the declarations, the new vehicle automatically has the same coverage as the vehicle it replaced. However, you are required to report a replacement vehicle within 30 days of acquisition only if you wish to add or continue physical damage insurance (Part D) on the replacement vehicle.

temporary substitute auto A nonowned auto or trailer that the insured is temporarily using because of mechanical breakdown, repair, servicing, loss, or destruction of a covered vehicle.

Third, a trailer owned by the named insured is also considered to be a covered auto. For example, you may be pulling a boat trailer that upsets and injures another motorist. The liability section of the PAP would cover the loss.

Finally, a **temporary substitute auto** *is a covered vehicle.* A temporary substitute auto is a nonowned auto or trailer that you are temporarily using because of mechanical breakdown, repair, servicing, loss, or destruction of a covered vehicle. Thus, if you drive a loaner car while your car is in the garage for repairs, it is insured for liability coverage under the PAP.

Insured Persons.   Four groups are insured under the liability section of the PAP.

First, the named insured and family members are insured for liability coverage The named insured also includes a spouse if a resident of the same household. Thus, the husband, wife, and children are covered while using any automobile, owned or nonowned. If the children are attending college, and are temporarily away from home, they are still insured under the parent's policy.

Second, any other person using the named insured's covered auto is insured provided that person can establish a reasonable belief that permission to use the covered auto exists. For example, Roger may have permitted his girlfriend, Tina, to drive his car several times over the past six months. If Tina takes Roger's car without his express permission, she is covered under his policy as long as she can show a reasonable belief that Roger would have given her permission to use the auto.

Third, any person or organization legally responsible for the acts of a covered person while using a covered auto is also insured. For example, if Claude drives his car on an errand for his employer, and he injures someone, the employer is covered for any suit or claim.

Finally, coverage applies to any person or organization legally responsible for the named insured's or family members' use of any automobile or trailer (other than a covered auto or one owned by the person or organization). For example, Claude may borrow the car of a fellow worker to mail a package for his employer. If Claude injures someone while driving that car, the employer is also covered for any suit or claim.

Part B: Medical Payments Coverage

medical payments coverage (Part B) That part of a personal auto policy that covers reasonable medical and funeral expenses incurred by a covered person within three years from the date of an accident.

Medical payments coverage (Part B) is an optional accident benefit that can be added to the PAP. Under this provision, the insurer will pay all reasonable medical and funeral expenses incurred by an insured for services rendered within three years from the date of the accident. Covered expenses include medical, surgical, x-ray, dental, and funeral services. The benefit limits typically range from $1,000 to $10,000 per person and apply to each insured who is injured in an accident. For example, if the parents and children are injured in an auto accident while on vacation, their medical expenses are covered up to the policy limits.

Part C: Uninsured Motorists Coverage

uninsured motorists coverage (Part C) That part of a personal auto policy that covers bodily injury (and property damage in some states) caused by an uninsured motorist, by a hit-and-run driver, or by a negligent driver whose insurance company is insolvent.

Some persons are irresponsible and drive without liability insurance. The **uninsured motorists coverage (Part C)** pays for the bodily injury (and property damage in some states) caused by an uninsured motorist, by a hit-and-run driver, or by a negligent driver whose company is insolvent.

The insurer pays compensatory damages that an insured is legally entitled to receive from the owner or operator of an uninsured motor vehicle because of bodily injury caused by an accident. Damages include medical bills, lost wages, and compensation for a permanent disfigurement resulting from the accident. Several important points must be emphasized with respect to this coverage.

■ *The coverage applies only if the uninsured motorist is legally liable.* If the uninsured motorist is not liable, the insurer will not pay for the bodily injury.

■ *The insurer's maximum limit of liability for any single accident is the amount shown in the declarations.* Furthermore, you cannot receive a duplicate payment for the same elements of loss under the uninsured motorists coverage and Part A (liability coverage) or Part B (medical payments coverage) of the policy.

■ *The claim is subject to arbitration if the insured and insurer disagree over the amount of damages or whether the insured is entitled to receive any damages.* Under this provision, each party selects an arbitrator. The two arbitrators select a third arbitrator. A decision by two of the three is binding on all parties.

Part D: Coverage for Damage to Your Auto

coverage for damage to your auto (Part D) That part of a personal auto policy that provides coverage for physical damage to or theft of the insured's automobile.

Coverage for damage to your auto (Part D) provides coverage for the physical damage or theft of your auto. In the insuring agreement, the insurer agrees to pay for any direct and accidental loss to a covered auto or any nonowned auto, including its equipment, less any applicable deductible. Two optional coverages are available. *A covered auto can be insured for both (1) a collision loss and (2) an other-than-collision loss (also called comprehensive).*

collision With respect to a personal auto policy, the upset of a covered auto or nonowned auto or its impact with another vehicle or object.

Collision Loss. **Collision** is defined as the upset of your covered auto or nonowned auto or its impact with another vehicle or object. The following are examples of a collision loss:

- Your car hits another car, a telephone pole, a tree, or a building.

- Your car is parked, and you find the rear fender dented when you return.

- You open the car door in a parking lot, and the door is damaged when it hits the vehicle parked next to you.

Collision losses are paid regardless of fault. It you cause the accident, your insurer will pay for the damage to your car, less any deductible. If some other driver damages your car, you can either collect from the negligent driver (or from his or her insurer), or look to your insurer to pay the claim. If you collect from your own insurer, you must give up legal rights to your insurer, who will then attempt to collect from the negligent driver who caused the accident. If the entire amount of the loss is recovered, you insurer will refund the deductible.

Other-Than-Collision Loss. The PAP can also be written to cover an **other-than-collision loss.** The PAP distinguishes between a collision loss and an other-than-collision loss. The distinction is important because some car owners do not desire collision coverage on their cars. Further, the deductibles under the two coverages may be different. Other-than-collision coverage is frequently written with a lower deductible.

Loss from any of the following perils is considered to be an other-than-collision loss:

other-than-collision loss Loss that may be covered by a personal auto policy; such losses include all physical damage losses except collision losses and other, specified losses.

- Missiles or falling objects

- Fire

- Theft or larceny

- Explosion or earthquake

- Windstorm

- Hail, water, or flood

- Malicious mischief or vandalism

- Riot or civil commotion

- Contact with a bird or animal

- Glass breakage

nonowned auto A private passenger auto, pickup, van, or trailer not owned by or furnished or made available for the regular use of the named insured or family member, while it is in the custody of or is being operated by the named insured or family member.

These losses are self-explanatory, but one comment is in order. Remember that colliding with a bird or animal is not a collision loss. Thus, if you hit a bird or a deer with your car, the physical damage to the car is considered to be an other-than-collision loss.

Nonowned Auto. The Part D coverages also apply to a nonowned auto. A nonowned auto is a private passenger auto, pickup, van, or trailer not owned by or furnished or made available for the regular use of the named insured or family member, while it is in the custody of or is being operated by the named insured or family member. A nonowned auto also includes a temporary substitute vehicle. For example, if Karen borrows Mike's car, Karen's collision coverage and other-than-collision coverage on her car also apply to the borrowed car. However, if Mike carries collision insurance on his car, his policy would pay first if a loss occurs. Karen's insurance would be excess over any physical damage insurance on the borrowed car.

The Part D coverages apply only if the nonowned auto is not furnished or made available for the regular use of the named insured or family member. You can occasionally drive a borrowed automobile, and your physical damage insurance will cover the borrowed vehicle. *However, if the vehicle is driven on a regular basis or is furnished or made available for your regular use, the Part D coverages do not apply.* The key point here is not how frequently you drive a nonowned auto, but whether the vehicle is furnished or made available for your regular use.

Deductible.   The collision coverage is typically written with a flat deductible of $250, or some higher amount. Coverage for other-than-collision losses is also normally written with a deductible. Deductibles are designed to reduce small claims, hold down premiums, and encourage the insured to be more careful in protecting the car from damage or theft.

Exclusions

As an informed consumer, you should be familiar with the major exclusions that appear in an auto insurance policy. The most important exclusions apply to liability coverage (Coverage A) and coverage for damage to your auto (Coverage D). They include the following:

■ *Use as a public or livery conveyance.* Liability coverage does not apply to any vehicle while it is being used as a public or livery conveyance, such as a public taxicab. The exclusion does not apply to a share-the-expense car pool.

■ *Vehicles used in the automobile business.* Liability arising out of the operation of vehicle in the automobile business is excluded. The automobile business refers to the selling, repairing, servicing, storing, or parking of vehicle designed for use mainly on public highways. Thus, if a mechanic has an accident and injures someone while road-testing your car, your liability coverage does not protect the mechanic.

■ *Using a vehicle without reasonable belief of permission.* If you use a vehicle without a reasonable belief that you have permission to do so, the liability coverage does not apply.

■ *Vehicles with fewer than four wheels.* Liability coverage does not apply to motorcycles, mopeds, motorscooters, minibikes, trailbikes, and similar vehicles.

■ *Vehicles furnished or made available for the named insured's or family member's regular use.* You can occasionally drive another person's car and still have coverage under your policy. However if the nonowned auto is driven regularly or is furnished for your regular use, your liability coverage does not apply. For example, if your employer furnishes you with a car, your liability coverage does not apply. However, for an additional premium, an endorsement can be added that would cover you while operating a nonowned car on a regular basis.

The preceding exclusions also apply to coverage for damage to your auto (Coverage D). In addition, certain physical damage losses to covered vehicles are excluded. The most important include the following:

■ *Damage from wear and tear, freezing, and mechanical or electrical breakdown.* The intent here is to exclude the normal maintenance cost of operating an automobile. The exclusion does not apply to the theft of a covered vehicle. For example, if the electrical system is damaged by a thief who hot-wires the car, the loss is covered.

■ *Certain electronic equipment.* Electronic equipment designed for the reproduction of sound, such as a stereo set and tape decks, is excluded. The policy also excludes a citizens' band radio, car telephone, personal computer, tapes, records, or other accessories. Coverage of excluded equipment can be obtained by an endorsement to the policy.

The proceeding exclusion does not apply to equipment designed for the reproduction of sound and accessories if the equipment is permanently installed in a covered auto or nonowned auto.

■ *Loss to a nonowned auto used without reasonable belief of permission.* Loss to a nonowned auto is not covered when it is used by the named insured or family member without a reasonable belief of permission.

■ *Awnings or cabanas.* Loss to awnings, cabanas, or equipment designed to create additional living facilities is also excluded. For example, adding such equipment to a van would not be covered. An endorsement can be added to cover such property.

■ *Radar detection equipment.* Loss to equipment for the detection or location of radar or laser is also excluded. The exclusion is justified since radar detection equipment is designed to circumvent state and federal speed laws.

■ *Custom furnishings or equipment.* Loss to custom furnishings or equipment in a van such as carpeting, furniture, bars, cooking and sleeping facilities, height-extending roofs, and custom murals or paintings is specifically excluded. However, a special customized equipment endorsement can be added that covers the excluded furnishings or equipment.

Other Policy Provisions

The PAP contains numerous additional policy provisions. Only two of them are discussed here.

Duties After an Accident or Loss. You should also know what to do if you have an accident or loss. You should first determine if anyone in the other vehicle is hurt. If someone is injured, call an ambulance. If there are bodily injuries, or the property damage exceeds a certain amount (such as $200), you are required to notify the police in most jurisdictions. You should give the other driver your name, address, and the name of your agent and insurer and request the same information from him or her. *Under no circumstance should you admit that you caused the accident.* The question of negligence and legal liability will be resolved by the insurers involved (or court of law if necessary) and not by you. If you admit that you are responsible for the accident, you prejudice your insurer's obligation and ability to defend you and jeopardize your insurance coverage.

Your agent should be promptly notified of the accident, even if there are no injuries or property damage. Failure to report the accident promptly to your insurer could jeopardize your coverage if you are later sued by the other driver. Finally, you should know how to file a valid claim if you have an auto accident. (see Insight 11.3)

Policy Territory. The PAP provides coverage only in the United States, its territories or possessions, Puerto Rico, and Canada. The policy also insures a covered auto while it is being transported between the ports of the United States, Puerto Rico, or Canada. For example, if you rent a car while vacationing in England, Germany, or Mexico, you are not covered. Additional automobile insurance must be purchased to be covered while driving in foreign countries.

Automobile Insurance and the Law

Although accident victims have bodily injuries or suffer property damage, they may recover nothing or receive less than full indemnifica-

11.3 How to File an Auto Insurance Claim

Auto Insurance Claims

Taking the time *now* to review the steps you should follow after an auto accident will help reduce the anxiety surrounding the incident and avoid costly and time-consuming mistakes.

Before You Have a Claim

Be sure you know the answers to these questions before you have to file a claim:

- *How much liability insurance do you have?* This coverage pays for damage you cause to another vehicle or injuries to other people.

- *Does your state have no-fault insurance?* What coverages does it provide?

- *If you have collision and/or comprehensive coverage, what is your deductible* (the amount you've agreed to pay out of your own pocket if you suffer a loss)?

At the Scene

- *Stop your car and get help for the injured.*
  Have someone call the police or highway patrol. Tell them how many people were injured and the types of injuries. The police can then notify the nearest medical unit. Give whatever help you can to the injured but avoid moving anyone so you don't aggravate the injury. Covering an injured person with a blanket and making that person comfortable usually is as much as you can do.

- *Provide the police with whatever information they require.*
  Ask the investigating officer where you can obtain a copy of the police report, which you may need to support any claim you submit to your insurance company.

- *Try to protect the accident scene.*
  Take reasonable steps to protect your car from further damage, such as setting up flares, getting the car off the road and calling a tow truck. If necessary, have the car towed to a repair shop. But remember, your insurance company probably will want to have an adjuster inspect it and appraise the damage before you order repair work done.

tion from the negligent drivers who caused the accident. To deal with this problem, the states have passed laws that provide some protection to accident victims from irresponsible and reckless drivers. These laws include financial responsibility laws, compulsory insurance laws, unsatisfied judgment funds, and no-fault automobile insurance.

Financial Responsibility Laws

financial responsibility law State law that requires persons involved in automobile accidents under certain circumstances to furnish proof of financial responsibility up to a minimum dollar limit or face having their driving privileges revoked or suspended.

Many states have financial responsibility laws that require motorists to furnish proof of financial responsibility up to certain minimum dollar amounts. A **financial responsibility law** is one that does not require proof of financial responsibility until the driver has his or her first accident, or until after conviction for certain offenses, such as driving under the influence of alcohol. If a motorist does not meet the financial responsibility law requirements, the state can revoke or suspend the motorist's driving privileges.

- *Make notes.*
  Keep a pad and pencil in your glove compartment. Write down the names and addresses of all drivers and passengers involved in the accident. Also note the license number, make and model of each car involved and record the driver's license number and insurance identification of each driver. Record the names and addresses of as many witnesses as possible, as well as the names and badge numbers of police officers or other emergency personnel. If you run into an unattended vehicle or object, try to find the owner. If you can't, leave a note containing your name, address and phone number.

Filing Your Claim

If your car is involved in an accident, if it is damaged by fire, flood or vandalism, or if it is stolen, put your insurance to work for you by following these steps in filing your claim:

- *Phone your insurance agent or a local company representative.* Do it as soon as possible even if you're far from home and even if someone else caused the accident. Ask your agent how to proceed and what forms or documents will be needed to support your claim. Your company may require a "proof of loss" form, as well as documents relating to your claim, such as medical and auto repair bills and a copy of the police report.

- *Supply the information your insurer needs.* Cooperate with your insurance company in its investigation, settlement or defense of any claim, and turn over to the company immediately copies of any legal papers you receive in connection with your loss. Your insurer will represent you if a claim is brought against you and defend you if you are sued.

- *Keep records of your expenses.* Expenses you incur as a result of an automobile accident may be reimbursed under your policy. Remember, for example, that your no-fault insurer usually will pay your medical and hospital expenses, and possibly such other costs as lost wages and at least part of your costs if you have to hire a temporary housekeeper.

- *Keep copies of your paper work.* Store copies of all paper work in your own files. You may need to refer to it later.

Source: Insurance Information Institute brochure. Reprinted with permission.

Evidence of financial responsibility can be provided by having automobile liability insurance with certain limits, such as $25,000/$50,000/$25,000. Other ways to satisfy the law include posting a bond, depositing money or securities in the amount required by law, or showing the person is a qualified self-insurer. Exhibit 11.5 shows the minimum liability insurance requirements in the various states.

Compulsory Insurance Laws

compulsory insurance law State law that requires the owners and operators of motor vehicles to carry liability insurance in certain minimum amounts in order for their vehicles to be registered or licensed.

The majority of states and the District of Columbia have enacted some type of compulsory insurance law as a requirement for driving within the states. A **compulsory insurance law** requires the owners and operators of motor vehicles to carry liability insurance with certain minimum limits before the vehicle can be registered or licensed. The law can also be satisfied by posting a bond that guarantees financial responsibility or by depositing money or other securities that can satisfy a judgment.

Exhibit 11.5

Automobile Financial Responsibility/Compulsory Limits

State	Liability Limits*	State	Liability Limits*
Alabama	20/40/10	Montana	25/50/10
Alaska	50/100/25	Nebraska	25/50/25
Arizona	15/30/10	Nevada	15/30/10
Arkansas	25/50/15	New Hampshire	25/50/25
California	15/30/5	New Jersey	15/30/5
Colorado	25/50/15	New Mexico	25/50/10
Connecticut	20/40/10	New York	10/20/5†
Delaware	15/30/10	North Carolina	25/50/10
D.C.	25/50/10	North Dakota	25/50/25
Florida	10/20/10	Ohio	12.5/25/7.5
Georgia	15/30/10	Oklahoma	10/20/10
Hawaii	20/10/25	Oregon	25/50/10
Idaho	25/50/15	Pennsylvania	15/30/5
Illinois	20/40/15	Rhode Island	25/50/25
Indiana	25/50/10	South Carolina	15/30/5
Iowa	20/40/15	South Dakota	25/50/25
Kansas	25/50/10	Tennessee	20/50/10
Kentucky	25/50/10	Texas	20/40/15
Louisiana	10/20/10	Utah	25/50/15
Maine	20/40/10	Vermont	20/40/10
Maryland	20/40/10	Virginia	25/50/20
Massachusetts	20/40/5	Washington	25/50/10
Michigan	20/40/10	West Virginia	20/40/10
Minnesota	30/60/10	Wisconsin	25/50/10
Mississippi	10/20/5	Wyoming	25/50/20
Missouri	25/50/10		

* The first two figures refer to bodily injury liability limits and the third figure to property damage liability. For example, 20/40/10 means coverage up to $40,000 for all persons injured in an accident, subject to a limit of $20,000 for each individual, and $10,000 coverage for property damage.

† 50/100 if injury results in death,

Source: *The Fact Book of 1995, Property/Casualty Insurance Facts*, NY: Insurance Information Institute, pp. 115–116. Reprinted with permission.

Unsatisfied Judgment Funds

unsatisfied judgment fund A fund established by a state to compensate accident victims who have exhausted all other means of recovery.

Five states—Maryland, Michigan, New Jersey, New York, and North Dakota—have established unsatisfied judgment funds for compensating innocent accident victims. An **unsatisfied judgment fund** is a fund established by the state to compensate accident victims who have exhausted all other means of recovery. To receive payment from the fund, the accident victim must obtain a judgment against the negligent motorist who caused the accident and must show that the judgment cannot be collected. Thus, there must be an unsatisfied judgment.

No-Fault Automobile Insurance

no-fault insurance A type of insurance providing that after an automobile accident, each party collects from his or her own insurer regardless of fault.

Because of dissatisfaction and defects in the traditional tort liability system for compensating accident victims, about half the states have enacted some type of no-fault law. **No-fault insurance** means that after an automobile accident involving a bodily injury, each party collects from his or her insurer regardless of fault. It is not necessary to determine who is at fault and prove negligence before a loss payment is made. Regardless of who caused the accident, each party collects from his or her own insurer.

A true no-fault law places some restriction on the right to sue the negligent driver who caused the accident. *If the claim is below a certain dollar threshold (such as $2,000), an injured motorist would not be permitted to sue but instead would collect from his or her own insurer.* However, if the bodily injury claim exceeds the threshold amount, the injured person has the right to sue the negligent driver for damages. In three states, a verbal rather than monetary threshold is used. A verbal threshold means a suit for damages is allowed only in serious cases, such as death, dismemberment, or disfigurement. If the injured person has a less severe injury than those listed, the injured person would not be permitted to sue but would collect from his or her insurer.

No-fault benefits are provided by adding an endorsement to an automobile insurance policy. Benefits are restricted to the injured person's *economic loss,* such as medical bills and lost wages. The injured person can sue for *noneconomic loss factors* (such as pain and suffering and inconvenience) only if the dollar threshold is exceeded or the verbal threshold is met. However, some states have enacted no-fault laws (called add-on plans) by which an injured person can collect benefits from his or her insurer and still retain the right to sue the negligent driver. Such laws, however, are not true no-fault laws since no restrictions are placed on the right to due.

The no-fault benefits typically paid include payment of medical bills up to some maximum limit, payment of a stated percentage of the injured person's earnings, essential services expenses (such as hiring someone to mow the lawn), funeral expenses, and survivors' loss benefits to eligible surviving family members. As stated earlier, no payments are made for pain and suffering.

Shopping for Auto Insurance

Auto insurance is expensive. Thus, you should be aware of the major rating factors that determine your premiums and what you can do to reduce the premiums. In addition, you should be aware of the sugges-

Exhibit 11.6

Accidents by Age of Drivers, 1993

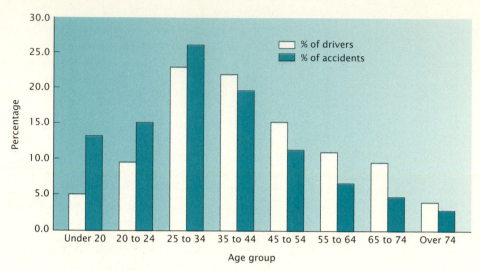

Source: Calculated from *The Fact Book 1995, Property/Casualty Insurance Facts* (New York: Insurance Information Institute, 1995), p. 86.

tions that informed consumers should follow when auto insurance is purchased.

Cost of Auto Insurance

Depending on where you live, your age, driving experience, and other factors, the annual cost of insuring your car can range from several hundred dollars to several thousand dollars.

Insurers use numerous rating factors to determine the actual premiums paid. *Territory* is one of the most important rating factors. Rates are substantially higher in territories that have more cars because of a higher probability of an accident. Each state is divided into rating territories—for example, a large city, part of a city, suburb, or rural area. City drivers normally pay higher rates than rural drivers because of the higher number of auto accidents in congested cities.

Age, sex, and marital status are also important in determining the total premium. Younger drivers under age 20 account for a disproportionate number of accidents and pay higher rates as a result (see Exhibit 11.6). In addition, the sex of the driver is important. Fatal accident rates are much higher for males than for females. Male drivers also have higher alcohol-related fatal accident rates than females. Marital status is also important because married male drivers as a group have relatively fewer accidents than unmarried drivers in the same age category.

Use of the automobile is another important rating factor. Insurers have various rating classifications, such as pleasure use, number of miles the car is driven to work, business use, farm use, and annual mileage. The greater the annual mileage driven, the higher the rates.

The year, make, and model of the auto have an important impact on total premiums. Premiums on a new car are substantially higher than on a car several years old. In addition, the damageability and repairability of the car are important rating factors for physical damage insurance. New cars are now rated based on the susceptibility to damage and the cost of repair.

The individual driving record is a very important rating factor. Your driving record will determine whether you will be insured at standard rates or at high-risk rates. If your driving record is poor, you may be denied coverage. In particular, you may be denied insurance because of a conviction for drunk driving, an excessive number of speeding tickets or accidents, driving on a suspended license, and homicide or assault involving an automobile.

Another rating factor is the *number of cars insured*—a multicar discount is usually given if the insured owns two or more automobiles. In addition, the insured may qualify for a rate discount or credit, such as a

---

Exhibit 11.7

Tips for Buying Auto Insurance

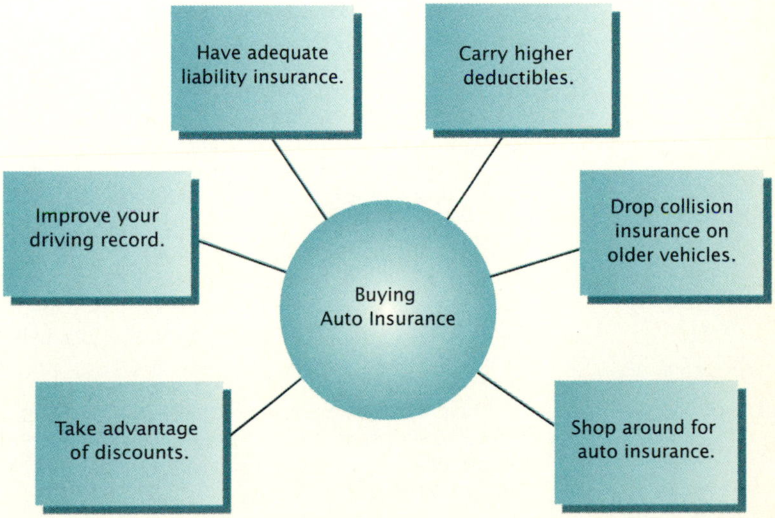

good student discount or a credit for taking an approved *driver education course.*

Suggestions for Buying Auto Insurance

As a careful insurance consumer, you should remember certain suggestions when an auto policy is purchased (see Exhibit 11.7).

Have Adequate Liability Insurance. The most important rule in purchasing auto insurance is to carry adequate liability insurance. If you carry minimum limits to satisfy the state's financial or compulsory insurance law, such as $25,000/$50,000/$25,000, you are seriously underinsured. Even if you carry higher limits of $100,000/$300,000/$50,000, you are still underinsured in most states. Damage awards in recent years have increased because of inflation, higher hospital and medical costs, higher wage losses, changing concepts of damages, and more liberal juries. A

Exhibit 11.8

**Automobile Insurance Premiums for Phoenix, Arizona
(six-month premiums)**

	Five Lowest-Price Policies	
Rank	**Name**	**Premiums***
1.	AIC Insurance Company	$505.66
2.	Amex AC	509.60
3.	United Services Auto. Assoc.	510.56
4.	Teachers Insurance Company	526.80
5.	Liberty Mutual Fire Ins. Co.	567.00
	Five Highest-Price Policies	
53.	Milwaukee Safeguard Insurance Company	$1,338.00
54.	Phoenix Indemnity Insurance Company	1,371.51
55.	Leader National Insurance Company	1,385.00
56.	Atlantic Casualty Company	1,462.00
57.	Acceptance Insurance Company	1,541.47

Note: The premiums shown are for six months based on the rates in effect as of February 29, 1996. The hypothetical driver is a married male, age 48, who drives 15 miles each way to work (30 miles round-trip). He drives a 1993 Ford Taurus LX, 4-door sedan with an automatic shift and has a clean driving record for the last three years.

*   The coverages are bodily injury liability, $100,000/$300,000 or a single limit of $300,000; property damage liability, $50,000; medical payments, $5,000; uninsured motorist (same limits as liability); collision, $200 deductible; and comprehensive, $100 deductible.

Source: Department of Insurance, State of Arizona, *Automobile Premium Comparison Survey,* Edition 1, April 1996.

Consider This

Another source of auto and homeowners insurance rates is Quicken InsureMarket at: http://www.insure-market. com/

negligent driver who is underinsured could have a deficiency judgment filed against him or her, by which both present and future income and assets could be attached to satisfy the judgment. This can be avoided by carrying adequate liability limits.

Carry Higher Deductibles.   Another important suggestion is to carry higher deductibles for collision and other-than-collision losses (also called comprehensive). Some insureds carry deductibles as low as $100, which is too low in view of the rapid inflation in automobile prices over time. Many insureds have $250 deductibles. However, increasing the deductible from $250 to $500 will reduce your collision and comprehensive cost by 15 to 30 percent.

Drop Collision Insurance on an Older Vehicle.   You should consider dropping collision insurance on your car if it is an older model with a low market value. The cost of repairs after an accident will often exceed the value of an older car, but the insurer will pay no more than its current market value (less the deductible). One rough rule of thumb is that when a standard-size automobile (such as a Chevrolet, Ford, or Dodge) is more than six years old, the physical damage insurance on the car should be dropped.

Shop Around for Automobile Insurance.   Another important suggestion is to shop carefully for automobile insurance. There is intense price competition among insurers. You should contact several insurers so that you can compare premiums. Several states publish shoppers' guides to help insurance consumers make better purchase decisions. For example, Exhibit 11.8 shows the five lowest- and five highest-cost auto policies in Phoenix, Arizona, based on a survey by the Arizona Department of Insurance. As this exhibit shows, there is wide variation in premiums among insurers for the same coverages.

Take Advantage of Discounts.   When you shop for auto insurance, you should determine whether you are eligible for one or more discounts. All insurers do not offer the same discounts, and certain discounts are not available in all states. However, common discounts include the following:

- Multicar discount—10 to 25 percent

- No accidents in three years—5 to 10 percent

- Drivers over age 50—5 to 15 percent

- Defensive driving course—5 to 10 percent

- Antitheft device—5 to 50 percent discount for comprehensive

- Automatic seat belt and air bag—20 to 60 percent for medical payments

■ Good student discount—5 to 25 percent

■ Auto and HO policy with same insurer—5 to 15 percent

■ College student away from home without a car—10 to 40 percent

Improve Your Driving Record. If you are a high-risk driver and are paying exorbitant premiums, a clean driving record over the last three years will substantially reduce your premiums. Meanwhile, other alternatives should be considered. Although physical damage insurance on a new or late-model car can easily double the premiums for a high-risk driver, an older car can be driven without collision insurance. You might also consider riding a motorcycle or bicycle or using mass transit. However, there is no substitute for a good driving record.

Finally, you should not drive when you are drinking. Drunk drivers account for a relatively high proportion of auto accidents in which someone is seriously injured or killed. A conviction for driving under the influence (DUI) will have a devastating impact on the premiums paid. Premiums can easily double or triple after a DUI conviction.

SUMMARY

■ Several groups of persons are insured under the homeowners policy. This includes the named insured and spouse, family members residing in the named insured's household, and other persons under age 21 in the care of an insured.

■ The homeowners policy is divided into two parts. Section I provides coverage on the dwelling, other structures. personal property, loss-of-use benefits, and additional coverages. Section II provides personal liability insurance and covers the medical expenses of others who may be injured while on the insured premises or by some act of the insured or by an animal owned by the insured.

■ HO-2 is a broad form that covers the dwelling and other structures, and personal property against loss from certain listed perils.

■ HO-3 is a special form that covers the dwelling and other structures against risk of direct physical loss to the described property. This means that all losses to the dwelling and other structures are covered except those losses specifically excluded. However, personal property is insured only on a named-perils basis.

■ HO-4 is a contents broad form policy for renters. HO-4 covers the personal property of tenants on a named-perils basis and also provides personal liability insurance.

■ HO-6 is a unit-owners form for condominium owners. HO-6 covers the personal property of the insured on a named-perils basis.

■ HO-8 is a modified coverage form for older homes. Losses to the dwelling and other structures are indemnified on the basis of actual cash value or the amount required to repair or replace the property using common construction materials and methods. Losses are not indemnified based on replacement cost.

■ The replacement-cost provision is one of the most valuable features in the homeowners policy. Losses to the dwelling and other structures are paid on the basis of replacement cost if the insured carries insurance at least equal to 80 percent of the replacement cost at the time of loss. Losses to personal property are paid on the basis of actual cash value. However, an endorsement can be added that covers personal property on a replacement-cost basis.

■ Section II provides personal liability insurance (Coverage E), which protects the insured against a claim or suit for damages because of bodily injury or property damage caused by the insured's negligence. The company will defend the insured and pay those sums that the insured is legally obligated to pay up to the policy limits.

■ Section II also provides medical payments to others (Coverage F), which pays the reasonable medical expenses of another person who may be accidentally injured on the premises, or by the activities of an insured, resident employee, or animal owned by or in the care of an insured. It is not necessary to prove negligence and establish legal liability before the medical expenses are paid.

■ Certain endorsements can be added to the homeowners policy, including an inflation-guard endorsement, earthquake coverage, personal property replacement-cost endorsement, and scheduled personal property endorsement.

■ Federal flood insurance is a government insurance program that provides flood insurance at subsidized rates to property owners in flood zones.

■ The personal umbrella policy is designed to provide protection against a catastrophic lawsuit or judgment. The policy provides excess liability insurance over basic underlying insurance limits.

■ The personal auto policy (PAP) provides the following basic coverages: Part A: liability coverage, Part B: medical payments coverage, Part C: uninsured motorists coverage, and Part D: coverage for damage to your auto.

- Liability coverage protects the insured from bodily injury or property damage liability arising out of the negligent operation of an automobile or trailer. A single limit of liability applies to both bodily injury and property damage. The coverage can also be written with split limits.

- A covered auto includes any vehicle shown in the declarations: newly acquired vehicles, a trailer owned by the insured, and a temporary substitute auto.

- Insured persons include the named insured and spouse, family members, other persons using a covered auto if there is a reasonable belief that permission to use the vehicle exists , and any person or organization legally responsible for the acts of a covered person.

- Medical payments coverage pays all reasonable medical, dental, and funeral expenses incurred by an insured person within three years from the date of the accident.

- Uninsured motorists coverage pays for the bodily injury of a covered person caused by an uninsured motorist, a hit-and-run driver, or a negligent driver whose insurer is insolvent.

- Coverage for damage to your auto pays for any direct physical loss to a covered auto or nonowned auto less any deductible. A collision loss is covered only if the declarations page indicates that collision coverage is in effect. Other-than-collision coverage can also be purchased.

- Financial responsibility laws require motorist to show proof of financial responsibility at the time of an accident involving bodily injury or property damage over a certain amount, for conviction of certain offenses, and for failure to pay a final judgment resulting from an automobile accident. Most motorists meet the financial responsibility law requirements by carrying adequate automobile liability insurance limits.

- Compulsory insurance laws require the owners and operators of automobiles to carry automobile liability insurance at least equal to a certain amount before the automobile can be registered or licensed.

- Five states have unsatisfied judgment funds to compensate accident victims who have exhausted all other means of recovery. The accident victim must obtain a judgment against the negligent driver who caused the accident and show that the judgment cannot be collected.

- No-fault automobile insurance means that after an automobile accident, involving a bodily injury, each party collects from his or her own insurer, regardless of fault. However, if the bodily injury exceeds the monetary threshold or meets a verbal threshold, the injured person has the right to sue the negligent driver.

■ Automobile insurance premiums are based on numerous rating factors. The most important factors include: territory; age, sex, and marital status; use of the auto; year make, and model; and individual driving record. Various discounts and rate credits may also be available.

■ Several suggestions should be followed when an auto policy is purchased: (1) have adequate liability insurance, (2) carry higher deductibles, (3) drop collision insurance on an older vehicle, (4) shop around for automobile insurance, (5) take advantage of discounts, (6) improve your driving record.

KEY CONCEPTS AND TERMS

Actual cash value
Additional living expense
"All-risks" basis
Collision
Compulsory insurance law
Coverage for damage to your auto (Part D)
Covered auto
Earthquake endorsement
Federal flood insurance
Financial responsibility law
Guaranteed replacement-cost endorsement
Homeowners 2 (broad form)
Homeowners 3 (special form)
Homeowners 4 (contents broad form)
Homeowners 6 (unit owners form)
Homeowners 8 (modified coverage form)
Inflation-guard endorsement
Liability coverage (Part A)
Medical payments coverage (Part B)

Medical payments to others
No-fault insurance
Nonowned auto
Other-than-collision loss
Peril
Personal auto policy (PAP)
Personal liability insurance
Personal property replacement-cost endorsement
Personal umbrella policy
Replacement cost
Schedule
Scheduled personal property endorsement
Self-insured retention
Single limit
Split limits
Temporary substitute auto
Uninsured motorists coverage (Part C)
Unsatisfied judgment fund

QUESTIONS FOR REVIEW

1. Identify the different types of homeowners policies, and identify the groups for which each form is designed.

2. Briefly describe the property coverages that are found in Section I of the homeowners policy.

3. Identify the Section I insured perils that apply to the following:
   a. Dwelling and other structures
   b. Personal property

4. Explain the liability coverages that are found in Section II of the homeowners policy.

5. Explain how the following would modify the coverage provided by the homeowners policy:
   a. Inflation-guard endorsement
   b. Earthquake endorsement
   c. Personal property replacement-cost endorsement
   d. Scheduled personal property endorsement

6. Briefly describe the following coverages:
   a. Federal flood insurance
   b. Personal umbrella policy

7. Identify the major coverages in the personal auto policy (PAP).

8. Who are the persons insured for liability coverage under the PAP?

9. Identify the major exclusions that are found in the PAP.

10. Briefly explain the characteristics of the following approaches for compensating injured automobile accident victims:
    a. Financial responsibility law
    b. Compulsory insurance law
    c. Unsatisfied judgment law
    d. No-fault automobile insurance

11. Identify the major rating factors that determine the cost of automobile insurance.

12. What suggestions should consumers follow when shopping for a homeowners policy and auto insurance?

PROBLEMS

1. James has his home and personal property insured under a Home-owners 3 policy. The dwelling is insured for $80,000. The replacement cost of the home is $100,000. The roof is severely damaged in a tornado. The actual cash value of the damaged roof is $10,000, and it will cost $18,000 to repair the damaged portion. Ignoring any deductible, how much will James collect under his policy?

2. Kristin purchased an unendorsed Homeowners 4 policy to cover her personal property. A fire damaged her apartment. A stereo system purchased two years ago for $500 was totally destroyed. The system was 20 percent depreciated when the loss occurred, and a comparable replacement system will cost $600. Ignoring any deductible, how much will Kristin collect from her insurer? Would your answer change if a personal property replacement-cost endorsement had been added to the policy? Explain.

3. Rachel has a personal auto policy with a liability limit of $100,000 per person. She also has a personal umbrella policy with a liability limit of $1 million and a self-insured retention of $500. How much will be paid by each policy if an injured motorist has a judgment of $250,000 against Rachel?

INTERNET EXERCISES

1. As noted in Chapter 8, the Insurance Information Institute provides information about homeowners and auto insurance for consumers online at:

   http://www.iii/org/

   Consumer information is also available from the Independent Insurance Agents of America. Visit the organization's Independent Insurance Network at:

   http://www.iiaa.iix.com/

   and select "Consumer Info" to see what's available.

2. What are the risks associated with owning your car in your zip-code area? Visit Quicken InsureMarket, "the Web's most complete insurance service," at:

   http://www.insuremarket.com/

   Choose "Risk Evaluator," follow the instructions, and find out.

CASE APPLICATIONS

Case 1

Kirsten has her home and personal property insured under an unendorsed Homeowners 3 (special form policy). The dwelling is insured for $60,000. Personal property is insured for $30,000. The replacement cost of the home is $100,000, and its actual cash value is $80,000, Indicate the extent to which each of the following losses would be covered under Kirsten's Homeowners 3 policy (ignore the deductible). Treat each event separately.

1. Lightning strikes the roof of the house and severely damages it. The actual cash value of the damaged roof is $10,000, and it will cost $16,000 to repair the damaged portion.

2. The hot water heater explodes and damages some furniture and other household items. The actual cash value of the damaged property is $1,000, and the cost of replacing the property is $1,600.

3. A burglar breaks into Kirsten's home and steals a coin collection valued at $5,000.

4. Kirsten entertained members of a local book club in her home and served the guests a buffet luncheon. Two guests became seriously ill and sued Kirsten, alleging that she served them contaminated food. The court awarded each guest damages of $60,000.

5. Kirsten has a German Shepherd guard dog to protect her house from intruders. The dog escaped from the house and attacked a runner who was running in the street near her house. The runner's medical bills are $900.

Case 2

Fred has a personal auto policy that provides the following coverages: $300,000 liability coverage, $5,000 medical payments coverage, $25,000 uninsured motorists coverage, $250 deductible for a collision loss, and a $100 deductible for an other-than-collision loss. Indicate the extent to which each of the following losses would be covered under Fred's personal auto-policy. Treat each event separately.

1. Fred fails to stop at a red light and negligently smashes into another motorist. The other driver's car, valued at $5,000 is totally destroyed. In addition, damages to Fred's car are $1,000.

2. Fred's daughter, Myra, attends college in another state and drives a family automobile. Myra lets her boyfriend drive the car, and he negligently injures another motorist. The boyfriend is sued for $10,000.

3. Fred's wife is driving a family car in a snowstorm. She loses control of the car on an icy street and smashes into the foundation of a house. The property damage to the house is $20,000. Damages to the family car are $5,000. Fred's wife has medical expenses of $3,000.

4. Fred's car is being repaired for faulty brakes. While road testing the car, a mechanic injures another motorist and is sued for $50,000.

5. Fred hits a steer crossing a highway. Damages to Fred's car are $700.

6. Fred's wife goes shopping at a supermarket. When she returns, she finds that the left rear fender has been damaged by another driver who did not leave a name. Damages to the car are $500.

Case 3

Kim, age 20, is a college student who recently purchased her first car from a friend who had financial problems. The vehicle is a high-mileage 1982 Toyota Tercel with a current market value of $1,000. Assume you are a financial planner and Kim asks your advice concerning the various coverages in the PAP.

1. Briefly describe the major coverages that are *available* in the PAP.

2. Which of the available coverages in part (1) should Kim purchase? Justify you answer.

3. Which of the available coverages in part (1) should Kim not purchase? Justify your answer.

4. Assume that Kim purchases the PAP coverages that you have recommended. To what extent, if any, would Kim's insurance cover the following situations?

   a. Danielle, Kim's roommate, borrows Kim's car with her permission and injures another motorist. Danielle is at fault.
   b. Kim is driving under the influence of alcohol and is involved in an accident where another motorist is seriously injured.
   c. During the football season, Kim charges a fee to transport fans from a local bar to the football stadium. Several passengers are injured when Kim suddenly changed lanes without signaling.
   d. Kim drives her boyfriend's car on a regular basis. While driving the boyfriend's car, she is involved in an accident where another motorist is injured. Kim is at fault.
   e. Kim rents a car in England where she is participating in a summer study program. The car is stolen from a dormitory parking lot.

SUGGESTIONS FOR ADDITIONAL READING

Chatzky, Jean Sherman. "Everything You Ever Needed to Know About Insurance—But Were Too Confused to Ask," *Smart Money* (October 1993), pp. 120–125.

Fire, Casualty & Surety Bulletins, Personal Lines Volume, Auto and Dwelling Sections. Cincinnati: National Underwriter Company. The bulletins are published monthly.

"A Guide to Auto Insurance," *Consumer Reports,* Vol. 60, No. 10 (October 1995), pp. 638–645.

"Homeowners Insurance," *Consumer Reports,* Vol. 58, No. 10 (October 1993), pp. 627–635.

Rejda, George E., Constance M. Luthardt, Cheryl L. Ferguson, and Donald R. Oakes. *Personal Insurance,* 3rd ed. Malvern, Pa.: Insurance Institute of America, 1997.

Rejda, George E. *Principles of Risk Management and Insurance,* 6th ed. Reading, MA: Addison Wesley Longman, 1998.

Reisman, Liz Comte, "Home Truths—By Taking a Few Hours to Shop Around for a New Policy, or Even by Just Reading the Fine Print on Your Current One, You Can Cut Your Home Insurance Bill by As Much As 50 Percent," *Smart Money,* Vol. III, No. XI (November 1994), pp. 105–111.

NOTES

1. This chapter is based on George E. Rejda, *Principles of Risk Management and Insurance,* 6th ed. (Reading, MA: Addison Wesley Longman, 1998); *Fire, Casualty & Surety Bulletins,* Personal Lines Volume, Auto and Dwelling Sections (Cincinnati National Underwriter Company); and the current edition of Homeowners 3 policy and 1994 edition of the Personal Auto Policy drafted by the Insurance Services Office (ISO). The ISO forms and various policy provisions are used with the permission of ISO.

2. "Homeowners Insurance," *Consumer Reports,* Vol. 58, No. 10 (October 1993), pp. 627–635.

Part Three

The Role of Investments in Financial Planning

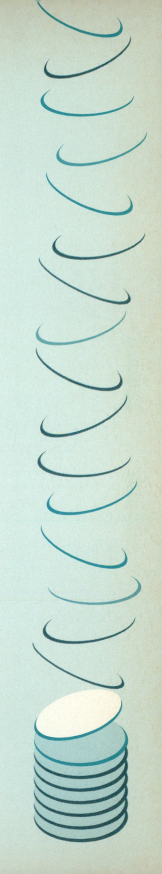

Chapter 12

Fundamentals of Investing

Learning Objectives

After studying this chapter, you should be able to:

- Define investment and differentiate between saving and investing.

- Describe the various types of investments, including common and preferred stock, bonds, mutual funds, real estate, options, and commodities.

- Explain the various investment objectives, including current income, preservation of purchasing power, capital appreciation, and tax avoidance.

- Explain the relationship between risk and return in investing.

- Discuss risk tolerance and the various types of risk that investors must consider when making investments.

- Explain asset allocation in relation to risk and the investor's life-cycle stage.

- Explain the various investment strategies, including buy and hold, market timing, diversification, dollar-cost averaging, value investing, and combination strategies.

- Discuss the various methods through which investors make investment transactions, cash versus margin trades, and sources of investment information.

"

In investing money, the amount of interest you want should depend on whether you want to eat well or sleep well.

—Kenfield Morley

Is the American Dream becoming a nightmare? Is the chance to accumulate wealth flitting away? Not at all. You can still accumulate substantial wealth—if you know how. After a rocky start, the decade of the '90s will be a decade of solid growth, filled with great opportunities for the savvy investor.

—Knight A. Kiplinger

"So where do we start?" That's the question Rob and Marla Nolan are trying to answer with respect to investments. The Nolans have paid off their credit card debt and their car loans, and they have accumulated enough savings to draw upon in case an emergency arises. After making their mortgage payment each month and paying their other bills, they have money left over. Although it is a nice problem to have, the Nolans are unsure what to do with the surplus. Although savings alternatives offer little risk, they also provide a low rate of return. Rob and Marla are thinking about investing the left over money. They are curious about what investment options are available, the characteristics of these investment options, investment strategies they can employ, and how to go about making investments. This chapter provides an overview of investment options, and the following three chapters discuss them further.

Nature of Investment

Earlier in this text, we discussed the nature of saving. In this chapter, we begin our discussion of investment. What is investment, and how does it differ from saving? **Investment** is the commitment of funds for the purpose of achieving some long-term goal or objective. Investment differs from saving in terms of the time horizon involved, the financial assets and instruments used, and the objectives of the individual.

investment The commitment of funds for the purpose of achieving some long-term goal or objective.

- Savers have shorter time horizons, whereas investors commit their funds for longer periods.

- Savers use the money market, the market for short-term deposits and short-term debt, to earn a return on their highly liquid assets. Investors use real property, capital market securities such as stocks and bonds, and other long-term commitments that may not be as liquid as short-term assets.

- Finally, the objectives of savers and investors differ. Savers tend to accumulate funds to address short-term goals, whereas investors have longer-term goals, such as retirement security or funding children's college expenses.

Consider This

Learn about some investment basics from the American Association of Individual Investors at: http://www.aaii.org/

Even though investment is designed to achieve long-term goals, you should not start an investment plan until you have accumulated adequate savings. As noted earlier, you should have an emergency fund to draw upon should you experience unexpected events (such as loss of a job or large car repair bills). But since investments generally provide a higher rate of return than savings, there is an opportunity cost involved with having too much of your wealth tied up in savings.

You should start investing as early as possible. Young investors have time on their side, as illustrated in Exhibit 12.1. You don't necessarily have to have large sums of money to begin investing, as discussed in Insight 12.1.

Types of Investment—a Brief Overview

Investors today have more investment choices available than ever before, from bonds backed by the U.S. government, to stocks in new enterprises emerging in China and the former Soviet Union, to commodity futures contracts. The characteristics of various investments are discussed in greater detail in the next three chapters; a brief overview and description are provided in this section. These investments include common stock; bonds; preferred stock; mutual funds; real estate; options; commodities; metals, art, and collectibles.

Insight 12.1 For Novice Investors on Small Budgets, There Are Plenty of Ways to Start Out

If you've only got a few hundred dollars, there are plenty of ways to get started as an investor. And I've used all too many of them.

Like a lot of investment novices, I didn't have much money when I started out, so I went on the prowl for low-rent ways to enter Wall Street. My ideal investment cost $500 or less. All other considerations were secondary.

I quickly discovered the National Association of Investors Corp. in Royal Oak, Mich., which helps its members enroll in dividend-reinvestment plans. With these plans, your quarterly dividends automatically buy additional shares, thus ensuring that you get the full benefit of stock-market compounding. I proudly plunked down $314 and bought a single share of each of six great and not-so-great U.S. corporations.

Not content with that, I began dabbling in mutual funds and soon owned a fistful, almost all with investment minimums of $500 or less. My money wasn't multiplying too quickly, but when it came to the number of accounts, my portfolio was going gangbusters.

Along the way, I learned a lot about investing, and even more about taxes. When my wife and I decided to buy a house, I sold many of our tiny investments. That year's tax return listed 12 separate capital gains, with a total profit of just $1,180.73. Even then, I still wasn't rid of all our puny accounts.

Sound like an odd way to start investing? My experience is hardly unique. Many investors, including many professionals, make terrible mistakes and pursue bizarre strategies when they first venture into the markets.

Take Richard Fontaine, a money manager I met early in my reporting career. At the time, I was greatly impressed as Mr. Fontaine described his initial foray onto Wall Street.

He began investing in the late 1970s, when he was an IBM salesman. Mr. Fontaine's strategy? He bought one or two shares of 180 different companies, and then got himself enrolled in each company's dividend-reinvestment plan.

Mr. Fontaine recently told me that he still owns all 180 stocks. "It's a bit of a pain in the

Exhibit 12.1

Starting to Invest Early Makes a Big Difference

Starting Age	Amount Invested Annually	Balance at Age 65, at Various Rates of Return		
		6%	10%	12%
25	$2,000	$309,524	$885,185	$1,534,183
35	$2,000	158,116	329,988	482,665
45	$2,000	73,571	114,550	144,105
55	$2,000	26,361	31,875	35,098
25	$4,000	616,048	1,770,370	3,068,366
35	$4,000	316,232	657,976	965,331
45	$4,000	147,142	229,100	288,210
55	$4,000	52,723	63,750	70,195

neck in terms of paperwork," he concedes. But Mr. Fontaine reckons it's been worth the hassles.

"I've learned a lot over the last 17 years," says the Towson, Md., money manager. "And I've made a lot of money." But Mr. Fontaine says only investment junkies should try to replicate his feat.

So what should you do? If you are a first-time investor who only has a few hundred dollars to play with, aim to buy a single stock fund, with a low investment minimum, that could become your portfolio's cornerstone.

Despite the fund industry's move toward higher investment minimums, there are still a handful of broadly diversified no-load funds that will let you open an account for $500 or less. Consider funds such as AARP Growth & Income Fund, Nicholas Fund,

Strong Total Return Fund and Vanguard STAR Fund.

But don't ignore funds with higher minimums. You can often get in for less than the regular minimum by opening an individual retirement account or agreeing to an automatic-investment plan. In addition, some funds will accept a smaller initial investment if you are setting up a custodial account for a child.

For instance, Vanguard Group regularly expects investors to pony up $3,000 to open an account. But the Valley Forge, Pa., fund group will let you open an IRA or a custodial account for just $500. Similarly, Baltimore's T. Rowe Price Associates, which usually demands a $2,500 initial investment, will let you open an IRA or a custodial account with $1,000.

T. Rowe Price also will waive its minimum entirely, provid-

ing you agree to invest at least $50 a month through its automatic-investment plan. With these plans, your monthly investment is deducted directly from your bank account or paycheck and deposited straight into the fund.

Other no-load fund groups offer a similar service. AARP Investment Program, Dreyfus Corp., Founders Funds, Gabelli Funds, Invesco Funds Group, Janus Funds, Jones & Babson, Neuberger & Berman Management, Strong Funds and Twentieth Century Investors will waive the minimums on some or all of their funds, providing you agree to invest at least $50 or $100 every month.

Source: Jonathan Clements, "For Novice Investors on Small Budgets, There Are Plenty of Ways to Start Out," February 28, 1995. Reprinted by permission of the *Wall Street Journal,* © 1995 Dow Jones & Company, Inc. All Rights Reserved Worldwide.

Common Stock

common stock Stock representing ownership of a corporation.

Shares of **common stock** represent ownership of a corporation. If a corporation has issued 100,000 shares of common stock and you own 1,000 shares, you own 1 percent (1,000/100,000) of the company.

Companies use common stock as a means of raising funds for many purposes, most often to fund investment in plant and equipment. For example, General Motors may decide to build a new production facility that will cost $50 million. To finance construction of the production facility, the company may decide to issue additional shares of common stock. General Motors receives funds only when new shares of common stock are issued. Once issued, there is an active secondary market for the shares of stock. This means that if you decide you no longer want to own General Motors common stock, you can sell your shares to another investor.

Because shares of common stock represent ownership interest in the company, investors share in the company's experience through share price increases and decreases, as well as dividend payments if the company pays dividends. Dividend payments are cash distributions made to shareholders of common stock, usually on a quarterly basis. Some companies pay large quarterly dividends, whereas others pay low dividends or no dividends. If the company performs well, the share price will increase to reflect the increased value of the underlying company. Conversely, if the company does not fare well, the share price will fall.

Stockholders delegate the authority to make day-to-day decisions to the company's managers. This delegation leads to more efficient decision making, plus the managers of the company may have greater expertise. As owners of the company, stockholders must approve major corporate decisions. They vote on these major issues by completing a form each year called a proxy statement. We will discuss investing in common stock in greater detail in Chapter 13.

Bonds

bond Interest-bearing debt instrument issued by a corporation or a government entity.

Rather than issuing shares of common stock as a means of raising funds to finance investment in plant and equipment, corporations can also borrow the money by issuing bonds. **Bonds** are debt instruments issued by corporations and government entities, usually in $1,000 denominations. Bonds have a fixed maturity date, and most bonds provide periodic interest payments to the bondholder. Upon maturity, the issuer of the bond must repay the money borrowed.

Suppose, for example, that instead of issuing shares of common stock to finance the new production facility, General Motors decided to borrow the money. It may decide to borrow the money for 20 years by issuing 20-year bonds. If you purchase one of these bonds, you are loaning money to General Motors in exchange for receiving interest each year and repayment of the loan 20 years from now.

Just as with common stock, General Motors receives the funds only when the bonds are issued. Rather than holding your bond for 20 years, you may decide to sell it to someone else before the bond matures. Many types of bonds are available, including corporate bonds, U.S. Treasury bonds, bonds issued by government agencies, and municipal bonds. Bonds will be discussed in greater detail in Chapter 13.

Preferred Stock

preferred stock Stock that entitles the holder to a fixed dividend that must be paid before any dividend is paid on common stock. Preferred stock is often called a hybrid security because it has characteristics of both common stock and debt.

Preferred stock is often called a hybrid financial security because it has characteristics of both common stock and debt. Like common stock, preferred stock does not have a maturity date though many new preferred stock issues can be retired ("called") by the issuer. Preferred stock provides a fixed, periodic dividend payment to the owner, similar to interest payments on bonds.

Instead of issuing common stock or bonds to finance the production facility, General Motors may decide to issue shares of preferred stock that will provide a $4 per share annual dividend to the owner. Although common stock may also provide a dividend to stockholders, common stock dividends are not guaranteed. Preferred stock is sometimes issued by corporations that do not want to borrow the funds and would rather not issue additional shares of common stock. A more extensive discussion of preferred stock is provided in Chapter 13.

Mutual Funds

mutual fund An organization that pools funds from many investors through the sale of shares and uses the funds to purchase financial securities issued by corporations and government entities.

Mutual funds are another popular investment alternative. A **mutual fund** is an organization that pools funds from many investors and uses the funds to purchase financial securities issued by corporations and government entities. Mutual funds invest in many different securities. This practice, known as diversification, reduces risk because if several securities do not perform well, other securities can offset their poor performance. You can purchase shares of a mutual fund just as you purchase shares of an individual company. Mutual fund investors may receive periodic dividends from the fund. In addition, if the value of the securities in the mutual fund increases, the price per share of the mutual fund increases. Of course, the value of the securities in the mutual fund could decrease, with the price per share of the mutual fund also decreasing.

Mutual funds present an excellent opportunity for investors since the funds are well diversified, professionally managed, and require low minimum investments. Mutual funds are available that invest in certain types of securities, such as growth stock funds and bond funds; other mutual funds are tailored to meet the specific investment objectives of certain investors, such as growth funds and income funds. Individual investors can match their investment goal with the fund objective. We will discuss this popular investment in greater detail in Chapter 14.

Real Estate

Another investment alternative is real estate. Recall that real estate is land and permanent attachments to the land. There are many ways to invest in real estate. As discussed in Chapter 7, the largest investment most individuals will ever make is the purchase of a home. Residential real estate remains one of the best investments individuals can make. In addition to providing for a basic need, shelter, residential real estate enjoys many tax advantages. After purchasing a principal residence, some individuals purchase a second home for tax and investment purposes. Some real estate investments, such as the purchase of an apartment building, provide current income to the purchaser through rental payments as well as the potential for price appreciation. There are other ways to invest in real estate, including the purchase of undeveloped land, the purchase of shares in a real estate investment trust (REIT), and the purchase of mortgage-backed securities. These investment alternatives are discussed in Chapter 15.

Options

option The right to buy or sell something at a given price during a specified period.

put option A right to sell shares of stock at a given price during a specified period.

call option The right to purchase shares of stock at a given price during a specified period.

An **option** is the right to buy or sell something at a given price during a specified period. An active market exists for options on shares of common stock. There are two types of options, puts and calls. A **put option** is the right to sell shares of stock at a given price during a specified period. A **call option** is the right to purchase shares of stock at the strike (or exercise) price, during a specified period. Options are known as derivative securities because they derive their value from another security.

To demonstrate how an options transaction works, suppose you believe that the price of General Motors common stock will increase during the next six months from the current price of $35 per share. Further assume that you can purchase a General Motors call option for $150 with a strike price of $37. This option permits you to purchase 100 shares of General Motors stock at a price of $37 per share. Further assume that the option will be "good" for the next six months. After you purchase this call option, you hope that the share price of General Motors will increase. The price of General Motors may never go above $35 per share while the option is valid, and the option may expire worthless. Suppose, however, that the price of General Motors increases to $40 per share five months later. Your call option gives you the right to purchase 100 shares of General Motors at $37 per share. If you exercise the option, you can realize an immediate $300 gain by purchasing 100 shares at $37 per share when the market price is $40 per share. Subtracting the cost of the option ($150), and ignoring transactions costs such as brokerage fees, your gain on this transaction is $150. We will discuss options in greater detail in Chapter 15.

Commodities

commodity A product or good.

A **commodity** is a product or good. Some transactions involving commodities require the actual delivery of the commodity at the agreed-upon price. Such a transaction occurs in what is known as the "spot," or cash, market.

There are situations, however, in which the producer or user of a commodity is concerned about the price of the commodity in the future. If you were a baker, for example, you would be very concerned about the price of wheat, a basic ingredient needed for baking, in the future. If the price of wheat were to increase significantly in the next six months, you might not be able to produce and sell your bread at a profit. By using a futures contract, you could protect yourself against adverse price movements.

futures contract A contract providing for the delivery of a specified amount of a commodity on a certain day at a specified price.

A **futures contract** provides for the delivery of a specified amount of a commodity on a certain day at a specified price. As with stocks and bonds, there is an active secondary market for futures contracts. Commodity futures contracts exist for a number of products, such as coffee, cotton, corn, gold, heating oil, pork bellies, orange juice, and wheat. There are also financial futures contracts, including futures contracts on currency, U.S. Treasury bills, and stock indexes.

hedger In the futures market for a commodity, a trader who is an actual producer or user of the commodity and who engages in trading in an attempt to reduce the negative impact of possible future price changes.

speculator In the futures market for a commodity, a trader who is neither a producer nor a user of the commodity but who engages in trading in an attempt to profit from commodity price movements.

There are two groups of traders in the futures market: hedgers and speculators. **Hedgers** are the actual producers and users of the commodity who are seeking to reduce the negative impact of possible future price changes. **Speculators,** who take the other side of the transaction, are traders who are neither producers nor users of the commodity. Speculators are risk takers who attempt to profit from commodity price movements. Futures contracts are characterized by the low initial deposit (margin) required, which is typically only 2 to 10 percent of the value of the underlying commodity contract. Few futures contracts actually involve the physical delivery of the commodity. Buyers and sellers simply make an offsetting transaction, and money rather than the commodity changes hands. A more extensive treatment of commodities and futures contracts is provided in Chapter 15.

Metals, Art, and Collectibles

Precious metals provide another investment opportunity. Gold, silver, and platinum are the most popular investment metals. The price of precious metals tends to increase when inflation is high or when there is economic and political uncertainty. There are a number of ways in which you can invest in precious metals, including the direct purchase of coins and bullion, and indirect investment through the purchase of mining company stocks and mutual funds that specialize in metals.

Investing in art combines the opportunity for price appreciation with the enjoyment of the artwork. You can purchase many types of art, including sculpture, paintings, etchings, photography, lithographs, and others. Art collectors may purchase the work of an unknown artist for pure enjoyment or with the hope that the artist will someday be discovered and the artwork will increase in value.

Antiques and collectibles provide another investment opportunity. The market for these items may involve individuals who own a single item or dealers who have an inventory. Like investment in art, antiques and collectibles permit the purchaser to enjoy possession of the asset, as well as providing the possibility of price appreciation. Often investment in collectibles develops from a hobby, such as coin collecting, stamp collecting, or collecting glassware from the Depression era.

Investing in metals, art, and collectibles is discussed in greater detail in Chapter 15.

Investment Objectives

With so many investment alternatives available, how do you decide where to invest your money? One factor to consider is your investment objective. Investment objectives may include generation of income, preservation of capital, capital appreciation, and tax avoidance.

Generation of Income

One investment objective may be to provide a periodic stream of income. Several investment alternatives are available that produce income:

- Investing in real estate that produces monthly rental payments
- Buying common stocks of companies that pay quarterly dividends
- Purchasing corporate bonds that provide semiannual interest payments

A group of investors for whom receiving periodic income is often an objective is retirees. They use income from investments to supplement income from other sources. On the downside, most income produced by such investments is currently taxable. However, many investors who prefer investment income to price appreciation no longer have an earned income. Such investors often face a lower marginal tax rate, so less of the income received is paid in taxes.

Preservation of Capital

Another investment objective is preserving the purchasing power of the capital. *Purchasing power* refers to the quantity of goods and services that can be purchased for a given amount of money. At first glance, you may wonder why investment is necessary to maintain the purchasing power of money. Why not simply store the wealth in a safe place? Storing wealth in a safe place does not guarantee preservation of purchasing power. If you place $10,000 in a safe-deposit box and do not withdraw any of the funds, ten years later you will still have $10,000. Unfortunately, the purchasing power of your stored wealth will have eroded over time because of inflation.

To preserve the purchasing power of your wealth, your rate of return must at least keep pace with inflation. We need only consider the high inflation experienced in the late 1970s and early 1980s to understand the importance of purchasing power preservation and earning at least the rate of inflation on your investments.

Capital Appreciation

The objective of many investors is capital appreciation. Capital appreciation means that the value of the investment increases over time. A major benefit of capital appreciation is that under the U.S. tax code, gains on investments are not taxed until the gain is actually realized. For example, if you purchased 100 shares of stock at a price of $20 per share (total investment of $2,000), and four years later the price per share is $30, your investment would have appreciated in value by $1,000 ($100 \times (30 - 20)$). You are not taxed on this capital gain, however, until you sell the stock. For this reason, investors who face high marginal tax rates often prefer investments that provide little or no current income, but that offer the potential for capital appreciation.

Tax Avoidance

tax avoidance A planned strategy of legally minimizing tax liability.

A final investment objective is tax avoidance, which should not be confused with tax evasion. **Tax avoidance** is a planned strategy of legally minimizing your tax liability. In contrast, tax evasion is the illegal practice of not paying taxes that are legally owed to the government. Tax avoidance may influence the types of investments held by the investor and when investment transactions occur. There are tax advantages associated with some investments. For example, as described earlier, if your stock appreciates in value, you are not taxed on the gain until you actually sell the stock and realize the gain. The same is true for real estate. Interest on municipal bonds is also exempt from federal income tax and is usually exempt from state income tax for residents of the state where the bond was issued. Other forms of current income from investments, such as dividends, interest, and rental income, are usually fully taxable, however.

The Risk–Return Relationship

Your objectives in investing, then, play a role in your choice of where to invest your money. Another important element in this selection is your attitude toward risk. Indeed, the relationship between risk and return should be one of your central considerations in investing. *Briefly, the relationship is this: The riskier the investment, the higher the investor's required expected rate of return.* Next, we examine this important relationship.

What is Investment Risk?

risk In the context of investment, the variability of investment outcomes.

In the context of investment, **risk** refers to the variability of investment outcomes. Some investments, such as one-year government bonds, provide a rate of return that is virtually guaranteed. Because you know what your return will be when you make such investments, the risk is very low. Other investments, in contrast, involve great uncertainty; in other words, they are **speculative.** An example of a speculative investment is purchasing the common stock of a new, unproven, company. When you invest in startup companies, you may hope to earn a high rate of return, but you have no way of knowing whether your hopes will be realized. Making such an investment is risky.

speculative Involving uncertainty.

Risk can be measured statistically in terms of the variability of the actual or expected return. Although describing the risk measurement technique is beyond the scope of this text, realize that assessing investment risk is not simply a matter of intuition. Researchers examining the historical relationship between risk and return have found that investments providing the lowest rates of return also exhibit the lowest risk. Conversely, investments providing the highest rates of return have, on average, exhibited the highest risk.

Risk Tolerance

risk tolerance Level of comfort with uncertainty.

risk averse Having a dislike for risk; tending to avoid or minimize risk.

Risk tolerance refers to an individual's level of comfort with uncertainty. Some people are risk neutral, or indifferent to risk. Others, those who are risk seeking, are quite comfortable bearing risk. Most of us, though, are **risk averse;** in other words, we don't like risk, and we attempt to avoid or minimize risk in our lives. In theory, the fact that most people are risk averse fits well with the historical risk-return relationship: Investors must be compensated for taking risk since they would prefer not to do so. The compensation is provided through a higher average rate of return.

Types of Risk

In analyzing an investment, investors must consider several types of risk, including business risk, inflation risk, financial risk, market risk, and liquidity risk.

business risk Uncertainty associated with the characteristics of a particular industry.

Business Risk. Business risk, as the name implies, is uncertainty associated with the characteristics of the industry in which the company operates. Business risk encompasses technological innovation, the degree of competition in the industry, production costs (for example, the size of fixed and variable costs), changing consumer tastes and preferences, and other factors that could affect a company's earnings.

In a stable business environment, the income of a company is less variable. However, because of business risk, operating income becomes more variable, increasing the degree of risk to the investor. The computer industry provides an excellent example. A computer manufacturer that is not keeping pace with the latest technological innovations will likely lose market share to competitors that are producing state-of-art computers. Likewise, an apparel manufacturer may lose market share and profits if consumer preferences change to other fashion styles.

inflation risk Uncertainty associated with the loss of purchasing power due to inflation.

Inflation Risk. Inflation risk is the risk associated with the loss of purchasing power. Purchasing power reflects the quantity of goods and services that can be obtained for a given unit of value. As inflation increases price levels, smaller quantities of goods and services can be purchased for the same unit of value. If the income and price appreciation from an investment do not keep pace with inflation, the standard of living attributable to the investment will decline. Consider an individual who retires at age 62 with a fixed pension benefit of $800 per month. Even if inflation is moderate, the purchasing power of $800 per month will decline significantly over the period of retirement. Some sources of retirement income are periodically increased to keep pace with inflation.

financial risk Uncertainty associated with profitability because of a company's fixed financial obligations.

Financial Risk. Financial risk is the risk associated with a company's fixed financial obligations, such as interest payments on debt and lease payments. Companies use several methods to finance their operations, including debt, common stock, and preferred stock. The proportions in which these instruments are used determine the firm's capital structure. Certain capital structures pose greater financial risk to investors than do other capital structures. For example, a company that uses a high proportion of debt financing faces greater financial risk than a firm that uses no debt. Why? Because regardless of the company's profitability, the bondholders must be paid interest on the money they have loaned the company. Certain other fixed financial obligations increase a firm's financial risk. These obligations include such things as preferred stock dividends, pension contributions, annual contributions earmarked to repay debt issues (called sinking fund payments), and lease payments.

market risk Uncertainty associated with price volatility of a firm's financial securities.

Market Risk. **Market risk** is the risk associated with price volatility of the firm's financial securities. The financial securities of some companies are more sensitive to external factors, such as general economic conditions, than are the securities issued by other companies. The prices of these securities tend to fluctuate to a higher degree because of this increased sensitivity. Technology stocks and financial stocks, for example, are more susceptible to market risk than are stocks issued by consumer products companies.

liquidity risk Uncertainty associated with ability of the holder of an investment asset to buy or sell the asset at a reasonable price within a short period.

Liquidity Risk. Liquidity is another important consideration. The **liquidity risk** of an investment refers to the investor's ability to buy and sell the asset at a reasonable price within a short period. Some investments are highly liquid. Widely traded common stocks and bonds, for example, have active secondary markets with many buyers and sellers. Some stocks and bonds are not widely traded and subject to greater liquidity risk. Real estate and art are other types of investments where liquidity risk is higher. A house in the "right" neighborhood may be sold easily at a fair price, whereas property in another area might prove to be illiquid. Artwork that one collector finds appealing may not appeal to others. Investors should consider how easy it would be to "reverse" the investment, and the cost involved in doing so, before making an investment.

Rates of Return

We have noted that riskier investments offer, on average, greater returns. The return, or rate of return, is simply what you receive in exchange for making the investment. Your return is made up of current income, price appreciation, or both.

Current income consists of periodic cash payments that the investor receives. Current income from an investment might take the form of rental income from real estate, interest payments from bonds, or dividend payments on stocks. Price appreciation occurs when an investment increases in value.

You can use the following equation to determine your rate of return on a one-year investment:

$$\frac{\text{Ending Value} + \text{Cash Flow} - \text{Original Investment}}{\text{Original Investment}} = \text{Total Return}$$

For example, if you purchase a share of stock for $50 and sell it for $55 one year later, you have benefited from $5 of price appreciation. Further assume that you received a $1 dividend payment on the stock. Your rate of return would be 12 percent, as shown here:

$$\frac{55 + 1 - 50}{50} = 12\%$$

Some investments, such as a piece of artwork or the purchase of raw, undeveloped land, provide only the potential for price appreciation. Other investments, such as the purchase of stocks and bonds, provide a combination of current income and possible price appreciation. The actual rate of return that you earn on an investment is a composite measure made up of both the income received (if any) and the increase (or decrease) in value of the investment.

Asset Allocation

asset allocation The assignment of investment dollars to different types of investments.

Asset allocation is the assignment of investment dollars to different types of investments. For example, one investor may allocate 70 percent of her investment dollars to common stock and 30 percent to corporate bonds, whereas another investor may place 10 percent of his investment funds in stocks, 60 percent in bonds, and 30 percent in real estate. Asset allocation is a critical choice, and the mix you select is affected by many variables. Risk tolerance is one factor; another is the position of the investor relative to his or her life-cycle. Asset allocation is also determined by an investor's objectives.

Asset Allocation and Risk

We noted earlier that risk tolerance is your comfort level with risk. The amount of risk that you are willing to tolerate with respect to your investments is determined by many factors, including your wealth, investment experience, job security, age, marital status, and the number of dependents you have. How much risk are you willing to accept? The risk assessment quiz provided in Insight 12.2 should help you measure your tolerance for risk. If you are very risk averse, you will allocate your investment dollars differently from a person who seeks, or is indifferent to risk.

Ranked on a continuum, the lowest-risk investment is U.S. government (treasury) securities. These securities are of low risk because the federal government backs them and has the authority to raise revenues to make required payments when they are due. Treasury securities are followed by corporate bonds, then preferred stock, then common stock, and finally the common stock of small companies.[1] Common stock is riskier because dividend payments are not guaranteed, and there is no specified future value of the security. Exhibit 12.2 shows some typical investment portfolios based on the investor's comfort level with risk.

Insight 12.2 How Much Risk Is Right? A Quick Quiz

Smart—and happy—investors know their risk comfort sense and make money in ways they feel at ease with. Here's a quiz to help you determine how much risk you can handle.

1. Your investment loses 15 percent of its value in a market correction a month after you buy it. Assuming that none of the fundamentals have changed, do you:
   ❑ a. Sit tight and wait for it to journey back up.
   ❑ b. Sell it and rid yourself of further sleepless nights if it continues to decline.
   ❑ c. Buy more—if it looked good at the original price it looks even better now.

2. A month after you purchase it, the value of your investment suddenly skyrockets by 40 percent. Assuming you can't find any further information, what do you do?
   ❑ a. Sell it.
   ❑ b. Hold it on the expectation of further gain.
   ❑ c. Buy more—it will probably go higher.

3. Which would you have rather done:
   ❑ a. Invested in an aggressive growth fund which appreciated very little in six months.

   ❑ b. Invested in a money-market fund only to see the aggressive growth fund you were thinking about double in value in six months.

4. Would you feel better if:
   ❑ a. You doubled your money in an equity investment.
   ❑ b. Your money-market fund investment saved you from losing half your money in a market slide.

5. Which situation would make you feel happier?
   ❑ a. You win $100,000 in a publisher's contest.
   ❑ b. You inherit $100,000 from a rich relative.
   ❑ c. You earn $100,000 by risking $2,000 in the options market.
   ❑ d. Any of the above—you're happy with the $100,000, no matter how it ended up in your wallet.

6. The apartment building where you live is being converted to condominiums. You can either buy your unit for $80,000 or sell the option for $20,000. The market value of the condo is $120,000. You know that if you buy the condo, it might take six months to sell, the monthly carrying cost is $1,200, and you'd have to borrow the down payment for

a mortgage. You don't want to live in the building—what do you do?
   ❑ a. Take the $20,000.
   ❑ b. Buy the unit and then sell it on the open market.

7. You inherit your uncle's $100,000 house, free of any mortgage. Although the house is in a fashionable neighborhood and can be expected to appreciate at a rate faster than inflation, it has deteriorated badly. It would net $1,000 monthly if rented as is; it would net $1,500 per month if renovated. The renovations could be financed by a mortgage on the property. You would:
   ❑ a. Sell the house.
   ❑ b. Rent it as is.
   ❑ c. Make the necessary renovations, and then rent it.

8. You work for a small, but thriving, privately held electronics company. The company is raising money by selling stock to its employees. Management plans to take the company public, but not for four or more years. If you buy the stock, you will not be allowed to sell until shares are traded publicly. In the meantime, the stock will pay no dividends. But when the

Asset Allocation Over the Life-Cycle

An extremely important determinant of asset allocation should be your stage in the life-cycle. As you pass through life, you will go through a number of "stages." Your investment

company goes public, the shares could trade for 10 to 20 times what you paid for them. How much of an investment would you make?

- ❑ a. None at all.
- ❑ b. One month's salary.
- ❑ c. Three months' salary.
- ❑ d. Six months' salary.

9. Your longtime friend and neighbor, an experienced petroleum geologist, is assembling a group of investors (of which he is one) to fund an exploratory oil well which could pay back 50 to 100 times its investment if successful. If the well is dry, the entire investment is worthless. Your friend estimates the chance of success is only 20 percent. What would you invest?

- ❑ a. Nothing at all.
- ❑ b. One month's salary.
- ❑ c. Three months' salary.
- ❑ d. Six months' salary.

10. You learn that several commercial building developers are seriously looking at undeveloped land in a certain location. You are offered an option to buy a choice parcel of that land. The cost is about two months' salary and you calculate the gain to be ten months' salary. Do you:

- ❑ a. Purchase the option.
- ❑ b. Let it slide; it's not for you.

11. You are on a TV game show and can choose one of the following. Which would you take?

- ❑ a. $1,000 in cash.
- ❑ b. A 50 percent chance at winning $4,000.
- ❑ c. A 20 percent chance at winning $10,000.
- ❑ d. A 5 percent chance at winning $100,000.

12. It's 1992, and inflation is returning. Hard assets such as precious metals, collectibles, and real estate are expected to keep pace with inflation. Your assets are now all in long-term bonds. What would you do?

- ❑ a. Hold the bonds.
- ❑ b. Sell the bonds, and put half the proceeds into money funds and the other half into hard assets.
- ❑ c. Sell the bonds and put the total proceeds into hard assets.
- ❑ d. Sell the bonds, put all the money into hard assets, and borrow additional money to buy more.

13. You've lost $500 at the blackjack table in Atlantic City. How much more are you prepared to lose to win the $500 back?

- ❑ a. Nothing—you quit now.
- ❑ b. $100.
- ❑ c. $250.
- ❑ d. $500.

- ❑ e. More than $500.

Your Score

Now it's time to see what kind of investor you are. Total your score, using the point system listed below for each answer you gave.

1. a-3, b-1, c-4
2. a-1, b-3, c-4
3. a-1, b-3
4. a-2, b-1
5. a-2, b-1, c-4, d-1
6. a-1, b-2
7. a-1, b-2, c-3
8. a-1, b-2, c-4, d-6
9. a-1, b-3, c-6, d-9
10. a-3, b-1
11. a-1, b-3, c-5, d-9
12. a-1, b-2, c-3, d-4
13. a-1, b-2, c-4, d-6, e-8

If you scored...

Below 21: You are a conservative investor, allergic to risk. Stay with sober conservative investments. 21 to 36: Your are an active investor, willing to take calculated, prudent risks to gain financially. 36 or more: You are a venturesome, agressive investor.

Source: *Donoghue's Money Letter*.

Exhibit 12.2

Typical Investment Portfolios
Based on an Investor's Comfort Level with Risk

Stock Investments
Diversified portfolio
of common stocks
Stock mutual funds

**Bonds and Other Fixed
Income Investments**
U.S. Treasury bonds
Corporate bonds
Municipal bonds
Mortgage-backed securities
Bond mutual funds

Cash Equivalent Investments
Money market funds
Short-term certificates of deposit
Treasury bills

Investor A

Investor A
Aggressive growth portfolio
Investor A has a high tolerance for risk and
invests very aggressively. The cash equivalent
portion of his portfolio is small and limited to
investments that can be easily liquidated,
should he need money. The balance is invested
in stocks, which gives him the chance for
higher returns—at the expense of more risk.

Investor B

Investor B
Growth portfolio
Investor B is after high returns but is not
as willing as Investor A to take investment
risks. She's still heavily invested in stocks,
but the fixed income portion of her portfolio
is somewhat larger than Investor A's and
includes bonds for stability.

Investor C

Investor C
Balanced portfolio
Investor C wants a blend of investment growth
capital preservation. He devotes a substantial
portion of his portfolio to fixed income and
cash equivalent investments. But to allow for
investment growth, he still keeps his portfolio
weighted toward stock investments.

Investor D

Investor D
Income-earning portfolio
Investor D is conservative. He's primarily
interested in receiving income, though he
wants his returns to keep pace with inflation.
The major portion of his portfolio is in fixed
income and cash equivalent investments, with
a high percentage in bonds. The balance of
his money is invested in stocks.

Investor E

Investor E
Safety-oriented portfolio
Investor E's main objective is to conserve her
principal, so she's extremely averse to risk.
Her portfolio reflects this attitude, with half
her investments in high quality bonds and a
lesser percentage in stocks and cash
equivalents.

Source: Charles Schwab Guide to Bonds and
Income Earning Investments, 1993, pgs. 3–4.

goals and asset allocation change as you pass through these life-cycle stages. Although these stages can be divided into any number of categories, we will consider five typical periods through which each individual-investor passes. They include childhood and adolescence, young adult, middle age, preretirement, and retirement.

Childhood and Adolescence. Individuals in this stage usually depend on parents or guardians for financial support. Children and adolescents usually do not have funds to invest. If, however, you are able to set up an investment plan for a child or adolescent, it is an excellent time to consider investments that can provide price appreciation.

Young Adult. In the young adult stage, many individuals complete their education, get their first "real" job, get married, start a family, and buy a house. Obviously, individuals in this stage have great demands on the income they earn. At the same time, salaries tend to be lower in entry-level positions and in the early years of a career.

If individuals in this stage have money available to invest, it is a good time to consider investments that offer growth and do not produce income, which is currently taxable. Common stocks are a good investment during this period since, historically, they have provided higher rates of return than bonds, preferred stock, and the various savings alternatives. Although stocks are riskier, you have time and the power of compounding on your side.

Middle Age. This period, for many individuals, is a prime investment period. Salaries tend to be higher than at the young adult stage, and some of the demands on income that were present during that time may no longer be present during middle age. This stage is still far enough away from retirement that investors can take a more aggressive approach to their investment mix.

Preretirement. The period before retirement is a critical time for investors. Many investors choose to lock-in some of their investment gains during this period by selling investments that have appreciated in value. For example, you may have stock that has significantly increased in value over the years since you purchased it. Since stock prices are not guaranteed, you may decide to sell some of the stock now in order to lock-in the gain. During the period before retirement, the goal of many investors changes from growth to income, and investors begin to restructure their holdings to reflect this change.

Retirement. Many retirees shift their asset allocation to more income-producing investments that are less risky during retirement. They use the income produced by these investments to supplement other sources

Insight   12.3 Smart Investing Through the Ages

■ 20s–30s

You've got to start somewhere. Investing just $100 a month may not seem like a lot. But if you start socking away that sort of money when you're in your 20s or early 30s, it can make a huge difference to your lifestyle when you finally quit the work force.

How come? Younger investors may not have much money. But they do have one big advantage: time.

According to T. Rowe Price Associates, if you invest $100 a month starting at age 30, by the time you retire at age 65 you would have over $177,000 in today's dollars. This presumes that you earn 7% a year, which is the historical rate of return achieved by stocks, after adjusting for inflation.

When you're in your 20s and 30s, "get into the habit of systematic saving," says John Cammack, a vice president with T. Rowe Price. "It's a wonderful discipline. You may see it as a sacrifice in your 20s and 30s, but you'll see it as your savior in your 50s and 60s."

For those who don't have a lot of money to invest, mutual funds are often an ideal invest-ment. Many funds demand investment minimums of $1,000 and below. Some will waive their minimums entirely, providing you agree to save $25, $50 or $100 every month through an automatic investment plan.

Younger investors who are saving for retirement should stash most of their money in stocks, say investment advisers. Lewis J. Altfest, president of L.J. Altfest & Co., suggests keeping 80% of one's portfolio in stocks, including a hefty stake in small-company stocks and foreign stocks.

Mr. Altfest also recommends stocks when saving for a child's college education.

But while stocks may be a fine investment when saving for retirement or a child's edu-cation, younger investors may want to be more conservative when it comes to investing their emergency money or saving for the down payment on a house.

"Before you start investing in stock mutual funds, you should get a reserve built up," says Robert Bingham, an investment adviser with San Francisco's Bingham, Osborn & Scarborough.

He thinks that investors should have an emergency fund equal to between three and six months' living expenses.

When saving to buy a house, investors should also favor con-servative investments, he says.

■ 40s–50s

Middle-aged investors often have awesome responsibilities. "These are people in the triple bind," says Cammack. "They have to prepare for their own retirement. They're probably knocking off a couple of col-lege educations. And they've got aging parents to look after."

Mr. Cammack says those in their 40s and 50s should care-fully consider how much money they can afford to spend on each of these items. And he thinks investors shouldn't short-change themselves, by skimping on their retirement savings.

Investment advisers note that investors sometimes under-estimate how much money they really need to retire.

To accumulate retirement savings, investment advisers often suggest that investors first try to make the maximum pos-sible contribution to their 401(k) plan and their individ-ual retirement account.

After that, they should consider putting money in a no-load, low-cost tax-deferred variable annuity.

For those who are struggling to save enough money for retirement, consider staying in the work force longer, says T. Rowe Price's Mr. Cammack. "There's tremendous leverage from delaying your retirement," he says. "If you delay your retirement from 62 to 65, it can change the amount of capital you need dramatically."

Investors in their 40s and 50s should consider putting 65% of their portfolio in stocks and 35% in bonds, says Lewis J. Altfest, president of L.J. Altfest & Co. "The 65% is for growth, and the 35% is for income and safety," he says.

If you are in one of the top income tax brackets, you may want to use municipal bonds for the fixed-income part of your portfolio. Municipal bonds kick off income that is exempt from federal taxes and, in some cases, from state and local taxes as well.

Smaller investors, or those planning to invest for a relatively short period of time, should probably stick with municipal bond funds, because of the high cost of trading in the muni market. But if you're making a long-term investment in munis, you may want to buy an individual bond and hold it to maturity, thereby saving on mutual fund expenses.

■ 60-Plus

Income-hungry retirees face some grim choices these days. Slumping interest rates have shoved money market fund yields below 3% and pushed 30-year Treasury bonds close to 7%. Yield-starved investors can't even find comfort in high-yield junk-bond funds, which these days are paying less than 9%.

"People who are in their 70s and 80s remember so many years of high interest rates," says John Blankinship Jr. of Blankinship & Foster, a Del Mar, Calif., investment adviser. "Where before they could live off their portfolio's current yield, now they can't."

The solution, says Mr. Blankinship, is to manage your portfolio for total return. A portfolio's total return is calculated by considering not only the income kicked off by the portfolio, but also any change in the value of the portfolio's investments. Financial advisers say the trick is to spur the growth in your portfolio's value, by keeping a healthy chunk of your assets in stocks.

Lewis J. Altfest, president of L.J. Altfest & Co., suggests that retirees keep 40% of their portfolio in stocks and 60% in bonds and money market instruments. If you do that, he says, you can spend all the income kicked off by your bonds and money market instruments without worrying that inflation will eat away at your standard of living.

How come? While the bonds are unlikely to generate any capital gains, the 40% stock position should provide enough growth for the portfolio's value to stay even with inflation, says Mr. Altfest.

Because retirees will have to periodically sell portions of their stock portfolio, they need to ensure that their stock investments don't bounce around in value too much. As a result, owning a broad mix of stocks is crucial, say investment advisers.

For retirees, holding down investment costs is also critical, especially when it comes to picking bond investments. With bond mutual funds, for instance, high annual expenses eat directly into a fund's yield, thereby reducing the amount of money available for a retiree to spend.

Source: Excerpted from Jonathan Clements, "Smart Investing through the Ages," June 11, 1993. Reprinted by permission of the *Wall Street Journal,* © 1993 Dow Jones & Company, Inc. All Rights Reserved Worldwide.

of retirement income, such as social security old-age benefits and private pension income. Although investment income is currently taxable, retirees no longer have work earnings, and their investment income may be taxed at a lower marginal rate than it would have been taxed before retirement.

Given recent retirement trends, many financial planners believe that there is still a place for investments that can provide price appreciation in a retiree's portfolio. On average, people are retiring earlier and living longer, creating a longer period of retirement. Since the money must last longer, there remains a need for growth.

These life-cycle stages may suggest a "cookie cutter" approach to investment allocation. However, it is important to remember that each investor has his or her own objectives, comfort level with risk, financial resources, and so on. Some asset allocation ideas for investors in three of the life-cycle stages just discussed are presented in Insight 12.3.

Investment Strategies

investment strategy An investment plan designed to bring about a desired investment result.

Regardless of life-cycle stage and tolerance for risk, most investments are not made randomly. Rather, the investor has an investment strategy that he or she follows. An **investment strategy** is an investment plan that is designed to bring about a desired investment result. Investors use a number of investment strategies, some of them simultaneously. These strategies include buy and hold, market timing, diversification, dollar-cost averaging, value investing, and combination strategies.

Buy-and-Hold

buy-and-hold strategy Investment strategy in which an investor makes an investment and then holds (does not sell) the investment asset for a long period.

The simplest investment strategy to understand and employ is buy-and-hold. Under the **buy-and-hold strategy,** an investor makes an investment and then does not sell it for a long time. The buy-and-hold strategy has at least three distinct advantages.

1. It is a low maintenance strategy. You are not constantly readjusting your portfolio by buying and selling.

2. The strategy minimizes transaction costs, such as brokerage fees, incurred when buying or selling securities.

3. The strategy delays taxation of investment gains since most gains are not taxed until the gain is realized.

If you use the buy-and-hold strategy, you will never miss an upturn in the value of the asset you are holding. Of course, you will not avoid downturns either. Studies have shown the buy-and-hold strategy to be very effective over time.

Market Timing

market timing Investment strategy in which an investor attempts to buy securities before a price increase and sell securities before a price drop.

A second strategy, in a sense the opposite of buy and hold, is market timing. **Market timing** means trying to buy securities before the price increases and trying to sell securities before the price falls. Market timers use a variety of indicators that they believe signal the proper time to buy or sell. This strategy requires greater maintenance, higher transaction costs, and earlier realization of capital gains than the buy-and-hold strategy. However, if you buy and sell at just the "right" time, you can do well.

The problem is knowing the right time to buy and sell. If you choose the wrong time to be out of the market, you can lose out on large gains. Missing just a few good days over a trading period can have a monumental effect, as shown in Exhibit 12.3. This exhibit shows the annual rate of return that you would have earned had you invested in the Standard & Poor's 500, a widely followed stock index, over the period 1986 though 1995. If you had been invested in the index every trading day over this period, your annual rate of return would have been close to 15 percent. However, if you were "out of the market" on the 10 "best" days, your annual return would have been 10.2 percent. If you missed the 20 best days, 7.3 percent; the 30 best days, 4.8 percent; and the 40 best days, 2.5 percent.

Exhibit 12.3

Market Timing Can Be Painful

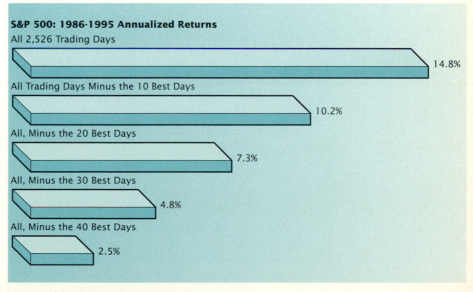

S&P 500: 1986-1995 Annualized Returns

All 2,526 Trading Days — 14.8%

All Trading Days Minus the 10 Best Days — 10.2%

All, Minus the 20 Best Days — 7.3%

All, Minus the 30 Best Days — 4.8%

All, Minus the 40 Best Days — 2.5%

Source: *Fidelity Forum*, Winter 1996, p. 8.

Diversification

diversification Investment in a number of different assets.

portfolio The combination of financial assets held by a particular investor.

A third strategy is diversification. You have probably heard the adage "don't put all your eggs in one basket." The same advice applies to your investments. Investing all of your wealth in a single asset or single type of asset can have disastrous results if the value of the asset declines sharply. **Diversification** means investing in a number of different financial assets. The combination of financial assets that you select is called your **portfolio.** For example, rather than investing $20,000 in a single common stock, perhaps you invest $5,000 in each of four different stocks. Should the price of one stock fall, your other three stocks may perform well enough to offset your losses on the stock that did not perform well.

Diversification sounds good in theory, and it has empirical support in practice. In his pioneering work, Harry Markowitz, a Nobel Prize winner in economics, showed how diversification can reduce portfolio risk. Markowitz used the variability of the rate of return on a portfolio of securities as the measure of risk. As the number of securities in the portfolio increases, the variability of the portfolio's rate of return decreases.[2]

Investors achieve maximum diversification benefits by combining financial securities from different industries and by investing in different types of financial securities. Holding a portfolio consisting of the stocks of several pharmaceutical companies is less risky than purchasing the common stock of a single pharmaceutical company. If you invest in one company, and that company does not perform well, you will lose money. A portfolio made up of stocks from many different industries is far less risky than a portfolio of stocks from the same industry.

correlation With regard to investments, the degree to which the prices or returns of two investments move together, up or down, over time.

Additional diversification benefits are achieved if you hold investments that do not have highly positively correlated returns. **Correlation** is the degree to which the prices or returns of two investments "move together," up or down, over time. The correlation between the prices or returns of two assets ranges from a score of 1, meaning perfect positive correlation, to a score of 2-1, meaning perfect negative correlation. A correlation of 0 means that the prices or returns are not correlated.

If the returns of two investments are highly positively correlated, they tend to move together in the same direction over time. For example, the rate of return on common stock is highly positively correlated with the rate of return on small company stocks. If returns are negatively correlated, it means that the returns tend to move in opposite directions. For example, when interest rates increase, the return on short-term treasury securities also increases. Higher interest rates, however, have a negative influence on the price of common stock.

By adding assets with low or negative correlations to your investment mix, you reduce risk. If one investment does not perform well, the other investments might perform better. As you might expect, however, it is difficult to find investments that have low or negative correlation. Exhibit 12.4 shows the correlation between various pairs of investment alternatives.

Dollar-Cost Averaging

In addition to diversification across companies, the investor should consider diversification across time. Suppose you inherited $100,000 and decided to invest the money in a mutual fund. As discussed earlier in this chapter, mutual funds invest in many different securities, so such an investment would provide diversification across securities. If you invest the entire $100,000 at one time, however, you may be buying at the wrong time—that is, when the price is high, just before a steep decline. You can reduce your risk of buying at the wrong time by investing smaller amounts at different times. For example, instead of investing the $100,000 at one time, you may decide to invest $10,000 every six months for five years. This strategy is called **dollar-cost averaging.** A more detailed example of dollar-cost averaging appears in Exhibit 12.5. The idea is to purchase fewer investment units when the price is high and more investment units when the price is low. Although this strategy is more expensive when you consider brokerage fees and other transaction costs, dollar-cost averaging provides diversification across time.

dollar-cost averaging
Investment strategy involving investing a set amount at regular intervals with the goal of diversifying purchases across time.

Exhibit 12.4

Asset Allocation: Searching for Opposites

A well-constructed bulletproof portfolio should include assets whose returns do not rise or fall in step with one another. To see whether two types of investments are closely entwined or move in opposite directions, find the point at which they intersect. Example: Returns of small-company stock are only slightly correlated with those of corporate bonds.

	Correlation in Returns					
	Corporate Bonds	Common Stocks	Small Stocks	International Stocks	International Bonds	Equity Reits
Treasury Bills	Very Low	Opposite	Opposite	Opposite	Opposite	Opposite
Corporate Bonds	—	Mod. Low	Low	Low	Mod. Low	Moderate
Common Stocks	Mod. Low	—	High	Moderate	Low	High
Small Stocks	Low	High	—	Moderate	Very Low	High
Internatl. Stocks	Low	Moderate	Moderate	—	Mod. High	Mod. High
Internatl. Bonds	Mod. Low	Low	Very Low	Mod. High	—	Mod. Low

Source: Adapted from Roger Gibson, *Asset Allocation: Balancing Financial Risk*, Business One Irwin. Reprinted with permission of The McGraw-Hill Companies.

Exhibit 12.5

Dollar-Cost Averaging

Dollar-cost averaging is a powerful investment strategy. By investing smaller amounts periodically, the investor achieves a lower overall cost per share since more shares are purchased when the price is low, and fewer shares are purchased when the price is high. An example will illus-

trate this concept. Suppose you wish to invest $2,400 in the stock of Universal Megatronics. You are concerned that you will make your investment at "the wrong time." Rather than investing $2,400 at one time, suppose instead that you invest $400 every other month.

Investment Date	Investment	Share Price	Shares Purchased
February 28	$400	$15	26.667
April 30	400	18	22.222
June 30	400	20	20.000
August 31	400	22	18.182
October 31	400	25	16.000
December 31	400	20	20.000

Total Investment = $2,400
Total Shares Purchased = 123.071
Ending Market Value (at $20 per share) = 123.071 × $20 = $2,461.42
Average Purchase Price per Share = ($2,400/123.071) = $19.50

Notice that the average purchase price during this period is $20 per share:
$15 + $18 + $20 + $22 + $25 + $20 = $1,200
$1,200/6 = $20.
Through dollar-cost averaging, however, you purchase more shares when the price is lower and fewer shares when the price is higher. Your average purchase price per share is only $19.50.

Value Investing

value investing Investment strategy involving investing in companies or industries that have fallen out of favor with other investors.

Some investors follow a strategy known as value investing. **Value investing** refers to investing in companies or industries that have fallen out of favor with other investors. Securities issued by such companies are likely to be selling at a low price relative to other securities. Value investors hope to purchase such securities at the depressed price and profit when the companies return to favor with investors. Value investing can be risky because some companies and industries remain out of favor with investors for long periods or never recover.

Combination Strategies

The investment strategies discussed here are not mutually exclusive—you can use some of these strategies in combination. For example, many investors successfully combine the buy-and-hold strategy with diversification. Such investors purchase securities in several different companies in different industries, and then hold the securities for many years. Another example is combining dollar-cost averaging with value investing. Under this strategy, called value averaging, investors periodically purchase shares of companies that are out of favor.

Markets and Market Efficiency

market A coming together of buyers and sellers for the purpose of making transactions.

Regardless of the investment strategy that you employ, you will have to buy and sell assets. Assets are bought and sold in markets. A **market** is simply the coming together of buyers and sellers for the purpose of making transactions. Thus a market exists wherever investment transactions occur. Some markets, like the New York Stock Exchange and the Chicago Board of Trade, are formal, centralized markets. Other markets, such as the market for the stock of many smaller companies, are less formal, and the transactions are performed at many locations. Some markets, such as the market for currencies, are global, whereas other markets, such as the market for real estate, are purely local.

efficiency With regard to markets, the degree to which the prices of assets traded in a market reflect all relevant information.

Regardless of the type of market, an important characteristic of the market is its degree of efficiency. **Efficiency** in this context refers to the degree to which the prices of assets traded in the market reflect all relevant information. Why is the efficiency of a market important to investors? Because buyers and sellers have a common goal: receiving the "best" price when they purchase or sell an asset. Sellers want to sell at the highest possible price, whereas buyers want to buy at the lowest possible price. If the market is efficient, the price of the asset reflects all relevant information pertaining to the asset. If markets are not efficient, individuals who possess superior information can use the information to earn higher investment returns. Empirical research has shown the security markets in the United States are highly efficient.

Investment Transactions

How do you actually go about making an investment? Can you make the investment directly or do you have to use an intermediary to arrange the purchase and sale? Do you have to pay cash or can you borrow a portion of the amount invested? Where do you get information on investment opportunities? We will answer these and other questions in this section.

Making Investment Transactions

You can make investment transactions in a number of ways, including using a broker, using a dealer, and performing direct transactions. Brokers handle most investment transactions.

broker An investment intermediary who links buyers and sellers and is paid a commission for arranging the exchange of the asset.

commission A per-trade fee for service.

full-service broker Broker that offers a complete range of services in addition to performing investment transactions.

discount broker Broker that charges lower commissions than a full-service broker but offers fewer services.

Brokers. A **broker** is an investment intermediary who links buyers and sellers and is paid a **commission**—a per-trade fee—for arranging the exchange of the asset. For example, if you want to purchase 100 shares of McDonalds common stock, you could call a stock broker who would match your request to purchase McDonalds stock with a seller who was willing to sell his or her shares of McDonalds.

There are two types of brokers: full-service brokers and discount brokers. **Full-service brokers** offer a complete range of services to their customers. For example, in addition to performing investment transactions, full-service brokerages have investment analysts who research financial securities and make recommendations on what to buy and sell. The investor pays for these services through higher commissions.

At the other end of the spectrum are discount brokers. **Discount brokers** are intermediaries who provide limited services, usually only the purchase and sale of securities, to their customers. Discount brokers charge lower commissions than full-service brokers charge, but provide fewer services.

With the growth of the Internet, many discount brokerages are offering their customers the option of online trading. In addition to easy access to information about your account, online trading commissions are very low. For example, one discount broker permits clients to electronically trade up to 1,000 shares of common stock for only $30.[3]

How do you go about selecting a broker? If you have friends or relatives who invest, you can ask who handles their accounts and what their experience has been with their brokers. Insight 12.4 describes suggestions for choosing a securities broker offered by the U.S. Securities and Exchange Commission (SEC), which regulates the securities industry. States have disciplinary reports available on brokers that note unresolved investor complaints, pending arbitration cases, pending civil cases, criminal charges, and criminal convictions that are being appealed. Exhibit 12.6 lists whom you should contact in your state to get this information.

With regard to selecting a broker, two primary considerations are the services offered by the broker and the cost to perform transactions. Obviously, a full-service broker will provide a wider range of services to you; however, you will pay more when you trade. A discount broker will cost less for you to use; however, the range of services provided is quite narrow. Other important considerations include the quality of service provided, research, the minimum amount needed to open an account, convenience, online trading availability, the interest rate paid on savings options provided by the broker, and the interest rate charged on loans from the broker.

Insight

12.4 Selecting Your Broker

Before making a securities investment, you must decide which brokerage firm—also referred to as a broker/dealer—and sales representative—also referred to as a stockbroker, account executive, or registered representative—to use. Before making these decisions, you should:

- THINK through your financial objectives and prepare a personal financial profile.

- TALK with potential salespeople at several firms. If possible, meet them face to face at their offices. Ask each sales representative about his or her investment experience, professional background, and education.

- FIND OUT about the disciplinary history of any brokerage firm and sales representative by calling 800-289-9999, a toll-free hot line operated by the National Association of Securities Dealers, Inc. (NASD). The NASD will provide information on disciplinary actions taken by securities regulators and criminal authorities. State securities regulators also can tell you if a sales representative is licensed to do business in your state.

- UNDERSTAND how the sales representative is paid; ask for a copy of the firm's commission schedule. Firms generally pay sales staff based on the amount of money invested by a customer and the number of transactions done in a customer's account. More compensation may be paid to a sales representative for selling a firm's own investment products. Ask what "fees" or "charges" you will be required to pay when opening, maintaining, and closing an account.

- DETERMINE whether you need the services of a full-service or a discount brokerage firm. A full-service firm typically provides execution services, recommendations, investment advice, and research support. A discount broker generally provides execution services and does not make recommendations regarding which securities you should buy or sell. The charges you pay may differ depending upon what services are provided by the firm.

- ASK if the brokerage firm is a member of the Securities Investor Protection Corporation (SIPC). SIPC provides limited customer protection if a brokerage firm becomes insolvent. Ask if the firm has other insurance that provides coverage beyond the SIPC limits. SIPC *does not* insure against losses attributable to a decline in the market value of your securities. For further information, contact SIPC at 805 Fifteenth Street, N.W., Suite 800, Washington, D.C. 20005-2207; or call 202-371-8300.

Remember, part of making the right investment decision is finding the brokerage firm and the sales representative that best meet your personal financial needs. Do not rush. Do the necessary background investigation on both the firm and the sales representative. Resist salespeople who urge you to immediately open an account with them.

Source: U.S. Securities and Exchange Commission.

Exhibit 12.6

What Your State Will Tell You About Your Broker

Use these phone numbers and addresses to obtain an employment and disciplinary report on a stockbroker. Nearly all 50 states and the District of Columbia say they will send out-of-state investors a report on a broker. So if you live in Louisiana, which withholds all disciplinary information, or in a state that deletes some information, call another state's securities department because all have access to the Central Registration Depository data base.

There is usually a charge for a report. In most instances, the cost is nominal, but Georgia charges a minimum of $10 and Michigan and Rhode Island

charge hourly fees ranging from $11 to $15. The NASD's reports are free. (The NASD is the National Association of Securities Dealers.)

Here's what you'll find in the state reports:

■ **Unresolved investor complaints.** Included by all states except Alaska, Connecticut, Illinois, Louisiana, Minnesota, Nevada, North Dakota, Rhode Island and Wisconsin and the District of Columbia.

■ **Pending arbitration cases.** Included by all states except Georgia, Hawaii, Illinois, Louisiana, Minnesota, Nevada, New York, Oregon, Rhode Island

and Wisconsin and the District of Columbia.

■ **Pending civil lawsuits.** Included by all states except Georgia, Hawaii, Illinois, Louisiana, Rhode Island and Wisconsin and the District of Columbia.

■ **Criminal charges.** Included by all states except Delaware, Hawaii, Illinois, Louisiana, Rhode Island and Wisconsin.

■ **Criminal convictions being appealed.** Included by all states except Delaware, Hawaii, Illinois, Louisiana, Oklahoma and Wisconsin.

ALABAMA
Office of Securities Commission
770 Washington Ave., Ste. 570
Montgomery, AL 36130
800-222-1253

ALASKA
Div. of Banking and Securities
P.O. Box 110807
Juneau, AK 99811
907-465-2521

ARIZONA
Securities Division
1300 W. Washington St., 3rd Fl.
Phoenix, AZ 85007
602-542-4242

ARKANSAS
Security Dept.
Heritage West Bldg.
201 E. Markham
Little Rock, AR 72201
(no phone requests)

CALIFORNIA
Department of Corporations
3700 Wilshire Blvd., Ste. 600
Los Angeles, CA 90010
213-736-2502

COLORADO
Division of Securities
1580 Lincoln St., Ste. 420
Denver, CO 80203
303-894-2320

CONNECTICUT
Dept. of Banking/Securities
and Business Investment Div.
260 Constitution Plaza
Hartford, CT 06103
860-240-8230

DELAWARE
Department of Justice
Securities Division
820 N. French St., 8th Fl.
Wilmington, DE 17801
302-577-2515

DISTRICT OF COLUMBIA
Division of Securities
450 5th St., N.W., Ste. 821
Washington, DC 20001
202-626-5109

FLORIDA
Office of Comptroller
Dept. of Banking and Finance
Division of Securities
LL22, The Capitol
Tallahassee, FL 32399
904-488-9530

GEORGIA
Business Services Regulation
2 Martin Luther King Jr. Dr.
West Tower, Ste. 802
Atlanta, GA 30334
404-656-2895

HAWAII
Business Registration Division
Dept. of Commerce and
Consumer Affairs
P.O. Box 40
Honolulu, HI 96810
808-586-2740

IDAHO
Department of Finance
P.O. Box 83720
Boise, ID 83720
208-332-8004

ILLINOIS
Securities Dept.
Lincoln Tower, Ste. 200
520 South Second St.
Springfield, IL 62701
217-782-2256

INDIANA
Secretary of State's Office
Securities Division
302 W. Washington St.,
Rm. E111
Indianapolis, IN 46204
317-232-6681

IOWA
Securities Bureau
Lucas Building, 2nd Fl.
Des Moines, IA 50319
515-281-4441

KANSAS
Office of the Securities
Commissioner
618 S. Kansas Ave., 2nd Fl.
Topeka, KS 66603
(no phone requests)

KENTUCKY
Dept. of Financial Institutions
477 Versailles Rd.
Frankfort, KY 40601
(no phone requests)

LOUISIANA
Securities Commission
Energy Centre
1100 Poydras St., Ste. 2250
New Orleans, LA 70163
(no phone requests)

MAINE
Securities Division
121 State House Station
Augusta, ME 04333
207-624-8551

MARYLAND
Division of Securities
200 St. Paul Place, 20th Fl.
Baltimore, MD 21202
410-576-6494

MASSACHUSETTS
Securities Division
One Ashburton Pl., Rm. 1701
Boston, MA 02108
800-269-5428

MICHIGAN
Registration Section
P.O. Box 30222
Lansing, MI 48909
517-334-6215

MINNESOTA
Department of Commerce
Securities and Licensing Div.
133 East Seventh St.
St. Paul, MN 55101
800-657-3602

MISSISSIPPI
Securities Division
P.O. Box 136
Jackson, MS 39205
800-804-6364

MISSOURI
Attn: Kathy Palmero
Division of Securities
P.O. Box 1276
Jefferson City, MO 65102
800-721-7996

MONTANA
no printed report
406-444-2040

NEBRASKA
Bureau of Securities
The Atrium, Ste. 311
1200 N St.
Lincoln, NE 68508
(no phone requests)

NEVADA
Sec. of State/Securities Div.
555 E. Washington Ave.,
Ste. 500
Las Vegas, NV 89101
800-758-6440

NEW HAMPSHIRE
Bureau of Securities Regulation
State House, Rm. 204
Concord, NH 03301
(no phone requests)

NEW JERSEY
Bureau of Securities
P.O. Box 47029
Newark, NJ 07101
(no phone requests)

NEW MEXICO
Securities Division
725 St. Michaels Dr.
Santa Fe, NM 87501
505-827-7140

NEW YORK
Andrew Kandel/Bureau Chief
Investor Protection & Securities
Attorney General's Office
120 Broadway
New York, NY 10271
(no phone requests)

NORTH CAROLINA
Attn: Sandra Strickland
Sec. of State/Securities Div.
300 N. Salisbury St., Ste. 100
Raleigh, NC 27603
919-733-3924

NORTH DAKOTA
Securities Commissioner's
Office
600 E. Blvd., 5th Fl.
Bismarck, ND 58505
701-328-2910

OHIO
Division of Securities
77 South High St., 22nd Fl.
Columbus, OH 43266
(no phone requests)

OKLAHOMA
Department of Securities
First National Center, Ste. 860
120 N. Robinson
Oklahoma City, OK 73102
405-280-7700

OREGON
Div. of Finance/Corp. Securities
350 Winter St., N.E., Ste. 410
Salem, OR 97310
503-378-4387

PENNSYLVANIA
Office of the Secretary
1010 N. 7th St., 2nd Fl.
Harrisburg, PA 17102
717-787-8061

RHODE ISLAND
Business Regulation/
Securities Div.
233 Richmond St., Ste. 232
Providence, RI 02903
401-277-3048

SOUTH CAROLINA
Sec. of State/Securities Div.
P.O. Box 11350
Columbia, SC 29211
(no phone requests)

SOUTH DAKOTA
Attn: Linda Todd
Division of Securities
118 W. Capitol Ave.
Pierre, SD 57501
605-773-4013

TENNESSEE
Securities Division
Broker Dealer Section, Ste. 680
500 James Robertson Pkwy.
Nashville, TN 37243
(no phone requests)

TEXAS
State Securities Board
Broker/Dealer Registration
P.O. Box 13167
Austin, TX 78711
512-305-8332

UTAH
Securities Division
160 East 300 S., Box 146760
Salt Lake City, UT 84114
801-530-6600

VERMONT
Dept. of Banking, Insurance
and Securities
89 Main St., Drawer 20
Montpeller, VT 05620
802-828-3420

VIRGINIA
Securities Division
P.O. Box 1197
Richmond, VA 23219
804-371-9686

WASHINGTON
Dept. of Financial Institutions/
Securities Div.
P.O. Box 9033
Olympia, WA 98507
(no phone requests)

WEST VIRGINIA
Securities Division, WW 118
Capitol Building
Charleston, WV 25302
304-558-2257

WISCONSIN
Commissioner of Securities
Div. of Market Licensing
P.O. Box 1768
Madison, WI 53701
608-266-3431

WYOMING
Attn.: Securities Division
Sec. of State, State Capitol
Cheyenne, WY 82002
307-777-7370

Source: Reprinted with permission from the July 1996 issue of *Kiplinger's Personal Finance Magazine.* Copyright © 1996 The Kiplinger
Washington Editors, Inc.

Dealers. Brokers facilitate trades without taking possession of the asset. **Dealers** buy and sell assets and are compensated through the difference between the price paid for the asset and the sales price. For example, an art dealer who specializes in prints may purchase an etching for $5,000 and then try to sell it for $6,000. Dealers are important in markets where there is less liquidity, such as the market for art, real estate, and collectibles.

dealer Intermediary who buys and sells assets and whose profit or loss is the difference between the price paid for the asset and the sales price.

Direct Transactions. Using a broker or dealer to perform an investment transaction involves the use of an intermediary—someone who arranges the sale or purchase of the asset. Some investment transactions can be performed directly between the buyer and seller. A **direct transaction** is the purchase and sale of an asset without the use of an investment intermediary. A "for sale by owner" real estate transaction, for example, does not involve a broker or dealer; the purchaser negotiates terms of sale directly with the owner of the property. Some transactions involving collectibles and artwork are directly carried out between the owner and prospective purchaser.

direct transaction The purchase and sale of an asset without the use of an investment intermediary.

A few companies permit investors to directly purchase their common stock, thus avoiding brokerage commissions. These stocks are called no-load stocks because the investor does not have to pay a fee (also known as a load) at the time of purchase. A list of some of these no-load stocks is provided in Insight 12.5.

These no-load stocks and many other stocks offer investors dividend reinvestment plans. A **dividend reinvestment plan (DRIP)** permits the investor to use the dividends to purchase common stock rather than receiving the dividend in cash. For example, an investor may be paid $25 in dividends at the end of the quarter. Instead of receiving the dividend in cash, the investor may reinvest the dividend in the company's common stock. If the stock sells for $50 per share at that time, the investor will purchase half a share ($25/$50). In addition to reinvesting dividends, most DRIPs accept voluntary cash investments, directly investing these payments at no cost or for a nominal fee. Using DRIPs is an excellent way to dollar-cost average your investment.

dividend reinvestment plan (DRIP) Plan by which an investor who owns common stock in a particular company can have dividends automatically used to purchase more stock in the company rather than receiving the dividends in cash. Most DRIPs also permit optional cash contributions.

Cash Transactions Versus Margin Trading

An actual investment—the purchase of an asset—can be made in two ways. Most investments are made on a cash basis, with the purchaser giving the seller the agreed-upon value in cash in exchange for the asset. The second method of investing, which is often used in purchasing common stock, is margin trading. In a **margin trade,** an investor borrows a portion of funds needed for a transaction from a stock brokerage firm, using the stock to secure the loan. The brokerage firm charges interest on the loan and may require additional funds from the investor if the price of the security declines.

margin trade Transaction in which an investor borrows from the stock brokerage a portion of the funds necessary to buy stock, using the stock to secure the loan.

Why do investors use margin trades? Some investors simply do not have enough cash at the time of investment to make a cash purchase. Alternatively, some investors hope to use the borrowed funds to increase their investment returns by being able to invest more. As we shall see, however, margin trading can also increase the investor's losses if the price of the security declines.

An example illustrating a cash trade and a margin trade is provided in Exhibit 12.7. In the example, an investor purchases 100 shares of Merck common stock selling for $80 per share. If a cash purchase is made, the total investment is $8,000. Alternatively, the investor may borrow up to 50 percent ($4,000) of the purchase price of the stock, as illustrated in the second column. The middle and bottom sections of Exhibit 12.7 show how the investor would fare if the price of Merck increases to $100 per share and if the price declines to $60 per share. As is clear from the exhibit, margin trading increases the variability of the investor's return.

Sources of Investment Information

Where can you get information about investments? Many resources are available in a number of media, including written, video, and online.

Written. Most bookstores have a section devoted to books on investments and investing. There are also personal finance magazines, such as *Kiplinger's* and *Your Money,* and business magazines, such as *Business Week* and *Money,* that frequently publish articles on investments. There are investment tracking services that are devoted to certain types of investments. For example, *Value Line* tracks common stocks, *Moody's* is devoted to bond issues, and *Morningstar* tracks mutual fund performance. The business section of your daily newspaper will provide current stock prices and some investment news. Some newspapers, such as the *Wall Street Journal, Barron's,* and *Investor's Business Daily* provide a wealth of information about financial markets and financial securities. A number of subscription newsletter services also provide investment information.

Video. There are television networks and television shows devoted to investments and the performance of financial markets. Some networks run a "ticker" at the bottom of the screen listing stock trades and provide a summary of market performance for the day. "Nightly Business Report" and "Wall Street Week" on public television are popular investment programs.

Online. With the growth of the Internet, a wealth of information about investments has become available online. Many companies have established sites at which investors can get company-related information.

Consider This

At the web site of the Securities and Exchange Commission, you can learn "What Every Investor Should Know" and find out how consumer complaints to the SEC are handled, among other things. Access the site at:
http://www.sec.gov/

Insight

12.5 To Build a Portfolio Cheaply, Consider No-Load Stocks

Readers write to us and call and send electronic mail, so we get to learn a lot about you. And this much is clear: Many of you are tight-fisted. Really tight-fisted.

In fact, some of you are so flinty, you won't even use a discount stockbroker. Which brings us to today's topic, no-load stocks, those shares you can buy directly from the issuing company without using a broker.

The number of no-load stocks is exploding, with 129 now available. The most startling addition came recently, when J.P. Morgan started offering 18 foreign stocks, all of which trade in the U.S. as American depositary receipts. Listed here are 90 no-load stocks that are nationally available.

How do the programs work? You buy your first shares from the company, with the initial minimum typically pegged at between $50 and $1,000. These shares are plunked in a dividend reinvestment plan, so that your dividends automatically buy additional shares.

You can also add to your account by sending in optional cash payments.

Now that so many no-load stocks are available, it's possible to build an entire portfolio. "You can do a nice job of diversification with 13 to 20 stocks," reckons Charles Carlson, editor of *DRIP Investor*, a Hammond, Ind., newsletter devoted to dividend reinvestment plans. "If the portfolio is a long-term growth portfolio, I would throw in a utility, an oil stock and three or four consumer product-related companies like Procter & Gamble and McDonald's."

Mr. Carlson continues: "I'd pick up a couple of telecommunications companies like AirTouch, Comsat and Ameritech. I would probably try to buy at least two foreign companies. I would also try to pick up a couple of the economically sensitive stocks, like Morton International and York International. You might also want to salt in a retailer, like Home Depot. Finally, you might want

a financial-services company, like Regions Financial or Dean Witter, Discover." Those looking for more income "might add a second oil stock or a few more utilities," Mr. Carlson suggests.

But don't buy too many no-load stocks, if you don't have the money to build up the accounts quickly. That's especially so with no-load stocks that charge fees. J.P. Morgan, for instance, levies a $15 annual account charge for each ADR, plus a $5 fee and 12 cents a share for each optional purchase. That won't seem significant once you have $2,000 or so invested. But for smaller accounts, the fees could prove punishing.

Fortunately, price competition may be at hand. Bank of New York, another ADR sponsor, expects to introduce no-load ADRs before year end, says Kenneth Lopian, a senior vice president. "I thought the fees were very high" for Morgan's program, sniffs Mr. Lopian. "I think we'll make it more attractive."

Ninety Stocks for Penny Pinchers

ABT Building Products	800-774-4117	Arrow Financial	518-745-1000
Advanta	800-774-4117	Atlantic Energy	609-645-4506
Aflac	800-774-4117	Atmos Energy	800-774-4117
AirTouch Communications	800-233-5601	Augat	617-575-3400
Amer. Recreation Centers	916-852-8005	Banco de Santander	800-711-6475
Ameriteck	888-752-6248	Bard (C.R.)	800-828-1639
Amoco	800-774-4117	Barnett Banks	800-328-5822

Bob Evans Farms	800-774-4117	McDonald's	800-774-4117
British Airways	800-711-6475	MidAmerican Energy	800-247-5211
British Telecommunications	800-711-6475	Mobil	800-648-9291
Cadbury Schweppes	800-711-6475	Morton International	800-774-4117
Capstead Mortgage	214-874-2323	National Westminster Bank	800-711-6475
Carpenter Technology	800-822-9828	Nippon Telegraph	800-711-6475
Central & South West	800-774-4117	NorAm Energy	800-843-3445
CMS Energy	800-774-4117	Norsk Hydro	800-711-6475
Comsat	301-214-3200	Novo Nordisk	800-711-6475
Conrail	800-243-7812	Oklahoma Gas & Electric	800-395-2662
Crown American Realty	800-278-4853	Oneok	800-395-2662
Dean Witter, Discover	800-228-0829	Pacific Dunlop	800-711-6475
DeBartolo Realty	800-850-2880	Pharmacia & Upjohn	800-774-4117
Dial	800-453-2235	Philadelphia Suburban	800-774-4117
DQE	800-247-0400	Piedmont Natural Gas	800-774-4117
DTE Energy	800-774-4117	Pinnacle West	800-774-4117
Duke Realty	800-774-4117	Portland General	503-464-8599
Eastern Co.	800-774-4117	Proctor & Gamble	800-742-6253
Empresa Nac. de Electricidad	800-711-6475	Rank Organisation	800-711-6475
Energen	800-774-4117	Reader's Digest	800-242-4653
Enron	800-662-7662	Regions Financial	800-446-2617
Exxon	800-252-1800	Reuters Holdings	800-711-6475
Fiat	800-711-6475	Scana	800-774-4117
First Commercial	501-371-6716	Sony	800-711-6475
First USA	800-524-4458	TDK	800-711-6475
General Growth Properties	800-774-4117	Telefonos de Mexico Series L	800-711-6475
Grand Metropolitan	800-711-6475	Tenneco	800-446-2617
Hawaiian Electric Industries	808-543-5662	Texaco	800-283-9785
Home Depot	800-774-4117	Tyson Foods	800-822-7096
Home Properties	716-546-4900	Urban Shopping Centers	800-774-4117
Houston Industries	800-774-4117	U S West Communications	800-537-0222
Illinova	800-750-7011	U S West Media Group	800-537-0222
Imperial Chemical Industries	800-711-6475	Wal-Mart Stores	800-438-6278
Integon	910-770-2000	Western Resources	800-774-4117
Interchange Fncl Services	201-703-2265	Wisconsin Energy	800-558-9663
Johnson Controls	414-228-2363	WPS Resources	800-236-1551
Kellwood	314-576-3100	York International	800-774-4117
Kerr-McGee	405-270-1313		
Madison Gas & Electric	800-356-6423		

Source: Jonathan Clements, "To Build a Portfolio Cheaply, Consider No-Load Stocks," July 5, 1996. Reprinted by permission of *The Wall Street Journal*, © 1996 Dow Jones & Company, Inc. All Rights Reserved Worldwide.

Exhibit 12.7

Margin Trading Example

Assume that Merck common stock is selling for $80 a share. An investor is considering the purchase of 100 shares. The investor can purchase the shares on a cash basis, or borrow up to 50 percent of the purchase price from the broker. Further assume that the broker charges 10 percent interest on the margin loan. What effect does borrowing have upon the investor's return on this investment?

	Cash Purchase	Margin Purchase
Initial investment	$8,000	$4,000
Amount borrowed from broker		4,000
Total invested (100 shares × $80)	$8,000	$8,000

What if the price of Merck is $100 per share one year later and the investor sells the stock at that time?

	Cash Purchase	Margin Purchase
Sales proceeds (100 shares × $100)	$10,000	$10,000
Less loan interest ($4,000 × .10)		400
Net proceeds	$10,000	$9,600
Less investment	8,000	8,000
Net gain on investment	$2,000	$1,600

Rate of return (net gain/amount invested)

$$\frac{\$2,000}{\$8,000} = 25\% \qquad \frac{\$1,600}{\$4,000} = 40\%$$

What if the price of Merck is $60 per share one year later and the investor sells the stock at that time?

	Cash Purchase	Margin Purchase
Sales proceeds (100 shares × $60)	$6,000	$6,000
Less loan interest ($4,000 × .10)		400
Net proceeds	$6,000	$5,600
Less investment	8,000	8,000
Net loss on investment	($2,000)	($2,400)

Rate of return (net loss/amount invested)

$$\frac{(\$2,000)}{\$8,000} = (25\%) \qquad \frac{(\$2,400)}{\$4,000} = (60\%)$$

As this example shows, margin trading can magnify investment gains and investment losses.

Rating services and reports from the Security and Exchange Commission (SEC) and other regulatory bodies are also available online. The Internet margin notes and exercises in Chapters 12 through 15 will give you some idea of the resources available for investors online.

SUMMARY

■ Investment is the commitment of funds in order to achieve some long-term goal. Investment differs from savings in several ways. Investment involves a longer time horizon, real property and capital market securities, and long-term objectives.

■ There are many investment alternatives, including common stock, bonds, preferred stock, mutual funds, real estate, options, commodities, art, metals, and collectibles.

■ Common stock represents ownership interest in a corporation. Bonds are debt securities issued by corporations and government entities. Preferred stock is a hybrid security, having characteristics of both common stock and debt.

■ Mutual funds are pools of funds that are invested in financial securities. Investors purchase shares of the mutual fund.

■ Real estate is land and permanent attachments to the land, such as buildings. There are many ways to invest in real estate. Some real estate investments have significant tax advantages.

■ An option is the right to buy or sell something at a given price during a specified period. An active market exists for options on shares of common stock. The right to purchase stock is a call option; the right to sell stock is a put option.

■ A commodity is a product or good. Some transactions in commodities involve the actual purchase and delivery of the good. Other transactions in commodities involve futures contracts. Futures contracts provide for the delivery of a specified quantity of a commodity on a certain day, for a specified price.

■ Hedgers use futures contracts to reduce the adverse impact of price fluctuations. Speculators seek to profit from commodity price movements.

■ Other types of investment include precious metals, art, and collectibles.

■ There are many investment objectives. Some common investment objectives include generation of income, preservation of capital, capital appreciation, and tax avoidance.

■ There is a tradeoff between risk and return. Low-risk investments, such as government securities, have historically provided low rates of return. As the degree of risk of an investment increases, the rate of return must also increase to compensate investors for bearing the higher degree of risk.

■ Risk tolerance refers to the individual's level of acceptance of uncertainty. Most people are risk averse. This means that the individual will attempt to avoid or at least minimize risk. Risk-neutral individuals are indifferent toward risk. Risk-seeking individuals are more willing to accept risk. The level of risk tolerance will affect your selection of investments.

■ Investors face a number of types of risk, including business risk, inflation risk, financial risk, market risk, and liquidity risk.

■ Business risk is the risk associated with a company's earnings. Earnings may vary because of competition, changes in the costs of raw materials and labor, and other factors.

■ Inflation risk is the risk associated with changes in purchasing power because of changes in the relative price level of goods and services.

■ Financial risk is the risk associated with fixed financial obligations. Companies that issue large amounts of debt have greater financial risk since they must pay interest on the debt.

■ Market risk is the risk associated with security price volatility. The securities issued by some companies are more sensitive to changes in external factors, such as changes in interest rates.

■ Liquidity risk refers to the ability to buy and sell an asset in a short time at a reasonable price. Some investments are highly liquid, whereas other investments are more difficult to buy and sell.

■ Your rate of return on an investment is determined by what you "receive in return" for making the investment. Many investments provide current income to the investor through dividends, interest, rental payments or other cash flows. The other component in the rate of return is price appreciation or depreciation.

■ Asset allocation refers to the relative mixture of investments. Asset allocation varies with the age, objectives, and degree of risk aversion of the investor.

■ There are several investment strategies, including buy-and-hold, market timing, diversification, dollar-cost averaging, value investing, and combination strategies.

■ Buy-and-hold is a low-maintenance strategy by which an investor purchases an asset and then does not sell it for a long time.

■ Market timing is a strategy by which an investor attempts to sell when the price is high and buy when the price is low.

■ Diversification means investing in several different assets rather than investing everything in a single asset. Diversification reduces risk.

■ Dollar-cost averaging is a strategy through which investors invest smaller dollar amounts more frequently. The strategy reduces risk since large purchases are never made at the "wrong" time.

■ Value investors invest in securities of companies or industries that are currently out of favor. When other investors are selling these shares, value investors purchase them.

■ Markets exist whenever buyers and sellers meet to perform transactions.

■ The efficiency of a financial market refers to the extent to which relevant information is reflected in the price of the assets.

■ Most investment transactions involve the services of an investment intermediary, either a broker or a dealer.

■ Brokers arrange the purchase of sale of securities without owning the securities traded. They are compensated through commissions. Full-service brokers provide a wide array of services to their customers. Discount brokers limit their services to the purchase and sale of securities.

■ Dealers purchase assets and then try to sell the assets for more than their purchase price.

■ Some investment transactions involve the direct purchase and sale of the asset without involvement of an intermediary.

■ Investment transactions may take place on a cash basis or be conducted through a margin trade. A margin trade involves borrowing a portion of the purchase price of the investment from the brokerage firm.

■ A variety of sources of information about investments is available, including written, video, and online information.

KEY CONCEPTS AND TERMS

Asset allocation
Bond
Broker
Business risk
Buy-and-hold strategy
Call option
Commission

Commodity
Common stock
Correlation
Dealer
Direct transaction
Discount broker
Diversification

Dividend reinvestment plan
  (DRIP)
Dollar-cost averaging
Efficiency
Financial risk
Full-service broker
Futures contract
Hedger
Inflation risk
Investment
Investment strategy
Liquidity risk
Margin trade
Market

Market risk
Market timing
Mutual fund
Option
Portfolio
Preferred stock
Put option
Risk
Risk averse
Risk tolerance
Speculative
Speculator
Tax avoidance
Value investing

QUESTIONS FOR REVIEW

1. How does saving differ from investing? What are some common investment objectives?

2. What are common stocks and bonds? How does common stock differ from preferred stock?

3. What is a mutual fund? How does a mutual fund provide diversification to an investor?

4. What is the relationship between the expected rate of return and the degree of risk of an investment?

5. What are the major types of risk that an investor should consider when making an investment?

6. What is meant by "asset allocation"? What is the relationship between asset allocation and the investor's stage in the life-cycle?

7. How does the buy-and-hold strategy differ from market timing?

8. What is diversification, and how does diversification reduce risk? What is meant by "diversification across time"?

9. What is meant by the "efficiency" of a market? Why is it important that security markets operate efficiently?

10. How does a broker differ from a dealer? What is the difference between a full-service broker and a discount broker?

PROBLEMS

1. Anil Srivana purchased 100 shares of common stock at a price of $64 per share in early January of 1997. The stock paid an 80 cents per share dividend in each of the four quarters of 1997. He sold the stock at the end of 1997, after receiving the four quarterly dividend payments, for $67 per share.

   a. How much dividend income did Anil receive in 1997?

   b. How much price appreciation did Anil realize when he sold his shares?

   c. What was Anil's total dollar return on his investment (dividend income plus price appreciation)?

   d. What was Anil's rate of return on this investment?

2. Susan Davis purchased a four-plex apartment building at a cost of $120,000. The apartments rent for $650 per month, and there were no vacancies during any of the 12 months she owned the building. At year end, she sold the building for $125,500.

   a. How much rental income did Susan receive during the year?

   b. How much did Susan gain when she sold the building for more than she originally paid for it?

   c. What was Susan's total dollar return on this investment (rental income plus the difference between the sales price and the purchase price)?

   d. What was Susan's rate of return on this investment?

3. Tameka Taylor would like to purchase 100 shares of QRB common stock. She called a broker to see what the commission would be on the purchase. The broker said that the commission would be $35 plus .7 percent (.007) of the total cost of the shares. QRB common stock sells for $40 per share. What will the broker's commission be if Tameka purchases 100 shares of QRB common stock?

INTERNET EXERCISES

1. As the chapter text pointed out, many publications are aimed at investors. Examples of financial and personal finance publications with online versions include *Kiplinger's*, *Money*, *Smart Money*, and *Worth* magazines, at the following addresses:

http://www.kiplinger.com/
http://www.money.com/
http://www.dowjones.com/smart/
http://www.worth.com/

You'll find that the sites don't simply reproduce the printed publications but add extras (for example, an interactive investment calculator at Kiplinger's). Check out these sites to discover the wealth of information available online for investors.

2. NASD Regulation, Inc., is an independent subsidiary of NASD, the National Association of Securities Dealers. Its job is self-regulation within the industry. Visit its site at:

http://www.nasdr.com/

to find out how to file a complaint against a securities broker.

CASE APPLICATIONS

Case 1

Tim and Mary Coyle just inherited $100,000. They are trying to decide what to do with the money and are considering four investment alternatives:

1. Purchase of "growth stocks." Growth stocks are the common stock of small, growing companies. Such stocks either do not pay dividends or pay very low dividends.

2. Investment in high-quality bonds issued by large U.S. corporations and U.S. government bonds.

3. Purchase of a vacation home on Cape Cod. They would use the home during summer months, and rent it to tenants from Labor Day to Memorial Day.

4. Purchase the paintings of several local "undiscovered" artists.

   a. Evaluate each of the investments from the standpoint of tax advantages, current income, and total rate of return.

   b. Evaluate each of the investments from the standpoint of inflation risk, market risk, and liquidity risk.

Case 2

Wendy Klein is a personal financial planner and investment advisor. Last week she was visited by three clients.

1. Jim and Christy Carson, a couple in their early 30s. Jim is a college professor and Christy is an insurance underwriter.

2. Tom and Cathy Lyons, a couple in their early 50s. Tom is an auto mechanic and Cathy is a registered nurse.

3. Mary Katherine Marshall, a recently widowed retiree, age 66.

Each client has $50,000 to invest, and each client has expressed the goal of "investing for retirement." Considering their life-cycle stage and objective, what investment advice should Wendy offer?

SUGGESTIONS FOR ADDITIONAL READING

Cheney, John M., and Edward A. Moses. *Fundamentals of Investing*. St. Paul, Minn.: West Publishing Company, 1992.

Cottle, Sidney, Roger F. Murray, and Frank E. Block. *Graham and Dodd's Security Analysis,* 5th ed. New York: McGraw-Hill, 1988.

Dolan, Ken and Daria Dolan. *Straight Talk on Money*. New York: Simon and Schuster, 1993.

Dunnan, Nancy. *Dun & Bradsteet Guide to $Your Investments$*. New York: HarperCollins Publishers, 1994.

Malkiel, Burton. *A Random Walk Down Wall Street*. New York: W.W. Norton & Company, 1996.

Miller, Theodore J. *Invest Your Way to Wealth*. Washington: The Kiplinger Washington Editors, Inc., 1994.

Morris, Kenneth M. and Alan M. Siegel. *The Wall Street Journal Guide to Understanding Personal Finance*. New York: Lightbulb Press, 1992.

Personal Financial Planning Guide. Ernst & Young. New York: John Wiley & Sons, 1995.

Sloane, Leonard. *The New York Times Personal Finance Handbook*. New York: Times Books, 1995.

Tyson, Eric. *Investing for Dummies*. Foster City, CA: IDG Books, 1996.

NOTES

1. The historical rate of return and standard deviation of a number of investment alternatives are compiled annually by Roger G. Ibbotson and Rex A. Sinquefield, and printed in their *Stocks, Bonds, Bills, and Inflation Yearbook,* published annually by Ibbotson Associates, Chicago.

2. The risk of a portfolio is measured by the standard deviation of the rate of return of the portfolio. As you add more securities to the portfolio, the standard deviation of the portfolio declines, unless there is perfect positive correlation between the portfolio and the security added to the portfolio.

3. Charles Schwab's eSchwab online trading option.

Chapter 13

Investing in Stocks and Bonds

Learning Objectives

After studying this chapter, you should be able to:

■ Describe the characteristics of common stock and explain the risks and rewards of investing in common stock.

■ Explain the differences between preferred stock and common stock, and discuss the various types of common stock.

■ Explain how common stock and preferred stock are issued, valued, and traded, and describe what causes stock prices to fluctuate.

■ Describe the basic characteristics of bonds and explain the risks and rewards of investing in bonds.

■ Identify the issuers of bonds and describe the characteristics of the bonds they issue.

■ Explain how bonds are issued, valued, and traded, and describe what causes bond prices to fluctuate.

■ Discuss important factors that you should consider when investing in stocks and bonds.

October. This is one of the particularly dangerous months to speculate in stocks. The others are July, January, September, April, November, May, March, June, December, August, and February.

—Mark Twain

If you'd know the value of money, go and borrow some.

—Ben Franklin in *Poor Richard's Almanac*

Meldrick could not sleep, so he decided to watch television. As he flipped from channel to channel, he saw, in rapid-fire, a home shopping show, a Smashing Pumpkins music video, a televangelist, a commercial for deodorant, and, finally, two people on a business show discussing investments. Meldrick owns 300 shares of stock in the aerospace company where he works through the company pension plan. He would like to start investing in stocks and bonds on his own, but as he told his wife, "I'm a mechanical engineer—not a Wall Street tycoon!"

Focusing on the business program, he heard the first commentator say, "I see interest rates falling this year, and that bodes well for bonds. I especially like munis and zeroes at this time."

The second commentator responded, "You're all wet on this one, Harold! While I agree inflation is under control, the stock market remains the place to be. Of course some of the small caps are selling at too high an earnings multiple, but if investors buy blue chips and rotate out of cyclicals, they'll be fine."

Meldrick turned off the television in disgust. Munis? Zeroes? Interest rates and bond prices? And what was that about blue chips, small caps, and rotating cyclicals? Huh? He wonders where he can find some basic, useful, information about investing in stocks and bonds.

As we pointed out in Chapter 12, corporations raise money by issuing shares of common stock and preferred stock and by borrowing through the issuance of bonds. Government entities issue bonds as well, to raise funds for such things as defense, roads, bridges, and schools. Stocks and bonds represent investment opportunities for individuals. These investments are created and traded in the capital markets. This chapter looks more closely at investing in stocks and bonds. We start with stocks, one of the most popular investment vehicles in the United States, and then consider bonds.

The Nature of Investment in Stock

What are you actually buying when you purchase a share of stock? How do stock investments produce returns for the investor? We consider these questions first, and then discuss the issuance and trading of stock, various types of common stock, and stock prices and valuation.

Ownership of Common Stock

In Chapter 12, we defined common stock as a financial security that represents ownership interest in a corporation. Common stock has no maturity, or expiration, date. When you buy a share of common stock, then, you are buying a "piece" of the company that, theoretically, you can own forever. Although stockholders have the right to vote on major corporate decisions, the authority to make most day-to-day decisions is delegated to the corporation's management team.

residual owner Shareholder in a corporation, also called residual claimant. Residual owners' claims on the corporation's assets are good only after all other obligations have been met.

Stockholders are actually designated the **residual owners** (or **residual claimants**) of the company. This means their claims on the corporation's assets are good only after all other obligations have been met. Suppose you own shares in a company that fails and goes into bankruptcy, and the company's assets are liquidated—turned to cash—to repay money that is owed. You can claim a share of any cash that remains after the creditors, bondholders, preferred stockholders, and others have been paid what they are owed. Similarly, other claims take priority over payment of dividends to holders of common stock. It's possible, then, that you might receive no return on a common stock investment. In contrast, however, if you own shares in a company that is doing well, the return on your investment may be very high. Chapter 12 pointed out that common stocks are a relatively risky investment. Uncertainty over the actual return that stockholders will earn helps explain why.

Ownership of Preferred Stock

Recall that preferred stock is a hybrid security, possessing characteristics of both common stock and debt. Like common stock, preferred stock has no maturity date although some preferred stock is **callable,** meaning that the issuer may choose to retire the stock by paying the owner a specified amount. Like debt, there is greater certainty that the periodic cash flows, in this case dividends, will be paid to the owner of preferred stock. Owners of preferred stock do not share in the risks and rewards of the corporation in the same way owners of common stock do. Instead, they receive fixed dividends that remain the same no matter how the company is doing. Most preferred stock is **cumulative,** meaning that any dividends not paid in previous periods on preferred stock must be paid in full before the company can pay dividends on common stock.

callable preferred stock Preferred stock that the issuer may choose to retire by paying the owner a specified amount.

cumulative preferred stock Preferred stock on which any dividends not paid in previous periods must be paid in full before the company can pay dividends on common stock.

Despite its higher predictability, investment in preferred stock is not without risk. First, there is the risk that the corporation that issued the preferred stock will not be able to make the dividend payments. The second risk involved with investing in preferred stock is the risk that the price of the security may decline after you purchase it. If you sell the preferred stock at that time, you will lose money on your investment.

The Rewards from Investment in Stock

The returns from investing in common and preferred stock can take two forms: dividends and price appreciation.

Dividends. As an owner of common stock, you may receive a quarterly dividend payment. Not all companies that issue common stock pay quarterly dividends. Common stock dividends are not guaranteed. A company may not be able to pay a dividend or may have to cut the dividend if profits for the period are not high enough. Or the company may wish to reinvest profits, using them to fund growth, rather than paying profits out to stockholders in the form of dividends. Dividends, then, can vary from company to company and from period to period. Utility companies, for example, are notorious for paying large quarterly dividends; whereas high-tech companies either pay low dividends or no dividends.

Preferred stock, as already mentioned, is much more predictable with respect to dividends. As a holder of preferred stock, you receive a fixed dividend, usually paid quarterly. For example, one category of General Motors preferred stock pays a 57-cent dividend each quarter. As noted, payment of dividends to those who hold preferred stock takes priority over payment of dividends to holders of common stock.

Price Appreciation. If the stock that you purchase increases in value, you can make money from this price appreciation by selling the stock. The price of common stock fluctuates more than the price of preferred stock. Recall that common stock dividends are not guaranteed. In addition, as residual claimants, owners of common stock share directly in the good fortune and bad fortune of the company. Owners of preferred stock receive the same dividend regardless of how the company fares. As the risk-return relationship discussed in the previous chapter predicts, the price of preferred stock does not fluctuate as widely as the price of common stock. Stock prices will be discussed in greater detail later in this chapter.

Tax Considerations

Dividends paid to owners of common stock and preferred stock are currently taxable income. If you own 100 shares of stock that pays a 50-cent dividend each quarter, you will receive $50 in dividends per quarter (.50 × 100), $200 in dividends for the year ($50 × 4). You must pay taxes on the $200 in dividend income.

Price appreciation is given favorable tax treatment under the tax code. Gains on stocks are not taxed unless the investor chooses to realize the gain, at which time only the gain itself is taxable. An example will clarify this important tax advantage. Assume that you paid $10 per share for 100 shares of stock in 1992, a total investment of $1,000 ($10 × 100). Today, the price per share of the stock is $34. Although your stock has increased in value, you are not required to pay taxes on the price appreciation until you sell the stock. If you sell the stock today, you will receive $3,400 ($34 × 100). However, only the $2,400 gain ($24 × 100) is taxable. Dividend income is taxed at the taxpayer's regular tax rate. The maximum tax rate for capital gains is currently 28 percent. Thus the investor would pay $672 in taxes (.28 × $2,400) on the capital gain. The ability to delay paying taxes until the gain is realized is an important tax advantage of stock ownership.

How Stock is Issued and Traded

As mentioned earlier, corporations issue stock to raise funds, and investors can purchase this stock as an investment. After stock is issued, there is an active secondary market for the shares.

Issuance of Stock by Corporations

initial public offering (IPO) A corporation's first issue of common stock.

Corporations issue stock when they first "go public." For example, a business may grow to the point where it decides to incorporate and to sell ownership rights, as represented by shares of stock, in the business. A company's first issue of common stock is called an **initial public offering (IPO).** Investment banks purchase the new shares from the company, which may use the proceeds for a number of purposes, such as constructing and equipping a new plant. The investment banks, in turn, sell the stock to interested investors.

primary market Market in which securities are sold by the issuing corporation.

Corporations that already have sold shares of stock may from time to time issue additional shares. Announcements that companies are issuing additional shares of stock frequently appear in the *Wall Street Journal* and other newspapers. An announcement that Cincinnati Bell is issuing additional shares of common stock is shown in Exhibit 13.1. Both IPOs and the issue of additional shares of stock are **primary market** transactions— that is, they are sales by the issuing company. When the shares are first sold, the issuer receives the money.

Other Stock Transactions

After issuing shares of stock, a corporation may alter the number of shares of stock outstanding. This is done through stock repurchases, stock splits, and stock dividends.

stock repurchase Buy-back of shares of stock by the issuing company.

Stock Repurchases. When a company conducts a **stock repurchase,** it buys back shares of common stock that it previously issued. Why would a company repurchase its shares? The company may have earned a profit from its operations, but not have a current need to invest in plant and equipment. Rather than paying large, currently taxable, dividends to stockholders, the company may decide to repurchase shares of stock.

Exhibit 13.1

Announcement of a Share Offering by ABC Company

This announcement is neither an offer to sell nor a solicitation
of an offer to buy any of these Securities.
The offer is made only by the Prospectus.

8,000,000 Shares

ABC Company

Common Shares

Price $75^3/_4$ a Share

Copies of the Prospectus may be obtained in any State from only such
of the undersigned as may legally offer these Securities in compliance
with the securities laws of such State.

Joint Book-Running Managers

Incorporated

Since the size of the company is still the same, but fewer shares of stock are outstanding after the stock repurchase, the price per share should increase. In this way, the company passes profits to stockholders through stock price appreciation that is not currently taxable rather than through dividends.

stock split An adjustment in the number of shares of stock outstanding by a corporation.

stock dividend A dividend paid in the form of additional stock, stated as a specified percentage of stock already held.

Stock Splits and Stock Dividends. Stock splits and stock dividends are often misunderstood financial transactions. When a company splits its stock or declares a stock dividend, it is simply adjusting the number of shares currently outstanding. For example, a company may declare a three for two stock split. This means that for every two shares of stock you have before the split, you will have three shares after the split. So if you owned 200 shares before the split, you will have 300 shares after the split. The same result could have been achieved through a stock dividend, which should not to be confused with cash dividends discussed earlier. Through a stock dividend, each investor receives a specified percentage of additional stock in the organization. For example, if a 10 percent stock dividend were declared, and you had 200 shares, you would receive an additional 10 percent of 200 shares, or 20 shares.

The reason that stock splits and stock dividends are often misunderstood is that some people believe that a stock split or stock dividend increases the value of the company. That is not true. Think of a pizza cut into two pieces. If you cut each piece in two again, you have increased the number of pieces, but you have not increased the amount of pizza that you have. As with the pizza, increasing the number of shares of stock does not increase the value of the company.

If stock splits and stock dividends do not increase the value of the company, why do they occur? Most investors trade stocks in 100-share units called round lots. To purchase 100 shares of a company that sells for $120 a share, you need $12,000 ($120 $\times$ 100). If the company splits its stock 3 for 1, the price would fall to $40 per share ($120/3), and a round lot would then cost $4,000 ($40 $\times$ 100), a much more manageable sum for many investors.[1]

secondary market Market in which securities are traded among investors; the issuing companies receive none of the proceeds.

The Secondary Market

After stocks have sold initially, they are traded in the **secondary market.** When stocks are traded in the secondary market, they are traded between investors—the issuing company receives none of the proceeds. Stocks are traded in three major markets in the United States.

- The New York Stock Exchange (NYSE) is a centralized market in New York City. The stock of many large companies is traded on the NYSE.

- The American Stock Exchange (ASE), a smaller exchange, is also based in New York City.

Consider This

You can access the stock exchanges online. You'll find the New York Stock Exchange at:

http://www.nyse.com/

and the American Stock Exchange at:

http://www.amex.com/

NASDAQ (the National Association of Securities Dealers Automated Quotations), a communications system linking dealers in the over-the-counter market, can be found at:

http://www.nasdaq.com/

over-the-counter (OTC) market A non-centralized secondary market dealing in securities not listed or traded on the New York Stock Exchange and the American Stock Exchange.

■ The **over-the-counter (OTC) market** is the third major secondary market in the United States. The OTC is not a centralized market—there is no trading floor where OTC stocks are traded. Rather, brokers and dealers who wish to buy and sell OTC stocks are connected through computers that show the latest offers to buy (bids) and to sell (asks). The OTC caters to small and medium-sized companies; however, some of the larger OTC companies, such as Intel and Microsoft, are also household names.

Types of Common Stock

Common stocks can be grouped into several broad, sometimes overlapping, categories. These categories are based on historical performance, the company's dividend policy, how the stock performs in relation to the economy, and the risk associated with investing in the stock. Here we discuss blue-chip stocks, income stocks, growth stocks, cyclical stocks, defensive stocks, and speculative stocks.

blue-chip stock Stock that has exhibited a record of solid performance over time.

■ **Blue-chip stocks** are stocks that have exhibited a record of solid performance over time. These are the common stocks of large, well-established, mature companies, such as AT&T, IBM, General Electric, and Exxon. Investors in such companies expect little price variability. However, because the companies are large and mature, the earnings growth rate may be less than that of smaller companies. The return provided by blue-chip stocks is a combination of moderate growth and dividend income.

income stock Stock that has relatively high dividend yield.

dividend yield Annual dividend divided by market price per share.

■ **Income stocks** are stocks that have relatively high dividend yields. The **dividend yield** is the annual dividend divided by the market price per share. These stocks are called income stocks because they provide high quarterly dividends to the purchaser, relative to the price per share. Stocks issued by utility companies, phone companies, and auto makers often have dividend yields in excess of 3 percent. Income stocks are favorites of retirees who use the quarterly dividends to supplement other sources of retirement income.

growth stock Stock issued by a company that has posted superior earnings growth; the stock is expected to provide above-average price appreciation.

■ **Growth stocks** are stocks issued by companies that have posted superior earnings growth and are expected to provide above-average price appreciation. Growth stocks have several identifying characteristics. First, these companies either do not pay dividends or pay very small dividends. Rather than paying dividends, growth companies retain the earnings and reinvest the earnings in the company. Second, the share price tends to be more volatile for growth stocks than for blue-chip and income stocks. Finally, many growth stocks are small and medium-sized companies that are traded over-the-counter rather than on the New York Stock Exchange.

cyclical stock Stock that moves in step with the business cycle.

■ **Cyclical stocks** are stocks that move in step with the business cycle. When there is an upswing in the economy, these stocks tend to perform well; when there is an economic downturn, they do not perform as well. We can identify cyclical stocks by considering consumer and business spending patterns. When the economy is performing well, more people are likely to be employed at better wages. Therefore, consumers have more disposable income for purchasing autos and durable goods, such as washers and dryers. Businesses also fare well in an economic upturn and purchase additional raw materials and use transportation to deliver the finished goods. In an economic downturn, there is less disposable income to purchase goods and services, a corresponding slump in consumer demand, and less business activity. Airline, trucking, chemical, hotel, steel, and consumer durables companies are the issuers of stocks that are classified as cyclical stocks.

defensive stock Stock that is immune or less susceptible to economic fluctuations.

■ **Defensive stocks** are stocks that are immune or less susceptible to economic fluctuations. In economic terms, the demand for the goods and services produced by the companies whose stock can be categorized as defensive can be described as inelastic (that is, not related to the level of consumer income). An excellent example is the common stock of some pharmaceutical companies. Whether the economy is in an upturn or downturn, individuals must take prescribed medication. The stocks of utility companies, grocery stores, and home products companies are also defensive stocks. Although such stocks do not perform as well as cyclicals during upturns, they hold their value better during economic downturns.

speculative stock Risky stock; the stock of a new, unproven company or a company out of favor with investors.

■ **Speculative stocks** are stocks of new, unproven companies or companies that are out of favor with investors. Investors sometimes purchase these stocks in the hope of earning a high rate of return. As the name implies, these are risky stocks to purchase. They are often touted for their potential, but just as often the forecast profits do not materialize. In addition, such stocks are often thinly traded, meaning that an investor may have difficulty selling his or her shares to another investor at a reasonable price.

Stock Prices and Valuation

The price of a share of stock is what you pay when you purchase the stock or what you receive when you sell the stock. But what does the price represent, how are stock prices determined, and why do stock prices fluctuate? We answer these questions in this section.

Exhibit 13.2

Quote for McDonald's Company Common Stock

Quote as it appeared in the *Wall Street Journal*, January 27, 1997:

52 Weeks Hi	Lo	Stock	Sym	Div	Yld %	PE	Vol 100s	Hi	Lo	Close	Net Chg
30	16	McDermott	JRM	—	—	cc	1047	26	$25^5/_8$	$25^5/_8$	$-^1/_4$
$23^1/_4$	16	McDermint	MDR	.20m	1.1	dd	2491	$17^3/_4$	$17^1/_2$	$17^3/_4$	—
$30^3/_4$	$25^1/_2$	McDermint pfA		2.20	7.4	—	17	$29^5/_8$	$29^1/_4$	$29^5/_8$	$-^1/_4$
$31^1/_4$	$29^3/_8$	McDermint pfB		2.60	8.7	—	10	$29^3/_4$	$29^3/_4$	$29^3/_4$	—
$37^1/_2$	$17^3/_4$	McDnInvst	MDO	.38	1.0	15	80	$37^1/_4$	$36^7/_8$	$36^7/_8$	$-^5/_8$
$54^1/_4$	41	McDonalds	MCD	.30	.6	21	28048	$46^3/_4$	$45^7/_8$	$46^5/_8$	$+^1/_8$
$26^3/_8$	$25^1/_4$	McDonalds dep pf		1.93	7.4	—	152	26	$25^7/_8$	26	$+^1/_8$
$26^7/_8$	25	McDonalds OUDS MCZ		2.09	8.2	—	106	$25^1/_2$	$25^3/_8$	$25^1/_2$	$+^1/_8$
n $25^1/_8$	$24^1/_4$	McDonalds sbob MCW		.29p	—	—	77	$24^5/_8$	$24^3/_8$	$24^3/_8$	$-^1/_8$
s $71^3/_4$	$42^1/_4$	McDonDoug	MD	.48	.7	19	7503	$68^1/_2$	$67^1/_2$	$68^3/_8$	$-^1/_2$

Reading the quote from left to right:

52 Week Hi and Lo:	McDonald's stock has traded as high as $54.25 and as low as $41 per share during the previous year.
Name of Company:	McDonald's, the fast-food restaurant chain.
Ticker Symbol:	The shorthand symbol for the company.
Dividend:	The dividend shown is the annualized dividend from the previous quarter. Since the entry is .30, it means McDonald's paid a 7.5-cent dividend per share in the previous quarter.
Dividend Yield:	The Yld % is the dividend yield. This value is the annual dividend divided by the closing price. The dividend yield is 0.6 percent (.30/$46.625).
P/E Ratio:	The price/earnings (P/E) ratio is the closing price divided by earnings per share. McDonald's is selling at 21 times earnings per share.
Volume:	Stock volume is quoted in hundreds of shares. During this trading day, 2,804,800 shares of McDonald's stock were traded.
Hi, Lo, Close:	These three entries tell the highest price, lowest price, and closing price of McDonald's for the trading day.
Net Change:	Net change tells how the closing price compares to the closing price from the previous day's trading. McDonald's closed up one-eighth of a dollar, or 12.5 cents per share.

Stock Prices

The financial page of your newspaper provides a listing of stock prices for many companies, along with some additional information. An annotated stock quote for McDonald's is provided in Exhibit 13.2.

What does the price of a share of stock actually represent? As we learned in Chapter 2, money has time value. The value of $1,000 to be received one year from today is less than $1,000 today. The same principle applies to stock prices. The price of a share of stock is the present value of future cash flows that investors expect to receive if they purchase the stock.

Stock Valuation

To value common and preferred stock, investors estimate future cash flows and assign an appropriate interest rate to use in determining the present value of the future cash flows.

Expected Cash Flows. The expected cash flows from preferred stock and common stock are dividend payments and the proceeds you will receive when you sell the stock. Preferred stock dividends are known with certainty. If you purchase preferred stock, you will receive a constant, periodic dividend. Since preferred stock does not have a maturity date, these dividends, in theory, will be paid forever. The expected cash flows from common stock vary. Some companies pay no dividends; others pay a constant dividend; still others periodically increase the dividends paid to stockholders. In addition to dividend payments, you will receive the price of the stock at the time you sell it.

Investor-Required Rate of Return. The second factor that determines the price of stock is the interest rate used to determine the present value of the future cash flows. We will give this interest rate a special name: *the investor-required rate of return.* In other words, we will discount the expected future cash flows at the rate of return that investors require for that particular security. The rate of return that investors require for a security is made up of several components:

■ Compensation to investors for not having use of their funds if they purchase the stock.

■ Compensation to investors for expected inflation. The investment should earn back at least the rate of inflation, or the investor loses purchasing power.

■ Compensation to investors for bearing risk. Some stocks, for example, blue chips, are of less risk than others, such as speculative stocks. Investors increase their required rate of return to reflect the risk that the expected cash flows may not be realized.

For example, assume that investors require a 3 percent return for not having use of their money and that expected inflation is 4.5 percent. To adjust for risk investors may add 2.5 percent to their required rate of return for an investment in a blue-chip stock, for a total of 10 percent (3% + 4.5% + 2.5%). Investors may add 7.5 percent to their required rate of return for an investment in a speculative stock to adjust for risk, for a total of 15 percent (3% + 4.5% + 7.5%). The higher the degree of risk, the higher the investor-required rate of return.

Pricing Stocks. To price stock, you must consider the expected cash flows, the investor-required rate of return, and the time value of money techniques from Chapter 2.

Pricing preferred stock. With preferred stock, the dividend payments are known in advance. The cash flows that an investor will receive from his or her ownership of preferred stock resemble a special type of annuity, called a **perpetual annuity,** or **perpetuity.** A perpetual annuity is an annuity that provides a constant payment with no maturity date. The valuation formula is as follows:

perpetual annuity, or perpetuity An annuity that provides a constant stream of payments with no maturity date.

$$\text{Price} = \text{Present Value} = \frac{\text{Annual Dividend}}{\text{Investor Required Return}}$$

Thus, if an investor requires a 10 percent return on a share of preferred stock that provides a $4 annual dividend, the most the investor should be willing to pay for the preferred stock is:

$$\text{Price} = \text{Present Value} = \frac{\$4}{.10} = \$40$$

Common stock. Common stock is more difficult to value because the future cash flows are not known in advance. Some companies pay no dividends, others pay constant dividends, and still others pay dividends that grow constantly.[2] Although we will employ different valuation formulas to price common stock, we will adhere to the same valuation principle: *The price of a financial security is the present value of the future expected cash flows discounted at the investor-required rate of return.* We will consider several cases for common stock:

■ *Case 1: Constant Dividend.* If the company pays a constant dividend, the perpetual annuity formula just presented for preferred stock may be employed.

■ *Case 2: Constant Growth.* If the earnings and dividends are growing at a constant rate, the constant growth model formula may be employed. This formula is:

$$\text{Price} = \text{Present Value} = \frac{\text{Dividend}_1}{\text{Investor Required Return} - \text{Growth Rate}}$$

So, according to the formula, the price is equal to the dividend forecast for next year (Dividend$_1$) divided by the difference between the investor-required rate of return and the growth rate.

An example will show how this formula can be applied. Suppose that a company just paid a $2.00 annual dividend, and that you expect dividends and earnings to grow at a constant rate of 8 percent. Next year's forecasted dividend is $2.16 ($2.00 × 1.08). If you require a 12 percent return on this stock, the most you should be willing to pay for a share is:

$$\text{Price} = \text{Present Value} = \frac{2.16}{.12 - .08} = \$54$$

■ *Case 3: Fixed Time Period.* Other valuation formulas may be applied, depending on the time horizon of the investor. For example, you may expect that a stock will provide a $2.00 dividend one year from today and that the stock will sell for $60 per share at that time. Given these expectations, what is the most you should be willing to pay for a share of the stock today if your required rate of return is 15 percent? Using the price equals present value formula, we have:

$$\text{Price} = \text{Present Value} = \frac{\$2 + \$60}{(1 + .15)} = \$53.91$$

Stock Price Movements. Given the valuation formulas just presented, it is not surprising what causes stock prices to fluctuate: changes in expected cash flows and changes in investor-required rates of return.

■ *Changes in expected cash flows.* A company's expected earnings may change for a number of reasons. For example, the company may introduce a new product that is very successful. The added sales may increase the earnings of the company. Alternatively, an economic slowdown may hurt sales if the company produces luxury items. These changes in earnings will affect the expected cash flows for common stock, which in turn, will cause the stock price to change. With preferred stock, the periodic dividend is fixed.

■ *Changes in investor-required rates of return.* Investors adjust their required rate of return for a number of reasons. For example, fears of inflation may subside, and investors may reduce their estimate of anticipated inflation accordingly. This would cause the investor-required rate of return to fall. Alternatively, the company may experience financial difficulty, and investors may increase their required rate of return to reflect the risk that the company may be unable to generate earnings.

The Stock Investment Decision

In this section, we discuss variables that you should consider when determining which stocks to purchase, where you can get information about stocks and the stock market, and how stocks are bought and sold.

Determining Which Stock to Buy

You should consider a number of variables when determining whether to invest in stocks and which stocks to purchase. Some of the important variables include risk, rate of return, income, taxes, life-cycle stage, transactions costs, and wealth.

Risk. You should consider your tolerance for risk when making an investment. Stocks of high-tech companies, for example, tend to be volatile, and you may not be willing to bear this risk. Conversely, you may be willing to accept a higher level of risk if you have less risk aversion. Some measures of risk and return are discussed in the following section.

Rate of Return. The rate of return that you earn on an investment is determined by your purchase price, dividend payments, and price appreciation. The risk–return relationship we discussed in the previous chapter holds for the various types of stocks. Blue-chip companies, for example, tend to offer a lower rate of return, but the risk associated with investing in these companies is also lower. Growth stocks, on average, provide higher rates of return, but the variability of the return is greater.

Income. If generating current income is your investment goal, you should consider stocks that have a high dividend yield. If you do not need income currently, you may opt for a growth stock and realize income later in the form of capital appreciation.

Taxes. Dividend income is currently taxable, whereas gains on stocks are not taxed until actually realized. This being the case, individuals who face high marginal tax rates often invest in stocks that do not pay dividends or that pay low dividends. Individuals who do not face high marginal tax rates often opt for income stocks since the tax penalty is lower.

Life-Cycle Stage. Your life-cycle stage should also be considered. For example, income stocks that offer little growth potential do not make sense for a person in his or her early 40s who has a high income and 20 years until retirement. Likewise, speculative stocks that do not provide income do not make sense for retirees on a fixed income.

Transactions Costs. Brokerage fees and other transactions costs are important, especially if you buy and sell frequently. Even if you use a discount broker, these costs can add up over time.

Wealth. As we discussed in the previous chapter, you should not consider investing unless you have first established a safety fund (enough to cover several months expenses) that can be drawn upon in case of emergency.

Exhibit 13.3

Stocks That Currently Compose the Dow Jones 30 Industrial Average

AT&T	Hewlett-Packard
Allied Signal	IBM
ALCOA	International Paper
American Express	Johnson & Johnson
Boeing	McDonald's
Caterpillar	Merck
Chevron	Minnesota Mining and Manufacturing
Coca Cola	Morgan (JP)
Walt Disney	Philip Morris
Du Pont	Procter & Gamble
Eastman Kodak	Sears
Exxon	Travelers
General Electric	Union Carbide
General Motors	United Technologies
Goodyear	WalMart

Your level of wealth will obviously influence your degree of risk aversion, which in turn affects your investment decision.

Getting Information About Stocks and the Stock Market

After each trading day, a summary of the day's trading activity is printed in the business section of many newspapers. In addition to individual stock performance, several indexes are computed to indicate how the market or various market segments of the market performed. The most-watched index is the Dow Jones Industrial Average (DJIA), an index of 30 large companies in a variety of industries. A list of stocks that compose the Dow 30 is provided in Exhibit 13.3. Other often-quoted indexes are the Dow Transportation Index, the Standard & Poor's 500, the NASDAQ Composite, and the Russell 2,000. Each index is designed to provide information about how a certain segment of the market performed.

In addition to the information provided on the financial pages, many sources of information are available about stocks and the stock market. A number of magazines and newspapers are dedicated to investments and personal finance. Other publications, such as *Moody's* and *Standard & Poor's,* provide information about stocks. You can also write to the company and request a copy of the latest quarterly and annual report.

The most frequently employed source of information about stocks is probably *Value Line Investment Survey.* Available at many libraries, *Value Line* is a loose-leaf service that provides a one-page summary of data on

Exhibit 13.4

Value Line Investment Service

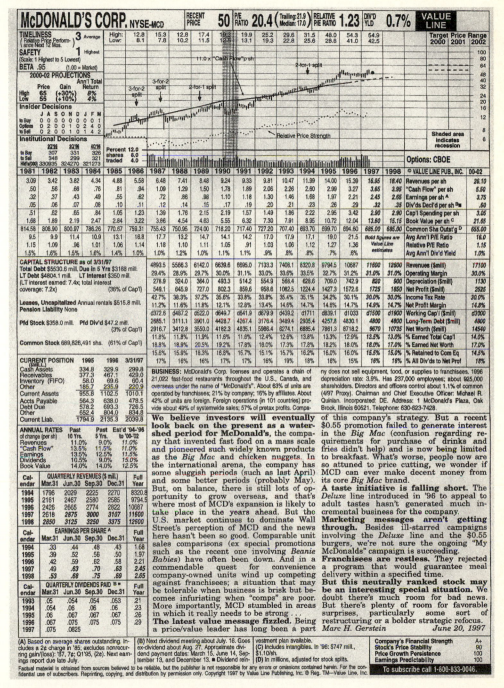

most major stocks. The reports for each stock are updated quarterly. The *Value Line* report for McDonald's Corporation is provided in Exhibit 13.4.

This exhibit displays a number of important ratios and statistics for each stock. Some of the important variables displayed include the following:

earnings per share (EPS)
The net earnings available to common stockholders after taxes divided by the number of shares of common stock outstanding.

■ EPS. The **earnings per share (EPS),** the net earnings available to common stockholders after taxes divided by the number of shares of common stock outstanding, are shown in the lower left-hand corner, just above the information about dividends. In 1996, earnings per share were $2.21, up from $1.68 in 1994. EPS is important because it shows how the company is doing in generating income for the stockholders.

price/earnings (P/E) ratio The ratio of share price to earnings per share.

■ P/E ratio. The **price/earnings (P/E) ratio,** the ratio of share price to earnings per share, is found at the top of the exhibit, in the middle. For McDonald's, this ratio is 20.4. This means that at the time, McDonald's is selling at 20 times its earnings per share. Should EPS estimates increase or decrease, this change will be magnified by this price to earnings multiple.

■ Dividend yield. Recall that the dividend yield is the annual dividend divided by the market price per share. The dividend yield is displayed in the upper right-hand corner, next to the page number. For McDonald's, the dividend yield at this time was 0.7 percent. The annualized dividend based on the last quarterly dividend paid by McDonald's is 33 cents, which when divided by the recent price of $50 (top of exhibit), produces a dividend yield of .7 percent.

beta A measure of risk that expresses the volatility of a security's returns in relation to the volatility of the market. A stock with a beta of 1.0 has the same volatility as the market.

■ Beta. **Beta** is a measure of risk that expresses the volatility of the security's returns in relation to the volatility of the overall stock market. Beta is displayed in the upper left-hand corner, right below the name of the stock. Betas less than 1.0 mean that the stock is less volatile than the market. A beta of 1.0 means that the stock is just as volatile as the market, and betas exceeding 1.0 mean that the stock is more volatile than the market. The beta of McDonald's is .95, slightly less risky than the market.

Making Stock Market Transactions

How do you actually go about purchasing stock? As discussed in the previous chapter, most stock transactions are handled through stock brokers. A broker will match your desire to purchase a stock for a specified price with a seller who is willing to sell the stock. The broker receives a fee, called a commission, for performing this service.

Most stock trades are conducted in 100-share units called round lots. If you trade in units other than 100 shares, the broker may charge an additional fee for this "odd-lot" trade. Commissions vary with the size of the trade (number of shares and price per share) and by the range of ser-

Insight   13.1   Investing Through Dividend Reinvestment Plans

Many stocks that pay dividends offer stockholders the option of using the dividend to purchase more stock rather than receiving the dividend in cash. But dividend reinvestment plans (DRIPs) do far more than simply invest dividends. Many plans offer the opportunity for you to purchase additional shares of stock by making optional cash contributions.

The beauty of this method of investing is that you are investing smaller amounts more frequently and, in many instances, avoiding brokerage and service fees. Although the dividends are reinvested, the investor must pay taxes on the dividend income.

To join a DRIP, you must be a stockholder. Most plans permit you to enroll in the DRIP if you have as few as one share of stock. The buy-direct companies listed in the previous chapters are an excellent starting point.

Other services exist that help you purchase your first share of stock at a reasonable price. One of the most popular is the National Association of Investors Corporation (NAIC). The NAIC charges members a $7 per-company fee, in addition to the price of one share, to establish a DRIP with any of more than 140 member companies. Once the investor is a shareholder of record, he or she can enroll in the DRIP and avoid most transaction costs. The address of the NAIC is:

National Association of
  Investors Corp.
711 W. 13 Mile Road
Madison Heights, MI 48071
Phone: 810-583-6242

Another possibility, if you know the company in which you want to invest, is to use a discount broker to make the initial purchase, then enroll in the DRIP.

Which companies offer DRIPs? There are directories of companies that offer DRIPs, such as *The Money Paper,* or you can simply use *Value Line.* If you look in the footnotes at the bottom of Exhibit 13.4, you will see the notation that McDonald's does offer a DRIP. You can write to the company and request a description of the plan. Review the plan to determine if there are fees and commissions on additional share purchases.

DRIPs offer many advantages, but there are also some drawbacks. Recordkeeping can be a problem since you are purchasing fractional shares and making at least four investments a year (dividends) in addition to any cash contributions you make. Furthermore, you may not be able to sell the shares at a specific time, and there may be a fee to sell your shares.

For investors who are interested in dollar-cost-averaging (discussed in Chapter 12), DRIPs are an excellent investment vehicle.

vices the broker provides. Brokers will also handle the sale of shares for you in a similar manner.

An increasing number of companies are permitting investors to purchase shares directly from the company. A listing of such companies appeared in the previous chapter. Buying direct from the company saves commission dollars. These "buy direct" companies and many others offer dividend reinvestment plans (DRIPs). In addition to reinvesting your dividends, most DRIPs permit investors to make period cash investments at no cost or for a nominal fee. Insight 13.1 discusses the benefits of investing through dividend reinvestment plans.

The Nature of an Investment in Bonds

Now we turn our attention to bonds. Private companies may decide to borrow money rather than issuing additional shares of stock. Government entities, since they cannot sell ownership rights, must resort to the issue of debt to raise additional funds if tax revenues are not sufficient. When they issue bonds, private companies and government bodies receive funds today in exchange for the promise of repayment at a later date. Thus, if you are a bondholder, you are in the position of a creditor. The issuer must repay the amount borrowed at a specified time (the *maturity date*) and may be required to make periodic interest payments. As with stocks, there is an active secondary market for bonds. The issuer receives an infusion of capital when the bonds are issued but no additional funds from secondary trades.

bond covenant, or indenture The written agreement under which a bond is issued, specifying the obligations of the issuer.

Legally, bonds create a contractual liability for the issuer. The bond agreement, called the **bond covenant** or **indenture,** places certain obligations on the issuer, including the periodic payment of interest and repayment of the maturity value when the bond issue matures. Failure to honor these contractual obligations can lead to default on the bond issue. Should the company fail, the bondholders have a claim against the assets of the firm that is superior to that of the stockholders.

The Rewards and Risks of Investment in Bonds

The rewards from bond investing are twofold. *First, if the bond is interest bearing, the bondholder receives periodic interest payments.* Some investors prefer these fixed, periodic payments to the variable returns offered by common stock. *The second reward from bond investing is the possibility of price appreciation.* Like stocks, bonds are traded in secondary markets. The prices of bonds fluctuate with interest rate changes, as you will see later in the chapter. An investor may purchase a bond, hold the bond for a time, and then sell it at a price higher than the original purchase price. The bondholder may also purchase the bond at a price less than the amount to be repaid at maturity and then hold the bond until it matures.

Investing in bonds also poses several risks. The first two risks are the failure of the issuer to pay interest when it is due and the failure of the issuer to repay the maturity value when it is due. Although the claims of debtholders take precedence over the claims of stockholders when a company goes bankrupt, bondholders may still receive less than the maturity value of their bonds. The third risk is that the price of the bond may fall below the price that you paid for the bond. For example, you may have purchased the bond for $1,020 shortly after it was issued. Suppose that five years later you decide to sell the bond and at that time the bond is selling for $960. If you sell the bond at that time, you will have lost $60 ($1,020 − $960) on your investment.

Historically, stock investments have provided a higher rate of return to investors than bond investments, though at a greater level of risk. If the goal is long-term investment, some advisors suggest that investing in bonds is short-sighted, as discussed in Insight 13.2.

Basic Characteristics of Bonds

Bonds have a number of distinguishing characteristics. We examine some of them next.

maturity date With regard to a debt issue, the date on which the borrower must repay the maturity value.

Maturity Date. Almost all bonds have a maturity date—that is, they are issued for a specified period. The **maturity date** is the date on which the borrower must repay the maturity value of the bonds. Just as you decide whether to take out a 15- or 30-year mortgage when you buy a home, or to borrow the money to purchase a car over three or four years, bond issuers must also decide for how long to borrow. For example, CocaCola may decide to borrow the money it needs to fund a production facility that will cost $100 million. Since this is a large sum to repay in a short time, CocaCola may decide to issue 20-year bonds. Common maturity dates for bonds are 5, 10, 20, and 30 years after the bonds are issued. Bonds are often quoted in terms of their maturity date. For example, a bond identified as a "22" will mature in 2022.[3]

maturity value, or par value With regard to a debt issue, the amount that must be repaid when the issue matures.

Maturity Value. The **maturity value** of a bond or debt issue, also called the **par value,** is the amount that must be repaid when the debt issue matures. The amount is usually $1,000 per bond for corporate bonds and higher for many government bonds. The maturity value should not be confused with the market price. As mentioned, bonds are traded in the secondary market after they have been issued. The market price is the current price of the bonds in the secondary market. The price can be greater than, less than, or equal to the maturity value of the bond.

Bond Interest Rates. Some investors find bonds particularly confusing because a number of different interest rates are quoted in discussions of bond investments: the coupon rate, the yield to maturity, the current yield, and the actual rate of return on a bond investment.

coupon rate Rate that determines the periodic interest payment on a bond.

■ The **coupon rate** determines the periodic interest payment provided by the bond. A bond with a coupon rate of 8.5 percent is referred to as an 8.5 percent coupon bond. To determine the periodic interest payment, multiply the coupon rate by the maturity value of the bond. For example, an 8.5 percent coupon bond would provide the purchaser $85 per year in interest (.085 × $1,000), provided the bond was issued with a $1,000 maturity value. Interest payments are usually made on a

yield to maturity With regard to a bond, the rate of return that will be earned by a bondholder who purchases the bond, holds it until it matures, and receives all the payments (interest and maturity value) associated with the bond.

current yield With regard to a bond, annual interest payment divided by current price.

actual rate of return With regard to a bond investment, the amount the holder receives divided by the amount the holder has invested.

semiannual basis, so this bond would provide two payments of $42.50 per year until the maturity date.

■ The **yield to maturity** of a bond is the rate of return that you will earn if you purchase the bond for a specified price, hold the bond until it matures, and receive all the payments (interest and maturity value) associated with the bond.

■ The **current yield** provided by a bond is simply the annual interest payment divided by the current price of the bond. For example, assume that an 8.5 percent coupon bond is currently selling for $1,030. The current yield of the bond would be 8.25 percent ($85/$1,030).

■ The **actual rate of return** on a bond investment is what you received from the investment divided by the amount you invested. This

Insight 13.2 A Tip for Longer-Term Investors: Choosing Bonds Is Shortsighted

Bonds are a poor investment. Bond funds are even worse.

All right, it's true that bad-mouthing the entire $7 trillion bond market and the $700 billion in bond-mutual funds is probably a trifle ill-tempered. But I do worry that a lot of the investors barreling back into bonds are making a big mistake.

It's not simply that these folks are buying after bonds have already rallied, though that's unfortunate. Rather, I fear that these newcomers don't fully appreciate the bond market's pitfalls.

Investors tend to view bonds as the great compromise, offering better yields than money-market funds without the risks that accompany stocks. But I reckon bonds are so treacherous that many investors would be better off biting the bullet and sticking their long-term savings into the stock market.

You think I'm wrong? Consider:

■ Bonds often sustain the sort of price swings usually associated with stocks. Yet unlike stocks, you don't earn healthy inflation-beating returns. Since 1925, stocks have outpaced inflation by seven percentage points a year, while bonds have beaten inflation by a meager two percentage points, according to Ibbotson Associates, a Chicago research firm.

■ Bonds are Uncle Sam's best friend. How so? Most of your gain consists of interest, which is immediately taxable unless you own municipal bonds. By contrast, stock-market profits come partly from price appreciation, which isn't taxed until you sell your securities. And when you do sell, this appreciation is taxed at the lower capital-gains rate.

■ Bonds are tricky to buy and sell. There's no central marketplace for bonds, as there is for stocks, so often you can't be sure that you're getting a decent price when you trade a bond. This is a big problem for individual investors, though bond-fund managers can also have a tough time getting good prices.

■ Bond investors often fail to earn handsome profits, even when they guess right on interest rates. Suppose you buy a long-maturity bond to lock in a fabulous yield. Interest rates subsequently fall. What happens next? The bond's issuer comes along and uses the bond's call provision to steal back the bond. Many corporate and municipal bonds can be paid off early, usually after just 10 years.

So we're agreed, there are a lot of problems with bonds. Maybe life is easier for bond-fund investors? You be the judge:

measure considers both interest payments that you receive and price appreciation (or loss) if you sell the bond before it matures. Your actual rate of return may differ from the yield to maturity if you sell the bond before it matures. As mentioned, you can sell the bond before it matures for more or less than the original purchase price.

Bond Ratings. Bonds are "rated" by a number of investment service companies. The two best-known bond rating agencies are Moody's and Standard & Poor's. These companies assess the bond issuer's ability to service the debt (pay interest) and to repay the maturity value when the bond issue matures. The greater the issuer's ability to make the scheduled payments, the higher the rating assigned. The top investment grade, triple a (AAA), is reserved for bond issues with the lowest risk of default. Lower ratings are assigned as the risk of default increases. Exhibit 13.5 provides a description and a comparison of Moody's and Standard & Poor's bond ratings.

Consider This

Both Moody's and Standard & Poor's maintain web sites. Visit them at:
http://www.moodys.com/
and
http://www.ratings.standardpoor.com

■ Bond-fund costs can decimate returns. Taxable-bond funds charge average annual expenses of 0.95%, while municipal-bond funds dun shareholders 0.81% annually, according to Chicago fund researchers Morningstar Inc. These fees come straight out of bond-fund dividends—a big hit now that most bonds yield less than 7%. To add insult to injury, many funds also levy a sales commission when you buy or sell shares.

■ You can't lock in a rate of return with a bond fund, as you can with an individual issue. For instance, imagine you want to invest some money for just five years. If you buy individual high-quality bonds that have good protection against calls and that mature in five years, you can be fairly confident about how much money you'll make. You know exactly how much you'll receive in interest each year and you know exactly how much you'll get

back when the bonds mature. Your only real worry is what rate of return you will earn when reinvesting your interest payments.

But if you stash your savings in a bond fund for the next five years, everything is up for grabs. After all, bond funds—unlike individual bonds—usually don't mature. If you purchase an intermediate-term bond fund, it will always be an intermediate-term bond fund. The fund just carries on, year after year, buying and selling intermediate-term securities. Result? You can't be sure how much income you'll get from the fund, nor is there any guarantee that at the end of five years your shares will be worth what you paid for them.

Granted, bond funds aren't always a bad deal. If you want to tap into esoteric securities, like high-yield junk bonds or emerging-market debt, funds make a lot of sense.

Bond funds are also convenient, with their low initial-investment minimums, check-writing privileges and automatic dividend reinvestment. But in all too many cases, these perks come with an awfully steep price tag.

The bottom line: Bonds are often a dicey investment, and buying them through mutual funds isn't an improvement. Sure, individual bonds are useful for locking in a rate of return, and bond funds can be a convenient way to invest.

But if you're truly a long-term investor, do yourself a favor: Take some of your bond-market money and sink it into stocks. The ride may be rougher, but at least you'll have a good shot at making some decent money.

Source: Jonathan Clements, "A Tip for Longer-Term Investors: Choosing Bonds Is Shortsighted," May 30, 1995. Reprinted by permission of *The Wall Street Journal*, © 1995 Dow Jones & Company, Inc. All Rights Reserved Worldwide.

Exhibit 13.5

Bond Ratings

	Standard & Poor's	Moody's
Highest quality	AAA	Aaa
Second-highest quality	AA	Aa
Upper-medium quality	A	A
Medium quality	BBB	Baa
Speculative	BB	Ba
Lower grade	B	B
Poor to default	CCC	Caa
Highly speculative	CC	Ca
Lowest grade	C	C
Issuer in default	D	—

Moody's and Standard & Poor's list each company's outstanding bond issues and provide a brief description of each debt issue. In February 1991, Mobil Corporation issued $200 million in debt that will mature in 2001. A description of this debt issue, rated Aa2 at the time by Moody's, is provided in Exhibit 13.6.

Bonds rated BB or lower by Standard & Poor's and Ba or lower by Moody's are called **junk bonds.** These bonds are also known as *high-yield bonds* because their prices are lower than that of other bonds with the same coupon rate. The reason the price is lower is that there is greater risk that the issuer will be unable to pay interest and the maturity value when the bonds mature. Although investing in junk bonds can provide a higher rate of return than investing in higher-rated bonds, there is significantly more risk.

Bonds receive low ratings for several reasons:

junk bond Bond rated BB or lower by Standard & Poor's and Ba or lower by Moody's; junk bonds offer potentially higher returns than higher-rated bonds but also involve significantly higher risk.

■ Recall that bond issues may be outstanding for 10, 20, 30, or more years. A bond may receive a good rating when it is first issued. Over time, however, the financial fortunes of the issuer may not go well, and the bond issue may be downgraded to reflect this added risk of default.

■ Some companies already experiencing financial difficulty issue bonds, and these bonds are assigned a speculative rating at the time the bonds are issued.

Exhibit 13.6

Moody's Description of a Debt Issue

> 4. Mobil Corp. 8 $^3/_8$% notes, due 2001:
>
> Rating = Aa2
>
> AUTH - $200,000,000.
> OUTSTG - Dec. 31, 1994, $200,000,000.
> DATED - Feb. 12, 1991. DUE - Feb. 12, 2001.
> INTEREST - Payable semiannually on each F&A 12,
> beginning Aug. 12, 1991.
> TRUSTEE - Chemical Bank.
> DENOMINATION - Fully registered, $1,000 and any
> multiple of $1,000. Transferable and exchangeable
> without service charge.
> CALLABLE - Not callable prior to maturity.
> SECURITY - Not secured. Rank equally with all other
> unsecured and unsubordinated indebtedness of Co.
> INDENTURE MODIFICATION - Indenture may be
> modified, except as provided, with consent of 66 $^2/_3$%
> of notes outstg.
> RIGHTS ON DEFAULT - Trustee, or 25% of notes
> outstg., may declare principal due and payable (30
> days' grace for payment of interest).
> PURPOSE - Proceeds from the sale of the debt securi-
> ties will be used for general corporate purposes.
> OFFERED - ($200,000,000) at 99.832 plus accrued
> interest (proceeds to Co., 99.332) on Feb. 1, 1991 thru
> Solomon Brothers Inc. and associates.

PRICE RANGE -	1994	1993
High	116	117$^1/_2$
Low.....................	101$^1/_4$	108$^1/_4$

Explanation of key points:

- Mobil issued $200 million in 8$^3/_8$ percent coupon bonds on February 12, 1991. The bonds mature in 2001.

- Moody's has assigned a rating of Aa2 to this debt issue.

- Interest is paid semiannually, on February and August 12.

- The bonds are not callable, nor are they secured.

- The bond indenture may be modified only if two-thirds of the notes outstanding agree to the change.

- If Mobil defaults, the trustee or 25 percent of the notes outstanding may declare the principal due and payable.

- The proceeds from the bond issue were used for general corporate purposes.

Source: Moody's Industrial Manual. Reprinted with permission.

■ Finally, the 1980s was a period of corporate restructuring. Many companies significantly increased the amount of debt they employed during this period. Since previously issued debt often had a claim on assets superior to the newly issued debt in case of default, and the amount of debt issued by the company increased, ratings agencies assigned lower ratings to many of these new issues.

Bond Features. Some important features that vary among bond issues include whether the bonds are secured or have a superior claim to other debt issues, whether they are callable, whether they are convertible, whether the bond pays periodic interest payments, and whether the bonds provide a fixed interest payment.

secured debt Debt for which specific assets have been pledged as collateral.

■ A **secured debt** issue has specific assets pledged as collateral for the debt. Another form of security a bond issue may provide is a priority claim over other bonds issued by the company. Although the claims of bondholders take precedence over the claims of stockholders should the firm be forced to liquidate, the bond agreement may also place restrictions on the financial decisions of the company in order to protect the interests of the bondholders. The Mobil Corporation bond issue summarized in Exhibit 13.6 indicates that the issue is not secured and ranks equally with the company's other unsecured debt issues.

call provision A provision by which the bond issuer can retire the debt issue before the scheduled maturity date.

■ Another characteristic of bonds is whether or not the bonds are callable. A **call provision** permits the company that issued the bonds to retire the debt issue before the scheduled maturity. Bonds that are issued with high coupon rates are often callable. An example will help clarify this practice. Assume that a company issued some 14 percent, 30-year, callable bonds in 1981. These bonds will mature in 2011 and require the company to pay $140 (.14 × $1,000) per bond per year in interest until the bonds mature. Further assume that interest rates decline significantly and that in 1998, the company could issue similar bonds with a 10 percent coupon. At that time, the company may choose to "call" in the outstanding bonds, repaying the maturity value early. If the company still needed to borrow, it could reissue some 10 percent coupon bonds, thus saving $40 per year ($140 − $100) per bond in interest expense. Although a call provision provides flexibility for the issuer, it also makes a bond riskier for the bond owner since the bond may be called away before the scheduled maturity date.

convertible bond Bond that can be exchanged for a specified number of shares of common stock of the issuing company.

■ Some bonds include a conversion provision. **Convertible bonds** can be exchanged for a specified number of shares of common stock of the issuing company. Convertibles give investors added flexibility. For example, suppose XYZ Company issues some 20-year, $1,000 maturity value, 6 percent coupon bonds that can be converted into 50 shares of XYZ common stock. At the time the bonds are issued, XYZ common stock may be trading for $14 per share. Converting the bond into 50 shares of XYZ stock at this time will provide a value of only $700 ($14 × 50). But suppose that three years go by and the stock price has increased to $25 per share. A bond can now be converted into 50 shares of XYZ stock worth $1,250 ($25 × 50). If the stock price does not increase to a point where conversion is profitable, the investor can continue to receive the scheduled interest payments and the maturity value when the bond matures. Of course, there is a cost to the investor for this added flexibility. Convertible bonds typically yield less than nonconvertible bonds of the same duration issued by the same company. Why do corporations issue convertible bonds? Since these bonds typically carry lower coupon rates, the cost to borrow is less than it is with nonconvertible bonds. In addition, some companies do not wish to issue additional shares of common stock at the present time. Many convertible bond issues are also callable.

zero coupon bond Bond that does not provide a periodic interest payment to the holder.

■ Not all bonds are interest bearing. **Zero coupon bonds** are bonds that do not provide a periodic interest payment to the bondholder. Corporations, the U.S. government, and municipalities issue zero coupon bonds. These bonds sell for less than their maturity value—significantly less if there is a long time until the bond matures. Although zero coupon bonds do not provide interest payments, the bondholder is required to pay taxes on the annual appreciation of the bond. Zero coupon bonds are well suited for tax-sheltered investments, such as IRAs and Keogh plans. By using zero coupon bonds in this way, the bondholder avoids paying taxes on interest not actually received. Zero coupon bonds are also an effective vehicle for accumulating funds for college. If the bonds are placed in the child's name, they are taxed at a lower rate.

■ A criticism of bond investments is that because bond payments (coupon interest and maturity value) are fixed, bond investments lose value over time to inflation. We discussed inflation risk in the previous chapter. To address this concern, the U.S. government began to issue inflation-indexed bonds in 1997. An inflation-indexed bond's maturity value and interest payments are adjusted to keep pace with the consumer price index (CPI).

For example, assume an inflation-indexed bond carries a 4 percent coupon rate per thousand dollars of maturity value. When issued, the bond will provide $40 in interest per year (.04 × $1,000). If inflation, as measured by the CPI, is 5 percent, the maturity value will be increased by 5 percent to $1,050. The new interest payment is 4 percent of the new maturity value, $42 (.04 × $1,050).

Who Issues Bonds?

As noted, both corporations and government entities issue bonds. Here we briefly discuss these issuers and point out some of the interesting characteristics of their bond issues.

Private Companies

corporate bond Bond issued by a private company.

Corporate bonds are issued by private companies to raise money to fund investments in plant and equipment or for other corporate financial needs. Corporate bonds have a special advantage to the company that issues them. Interest payments to bondholders are tax deductible expenses for corporations. Thus, corporations are permitted to offset interest paid to bondholders against taxable income, thereby reducing taxable income, which in turn reduces the company's tax liability. So the true cost of corporate borrowing is lower than the coupon rate of a bond issue, after you consider tax savings. Although interest is a tax deductible business expense, dividends on preferred and common stock are not tax deductible for the corporation.

Government Entities

government bond Bond issued by a government entity.

Government bonds represent borrowing by the government (federal or local) or by another government entity, such as an agency or political subdivision. Borrowing may be necessary because tax revenues are not sufficient to finance authorized spending.

Consider This

Get news about U.S. government notes and bonds from the Treasury Department at: http://www.publicdebt.trea s.gov/

The Federal Government. The U.S. government borrows money through both short-term and longer-term securities. Short-term borrowing is done through the issue of Treasury bills (T-bills). T-bills, a savings alternative, were discussed in Chapter 3. The U.S. government also borrows money for longer time periods through the issue of Treasury notes and Treasury bonds. **Treasury notes** are "intermediate" term securities, with maturities that range from 2 to 10 years. Treasury notes are issued in $1,000 and $5,000 denominations. **Treasury bonds** are long-term securities, with maturities over 10 years. Treasury bonds are issued in $1,000 minimums, with $5,000, $10,000, $50,000, $100,000, and $1 million denominations available. These debt securities are not rated by the ratings services. Since they are obligations of the federal government, they are considered risk-free.

Treasury note An intermediate-term debt security issued by the U.S. government.

Treasury bond A long-term debt security issued by the U.S. government.

Some U.S. government agencies also issue debt securities. **Agency bonds** are bonds issued by U.S. government agencies that are almost as safe as U.S. Treasury securities and provide higher yields. Some agency

agency bond A bond issued by a U.S. government agency, such as the Federal Housing Administration or the Government National Mortgage Association.

bonds, such as bonds issued by the Federal Housing Administration and Government National Mortgage Association, are fully guaranteed by the U.S. government. Other government agency bonds are not guaranteed or only partially guaranteed. Some other issuers of agency bonds include the Tennessee Valley Authority, the Student Loan Marketing Association, the Federal National Mortgage Association, and the Federal Home Loan Mortgage Corporation.

municipal bond Bond issued by a city, state, county, or other political unit.

State and Local Government. Municipal bonds are bonds issued by cities, states, counties, and other political units. Revenues raised through issuing municipal bonds are used to fund local projects, such as the construction of a bridge, sewage treatment plant, or highway. Municipal bonds (called munis) are issued in units of $5,000 or more.

Munis have a distinguishing feature—interest payments to the bondholder do not represent taxable income for federal tax purposes. In addition, the interest income is not taxable at the state level in most states. Since the yield is tax exempt in most instances, munis can pay a lower interest rate. Investors are willing to accept the lower rate if it is competitive with fully taxable bonds on an after-tax basis.

You can determine the fully taxable equivalent yield through this relationship:

$$\text{Fully Taxable Equivalent Yield} = \frac{\text{Municipal Bond Yield}}{(1 - \text{Marginal Tax Rate})}$$

Thus, a municipal bond yielding 7 percent would be equivalent to a fully taxable bond yielding 10 percent if the investor's marginal tax rate was 30 percent:

$$\text{Fully Taxable Equivalent Yield} = \frac{.07}{(1 - .30)} = 10.00\%$$

Historically, the default rate on municipal bonds has been very low. Given that government entities can become insolvent (for example, Orange County, California, in 1994), some issuers purchase private insurance coverage that will provide the required payments to bondholders if the issuer defaults. A table of taxable equivalent yields for municipal bonds is provided in Exhibit 13.7.

Bond Trading and Bond Prices

As noted, there is an active secondary market for bonds. In this section, we discuss where bonds are traded, how to read bond quotations, and how bonds are priced.

Exhibit 13.7

Taxable Equivalent Yield Table for Municipal Bonds

Taxable Equivalent Yield Table								
		Highest Marginal Tax Rates						
	Federal	CA	CT	MA	NJ	NY	NYC	OH
State Rate		11.0%	4.50%	12.0%	6.65%	7.88%	12.34%	7.50%
Combined State and Local Rate	39.60%	46.24%	42.32%	46.85%	43.62%	44.36%	47.05%	44.13%
Tax Exempt Yields	Taxable Equivalent Yields							
	Exempt from Federal Tax Only	Exempt from Federal, State, and Local Taxes						
4.00%	6.62%	7.44%	6.93%	7.53%	7.09%	7.19%	7.55%	7.16%
4.50	7.45	8.37	7.80	8.47	7.98	8.09	8.50	8.05
5.00	8.28	9.30	8.67	9.41	8.87	8.99	9.44	8.95
5.50	9.11	10.23	9.54	10.35	9.75	9.88	10.39	9.84
6.00	9.93	11.16	10.40	11.29	10.64	10.78	11.33	10.74
6.50	10.76	12.09	11.27	12.23	11.53	11.68	12.28	11.63
7.00	11.59	13.02	12.14	13.17	12.42	12.58	13.22	12.53
7.50	12.42	13.95	13.00	14.11	13.30	13.48	14.16	13.42
8.00	13.25	14.88	13.87	15.05	14.19	14.38	15.11	14.32

Notes: Taxable equivalent yields apply to investors subject to the highest marginal tax brackets. State tax rates given were effective as of August 1, 1994 and are subject to change. The combined federal and state tax rate reflects the deduction of state and local taxes on federal returns.

Source: *Guide of Bonds and Income Earnings Investments*, Charles Schwab & Co., Inc., 1995. Reprinted with permission.

Bond Market and Bond Quotations

Bonds are traded on the New York Stock Exchange, the American Stock Exchange, and the over-the-counter (NASDAQ) market. Just as there are stock indexes that measure performance of a group of stocks, there are also bond indexes, such as the Lehman Brothers Long Bond Index, that measure bond prices for groups of bonds.

Bond trading activity for most larger bond issues, for U.S. government and agency bonds, and for some representative municipal bond issues is reported daily in the *Wall Street Journal* and other business publications. A quotation for the Mobil bond displayed in the Moody's exhibit earlier in this chapter and an explanation of the information presented in the quotation appear in Exhibit 13.8.

Exhibit 13.8

Quote for Mobil Company Bond

Quote as it appeared in the *Wall Street Journal*, January 27, 1997:

Bonds	Cur Yld	Vol	Close		Net Chg
Mascotch 03	cv	32	88	+	$^1/_2$
Maxus $8^1/_2$08	8.7	80	$98 ^1/_8$	–	$1 ^1/_8$
McDnl $6^3/_4$03	6.8	27	100		...
MerLyCo 98	...	100	103		
Metrom $9^1/_8$97	9.9	12	$99 ^1/_2$	–	$^1/_{16}$
Metrom $9^1/_2$98	9.5	1	$100 ^1/_4$	–	$^3/_4$
MichB $7^3/_4$11	7.6	5	$101 ^5/_8$		...
MPac $4^3/_4$20f	...	2	64	–	$1 ^7/_8$
Mobil $8^3/_8$01	7.9	62	$106 ^1/_2$	–	$^3/_4$
Mott 21.13	...	54	79	–	2
Nabis 8.3s99	8.0	110	$103 ^1/_2$	–	$^1/_2$

Reading the quote from left to right:

Name of Company:	Bonds issued by Mobil, the large oil company.
Coupon Rate:	This bond has an $8^3/_8$ percent coupon. It will pay the bondholder $83.75 in interest each year (.08375 × $1,000) until it matures.
Maturity Date:	This bond issue will mature in 01, meaning the year 2001.
Current Yield:	The current yield is the annual interest payment divided by the closing price. The current yield is 7.86 percent ($83.75/$1,065), which is rounded to 7.9% in the exhibit.
Volume:	The dollar value of Mobil bonds traded during the trading day. To learn the dollar value, add three zeroes to 62. In other words, $62,000 worth of Mobil bonds were traded.
Closing Price:	Bond prices are quoted per hundred dollars of maturity value. So 106.5 would be $1,065.00 per $1,000 maturity value.
Net Change:	Net change is quoted in terms of the bond's par value, $1,000. So a decline of three-fourths percent would be a drop of $7.50 per bond (.0075 × $1,000) between the previous day's closing price and today's closing price.

Bond Valuation

How are bond prices determined? The same general rules used to price shares of preferred stock and common stock also apply to bonds. *The price of a bond is equal to the present value of the expected future payments, discounted at the investor-required rate of return.*

Expected Cash Flows. Unlike common stock, where the future cash flows are not known with certainty, the expected cash flows from a bond are known in advance. If you purchase an interest-bearing bond, you will receive periodic interest payments and the maturity value when the bond matures, provided the issuer does not default.

Consider an example. Suppose ConAgra issues some 20-year, 10 percent coupon bonds to fund the acquisition of a frozen foods company. If you purchase a newly issued ConAgra bond, you are entitled to receive $100 in interest (.10 × $1,000) per year for 20 years and $1,000 when the bond matures in 20 years. You will receive these cash flows unless ConAgra defaults.

Investor-Required Rate of Return. The second factor that determines the price of a bond is the investor-required rate of return. The rate of return that investors require is made up of several components, as discussed earlier in this chapter:

■ Compensation for not having use of their funds

■ Compensation for expected inflation

■ Compensation for risk

For example, assume that investors require a 3 percent return for not having use of their money. Further assume that expected inflation is 4.5 percent and that investors add 1.5 percent to their required return to reflect the risk that ConAgra may default on the bond issue. The investor-required rate of return for this bond, then, is 9 percent (3% + 4.5% + 1.5%).

Pricing a Bond. To price a bond, you must consider the expected cash flows, the investor-required rate of return, and the time value of money techniques from Chapter 2. The interest payments from a bond are in the form of an ordinary annuity, and the maturity value is a single amount. The formula for pricing a coupon bond is:

$$\frac{\text{Bond}}{\text{Price}} = \frac{\text{Coupon}}{\text{Payment}} \times \frac{\text{Present Value}}{\text{Annuity Factor}} + \frac{\text{Maturity}}{\text{Value}} \times \frac{\text{Present Value of}}{\text{Future Amount Factor}}$$

If the investor-required rate of return on the ConAgra bond is 9 percent, the most you should be willing to pay for a newly issued ConAgra bond is:

$$\frac{\text{Bond}}{\text{Price}} = \$100 \times \frac{\text{Present Value Annuity}}{\text{Factor (9\% i, 20 N)}} + \$1,000 \times \frac{\text{Present Value of Future}}{\text{Amount Factor (9\% i, 20 N)}}$$

Bond Price = $100 × 9.1285 + $1,000 × .1784

Bond Price = $912.85 + $178.40 = $1,091.25

premium With regard to bonds, the amount by which a bond's selling price exceeds its maturity value.

discount With regard to bonds, the amount by which a bond sells below its maturity value.

Notice that the price of the ConAgra bond is more than $1,000. Bonds selling for more than their maturity value are said to be selling at a **premium.** A bond that sells for less than its maturity value is described as selling at a **discount.**

Bond Price Movements. Just as stock prices change, so to do bond prices. As the expected cash flows from a bond are fixed, changes in investor-required rates of return cause bond prices to fluctuate. Investors constantly readjust their required rate of return based on interest rate changes and the risk of default. *The relationship between bond prices and interest rates is inverse: When interest rates increase, bond prices fall; when interest rates decrease, bond prices rise.*

To verify the preceding statement, recalculate the price of the Con-Agra bond using a required rate of return of 12 percent and a required rate of return of 8 percent. You will find that with a 12 percent required rate of return, the price of the bond falls to $850.61; whereas if the required rate of return is 8 percent, the price of the bond increases to $1,196.36. If the coupon rate exceeds the investor required return, as in the previous example, the bond sells at a premium. If the coupon rate is less than the investor-required return, the bond sells at a discount. If the two rates are equal, the bond sells at its maturity value. Exhibit 13.9 shows how the price of a bond varies over time with interest rate changes.

The size of bond price movements is also related to the time until the bond matures. Bonds that are closer to maturity are less affected by changes in investor-required rates of return than are bonds that have many years until maturity. This is true because with shorter-term bonds, fewer cash flows remain and the discounting is done over fewer years. The reverse is true for bonds with a longer time until maturity. Exhibit 13.10 shows the relationship between bond prices, time to maturity, and change in investor required rates of return.

Investing in Bonds

Suppose you decide to invest in bonds. How do you go about buying and selling bonds, and what types of bonds should you consider?

Buying and Selling Bonds

Newly issued bonds and outstanding bonds can be purchased through stockbrokers and are available from some banks. Newly issued U.S. Trea-

Exhibit 13.9

Bond Prices Vary Inversely with Market Interest Rates

As you can see, if interest rates drop to 5 percent three years after you buy a 15-year $1,000 bond paying 8 percent, it becomes more valuable to prospective investors and its market value rises to $1,268. Conversely, if interest rates rise to 13 percent three years after you buy your bond, it becomes less valuable to investors and will probably sell for about $739. (Of course, if you hold it to maturity, you'll receive its full face value, regardless of interest rates.)

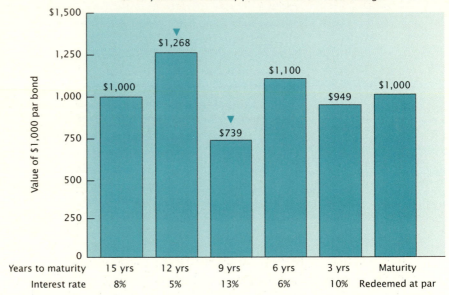

How the value of a $1,000-8% coupon bond changes during its 15-years until maturity period as interest rates change.

Years to maturity	15 yrs	12 yrs	9 yrs	6 yrs	3 yrs	Maturity
	$1,000	$1,268	$739	$1,100	$949	$1,000
Interest rate	8%	5%	13%	6%	10%	Redeemed at par

Value of $1,000 par bond

Source: *Guide of Bonds and Income Earnings Investments*, Charles Schwab & Co. Inc., 1993, p. 7. Reprinted with permission.

sury notes and bonds can be purchased directly from Federal Reserve Banks without commission. If you decide to sell a bond before it matures, whether it is a corporate or a government issue, you can sell the bond through a broker who will match you with a purchaser.

Selecting Bonds

You should concern yourself with a number of factors when making an investment in bonds. Investors should consider the degree of risk, the rate of return, tax consequences, time to maturity, and other factors.

Risk. U.S. Treasury securities are not rated because they are considered risk-free. Other issues are rated based upon the ability of the issuer to pay interest and the maturity value. Bonds range from high quality, low risk, to low quality, high risk. You should determine your level of comfort with risk before purchasing a bond.

Exhibit 13.10

Bond Prices Vary Directly with Time Until Maturity

This chart shows the impact of a 1 percent fluctuation in market interest rates on bonds with different maturities. With a short-term bond, the market value of a $1,000 investment rises or falls about 2 percent in response to a 1 percent interest rate change. With a long-term bond, the market value of the same $1,000 investment fluctuates more dramatically.

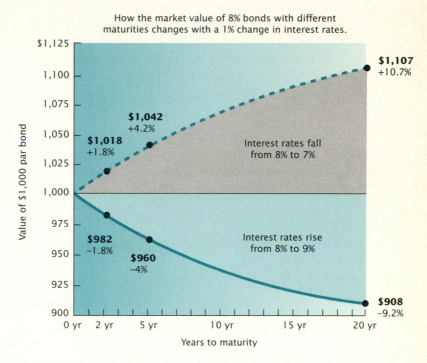

How the market value of 8% bonds with different maturities changes with a 1% change in interest rates.

Source: *Guide of Bonds and Income Earnings Investments*, Charles Schwab & Co., 1993, p. 7. Reprinted with permission.

Rate of Return. The rate of return provided by the bond is obviously related to the degree of risk that you are willing to bear. Even though government-issued bonds offer lower rates of return than corporate issues, these bonds are also of lower risk.

Tax Consequences. Interest received and capital gains from corporate bonds are fully taxable. Municipal bonds are exempt from federal taxes and are usually exempt from state and local taxes in the jurisdiction where they are issued. Many federal government issues are exempt from state and local taxes.

Other Factors. Some investors like to purchase municipal bonds as a means of investing in local community projects. The size of the initial investment required may also be a consideration. For example, corporate bonds trade in units of $1,000, whereas municipal bonds trade in units of $5,000 or more. Finally, you should consider the characteristics of the bond (callable, convertible, secured, and so forth).

SUMMARY

■ Common stock represents ownership interest in a company. Common stockholders are the residual owners of the company. Preferred stock is a hybrid security, sharing characteristics of common stock and bonds.

■ Preferred stock provides a fixed periodic dividend payment and limited price appreciation potential. Common stock may or may not pay dividends.

■ The rewards of stock ownership are current income if the stock pays dividends and potential capital gains if the share price increases in value.

■ The risks of stock investment are loss of current income if dividends are not paid and loss of value if the price of the stock declines.

■ Common stock and preferred stock do not have a maturity date. However, some preferred stock is callable, and some companies may choose to repurchase shares of common stock.

■ Dividends on common stock and preferred stock are usually paid quarterly. Preferred stock is usually cumulative, meaning that dividends owed preferred stockholders must be paid before dividends can be paid to common stockholders.

■ Cash dividends paid to stockholders are currently taxable income. Gains on stock are not taxed until the gain is actually realized.

■ When stock is initially issued, the company receives funds. This is a primary market transaction. After shares have been issued, they are traded between investors, and the company receives no funds. These are secondary market transactions.

■ Companies adjust the price of their stock through stock dividends and stock splits. Stock splits and dividends do not increase the value of the stock. Stock splits and dividends are used to keep the price of the stock in a preferred trading range.

■ There are several types of stocks, including blue-chip stocks, income stocks, growth stocks, cyclical stocks, defensive stocks, and speculative stocks.

■ Blue-chip stocks are high-quality shares of established, mature companies. These low-risk stocks provide dividends and moderate growth.

■ Income stocks are stocks that provide a high dividend yield.

■ Growth stocks are stocks in companies that are expected to have earnings growth exceeding other stocks.

■ Cyclical stocks are stocks that move with the business cycle. During economic upturns, these stocks perform well. During economic downturns, these stocks do not perform well.

■ Defensive stocks are stocks in companies that have stable demand for their goods and services. The performance of such stocks is more immune to economic fluctuations.

■ Speculative stocks are higher-risk stocks in unproven companies or companies out of favor with investors.

■ The price of common stock is the present value of the future cash flows associated with the common stock. Expected future cash flows and investor-required rates of return determine stock prices. Stock prices change because of changes in expected cash flows and changes in investor-required rates of return.

■ Earnings per share (EPS) is the earnings available to common stock-holders after expenses, taxes, and preferred dividends have been paid, divided by the number of shares of common stock outstanding.

■ A stock's price to earnings (P/E) ratio is the market price per share divided by earnings per share (EPS). The P/E ratio tells investors at how many times EPS the stock is currently selling.

■ The dividend yield for a stock is the annual dividend divided by the price per share.

■ Beta is a measure of the riskiness of the stock in relation to the volatility of the market.

■ Bonds are debt securities that represent borrowing by corporations and government entities.

■ The rewards of investing in bonds are current income from interest payments and price appreciation if you sell the bond for more than you paid for it or if you pay less than the maturity value for the bond and hold the bond until maturity.

■ Several risks are inherent in purchasing a bond. First, there is default risk. The issuing company or government entity may fail to pay the interest and maturity value. Second, there is price risk. Adverse interest rate movements may cause the price of the bond to fall.

■ The maturity date of a bond is when the bond matures and the issuer must pay the maturity (par) value to the bond owner.

■ A number of interest rates are associated with bonds:(1) The coupon rate determines the periodic interest payment that the bond issuer (borrower) must pay. (2) The yield to maturity is the rate of return that an investor will earn if he or she purchases the bond at a specified price today, holds the bond until it matures, and receives all payments. (3) The current yield is the annual interest payment provided by the bond divided by the current price. (4) The actual rate of return an investor earns on a bond investment may differ from the yield to maturity if the investor sells the bond before it matures.

■ Bond rating agencies assign grades to debt issues based upon the ability of the issuer to pay interest and principal. The lower the bond rating, the higher the investor-required rate of return on the bond issue.

■ Junk bonds are bonds that do not receive investment-grade ratings from the ratings services.

■ A secured debt issue has specific assets pledged as collateral for the debt.

■ A callable bond can be retired prior to the scheduled maturity date if the issuer chooses to exercise this right.

■ Convertible bonds can be switched to a specified number of shares of common stock of the issuer if the bondholder chooses to exercise this right.

■ Zero coupon bonds are bonds that do not provide periodic interest payments to the bondholder.

■ Corporations borrow money by issuing bonds. Interest paid on corporate bonds is a tax deductible expense for corporations.

■ The U.S. government borrows money on a short-term basis through the issue of Treasury bills. Longer-term borrowing is done through the issue of Treasury notes and Treasury bonds. Agencies of the U.S. government also borrow money through the issue of bonds.

■ Cities, states, counties, and other political divisions issue municipal bonds. Interest income is exempt from federal income tax and state income tax in most states.

■ The price of any bond is the present value of the future payments the bondholder will receive, discounted at the appropriate investor-required rate of return.

■ Once issued, the coupon rate of a bond does not change. Changes in investor-required rates of return make bond prices fluctuate.

■ There is an inverse relationship between bond prices and changes in investor-required rates of return. Bonds selling for more than their maturity value are selling at a premium; bonds selling for less than their maturity value are selling at a discount.

KEY CONCEPTS AND TERMS

Actual rate of return
Agency bond
Beta
Blue-chip stock
Bond covenant (indenture)
Callable preferred stock
Call provision
Convertible bond
Corporate bond
Coupon rate
Cumulative preferred stock
Current yield
Cyclical stock
Defensive stock
Discount
Dividend yield
Earnings per share (EPS)
Government bond
Growth stock
Income stock
Initial public offering (IPO)

Junk bond
Maturity date
Maturity (par) value
Municipal bond
Over-the-counter (OTC) market
Perpetual annuity (perpetuity)
Premium
Price/earnings (P/E) ratio
Primary market
Residual owner (claimant)
Secondary market
Secured debt
Speculative stock
Stock dividend
Stock repurchase
Stock split
Treasury bond
Treasury note
Yield to maturity
Zero coupon bond

QUESTIONS FOR REVIEW

1. What are the differences between common stock and preferred stock?

2. What does it mean if preferred stock is:
   a. callable
   b. cumulative

3. What are the two ways in which you can profit from purchasing preferred and common stock?

4. What types of common stock are available to investors?

5. What do stock prices represent? How do you determine the price of common stock and preferred stock?

6. With regard to common stock, what do each of the following variables measure:
   a. earnings per share (EPS)

 b. P/E ratio

 c. dividend yield

 d. beta

7. With regard to corporate bonds, explain the meaning of each of the following:

 a. selling at a discount versus selling at a premium

 b. coupon rate versus yield to maturity

 c. secured debt versus unsecured debt

 d. bond rating

8. Besides corporate bonds, what other types of bonds are available to investors?

9. What special tax benefit is available to purchasers of municipal bonds? How is the fully taxable equivalent yield for tax-free municipal bonds calculated?

10. How is the price of a bond calculated? What is the relationship between changes in market-required rates of return and bond prices?

PROBLEMS

1. Marta purchased 300 shares of RPM stock. The stock pays a 12 cent per share dividend each quarter. How much dividend income will Marta receive this year from her RPM stock?

2. Kelly purchased 100 shares of Colgate Palmolive stock six years ago at a price of $42.50 per share. If she sells the stock this year for $88.00 per share:

 a. What is Kelly's capital gain on this investment?

 b. If Kelly's gain is taxed at 28 percent, how much will she have to pay in taxes on the gain?

3. SLD stock sells for $40 per share. The expected annual dividend for next year is $1.20. SLD earnings per share (EPS) is $2.50.

 a. What is the SLD's dividend yield?

 b. What is SLD's price/earnings (P/E) ratio?

4. Lu Ann is considering the purchase of a corporate bond. The bond has a 10 percent coupon bond that matures in 10 years ($1,000 maturity value).

   a. What annual interest payment should Lu Ann expect from the bond?

   b. What is the most that Lu Ann should be willing to pay for the bond if her required rate of return is:

      (1) 8 percent

      (2) 10 percent

      (3) 12 percent

INTERNET EXERCISES

1. EduStock is an educational site that explains how the stock market works. Visit the site at:

   http://tqd.advanced.org/3088

   and perform the interactive stock market simulation.

2. The World Wide Web includes many large and information-rich sites where investors can conduct research on corporations, track the markets and the value of their investments, and so forth. Examples include the following:

   ■ InvestorGuide at:

   http://www.investorguide.com/

   ■ NETworth (choose Equities Center for stocks) at:

   http://networth.galt.com/

   ■ StockSmart at:

   http://www.stocksmart.com/

   ■ *Research* magazine's InvestorNet at:

   http://www.researchmag.com/

   ■ The PAWWS Financial Network at:

   http://www.pawws.com/

   ■ InvesTools at:

   http://www.investools.com/

Visit the various parts of these sites to get an idea of the vast amount of information available for investors on the web. (Some sites, such as InvesTools, charge for some of their services, but you can browse to see what's available for free.)

CASE APPLICATIONS

Case 1

Paula Fredricks is a financial planner. A number of clients have questions about investing in stocks and bonds. What types of stocks or bonds should Paula recommend to each of these clients? Explain your answer.

a. Rueben Jones is a retiree. He would like to invest in stocks. His primary goal is large quarterly dividend checks that he can use to supplement his social security and private pension income.

b. Francois Pascal is tired of the low rate of return she has been earning on her savings account. She would like to invest in bonds, but is very risk averse.

c. Yul Kim has high work earnings and faces the highest marginal tax rate. He would like to invest in bonds, but does not want to receive any taxable interest income.

d. Michael Barnes believes that the economy will soon begin a period of record growth. He would like to profit from the growth by buying stocks that are currently selling at low prices, relative to their historic performance.

e. Amanda Taylor is "bearish" on the economy. She would like to invest in stocks, but is concerned that an economic slow-down will hurt stock prices. She would like to invest in companies that can "hold their own" during a recession.

Case 2

Charles Evert has a portfolio of stocks and bonds. The portfolio consists of:

■ 100 shares of ABC common stock. ABC pays a 50 cent per quarter dividend. ABC stock sells for $65 per share.

■ a $1,000, 8% coupon bond issued by LMN Company. The bond is currently selling at its maturity value, $1,000.

■ 100 shares of XYZ preferred stock. XYZ preferred stock pays a 75 cent per quarter dividend. XYZ preferred stock sells for $30 per share

a. What is the total market value of Charles Evert's stock and bond portfolio?

b. How much investment income will Charles receive from the portfolio this year?

c. The LMN bond that Charles owns is yielding 8%. The marginal tax rate Charles faces is 25%. What rate of return must a municipal bond provide to equal the after-tax yield provided by the LMN Company bond?

SUGGESTIONS FOR ADDITIONAL READING

Cheney, John M. and Edward A. Moses. *Fundamentals of Investing.* St. Paul, Minn.: West Publishing Company, 1992.

Cottle, Sidney, Roger F. Murray, and Frank E. Block. *Graham and Dodd's Security Analysis,* 5th ed. New York: McGraw-Hill, 1988.

Dolan, Ken and Daria Dolan. *Straight Talk on Money.* New York: Simon and Schuster, 1993.

Dunnan, Nancy. *Dun & Bradsteet Guide to $Your Investments$.* New York: HarperCollins Publishers, 1994.

Malkiel, Burton. *A Random Walk Down Wall Street.* New York: W.W. Norton & Company, 1996.

Miller, Theodore J. *Invest Your Way to Wealth.* Washington: The Kiplinger Washington Editors, Inc., 1994.

Morris, Kenneth M. and Alan M. Siegel. *The Wall Street Journal Guide to Understanding Personal Finance.* New York: Lightbulb Press, 1992.

Personal Financial Planning Guide. Ernst & Young. New York: John Wiley & Sons, 1995.

Sloane, Leonard. *The New York Times Personal Finance Handbook.* New York: Times Books, 1995.

Wurman, Richard Saul, Alan Siegel, and Kenneth M. Morris, *The Wall Street Journal Guide to Understanding Money & Markets.* New York: HarperCollins Publishers, 1990.

NOTES

1. If a successful company does not periodically adjust its stock price through stock splits and stock dividends, the price of 100 shares, let alone one share, may not be affordable. An excellent example is billionaire investor Warren Buffet's company,

Berkshire Hathaway. This company, traded on the New York Stock Exchange, has not split. As the time of this writing, a single share sells for more than $46,000!

2. Companies are reluctant to make significant changes in their dividend policy. Investors purchase shares in companies that offer dividend policies that match their preferences. The last thing an individual facing a high marginal tax rate wants is for a growth stock to begin to pay large dividends. Many retirees depend on income stocks with large dividend payouts.

3. Bonds maturing in 2007 are sometimes called "James" bonds since their maturity, 007, has the same code name as the fictional government agent.

Chapter 14

Investing in Mutual Funds

Learning Objectives

After studying this chapter, you should be able to:

- Discuss the nature of mutual funds, including their organization, composition, net asset value, and closed-end versus open-end funds.

- Explain how mutual fund investors earn money and the advantages and disadvantages of investing in mutual funds.

- Explain the costs of mutual fund investing, including the various fees that mutual funds charge.

- Describe how mutual fund transactions are performed, how performance of mutual funds is measured, and the tax implications of investing in mutual funds.

- Discuss the investment objectives and the types of securities held by the various types of mutual funds.

- Explain how to select a mutual fund that is right for you.

 Mutual Funds: The Best Investment Idea Anyone Ever Had

—Theodore J. Miller, *Kiplinger's
Invest Your Way to Wealth*

*Small investors turn to mutual fund managers in hopes of
earning superior gains in today's financial markets.
Too bad the vast majority of funds aren't
able to beat the market averages.*

—*Money Magazine*

505

D r. Larry Martin had not stayed up all night since studying for the biology final exam when he was an undergraduate in college. But he had to know. He just *had* to know.

He shuffled some papers and jotted down some information. His fingers flew from key to key on his calculator. He had been at it for four hours solid. But he had to know. He just *had* to know.

He entered the final information in his calculator, took a deep breath, and performed the final calculation. Then he uttered a single word, "Darn."

You see, Dr. Martin takes three to four hours per week from his busy schedule to manage his investment portfolio. He buys and sells stocks and bonds, tracks their performance, and keeps meticulous records of his transactions.

But guess what: He would have earned a 4 percent higher rate of return last year by simply investing his money in a portfolio of stocks that match one of the major stock market indexes. He could have saved time, avoided brokerage fees, let someone else generate records for him through monthly account statements, and earned a higher rate of return. Such investment portfolios, and many others, are available to investors through mutual funds, the subject of the chapter.

Many investors lack the knowledge, capital, or time necessary to select individual financial securities for investment and to diversify their investments across securities and across time. For these investors, mutual funds provide an excellent investment opportunity. More than 8,000 mutual funds are available for investment. First offered in the United States in 1924, today mutual funds boast assets of more than $3.5 trillion.[1] In this chapter, we examine the nature of mutual funds, mutual fund performance, and the various types of mutual funds that are available to investors.

What Are Mutual Funds?

Recall from Chapter 12 that mutual funds are investment companies that accept funds from many investors who have similar investment objectives and use the pooled funds to purchase a diversified portfolio of securities. For example, bond funds restrict investment to bonds, equity funds invest in stock, and balanced funds invest in both stocks and bonds. In exchange for the investment, the investor is credited with a number of shares in the mutual fund. The price of mutual fund shares fluctuates with the performance of the securities owned by the fund. The owner of the mutual fund shares may sell his or her shares of the mutual fund at any time.

Administration of Mutual Funds

Management companies (such as Dreyfus, Fidelity, and T. Rowe Price) administer mutual funds. These companies have investment advisors who analyze investments and make recommendations, and fund managers who decide when to buy and sell securities. Each mutual fund is designed and managed to meet the investment objectives of a specified group of investors. Common investment objectives of mutual funds include current income, capital appreciation, income and appreciation, conservation of principal, and tax avoidance. Exhibit 14.1 presents information about one of the largest mutual funds, the Fidelity Magellan Fund, administered by Fidelity Investments. Note in the upper left-hand corner that this fund's objective is growth.

Composition of Mutual Funds

portfolio composition
The combination of individual securities in a portfolio.

Although sometimes viewed as monoliths, mutual funds are made up of many individual security investments. **Portfolio composition** refers to the individual securities in the portfolio. Referring to Exhibit 14.1, the portfolio composition of the Fidelity Magellan mutual fund is described just above the Morningstar logo at the bottom of the page. Under "Composition," we learn that as of January 1997, Fidelity Magellan had 5.7 percent of assets in cash, 93.5 percent in stocks, and 0.8 percent in bonds. In the lower right-hand corner, the sector weightings are provided. We see that of the stocks in the portfolio, cyclical industrial companies had the highest weighting (23.2 percent), followed by services (16.3 percent) and energy (16.1 percent). Under "Portfolio Analysis," we learn that Fidelity Magellan held 529 different stocks and 26 fixed-income (bonds, for example) securities. The largest individual security positions were in U.S. Treasury notes (2.90 percent), Caterpillar (2.01 percent), and CSX (1.53 percent). The fund manager, Robert E. Stansky, listed in the left-hand column just below the description of the fund, is free to buy and sell securities at any time. If the fund manager invests in securities that perform well, the portfolio will also perform well. If the securities selected do not perform well, the overall performance of the portfolio will also be unfavorable.

Mutual Fund Share Prices: The NAV

net asset value (NAV)
The per unit price of a mutual fund—the price at which shares are purchased and redeemed.

One of the most quoted values with regard to mutual funds is the net asset value. The **net asset value (NAV)** of a mutual fund is the per unit price of the fund—the price at which shares are purchased and redeemed. The net asset value is determined by summing the market value of the assets in the mutual fund portfolio, subtracting relevant fees and expenses, and dividing by the number of mutual fund shares outstanding.

Exhibit 14.1

Fidelity Magellan Fund Information

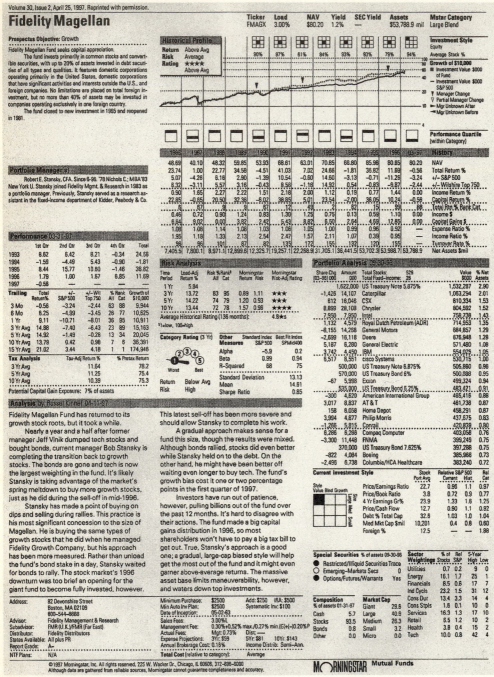

Source: Reprinted by permission of Morningstar, Inc.

If the securities in the fund perform well, their value will increase, and the NAV will rise. If the fund does not perform well, the NAV will decline. The NAV of the Fidelity Magellan Fund, at this time $80.20, is provided at the top of the page, just above the chart. In the table below the chart, the historical NAV of the Magellan Fund from 1985 to 1996 is provided. An investor's return is determined by the change in the NAV plus any income distributed by the fund to the mutual fund share-holders.

Closed-End Versus Open-End Funds

closed-end fund A mutual fund that issues a fixed number of shares; after the shares have been sold, the fund is closed and will nei-ther buy back shares nor issue additional shares.

There are two basic categories of mutual funds: closed-end funds and open-end funds. **Closed-end funds** make an initial offering of a fixed number of shares; after this offering, the fund is closed and will neither buy back shares nor issue additional shares. There is an active secondary market for closed-end fund shares, with most closed-end fund companies listed on the New York Stock Exchange. Closed-end fund shares may sell for more or less than the net asset value, depending on supply of and demand for shares of the fund, investor perceptions, and value of the underlying securities.

open-end fund A mutual fund that stands ready to repurchase shares and to issue new shares.

Open-end funds are the dominant form of mutual fund. **Open-end funds** stand ready to repurchase shares and to issue new shares. As many new shares will be issued as demand from investors dictates. Open-end shares are highly liquid, and transactions are based on the net asset value of the fund at the time of the transaction. Occasionally, an open-end fund will stop issuing shares once the fund has reached a specified size. As noted in the upper left-hand corner of Exhibit 14.1, Fidelity Magellan closed to new investment in 1965 and reopened in 1981.

Unit Investment Trusts

unit investment trust A pool of bonds or mort-gage-backed securities assembled by a brokerage house.

An investment vehicle that is similar to a mutual fund is the unit invest-ment trust. A **unit investment trust** is a pool of bonds or mortgage-backed securities assembled by a brokerage house. The brokerage then sells portions of the trust to investors. There are two major differences between unit investment trusts and mutual funds. First, there is no "active" management of the unit investment trust. Once assembled, the trust "runs its course," continuing to operate until all the securities in the portfolio mature or the trust is liquidated. Second, it may be difficult to obtain information about the trust at the time of the purchase.

Sources of Information About Mutual Funds

Investors have a number of sources of information about mutual funds available to them.

Consider This

Learn the basics about mutual funds, track prices and performance, and get lots of other information at the Mutual Fund Investor's Center at:

http://www.mfea.com/

Insight   14.1   Getting the Most from a Prospectus

When you purchase shares of a mutual fund, the Securities and Exchange Commission requires that a prospectus describing your investment choice be made available to you.

Here is a list of some of the most important aspects of a prospectus:

Objectives and Strategies— One of the most important roles of the prospectus is to define the investment objectives of a fund and set out its specific strategies. The fact that every mutual fund has a stated objective is one of the important differences between purchasing a mutual fund versus purchasing an individual stock. The first thing to do when you have a fund prospectus in hand is to ask yourself, "Is this fund's objective my objective?" If not, you'll want to continue your search for a suitable fund. If it does match, read on to find out if you are comfortable with the specific strategies the fund will employ and whether you like the features the fund has to offer.

The fund's objective and strategies, as stated in the prospectus, are designed to provide an investor with a clear sense of how much risk and how much potential return a fund manager will seek and the types of securities in which the portfolio will invest.

All funds focus on achieving some measure of one or more of three basic objectives:

- Stability: Protecting your principal—the amount you invest—from risk of loss

- Growth: Increasing the value of your principal through increases in your share price

- Income: Generating a stream of income payments through interest or dividend payments from the securities in the portfolio

In general, when you make an informed decision to assume some risk, you create the opportunity for greater reward. Because of this tradeoff, no fund can maximize all three goals simultaneously, but will often mix and match them, depending on the type of fund.

The fund's specific investment strategies are discussed in the section entitled "Investment Policies." This section describes the fund's personality—the types of securities (stock, bond, or money market) it invests in to pursue its objective. This section will also identify the quality level of the securities the fund purchases, the types of issues involved (for example, Fortune 500 companies; small, younger companies; municipal authorities; governments), and the types of transactions and investment techniques the fund managers will use in pursuing the fund's objective.

Risks involved—The prospectus also describes the principal risks associated with investing in a certain type of mutual fund in general, and the fund you're reading about in particular. Whenever you invest in a security, a tradeoff exists: If you want to achieve a level of return, you need to invest in a fund with a corresponding level of risk. Only you can decide what level of risk is appropriate for you.

All fees charged—At the front of the prospectus is a table showing any and all fees the fund

---

prospectus A disclosure document describing the operations of a mutual fund, including important financial data about the fund.

■ Each mutual fund has a prospectus. A **prospectus** is a disclosure document describing the operations of the fund, including important financial data about the fund. Some tips for getting the most from a mutual fund prospectus are discussed in Insight 14.1.

■ In addition to the prospectus, investment companies prepare annual reports and other reports about the company and the various funds offered.

charges. This table is divided into three sections: *transaction expenses* a fund will charge, including any sales commissions, reinvestment charges, redemption fees, and costs to exchange shares; *management fees,* any "12b-1" fees (12b-1 fees are asset-based fees that are generally assessed annually by certain funds to support marketing and distribution efforts), other expenses, and a *hypothetical example* that provides the total dollar amount of expenses the fund would charge an investor over one-, three-, five-, and 10-year periods.

Financial Highlights—Like the fee tables, this condensed financial statement also appears in the front section of every prospectus. In tabular form, year by year, this section includes the following:

- Total return: The most common yardstick used to measure the performance of a fund. Total return is based on a combination of capital return plus income and capital gain distributions, if any, expressed as a percentage gain or loss in value.
- Net distributions made by fund: The total dollar amount of income per share that the fund distributed in income and/or capital gains to shareholders each year for the last ten years (or, if the fund is less than ten years old, for the life of the fund).

- Change in net asset value: This listing tells you how the fund's net asset value (share price) has fared from year to year, adjusted for any distributions.

- Ratio of operating expenses to average net assets: The total of a fund's operating expenses divided by the average net assets under management for that year. This figure provides a useful and consistent way to compare expenses among two or more funds.

- Portfolio turnover rate: A measure of the buying and selling activity in the fund's investment portfolio. This figure can be another clue to a fund's expense level, because a fund with a higher turnover rate will tend to have higher expenses.

Minimum initial investment amount—Minimums vary among fund families. Often, the minimum initial investment requirement for opening an IRA account will be lower.

Services available and how to purchase, exchange, and sell shares—It can pay to review this section early for the services you'll need later, such as automatic investing, telephone redemption, and the various ways to buy or sell fund shares.

Fund reports fill out the picture—Once you've decided to invest in a fund, you will continue to receive detailed information about your investment choice. As a source of information about the progress of a particular fund, the fund's annual and semiannual reports are second only to the prospectus in importance. Issued at least twice a year, and in the case of certain funds, quarterly, the fund report describes how well a fund performed during the period covered. The fund report also discusses the fund's investment strategies and specific changes in the portfolio and, perhaps most important, places the fund's performance in the context of current economic and market activity.

Source unknown.

■ A number of investment services also track mutual fund performance. Two widely used investment services are *Value Line* and *Morningstar.* A *Morningstar* exhibit for one of the largest mutual funds, Fidelity's Magellan Fund, is shown in Exhibit 14.1. Many libraries subscribe to these frequently-updated references.

■ Personal finance magazines (such as *Kiplinger's,* and *Smart Money*) also cover mutual funds and report mutual fund performance.

■ As with other areas of personal finance, more and more information about mutual funds is becoming available on the Internet. In fact, you can access many mutual fund investment companies directly via the Internet.

Should You Invest in Mutual Funds?

Are mutual funds the right investment for you? In this section, we discuss how you can earn money by purchasing shares of a mutual fund and the advantages and disadvantages of mutual fund investing.

How Mutual Fund Investors Earn Money

Mutual fund investors can earn money from their investment in three ways:

■ A fund may receive income in the form of dividends and interest on the securities it owns. A fund will pay its shareholders nearly all the income it has earned in the form of dividends.

■ The value of the securities a fund owns may increase. When a fund sells a security that has increased in value, the fund realizes a capital gain. At the end of the year, most funds distribute these capital gains (less any capital losses) to investors.

■ If a fund does not sell the securities that have increased in value, the price of its shares (its NAV) increases. A higher NAV reflects the higher value of each investor's shares. An investor who sells shares that have increased in value makes a profit (also a capital gain).

Usually mutual funds give investors a choice: The fund will pay you dividends and capital gains in cash, or you can have them reinvested in the fund and purchase more shares.[2]

Advantages of Investing in Mutual Funds

Mutual funds provide a number of advantages to investors.

■ A major advantage is instant diversification since the assets are invested in many different securities. The risk to the purchaser is reduced through this portfolio diversification.

■ Initial investment requirements of many mutual funds are low, with some funds accepting less than $1,000. Many funds will also accept small additional investments.

■ The ability to make additional purchases of mutual fund shares by reinvesting income (dividends) and capital gains distributions is another advantage. Not only is reinvestment convenient, but mutual fund investors also reduce their risk through dollar-cost averaging. Recall that dollar-cost averaging is a strategy through which smaller investments are made periodically at many different prices. The result is a lower average cost per share than if a single large purchase was made at the "wrong time."

■ Purchase and sale of mutual fund shares is relatively simple and often can be done by mail or through a phone call.

■ Individuals with investment expertise manage mutual fund assets.

■ Most mutual fund companies offer a "family of funds." A **family of funds** is a group of mutual funds with different objectives and asset composition under the management of the same investment company. If your objectives change or if you are not satisfied with the performance of one fund, you can easily switch to another fund.

family of funds A group of mutual funds with different objectives and asset compositions under the management of the same investment company.

Disadvantages of Investing in Mutual Funds

There are also some disadvantages associated with mutual fund investments.

■ Mutual funds are characterized by a number of fees, which we discuss in the next section.

■ Even though mutual funds are diversified and managed by investment professionals, it is possible to lose money because of poor decisions by the fund manager.

■ The mutual fund's rate of portfolio turnover may be high. **Portfolio turnover** is the amount of financial securities sold in one year versus the total assets of the fund. A high rate of turnover means higher transactions costs for the fund and possibly larger taxable capital gains distributions to mutual fund shareowners.

portfolio turnover The amount of financial securities sold by a mutual fund in one year versus the total assets of the fund.

Costs of Investing in Mutual Funds

As just noted, mutual funds are characterized by a number of fees, sometimes called *loads,* including purchase fees, sales fees, management fees, promotional fees, tax loads, and reinvestment loads.

Purchase and Sales Fees

front-end load A charge levied at the time of purchase.

Many mutual funds charge purchase fees. A **front-end load** is a charge levied at the time of purchase. For example, if the front-end load is 3 percent of the amount invested, and you invest $1,000, the purchase fee is $30 (3% × $1,000). The net proceeds, $970, are actually invested, not the gross amount. The average purchase charge for front-end loaded mutual funds is 4 to 5 percent. Some funds use a sliding scale under which the size of the front-end load decreases with the size of the investment.

sales charge A load levied at the time the mutual fund shares are redeemed. Also called a redemption fee or back-end load.

As an alternative to purchase fees, some mutual funds levy sales charges at the time of sale. A **sales charge** (also called a **redemption fee** or **back-end load**) is a load levied at the time the mutual fund shares are redeemed. Thus, if the gross proceeds from the sale of your mutual fund shares are $50,000, you may net only $49,000 if there is a 2 percent sales (redemption) fee. With some funds, the back-end load disappears with the passage of time. For example, a fund may levy a 4 percent redemption fee if you sell your mutual fund shares within three years of purchasing the shares and no fee if you sell your shares after three years. Some mutual funds have both a front-end load and a sales charge.

no-load mutual fund Mutual fund that does not charge purchase fees.

You may have heard of **no-load mutual funds.** These are mutual funds that do not charge purchase fees.[3] No-load mutual funds do not employ salespeople, as many load funds do, to market the funds. Rather, interested investors can learn about the funds through the financial press and other avenues.[4] Although there are no purchase fees, no-load funds do charge other fees, such as sales (redemption) fees, management fees, and promotional fees. We describe the latter two fees later in this section.

The issue of investment performance of load versus no-load funds naturally arises. Why should you pay a purchase fee for a load fund if there is no benefit in doing so? A recent study (see Insight 14.2) found that over a five-year period, investors in no-load and low-load (3 percent or less) mutual funds earned a 42.0 percent return, whereas investors who bought load funds earned only 34.6 percent over the same period.[5] As noted in Insight 14.2, these figures do not reflect purchase and sales charges, but they do reflect other fees. A few words of explanation are needed, however. No-load investors tended to be more aggressive, investing more of their money in mutual funds that invest in common stock. Load fund investors tended to be less aggressive, investing a higher percentage of their money in mutual funds with higher percentages invested in bonds and money market instruments. Investors who purchased load funds also tended to be older, which often contributes to a more conservative investment approach.

Management Fees

management fees Fees assessed by a mutual fund to compensate the professionals who make the investment decisions and to cover the cost to the fund of securities transactions and basic overhead.

Management fees are assessed to compensate the professionals who make the investment decisions and to cover the cost to the fund of securities transactions and basic overhead costs. Management fees are assessed whether or not there is a front-end load or a sales charge. The average management fee is between .5 and 1 percent of the mutual fund's assets. The fee may be assessed as a flat percent of fund assets or may be based on a sliding scale that decreases as the size of the fund increases.

Promotional Fees

12(b)-1 fee A fee that may be assessed by a mutual fund to cover the cost of advertising and promoting the fund.

Another fee that may be assessed is a **12(b)-1 fee,** which covers the cost of advertising and promoting the mutual fund. This fee takes its name from a 1980 Security and Exchange Commission regulation that permits a mutual fund to deduct these fees directly from the assets of the plan. These fees are usually between one fourth and one half of 1 percent of plan assets. Given the level of competition among mutual funds, marketing efforts are important in attracting additional capital for investment.

Tax Loads

tax load A built-in tax liability that is part of a mutual fund's net asset value; it consists of realized but not yet distributed capital gains and unrealized capital gains.

An additional fee that mutual fund investors may not be aware of is the mutual fund's tax load. **Tax loads** are built-in tax liabilities that are part of a mutual fund's net asset value. They consist of realized but not yet distributed capital gains and unrealized capital gains. For example, assume that you purchase a mutual fund share in October and the NAV is $50. Further assume that the mutual fund sells some securities that have appreciated in value and that the fund distributes the capital gain in December, when the NAV of the fund has fallen to $45. Interestingly, you will have to pay taxes on the capital gains distribution from the mutual fund even though your NAV declined by 10 percent since you invested in the fund. Although the gain in value of individual securities in the fund may have occurred long before you owned shares of the fund, investors who are fund owners when realized capital gains are distributed must pay tax on the gain. A goal of mutual fund investors is price appreciation, but you should be aware of unrealized capital gains and realized but not distributed capital gains when you purchase mutual fund shares. These capital gains are usually distributed near year end, and are common when there has been a significant increase in the value of the securities in the fund during the year.[6]

Reinvestment Loads

reinvestment load A fee charged by a mutual fund for the reinvestment of dividends or capital gains distributions.

Mutual fund investors can often make additional purchases through reinvestment of income or capital gains distributed by the mutual fund. For example, a mutual fund shareholder may elect to reinvest a $250 dividend paid by the mutual fund rather than to receive a cash dividend. Usually dividends and capital gains can be invested without a fee. However, some mutual funds levy a **reinvestment load,** a fee charged for the reinvestment of dividends or capital gains distributions.

Insight   14.2   No-Load Mutual–Fund Shareholders Find Rewards in a Riskier Strategy

No-load mutual-fund investors get better results. Period.

Surprised? You shouldn't be. Folks who avoid brokers, and buy no-load funds instead, don't just save on commissions. They also put far more money into stock funds, which translates into higher long-run returns. Indeed, no-load fund investors have almost half their money in stocks, compared with less than a third for those who buy through brokers.

In recent years, this riskier strategy has been well rewarded. For proof, consider some numbers that were calculated for *The Wall Street Journal* by Chicago fund researchers Morningstar Inc. To get a handle on how good investors are at picking funds, Morningstar calculated asset-weighted returns for load and no-load fund investors.

What are asset-weighted returns? Imagine you want to know how well your portfolio

has performed. Maybe you own a technology fund, which has soared 50% in 1995. That's impressive, but the impact on your investment performance would have been modest if you had only 5% of your money in the fund. In fact, if the rest of your portfolio was in a money-market fund, your overall performance would have been thoroughly mediocre.

Using the same concept, Morningstar computer whiz Paul Gozali calculated two sets of asset-weighted returns, one for all the funds owned by no-load fund shareholders and the other for funds owned by load investors. He looked at returns for the five years ended December 1994, with each quarter's fund results weighted by fund assets at the beginning of that particular three-month stretch.

Stock funds with up-front sales charges of 3% or less, such as Fidelity Investments' low-

load stock funds, were included in the no-load category. The study assumed municipal-bond funds were owned by a person in the 31% tax bracket, and the dividends were adjusted upward accordingly. The calculations include institutional funds, such as those offered through 401(k) plans.

Result? based on the asset-weighted performance for stock, bond and money-market funds combined, no-load fund investors earned 42% for the five years ended December 1994, compared with 34.6% for those who bought load funds. These figures don't reflect upfront and back-end sales charges, which would further depress load-fund performance.

The numbers do, however, take into account annual fund expenses, which explains part of the performance gap. In recent years, the difference between load and no-load fund expenses

---

As you can see, many types of fees can be charged by mutual funds. Although the various fees may seem trivial, any fee that is charged reduces the investor's total return. Average mutual fund fees have increased significantly in recent years. In 1980, investors paid an average of $71 in fees for every $10,000 invested in mutual funds. By 1995, the average fees paid per $10,000 invested had increased to $99, according to one authority.[7] Although some expenses, such as front-end loads, are paid only once, other expenses, such as 12(b)-1 and management fees, are annual charges. Some suggestions for lowering the cost of mutual fund investing, thereby increasing your returns, are provided in Insight 14.3.

has widened as many load funds have tacked on annual 12b-1 fees, which are often used to reimburse brokers.

But while expenses explain part of the performance gap, a critical factor is the willingness of no-load shareholders to invest heavily in stocks. As of year-end 1994, for instance, no-load fund investors had 49.2% of their money in stock funds, 27.5% in bond funds and 23.3% in money funds, according to the Investment Company Institute, the trade group for the fund industry. By contrast, the mix for those who buy through brokers was 31.7% stock funds, 34.7% bond funds and 33.7% money funds.

The greater aggressiveness of no-load fund investors is nothing new. A decade ago, both load and no-load investors were fairly timid, with more than half their fund portfolios in money-market funds. Even then, however, no-load fund shareholders were noticeably more adventurous, with 28% of their money in stock funds at year-end 1984, compared with 19% for load fund investors.

Morningstar's findings don't jibe with an earlier study conducted by Dalbar Inc., a Boston research firm. Using a different methodology and looking at a different time period, Dalbar found that investors in load stock funds made more money than their no-load brethren. The firm found that load bond investors also got better results. But when it came to money-market funds, the edge went to the no-load camp.

Dalbar's study, however, didn't consider the radically different mix of stock, bond and money funds owned by load and no-load fund investors. "There's no question that the no-load investor is more aggressive," concedes Louis Harvey, Dalbar's president.

If no-load investors are bigger risk takers than their load-fund brethren, there's a good reason. Neal Litvack, a Fidelity executive vice president, says Fidelity's market research indicates that investors who buy through a broker tend to be older, which may explain their greater caution.

Mr. Litvack adds that these brokerage-house customers will typically own some individual stocks, so they may be taking more risk than it appears. Nonetheless, he says buyers of load funds tend to be more conservative.

Morningstar President Don Phillips notes that brokerage firms also are more likely to deal with less experienced shareholders. "The reluctant investors who left their bank kicking and screaming probably got introduced to funds by a broker," he says. Their first stop? Often, it's a load bond fund, not a stock fund.

Source: Jonathan Clements, "No-Load Mutual-Fund Shareholders Find Rewards in a Riskier Strategy," September 19, 1995. Reprinted by permission of *The Wall Street Journal,* ©1995 Dow Jones & Company, Inc. All Rights Reserved Worldwide.

Tax Implications of Investing in Mutual Funds

Next we will examine the tax treatment of mutual fund investments. First, we will consider capital gains; then, we will consider dividend income distributions; and finally, we will consider two problem areas.

Capital Gains. Just as with other types of investments, it is important to keep track of how much you invested in a mutual fund and any related transactions costs. These amounts are subtracted from the net proceeds when you sell your shares to determine whether you gained or lost money. Any gain that you realized is taxed currently at a maximum rate of 28 percent.

Insight   **14.3 Increase Your Returns by Cutting Fund Expenses**

The only sure-fire way to raise your investment returns is to lower your expenses. "If you pay 1% less in fees, you earn an additional 1% risk-free on your portfolio each year," says Don Phillips, president of Morningstar Inc., a Chicago mutual-fund tracking service.

But keeping costs down is getting harder and harder. Mutual-fund expenses have soared in recent years. Investors today pay $99 for each $10,000 invested in funds, up from $71 in 1980, according to Morningstar data.

Figuring out how much you really pay for your funds is more difficult. Many funds have dropped or lowered conspicuous upfront commissions in recent years and are recouping the cost by charging higher annual fees, which are less obvious. So while it always makes sense for cost-conscious investors to avoid paying commissions, they need to zero in on a fund's annual expenses, too.

There are several ways to lower fund cost—and increase returns:

Aim Low: One way to get a handle on a fund's expenses is to look at its so-called annual expense ratio, listed in *The Wall Street Journal*'s mutual-fund tables on Fridays. That figure tells you roughly what portion of the potential returns in your mutual-fund account went to cover a fund's fees during the previous year. For example, if

your stock fund gained 20% over the past year but has an expense ratio of 2%, it earned about 22% before expenses.

Many funds have different classes of shares, each with its own pricing structure. You can compare the costs of share classes by looking in the expense table listed in the fund prospectus. A brand-new fund won't have a historical expense ratio, but you can get an estimate of its fees in the prospectus.

How much should you pay? Stock funds charge 1.35% on average, which means you pay annual fees of $135 for each $10,000 invested in the average stock fund. Taxable bond funds charge 0.97% on average, or $97 for each $10,000 in an account.

Look Out for Hidden Costs: A few of the fees that fund investors pay aren't reflected in the annual expenses. For example, most investors don't know what they pay to cover the commissions and trading costs their funds incur. That is because these costs are deducted from a fund's assets and aren't part of its fees.

Number-crunchers at Morningstar estimate that the average fund loses three-tenths of 1% of its value in commissions. That figure could be as high as 1% or more in funds that trade frequently, says Morningstar's Mr. Phillips.

Other things being equal, choose funds that trade the investments in their portfolios less fre-

quently. You can get an idea of how often a fund trades securities by asking your broker or a shareholder service representative for its turnover. Turnover measures roughly how often a fund changes the investments in its portfolio, so a turnover of 80% means a fund replaced about 80% of its portfolio last year.

If you would prefer to know precisely how much you lost to a fund's trading costs last year, consult the Morningstar Mutual Funds report, available in the reference section of many local libraries.

Be sure to look at the sales commissions you pay when you buy or sell fund shares, and any small-account fees. Loads have been shrinking, but small-account fees have been spreading.

Don't Overpay for Conveniences: The small but growing number of "no-fee" fund supermarkets have attracted thousands of bargain-shoppers during the past few years, in part because they are so convenient. The supermarkets offered by discount brokerage firms like Charles Schwab Corp. and Fidelity, for instance, allow investors to choose from hundreds of mutual funds without having to pay a load or transaction fee.

That sounds like a steal—until you consider the extra amount you pay for funds offered for sale. Funds at the three biggest no-fee supermarkets charge at least 50%

more than do other funds, according to an analysis by Morningstar reported in this newspaper earlier this week.

But there are a few ways to enjoy the all-in-one convenience offered by a mutual-fund supermarket without getting gouged. One is simply to choose the lowest-cost funds available in those programs. Another option that makes sense for long-term investors with sizable balances is to pay the supermarket operators a trading fee in order to buy low-cost funds that aren't on the no-transaction-fee menu.

Own Bonds Instead of Bond Funds: The continuing fees you pay for bond funds can really add up over the years.

When you buy corporate or municipal bonds, be sure to haggle over the spread that brokers earn on the sale. Mr. Costello suggests paying a spread of between one-quarter and half of one percent. You can buy Treasury securities without a broker through the Treasury Department's Bureau of the Public Debt or your nearest Federal Reserve Bank or branch.

Fork Over Less for Advice: Thousands of brokers and financial advisers who once earned commissions each time they sold a fund are now charging annual fees of 1% to 2% of the total value of an investor's account.

Most simply divide your account among different types of stock and bond funds, then rebalance the mix when it is out

How Fees Add Up

Here's an example of roughly how much an investor would have lost to annual fund fees and other costs if he had $10,000 in each of three popular mutual funds and paid a planner or broker 1.5% to manage the account. Grand total: $913.

	Berger One Hundred	Mutual Beacon	IAJ INT'L
Fund expenses*	$170	$75	$172
Fund brokerage costs†	13	22	67
TOTAL MUTUAL FUND FEES	183	97	239
Wrap or advisory fees (per fund)	150	150	150
TOTAL ANNUAL COST	333	247	389

* Based on the funds' published expense ratios, provided by Lipper Analytical Services Inc.
† Data from Morningstar Inc.

of whack. Is this basic service worth a fee of 2% a year? "I don't think so," Mr. Costello says. "Even 1% is too much if you have an account of more than $150,000 or more."

Many people can do that on their own. If you really feel you need help, you might save money by asking a financial planner to review your investments once or twice a year for a flat fee of, say, $100 to $125 an hour. If you decide to pay a percentage of your assets instead, be sure to negotiate the annual advisory or "wrap" fee.

Either way, ask the planner or broker to bill you, instead of allowing him to deduct his fee directly from your account. When you pay out of pocket, the cost of the service is less likely to slip your mind, Mr. Costello says.

Buy Low-Cost Load Funds on the Cheap: San Diego discount-brokerage firm Jack White & Co. offers a little-known way to do this. In its Connect program, White matches buyers and sellers of load funds with one another. Buyers pay $200 in lieu of the front-end sales charge on a fund. Sellers receive a $100 premium on their shares.

Add Up Your Fees at Least Once a Year: One of the reasons why people overpay for funds is that they never see exactly how much they have paid, in dollar terms. Many mutual-fund fees "are so seamless," Mr. Phillips says. "It's almost as if they weren't real."

Source: Vanessa O'Connell and Ellen E. Schultz, "Increase Your Returns by Cutting Fund Expenses," December 1, 1995. Reprinted by permission of *The Wall Street Journal*, ©1995 Dow Jones & Company, Inc. All Rights Reserved Worldwide.

Managers of the mutual fund may also sell securities that have appreciated in value. If the mutual fund distributes these capital gains to shareholders, they are taxed as capital gains rather than ordinary income. They are considered long-term gains regardless of how long the investor has owned shares in the fund. Capital gains are taxable income whether the shareholder takes the capital gain in cash or reinvests it.

Dividend Income. The taxation of dividends distributed by the mutual fund must also be considered. Although the source of income that some mutual funds distribute is interest income, when distributed from a mutual fund, it is considered dividend income for tax purposes. Ordinary dividends represent taxable income in the year the dividend is paid, whether the mutual fund shareowner receives the dividends in cash or reinvests the dividend. One exception is income distributed by municipal bond funds, which is exempt from federal income taxes and often from state income taxes.

Problem Areas. Two areas where questions often arise with regard to the tax treatment of mutual funds are the movement of funds from one mutual fund to another and the partial sale of mutual fund holdings. Unfortunately, it is not possible to simply transfer money from one mutual fund to another, even if the funds are members of the same mutual fund family, without tax implications. *When leaving a mutual fund, your shares must be sold and a new purchase made in another mutual fund. If there is a gain or loss on the sale, that gain or loss must be reported for tax purposes.*

The partial sale of mutual fund shares also creates tax questions. Suppose that you purchased 100 shares of a mutual fund in 1993, another 100 shares in 1995, and that by reinvesting dividends, you own an additional 25 shares. Further assume that you need some money and that, in 1997, you decided to sell 100 shares. Which 100 shares did you sell? Obviously, if you sold the shares that you bought at the lowest price, it will create the largest taxable gain and the largest tax liability. You are permitted to direct the mutual fund to sell specific mutual fund shares under the current tax code. Then you can match the purchase information for these shares with the sales information to determine the income tax consequences of the sale. If you do not direct the sale of specific shares, the shares that you first purchased will be deemed the shares that you sold. Obviously, it is important to keep good records of your mutual fund purchases and sales for tax purposes.

How Mutual Fund Transactions are Performed

We mentioned earlier that purchase and sale of mutual fund shares is relatively simple. How are mutual fund transactions actually performed?

Trading Closed-End Funds

Closed-end funds, as you may recall, have a fixed number of shares. These funds are traded on the stock exchanges just like the individual securities that compose the funds. Security brokers and dealers perform the purchase and sale of closed-end fund shares for investors and are compensated through commissions and fees. Remember that closed-end funds do not repurchase shares, so it is necessary to use a broker or dealer when you want to buy or sell shares of a closed-end fund.

Trading Open-End Funds

The steps involved in purchasing shares in an open-end mutual fund depend on whether the mutual fund is a load fund or a no-load fund.

Load funds are marketed in a number of ways. Some funds employ salespeople or market their funds through authorized brokers. Some load funds are also available through banks and discount brokers.

With no-load and low-load funds, you will have to do more of the work yourself. Since there is no salesperson, you will need to find a desirable fund and contact the fund directly. You can either write to the fund company or call them to request information about the fund, including a prospectus. Information about no-load funds is also available through investment tracking services, such as *Value Line* and *Morningstar,* and through financial publications, such as *Your Money, Kiplinger's,* and *Smart Money.* After you contact the fund, you will be sent a prospectus and an enrollment/order form. To make your first purchase, simply complete the form and return it to the fund, along with your initial investment. After making the initial investment, you can purchase additional shares through voluntary investments and by reinvesting capital gains and income distributions. Open-end mutual funds will repurchase shares at the NAV.

Consider This

Mutual Funds Interactive provides a wealth of information on investing in mutual funds, including expert commentary and links to useful fund-related sites, at:

http://www.brill.com/

Mutual Fund Performance

How can investors track the performance of mutual funds? As with stocks and bonds, daily mutual fund quotations appear in the business section of most major newspapers. The information usually provided includes the name of the fund, the net asset value (NAV), the increase or decrease in the NAV from the previous closing price, the objective of the fund, the performance of the fund for the year and over previous time periods, the front-end load (if any), and annual expenses as a percent of assets. Some quotations also include a relative ranking of the fund versus the performance of other funds that have a similar investment objective. Exhibit 14.2 illustrates how to read mutual fund quotations.

Although daily price fluctuations of a mutual fund can be considered, the performance record of a mutual fund over longer periods of time is of greater interest to mutual fund owners and prospective purchasers. In examining mutual fund performance, the two most important measures to consider are the total rate of return earned by the fund and the degree of risk of the fund.

The Rate of Return

total rate of return The rate of return generated through dividend payments, capital gains distributions, and price appreciation.

The relevant return measure is the fund's total rate of return. The **total rate of return** is the rate of return generated through dividend payments, capital gains distributions, and price appreciation. The total return over various time periods is often included in mutual fund price quotations, as it is in Exhibit 14.2. Your actual total rate of return may vary from the published return, depending on when you bought shares of the fund, whether you have reinvested your dividends and capital gains distributions or taken them in cash, and the fee structure of the fund. When appraising mutual fund performance, it is important to consider both the rate of return earned in recent years and the long-term rate of return provided by the fund.

Degree of Risk

What is the relevant risk measure for a mutual fund? For individual securities, the relevant measure of risk is the standard deviation of the returns generated by the security. However, when securities are combined in a portfolio, the relevant measure of risk is the beta coefficient of the security or fund. Recall from Chapter 13 that beta is a measure of relative price volatility. Beta tells you how much the returns of a security or a fund are expected to fluctuate in relation to changes in the rate of return of a market portfolio of assets. By definition, the beta of the market portfolio is 1.0. A security or fund with a beta greater than 1.0 is more volatile than the market, whereas a security or fund with a beta less than 1.0 is less volatile than the market. Referring once again to Exhibit 14.1, it is indicated almost exactly in the middle of the exhibit that the Fidelity Magellan Fund has a beta of 0.99. That means the fund is .01 (1 percent) less volatile than the market portfolio; so if the market advances or declines by 10 percent, we should expect the Magellan Fund to advance or decline by slightly less than 10 percent.

In addition to the fund's beta coefficient, some more specialized measures of risk are available. Some tracking services monitor the riskiness of the fund's return when the market as a whole is rising versus the riskiness of the fund's returns when the market is falling. Relative riskiness

Exhibit 14.2

Understanding Mutual Fund Quotations

Data come from two sources. The daily Net Asset Value (NAV) and Net Change calculations are supplied by the National Association of Securities Dealers (NASD). The NASD requires a mutual fund to have at least 1,000 shareholders or net assets of $25 million before being listed. Performance and cost data come from Lipper Analytical Services Inc.

Though verified, the data cannot be guaranteed by Lipper or its data sources. Double-check with funds before investing.

Performance calculations assume reinvestment of all distributions, and are after subtracting annual expenses. But figures don't reflect sales charges ("loads") or redemption fees.

These expanded tables appear Fridays. Other days, you'll find net asset value and the daily change and year-to-date performance.

● **NET ASSET VALUE CHANGE**

Gain or loss, based on prior day's NAV.

● **TOTAL RETURN**

NAV change plus accumulated income for the period, in percent. Assumes reinvestment of all distributions. Percentages are annualized for periods exceeding one year. Calculations are based on latest data from fund.

● **NET ASSET VALUE**

Per-share value calculated by the fund.

● **COMPANY**

Fund families in bold face.

● **ANNUAL EXPENSES**

Shown as a percentage, based on fund annual report. Covers all asset-based charges including distribution (12b-1) fees.

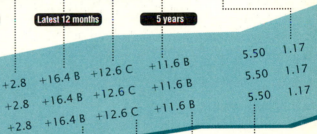

				4 weeks		3 years	
			Year-to-date		Latest 12 months		5 years	
XYZ Mutual:								5.50	1.17
								5.50	1.17
8.43	−0.09	Bond p	IB	+16.4	+2.8	+16.4 B	+12.6 C	+11.6 B	5.50	1.17
8.43	−0.09	Growth	GR	+16.4	+2.8	+16.4 B	+12.6 C	+11.6 B	
8.43	−0.09	Midcap Stock	MC	+16.4	+2.8	+16.4 B	+12.6 C		

● **FUND OBJECTIVE**

● **MAXIMUM INITIAL SALES COMMISSION**

In percent. Based on prospectus.

● **FUND NAME**

● **RANKING**

Compares performance among funds with same investment objectives and then ranked for time periods listed. Performance is measured from either the closest Thursday or month-end for periods of more than three years. **A**=top 20%; **B**=next 20%; **C**=middle 20%; **D**=next 20%; **E**=bottom 20%.

measures are also assigned based on the fund's stated objectives. Relative risk measures for mutual funds are provided in *Kiplinger's* and other personal finance publications.

Combining these two measures—risk and return—provides an excellent composite measure of mutual fund performance. A fund's actual rate of return can be compared to the expected rate of return given the level of risk that was undertaken. This concept, risk-adjusted performance, is often overlooked by investors, who too often consider only the rate of return earned on an investment. However, the degree of risk must also be considered. A mutual fund manager who earned a 12 percent return at a lower degree of risk has "outperformed" another manager who also earned a 12 percent return but who undertook a significantly greater level of risk.

Types of Mutual Funds

Many different types of mutual funds are available. The wide range of funds permits investors to match their investment objectives with the stated objectives of the fund. Next we briefly describe each of the major types of mutual funds. Then we discuss some guidelines for choosing the fund that's right for you.

Growth Funds

growth fund Mutual fund that emphasizes capital appreciation rather than current income.

long-term growth fund Mutual fund that invests in large, mature companies that are expected to perform well without undue risk to the purchaser.

aggressive growth fund Mutual fund whose investments are more speculative than those of long-term growth funds—for example, new companies that have just "gone public" and small companies that have yet to establish a record of performance.

income fund Mutual fund that emphasizes current income rather than capital appreciation.

A goal of many investors is growth in the value of their investment. **Growth funds** are mutual funds that emphasize capital appreciation rather than current income. Growth funds can be divided into two categories: long-term growth funds and aggressive growth funds. **Long-term growth funds** invest in large, mature companies that are expected to perform well without undue risk to the purchaser. Examples of long-term growth funds include Longleaf Partners, Fidelity Blue Chip Growth, and Harbor Capital Appreciation. **Aggressive growth funds** seek higher rewards but also accept more risk. Aggressive growth funds invest in new companies that have just "gone public," small companies that have yet to establish a record of performance, and other, more speculative investments. The AIM Aggressive Growth Fund, Janus Mercury Fund, and Franklin Small Cap Growth Fund are examples of aggressive growth funds.

Income Funds

Income funds are mutual funds that emphasize current income rather than capital appreciation. Some investors, especially retirees who have a fixed-income and face a low marginal tax rate, prefer current income to capital appreciation. Current income from such funds can be used to supplement other sources of retirement income. Some income funds invest in government and corporate bonds. Other income funds invest in stocks with high dividend yields. Income mixed (or balanced) funds invest in government and corporate bonds as well as stock issues, generating income from both interest payments and dividends. Some mutual funds that emphasize current income include Smith Barney Equity Income, USAA Income, and Oppenheimer Equity Income.

Growth and Income Funds

growth and income fund Mutual fund that combines the objectives of current income and capital appreciation.

Some investors desire a mix of current income with capital appreciation potential. **Growth and income funds** combine these objectives by purchasing common stock in companies that have a proven record of dividend payments and also have growth potential. Investors receive a steady stream of dividend income and at the same time are provided long-term capital gains income. Examples of funds that combine these objectives include Kent Growth and Income, Mutual Beacon, and Principal Preservation S&P 100 Plus.

Balanced Funds

balanced fund Mutual fund that combines the objectives of maintaining principal, generating income, and providing long-term growth.

Another common offering is a balanced fund. **Balanced funds** are mutual funds that have several objectives. These funds attempt to maintain principal, generate income, and provide long-term growth. In order to satisfy all these objectives, balanced funds not only diversify across companies but also across types of financial securities. Balanced funds invest in common stocks, preferred stocks, and bonds. Such funds are conservative investments, providing steady returns to purchasers without large swings in performance. Some balanced funds are Twentieth Century Balanced, Vanguard Wellington, and Eclipse Balanced.

Some critics have argued that balanced funds, along with some other types of funds described next, should be avoided by most investors. The perceived shortcomings of the funds are outlined in Insight 14.4.

Index Funds

index fund Mutual fund that attempts to match the performance of a known index by purchasing the same securities that comprise the index in the same relative weights.

The rate of return on investment indexes such as the Standard & Poor's 500, the Dow Jones 30 Industrial Average, and the Russell 2,000 is often used as a benchmark for comparing mutual fund performance. Over time, these indexes have posted solid gains. An **index fund** is a mutual fund that attempts to match the performance of a known index by purchasing the same securities that compose the index in the same relative weights. An S&P 500 index fund, for example, would own the same 500 securities that compose the S&P 500 index. Obviously, such funds, properly weighted, will mimic the index in terms of both risk and return.

Index funds also offer two cost savings to investors. Part of a mutual fund's expenses consist of costs incurred to research investment alternatives. Index funds do not have these expenses since the stocks bought and sold are simply those that comprise the index. Second, since index funds tend to buy and hold shares for long periods, transactions costs and portfolio turnover are reduced. Some popular index funds include Fidelity's Market Index Fund, Schwab-1,000, and Vanguard Index Trust 500.

Asset Allocation Funds

asset allocation fund Mutual fund in which the investment mix varies according to the fund manager's expectations.

Whereas index funds are an example of the buy-and-hold strategy discussed earlier, asset allocation funds (also called *flexible portfolio funds*) embody the market timing strategy. **Asset allocation funds** are mutual funds in which the investment mix varies based on the fund managers' expectations. For example, if the fund manager thinks that stocks and bonds will perform well in the near term, additional investments are made in stocks and bonds. If the fund manager turns "bearish" on stocks and bonds, these securities are sold, and a larger position in cash or cash-equivalents is maintained. Although asset allocation funds are relatively new, the same criticism of market timing with individual securities can also be levied against market timing with mutual funds: It is difficult to consistently predict market movements. Research has shown that it is difficult for market-timers to beat a simple buy-and-hold strategy.

Life-Cycle Funds

life-cycle fund Mutual fund that invests in a broad array of securities; the investment mix varies slightly in response to expected investment performance; similar to, but more conservative than, an asset allocation fund.

Closely related to asset allocation funds are a relatively new type of mutual fund called life-cycle funds. A **life-cycle fund** is a mutual fund that invests in a broad array of securities. Fund managers slightly alter the investment mix in response to expected investment performance. For example, a life-cycle fund may have 50 percent of its assets invested in equities. If the fund managers expect equity returns to increase in the next six months, an additional 5 to 10 percent of fund assets would be invested in equities. Although life-cycle funds are similar to asset allocation funds, the changes in the investment mix are more conservative. Returns of life-cycle funds exhibit less variability than the returns of asset allocation funds.

Sector Funds

sector fund Mutual fund that concentrates investment in a single area (or sector) of the economy.

Sector funds are mutual funds that concentrate investment in a single area (or "sector") of the economy. Sector funds are riskier than some other types of mutual funds because they are not diversified across several industries, and stock returns of companies in the same industry tend to be highly correlated. Funds that concentrated in pharmaceutical companies and medical care, for example, experienced sharp price declines when President Clinton's health care reform proposal was being debated. When it became clear that a reform bill would not be enacted, these funds rallied.

If you choose the "right" sector, sector funds offer significant rewards; however, if you choose the "wrong" sector, you cannot count on performance of stocks in other industries to offset the poor performance in the sector you selected. Sector funds can be used as one part of a diversified portfolio; however, holding sector funds in isolation is a risky investment strategy. Examples of sector funds include Putnam Health Sciences, Kemper Technology, and Seligman Communication & Info A.

International and Global Funds

global equity fund Mutual fund that invests in the stock of U.S. companies and companies based in other nations.

international equity fund Mutual fund that invests all or almost all of the fund assets in the stock of companies located in other countries.

global bond fund Mutual fund that invests in debt securities issued by U.S. companies and foreign companies.

For additional diversification benefits, some investors look outside the United States. A number of mutual funds are available that hold securities issued by foreign countries. Investors interested in common stock can purchase global equity funds and international funds. **Global equity funds** invest in the stock of U.S. companies and companies based in other nations. **International equity funds** invest all or almost all of the fund assets in the stock of companies located in other countries. Global bond funds are available for mutual fund investors who desire current income. **Global bond funds** invest in debt securities issued by U.S. companies and foreign companies. Some global and international funds include Harbor International, Scudder Global, GAM Global, and Ivy International.

Investors interested in international funds must consider a type of risk not faced by investors in domestic funds: exchange rate risk. This is the risk that the value of the relevant foreign currency will fall in comparison to the value of the U.S. dollar. Should this occur, the value of the fund will fall. Conversely, if the value of the foreign currency increases compared to the U.S. dollar, mutual funds holding securities issued by the foreign country will benefit from this increase.

Municipal Bond Funds

municipal bond mutual fund Mutual fund that purchases municipal bonds issued in states and cities across the country or specializes in municipal bonds issued by political subdivisions in a single state.

Earlier in this section, we mentioned government and corporate bond funds as one type of income fund. Among the other types of mutual funds that specialize in bonds are municipal bond funds. **Municipal bond mutual funds** purchase municipal bonds issued in states and cities across the country or specialize in municipal bonds issued by political subdivisions in a single state. As you may recall, municipal bonds are tax-advantaged in that interest income is exempt from federal income tax and often exempt from state income tax. This favorable tax

Insight 14.4 Within the Families of Mutual Funds, These Are Relatives Worth Avoiding

Some mutual funds are in a class of their own—the wrong class.

If you're shopping for funds, there are dozens of different types to choose from. But some categories I wouldn't touch:

Balanced Funds These aren't a bad bet for novice investors on modest budgets. But if you have more than a few thousand dollars to invest, I would look elsewhere.

How come? Balanced funds aim to provide one-stop shopping by combining stocks and bonds in a single portfolio. Trouble is, the stock portion typically gets invested in blue-chip shares, while the bond section is given over to high-quality taxable bonds.

What if you'd be better off with municipal bonds, because of your lofty tax bracket? What if you want a more diversified stock portfolio, including small-company shares and for-

eign securities? What if the fund manager changes the stock-bond mix, so that the fund is too meek or too aggressive for your taste? You start to see the problems.

Moreover, balanced funds charge annual expenses averaging 1.27%, barely less than the 1.38% levied by pure U.S. stock funds. So balanced funds are a bargain? Not at all, when you consider that 40% to 50% of a balanced fund is given over to bonds, and there are plenty of bond funds that charge far less than 1% a year.

Asset-Allocation Funds If you want a fund that does it all, you might try digging among the asset-allocation funds. Often included in the category are the new life-cycle funds, which do a much better job of providing one-stop shopping than traditional balanced funds.

But pick carefully. Many asset-allocation funds are

either market timers or market timers in drag. "There are only a few hard-core market-timing asset-allocation funds," says Catherine Voss Sanders, editor of Morningstar Mutual Funds, a Chicago newsletter. "Most see themselves as asset allocators who aren't making all-or-nothing bets."

But whether they call themselves market timers or asset allocators, these funds are basically doing the same thing: They're trying to make money by guessing which way markets are headed. Many experts believe it's all but impossible to make such predictions. Indeed, few of these funds have covered themselves with glory, and I doubt the record will get much better.

Global Funds If you invest in foreign stocks, you can buy either an international fund or a global fund. International funds invest exclusively abroad, while global funds buy a mix of

---

treatment also applies to municipal bond mutual funds. Although the rate of return on a municipal bond fund may appear low compared to other mutual funds, you must remember that returns quoted for other funds are fully taxable. SAFECO Municipal Bond, Blanchard Flexible Tax Free, and Nuveen Municipal Bond are examples of these funds.

High-Yield (Junk) Bond Funds

high-yield (junk) bond fund Mutual fund that invests in debt securities rated BB or lower by Standard & Poor's, and Ba or lower by Moody's.

Aggressive investors may consider the purchase of shares in a high-yield bond fund. **High-yield (junk) bond funds** are mutual funds that invest in debt securities rated BB or lower by Standard & Poor's, and Ba or lower

U.S. and foreign shares.

I much prefer international funds, because you know exactly how much foreign exposure you're getting. Global funds, meanwhile, are all over the map. G.T. Global Growth & Income Fund has 85% of its money abroad, for instance, while Keystone Global Opportunities Fund has 58% in U.S. securities.

Global funds are also a pricey bunch, according to Morningstar. They levy average expenses of 1.95%, far above the 1.71% average for international funds.

Foreign-Bond Funds Scott Lummer, a managing director with Ibbotson Associates, a Chicago research firm, says that if you want money abroad, consider skipping foreign-bond funds and buying a foreign-stock fund instead.

Why? When foreign bonds do well, because of a weakening dollar or falling foreign interest rates, foreign stocks are likely to do even better. In addition, Mr. Lummer says, foreign-stock funds are often a better way to diversify a U.S. portfolio.

Many investors put money abroad because foreign securities sometimes provide offsetting gains when U.S. investments get whacked. That happens partly because foreign markets don't move in sync with the U.S. and partly because of currency swings.

But with foreign-bond funds, you can lose part of this diversification advantage because the funds typically do a lot of currency hedging. At the beginning of this year, for instance, Scudder International Bond Fund had eliminated much of its currency exposure. Result? When the dollar collapsed in early 1995, the fund hardly benefited.

A Scudder spokeswoman says that the fund's managers hedged a portion of their currency exposure because they felt the dollar was too cheap. "That proved to be premature," she says. "But we've continued to hedge and, over the long run, we think that'll benefit shareholders."

Sector Funds If you like Vegas, you'll love sector funds, which invest all their money in one market sector, such as gold, energy or technology. These single-industry crapshoots can make you a mint, or cost you your shirt.

But whatever happens, the ride will be rough, which can be unnerving for all but the most hardened investors. And sector funds sure aren't cheap. They levy hefty average annual expenses of 1.64%, and many also charge a sales commission. Just say no.

Source: Jonathan Clements, "Within the Families of Mutual Funds, These Are Relatives Worth Avoiding," August 22, 1995. Reprinted by permission of *The Wall Street Journal*, ©1995 Dow Jones & Company, Inc. All Rights Reserved Worldwide.

by Moody's. On the positive side, these funds offer the possibility of earning a higher rate of return than other investments offer. From a risk perspective, holding a portfolio of junk bonds is less risky than holding a single junk bond. In addition, these funds are actively managed, and fund managers may sell off lower-quality issues. On the negative side, however, investors must remember that the ratings assigned to the securities that compose junk bond portfolios were not assigned by accident. Although high-yield bonds have the potential of providing higher rates of return than higher-quality bond issues, the risk of default by the bond issuer must also be considered. PIMCO High Yield, Columbia High Yield, and Invesco High Yield are examples of this type of fund.

Money Market Mutual Funds

money market mutual fund Mutual fund that invests in short-term financial instruments that are traded in the money market rather than investing in capital market securities.

We briefly discussed money market mutual funds in Chapter 3, which examined savings alternatives. Money market mutual funds are suitable for savers who desire safety and immediate access to their funds. Rather than investing in capital market securities, **money market mutual funds** invest in short-term financial instruments that are traded in the money market. Such funds are usually not appropriate for investment purposes since returns on savings instruments, on average, are lower than returns on investment alternatives. Some money market mutual funds include Fidelity Spartan, Dreyfus Basic, and Olde Premium Plus.

Precious Metals Funds

precious metals mutual fund Mutual fund that invests directly or indirectly in precious metals, including gold, silver, and platinum.

Precious metals funds are mutual funds that invest directly or indirectly in precious metals, including gold, silver, and platinum. Such funds purchase shares of companies that engage in exploring for, mining, and processing precious metals, as well as making direct investments in the metals themselves. These funds are risky, and their recent performance has not been favorable. Examples of precious metals funds include Lexington Gold Fund, Van Eck Gold/Resources A, and United Services World Gold.

Ginnie Mae Funds

Ginnie Mae fund Mutual fund that invests primarily in mortgage-backed securities issued by the Government National Mortgage Association (GNMA, or "Ginnie Mae") and in other mortgage-backed securities.

Ginnie Mae funds are mutual funds that invest primarily in mortgage-backed securities issued by the Government National Mortgage Association (GNMA, or "Ginnie Mae") and in other mortgage-backed securities. The GNMA purchases government-insured FHA and VA mortgage loans from real estate lenders, pools these mortgages, and sells securities backed by the mortgages to investors. Principal and interest payments are made to the fund rather than individual investors, and the fund distributes income to mutual fund shareholders. Although the U.S. government guarantees the mortgages, there are risks in purchasing shares in a Ginnie Mae fund. The yield is not guaranteed, and there are fluctuations in the price of Ginnie Mae fund shares. As you might suspect, these share prices are highly influenced by changes in interest rates. Nevertheless, Ginnie Mae funds provide an excellent opportunity for individual investors to participate in the mortgage-backed securities market. Many mutual fund companies offer Ginnie Mae funds, including T. Rowe Price, Vanguard, Lexington, and Fidelity.

Social Choice Mutual Funds

Some investors would like their investments to reflect their personal beliefs and ethical principles. They might prefer to avoid investing in companies that produce alcohol, tobacco products, or weapons; companies that engage in gambling; companies and industries that damage the environment; companies that experiment on animals; or companies that have operations in countries in which there are human rights abuses. Responding to demands from this group of investors, some mutual fund companies have established "social choice" mutual funds. **Social choice mutual funds** are funds that restrict investment to companies their investors deem socially responsible. Such funds may adhere to a policy of investing in environmentally friendly companies only, companies that do not manufacture products investors believe to be objectionable, and companies that provide equal employment opportunities. The mutual fund prospectus lists the screens that are used when these funds purchase securities. Examples of social choice mutual funds include Dreyfus Third Century Fund, The Pax World Fund, and Calvert Social Investment Fund.

social choice mutual fund Mutual fund that restricts investments to companies their investors deem socially responsible.

Value Mutual Funds

In Chapter 12, we discussed the relationship between risk and return. The highest-risk companies are those that are experiencing financial difficulty. However, these companies also present the opportunity to earn high returns. Holding securities of one company that is experiencing financial problems is very risky. However, some mutual funds provide the opportunity to diversify across financially troubled and unproven companies. **Value mutual funds** purchase financial securities of companies that are experiencing financial difficulty, new and unproven companies, and companies in depressed industries. Such funds are also known by the colorful name "vulture funds." Although these funds have the possibility of providing an above-average return, like high-yield bond funds, they are also risky.

value mutual fund Mutual fund that purchases financial securities of companies that are experiencing financial difficulty, new and unproven companies, and companies in depressed industries.

Finally, there are mutual funds that specialize in real estate investments. Another type of real estate investment that is similar to a mutual fund is called a real estate investment trust (REIT). We discuss these investment alternatives in Chapter 15.

Choosing the Mutual Fund That's Right for You

Obviously, many types of mutual funds are available to investors. The question naturally arises, which mutual fund is best for you? The best answer is "it depends." Given the variety of funds available, you must match your objective, risk tolerance, and time horizon with the mutual fund. Some guidelines for choosing a type of fund based on the risk and reward tradeoff and your time frame are presented in Exhibit 14.3.

Once an investor selects the type of fund in which to invest, he or she must consider past performance, riskiness, asset composition, sales charges, management fees, the quality of management, and other factors before making an investment. Although holding shares of a single mutual fund is less risky than purchasing stock in a single company, investors should also consider the benefits of diversification across several different mutual funds.

As one of the quotations at the beginning of this chapter suggests, mutual funds present an excellent investment opportunity, especially for novice

Exhibit 14.3

Selecting the Proper Mutual Fund: Risk, Reward, and Time

Type of Fund	Share Price Fluctuation	Potential for Current Income	Potential for Growth
Money Market Fund	None	Moderate	None
Income Fund	Low to moderate	High	Low
Growth and Income Fund	Moderate	Moderate	Moderate
Growth Fund	High	Low	Moderate to high

If your time frame is	And you can accept	Then consider a
Less than 2 years	No risk to principal	Money market fund
	Some risk to principal in exchange for a slightly higher yield	Short-term bond fund
2–4 years	No risk to principal	Money market fund
	Some risk to principal in exchange for a slightly higher yield	Short-term bond fund
	Moderate risk with some growth potential	Intermediate-term bond fund or growth and income fund
4–6 years or more	No risk to principal	Money market fund
	Some risk to principal in exchange for a slightly higher yield	Short- or intermediate-term bond fund
	Moderate risk with moderate growth potential	Growth and income fund
	Market-sensitive price fluctuations in exchange for highest growth potential	Growth fund

Source unknown.

investors. Although mutual funds provide diversification and professional management, investors must be careful when selecting a fund to match the objective of the fund with their own objectives. The appendix at the end of this chapter provides some excellent guidelines for mutual fund investors.

SUMMARY

■ Mutual funds are investment companies that accept funds from many investors who have similar interests and use the pooled funds to purchase a diversified portfolio of securities.

■ Mutual funds are administered by management companies. Each fund is managed to meet the specific objectives of a specified group of investors.

■ The portfolio composition is the individual securities in the portfolio. The types of securities selected vary with the objectives of the fund.

■ The per unit price of a mutual fund is the net asset value (NAV). The NAV is the total value of the securities in the fund less expenses, divided by the number of mutual fund shares outstanding.

■ There are three categories of mutual funds: closed-end funds, open-end funds, and unit investment trusts.

■ Closed-end mutual funds have a limited number of shares. Shares of these funds are traded on the stock exchanges. Closed-end funds do not repurchase shares or issue additional shares.

■ Open-end funds are mutual funds that constantly issue new shares and stand ready to purchase shares already issued.

■ Unit investment trusts are mutual fund investments put together by brokerage houses. Unit investment trusts package existing securities (usually bonds) and sell portions of the trust to investors.

■ Investors can obtain information about mutual funds by reviewing the annual report, mutual fund prospectus, or the exhibit in *Value Line* or *Morningstar*.

■ Mutual fund investors can earn money from their investment through dividends and interest, capital gains distributions, and an increase in the NAV of the fund.

■ Mutual funds have a number of advantages to purchasers, including diversification across assets, low initial and additional investments, ease in buying and selling mutual fund shares, professional management, and the ability to switch to another member of the same mutual fund family.

■ Mutual funds also have some disadvantages, including a variety of fees the investor must pay, transactions costs, and poor performance because of bad investment decisions.

■ A number of different types of fees are associated with mutual funds, including front-end loads (purchase charges) levied at the time of purchase; sales (redemption) charges levied when the mutual fund is sold; management fees that are assessed to compensate fund managers, to cover the cost of securities transactions, and to defray basic overhead costs; 12(b)-1 fees that are assessed to cover the marketing and promotional expenses of the fund; tax loads, which are built-in tax liabilities that mutual fund purchasers may have to pay even though the gain occurred before they owned shares in the mutual fund; reinvestment loads, which are fees charged on reinvested income and capital gains distributions.

■ The tax treatment of mutual fund investments follows the same tax principles of other investments. Income that is distributed is currently taxable whether the dividend is reinvested or taken in cash.

■ Capital gains distributions from the mutual funds are taxed as capital gains rather than ordinary income. If the mutual fund investor sells his or her shares, any gains and losses are taxed as capital gains and losses rather than as ordinary income.

■ Closed-end funds are purchased through stock brokers and dealers.

■ Load open-end funds can be purchased from a salesperson who represents the fund, as well as through banks and discount brokers.

■ You can purchase no-load and low-load funds by contacting the fund directly and requesting information about the fund. You can buy and sell shares directly from the investment company.

■ To analyze the performance of mutual funds, you should consider both the total rate of return and the riskiness of the fund.

■ The total rate of return is the rate of return provided through dividend payments, capital gains distributions, and price appreciation.

■ The relevant risk measure for a mutual fund is the fund's beta coefficient. Beta measures the volatility of a fund's returns in relation to the returns of the market portfolio. Other relative measures of riskiness are also available.

■ Growth funds emphasize capital appreciation rather than current income.

■ Income funds emphasize current income rather than capital appreciation.

■ Growth and income funds provide both current income and capital appreciation potential.

■ Balanced funds attempt to maintain principal, generate income, and provide long-term growth.

■ Index funds attempt to match the performance of a well-known market index, such as the Standard & Poor's 500.

■ Asset allocation funds switch investment vehicles and the investment mix based upon the fund manager's expectations.

■ Life-cycle funds invest in an array of securities and slightly alter the investment mix based upon the fund manager's expectations.

■ Sector funds concentrate investment in a single area or sector of the economy.

■ Global bond funds and global equity funds invest in securities issued by companies in foreign countries.

■ Municipal bond funds invest in tax-exempt bonds issued by cities, counties, and other political subdivisions.

■ High-yield (junk) bond funds invest in debt securities that have been assigned low-quality ratings by the ratings services.

■ Money market mutual funds invest in short-term financial instruments traded in the money market.

■ Precious metals funds invest directly or indirectly in gold and other valuable metals.

■ Ginnie Mae funds invest primarily in mortgage-backed securities issued by the Government National Mortgage Association and in other mortgage-backed securities.

■ Social choice funds invest in environmentally friendly companies; companies that do not produce alcohol, tobacco products, or weapons; and companies that do not participate in activities that some investors find objectionable.

■ Value funds invest in financially troubled companies, new and unproven companies, and companies in depressed industries.

KEY CONCEPTS AND TERMS

Aggressive growth fund	International equity fund
Asset allocation fund	Life-cycle fund
Back-end load	Long-term growth fund
Balanced fund	Management fees
Closed-end fund	Money market mutual fund
Family of funds	Municipal bond mutual fund
Front-end load	Net asset value (NAV)
Ginnie Mae fund	No-load mutual fund
Global bond fund	Open-end fund
Global equity fund	Portfolio composition
Growth and income fund	Portfolio turnover
Growth fund	Precious metals mutual fund
High-yield (junk) bond fund	Prospectus
Income fund	Redemption fee
Index fund	Reinvestment load

Sales charge	Total rate of return
Sector fund	12(b)-1 fee
Social choice mutual fund	Unit investment trust
Tax load	Value mutual fund

QUESTIONS FOR REVIEW

1. Describe how mutual funds are organized and what is meant by "portfolio composition."

2. Explain the difference between a closed-end fund and an open-end fund.

3. What are the advantages of investing in mutual funds? What are the disadvantages of investing in mutual funds?

4. What are the different types of fees that are charged in conjunction with the purchase, sale, and ownership of mutual funds?

5. Explain the tax treatment of mutual fund dividend income distributions and capital gains distributions. Are dividend income and capital gain distributions taxable if they are reinvested?

6. How are mutual fund shares bought and sold?

7. What two measures should be considered when appraising the performance of a mutual fund?

8. How do the objectives and the securities purchased differ between growth funds and income funds?

9. What are index funds? What are sector funds? Which of these two types of funds offers investors the greater possible reward? Compare the diversification provided by each type of fund.

10. How do money market mutual funds differ from other mutual funds? Why are value funds and high-yield bond funds riskier than money market mutual funds?

PROBLEMS

1. The value of the assets that compose Ajax Mutual Fund is $100 million. Currently, there are 125,000 shares outstanding. Ignoring any fees and expenses, what is the net asset value (NAV) of this fund?

2. Josephina purchased 300 shares of Gauntlet Growth Fund six years ago at a net asset value of $33.50 per share. This year she decided to sell her 300 shares. The NAV per share had increased to $74.75 per share. Ignoring any expenses, what is Josephina's taxable gain on this sale?

3. Bill and Jill each decided to start investing in mutual funds. Each plans to invest $500 per quarter in a growth fund. Bill's fund has a 4 percent front-end load. Jill's fund is a no-load fund. Assuming that each investor sticks to the plan of investing $500 per quarter, how much more will Jill have invested in her fund after 10 years?

4. Parker Aggressive Growth Fund had a total year-end value last year of $42.85 million.
   a. Gerilyn Evans is the portfolio fund manager of Parker Aggressive Growth Fund. Her management fee is .65 percent of the year-end balance. How much will Gerilyn receive as a management fee?
   b. Parker Aggressive Growth Fund levies a 12(b)-1 fee equal to .25 percent of the year-end balance. How much will the fund be assessed for 12(b)-1 fees?

5. Madeline would like to invest in mutual funds. She has asked for your assistance in evaluating investment alternatives.
   a. Which of the following growth funds would you recommend:

	Fund A	Fund B
Historical return	15.70%	15.70%
Beta coefficient	1.40	1.10

   b. Which of the following balanced funds would you recommend?

	Fund C	Fund D
Historical return	8.20%	9.60%
Beta coefficient	.90	.90

INTERNET EXERCISES

1. NETworth is a megasite for investment research. You can, for example, sort through thousands of mutual funds according to criteria of your choice and then get more information on the funds. Go to this site at:
   http://networth.galt.com/

   Use the screening engine to find some funds that meet your investment criteria. Then find out more about the funds. You may have to register to get to some parts of the site, but registration is free.

2. The chapter noted that many mutual fund companies have World Wide Web sites. American Century (formerly Twentieth Century), Dreyfus, Fidelity, Janus, Putnam, T. Rowe Price, and Vanguard are a just few examples. Visit their sites at:
   http://www.americancentury.com/
   http://www.dreyfus.com/
   http://www.fid-inv.com/
   http://www.janusfunds.com/

http://www.putnaminv.com/

http://www.troweprice.com/

http://www.vanguard.com/

Compare the information and services available at these sites for mutual fund investors.

CASE APPLICATIONS

Case 1

Philip Wong is attempting to make an investment decision. He would like to invest in mutual funds. His broker mentioned three alternatives: open-end investment companies, closed-end investment companies, and unit investment trusts.

1. If Philip desires additional information about specific funds, which two types of funds have the most available information?

2. Which of these types of funds constantly issues new shares? Which type of fund, as a consequence of its design, will not last indefinitely?

3. Which of these funds are professionally managed?

Case 2

Jolene Foster is a financial advisor. Recently, a number of her clients have sought advice regarding the purchase of mutual funds. Based on the stated investment objective of each client, what type of mutual fund should Jolene recommend each client purchase?

1. Steve and Valerie Davis, a young couple with a high annual income, are interested in stocks that will appreciate significantly over time. They are willing to take greater risk in exchange for the opportunity to receive higher gains, and they do not desire current income.

2. Walter Collins, an environmentalist, wants to invest in securities issued by companies that strictly adhere to environmental guidelines. In addition, he does not want to invest in alcohol, tobacco, gambling, and defense companies.

3. Rick and Eileen Barnes are self-described "techies." They are convinced that technology stocks are an excellent investment. They would like to diversify their investment across technology companies.

4. Helen Greenberg prefers to invest in mutual funds that purchase both stocks and bonds.

5. Maria Gonzales is interested in investing in tax-free debt securities issued by the city in which she lives. She wonders if a mutual fund is available with this specialization.

6. David Smith would like to invest in a mutual fund in which the investment mix was slightly altered based upon expected performance of alternative investments. His prior experience with asset allocation funds has been unfavorable, and he desires less volatility.

7. Monique Richards would like to invest in government-backed mortgages. Unfortunately, she does not have $25,000 to purchase a Ginnie Mae certificate.

8. Ralph and Kathy Svenningsen would like a portfolio of stocks with the same risk and return pattern of the Standard & Poor's 500.

9. A self-described contrarian, Marilyn Van Dreesen would like to invest in companies that have depressed stock prices and in industries that are currently out of favor with other investors.

Case 3

Bayless Investment Company offers a family of mutual funds. One fund, the Bayless Equity Income Fund, is comprised of common stock issues that pay high dividends. Major stock holdings of this fund include phone companies, natural gas companies, petroleum companies, electric companies, and "mature" companies. The following questions refer to the Bayless Equity Income Fund.

1. The net asset value (NAV) of the Bayless Equity Income Fund recently was $46.75. At that time, there were 400,000 shares of the fund outstanding. What is your best estimate of the total market value of the Bayless Equity Income Fund?

2. The beta coefficient of the Bayless Equity Income Fund is .80. If the stock market rises by 8 percent, what is the Bayless Equity Income Fund expected to do?

3. Bayless Equity Income Fund carries a 4 percent sales load. Management fees are .40 percent of year-end assets. The fund has a 12(b)-1 fee of .25 percent of year-end assets. The fund charges a 5 percent sales fee if you sell shares during the first year, 4 percent during the second year, and so on, with the sales load disappearing after five years.

   a. Reggie Adams sold his 500 shares of Bayless Equity Income Fund after owning the shares for three and a half years. The sales price per share was $46.75. How much of the net proceeds will Reggie pay in sales fees? If Reggie paid $32.50 per share when he bought the 500 shares, what was Reggie's capital gain on this investment?

   b. Brittany Williams invests $500 each quarter in the Bayless Equity Income Fund. How much does Brittany pay in sales charges each year? What is her net investment in the fund each year?

   c. The NAV of Bayless Equity Income Fund was $42.125 last year at year end. At that time, there were 376,000 shares of the fund outstanding. Calculate last year's management fee and 12(b)-1 fee based upon the year-end value of the fund.

SUGGESTIONS FOR ADDITIONAL READING

Cheney, John M., and Edward A. Moses. *Fundamentals of Investing.* St. Paul, Minn.: West Publishing Company, 1992.

Cottle, Sidney, Roger F. Murray, and Frank E. Block. *Graham and Dodd's Security Analysis,* 5th ed. New York: McGraw-Hill, 1988.

Dolan, Ken and Daria Dolan. *Straight Talk on Money.* New York: Simon and Schuster, 1993.

Dunnan, Nancy. *Dun & Bradstreet Guide to $Your Investments$.* New York: Harper-Collins Publishers, 1994.

Malkiel, Burton. *A Random Walk Down Wall Street.* New York: W.W. Norton & Company, 1990.

Miller, Theodore J. *Invest Your Way to Wealth.* Washington: The Kiplinger Washington Editors, Inc., 1994.

Morris, Kenneth M. and Alan M. Siegel. *The Wall Street Journal Guide to Understanding Personal Finance.* New York: Lightbulb Press, 1992.

O'Connell, Vanessa. "Life-Cycle Funds Simplify Investment Choices." *Wall Street Journal,* August 4, 1995, pp. C1, C21.

Personal Financial Planning Guide. Ernst & Young. New York: John Wiley & Sons, 1995.

Sloane, Leonard. *The New York Times Personal Finance Handbook.* New York: Times Books, 1995.

Tyson, Eric. *Mutual Funds for Dummies.* Foster City, CA: IDG Books, 1995.

NOTES

1. Charles Gasparino, "Mutual-Fund Firms Eager to Give Advice," *Wall Street Journal,* February 21, 1997, pp. C1, C23.

2. This section is based on "Invest Wisely: An Introduction to Mutual Funds," advice from the U.S. Securities and Exchange Commission, October 21, 1996.

3. By a strict definition, no-load funds do not charge purchase fees. Some authors distinguish between low-load mutual funds (under 3 percent) and no-load mutual funds. Other authors classify funds that have a load of 3 percent or less as no-load funds.

4. Some brokerages also make no-load funds available. Charles Schwab, for example, offers more than 90 mutual funds with no loads or transaction fees.

5. Jonathan Clements, "No-Load Mutual-Fund Shareholders Find Rewards in a Riskier Strategy," *Wall Street Journal,* September 19, 1995, p. C1.

6. For an expanded discussion, see "Tax Loads: A Little Known Burden of Mutual Fund Investors," *Mutual Funds,* December 1994/January 1995, pp. 35–36.

7. Vanessa O'Connell and Ellen Schultz, "Increase Your Returns by Cutting Fund Expenses," *Wall Street Journal,* December 1, 1995, pp. C1, C16.

Appendix

The 25 Facts Every Mutual Fund Investor Should Know

Mutual funds are meant to provide a simple way for small investors to buy into the stock and bond markets.

But fund investing isn't always that simple. Here are 25 facts that every mutual fund investor ought to know.

1 Past stock fund performance is often a rotten guide to future results.

"Good past performance indicates that a fund did something good at some time—and that's it," says Kurt Brouwer, president of Brouwer & Janachowski, a San Francisco investment adviser.

He notes that a fund's brilliant track record may have been built by a fund manager who has since quit, or might be the result of one or two spectacular years that are unlikely to be repeated. Alternatively, the fund may have done well over the past three or five years because the fund's investment style has been in vogue—and is on the verge of going out of favor.

2 Even bad funds sometimes rank as No. 1 performers.

According to Lipper Analytical Services Inc., Nautilus Fund was the top-performing mutual fund in 1980, Lexington Strategic Investments claimed that honor in 1979, 44 Wall Street Fund in 1975 and Sherman Dean Fund in 1974. All four funds rank among the nation's worst long-term performers.

"Long-term losers are frequently No. 1 performers over short time periods," says John Rekenthaler, editor of Morningstar Mutual Funds, a Chicago newsletter. "By choosing the proper category and the proper time period, virtually any fund in existence can claim to be No. 1."

3 Even the best funds have their bad years.

Most stock funds pursue a single investment style. They might, for instance, favor growth companies, which have rapidly increasing profits, or value stocks, which appear cheap based on corporate assets or current earnings. If a fund's investment style is out of favor, it is likely to lag behind the market. That's what happened recently to the value-oriented Vanguard Windsor Fund.

"John Neff over at Windsor Fund had a terrible year in 1990," notes Gerald Perritt, editor of the Mutual Fund Letter, a Chicago newsletter. "If you had sold the fund, you would have been sorry. This is a man with a great track record."

4 Stock funds that get hit hard in market crashes aren't necessarily bad investments.

Pasadena Growth Fund and Twentieth Century Giftrust

Investors got pounded in the 1990 bear market. Brandywine Fund, Kaufmann Fund and Twentieth Century Ultra Investors were pummeled in the 1987 stock market crash. If you skipped these funds because of their rotten bear market performance, you would have been making a grave mistake. All of these funds rank among the fund industry's top long-term performers.

5 Most stock funds fail to beat the market.

According to Lipper Analytical, stock funds returned 13.5% a year over the 10 years through December, compared with 16.2% for the Standard & Poor's 500-stock index.

Funds charge annual expenses, they incur costs when they trade stocks and they generally keep at least 5% of assets in cash to meet redemptions, which acts as a drag on fund performance during bull markets. "All these things chip away at returns," says Mr. Perritt.

6 Owning an S&P 500 index fund doesn't mean you've indexed the market.

Many investors have taken to buying index funds, which simply buy the stocks that make up a particular stock market index and thereby seek to replicate the index's performance. But virtually all money invested in index funds is in S&P 500 stock index funds.

"People confuse indexing with indexing the S&P 500," says Morningstar's Mr. Rekenthaler. "A lot of people think the two are synonymous."

They aren't. The S&P 500 includes only U.S. large-company stocks that make up about 70% of the dollar value of the U.S. stock market. Analysts say investors should also consider indexing small-company stocks and foreign stocks.

7 Not all growth funds buy growth stocks.

Mutual fund companies classify stock funds with labels such as "equity-income," "growth" or "growth-and-income." But these classifications reflect a fund's investment goals. They don't tell you what investment style is used by a fund.

Funds classified as "growth funds," for instance, pay scant attention to a stock's dividend yield and instead emphasize potential share-price appreciation when picking stocks. Despite their name, growth funds don't necessarily buy growth stocks, which are those that have rapidly increasing earnings.

8 Mutual fund names are often misleading.

Consider a few examples. Dean Witter American Value Fund buys growth companies, not value stocks. The Strong funds don't necessarily have strong results: they are named after founder Dick Strong. Vanguard Windsor II isn't run by John Neff, the celebrated manager who runs Vanguard Windsor. Bond funds can use "government" in their name even if they have 35% of their assets invested in securities other than government bonds.

9 Bond funds with high yields don't necessarily generate high returns.

Many investors shop for bond funds based on yield. But yield is only one component of a fund's total return. The other component—what happens to a fund's share price—can be even more important. High-yield junk bond funds started 1990 with average yields of 13.6%. But because of falling fund share prices, the funds lost 11.1% over the next 12 months.

"If you see a fund with a good dividend yield, you should check to see what the total return has been," says Mr. Rekenthaler. "Yield is open to manipulation in a way that total return isn't."

10 Well-run bond funds often cut their dividends.

When a corporation cuts the dividend on its stock, it's usually a sign of trouble. That isn't the case with bond funds. In periods of falling interest rates, a prudent fund manager may choose to buy lower-yielding securities rather than risk a loss of capital in an effort to maintain the fund's dividend rate.

Conversely, some poorly run funds take inordinate risks in an effort to maintain a particular monthly dividend. That high dividend rate may come at the expense of a falling fund share price.

11 Costs are a key factor in determining differences in bond fund performance.

Bond funds with low annual expenses almost always do better than high-expense funds. For proof, consider some figures calculated by fund researchers CDA/Wiesenberger. The Rockville, Md., firm took the 108 intermediate- and long-term government bond funds that have been around for the past five years and divided them into four equal-size groups, depending on their average annual expenses over the past five years.

The 25% of funds with the lowest average expenses were the best performers, returning an average 9.9% a year over the five years ended December. The 25% with the highest expenses had the poorest performance, gaining an average 8.7% annually.

12 Money-market funds aren't risk-free.

Money as is funds seek to maintain a fixed $1 share price. But that share price isn't guaranteed. In recent years, some fund companies have had to buy defaulted commercial paper from their money funds to maintain the $1 share price.

But fund companies are under no obligation to do this; one day a fund company may decide it can't afford to bail out its money fund.

In addition, money funds generate rotten long-run returns and are susceptible to sharp drops in their dividend payout. In 1992, for instance, yields on taxable money funds dropped to 2.8% from 4.5%.

13 You don't need a broker to buy mutual funds.

If you go to a broker, financial planner, insurance agent or a bank, you're likely to end up buying load funds, which charge sales commissions of as much as 8.5%. You can avoid those sales charges by investing in no-load funds, which can be bought directly from fund companies and don't charge a commission. But if you buy no-load funds, you have to be willing to make your own investment decisions.

14 There's no difference in the average performance of load and no-load funds.

According to CDA/Wiesenberger, no-load stock funds returned an average 14.3% a year over the five years ended December, while load funds gained 14.4%. These figures, which are for diversified U.S. stock funds, don't reflect the impact of sales charges. "If you factor in the sales commission, an investor is probably going to be better off in a no-load fund," says Stephen Savage, CDA/

Wiesenberger's managing editor.

15 A fund that doesn't charge a front-end sales commission isn't necessarily a no-load fund.

Some broker-sold funds don't charge an upfront sales commission. Instead, they nick you every year with a "12b-1" marketing and distribution fee, or they hit you with a back-end sales commission when you sell. "That one shocks a lot of people," says Morningstar's Mr. Rekenthaler. "It's the roach motel style of investing: Once you check in, you can't check out—unless you pay 5%."

16 Even if you don't go through a broker, you can still end up paying a sales charge.

Fidelity Investments and Dreyfus Corp. sell most of their funds directly to the public. Nonetheless, some of their stock funds charge sales commissions. With most Fidelity funds, you can get around the sales charge by buying the fund through a retirement account.

17 You can often get into funds for less than the published investment minimum.

Fund companies such as Janus Group, T. Rowe Price Associates and Twentieth Century Investors will waive their investment minimums and let you open an account with no money down, providing you agree to invest $25 or $50 every month through an automatic investment plan. With these

plans, money is moved directly from your paycheck or bank account into a mutual fund.

Investors can also get into funds for less than the usual minimum if they open a retirement account like a Keogh plan or individual retirement account. For instance, Fidelity, T. Rowe Price and Vanguard Group, which regularly demand minimums of $2,500 or $3,000, will let you open an IRA with $500.

18 If you want to avoid tax nightmares, never sell a fund in dribs and drabs.

Tax rules for accounting for mutual fund capital gains and losses can be extremely confusing, especially if you sell only a portion of your fund holdings. As a result, fund investors intent on selling should try to redeem their fund holdings all at one time.

"I don't think there's anybody alive who can figure out what the cost basis is when you sell a mutual fund, especially if you've bought and sold the fund at various times in the past," says Mutual Fund Letter's Mr. Perritt.

19 If you buy a stock fund in December, you could get a nasty surprise.

Stock funds typically make a single capital gains distribution each year, usually in late December. If you buy a fund just before the distribution date, you have to pay taxes on the distribution, even though you have only just bought the fund.

20 Many municipal bond fund owners would be better off in a taxable bond fund.

"There are people in muni bond funds who don't belong there," says Lewis Altfest, president of L.J. Altfest & Co., a New York investment adviser. "If you're in the 15% tax bracket and your state taxes aren't very high, then you shouldn't be in a muni bond fund."

21 Most mutual fund investors are wimps.

Despite the superior long-run returns generated by stock funds, fund shareholders are most heavily invested in bond and money-market funds. At year end, for instance, stock funds accounted for 30% of the fund industry's $1.6 trillion in assets, compared with 34% for money-market funds and 36% for bond funds.

"That's not a good longer-term asset allocation," says Mr. Altfest. "Most people should have 50% or more of their money in stock funds, even if they're at retirement."

22 Most stock fund investors own the wrong mix of funds.

Stock fund investors keep the bulk of their money in funds

that own U.S. large-company stocks. According to Lipper Analytical, mutual fund investors have 6.4% of their stock market money in small-company stock funds, 7.3% in sector funds and 9.1% in foreign-stock funds; a whopping 77.2% is in large-company stock funds.

Stock-fund investors "should be broadening into the international arena," says Mr. Altfest. "They should have a stronger representation in the small-cap area. And they should not be in sector funds."

23 Risky funds aren't so risky if they're part of a fund portfolio.

Emerging markets funds, foreign-stock funds and small-company stock funds offer the prospect of handsome gains over time. But these funds also tend to bounce around sharply in share price. By mixing together these and other stock funds, however, you can make those share price gyrations more bearable, while still getting the handsome long-term gains.

Because of this phenomenon, "if you're a conservative investor, you don't have to buy just conservative investments," says Kenneth Gregory, editor of the No-Load Fund Analyst, a San Francisco newsletter.

24 If you own more than a dozen funds, you probably own too many.

Most investors buy funds on an ad hoc basis, so that they end up with a host of different funds, many of which use the same investment style. The solution, say analysts, is first to decide that you want to own, say, a government bond fund, an international-stock fund and a large-company stock fund. Once you have settled on a mix, you then buy the best possible funds to build your desired portfolio.

25 If the stock market crashes, it's probably too late to sell your mutual funds.

If the stock market suddenly goes into a tailspin, don't rush to sell your shares. Even if you immediately put in a sell order, your shares won't be sold until the end of the day, at which point the share price you get will reflect that day's trading activity.

"That lesson was brought home to a lot of people on Oct. 19, 1987," notes Sheldon Jacobs, editor of the No-Load Fund Investor, a Hastings-on-Hudson, N.Y., newsletter. "People who sold out that day pretty much got the absolute bottom."

Source: Jonathan Clements, "The 25 Facts Every Mutual Fund Investor Should Know," March 5, 1993. Reprinted by permission of *The Wall Street Journal,* ©1993 Dow Jones & Company, Inc. All Rights Reserved Worldwide.

Chapter 15

Other Investments

Learning Objectives

After studying this chapter, you should be able to:

■ Describe the characteristics of stock options and the advantages and disadvantages of stock options contracts.

■ Describe the characteristics of futures contracts and the advantages and disadvantages of futures contracts.

■ Explain the methods of investing directly in real estate, including the purchase of raw land, residential property, and commercial property.

■ Describe the methods of investing indirectly in real estate, including real estate investment trusts (REITs), mortgage-backed securities, collateralized mortgage obligations (CMOs), real estate mutual funds, and real estate-related companies.

■ Discuss investment in metals, art, and collectibles.

> *There are two times in a man's life when he should not speculate: when he can't afford it, and when he can.*
>
> —Mark Twain
>
> *Variety is the very spice of life.*
>
> —William Cowper, *Olney Hymns*

Douglas and Tina Webster have always been buy-and-hold common stock investors. They buy shares of stock in good companies and hold on to the shares for long periods. Although their strategy has been profitable in the past, they have begun to consider some other types of investments.

Tina recently completed an art appreciation class at the local community college. "You don't frame stock certificates and put them on the wall," Tina said. "I discovered some artists that I really like and was surprised to learn that we can afford their lithographs and etchings."

Douglas prides himself on the ability to select stocks. Recently, he played "what if" with a couple of stocks. He correctly predicted most of the short-term price increases and decreases in the share prices. Douglas would like to profit from these short-term stock price movements and is considering using options on stocks for this purpose.

Douglas and Tina are also considering purchasing land as an investment. There is a two-acre tract of land adjacent to their subdivision that has yet to be developed. The Websters are thinking about buying the land and selling it in several years, after the land has appreciated in value.

"You know," Tina said, "there are a lot of investment opportunities out there!"

Even though stocks, bonds, and mutual funds are the most widely used investment vehicles, many other investment alternatives are available. In this chapter, we examine several of these alternatives: options, commodities and futures, real estate, metals, art, and collectibles. Whereas some of these investments can actually be used to reduce risk, others are of greater risk because of the degree of leverage employed or because once you own the asset it may be difficult to find someone to buy it from you.

Stock Options

derivative A financial instrument that derives its value from another asset.

Options and futures contracts are known as derivatives. A **derivative** is a financial instrument that derives its value from another asset. Recall from Chapter 12 that an *option* is the right to buy or sell an asset at a given price during a specified period. Types of options traded include options on shares of stock, interest rate options, currency options, stock index options, and several others. Since most individual investors are not involved with these more exotic forms of options, we confine our treatment here to options on shares of common stock.

Basic Definitions

stock option A contract that permits its owner to buy or sell 100 shares of stock at a specified price during a specified period.

A **stock option** is a contract that permits its owner to buy or sell 100 shares of stock at a specified price during a specified period. As noted in

writing an option Selling an option to a buyer.

strike (exercise) price The price per share at which stock can be bought or sold under an option.

premium The price the buyer pays for the option and the price the seller receives.

in the money Description of an option that can be exercised at a profit.

at the money Description of an option that is at a break-even point; exercising it will produce neither a profit nor a loss.

out of the money Description of an option whose exercise would produce a loss.

Chapter 12, a *call option* is the right to purchase shares of stock at a given price during a specified period, and a *put option* is the right to sell shares of stock at a given price during a specified period. In options terminology, **writing an option** means selling an option to a buyer. The **strike price,** or **exercise price,** is the price per share at which the stock can be bought or sold under the option. The **premium** is the price the buyer pays for the option and the price the seller receives.

Based on the exercise price and the underlying price of the stock, the option is either "in the money," "at the money," or "out of the money." If an option is **in the money,** it currently can be exercised at a profit. For example, if you have the right to purchase stock for $40 a share when the price of the stock is $44 per share, you can make $4 per share by exercising your option and then selling the stock immediately. An option **at the money** will not produce a gain or a loss if you exercise it—it's at a break-even point. If an option is **out of the money,** currently it can only be exercised at a loss. For example, if you have the right to sell stock for $90 per share and the market price is $94 per share, you cannot make money by exercising your option. Remember that an in the money option may later become an out of the money option if the price of the underlying security moves in the wrong direction. The reverse is also true—you may be able to exercise an option that is currently out of the money at a later date for a profit.

How Stock Options are Traded

Suppose you were convinced that the price of General Electric (GE) stock was going to increase from the current price of $102 per share over the next three months. You want to profit if GE stock increases in value, but you prefer not to actually own the stock. How can you make a profit if the price of GE stock moves in line with your expectations? You could call a broker and ask the broker to purchase a GE call option for you at a strike price of $106 per share. As owner of this option, you have the right to purchase shares of GE stock during a specified period at a price of $106 per share. After you purchase the option, you hope that the price of GE will increase to more than $106 per share. If you decide to sell the option before it expires, there is an active secondary, with prices quoted on the financial page. A guide to understanding option quotations is provided in Exhibit 15.1.

Option Prices

Several factors influence the price of an option.[1]

■ The first is the price of the underlying security in relation to the strike price of the option. An option that is in the money is more valuable than an option that is out of the money.

■ Another factor is the expiration date of the option. Obviously, an option that is $2 out of the money with 60 days before expiration is more valu-

Exhibit 15.1

Understanding Options Quotations

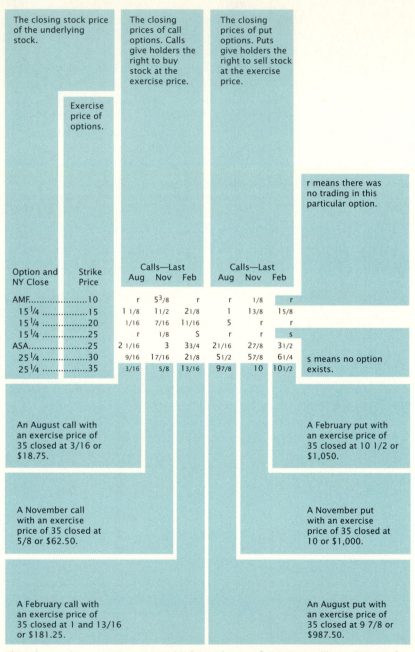

The closing stock price of the underlying stock.

The closing prices of call options. Calls give holders the right to buy stock at the exercise price.

The closing prices of put options. Puts give holders the right to sell stock at the exercise price.

Exercise price of options.

r means there was no trading in this particular option.

Option and NY Close	Strike Price	Calls—Last Aug	Nov	Feb	Calls—Last Aug	Nov	Feb
AMF	10	r	5 3/8	r	r	1/8	r
15 1/4	15	1 1/8	11/2	21/8	1	13/8	15/8
15 1/4	20	1/16	7/16	11/16	5	r	r
15 1/4	25	r	1/8	S	r	r	s
ASA	25	2 1/16	3	33/4	21/16	27/8	31/2
25 1/4	30	9/16	17/16	21/8	51/2	57/8	61/4
25 1/4	35	3/16	5/8	13/16	97/8	10	101/2

s means no option exists.

An August call with an exercise price of 35 closed at 3/16 or $18.75.

A February put with an exercise price of 35 closed at 10 1/2 or $1,050.

A November call with an exercise price of 35 closed at 5/8 or $62.50.

A November put with an exercise price of 35 closed at 10 or $1,000.

A February call with an exercise price of 35 closed at 1 and 13/16 or $181.25.

An August put with an exercise price of 35 closed at 9 7/8 or $987.50.

This is how trading in options is reported in financial pages of newspapers. The explanation of each item is contained in the box surrounding it.

Source: *The Merrill Lynch Guide to Writing Stock Options*, 1982, p. 3. Reprinted with permission.

able than an option that is $2 out of the money that expires tomorrow. Given that 60 days remain on the former option, there is still the possibility that the option will be in the money before it expires.

■ The volatility of the price of the underlying stock also influences the price of the option. Greater volatility is a favorable factor since it means there is greater probability that the option will be in the money at some point before expiration.

■ Finally, the supply and demand for stock options influence the price. Options in short supply, relative to the demand, will be bid up in price, whereas options in large supply relative to the demand will decrease in price.

The Two Sides of an Options Transaction

Let's consider each side of a call option and a put option transaction to understand what the writer and purchaser hope will happen with respect to the price of the underlying stock.

Call Options. People who buy call options believe that the price of the stock will increase. For example, a call option may be available with a strike price of $60 per share on stock that currently sells for $55 per share. Obviously, the call is not in the money. However, if the price of the underlying stock increases to $64 per share, the call option is in the money. The call writer may have two objectives. One objective is profit. If the stock price does not increase to where the option is in the money, the writer profits from collecting the premium. The writer may also already own the stock and may write the call option to reduce downside risk, promising to sell the stock at a specified price while keeping the call premium.

Put Options. Now let's consider a put option transaction. If you buy a put option, you have the right to sell 100 shares of stock at a specified price during a specified period. Put buyers hope that the price of the stock will decrease. For example, a buyer may pay a premium for the right to sell stock at a strike price of $50 per share when the current price is $54 per share. If the price drops to $46 per share, the put option is in the money. The put writer may have two motivations for selling the put option. He or she may believe that the price will not decline, hence a profit can be made from selling the put for a premium. Alternatively, the put writer may desire to own the stock, but at a lower price than the current market price.

Stock Option Strategies

Many strategies can be employed using stock options. Some strategies are used by individuals who currently own the underlying stock, and others are used by individuals who do not own the stock and who wish to earn a premium from writing the option or to make money from a stock price movement by purchasing the option. A brief look at two simple options strategies will show how these instruments can be used.

Writing Covered Calls. The first strategy we will consider is writing a covered call. A **covered call option** is a call option written on a stock that is already owned by the call writer. For example, you may own 100 shares of XYZ stock, with a current price of $60 per share. In exchange for a premium, you may sell the right to purchase your 100 shares of XYZ stock at a price of $64 per share. If the price of XYZ stock drops or does not increase to where the option could be exercised at a profit, you keep your stock and the option premium. If the price increases, the stock may be called away from you. This technique limits your upside potential because, if the price increases substantially, the stock will be called away from you for $64 per share. This strategy also provides additional income if the price does not increase to where it would be profitable for the call option to be exercised.

covered call option A call option written on a stock that is already owned by the call writer.

Buying Puts as "Insurance." A second strategy involves buying put options as insurance against a decline in the price of stock you already own. For example, the current price of your 100 shares of stock may be $43 per share. You may purchase a put option with a strike price of $40 per share in exchange for a premium. If the price increases, you have lost the premium, but the price of your stock has increased. Now let's assume the stock price drops to $33 per share. In the absence of the put, you have lost, on paper, $10 per share ($43–$33). However, as the owner of the put option, you own the right to sell 100 shares at $40 per share. That option is now in the money by $7 per share ($40–$33). You can either sell the stock you own or sell the option. Using put options is this way protects the investor from losing more money if the price of the stock declines.

Advantages and Disadvantages of Investing in Stock Options

A number of advantages are associated with stock options:

■ The option writer receives a cash inflow (the premium) when a stock option is sold.

■ Stock options can be used to protect against adverse price movements if the option writer owns the stock.

■ Using options does not tie up large sums of money, as does the outright purchase and ownership of common stock.

■ Finally, options are liquid securities. An option owner can sell the option or exercise the option if it is in the money.

There are, of course, some disadvantages associated with stock options:

■ You may pay a premium for an option, and the option may expire worthless.

■ Stock that you may desire to keep may be called away from you, or someone may "put" shares to you at a price above the current market price of the stock.

■ Finally, the commissions paid on options contracts are higher (proportionately) than commissions paid when buying and selling the actual shares of underlying security. Options commissions range from about 5 to 10 percent of the option premium.

Commodities and Futures Contracts

spot price The price today of a commodity.

Recall that a *commodity* is a product or good—for example, corn, wheat, metals, and petroleum products. People who produce and use these commodities know the price today, called the **spot price.** However, they face uncertainty with respect to the price of these products and goods in the future. Consider a corn grower and a cereal producer. The corn grower is uncertain what the market price of corn will be at harvest time. The cereal producer may have orders for thousands of boxes of cereal made from corn and may fear that corn prices will increase in the future. The corn grower and the cereal manufacturer may enter into futures contracts to reduce the riskiness of their positions with respect to adverse movements in the price of corn.

As noted in Chapter 12, a *futures contract* is an agreement between two parties to trade a specified quantity of a commodity at a future date at a price agreed upon today. An active secondary market exists for futures contracts. Traders buy and sell commodity futures contracts for a number of products and goods, such as coffee, cotton, soybeans, corn, gold, heating oil, pork bellies, orange juice, and wheat. There are also financial futures contracts, including futures contracts on the British pound, the Japanese yen, U.S. Treasury bills, the Standard and Poor's 500 stock index, and the New York Stock Exchange Composite Index. The financial pages list futures prices for specified quantities of various commodities based upon the delivery date. An annotated futures quotation from the *Wall Street Journal* is provided in Exhibit 15.2.

Who Trades Futures Contracts?

Two groups of individuals trade in the futures market, hedgers and speculators. *Hedgers* are producers and users of the commodity who are seeking to reduce the adverse impact of possible future price changes. Thus, in our previous example, the corn grower and the cereal maker would

Exhibit 15.2

Reading Futures Tables

The tables on futures markets show opening and closing prices, price history, and volume of sales every day. Because the futures markets reflect current political and economic conditions, the charts also provide interesting commentary on the state of the economy and the way people feel it's headed.

Open is the opening price for sugar on the previous trading day. Depending on what's

happened in the world overnight, the opening price may not be the same as the closing price the day before. Since prices are cents per pound, the 21.43 means sugar opened for sale at 21.43¢ per pound. Multiplying this amount by 112,000 pounds (the number of pounds in the contract) equals $24,001.60 per contract.

High, low and **settle** report the contract's highest, lowest and

closing prices for the previous trading day. Taken together, they're a good indication of the commodity's market **volatility** during the trading day. Here, the opening price of a sugar contract was also the lowest. The contract settled at its closing price of 21.51¢, up .09¢ from the closing price the previous day.

Change compares the closing price given here with the previous closing price. A plus (+) indi-

cates prices ended higher and a minus (-) means prices ended lower. In this case, sugar for July delivery settled .04¢ higher than the previous day.

The **month of the contract** is the month in which it expires. Ja94 indicates this contract will expire on the third Friday of January, 1994. When the expiration date arrives, the contract is dropped from the table.

The expiration cycles

for each commodity usually correspond with activity in that commodity. For example, trading in grains follows the cycle of planting, harvesting and exporting.

Lifetime highs and **lows** show volatility over the lifetime of a particular contract. Prices for brent crude oil have been more volatile than sugar prices-meaning the investment risks are higher but the chances of making a lot of money

are also higher.

Open interest reports the total number of outstanding contracts-that is, those that have not been canceled by offsetting trades. Generally, the further away the expiration date, the smaller the option interest because there's not much trading activity. In the case of grains and oilseed, however, there is increased activity in the months the new crop will be harvested.

FUTURES PRICES

Tuesday, June 29, 1993

Open Interest Reflects Previous Trading Day.

	Open	High	Low	Settle	Change	Lifetime High	Lifetime Low	Open Interest
SUGAR-DOMESTIC (CSCE)-112,000 lbs.; cents per lb.								
Sept	21.43	21.51	21.43	21.51	+ .09	21.99	21.15	2,656
Nov	21.55	21.60	21.55	21.60	+ .05	21.95	21.25	2,702
Ja94	21.61	21.70	21.69	21.69	+ .02	21.92	21.35	793
Mar	21.66	21.73	21.72	21.73	+ .02	21.81	21.35	1,992
May	21.74	21.82	21.82	21.78	− .05	21.90	21.35	1,207
July	21.84	21.90	21.89	21.89	+ .04	21.90	21.55	866
Sept		....		21.95	+ .01	21.90	21.80	345

Est vol 531; vol Mon 430; open int 10.611. -189.

	Open	High	Low	Settle	Change	Lifetime High	Lifetime Low	Open Interest
COTTON (CTN)-50,000 lbs.; cents per lb.								
July	55.05	55.15	54.30	54.40	− .47	65.80	53.00	361
Oct	57.31	57.40	56.75	56.77	− .50	64.40	54.40	5,715
Dec	57.25	57.35	56.80	56.82	− .36	64.25	54.60	21,901
Mr94	58.33	58.40	57.85	57.85	− .38	64.00	55.62	3,343
May	58.96	59.00	58.50	58.50	− .45	64.50	58.20	894
July	59.70	59.70	59.10	59.10	− .50	64.50	58.86	700

Est vol 3,500; vol Mon 3,557; open int 33,075, -21.

	Open	High	Low	Settle	Change	Lifetime High	Lifetime Low	Open Interest
ORANGE JUICE (CTN) - 15,000 lbs.; cents per lb.								
July	115.00	120.50	114.50	120.50	− 4.35	130.00	72.50	3,613
Sept	119.10	124.40	118.50	124.25	− 4.30	124.40	75.10	11,429

	Open	High	Low	Settle	Change	Lifetime High	Lifetime Low	Open Interest
BRENT CRUDE (IPE) 1,000 net bbls.; $ per bbl.								
Aug	17.56	17.75	17.53	17.66	+ .14	19.91	17.33	61,011
Sept	17.76	17.95	17.76	17.84	+ .09	19.58	17.57	18,539
Oct	17.97	18.03	17.97	18.02	+ .02	19.58	17.71	10,452
Nov	18.13	18.20	18.13	18.18	+ .01	19.44	17.86	3,922
Dec	18.30	18.40	18.27	18.30	+ .05	19.38	18.03	5,259
Ja94	18.40	18.43	18.39	18.44	+ .05	19.35	18.18	3,571
Feb		....		18.45	+ .05	19.30	18.82	1,107
Mar		....		18.48		18.97	18.25	1,758

Est vol 23,898; vol Mon 16,764; open int 105,799, -1,596.

	Open	High	Low	Settle	Change	Lifetime High	Lifetime Low	Open Interest
GAS OIL (IPE) 100 metric tons; $ per ton								
July	163.00	164.25	163.00	163.75	+ .50	182.50	161.00	19,757
Aug	165.00	165.75	165.00	165.75	+ .50	183.25	162.50	14,665
Sept	167.25	168.25	167.25	167.25	+ .50	182.25	162.25	7,609
Oct	170.00	170.50	170.00	170.25	+ .25	184.00	163.00	8,355
Nov	172.25	173.25	172.25	172.25	....	186.00	169.00	5,027
Dec	174.50	174.75	174.25	174.50	....	186.00	171.50	5,538
Ja94	175.50	175.75	175.25	175.75	− .25	187.00	173.30	4,145
Feb		....		174.50	− .75	181.50	174.50	842
Mar		....		17				
Apr		....						

The **product** is listed alphabetically within its particular grouping. Cotton is listed under the heading Foods & Fibers. Generally, detailed information is given in these charts for the most actively traded futures contracts. Activity for additional contracts is summarized at the end of the column under the heading **Other Futures**.

The **exchange** on which a particular con-

tract is traded appears. Here CTN is The New York Cotton Exchange. Some commodities, like wheat and corn, trade on more than one exchange. The exchange whose activity is watched most closely is the one which is shown.

The **size of each contract** reflects the bulk trading unit used during the normal course of commercial business. One cotton contract

covers the rights to 50,000 pounds of cotton. The **price per unit** is expressed in either dollars or cents per unit, depending on the commodity. Here, it's cents per pound. To find the total cost of the contract, multiply the price per unit by the number of units. The July cotton contract closed at $27,200 (50,000 × 54.40¢).

Est. vol., vol. Mon. and **open int.** are cumu-

lative daily figures for all the contracts in each commodity combined. The estimated volume for brent crude is 23,898 trades. The volume Monday was 16,764. The −1.596 shows the decrease in the open interest. Those contracts were canceled by offsetting trades.

The **Dow Jones Futures** and **Spot** (cash market) **Indexes** provide an overall indication of the direction of the futures market.

The **Commodity Research Bureau Futures Price Index** is the most

closely watched futures market indicator. It is also referred to frequently in discussions of inflation. If the price of raw materials is rising, then the price of manufactured goods will probably rise as well.

COMMODITY INDEXES

Thursday, September 2, 1993

	Close	Net Chg.	Yr. Ago
Dow Jones Futures	126.04	+0.47	116.17
Dow Jones Spot	122.60	−0.19	118.32
Reuter United Kingdom	1628.1	+ 1.3	1514.0
C R B Futures*	215.66	−0.01	202.47

*Division of Knight-Ridder.

seek to hedge their risky position through the use of futures contracts. Speculators are neither producers nor users of the commodity. *Speculators,* who take the other side of a futures transaction, are risk takers who attempt to profit from commodity price movements. A sample futures transaction will show how futures contracts can reduce risk for a commodity producer or user.

Consider the corn grower who estimates in May that this year's crop output will be 20,000 bushels of corn, with harvest completed by December. The corn grower actually owns the commodity, which is called a "long position" in futures parlance. Checking the futures price, the corn grower notices that December corn is $2.90 per bushel. The corn grower would like to lock in the $2.90 per bushel price, and can do so through the appropriate use of futures contracts. Since corn futures contracts are traded in 5,000-bushel units, the farmer would sell four contracts totaling 20,000 bushels on the futures market. In December, the corn grower would purchase four contracts at the current market price to offset his futures position. As demonstrated in Exhibit 15.3, it doesn't matter if the price of corn has increased or decreased by December. By using futures contracts, the farmer has locked in total revenue of $58,000.

Speculators, on the other hand, do not own the commodity. They make futures transactions hoping to make money rather than to offset risk. For example, a speculator may purchase a corn futures contract hoping there will be a drought in corn-producing states. If the speculator is correct, the supply of the commodity will be low, and the price of the contract will increase. If there is a bumper corn crop, however, the price of corn and the value of the futures contract will fall, and the speculator will lose money.

Futures Markets and Transactions

Consider This

Visit the Chicago Board of Trade at:

http://www.cbt.com/

Futures contracts are bought and sold in markets based in several cities. These markets specialize in various commodities. For example, the Chicago Board of Trade specializes in contracts involving grain and other commodities, whereas the Commodity Exchange (COMEX) in New York specializes in precious metals and the other commodities.

Futures transactions are characterized by a high degree of leverage. This means that you are required to pay only a small fraction of the cost of the contract at the time of purchase, typically, only 2 to 10 percent of the contract's value. For example, corn is traded in units of 5,000 bushels. If the price of corn is $3.00 a bushel, and an initial margin of 10 percent is required, you will pay $1,500 (5,000 × $3.00 × .10) at the time you purchase a corn futures contract. If the price of the commodity drops, the investor may be called upon to add additional margin funds.

Few futures contracts actually involve the delivery of the commodity at the expiration of the contract. So a speculator need not worry about a

---

Exhibit 15.3

Using Futures Contracts to Hedge Price Risks

If spot price of corn drops to $2.50 per bushel in December:

Revenue from sale of corn:	20,000 × 2.50	=	$50,000
Sale of four contracts at 2.90:	58,000		
Purchase of four contracts at 2.50:	50,000		
Gain on futures transaction:			8,000
Total revenue			**$ 58,000**

If spot price of corn increases to $3.00 per bushel in December:

Revenue from sale of corn:	20,000 × 3.00	=	$60,000
Sale of four contracts at 2.90:	58,000		
Purchase of four contracts at 3.00:	60,000		
Loss on futures transaction:			(2,000)
Total revenue			**$ 58,000**

---

truckload of pork bellies or orange juice showing up at his or her home. Buyers and sellers simply make an offsetting transaction, as illustrated in Exhibit 15.2, and money rather than the commodity changes hands.

Price Changes

A number of factors cause the price of commodities and futures contracts to change. Three of the most important are supply and demand, new information, and speculator activity.

Supply and Demand. When the supply of a commodity increases relative to the demand for the commodity, the price falls. For example, if there is a bumper crop of wheat, and the demand is constant, the price will fall. If demand increases while supply remains the same, the price increases. For example, the quantity of heating oil may be constant. If a "cold spell" grips New England, the price of heating oil may be bid up as suppliers purchase heating oil to service their customers.

New Information. New information is constantly being released, and commodity and futures prices adjust accordingly. If the government releases information that housing starts are down, less lumber will be needed, and the price of the commodity and the futures contract will fall. If an early freeze hits Florida damaging the orange crop, the price of orange juice and orange juice futures will increase.[2]

Speculator Activity. Trading by speculators can also cause changes in commodity prices. A rumor may spread, for example, that an agreement to sell wheat to China will be announced shortly. Reacting to the rumor, speculators may bid the price of wheat contracts higher.

Advantages and Disadvantages of Futures Contracts

Futures contracts offer several advantages:

- Producers and users of commodities can hedge their price risk through the use of futures contracts.

- Since the initial margin is low, establishing a hedge position is not expensive. In addition, if the price of the commodity increases, you can make a lot of money for your small investment.

- Few futures contracts actually involve the physical delivery of the commodity since the producer or user can simply make an offsetting transaction at the expiration of the contract.

- Speculators can profit from futures contracts by choosing the "right" side of a futures contract.

Disadvantages are also associated with futures trading:

- A hedger may forego profits that could have been earned if the position was not hedged.

- Speculators can lose money in the futures market by selecting the "wrong" side of the transaction.

- The high degree of leverage employed increases risk. You can also lose a lot of money for your small investment.

Real Estate Investments

Purchasing residential real estate addresses a primary need: shelter. Investors may also choose to invest in real estate to generate current income, capital appreciation, or a combination of these objectives. There are several ways to invest in real estate, both direct and indirect.

Direct Investment in Real Estate

Methods of direct investment in real estate include the purchase of raw land, residential rental property, and commercial property.

Purchase of Raw Land. One investment option is the purchase of raw, undeveloped land. Raw land can generate both current income and price appreciation. For example, an investor may purchase land and use the land to grow crops for sale, or rent the land to someone else to farm. Raw land also has the potential for price appreciation. For example, an investor may purchase wooded land close to a popular real estate development in the suburbs. As the suburb grows, the real estate may become a prime location for additional home construction. As with other types of real estate purchases, the location of the land is an important consideration.

There are three important considerations when purchasing raw land: zoning restrictions, wetlands, and pollution exposures.

■ **Zoning restrictions** are local limitations placed upon the usage of property for a certain purpose.

■ **Wetlands** are swamps, marshes, bogs, and other areas that are subject to saturation by water. Federal law and some state laws restrict the usage of property that has been designated wetlands.

■ Investors should also consider pollution exposures when purchasing land. Land should be inspected before purchase to check for hazardous materials.

Purchase of Land with Structures. A second real estate investment alternative is the purchase of land with structures. The structure could be a home, duplex, apartment building, or a structure designed for commercial purposes. The structure can be used to generate rental income and may also appreciate in value. Purchasing residential or commercial rental property creates a number of responsibilities for the purchaser. The owner is responsible for repairs and maintenance, property taxes, finding tenants, and insurance. In addition to the risk of physical damage to the property, the owner has a liability exposure. What factors should you consider when selecting commercial real estate? Insight 15.1 provides a checklist of considerations.

Indirect Investment in Real Estate

You can invest indirectly in real estate through real estate investment trusts (REITs), mortgage-backed securities, collateralized mortgage obligations (CMOs), real estate mutual funds, and real estate–related companies.

Real Estate Investment Trusts (REITs). The first indirect investment method we will consider is real estate investment trusts. **Real estate investment trusts (REITs)** are closed-end investment companies that use borrowed funds and equity funds from investors to purchase proper-

zoning restriction Local limitation placed on the usage of property for a certain purpose.

wetlands Swamps, marshes, bogs, and other areas that are subject to saturation by water.

real estate investment trust (REIT) Closed-end investment company that uses borrowed funds and equity funds from investors to purchase properties or mortgages on property.

15.1   Rental Real Estate Checklist

Successful investment in rental real estate requires, among other things, buying the right property at the right time, judging carefully how much money to put down and knowing how to deal with tenants. Stick with what you know best. For most of us, that means residential real estate, mainly one- or two-family homes. Select properties for investment in much the same way you would if you were buying your own home.

■ *Pick a property that's typical,* not one so special that it will appeal only to a limited number of tenants.

■ *Invest close to home*—no more than 30 to 40 minutes of driving time from your own home. That makes it easier to check up on your property and your tenants. Also, you're more likely to be aware of important developments in your own community than you are someplace hundreds of miles away.

■ *Look for neighborhoods relatively free of crime and drugs,* and close to public transportation, good schools, shopping and recreational facilities.

■ *Compare prices of similar properties* to make certain the property you're considering isn't overpriced.

■ *Be skeptical of a seller's assurance that you can raise the rent once you take over.* Base your rental income assumptions on your own research. Search for properties that can generate monthly rents of at least 1% of market value.

■ *Examine existing leases* before closing so you know how long they have to run, who the tenants are and how long they've been there.

■ *Be wary of property on which maintenance has been put off.* Have the property inspected, and make any purchase offer contingent on an inspection satisfactory to you.

■ *Check for local code violations.* You don't want to get stuck with the expense of correcting them.

■ *Make your purchase offer contingent* on inspecting and approving the last two or three years of the seller's Schedule 1 from his or her federal tax return.

Source: unknown.

ties or mortgages on property. Equity funds are raised through the issue of certificates of ownership (shares), and once issued, the shares of the REIT are traded just like shares of stock.

A REIT is similar to a mutual fund, and if properly designed, it enjoys the same tax advantage. Ordinarily, corporate income is taxed twice—once at the corporate level and once when the income is distributed to shareholders. Income generated by a REIT is taxed only when distributed to shareholders if certain requirements are satisfied. To qualify, (1) the REIT must have at least 100 shareholders, and the shares must be transferable; (2) at least 95 percent of the income earned by the REIT must be distributed to the shareholders each year; and (3) the REIT's income must accrue primarily through income (interest, dividends, rental income, and so on) rather than capital gains.

There are three types of REITs: equity REITs, mortgage REITs, and hybrid REITs.

equity REIT REIT that invests directly in real estate.

■ **Equity REITs** invest directly in real estate. For example, an equity REIT may purchase strip malls, shopping centers, and apartment buildings. The tenants of the property pay rent for the use of the space, and the equity REIT distributes this income to shareholders. Equity REITs also provide an opportunity for investors to profit through capital gains. For example, an equity REIT may profit from the sale of an office complex that has appreciated in value since the REIT originally purchased the complex.

mortgage REIT REIT consisting of a portfolio of real estate loans.

■ **Mortgage REITs** are portfolios of real estate loans. The value of a mortgage REIT is especially sensitive to interest rate fluctuations.

hybrid REIT REIT that invests in both property and mortgages.

■ **Hybrid REITs** invest in both property and mortgages.

mortgage-backed security Debt issue backed by a pool of mortgages.

Mortgage-Backed Securities. A second method of investing indirectly in real estate is through the purchase of mortgage-backed securities. **Mortgage-backed securities** are debt issues that are backed by a pool of mortgages. The federal government is involved in the private mortgage market through the purchase of mortgages. Government involvement is necessary to provide a national secondary market for mortgages and to smooth regional variations in mortgage lending. Government-chartered agencies purchase mortgages, pool the mortgages, and then sell shares of the pool to investors. Three government-chartered organizations and government agencies are involved in the mortgage-backed security arena, each known by a nickname: the Government National Mortgage Association (GNMA, also known as "Ginnie Mae"), the Federal Home Loan Mortgage Corporation (FHLMC, also known as "Freddie Mac"), and the Federal National Mortgage Association (FNMA, also known as "Fannie Mae").

GNMA (Ginnie Mae) The Government National Mortgage Association, a wholly-owned U.S. government corporation, part of the Department of Housing and Urban Development (HUD), that buys mortgages and sells mortgage-backed securities.

■ The **GNMA (Ginnie Mae),** the largest of the three organizations, is a wholly-owned U.S. government corporation that is part of the Department of Housing and Urban Development (HUD). Ginnie Mae helps stimulate housing activity by purchasing mortgages, combining the mortgages into large portfolios, and then selling units of the portfolio. Ginnie Mae concentrates its efforts in the government-backed or guaranteed mortgage area, purchasing Federal Housing Administration (FHA) and Veteran's Administration (VA) mortgages. Ginnie Mae certificates are backed by the full faith and credit of the U.S. government and pay interest and principal on a monthly basis. In addition to the government guarantee, there is an active secondary market for Ginnie Mae certificates.

FHLMC (Freddie Mac) The Federal Home Loan Mortgage Corporation, a government-chartered, publicly held corporation that buys mortgages and sells mortgage-backed securities.

■ The **FHLMC (Freddie Mac)** is a government-chartered, publicly held organization that began to operate in 1970. Freddie Mac provides additional liquidity in the conventional mortgage market by purchasing conventional mortgages, pooling them, and issuing a variety of securities secured by the pooled mortgages. Unlike Ginnie Mae certificates, Freddie Mac securities are not officially backed by the federal government, which makes them somewhat riskier than Ginnie Maes. Freddie Macs provide a slightly higher yield to compensate for the added risk.

FNMA (Fannie Mae) The Federal National Mortgage Association, a government-chartered, privately owned corporation that buys mortgages and sells mortgage-backed securities.

■ The **FNMA (Fannie Mae)** is a privately owned, federally chartered corporation that was established in 1938 with the goal of providing additional liquidity in the mortgage market. Although federally chartered, Fannie Mae shares trade on the New York Stock Exchange. Fannie Mae is authorized to purchase and sell FHA-insured, VA-guaranteed, and conventional mortgage loans. Most of Fannie Mae's operations are in the conventional mortgage area. Fannie Mae assembles large portfolios of purchased mortgages and issues mortgage-backed securities against these portfolios. Fannie Mae's mortgage-backed securities are guaranteed by Fannie Mae, but not backed "by the full faith and credit of the United States." However, these securities carry Moody's and Standard & Poor's highest rating.

Ginnie Mae, Freddie Mac, and Fannie Mae assemble portfolios of purchased mortgages worth $1 million or more and then sell "participation certificates" in units of $25,000. The portion of the monthly payment attributable to interest is taxed as ordinary income, whereas the balance is considered a return of principal and therefore is not taxable. Over time, these portfolios are liquidated as the mortgages are paid off. Although there is little default risk in investing in mortgage-backed securities, the yield is not guaranteed, and the value of the securities is sensitive to fluctuating interest rates. Price quotes for these securities are provided in the *Wall Street Journal* and other financial publications. Given the high minimum trading unit, these certificates are often purchased by insurance companies and institutional investors.

collateralized mortgage obligation (CMO) A bond issued against a pool of mortgage-backed securities.

Collateralized Mortgage Obligations (CMOs). A shortcoming of these mortgage-backed securities is that early repayment of the mortgage creates uncertainty with respect to the payments to the mortgage-backed security holder. **Collateralized mortgage obligations (CMOs)** were introduced in 1983 as a remedy for this problem. A collateralized mortgage obligation is a bond issued against a pool of mortgage-backed securities. The bonds are divided into different classes (called tranches) based on the duration of the bond. Each bond pays interest to the CMO holder; however, principal is passed along to the bondholders with the shortest maturity only. After that class of bondholders is repaid, principal is passed along to bondholders in the next shortest maturity class, and so on, until all payments have been made. Since CMOs are sold in $1,000 units, they are more easily purchased than are the $25,000 units of mortgage-backed securities. Lack of liquidity and transactions costs are two problems associated with investing in CMOs.

Real Estate Mutual Funds. A few mutual fund families are available that specialize in real estate investments. Some funds limit investment to U.S. real estate, whereas others invest in real estate in other countries. In addition, Ginnie Mae mutual funds are available. These funds are especially attractive to small investors interested in mortgage-backed securities since they provide the opportunity to invest in Ginnie Mae certificates at amounts far below the $25,000 minimum investment for individual Ginnie Mae certificates.

Real Estate–Related Companies. A final method of investing in real estate indirectly is by purchasing financial securities issued by real estate–related companies. Some companies, by their very nature, have significant real estate holdings. Paper companies, mining companies, and energy companies, for example, may own large tracts of land from which natural resources are harvested. Home-building companies may own tracts of land that are being developed for residential usage. Other companies that may own real estate include railroads, agricultural products companies, and conglomerates. Many insurance companies have large positions in real estate, both through direct investment and through mortgage-backed security holdings. The financial statements of real estate–related companies must be examined to determine the type and extent of real estate holdings, and the likely benefit of these holdings to the company and its security holders.

Metals, Art, and Collectibles

Our treatment of investments would be not complete without a discussion of metals, art, and collectibles.

Investing in Metals

Gold, silver, and platinum are the most popular metals for investment purposes. The conventional wisdom is that precious metals provide a hedge against inflation. Metals are also thought of as a "doomsday"

Insight   15.2 Put It in the Attic—Some Hints for Collectors

Found money. In just a generation, that's exactly what collectibles have become. Items deemed nearly worthless in the not-so-distant past—Pez dispensers, baseball cards, James Bond novels—are suddenly selling for thousands of dollars.

Indeed, that everyday clutter gathering dust in your attic or awaiting sale at a flea market may very well escalate in price. But how can you decide what's worth seeking out and saving?

Experts suggest collectors on a shoestring look to today's versions of yesterday's skyrocketing collectibles: Power Rangers costumes could be the Star Wars play sets of 2010. Or you could find a niche—such as medical photography—that's lagging behind the boom in a hot field, or explore an area—such as space collectibles—that didn't exist a few generations ago.

Here are some sectors where you can still do some cheap shopping.

Pop-Culture Kitsch

You might not want to spend $10,000 on a 1939 "Gone With the Wind" movie poster, but posters from 1994's "Forrest Gump" are changing hands at a mere $10. Posters from such Oscar-winning films have shown appreciation in recent years. A 1964 "My Fair Lady" poster, with Audrey Hepburn, now costs $500, up from $50 five years ago.

Other good bets include posters from the complete "Rocky" series and from such 1980s action films as "The Terminator," says Bruce Hershenson, a movie-poster dealer in West Plains, Mo.

At his home in Chicago, collector and dealer Mike Gidwitz socks away McDonald's Happy Meals toys, as well as plastic watches decorated with licensed characters—Barbie, Fred Flintstone, Teenage Mutant Ninja Turtles and the like. He is betting that these trinkets, like lunch boxes and Pez dispensers before them, will be hot in coming years.

Sports and Medical Photography

Some sizzling fields have sectors that haven't yet joined the race. Fashion photography, surrealist photography and 19th-century photography have all taken off. But sports and medical photography are just starting to.

In June 1995, Robert Edwards Auctions of Hoboken, N.J., sold a 1913 photograph of Tris Speaker, a member of the baseball Hall of Fame, for $246. A collection of 34 photographs of Hall of Famers from 1910 to 1930 went for $2,400, or just over $70 apiece. (The collection included two pictures of Babe Ruth.)

Medical photography, once a cult collecting field favored by doctors, joined the mainstream last year with a major show in Paris and the publication of a history of the field. In October 1995, a life-size 1960s X-ray of a human head and torso brought $1,610 at Swann Galleries in New York. Collectors also seek old photographs of diseased people, which, unlike such pictures today, often show faces. And they're interested in pictures of doctors at work, many of which feature outdated equipment or techniques.

Space Memorabilia

The silver anniversary of Neil Armstrong's 1969 walk on the moon stirred interest in the market for space memorabilia. So has the movie "Apollo 13."

Recent auctions of space memorabilia—both commemorative items and those that have actually flown in space—show how popular space collectibles can be. At the end of 1993, after the fall of communism and the need for cash had persuaded former Soviet ministries, space organizations, scientists and cosmonauts to sell flight suits, letters, diaries and even space hard-

(continued)

ware, a sale at Sotheby's auction house in New York fetched $6.8 million. A congratulatory 1961 telegram to Yuri Gagarin, the first man in space, from then-Soviet premier Nikita Khrushchev brought $68,500, far higher than the estimated sale range of $2,000 to $3,000.

Not every space item is so costly. Several freeze-dried packets of astronaut "training meals," despite never having made it into orbit, brought $80 at a Beverly Hills auction earlier this year.

Prices of items that have been in space are likely to rise, say dealers in memorabilia, because museums, as well as collectors, will want them. And, needless to say, the supply is limited. Right now, watch prices start at about $3,000.

But because this is a young collecting field, there's a chance it won't take off—so it's best to focus on items with broad appeal. Chess sets, pens and watches that have been in space, for example, can be resold to chess, autograph and watch collectors, as well as to space-memorabilia collectors.

Before you spend money, make sure material that was in flight can be traced back to the astronaut or otherwise documented—the National Aeronautics and Space Administration won't authenticate space memorabilia.

Olympiana

The Olympic collecting tradition dates back to 1896. Prices for Olympic memorabilia run the gamut. Programs from the closing ceremonies of the 1994 Winter Games in Lillehammer,

Norway, sell for around $25. The black mourning banners that draped the athletes' village in Munich after the 1972 massacre of Israeli athletes run about $300. Gold medals, which rarely hit the collectibles market, bring about $3,000 when they do.

Currently in demand, and expensive, is memorabilia from the 1904 St. Louis Olympics. That's because the 1904 Games were an adjunct to the World's Fair, so World's Fair collectors covet the same items. Scarce, too, are medals from the first Winter Games—practically all that remains from those Games, in 1924 in Chamonix, France.

Source: Alexandra Peers, "Put It in the Attic Will Today's Space Memorabilia be Tomorrow's Pez Dispensers? Some Hints for Collectors," December 8, 1995. Reprinted by permission of *The Wall Street Journal*, ©1995 *Dow Jones & Company, Inc. All Rights Reserved Worldwide.*

investment—meaning that in periods of political or economic chaos, precious metals increase in value. There are a variety of methods of investing in precious metals, including the direct purchase of coins and bullion and indirect investment through the purchase of mining company stocks and mutual funds that specialize in metals.

Investing in Art

Investing in art provides the opportunity for aesthetic enjoyment of the artwork, as well as the possibility of price appreciation. For art investments, the latter concern is often secondary. Many art investors are satisfied if their investments appreciate at the rate of inflation.

The adage "buy something you like" definitely applies to art investments. Many types of art can be purchased, including sculptures, paintings, etchings, photographs, lithographs, and other forms of artistic expression. Works by well-known artists often start at prices well beyond

Consider This

Interested in art? You can visit a number of art museums online. For example,

visit the Louvre at: http://mistral.culture.fr/louvre/

and the Metropolitan Museum of Art at: http://www.metmuseum.org/

what most individual investors can afford, but museum-quality etchings and lithographs from some well-known artists are more affordable. Multiple images were usually produced, and the prints signed and numbered. Some art collectors purchase the works of "unknown" artists for enjoyment or in the hope that someday the artist will be "discovered." Unfortunately, the works of many artists to do not appreciate significantly until after the artists have died. Investments in art are less liquid than other investments since each work of art is heterogeneous and there may not be a ready market of buyers and sellers. Storage, security, and insurance are additional concerns when investing in art.

Investing in Collectibles

Antiques and collectibles provide another investment opportunity. The seller of collectibles may be an individual who owns a single item or a dealer who has an inventory of the collectibles. Like investment in art, antiques and collectibles permit the purchaser to enjoy possession of the asset, as well as providing the possibility of price appreciation. Often, investment in collectibles develops from a hobby, such as coin collecting, stamp collecting, or collecting glassware from the Depression era. Some hints for collectors are provided in Insight 15.2.

SUMMARY

- Options and futures contracts are known as derivatives because they derive their value from another asset, such as the price of common stock or the value of a commodity.

- A stock option gives the holder the right to buy or sell 100 shares of stock at a specified price during a specified time period. The specified price is called the strike or exercise price.

- A call option is the right to buy stock; a put option is the right to sell stock.

- Stock options may be in the money, at the money, or out of the money. These mean, respectively, that the option can be exercised for a profit, at no loss or gain, and for a loss.

- Several factors influence the value of a stock option, including the price of the underlying security in relation to the strike price, the time until the option expires, the volatility of the underlying stock, and the supply of and demand for options on the underlying stock.

- Stock options have several advantages: an option writer receives income when the option is written, the option can be used as a hedge against adverse price movements, options do not tie up large sums of money, and there is an active secondary market for options.

■ Stock options have several disadvantages: an investor may pay a premium for an option and the option may expire worthless, stock that you would like to keep may be called away from you, someone may "put" shares to you at a price above the current market price, and commissions must be paid on options transactions.

■ A commodity is a product or good. A futures contract is an agreement between two parties to trade a specified quantity of a commodity at a future date at a price agreed upon today.

■ There is an active secondary market for futures contracts. Futures are also available on financial securities and stock indexes.

■ There are two groups of traders in the futures market. Hedgers are attempting to reduce their risk through futures contracts by locking-in a future price today. Speculators are risk takers who attempt to profit from commodity price movements.

■ Futures prices are affected by the supply and demand for the underlying commodity, new information, and speculator trading activity.

■ Futures have several advantages: traders who have a "long" position in a commodity can hedge the price risk in an economical way, the initial margin requirement is low, few contracts involve the physical delivery of the commodity, and speculators can use futures to make profits.

■ Futures have several disadvantages: traders in a "long" position may have fared better financially without locking-in a futures price, speculators can lose money, and the high degree of leverage may produce large losses.

■ Investors can invest in real estate directly through the purchase of raw land and land with structures.

■ Investors can invest indirectly in real estate through real estate investment trusts, mortgage-backed securities, real estate mutual funds, and real estate–related companies.

■ Real estate investment trusts (REITs) are closed-end investment companies that use borrowed funds and equity funds from investors to purchase properties and mortgages on properties.

■ Mortgage-backed securities are debt issues that are backed by a pool of mortgages. The federal government is involved in this market through government-chartered agencies, including the Government National Mortgage Association (Ginnie Mae), the Federal Home Loan

Mortgage Corporation (Freddie Mac), and the Federal National Mortgage Association (Fannie Mae).

■ Collateralized mortgage obligations (CMOs) are bonds issued against pools of mortgage-backed securities. The bonds are of different duration, and those holding bonds of the shortest duration receive repayment of principal first.

■ Gold, silver, and platinum are the most popular investment metals. Investors can invest in metals through coins, bullion, and the purchase of stocks and mutual funds specializing in metals.

■ Art and collectibles provide the opportunity for aesthetic enjoyment as well as price appreciation. These investments are characterized by a lower degree of liquidity than other types of investments.

KEY CONCEPTS AND TERMS

At the money
Collateralized mortgage obligation
  (CMO)
Covered call option
Derivative
Equity REIT
FHLMC (Freddie Mac)
FNMA (Fannie Mae)
GNMA (Ginnie Mae)
Hybrid REIT
In the money
Mortgage-backed security

Mortgage REIT
Out of the money
Premium
Real estate investment trust
  (REIT)
Spot price
Stock option
Strike (exercise) price
Wetlands
Writing an option
Zoning restriction

QUESTIONS FOR REVIEW

1. What are stock options? What do put options and call options permit the owner to do?

2. Price movements of the underlying stock are important to writers and buyers of puts and calls. Explain what price movement is desirable for: a call writer, a call buyer, a put writer, a put buyer.

3. What are the advantages and disadvantages of using stock options?

4. What are futures contracts?

5. How do hedgers differ from speculators?

6. How does the basic law of supply and demand affect futures prices?

7. Besides purchasing a first or second home, what are the methods of direct investment in real estate? What are the indirect methods of investing in real estate?

8. What are real estate investment trusts (REITs)? What are mortgage-backed securities?

9. What are the methods through which investors can invest in metals?

10. Why is liquidity a greater concern with respect to investment in art and collectibles than it is with respect to stocks and bonds?

PROBLEMS

1. Julie paid $200 for a call option with a strike price of $36 per share. The price of the stock has increased to $41.50. How much will Julie earn (net of the premium she paid) if she exercises the option today?

2. Shirley purchased a put option for $300. The option has a strike price of $40.
   a. If the price of the underlying stock is $45, is Shirley's option in the money, at the money, or out of the money?
   b. If the price of the underlying security is $36 per share, how much will Shirley earn (net of the premium) if she exercises her option today?

3. Toby is a wheat farmer from Kansas. He seeks to hedge the price risk associated with his wheat crop. Currently, the price per bushel of wheat is $5.50. One wheat futures contract is for 5,000 bushels. How much initial margin per contract will Toby be required to post if 8 percent of the value of the contract is required?

INTERNET EXERCISES

1. Information about futures and options is available from INO Global Markets at:

   http://www.ino.com/

   In the "Exchange Directory," you'll find a listing of major worldwide exchanges that trade futures or options, with links to many. For example, you can visit the Minneapolis Grain Exchange (MGEX), the New York Mercantile Exchange (NYMEX), and the Coffee, Sugar, and Cocoa Exchange (CSCE). Browse this site for a glimpse at the world of futures and options trading.

2. As you might expect, the World Wide Web is an increasingly popular forum for buyers and sellers of collectibles. An online magazine for collectors of such things as sports trading cards and comic books is the World-Wide Collectors Digest at:

   http://www.wwcd.com/

   Visit the site to get an idea of what kinds of things are considered collectible.

CASE APPLICATIONS

Case I

In each of the following scenarios, discuss which type of option (call or put) should be employed, and discuss how the option could achieve the desired result.

1. Franklin Evans believes the price of IBM common stock will increase significantly in the next six months.

2. David Chu believes the price of General Electric stock will decline significantly in the next six months.

3. Madeline James owns 100 shares of AT&T stock. She seeks to generate income by writing an option while hedging against a possible price decline.

4. Gail Hernandez owns 100 shares of Dow Chemical stock. She is concerned that the price of Dow Chemical stock will decline significantly. She seeks downside protection through the purchase of an option.

Case II

Anderson Oil Company is a fuel delivery company operating in three New England states. During the summer months, thousands of customers place heating oil orders with Anderson at agreed-upon prices, with delivery of the heating oil in the late fall or early winter. Anderson is concerned that fuel oil prices will increase between the order date and the delivery date.

1. Explain how Anderson Oil Company can use fuel oil futures to reduce its price risk.

2. How do speculators lose by taking the "wrong" side of a futures contract?

Case III

Olivia Williams is considering a number of investments, including:

- Purchase of undeveloped building lots

- Purchase of a painting by an unknown 18th-century German artist

- Purchase of a Ginnie Mae certificate

- Purchase of an eight-unit apartment complex

- Purchase of gold coins

- Purchase of shares in a real estate mutual fund

Evaluate each of these investments according to the following criteria:

1. Riskiness of the investment

2. How the return on her investment will be provided (income, price appreciation, or both)

3. Liquidity of the investment

SUGGESTIONS FOR ADDITIONAL READING

Bartlett, William W. *Mortgage-Backed Securities—Products, Analysis, Trading.* New York: New York Institute of Finance, 1988.

Bloch, H. I., and Grace Lichtenstein. *Inside Real Estate—The Complete Guide to Buying and Selling Your House, Co-op, or Condominium.* New York: Grove and Weidenfeld, 1987.

Cheney, John M., and Edward A. Moses. *Fundamentals of Investing.* St. Paul, Minn.: West Publishing Company, 1992.

Dunnan, Nancy. *Dun & Bradstreet Guide to $Your Investments$.* New York: Harper-Collins Publishers, 1994.

Ficek, Edmund F., Thomas P. Henderson, and Ross H. Johnson. *Real Estate Principles and Practices,* 6th ed. New York: MacMillan Publishing Company, 1994.

Galaty, Fillmore, W., Willington H. Allaway, and Robert C. Kyle. *Modern Real Estate Practice,* 13th ed. Chicago: Dearborn Financial Publishing, 1994.

Johnson, R. Stafford, and Carmelo Giacatto. *Options and Futures.* St. Paul: West Publishing Company, 1995.

Merrill Lynch. *The Merrill Lynch Guide to Writing Stock Options,* 1982.

Miller, Theodore J. *Invest Your Way to Wealth.* Washington: The Kiplinger Washington Editors, Inc., 1994.

Morris, Kenneth M. and Alan M. Siegel. *The Wall Street Journal Guide to Understanding Personal Finance.* New York: Lightbulb Press, 1992.

NOTES

1. The actual price of an option can be determined through the application of the Black–Scholes option pricing model. This advanced topic is left to an investment or futures and options course.

2. Futures markets are so efficient, in fact, that some consider futures traders better weather forecasters than meteorologists.

Part Four

Retirement Planning and Estate Planning

Chapter **16**

Retirement Planning

Learning Objectives

After studying this chapter, you should be able to:

▪ Explain the problem of retirement in the United States.

▪ Describe the basic steps for determining the amount to save for retirement.

▪ Explain the major characteristics of defined-contribution pension plans, defined-benefit pension plans, profit-sharing and thrift plans, and Section 401(k) plans.

▪ Describe the major characteristics of the individual retirement account (IRA).

▪ Identify the major types of individual annuities that can be used to provide retirement income.

▪ Describe the major benefits under the social security program.

Retirement at age 65 is ridiculous. When I was 65, I still had pimples.

—George Burns

When some fellers decide to retire, nobody knows the difference.

—Kin Hubbard

A merican workers dream of financial independence and a comfortable retirement. Some workers retire early because they dislike their jobs, wish to travel, or start a second career. Other workers have no choice but are forced into retirement because of permanent downsizing of the labor force by corporations. Still other workers substantially underestimate the amount of money needed for a comfortable retirement. They erroneously believe that benefits from social security and an employer-sponsored retirement plan will provide all the income needed for a comfortable retirement. However, as discussed later, many workers are not saving enough to maintain their present standard of living during retirement. Finally, some workers may delay preparing for retirement until their late 40s or early 50s, which may not provide sufficient time to accumulate a sizable retirement fund.

This chapter discusses the important and timely topic of retirement planning. We emphasize five major areas. The first part of the chapter discusses the retirement problem in the United States and whether younger workers are saving enough for a comfortable retirement. The second part explains the steps in determining how much to save and invest for retirement. The third part describes the basic characteristics of tax-deferred retirement plans that receive favorable income tax treatment. The fourth part discusses the different types of individual annuities that can be used to provide supplemental retirement income. The chapter concludes with a discussion of the social security program, which provides an important base of retirement income to most retired workers.

Problem of Retirement

When workers retire, they lose their earned income. Unless they have adequate replacement income from other sources, they will be economically insecure. In addition, retirees often incur substantial medical expenses and may require long-term care in a nursing facility.

The retirement problem in the United States consists of the following: (1) growing proportion of older people, (2) longer retirement period, (3) insufficient income during retirement, (4) poor health, and (5) additional complicating factors.[1]

Growing Proportion of Older People

The proportion of older people in the population has increased dramatically over time. The age 65 and older group increased from 9.3 percent of the population in 1960 to 12.8 percent in 1995 and is projected to increase to 16.4 percent by 2020.[2] Thus, roughly one in six people in the

Consider This

Up-to-date information on the age and income of the U.S. population is available from the U.S. Census Bureau at:

http://www.census.gov/

population in the future will be age 65 and older. Unless they have adequate replacement income from social security, private pensions, and accumulated savings, they will experience a reduction in their standard of living after retirement.

Longer Retirement Period

A longer retirement period is another part of the retirement problem. Most workers are spending a relatively longer period of their adult lives in retirement and a relatively shorter period in productive employment. The longer retirement period is due to two factors: (1) early retirement and (2) longer life expectancy.

The majority of workers in the United States retire early before age 65. In 1993, only about 16 percent of the men and 8 percent of the women age 65 and older were participating in the labor force.[3] In addition, life expectancy has increased. The life expectancy for males age 65 increased from 13.1 years in 1970 to an estimated 15.2 years in 1994, while the life expectancy for females the same age increased from 17.1 years in 1970 to an estimated 19 years in 1994.[4] The combined effects of early retirement and longer life expectancy can substantially aggravate the problem of insufficient income during retirement. Because of a shorter period of productive employment, many older workers may not save enough during their working years to maintain a decent standard of living during the longer retirement period.

Insufficient Income During Retirement

Because of insufficient income, the financial position of many retired workers is unsatisfactory. Older retired workers are a financially diverse group, and total money incomes received are far from uniform. *In 1994, about 48 percent of the nonmarried persons age 65 and older had total money incomes under $10,000. About 7 percent of the married couples age 65 and older had total money incomes under $10,000.*[5] Because of the relatively small amount of income, older retired persons in these units were exposed to considerable economic insecurity. At the other extreme, only 3 percent of the nonmarried persons and 17 percent of the married couples age 65 and older had total money incomes of $50,000 or more.[6] The higher money income allowed these individuals to enjoy a substantially higher standard of living. *However, in 1994, the median money income for all people aged 65 and older was only $15,094.*[7] This amount is relatively small and may be insufficient for people with substantial additional expenses, such as high uninsured medical bills, care in a long-term nursing facility, or high property taxes.

In addition, the amount of financial assets owned by older workers on the threshold of retirement is relatively small, especially for some minority groups. In one study, the Rand Corporation analyzed the amount of financial assets owned by older households and individuals ages 51 to 61. *For 1993, the median amount of financial assets owned by middle-aged white households was only $17,300. For middle-aged black households, the median amount of financial assets was only $400, and for Hispanic households, only $150.*[8] These amounts are relatively small and provide only a limited amount of additional income to supplement social security and other retirement benefits.

Poor Health

Retired workers age 65 and older generally are in poorer health than the nonaged population. Many older persons suffer from chronic diseases, such as heart disease and arthritis, see physicians more frequently, and have longer hospital stays. Although Medicare covers virtually all retired people age 65 and older, the program does not cover all medical bills. Medicare pays less than half of the total medical expenses incurred by the elderly as a group. In addition, some retirees do not have a Medicare supplement policy that would cover part or all of the expenses not covered by Medicare. The financial burden on this group can be especially heavy.

Many retired persons also require long-term care in a nursing home, and the cost is staggering. Long-term care in a nursing home can easily exceed $40,000 annually. However, Medicare does not cover long-term care in a nursing facility. As a result, the financial assets of most older patients in long-term care nursing homes are quickly depleted. These patients may then be forced to apply for coverage under the Medicaid program, which is a welfare program and should not be confused with Medicare.

Additional Complicating Factors

A comfortable retirement is becoming more difficult to attain because of additional complicating factors. First, social security retirement benefits provide only a minimum floor of income. You will be exposed to considerable economic insecurity during your retirement years if you rely primarily on social security benefits as your major source of income. In 1997, the maximum monthly benefit for a retired worker at age 65 was $1,326; however, the average monthly benefit was only $745.

Second, middle-aged workers with dependent children must often provide financial assistance and physical care to sick elderly parents. The caretakers, usually females, typically provide help in eating, bathing, and other activities of daily living. The financial assistance provided may reduce the amount of savings available for retirement. In addition, the psychological and physical burden of caring for a sick

Consider This

The American Association of Retired Persons (AARP) is a large and powerful organization made up of members of the retired population. You can find its site at:

http://www.aarp.org/

parent often is so great that some employees are forced to drop out of the labor force. Again, saving for retirement is reduced because of the loss of earned income.

Finally, property taxes on homes have soared over time. States typically provide partial or complete tax relief to older low-income homeowners. However, middle-income retired homeowners may be ineligible for such tax relief, and the property tax burden on them can be especially heavy.

Planning for Retirement

Planning for retirement requires an understanding of certain important factors, including (1) reexamination of traditional retirement strategies, (2) inadequate savings for retirement by most younger workers, (3) barriers to saving for retirement, and (4) saving and investing strategies for retirement.

Reexamination of Traditional Retirement Strategies

Retirement planning for the next century requires a reexamination of traditional retirement strategies. Some retirement experts believe that retirement in the future will be substantially different from retirement today. In the future, many workers will not stop working at age 65 or at some earlier age; they will not neatly divide their lives into working years and retirement years, and relatively few retirees will move to Florida or Arizona for a life of sunshine, golf, and fishing. Instead, workers in the future will have a succession of jobs and careers interrupted by greater leisure time.[9]

Workers planning to retire in the next century should reexamine their retirement plans because of several emerging trends. First, because of insufficient financial assets, some workers will be unable to retire because they have not saved enough for a comfortable retirement.

Second, some married couples delay having children, and they may be faced with huge college bills when they are approaching their 60s. As a result, early retirement may not be possible, and retirement may have to be delayed.

Third, as we stated earlier, future retirees will live longer. Many older persons in the next century will survive into their 90s. Many of them will not have sufficient financial assets to support a comfortable retirement at that time, and some older retirees will outlive their savings. Moreover, the longer the retirement period, the greater will the effects of inflation erode the real purchasing power of the retirement benefits.

In addition, traditional defined-benefit pension plans (discussed later) that provide guaranteed retirement benefits have declined in importance. In order to limit pension contributions, many employers have replaced traditional defined-benefit pension plans with other types of retirement plans, such as Section 40l (k) and defined-contribution plans (also discussed later). Under such plans, retirement benefits are not guaranteed but depend on the level of funding and investment results. These plans allow employees to determine how the retirement contributions are invested. Some employees may not invest wisely or may invest too conservatively. As a result, future retirement benefits may be inadequate.

Finally, most workers will change jobs several times during their working careers, and workers employed by only one employer during their working careers will be in the minority. If you change jobs frequently before your benefits are fully vested (discussed later), your retirement benefits will be substantially reduced. Further, employer contributions into your retirement plan will terminate. As a result, retirement benefits from a private pension may be inadequate for many retirees.

Because of the preceding trends, some workers will have a strong financial need to continue working rather than retire. If they should retire, they may be faced with a reduced standard of living.

Inadequate Saving by Younger Workers

The majority of younger workers are saving an inadequate amount for retirement. Several studies point out the magnitude of the problem. One study of the baby boom generation (those born between 1946 and 1964) by Merrill Lynch showed that the baby boomers must nearly triple their rate of saving or face the prospect of delaying retirement, accepting a lower standard of living after retirement, or foregoing retirement altogether.[10] Another study sponsored by the Oppenheimer Management Corporation showed that, as things now stand, most Americans will have only one third to one half of the annual income needed to retire comfortably.[11] Finally, a study by the Public Agenda Foundation, a nonprofit organization, concluded that almost one third of all Americans have saved nothing or almost nothing for retirement.[12] Thus, the various studies show that undersaving for retirement is a serious problem.

Barriers to Saving for Retirement

The Public Agenda Foundation also identified several important barriers to saving for retirement.[13] They are summarized as follows:

1. *Retirement is not a high-priority goal for most people.* Most people are overwhelmed by work, by payment of bills, and by health-care costs.

Thirty-six percent stated they never think or seldom think about retirement planning.

2. *Many workers do not earn enough to save for retirement.* About one third believe they cannot save more for retirement because they lack the money to do so.

3. *Many Americans lack knowledge about retirement planning.* Seven in ten Americans did not know how much money they would need for retirement. Thirty-seven percent substantially underestimated the amount of money needed for retirement.

4. *Many Americans resist cutting back to save for retirement.* Some Americans struggle to make ends meet and have great difficulty saving for retirement. However, many middle-class Americans strongly resist cutting back on luxuries or nonessentials to save for retirement. About two-thirds of the respondents (68 percent) indicated they could save more for retirement by eating out less often, but only 18 percent of this group stated they are likely to do so.

5. *The public takes a conservative approach to retirement.* Many persons invest too conservatively for retirement and are frightened by the stock market and its volatility.

6. *Personality is also important in retirement planning.* The report identified four types of personalities:

■ *Planners.* Planners (about 21 percent of Americans) are in control of their financial affairs. They are more likely to save money than are other Americans. More than two thirds of the planners (68 percent) save regularly for retirement.
■ *Strugglers.* Strugglers (about 25 percent of Americans) have great difficulty in making ends meet. Only 20 percent of the strugglers save regularly.
■ *Deniers.* Deniers (about 19 percent of Americans) typically refuse to deal with retirement. They are less likely to save regularly, to have a retirement plan, or to give up extras to save for retirement.
■ *Impulsives.* Impulsives (about 15 percent of Americans) seek immediate gratification by spending today and forgetting about retirement. They are less likely to save regularly according to a plan and are more likely to acknowledge they have fallen behind financially.

Saving for Retirement

To reach your retirement goal, you need to know the amount to save each month or year. Many financial organizations have prepared simple and convenient worksheets to help you calculate the amount needed to attain your retirement income and annual savings goals (see Exhibit 16.1).

For example, referring to Exhibit 16.1, assume that Susan, age 37, wants to retire in 25 years. She must first estimate the amount of her annual retirement expenses. Pension experts believe that a replacement rate of 60 to 80 percent of your present income will provide a reasonable

---

Exhibit 16.1

Calculate Your Retirement Income and Annual Savings Goal

Use this Planner Page to help you determine the amount of money you will need to save annually to ensure the retirement income you are projecting for yourself. Follow the example on the right as a guide. Make a copy of this page before you begin, for easier updating.

Your Projections	Use the shaded area for your answers.	Example: Susan plans to retire in 25 years	
1. Annual retirement expenses	$	$60,000	Susan estimated her annual retirement expenses to be $60,000.
2. Retirement income a. Social security income	$	$10,000	Susan estimates $10,000 from social security. She has estimated another $10,000 to come from her defined-benefit plan.
b. Other income (defined-benefit plans, post-retirement income, rents, royalties)	$	$10,000	
3. Total income (Add lines 2a and 2b)	$	$20,000	Susan's total projected income is $20,000.
4. Income shortfall (Line 1 minus line 3)	$	$40,000	By subtracting her retirement income from her retirement expenses, Susan found a shortfall of $40,000.
5. Total assets needed at retirement (From Table 1)	$	$1,066,335	Since Susan is retiring in 25 years, Table 1 shows that she'll need total assets of $1,066,335 saved by the time she retires. Inflation is considered in this amount.
6. Amount you have saved already for retirement a. IRAs/Keoghs	$	$10,000	Susan has saved $10,000 in her IRA.
b. Employer-sponsored retirement plans	$	$21,000	She also has $21,000 in her company retirement program.
c. Other investments/savings (stocks, bonds, CDs, mutual funds, money market funds, etc.)	$	$40,000	This is the value of Susan's brokerage portfolio.
d. Equity in home (optional)	$	0	
7. Total amount saved (Add lines 6a through 6d)	$	$71,000	Combining the assets listed in line 6, Susan has saved this amount.
8. Value of current savings at retirement a. Portfolio Compounding Factor (From Table 2)	$	6.85	In Table 2, Susan has determined the factor selecting 8% as her rate of return. 6.85 times $71,000 is $486,350.
b. Multiply total from line 7 by line 8a	$	$486,350	
9. Asset shortfall at retirement (Line 5 minus line 8b)	$	$579,985	By subtracting $486,350 from $1,066,335, Susan estimated that $579,985 is the amount she must have saved by the time she retires.
10. Annual savings needed* (From Table 3)	$	$6,000	In order to meet this goal, Table 3 suggests that Susan save approximately $6,000 per year for the next 25 years.

*This amount could include any retirement accounts you may currently be contributing to, such as IRAs or 401(k)s. It could be reduced by an employer contribution.

estimate of your retirement expenses. Living expenses generally are lower at retirement; the mortgage on the house may be paid off; college tuition payments for the children may not be required; work-related expenses are not being incurred; and social security payroll taxes are not being paid. In this case, Susan estimates she will need $60,000 annually when she retires.

Exhibit 16.1 (continued)

Calculate Your Retirement Income and Annual Savings Goal

Use these tables to help complete the Planner Page. They will help you calculate the amount of money you'll need to save for retirement.

Table 1: Total Assets Requirement (needed at retirement)

If Your Income Shortfall Is	Years to Retirement							
	5	10	15	20	25	30	35	40
$ 5,000	60,833	74,012	90,047	109,556	133,292	162,170	197,304	240,051
$10,000	121,665	148,024	180,094	219,112	266,584	324,340	394,609	480,102
$15,000	182,498	222,037	270,142	328,668	399,875	486,510	591,913	720,153
$20,000	243,331	296,049	360,189	438,225	533,167	648,680	789,218	960,204
$25,000	304,163	370,061	450,236	547,781	666,459	810,849	986,522	1,200,255
$30,000	364,996	444,073	540,283	657,337	799,751	973,019	1,183,827	1,440,306
$40,000	486,661	592,098	720,377	876,449	1,066,335	1,297,359	1,578,436	1,920,408
$50,000	608,326	740,122	900,472	1,095,562	1,332,918	1,621,699	1,973,044	2,400,510

Table 2: Portfolio Compounding Factor (compounded annually)

Years to Your Goal	Rate of Return					
	5%	6%	7%	8%	9%	10%
5	1.28	1.34	1.40	1.47	1.54	1.61
10	1.63	1.79	1.97	2.16	2.37	2.59
15	2.08	2.40	2.76	3.17	3.64	4.18
20	2.65	3.21	3.87	4.66	5.60	6.73
25	3.39	4.29	5.43	6.85	8.62	10.83
30	4.32	5.74	7.61	10.06	13.27	17.45
35	5.52	7.69	10.68	14.79	20.41	28.10
40	7.04	10.29	14.97	21.72	31.41	45.26

Table 3: Annual Savings Requirement (needed to reach savings goal)

If Your Income Shortfall Is	Years to Retirement							
	5	10	15	20	25	30	35	40
$ 25,000	4,095	1,569	787	436	254	152	92	56
$ 50,000	8,190	3,137	1,574	873	508	304	184	113
$100,000	16,380	6,275	3,147	1,746	1,017	608	369	226
$150,000	24,570	9,412	4,721	2,619	1,525	912	553	339
$200,000	32,759	12,549	6,295	3,492	2,034	1,216	738	452
$300,000	49,139	18,824	9,442	5,238	3,050	1,824	1,107	678
$500,000	81,899	31,373	15,737	8,730	5,084	3,040	1,845	1,130
$750,000	122,848	47,059	23,605	13,095	7,626	4,559	2,767	1,695

Assumptions: Tax-deferred income, no depletion of principal, annual return on assets: 8%, annual inflation: 4%. annual savings made at the end of each year (Table 3)

Source: *Your Personal Guide to Retirement Planning*, Charles Schwab & Co., Inc., 1995, pp. 6–7. Reprinted with permission.

Susan next estimates the amount of retirement income she will receive from social security and from her employer's retirement plan. Estimated social security benefits can be obtained by calling 800-772-1213 and asking for a *Request for Earnings and Benefit Estimate Statement.* After filling out the form, Susan received an estimate of future social security retirement benefits stated in today's dollars. She also contacted the employee benefits office in her company and received an estimate of the amount of retirement income from her employer's retirement plan. Susan expects to receive $10,000 from social security and $10,000 from her employer's retirement plan.

Susan must next determine any income shortfall. In her case, the income shortfall is $40,000. Since Susan will be retiring in 25 years, she will need total assets of $1,066,335 at retirement to cover this shortfall (see Exhibit 16.1, Table 1). This figure takes into consideration inflation, life expectancy, and an annual return of 8 percent on assets.

Susan's present savings are only $71,000. Based on an annual return of 8 percent, this amount will accumulate to $486,350 in 25 years. If this figure is subtracted from $1,066,335, Susan must have an additional $579,985 at retirement. To meet her goal, she must save approximately $6,000 annually for the next 25 years.

Investing for Retirement

After determining the amount needed for retirement, you must invest the funds to reach your retirement goal. Two principles should be stressed at this point: (1) start investing early, and (2) do not invest too conservatively.

A delay in saving for retirement can be financially costly. For example, if Jennifer, age 25, saves $500 monthly in a tax-deferred retirement plan earning 8 percent; she would have $478,683 at age 50. If she delays until age 30 to save the same monthly amount, she would have only $296,474 at age 50, or about 38 percent less (see Exhibit 16.2).

In addition, do not invest too conservatively. Many younger workers make the common mistake of investing a large part of their retirement funds in fixed income investments, such as certificates of deposit, money market accounts, or bond mutual funds. There is little or no opportunity for sizable capital gains by following such a conservative strategy. *The desire to play it safe and preserve capital can be especially costly to younger workers in the long run.* For example, a $10,000 investment in a time certificate of deposit earning 4 percent interest would accumulate to $21,911 in 20 years. If the funds were invested instead in a growth mutual fund or growth common stocks earning 10 percent, the same investment would accumulate to $67,275, or 207 percent more (see Exhibit 16.3).

Mutual funds and common stocks that emphasize growth are extremely important in investing for retirement, especially for younger

Exhibit 16.2

The Cost of Waiting to Invest Retirement Funds

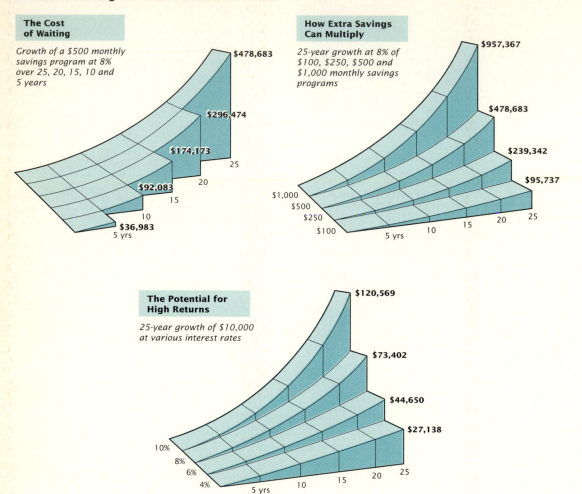

The Cost of Waiting

Growth of a $500 monthly savings program at 8% over 25, 20, 15, 10 and 5 years

$478,683
$296,474
$174,173
$92,083
$36,983

25
20
15
10
5 yrs

How Extra Savings Can Multiply

25-year growth at 8% of $100, $250, $500 and $1,000 monthly savings programs

$957,367
$478,683
$239,342
$95,737

$1,000
$500
$250
$100

5 yrs   10   15   20   25

The Potential for High Returns

25-year growth of $10,000 at various interest rates

$120,569
$73,402
$44,650
$27,138

10%
8%
6%
4%

5 yrs   10   15   20   25

Note: The costs of investing and taxes are ignored.
Source: *American Tragedy, American Dream,* Oppenheimer Funds, Inc., March 1994, p. 8. Reprinted with permission.

workers. The following steps may help you determine how the retirement funds should be invested:

1. *Select an initial allocation of assets among stocks, bonds, and cash reserves.* The asset mix depends on your investment objectives and time horizon. Younger workers should invest more of their retirement funds in common stocks because the longer you have to invest, the greater is the risk you can assume (see Exhibit 16.4). A simple rule for determining the proportion of assets to invest in stocks is to subtract your age from 100. *Remember, it is your asset mix, rather than selection of individual securities, that tends to have a greater long-run impact on your investing success.*

Exhibit 16.3

How Money Grows Over Time

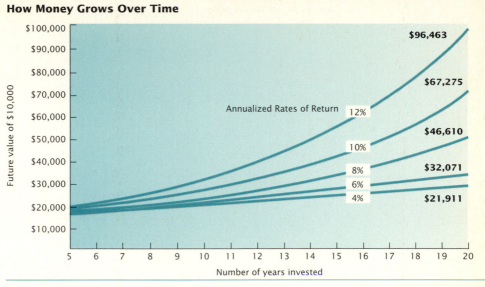

Note: Chart is intended for hypothetical illustration only, and not to project the future performance of any investments. No adjustments have been made for income taxes.
Source: *Your Personal Guide to Retirement Planning*, Charles Schwab & Co., Inc., 1995, p. 14. Reprinted with permission.

2. *Modify your asset allocation if necessary to reflect your tolerance for risk and personal financial situation.* Asset allocation is an individual decision. If you invest heavily in common stocks or aggressive growth mutual funds, you must be willing to tolerate sharp swings in stock prices. Depending on your investment temperament, you may be more comfortable with less risk. In addition, your personal financial situation may require a low-risk approach to retirement investing.

3. *Identify the mutual funds or individual stocks to use in your program.* The research reports by *Morningstar* and *Value Line* can be especially helpful in this regard. These reference materials are usually available in your local public library. Valuable information is provided on aggressive growth funds, growth funds, growth and income funds, balanced funds, index funds, international funds, and individual common stocks. Part of your funds should be invested in international mutual funds or stocks. One suggestion is that 20 to 30 percent of your stock portfolio should be invested in international funds or stocks.

4. *Consider a strategy of dollar-cost averaging by which a fixed amount is invested on a regular basis, regardless of market conditions.* As a result, the average cost per share will be less than the average market price. However, keep in mind that dollar-cost averaging does not guarantee a profit or protect against a loss in a declining market. Thus, you need to consider your temperament and willingness to continue investing during periods of declining market prices.

Exhibit 16.4
Choosing an Asset Allocation for Retirement Funds

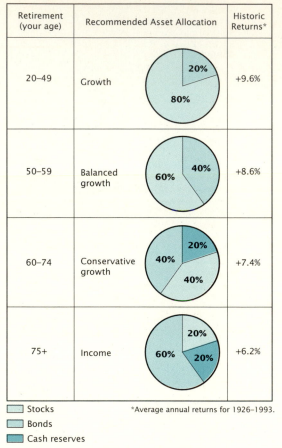

Retirement (your age)	Recommended Asset Allocation		Historic Returns*
20–49	Growth	20% / 80%	+9.6%
50–59	Balanced growth	40% / 60%	+8.6%
60–74	Conservative growth	20% / 40% / 40%	+7.4%
75+	Income	20% / 20% / 60%	+6.2%

☐ Stocks
☐ Bonds
☐ Cash reserves

*Average annual returns for 1926–1993.

5. *Consider the impact of inflation after you retire.* Inflation can substantially reduce the purchasing power of investment income. This means you should not have all of your retirement assets in fixed income investments after you retire (see Exhibit 16.5). Depending on your tolerance for risk, at least 20 percent to 40 percent of your retirement funds should be invested in common stocks or common stock mutual funds after you retire. Common stock prices generally will keep pace with or exceed the rate of inflation in the long run.

In addition, take advantage of any tax-deferred retirement plan sponsored by your employer, such as a Section 401(k) plan, and contribute the maximum allowed. Tragically, in 1993, one-third of the employees who

Exhibit 16.5

Loss of Purchasing Power with Fixed Annual Payments

Years

Note: Assumes $100,000 invested in 20-year bond with 7% coupon.
Source: *Part 3, Investing Your Retirement Assets*, T. Rowe Price Associates, Inc., 1994, p. 2. Reprinted with permission.

were eligible for 40l (k) plans did not participate. These plans provide enormous tax advantages, and you should participate and contribute the maximum allowed before you consider other investments for retirement. We discuss tax-deferred retirement plans in the following section.

Finally, if you are in your 20s. you should be saving part of your income for retirement. The advantages of starting early are great (see Insight 16.1

Tax-Deferred Retirement Plans

tax-deferred retirement plan Retirement plan that receives favorable income tax treatment.

Tax-deferred retirement plans are retirement plans that receive favorable income tax treatment. The employer's contributions are not taxed as income to the participating employees; investment earnings accumulate income-tax free; and the contributions are not taxed until the employee actually retires or receives the funds. Tax-deferred plans are typically sponsored by employers and are designed to supplement social security benefits. The additional income from a tax-deferred retirement plan can mean the difference between a higher standard of living and a much lower standard of living during your retirement years.

In the following section, we discuss the major types of tax-deferred retirement plans used today.[14] They include (l) private pension plans, (2) profit-sharing and thrift plans, (3) Section 401(k) plans, (4) Keogh plans for the self-employed, (5) individual retirement accounts (IRAs), (6) simplified employee pension (SEP) plans, and (7) SIMPLE retirement plans.

Ah, to be young again. Really young.

If you're in your 20s, ignore all the nonsense you hear about picking hot stocks, beating the market and spotting the next superstar fund manager. Instead, if you sincerely want to be rich, focus on socking away as much money as you can, and the sooner the better.

Absurdly simple advice? It certainly is. But consider the benefits:

You'll Get More for Less

Imagine you want to accumulate $1 million in retirement savings by the time you turn 65, and that your investments earn 8% a year.

If you put off saving until you're 45, you'll have to sock away some $21,900 a year, according to T. Rowe Price Associates. But if you begin at 25, you'll need to make an annual investment of just $3,900.

You Can Take Greater Risks

The sooner you start saving, the longer your time horizon, which means you can load up on stocks because you'll have plenty of time to ride out the market's ups and downs.

Moreover, as your wealth grows, you'll be able to take additional risks, even with money that's earmarked for financial emergencies.

How so? If you've got a substantial portfolio that's heavily invested in stocks, you'll always have enough money to cover a stint of unemployment or a substantial house repair, even if you have to sell some stocks during a fierce bear market.

By contrast, if you have little money but much of it is invested in stocks, a big market drop could leave you in deep trouble, especially if the market debacle coincides with a pressing financial need.

You'll Save on Insurance

Because of the risk that your family could suffer financially if you became disabled or died, you need to have both disability insurance and life insurance.

But if you start saving aggressively as soon as you get out of school, both policies may--depending on your family situation--become unnecessary by the time you are in your early 40s, says Alan Cohn, a financial planner in Bala Cynwyd, Pa.

Once you've accumulated enough money to carry your family through a prolonged illness, you may want to ditch your disability insurance or cut back your coverage, Mr. Cohn argues. Similarly, he says you may eventually be able to drop your life insurance, unless you need it for estate-planning purposes.

You'll Get Free Money

Those who start saving when they're young can take full advantage of retirement accounts, especially the 401(k) retirement plans now offered by many companies.

The demise of the traditional company pension and its replacement by 401(k) plans has meant that the burden of saving and investing for retirement has been shifted from employers to employees. But therein lies a great opportunity. For those who make full use of 401(k) plans, the payoff can be enormous.

"Some companies will match employee contributions dollar-for-dollar, while others will kick in $1 for every $3 contributed," says Michael Ceaser, a financial planner in Taylor, Mich. "But even if the company has no matching program, it's still a great wealth-building tool, because of the initial tax deduction and the ongoing tax deferral."

You Could Retire Early

If you want to take early retirement at, say, age 55, "at the very latest, I think you'd have to start saving by your early 30s," Mr. Ceaser says. "People don't realize what it takes to retire early."

But even if you don't want to quit the work force when you're 55, saving when you're younger will ease your financial worries and give you some flexibility, especially if you decide to go back to school or switch careers late in life.

Delaying saving for retirement, meanwhile, can be a financial disaster. Mr. Ceaser has worked with many clients who were laid off by local phone, steel and car companies. These folks had banked on saving heavily for retirement in the last 10 or 15 years before they quit their jobs.

It didn't work out that way. "In the years when they thought they would accumulate a lot for retirement, they found that they didn't have any job at all," Mr. Ceaser says. "They're really in desperate straits."

Source: Jonathan Clements, "A Word to 20-Somethings Aiming to Retire Rich: Start Saving Now," August 1, 1995. Reprinted by permission of *The Wall Street Journal*, © 1995 Dow Jones & Company, Inc. All Rights Reserved Worldwide.

Private Pension Plans

Many employers have private pension plans that pay retirement benefits to retired workers and their dependents. Private pension plans that meet certain federal requirements receive favorable income tax treatment.

Eligibility Requirements.   Most private pension plans have a minimum age and service requirement before the employees can participate in the plan. *Under present law, all employees eligible for plan coverage who are at least age 21 and have completed one year of service must be allowed to participate in the plan.* One exception is that the plan can require two years of service if there is 100 percent immediate vesting (discussed later) upon entry into the plan.

Types of Pension Plans.   There are two basic types of pension plans: (1) defined-contribution plans and (2) defined-benefit plans.

> **defined-contribution plan** Pension plan for which the contribution rate is fixed but the retirement benefit is variable.

A **defined-contribution plan** is a plan for which the contribution rate is fixed, but the retirement benefit is variable. For example, assume that Michelle, age 25, contributes 6 percent of her salary into a retirement plan, which is matched by an identical contribution from her employer. Although the contribution rate is known, the retirement benefit will vary depending on her earnings, investment results, and age of retirement.

> **defined-benefit plan** Pension plan in which the retirement benefit is known in advance but the contributions vary depending on the amount necessary to fund the benefit.

A **defined-benefit plan** is a plan in which the retirement benefit is known in advance, but the contributions will vary depending on the amount necessary to fund the desired benefit. For example, Tyrone, age 50, may be entitled to a retirement benefit at age 65 equal to 50 percent of his three highest consecutive years of earnings. An actuary then determines the annual amount that must be contributed to the plan to produce the desired benefit. Because of actuarial considerations, defined-benefit plans are more complicated and expensive to administer and fund than defined-contribution plans. As a result, defined-benefit plans have declined in importance in recent years.

Retirement Ages.   Private pension plans typically have three retirement ages. The **normal retirement age** is the age that a worker can retire and receive a full, unreduced benefit. The normal retirement age in most plans today is age 65. Under current law, with certain exceptions, a private pension plan cannot impose a mandatory retirement age.

> **normal retirement age** The age at which a worker can retire and receive a full, unreduced benefit.

> **early retirement age** The earliest age at which a worker can retire and receive a retirement benefit.

An **early retirement age** is the earliest age that workers can retire to receive a retirement benefit. The majority of employees retire before age 65. For example, a plan may permit a worker with ten years of service to retire at age 55. If a worker retires early, the retirement benefits under a defined-benefit plan are actuarially reduced because they must be paid over a longer period.

The **late retirement age** is any age beyond the normal retirement age. A relatively small number of older employees continue working beyond the normal retirement age. Under federal law, with certain exceptions, older workers can delay retiring with no maximum age limit as long as they can do their jobs.

Vesting Provisions.   To receive favorable tax treatment, private pension plans must meet certain vesting requirements. **Vesting** refers to the employee's right to the benefits attributable to the employer's contributions if employment is terminated prior to retirement. The purposes of vesting are to reduce labor turnover and reward long-service employees. Employees are always entitled to a refund of their contributions plus any investment earnings upon termination of employment. However, the right to the employer's contributions, or benefits attributable to the contributions, depends on the extent to which vesting has been attained.

To receive favorable tax treatment, a private pension plan must meet one of the following minimum vesting standards:

1. *Five-year rule.* Under this rule, the worker must be 100 percent vested after five years of service.

2. *Three-to-seven-year rule.* Under this rule, the rate of vesting must meet the following minimum standard:

Years of Service	Percentage Vested
3	20
4	40
5	60
6	80
7	100

Limits on Contributions and Benefits.   Under current law, there are certain annual limits on contributions and benefits. Under a defined-contribution plan, for 1997, the maximum annual contribution to an employee's account is limited to 25 percent of compensation, or $30,000, whichever is less. The maximum amount of annual compensation that can be counted in the contribution or benefit formula is $160,000 (indexed for inflation).

Under a defined-benefit plan, for 1997, the maximum annual pension that can be funded is limited to 100 percent of the participant's average compensation for his or her three highest consecutive years of compensation, or $125,000, whichever is lower. This latter figure is indexed for inflation.

Participants in defined-benefit plans are protected against the loss of benefits up to certain limits if the pension plan should terminate. The **Pension Benefit Guaranty Corporation (PBGC)** is a federal corporation that guarantees the payment of vested benefits up to $2,761.36 monthly (1997) if a private pension plan is terminated. The monthly limit is adjusted annually.

Early Distribution Penalty.   There is a 10 percent tax penalty if the funds are withdrawn before age 59¹/₂. An ordinary income tax must also be paid on the distribution plus a penalty tax of 10 percent. However, the 10 percent penalty does not apply to death or total and permanent disability of the employee; substantially equal payments that are paid over the worker's life expectancy; medical expenses that are deductible under the Internal Revenue Code; and certain other exceptions.

Profit-Sharing and Thrift Plans

profit-sharing plan A defined-contribution plan in which an employer contributes part of its profits to eligible employees.

Many employers have profit-sharing and thrift plans to provide retirement income to eligible employees. A **profit-sharing plan** is a defined-contribution plan to which an employer contributes part of the profits to eligible employees. Employers establish profit-sharing plans for several reasons. Eligible employees are encouraged to work more efficiently; the employer's cost is not affected by the age or number of employees; and there is greater flexibility in employer contributions. If there are no profits, there are no contributions.

The profit-sharing contributions can be discretionary based on an amount determined annually by the board of directors, or they can be based on a formula, such as a certain percentage of profits above a certain level. There are annual limits, however, on the amount that can be contributed into an employee's account. In 1997, the maximum annual contribution is limited to 15 percent of employee compensation or $24,000, whichever is lower (13.04 percent if self-employed).

The profit-sharing funds are typically distributed to the employees at retirement, death, disability, termination of employment (only the vested portion), or after a fixed number of years, which must be at least two years.

A 10 percent tax penalty applies to a distribution to a participant under age 59¹/₂. To avoid the tax penalty, many plans have loan provisions that permit employees to borrow from their accounts.

thrift plan A defined-contribution plan to which eligible employees voluntarily contribute; the employer contributes an amount that is typically some fraction of the employee's contribution.

Many employers also have thrift plans or savings plans for their employees. A **thrift plan** is a defined-contribution plan in which eligible employees voluntarily contribute to the plan; the employer also contributes, which is typically some fraction of the employee's contribution. For example, if the employee contributes $1, the employer contributes 25 or 50 cents. The purposes of thrift plans are to encourage employees to save, to provide retirement income, and to retain valuable employees.

Employees typically have a choice of the percentage of salary they wish to contribute into the plan, such as 1 to 6 percent of salary. The plan may also allow for additional contributions that are not matched by the employer, such as 10 percent of salary.

Section 401(k) Plans

Section 401(k) plan A plan in which part of an eligible employee's pay is deferred and invested rather than being paid as cash; taxes on the contributions and the investment earnings are paid when the funds are withdrawn.

Section 40l(k) plans are becoming increasingly popular as a tax-deferred savings plan. A **Section 40l (k) plan** is a cash or deferred arrangement that allows eligible employees to defer part of their before-tax pay rather than receive the pay as cash. The amount of salary deferred is then invested in the employer's 401(k) plan. A Section 40l (k) plan can be established that involves only employer contributions, both employer and employee contributions, or only employee contributions.

Annual Limit on Elective Deferrals.   Eligible employees can voluntarily elect to reduce their salary if they participate in a Section 401(k) plan. The amount of salary deferred is then invested in the employer's 401(k) plan. For 1997, the maximum salary that can be deferred is limited to $9,500 (indexed for inflation). The salary deferred is not taxed as income until the funds are actually received. However, social security taxes must still be paid on the amount of salary deferred.

Limitations on Distributions.   The tax law also places limitations on the distribution of funds under a 40l (k) plan. A 10 percent penalty tax applies to any distribution of funds to a participant under age 59½. The amounts withdrawn are also taxed as ordinary income.

The plan may permit the withdrawal of funds for a financial hardship, such as a down payment on a home, paying college tuition, or paying medical expenses deductible under the Internal Revenue Code. The 10 percent penalty tax also applies to any withdrawal of funds because of a financial hardship if the employee is under age 59½. However, 401(k) plans frequently contain a loan provision that allows the funds to be borrowed without a tax penalty.

Despite the tax penalty and ordinary income tax on a premature distribution, many employees are now using their 401(k) funds and other retirement funds for purposes other than retirement, such as education, medical bills, home purchases, and vacations. As a result, employees who take money out of their 401(k) plans early will receive a substantially lower amount of retirement income and may be exposed to considerable economic insecurity during their retirement years.

Keogh Plans for the Self-Employed

Sole proprietors and partners can also establish a tax-deferred retirement plan and enjoy most of the tax advantages now available to participants

Keogh plan A retirement plan that allows self-employed persons to make tax-deductible contributions to a qualified defined-contribution or defined-benefit pension plan.

in a qualified corporate pension plan. A **Keogh plan** is a retirement plan that allows self-employed persons to make tax-deductible contributions to a qualified defined-contribution or defined-benefit pension plan. The pension contributions and investment earnings are not taxed until the funds are actually distributed.

Certain annual limits on contributions and benefits apply. If the plan is a defined-contribution pension plan, for 1997, the maximum annual contribution is limited to 20 percent of net earnings or $30,000, whichever is lower. For purposes of determining net earnings, one half of the social security self-employment payroll tax must be deducted from net earnings. For example, after deducting one half of the social security payroll tax, Stephanie has net self-employment earnings of $50,000. She can make a maximum tax-deductible contribution of $10,000 into the plan.

If the plan is a defined-benefit pension plan, for 1997, self-employed individuals can fund for a maximum annual benefit equal to 100 percent of the average of the three highest consecutive years of compensation but not to exceed $125,000 (indexed for inflation). For example, assume that Jennifer, age 50, has a defined-benefit plan that will provide a retirement benefit at age 65 equal to 50 percent of her net income. If her average net income for the three highest consecutive years is $50,000, she can fund for a maximum annual benefit of $25,000. An actuary then determines the amount that she can contribute annually to reach her goal. Based on 7 percent interest and certain actuarial assumptions, Jennifer could contribute $10,847 each year into the plan.

Keogh plans contain several additional provisions. All employees at least age 21 with one year of service must be included in the plan; annual reports must be filed with the Internal Revenue Service (IRS Form 5500 Series), and the 10 percent penalty tax applies to the withdrawal of funds prior to age 59½.

Individual Retirement Accounts

individual retirement account (IRA) A retirement plan that allows workers with earned incomes to make annual contributions up to certain limits; earnings from the IRA are not taxed until they are withdrawn.

Workers with earned income can also establish an individual retirement account. An **individual retirement account (IRA)** allows workers with earned income to make annual contributions into a retirement plan up to certain limits with favorable tax advantages. An IRA can provide additional retirement income to supplement social security and private pension benefits.

Eligibility Requirements.   There are two basic eligibility requirements for IRAs. First, you must have taxable compensation during the year from personal services; investment income does not qualify. Second, you must be under age 70½. You cannot make any contributions to an IRA for the year in which you reach age 70½ and any later year.

Exhibit 16.6

Early-Start IRAs Pay Big Dividends

Age	Investor A		Investor B		Investor C	
	Contribution	Year-End Value	Contribution	Year-End Value	Contribution	Year-End Value
8	0	0	0	0	0	0
9	0	0	0	0	0	0
10	0	0	0	0	0	0
11	0	0	0	0	0	0
12	0	0	0	0	0	0
13	0	0	0	0	0	0
14	0	0	0	0	$2,000	$2,200
15	0	0	0	0	2,000	4,620
16	0	0	0	0	2,000	7,282
17	0	0	0	0	2,000	10,210
18	0	0	0	0	2,000	13,431
19	0	0	$2,000	$2,200	0	14,774
20	0	0	2,000	4,620	0	16,252
21	0	0	2,000	7,282	0	17,877
22	0	0	2,000	10,210	0	19,665
23	0	0	2,000	13,431	0	21,631
24	0	0	2,000	16,974	0	23,794
25	0	0	2,000	20,872	0	26,174
26	$2,000	$2,200	0	22,959	0	28,791
27	2,000	4,620	0	25,255	0	31,670
28	2,000	7,282	0	27,780	0	34,837
29	2,000	10,210	0	30,558	0	38,321
30	2,000	13,431	0	33,614	0	42,153
31	2,000	16,974	0	36,976	0	46,368
32	2,000	20,872	0	40,673	0	51,005
33	2,000	25,159	0	44,741	0	56,106
34	2,000	29,875	0	49,215	0	61,716
35	2,000	35,062	0	54,136	0	67,888
36	2,000	40,769	0	59,550	0	74,676
37	2,000	47,045	0	65,505	0	82,144
38	2,000	53,950	0	72,055	0	90,359
39	2,000	61,545	0	79,261	0	99,394
40	2,000	69,899	0	87,187	0	109,334
41	2,000	79,089	0	95,905	0	120,267
42	2,000	89,198	0	105,496	0	132,294
43	2,000	100,318	0	116,045	0	145,523
44	2,000	112,550	0	127,650	0	160,076
45	2,000	126,005	0	140,415	0	176,083
46	2,000	140,805	0	154,456	0	193,692
47	2,000	157,086	0	169,902	0	213,061
48	2,000	174,995	0	186,892	0	234,367
49	2,000	194,694	0	205,581	0	257,803
50	2,000	216,364	0	226,140	0	283,358
51	2,000	240,200	0	248,754	0	311,942
52	2,000	266,420	0	273,629	0	343,136
53	2,000	295,262	0	300,992	0	377,450
54	2,000	326,988	0	331,091	0	415,195
55	2,000	361,887	0	364,200	0	456,715
56	2,000	400,276	0	400,620	0	502,386
57	2,000	442,503	0	440,682	0	552,625
58	2,000	488,953	0	484,750	0	607,887
59	2,000	540,049	0	533,225	0	668,676
60	2,000	596,254	0	586,548	0	735,543
61	2,000	658,079	0	645,203	0	809,098
62	2,000	726,087	0	709,723	0	890,007
63	2,000	800,896	0	780,695	0	979,008
64	2,000	883,815	0	858,765	0	1,076,909
65	2,000	973,704	0	944,641	0	1,184,600
Less total invested:		(80,000)		(14,000)		(10,000)
Equals net earnings:		893,704		930,641		1,174,600
Money grew:		11-fold		66-fold		117-fold

Note: Interest assumption is 10 percent.

Source: Excerpted from *Mutual Funds Magazine*, April 1995, p. 42. Reprinted through the courtesy of the Editors of Mutual Funds Magazine, © The Institute for Econometric Research, Inc., 1997, 2200 SW 10th St., Deerfield Beach, FL 33442, 1-800-442-9000.

spousal IRA An IRA that includes a nonworking spouse.

Contribution Limits.   Annual IRA contributions are limited to a maximum of $2,000, or 100 percent of your taxable compensation, whichever is less. If you have a nonworking spouse **(spousal IRA),** the annual maximum is increased to $4,000. The IRA contributions can accumulate to sizable amounts, especially if the plan is started at an early age (see Exhibit 16.6)

Tax Deduction of IRA Contributions.   IRA contributions are fully deductible in two general situations. First, workers who are not active participants in an employer-sponsored retirement plan can make fully deductible IRA contributions up to the maximum limit of $2,000 ($4,000 for a spousal IRA). Second, even if covered by an employer's retirement plan, a full deduction is allowed if the worker's annual adjusted gross income is $25,000 or less ($40,000 or less for a married couple filing jointly).

Workers covered by a retirement plan who have an adjusted gross income between $25,000 and $35,000 annually ($40,000 to $50,000 for married couples) can receive a partial deduction. For example, if you earn $30,000, you can contribute $2,000 annually into the plan, but the maximum deduction is limited to $1,000.

Finally, workers with an annual adjusted gross income of $35,000 or more ($50,000 or more for married couples) can make annual IRA contributions up to the maximum limit but cannot deduct the amounts contributed. However, the investment income accumulates income-tax free until withdrawn, which can provide a financial advantage.

Withdrawal of Funds.   Funds deposited into an IRA generally cannot be withdrawn before age 59½ without incurring a penalty tax of 10 percent on the amount withdrawn. However, the penalty tax does not apply to distributions that result from death; disability; substantially equal payments paid over your life expectancy, or the life expectancy of you and your beneficiary (or joint life expectancies); and certain other exceptions.

The distribution of funds must start no later than April 1 of the year following the calendar year in which you attain age 70½. Certain minimum distributions rules must be followed. All distributions are taxed as ordinary income except for any nondeductible contributions that are received income-tax free. The Internal Revenue Service has prepared a detailed worksheet for determining the taxable and nontaxable portion of the total distribution.

Finally, if you leave your job and receive a cash distribution from your employer's retirement plan, the employer is required to deduct 20 percent for federal income tax purposes. The tax deduction and 10 percent penalty if under age 59½ can be avoided if you ask your employer to transfer the pension distribution directly into an IRA account (called a rollover IRA). The tax advantages of transferring the assets directly into an IRA are substantial (see Exhibit 16.7).

Types of IRAs. There are two principal types of IRA plans: (1) individual retirement account, and (2) individual retirement annuity.

An individual retirement account is a trust or custodial account established in the United States for your exclusive benefit or for the benefit of your beneficiaries. An IRA can be established with a bank, insured credit union, savings and loan institution, mutual fund, stock brokerage firm, or a person who is eligible to be a trustee or custodian. No more than $2,000 can be deposited annually into the account of any individual, and all contributions must be made in cash.

An IRA can also be established by purchasing an individual retirement annuity from a life insurer. An individual retirement annuity is designed to provide retirement income that cannot be outlived. The annuity purchased from a life insurer must meet certain requirements. The contract must be nontransferable by the owner. In addition, the annuity must have flexible premiums so that if your earnings change, the IRA contributions can also be changed.

IRA Investments. The IRA contributions can be invested in a wide variety of investments, which include certificates of deposit, mutual funds,

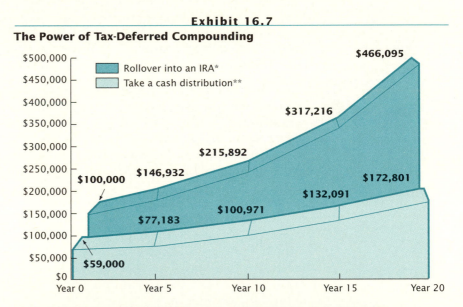

Exhibit 16.7

The Power of Tax-Deferred Compounding

We have assumed a 45-year-old individual (31% tax bracket) with a $100,000 distribution. Both accounts hypothetically earn 8% annually. In the rollover IRA account, the 8% earnings compound annually; in the taxable account, the 8% earnings are taxed at 31% annually, making the real rate of return in this account only 5.52%.
  *Assumes a direct rollover of entire $100,000 distribution.
 **Assumes $100,000 distribution taken as cash. Reflects 20% tax withholding, 10% early distribution penalty and additional federal taxes at year-end. Remaining $59,000 invested in a taxable account.

Source: *Making the Most of Your Retirement Plan Payout*, Charles Schwab & Co., Inc., 1995, p. 6. Reprinted with permission.

16.2   Getting the Most from Your IRA

Once you're committed to putting the IRA in your personal portfolio, you'll want to make sure you get the most from the account. Several strategies, suggested by financial experts, will help you maximize the already powerful benefits of an IRA.

■ *Set up an automatic contribution plan with the bank, credit union, brokerage house, mutual fund or insurance company where your IRA is invested.* You'll assure yourself of making the maximum annual contribution with little or no possibility that you'll find other uses for those funds.

■ *Fund your IRA as fully as possible even if automatic contributions are out of the question.* Some investors think they must contribute $2,000 or nothing. That is not true; $2,000 is only the ceiling for contributions. If you can afford only a lesser amount, contribute that. You may even skip a year if your financial situation is really tight, but that would be a pity considering you will never be able to make up for the opportunity you've lost. If you earn only $2,000 or less, you can contribute everything you earn.

■ *If you opt to make contributions on your own, make them early in the year to get the most earning power for your money.* However, IRS rules allow you to make contributions to an IRA as late as April 15 of the year after you earned the money.

■ *If you're looking for an easy way to contribute to your IRA, file your taxes early and contribute your tax refund (assuming, of course, you're entitled to one) to your IRA,* as long as you make the contribution before April 15.

■ If you have IRAs in many different institutions (you are allowed as many IRAs as you want as long as the total annual contribution is no more than $2,000), *consider consolidating them into one account at one institution.* You'll save on paperwork and fees; you may also squeeze a higher total return from a larger lump sum than from several smaller, less significant account balances.

■ *If you choose to move your IRA from one institution to another, you may transfer it or roll it over.* A transfer moves your funds directly from the old institution to the new one with no effort and minimal paperwork for you. Your funds stay intact because you have no access to them. A rollover, by contrast, puts more burden on you because you take possession of the funds from the old account and are responsible for reinvesting them within a 60-day time limit. Rolling over an IRA account takes a fair amount of self-discipline; you may be tempted to "sneak out" some funds while the money passes through your hands. An incomplete reinvestment of all funds from the old account or a missed deadline for reinvesting funds counts as a permanent withdrawal on which taxes and possible penalties are due.

Source: "Getting the Most from Your IRA." Reprinted from *USAA Magazine,* February 1995, p. 22. USAA, San Antonio, TX © 1995. Emphasis added.

individual stocks and bonds in a self-directed brokerage account, and gold and silver coins issued by the federal government. However, the contributions cannot be invested in collectibles, such as baseball cards or antiques. In addition, no part of the contributions can be used to purchase a life insurance policy.

Finally, to maximize the investment returns from your IRA contributions, you should follow certain investment strategies (see Insight 16.2).

Simplified Employee Pension Plans

simplified employee pension (SEP) A plan by which an employer contributes to an IRA for each covered employee.

A **simplified employee pension (SEP)** is a plan in which the employer contributes to an IRA established for each covered employee. The purpose is to reduce the paperwork for employers who wish to cover employees in a qualified pension plan.

Contribution Limits.   Under an SEP plan, each employee establishes and owns an individual IRA plan (called an SEP-IRA) and has fully vested rights. In 1997, annual employer tax-deductible contributions to a SEP-IRA were limited to 15 percent of employee compensation or $24,000, whichever is less (13.04 percent if self-employed).

Eligible Employees.   The SEP plan must cover all employees who are (1) at least age 21 and have worked for the employer during at least three of the immediately preceding five years, and (2) have received from the employer at least $400 in compensation in the tax year. This latter figure is annually indexed for inflation.

SIMPLE Plans

SIMPLE plan A plan that allows eligible employees to contribute a percentage of salary up to a certain limit; the employer may either match each employee's contribution or provide a flat-rate contribution for all eligible employees. SIMPLE stands for Savings Incentive Match Plan for Employees.

In 1996, federal legislation created a new retirement plan for employers with 100 or fewer employees known as the Savings Incentive Match Plan for Employees (SIMPLE). Under a **SIMPLE plan,** eligible employees can elect to contribute a percentage of salary into the plan but not to exceed $6,000 annually (indexed for inflation in increments of $500). The employer has the option of either matching the employee's contribution on a dollar-for-dollar basis up to 3 percent of salary or providing a nonelective contribution of 2 percent of salary for all eligible employees. Under a SIMPLE plan, employers are exempt from complex nondiscrimination rules that apply to qualified pension plans.

Individual Annuities

Individual annuities can also be purchased to provide additional retirement income. Although the premiums are not deductible for income-tax purposes, the investment income accumulates on a tax-deferred basis until the funds are actually received.

What is an Annuity?

annuity A periodic payment to an individual that continues for a fixed period or for the duration of a designated life or lives.

An **annuity** can be defined as a periodic payment to an individual that continues for a fixed period or for the duration of a designated life or lives. The **annuitant** is the person who receives the periodic payments or whose life governs the duration of payments.

The fundamental purpose of a life annuity is to provide a lifetime income to an individual that cannot be outlived. An annuity is designed to liquidate a principal sum and provides protection against the economic problems associated with living too long. It provides protection against the loss of income because of excessive longevity and the exhaustion of one's savings.

annuitant Person who receives the periodic payments composing an annuity or whose life governs the duration of payments.

Types of Annuities

Life insurers sell a wide variety of annuities. For the sake of convenience, the different types of annuities can be classified as follows:

1. Time when payments begin

■ Immediate annuity
■ Deferred annuity

2. Nature of the insurer's obligation

■ Life annuity (no refund)
■ Life annuity with guaranteed payments
■ Installment or cash refund annuity
■ Joint-and-survivor annuity

3. Fixed or variable benefits

■ Fixed annuity
■ Variable annuity

1. Time When Payments Begin.   Annuities can be classified according to the time the payments begin. The payments can start immediately or be deferred until some later date.

immediate annuity An annuity in which the first payment is due one payment interval from the date of purchase.

1. *Immediate annuity.* An **immediate annuity** is one where the first payment is due one payment interval from the date of purchase. If the income is paid monthly, the first payment starts one month from the purchase date. For example, assume that Marcia, age 65, purchases a life annuity with a lump sum payment of $100,000. She would receive the first monthly payment of $758 one month later.

deferred annuity An annuity that provides income at some future date.

2. *Deferred annuity.* A **deferred annuity** provides income at some future date. Several types of deferred annuities are sold today. A popular

retirement annuity A deferred annuity intended to accumulate a sum of money for retirement purposes.

single-premium deferred annuity A deferred annuity purchased with a lump sum.

flexible-premium annuity A deferred annuity permitting purchase through flexible premiums.

life annuity (no refund) Annuity that provides income to the annuitant only during the annuitant's lifetime. Payments cease at the annuitant's death.

life annuity with guaranteed payments Annuity that pays a life income to the annuitant with a certain number of guaranteed payments.

installment refund annuity Annuity that, if the annuitant dies before receiving total payments equal to the cost of the annuity, continues to make payments to a beneficiary.

cash refund annuity Annuity that, if the annuitant dies before receiving total payments equal to the cost of the annuity, makes a lump-sum payment to a beneficiary.

joint-and-survivor annuity Annuity based on the lives of two or more annuitants; payments are made until the death of the last annuitant.

fixed annuity Annuity that makes payments of a guaranteed fixed amount during the annuitant's lifetime.

variable annuity Annuity that makes payments that vary in amount depending on investment performance.

form of a deferred annuity is a **retirement annuity,** which is essentially a plan for accumulating a sum of money for retirement purposes. The premiums less expenses are accumulated at interest prior to retirement. At the retirement date stated in the policy, the annuitant can receive the funds in a lump sum or have the accumulated sum paid out as income under one of the annuity options stated in the contract.

A deferred annuity can be purchased with a lump sum, or the contract may permit flexible premiums. A deferred annuity purchased with a lump sum is called a **single-premium deferred annuity.**

The deferred annuity can also be purchased with flexible premiums. A **flexible-premium annuity** permits the annuity owner to vary the premium deposits. There is no requirement that a specified amount must be deposited each year. The amount of retirement income will depend on the accumulated sum at retirement.

2. Nature of the Insurer's Obligation. Annuities can also be classified in terms of the insurer's obligation. Payments may be made only during the lifetime of the annuitant, or the annuity may guarantee a certain number of payments.

A **life annuity (no refund)** provides a lifetime income to the annuitant only while he or she is alive. No further payments are made after the annuitant dies. A **life annuity with guaranteed payments** pays a life income to the annuitant with a certain number of guaranteed payments, such as 5, 10, 15, or 20 years.

An **installment refund annuity** pays a life income to the annuitant. However, if the annuitant dies before receiving total payments equal to the cost of the annuity, the payments continue to the beneficiary until they equal the sum of the premiums paid. A **cash refund annuity** is another version of this annuity. If the annuitant dies before receiving total payments equal to the cost of the annuity, the balance is paid in a lump sum to the beneficiary.

Finally, a **joint-and-survivor annuity** is based on the lives of two or more annuitants, such as a husband and wife. Annuity payments are paid until the death of the last annuitant.

3. Fixed or Variable Benefits. Annuities can also be classified as fixed or variable. A **fixed annuity** is an annuity that pays a guaranteed fixed amount during the annuitant's lifetime. Because the periodic payments are fixed, there is no protection against inflation, which reduces the real purchasing power of the benefits during retirement.

In contrast, a **variable annuity** pays periodic payments that vary depending on the investment results of the fund in which the premiums are invested. The fundamental purpose of a variable annuity is to provide an inflation hedge by maintaining the real purchasing power of the benefits during retirement.

accumulation units Units purchased by periodic premium contributions to a variable annuity. Value of each unit depends on market conditions.

annuity units Accumulation units are converted to annuity units to determine the amount of retirement benefits. Value of each annuity unit depends on market conditions.

Variable annuity premiums are typically invested in common stocks or other investments. During the period prior to retirement, the premiums are used to purchase **accumulation units** whose value changes periodically depending on the investment results of the fund. At retirement, the accumulation units are then converted into **annuity units** whose value determines the amount of the retirement benefits that the annuitant will receive. The number of annuity units remains constant, but the value of each unit changes periodically depending on the value of the underlying securities. For example, assume that an annuitant has 100 annuity units and that the annuity unit is initially valued at $5. Monthly income of $500 will be paid. During the second month, if the annuity unit increases to $5.10 because of an increase in common stock prices, the monthly income will increase to $510. Likewise, during the third month, if the annuity unit declines to $4.90 because of a stock market decline, the monthly income will decline to $490.

How effective are variable annuities as an inflation hedge? *In general, variable annuities have been effective in maintaining the real purchasing power of the benefits because the investment returns of most variable annuities have increased more rapidly than increases in the Consumer Price Index (CPI).* A study of variable annuities by Morningstar showed that over a 10-year period ending May 1993, diversified U.S. equity variable annuities earned an average annual total return of 11.35 percent. However, during the same period, the average annual inflation rate as measured by the Consumer Price Index was only 3.8 percent.[15] Thus, variable annuities provided an effective inflation hedge during that period.

On the negative side, however, many variable annuities have relatively high annual expense rates, which can be a costly drag on performance if the wrong annuity is purchased. Average total fund expenses for variable annuities frequently exceed 2 percent (see Exhibit 16.8). Annual expense charges include a mortality and expense risk charge that compensates the insurer for assuming certain risks, a charge for administrative expenses, an investment manager's fee, and an annual contract fee. In addition, a surrender charge that declines over time will substantially reduce the amount of cash if the annuity is surrendered for its cash value during the first five to ten years after the purchase date.

Consider This

Social Security Online is the official web site of the Social Security Administration. Visit the site at:

http://www.ssa.gov/

Old-Age, Survivors, Disability, and Health Insurance (OASDHI)

One of the most important programs in the United States is the Old-Age, Survivors, Disability, and Health Insurance program (OASDHI), commonly known as social security. Most retired workers age 62 or older are receiving

Exhibit 16.8

Annuity Funds' Average Performance and Fees

Type of Fund	Average Fund Expense	Average Total Expense	1st Qtr. Total Return	One-Year Total Return	Three-Year Annualized Return	Five-Year Annualized Return
Aggressive growth	0.94%	2.18%	5.80%	30.47%	18.20%	20.47%
Balanced	0.80	2.07	2.38	18.82	8.58	9.84
Corporate bond	0.69	1.93	−1.90	9.84	4.54	7.27
Government bond	0.64	1.90	−2.25	8.61	4.00	6.91
Growth	0.85	2.09	5.18	29.21	13.39	13.57
Growth and income	0.65	1.91	4.78	27.56	13.98	14.02
High-yield bond	0.80	2.10	2.62	15.19	8.76	13.83
International bond	1.10	2.39	−0.82	9.96	4.59	5.27
International stock	1.15	2.40	5.08	17.45	12.10	8.24
Money market	0.53	1.80	0.92	4.17	3.02	2.99
U.S. diversified equity avg.	0.81	2.06	5.18	28.92	14.28	14.70
Fixed-income avg.	0.73	1.99	−1.84	9.50	4.40	7.01

Note: Returns for periods ended March 29, 1996

Source: "Annuity Funds' Average Performance and Fees," April 4, 1996. Reprinted by permission of *The Wall Street Journal,* © 1996 Dow Jones & Company, Inc. All Rights Reserved Worldwide.

valuable retirement benefits through Social Security. The program also provides valuable survivor benefits, disability income benefits, and Medicare benefits to eligible beneficiaries. Roughly one in six Americans receives a monthly cash benefit.[16]

Covered Occupations

Virtually all occupations in the private sector are covered under the social security program. Federal civilian workers hired after 1983 are covered on a compulsory basis. State and local government employees can be covered by a voluntary agreement between the state and federal government. However, as of July 1, 1991, all government employees who are not participating in a public employee retirement plan are covered on a compulsory basis. Employees of nonprofit charitable, educational, and religious organizations are covered if they are paid at least $100 during the year. Self-employed workers with annual net earnings of $400 or more are also covered on a compulsory basis.

Determination of Insured Status

To become eligible for benefits, you must have a certain number of social security credits for work in covered employment. For 1997, you receive one credit for each $670 earned in covered employment. A maximum of four credits can be earned each year. The amount of covered earnings required to earn one credit will automatically increase each year as average wages in the national economy rise.

fully insured Status of one who has earned at least 40 social security credits.

Fully Insured.   To be eligible for retirement benefits, you must be fully insured. You are **fully insured** for retirement benefits if you have 40 credits. However, for people born before 1929, fewer credits are required, as shown here:

Year of Birth	Credits Needed
1929 or later	40
1928	39
1927	38
1926	37
1925	36
1924	35

currently insured Status of one who has earned at least 6 social security credits during the last 13 calendar quarters ending with the quarter of death, disability, or entitlement to retirement benefits.

Currently Insured.   You are **currently insured** if you have earned at least 6 credits during the last 13 calendar quarters ending with the quarter of death, disability, or entitlement to retirement benefits.

disability insured Number of credits required to be eligible for disability benefits. Number of credits depends on age.

Disability Insured.   The number of credits required to be **disability insured** depends on your age when you become disabled. If you are age 31 or older, you must have earned a certain number of credits, as shown by the following:

Disabled at Age	Credits Needed
31 through 42	20
44	22
46	24
48	26
50	28
52	30
54	32
56	34
58	36
60	38
62 or older	40

In addition, at least 20 of the credits must be earned during the past 10 years immediately before you became disabled.

Younger workers under age 31 can acquire a disability-insured status with fewer credits. If you become disabled before age 24, you must have earned six credits during the three-year period ending when your disability begins. For ages 24 through 30, you must have worked half the time between age 21 and the time you become disabled. For example, a worker who becomes disabled at age 27 needs credit for three years of work out of the past six years.

Social Security Benefits

The social security program has four principal benefits: (1) retirement benefits, (2) survivor benefits, (3) disability benefits, and (4) Medicare.

Retirement Benefits.   Workers who are fully insured can receive a full benefit at the normal retirement age (also called the full retirement age), which is currently age 65. However, the normal retirement age will gradually increase in the future to age 66 and then to age 67 (see Exhibit 16.9). A full retirement benefit is payable at age 65. However, workers can retire as early as age 62 and receive reduced benefits. The full retirement benefit is reduced 20 percent at age 62. The spouse of a retired worker can also receive benefits if he or she is at least age 62 and has been married to the worker for at least one year. The spouse's benefit at age 65 is 50 percent of the retired worker's full benefit and is reduced to 37.5 percent at age 62. The spouse of a retired worker may also be eligible for retirement benefits based on his or her own earnings. In such cases, in effect, the higher of the two benefits is paid.

Exhibit 16.9

Future Increases in the OASDI Normal Retirement Age

Year of Birth	Year of Attainment of Age 62	Normal Retirement Age
1937 and before	1999 and before	65
1938	2000	65,2 mo.
1939	2001	65,4 mo.
1940	2002	65, 6 mo.
1941	2003	65, 8 mo.
1942	2004	65, 10 mo.
1943–54	2005–16	66
1955	2017	66, 2 mo.
1956	2018	66, 4 mo.
1957	2019	66, 6 mo.
1958	2020	66, 8 mo.
1959	2021	66, 10 mo.
1960 and later	2022 and later	67

Source: G. E. Rejda, *Principles of Risk Management & Insurance* 5/E (table 23.1, p. 491). © 1995 HarperCollins College Publishers. Reprinted by permission of Addison Wesley Longman, Inc.

Retirement benefits can also be paid to unmarried children of a retired worker who are under age 18, to unmarried disabled children age 18 or older if they were severely disabled before age 22, and to a spouse at any age who is caring for an eligible child under age 16 (or disabled before age 22).

Retirement Benefit Amount.   The monthly retirement benefit is based on the worker's **primary insurance amount (PIA).** The PIA is the benefit paid to a worker at the normal retirement age or to a disabled worker. The PIA, in turn, is based on the worker's average indexed monthly earnings, which is a method that updates the worker's earnings based on increases in average wages in the national economy. The indexing of covered wages results in a relatively constant replacement rate so that workers retiring today and in the future will have about the same proportion of their work earnings restored by social security benefits.

primary insurance amount (PIA) The social security benefit paid to a worker at the normal retirement age or to a disabled worker.

Exhibit 16.10 shows approximate monthly benefits at age 65 for you and your spouse. It is assumed that you have worked steadily and received pay raises at a rate equal to the U.S. average throughout your working career. It is also assumed that your earnings, and the general level of wages and salaries in the country, will stay the same until you retire. This way, *the table shows the value of your benefits in today's dollars.* Your spouse may qualify for a higher retirement benefit based on her or his own work record.

delayed retirement credit Social security credit available to workers who delay retiring beyond the normal retirement age.

In addition, a **delayed retirement credit** is available to workers who delay retiring beyond the normal retirement age. The delayed retirement credit applies to the period beyond the normal retirement age and up to age 70. For people attaining age 65 in 1997, the primary insurance amount is increased 5 percent for each year of delayed retirement (prorated monthly). The credit will gradually increase in the future to a maximum of 8 percent for workers who were born in 1943 or later.

Finally, the monthly cash benefits are automatically indexed each year for changes in the cost of living, which maintains the real purchasing power of the benefits. This is a valuable benefit because relatively few public or private retirement plans are completely indexed for inflation.

earnings test (retirement test) Test by which monthly cash social security benefits are reduced or terminated if earned income exceeds the maximum annual limit.

Earnings test.   The social security program has an **earnings test (retirement test)** by which the monthly cash benefits are reduced or terminated if earned income exceeds the maximum annual limit. The purposes of the earnings test are to restrict payment of monthly cash benefits only to beneficiaries who have lost their earned income and to hold down the cost of the program.

In 1997, beneficiaries ages 65 through 69 can earn a maximum of $13,500 with no loss of benefits. One dollar of benefits is withheld for each three dollars of earnings above the annual exempt amount.

Exhibit 16.10

Monthly Benefits at Age 65

Your Age in 1997	Who Receives Benefits	Your Present Annual Earnings				
		$15,000	$24,000	$36,000	$48,000 and up	$65,400
65	You	$640	$864	$1,147	$1,236	$1,326
	Spouse	320	432	573	618	663
64	You	629	850	1,129	1,220	1,315
	Spouse	314	425	564	610	657
63	You	629	851	1,131	1,225	1,326
	Spouse	314	425	565	612	663
62	You	636	859	1,144	1,243	1,350
	Spouse	318	429	572	621	675
61	You	637	861	1,146	1,249	1,363
	Spouse	318	430	573	624	681
55*	You	606	821	1,091	1,213	1,355
	Spouse	298	404	537	597	667
50*	You	603	817	1,083	1,215	1,384
	Spouse	296	401	531	596	679
45*	You	607	824	1,087	1,223	1,414
	Spouse	298	404	534	600	694
40*	You	589	801	1,053	1,185	1,377
	Spouse	286	389	512	576	669
35*	You	571	777	1,018	1,147	1,335
	Spouse	274	373	489	551	641
30*	You	575	783	1,022	1,152	1,340
	Spouse	276	376	491	554	644

*These amounts are reduced for retirement at age 65 because the normal retirement age is higher for these persons.
Source: William M. Mercer, *1997 Guide to Social Security and Medicare*, p.11. Reprinted with permission.

A different exempt amount applies to beneficiaries under age 65. In 1997, beneficiaries under age 65 can earn $8,640 with no loss of benefits. One dollar of benefits is withheld for each two dollars of earnings above the exempt amount. Thus, the loss of benefits for beneficiaries under age 65 is more severe. The annual exempt amount is adjusted each year to keep pace with increases in average wages in the national economy.

The earnings test has three major exceptions. First, beneficiaries age 70 and older can earn any amount and receive full benefits. Second, the earnings test does not apply to investment income, dividends, interest, rents, pension benefits, or annuity payments. Finally, a special monthly earnings test is used for the initial year of retirement if it produces a more favorable result than the annual test. For the initial year of retirement, regardless of total earnings for the year, full benefits are paid to a beneficiary who does not earn more than one-twelfth of the annual exempt amount. The purpose of the special test is to pay full benefits, starting with the first month of retirement, to the worker who retires in the middle or near the end of the year and has earned income in excess of the annual exempt amount.

Survivor Benefits.   Survivor benefits can be paid to eligible dependents of a deceased worker who is either fully or currently insured. For certain survivor benefits, a fully insured status is required.

Survivor benefits can be paid to unmarried children under age 18, to unmarried children age 18 or older who were severely disabled before age 22, and to a surviving spouse who is caring for an eligible child under age 16. In addition, if certain requirements are met, survivor benefits can be paid to a surviving spouse age 60 or older, to a disabled widow or widower ages 50 to 59, and to dependent parents age 62 or older. A lump-sum death benefit of $255 is also paid if there is an eligible surviving spouse or child entitled to benefits.

The value of social security survivor benefits is substantial. For an average wage earner who dies and leaves a spouse and two children, the value of the survivor benefits is equivalent to a $295,000 life insurance policy.[17] The benefits, however, are paid monthly and not in a lump sum.

Disability Benefits.   Disability income benefits can be paid to disabled workers and eligible dependents if certain eligibility requirements are met. The worker must be disability-insured, satisfy a full five-month waiting period, and meet the definition of disability under the law. As we noted in Chapter 10, the worker must have a physical or mental condition that prevents him or her from doing any substantial gainful work and is expected to last at least 12 months or result in death.

We discussed the disability income program under social security in Chapter 10, so additional treatment is not needed here.

Medicare Benefits.   The fourth principal social security benefit is Medicare. Almost all people age 65 or older are eligible for Medicare. Medicare benefits are also available to disabled persons under age 65 who have been entitled to disability benefits for at least 24 months. Persons under age 65 who need long-term kidney treatment are also covered.

Medicare consists of two programs: (1) **Hospital Insurance (Part A)** and **Supplementary Medical Insurance (Part B).**

Hospital Insurance (Part A) That part of Medicare that pays for inpatient hospital care, care in a skilled nursing facility and other benefits.

1. *Hospital Insurance (Part A).* Part A of Medicare provides several important benefits. *Inpatient hospital care* is provided for up to 90 days. For the first 60 days, all covered charges are paid in full except for an inpatient deductible ($760 in 1997). For the 61st through 90th day, the patient must pay a daily coinsurance charge ($190 in 1997). The deductible and coinsurance charges are automatically adjusted each year to reflect changes in hospital costs.

Care in a *skilled nursing facility* is also covered for up to 100 days. The patient must be hospitalized for at least three days to be eligible for coverage, and confinement must be for medical reasons. Custodial care is not covered. The first 20 days of covered services are paid in full. For the next 80 days, the patient must pay a daily coinsurance charge ($95 in 1997). Long-term care and custodial care are not covered.

An unlimited number of *home health-care visits* by visiting nurses, physical therapists, speech therapists, and other health professionals is also covered. The patient's physician must establish a treatment plan. However, custodial care is not covered.

Hospice benefits for terminally ill beneficiaries are also covered. A hospice program provides inpatient, outpatient, and home-care services to terminally ill beneficiaries, such as cancer patients. Emphasis is on pain reduction, control of symptoms, and counseling, but curative treatment is not provided. Hospice benefits are limited to 210 days unless a physician recertifies the patient as terminally ill.

Supplementary Medical Insurance (Part B) That part of Medicare that covers physicians' fees and other medical services.

2. *Supplementary Medical Insurance (Part B).* Part B of Medicare is a voluntary program that covers physicians' fees and other related medical services.

Physician's services are covered in the doctor's office, hospital, and elsewhere. *Outpatient hospital services* for diagnosis and treatment are also covered, such as care in an emergency room or outpatient clinic. An unlimited number of *home health-care visits* is also covered under Part B if the beneficiary is not covered under Part A. Finally, *other medical and health-care services* are covered, including diagnostic tests, x-rays, durable medical equipment used at home, and numerous other services.

Part A pays 80 percent of the approved charges for covered medical services after the beneficiary pays a calendar-year deductible of $100.

Part B beneficiaries must pay a monthly premium for the benefits provided, which is supplemented by the federal government out of its general revenues. In 1997, the monthly premium was $43.80. The monthly premium is adjusted each year for changes in the cost of medical care.

Medigap Policies

Medigap policy Insurance policy that pays part or all of the costs not covered by Medicare.

Because of deductibles and cost-sharing provisions, limitations on approved charges, various exclusions, and limited coverage for care in a nursing facility, Medicare pays less than half the medical expenses incurred by the aged (which includes custodial nursing home costs as medical expenses). As a result, most aged people have purchased a **Medigap policy** that pays part or all of the costs not paid by Medicare.

Federal law strictly regulates the sale of Medicare supplement policies. Insurers can sell only a maximum of ten standard policies developed by the National Association of Insurance Commissioners. Each policy has a letter designation ranging from A through J. The basic policy has a core package of benefits. The remaining policies have a different combination of benefits, but they all include the core package of benefits. Insurers are not allowed to change the letter designations or the various combinations of benefits.

Insurers are required to have an open enrollment period of six months for beneficiaries who enroll in Medicare Part B. This means that beneficiaries age 65 or older cannot be refused coverage or charged higher premiums if they enroll during the open enrollment period. However, insurers can exclude preexisting conditions for six months even though coverage is guaranteed during the open enrollment period.

Financing Social Security

The monthly cash benefits are financed by a payroll tax paid by covered employees, employers, and the self-employed; interest income on the trust-fund investments; and a relatively small amount of revenue from taxation of part of the monthly benefits.

In 1997, a covered employee and employer each paid a payroll tax of 7.65 percent on a maximum taxable earnings base of $65,400. The self-employed paid a rate of 15.3 percent on the same earnings base. However, the self-employed are allowed certain deductions, which reduce the effective tax rate. The maximum taxable earnings base will automatically increase in the future if monthly benefits are increased based on the cost-of-living provisions. The increase in the earnings base is based on changes in average wages in the national economy.

Hospital Insurance (Part A) of Medicare is financed by a payroll tax of 1.45 percent, which is part of the 7.65 percent tax discussed earlier. The self-employed pay 2.90 percent. The Hospital Insurance payroll tax applies to all earned income, including earnings in excess of the maximum taxable wage base. Finally, as noted earlier, Supplementary Medical Insurance (Part B) is financed from monthly premiums and general revenues of the federal government.

Critics of social security believe they will never receive in retirement benefits the amounts paid into the program. Exhibit 16.11 shows the length of time it takes new retirees to recover the value of their own taxes.

Taxation of Benefits

About 20 percent of the beneficiaries who receive monthly cash benefits must pay an income tax on part of the benefits.[18] The amount of benefits subject to taxation depends on your total combined income. Combined

---

Exhibit 16.11

How Long Does It Take to Recover Your Social Security Taxes?

A study by Robert J. Myers and Bruce D. Schobel determined the time period required for a retired person to collect retirement benefits that are at least equal to the accumulated value of the taxes paid to the normal retirement age. The authors consider only the OASI taxes paid by employees. DI taxes and HI taxes are not considered since it is assumed that workers have received protection under both programs for the taxes paid. *The payback period for workers who retired in 1991 is 68 months for average earners and 82 months for maximum earners. By 2027, the payback period will increase to about 8 1/2 years for average earners and 13 1/2 years for maximum earners.* Average earners are workers who earn wages equal to the national average wage each year. Maximum earners are workers who earn wages equal to the maximum taxable OASDI earnings base each year.

Number of Months Required to Recover Accumulated OASI Taxes

Year of Retirement at NRA	Average Earner		Maximum Earner	
	Men	Women	Men	Women
1960	10	10	12	12
1970	21	21	24	24
1980	28	28	30	30
1991	68	68	82	82
2002	95	95	119	119
2009	105	105	135	135
2020	107	107	152	152
2027	103	103	160	160

Note: The taxes accumulated during the preretirement period are based on the annual average interest rate payable on new special investment issues of the Social Security trust funds: an assumed rate of 2.25 percent for 1937–50, actual experience for 1951–90, and nominal interest rates projected for the future under the intermediate assumptions contained in the 1991 Board of Trustees report. The above figures do not reflect any interest earnings on the accumulated taxes after retirement or any cost-of-living increases in monthly benefits.

Source: Adapted from Robert J. Myers and Bruce D. Schobel, "An Updated Money's-Worth Analysis of Social Security Retirement Benefits," *Transactions of the Society of Actuaries,* 44 (1992), Table 5. Reprinted with permission from the Society of Actuaries, Schaumburg, IL. Copyright © 1993 Society of Actuaries.

income includes earnings, pension income, dividends, and taxable interest from investments and other sources *plus* tax-exempt interest *plus* half of your social security benefits. If you file a federal tax return as an individual and your combined income is between $25,000 and $34,000, up to 50 percent of your benefits is subject to taxation. If your combined income exceeds $34,000, up to 85 percent of your benefits is subject to taxation.

If you file a joint return and you and your spouse have a combined income between $32,000 and $44,000, up to 50 percent of the benefits is subject to taxation. If your combined income exceeds $44,000, up to 85 percent of the benefits is subject to taxation.

At the end of each year, you will receive a form from the Social Security Administration (SSA-1099) that shows the amount of social security benefits received. The Internal Revenue Service has prepared detailed worksheets to determine the amount of such benefits, if any, to include in your taxable income.

Getting Your Money's Worth

A highly controversial issue is whether younger workers will get their money's worth under the social security program in the future.

An important study by Robert J. Myers, former chief actuary of the Social Security Administration, and Bruce D. Schobel, a private insurance actuary, sheds considerable light on this question. The authors considered only that portion of the total payroll tax that is used for retirement and survivor benefits (OASI). Disability income (DI) taxes and Hospital Insurance (HI) taxes were not considered since it is assumed that the worker has received equivalent DI and HI protection for the taxes paid.

In the study, the authors compare (1) the value of the OASI taxes accumulated at interest to the normal retirement age with (2) the present value of the retirement benefits paid to workers at that same normal retirement age. Data for both average and maximum wage earners are presented. An average worker is one with earnings equal to the Social Security Administration's national average wage. A maximum earner is one who pays taxes on the maximum taxable social security earnings base. The interest rate credited to the accumulated OASI taxes prior to the normal retirement age is based on the average yearly interest rate payable on new special issue investments of the social security trust funds. Finally, the authors use a "real interest rate" of 2 percent to determine the present value of the retirement benefits at the normal retirement age. The authors believe that 2 percent interest is a good approximation of the real interest rate relative to the Consumer Price Index and thus implicitly adjusts for benefit increases after the normal retirement age.

Exhibit 16.12

Ratio of Present Value of Social Security Retirement Benefits to Accumulated Value of OASI Taxes

	Year of Retirement at Normal Retirement Age				
	1991	2002	2009	2020	2027
Average Earner					
Men	232%	171%	152%	152%	154%
Women	281%	204%	182%	182%	185%
Maximum Earner					
Men	192%	136%	117%	106%	99%
Women	232%	162%	141%	127%	118%

Note: Only OASI taxes paid by the employee are considered. Taxes accumulated during the preretirement period are based on the average interest payable on new special investment issues of the Social Security trust funds: an assumed rate of 2.25 percent for 1937–50, actual experience for 1951–90, and nominal interest rates projected for the future under the intermediate assumptions contained in the 1991 Board of Trustees report. The present value of the retirement benefits at the normal retirement age is based on a real interest rate of 2 percent.

Exhibit 16.12 presents the results of the study, which shows the ratio of the present value of social security retirement benefits to the accumulated value of OASI taxes. For the average earner who retired in 1991, the ratio of the present value of the benefits to the accumulated taxes was 232 percent for men and 281 percent for women. *The value of the benefits was 2.32 times the value of a male worker's taxes and 2.81 times the value of a female worker's taxes.* The ratio for females is higher because of a higher life expectancy. Thus, workers who retired in 1991 received a good deal from social security because the value of their benefits substantially exceeded the value of their taxes.

The actuarial bargain enjoyed by recently retired workers will decline substantially for future retirees, who will still get a good deal under social security but not as much as present retirees. *For workers who will retire in 2027, the value of the benefits will be 1.54 times the value of the taxes for males with average earnings and 1.85 times for females with average earnings.* However, the ratios for males with maximum earnings will decline sharply in the future and fall slightly below the break-even point of 100 percent. Females with maximum earnings will still get a good deal because of a higher life expectancy.

In summary, with the major exception of males with maximum earnings who retire in 2027, most workers who retire in the future will get their money's worth based on their own taxes. Females will get a better deal because of a higher life expectancy. In addition, when one considers that the benefits are annually adjusted for inflation; that the program reduces or eliminates the financial support of aged parents by the children; that the value of the survivor benefits is substantial; and that individual underwriting is not used, most workers will get their money's worth under the program.

SUMMARY

- The retirement problem in the United States consists of a growing proportion of older retired persons, a longer period of retirement, insufficient income for many retired workers, poor health of some retired persons, and additional complicating factors.

- A rethinking of traditional retirement strategies is needed because some workers will be unable to afford to retire; many married couples delay having children and will be faced with large college bills as they approach retirement; future retirees will live longer; traditional defined-benefit pension plans that provide guaranteed benefits have declined in importance; and most workers will change jobs several times during their working careers, which will reduce their retirement benefits.

- Most younger workers are substantially undersaving for their retirement. Worksheets can be used to determine how much to save for retirement.

- There are six important barriers to saving for retirement. Retirement is not a high priority for most persons. Many workers do not earn enough to save for retirement. Many Americans lack knowledge about retirement planning. Many Americans resist cutting back to save for retirement. The public takes a conservative approach to retirement. Individuals with some types of personalities are not likely to save much for retirement.

- Two important principles should be followed in the investment of retirement funds: start investing early and do not invest too conservatively.

- The allocation of assets among stocks, bonds, and cash reserves depends on your investment objectives and time horizon.

- All employees who are at least age 21 and have one year of service must be allowed to participate in a qualified private pension plan.

- A pension plan has a normal retirement age, an early retirement age, and a late retirement age.

- There are two basic types of pension plans. Under a defined-contribution plan, the contribution rate is fixed, but the retirement benefit is variable. Under a defined-benefit plan, the retirement benefit is known in advance, but the contributions needed to fund the benefit will vary.

- A qualified private pension plan must meet one of two minimum vesting standards: the five-year rule or the three-to-seven-year rule.

- For 1997, the maximum annual contribution to a defined-contribution pension plan is limited to 25 percent of compensation or $30,000, whichever is less.

- For 1997, the maximum annual benefit that can be funded in a defined-benefit plan is limited to 100 percent of the worker's three highest consecutive years of compensation or $125,000 (indexed for inflation), whichever is lower.

- A profit-sharing plan is a defined-contribution plan to which an employer contributes part of the profits to eligible employees. For 1997, the maximum employer contribution is limited to 15 percent of compensation or $24,000, whichever is lower.

- A thrift plan is a defined-contribution plan to which eligible employees voluntarily contribute; the employer also contributes, which is typically some fraction of the employee's contributions.

- A Section 40l (k) plan is a cash or deferred arrangement that allows eligible employees to defer part of their before-tax pay rather than receive the pay as cash. The amount of salary deferred is then invested in the employer's 401(k) plan. For 1997, the maximum salary reduction is limited to $9,500 (indexed for inflation).

- A self-employed individual can establish a Keogh plan and receive favorable federal income tax treatment. The maximum annual contribution to a defined-contribution plan is limited to 20 percent of net income (after subtracting half the social security self-employment tax) or $30,000, whichever is lower.

■ The maximum annual contribution to an individual retirement account (IRA) is $2,000 or 100 percent of compensation ($4,000 for a spousal IRA), whichever is less.

■ The full IRA deduction is available only for persons who are not active participants in an employer-sponsored retirement plan, or whose adjusted gross income is $25,000 or less ($40,000 or less for married couples filing jointly).

■ A partial IRA deduction may be allowed depending on the amount of annual earnings.

■ A simplified employee pension (SEP) is essentially an employer-sponsored IRA that is designed to reduce paperwork. For 1997, the maximum annual employer contribution is limited to 15 percent of employee compensation or $24,000, whichever is less.

■ A SIMPLE retirement plan is designed for smaller employers. Eligible employees can contribute a percentage of annual salary into the plan but not to exceed $6,000 annually (indexed for inflation). The employer has the option of matching the employee's contribution up to 3 percent of salary or providing a nonelective contribution of 2 percent of salary for all eligible employees.

■ An annuity is a plan that provides periodic payments to an individual for a fixed period or for the duration of a designated life or lives. The purpose is to provide income to an individual that cannot be outlived.

■ Annuities can be classified based on the following: (1) time when payments begin: immediate annuity, fixed annuity; (2) nature of insurer's obligation: life annuity (no refund), life annuity with guaranteed payments, installment or cash refund annuity, joint-and-survivor annuity; (3) fixed or variable benefits: fixed annuity, variable annuity.

■ The social security program is important in retirement planning. The program provides four principal benefits: retirement benefits, survivor benefits, disability income benefits, Medicare benefits.

■ Medigap policies are designed to supplement the benefits available under the Medicare program. There are ten standard Medicare supplement policies.

KEY CONCEPTS AND TERMS

Accumulation units

Annuitant

Annuity

Annuity units

Cash refund annuity

Currently insured

Deferred annuity

Defined-benefit plan

Defined-contribution plan

Delayed retirement credit

Disability insured

Early retirement age

Earnings test (retirement test)

Fixed annuity

Flexible-premium annuity

Fully insured

Hospital Insurance (Part A)

Immediate annuity

Individual retirement account (IRA)

Installment refund annuity

Joint-and-survivor annuity

Keogh plan

Late retirement age

Life annuity (no refund)

Life annuity with guaranteed payments

Medigap policy

Normal retirement age

Pension Benefit Guaranty Corporation (PBGC)

Primary insurance amount (PIA)

Profit-sharing plan

Retirement annuity

Section 401(k) plan

SIMPLE plan

Simplified employee pension (SEP)

Single-premium deferred annuity

Spousal IRA

Supplementary Medical Insurance (Part B)

Tax-deferred retirement plan

Thrift plan

Variable annuity

Vesting

QUESTIONS FOR REVIEW

1. Explain the nature of the retirement problem in the United States.

2. Why will retirement planning for the next century require a reexamination of traditional retirement strategies?

3. Identify the important barriers to saving for retirement.

4. Describe how retirement funds should be invested.

5. Briefly describe the major characteristics of the following types of tax-deferred retirement plans.
   a. Defined-contribution pension plan
   b. Defined-benefit pension plan
   c. Profit-sharing and thrift plans
   d. Section 401(k) plan
   e. Keogh plans for the self-employed

6. Explain the major characteristics of individual retirement accounts (IRAs).

7. Describe the basic characteristics of a simplified employee pension (SEP).

8. Identify the major types of individual annuities sold today.

9. Explain the meaning of fully insured, currently insured, and disability insured under the social security program.

10. Briefly describe the major benefits under the social security program.

11. Why do the majority of Medicare beneficiaries purchase Medigap policies?

PROBLEMS

1. Jennifer, age 27, earns $40,000 annually and plans to retire in 35 years. She would like to receive $30,000 annually after she retires. She estimates she will receive annual benefits of $12,000 from social security and $8,000 from her employer's retirement plan. She has present savings of $4,000 in her employer's retirement plan and $2,397 in an individual retirement account (IRA). Using the worksheet in Exhibit 16.1, calculate the approximate amount she must save each year to reach her goal. In your calculations, assume an annual rate of return of 8 percent.

2. Marcia, age 25, earns $23,000 annually and is also participating in her employer's retirement plan. What is the maximum tax-deductible contribution, if any, that she can contribute to an individual retirement account (IRA)?

3. Travis, age 22, recently graduated from college and obtained a position as a tax accountant at an annual salary of $40,000. He will not be eligible to participate in his employer's pension plan for one year. What is the maximum tax-deductible contribution, if any, that he can contribute to an individual retirement account (IRA)?

4. Megan, age 35, is self-employed as a freelance writer. After deducting half the social security self-employment payroll tax, she had net earnings of $60,000 during the current tax year. What is the maximum tax-deductible contribution she can contribute to a defined-contribution Keogh plan?

5. Scott is self-employed and has two employees working for him. He would like to establish a SEP-IRA for his employees. Employee A earns $25,000 annually, and employee B earns $35,000. What is the maximum tax-deductible contribution he can contribute into the plan on behalf of the two employees?

6. James, age 63, is currently receiving social security retirement benefits. He receives an annual pension of $10,000 from his former employer. He also receives $2,000 each year in bond interest and common stock dividends. He recently returned to work on a part-time basis. His earned income exceeded the annual limit under the earnings test by $3,000. What is the amount of social security benefits, if any, that he will lose under the earnings test? Explain your answer.

INTERNET EXERCISES

1. LifeNet is a web site devoted to information on life insurance, retirement and estate planning, and other financial topics. Go to the site at:

   http://www.lifenet.com/

   Choose "Retirement Planning" and work through the "Retirement Cash Flow Analyzer," which includes a calculator to help you determine your retirement income needs. You might also check out SavingsNet at:

   http://www.savingsnet.com

   and look at the "Retirement Zone."

2. Some of the investment sites listed in the Internet Exercises for Chapter 13 also contain information on retirement planning. For example, go to Research magazine's site at:

   http://www.researchmag.com/

   Choose "InvestorNet," then "Retirement Planning." You should find useful articles, checklists, and worksheets. If possible, download a worksheet to your printer.

3. The Pension and Welfare Benefits Administration is an agency within the U.S. Department of Labor that "protects the integrity of pensions, health plans, and other employee benefits." Find out more about the agency at:

   http://www.dol.gov/dol/pwba/

CASE APPLICATIONS

Case I

Kelly, age 25, earns $25,000 as a marketing research analyst for a large public relations firm. She enjoys her life as a single woman and frequently goes out with friends to restaurants, bars, and movies. She belongs to a health club and is active in sports. She plans to take a vacation to the Bahamas. She usually pays her expenses by using credit cards. Her credit card debts presently total $12,340. The annual percentage rate (APR) on her credit card debt ranges from 18 to 21 percent. Kelly usually makes only minimum monthly payments to keep the accounts current. In addition, Kelly's company has a qualified Section 401 (k) plan for eligible employees. For each dollar contributed by the employees, the company contributes 25 cents. Although the plan has a maximum contribution rate of 6 percent, Kelly is contributing only 3 percent of her salary into the plan. The contributions are invested in a fixed-income account, which is currently yielding 6 percent interest. She has no other savings plan established. Kelly recently attended a public lecture on financial planning and would like to set up a financial plan for retirement. She would like to retire early at age 55 and travel extensively after retirement.

1. Is Kelly's goal of early retirement realistic based on her present saving and spending habits? Explain your answer.

2. Is Kelly eligible to set up an individual retirement account (IRA)? Explain your answer.

3. What financial consequence will Kelly face at retirement if she continues to invest all Section 401 (k) contributions into a fixed-income account?

4. Design a more realistic retirement plan so that Kelly can retire at age 62. In your plan design and recommendations, be certain to discuss the following:

   a. Reduction or elimination of credit card debts

   b. Appropriateness of the present percentage of her salary deferred

   c. Investment of Section 401 (k) contributions

Case II

Ron Lukens, age 47, earns $75,000 annually as a pipeline specialist for a utility company. His wife, Kay, age 46, is self-employed and has net earnings of $20,000 as a part-time freelance writer. Ron contributes 6 percent of his salary into a qualified defined-contribution pension plan, which is matched by a 6 percent contribution from the company. The current value of Ron's account is $200,000. About three fourths of the assets are invested in a fixed-income account; the remaining one fourth is invested in a conservative common stock fund. Kay has no retirement plan at the present time. A son, age 18, will be starting college next fall. The couple is buying their home and presently owe $90,000 on a 9½ percent mortgage that has 20 years to run. Ron would like to like to retire at age 62, but he believes that paying for his son's college education will make it difficult to save large amounts out of his present income.

Assume that you are a financial planner who is asked to give advice to the Lukens concerning their retirement plans. Answer the following questions:

1. Explain to Ron how the retirement income from his pension plan might be increased without a corresponding increase in pension contributions.

2. Identify two retirement plans for which Kay is eligible. For each plan, indicate the maximum annual amount that could be contributed.

3. Is Ron eligible to establish an individual retirement account (IRA)? Explain your answer.

4. Would a variable annuity be appropriate for Ron or Kay, or both, in their present financial position? Explain your answer.

5. What additional advice can you give the Lukens concerning their retirement plans?

SUGGESTIONS FOR ADDITIONAL READING

Asinoff, Lynn. "Still Working, Planning for Retirement Requires a Whole New Way of Thinking," *Wall Street Journal* (December 9, 1994), p. R18.

Blair, Dennis T. and Andrea T. Sellars. "Retirement Planning: More Than Investment Education," *Journal of the American Society of CLU & ChFC,* Vol. XLIX, No. 3 (May 1995), pp. 64–71.

Chandler, Darlene K. *The Annuity Handbook, A Guide to Nonqualified Annuities.* Cincinnati, Ohio: The National Underwriter Company, 1994.

The Charles Schwab Guide to Retirement Planning. New York: Charles Schwab & Co., 1994.

Facts on Funds for Your Retirement. Valley Forge, Pa.: The Vanguard Group, 1994.

Farkas, Steve and Jean Johnson. *Promises to Keep, How Leaders and the Public Respond to Saving and Retirement.* New York: Public Agenda, 1994.

The Growing Retirement Savings Crisis: Companies May Be a Key Factor in the Solution. New York: Merrill Lynch, Pierce, Fenner & Smith, Inc., 1992.

Is The Baby Boom Generation Preparing Adequately For Retirement? Summary Report. New York: Merrill Lynch & Co., 1993.

The Merrill Lynch Baby Boom Retirement Index. New York: Merrill Lynch, Pierce, Fenner & Smith, Inc., 1994.

Pollan, Stephen M. and Mark Levine. "The Rise and Fall of Retirement," *Worth,* Vol. 3, No. 10 (December January 1995), pp. 64–74.

"Problem of Old Age," in George E. Rejda, *Social Insurance and Economic Security,* 5th ed. Englewood Cliffs, N.J.: Prentice-Hall, 1994, pp. 69–101.

Rejda, George E. *Principles of Risk Management and Insurance,* 6th ed. Reading, MA: Addison Wesley Longman, 1998, Chapters 18, 22, 23.

Retirement Planning Guide, A Fidelity Common Sense Guide. Dallas, Tex.: Fidelity Distributors Corporation, 1994.

Stewart, James B. "Invest for Retirement," *Smart Money,* Vol. 11, No. 6 (November 1993), pp. 89–105.

NOTES

1. George E. Rejda, *Social Insurance and Economic Security,* 5th ed. Englewood Cliffs, N.J.: Prentice-Hall, 1994, pp. 69–85.

2. U.S. Congress, House, Committee on Ways and Means, *Overview of Entitlement Programs, 1994 Green Book, Background Material and Data on Programs Within the Jurisdiction of the Committee on Ways and Means.* Washington, D.C.: U.S. Government Printing Office, 1994, Table I-3, p.1217.

3. Ibid., Table A-3, p. 856.

4. *1995 Annual Report of the Board of Trustees of the Federal Old-Age and Survivors Insurance and Disability Insurance Trust Funds* (April 3, 1995).

5. Susan Grad, *Income of the Population 55 or Older, 1994.* Washington, D.C.: U.S. Government Printing Office, 1996, pp. 36–37.

6. Ibid.

7. Ibid., p. 35.

8. James P. Smith, *Documented Briefing, Unequal Wealth and Incentives to Save.* Santa Monica, Calif.: RAND, 1995, p. 10.

9. See Lynn Asinoff, "Still Working, Planning for Retirement Requires a Whole New Way of Thinking," *Wall Street Journal* (December 9, 1994), p. R18.

10. *Confronting the Savings Crisis, Perceptions and Attitudes About Retirement and Financial Planning.* New York: Merrill Lynch & Co., 1995, p. 6.

11. John L. Buckman, "Part I, Countdown to Retirement," *Barron's* (August 30, 1993), p. 24.

12. Steve Farkas and Jean Johnson, *Promises to Keep, How Leaders Respond to Saving and Retirement.* New York: Public Agenda 1995, p. 6.

13. Ibid., pp. 6–7.

14. This section is based on George E. Rejda, *Principles of Risk Management and Insurance,* 5th ed. New York: HarperCollins Publishers, 1995, Chapter 22.

15. Ibid., p. 346.

16. The following section on the social security program is based on Rejda, *Principles of Risk Management and Insurance,* pp. 486–502.

17. Social Security Administration, *Basic Facts About Social Security,* SSA Publication No. 05-10080 (August 1995), p. 2.

18. Social Security Administration, *Retirement,* SSA Publication No. 05-10035 (July 1995), p. 13.

Chapter **17**

Estate Planning

Learning Objectives

After studying this chapter, you should be able to:

- Describe the objectives of estate planning.

- Explain the problem of estate shrinkage.

- Identify the steps in the estate-planning process.

- Explain the basic tools of estate planning, which include a will, marital deduction, gifts, trusts, and life insurance.

- Show how a living trust can reduce probate expenses.

- Explain how a credit shelter trust (bypass trust) can substantially reduce the federal estate tax.

- Design an estate plan that will accomplish your estate objectives.

To kill a relative of whom you are tired is something. But to inherit his property afterwards, that is genuine pleasure.

—Honore de Balzac

A man left the bulk of his fortune to his lawyers. If everybody did this, a lot of time would be saved.

—London Opinion

I f you are successful in your saving and investing program, you will accumulate a sizable estate. However, if you do not have an effective estate plan for the conservation and distribution of your assets when you die, you may be shortchanging your heirs. Estate planning is an important part of a total financial plan because it involves the distribution of your property to family members or to other groups, such as churches, colleges, and charities. Estate planning is used to distribute property to your heirs according to your wishes, to conserve estate assets, to minimize estate taxes, and to meet other important financial goals and objectives.

This chapter discusses the fundamentals of estate planning. We emphasize three major areas. The first part of the chapter discusses the basic objectives of estate planning, which include the distribution of property to designated heirs, reducing probate expenses and estate taxes, and providing liquidity to the estate. The second part discusses the basic tools of estate planning, which include a will, marital deduction, gifts, trusts, and life insurance. The chapter concludes with a discussion of certain basic strategies for reducing the federal estate tax and state death taxes.

Consider This

An extensive list of links to web sites on estate planning is provided by FindLaw Internet Legal Resources at:

http://www.findlaw.com/

Go to "Legal Subject Index" and then to "Probate, Trusts & Estates."

Fundamentals of Estate Planning

Objectives of Estate Planning

Estate planning is a process for the conservation and distribution of a person's property and wealth. As such, an effective estate plan has certain fundamental goals and objectives. They are summarized as follows:

- Conserve estate assets both before and after death.

- Distribute property according to the individual's wishes.

- Minimize federal estate and state death taxes.

- Minimize income taxes.

- Minimize probate costs in the settlement of an estate.

- Provide liquidity to the estate.

- Provide for the family's financial needs or other special needs.

The first objective is to conserve estate assets both before and after the decedent's death. Without an effective estate plan, assets may have to be sold to pay federal estate taxes and the costs of settling the estate. We discuss the problem of estate shrinkage later in the chapter.

The second objective is to distribute property according to the individual's wishes. This objective involves the creation of a will or trusts by which property can be distributed efficiently to the designated heirs, which may include a surviving spouse, children, grandchildren, charities, or other parties.

The third objective is to minimize the federal estate tax and state death taxes. Various techniques are available to reduce or eliminate the federal estate tax that may be payable. In addition, the states also impose inheritance and estate taxes that can reduce the amount available for distribution to the heirs.

The fourth objective is to minimize income taxes. A deceased person may have accumulated large amounts of money in a tax-deferred qualified retirement plan, Section 401(k) plan, profit-sharing plan, or individual retirement account (IRA). Proper planning can minimize the income tax that must be paid on the amounts distributed to the heirs from qualified retirement plans.

probate The process of proving the validity of a will in a court of law and executing its provisions under the supervision of the court.

Another objective is to minimize probate costs of settling an estate. **Probate** refers to the process of proving the validity of a will in a court of law and executing its provisions under the supervision of the court. Probate costs include attorney fees, which can be an hourly charge or a percentage of the probate estate, fees for administrators and appraisers, and court costs. An effective estate plan can minimize probate expenses.

Still another objective is to provide liquidity to the estate. Large amounts of cash may be needed for administrative and funeral expenses, payment of probate expenses, and payment of federal estate and state death taxes. Without sufficient liquidity, valuable estate assets may have to be sold in an unfavorable market, which results in shrinkage of the estate.

A final objective is to provide for the family's financial needs or other special needs. The plan should provide for periodic income to a surviving spouse and minor children. The plan should also consider any special needs such as the sale or continuation of a family business, financial support for a physically or mentally challenged child, or inability of a spendthrift heir to manage large amounts of money. A properly designed and effective estate plan will accomplish all the preceding objectives as well as provide other benefits (see Exhibit 17.1).

The Problem of Estate Shrinkage

estate shrinkage The decline in the value of an estate after an individual dies because of failure to develop an effective estate plan.

We noted earlier that an important estate-planning objective is to reduce or eliminate estate shrinkage. **Estate shrinkage** refers to the decline in the value of an estate after an individual dies because of failure to develop an effective estate plan. As a result, surviving family members

Exhibit 17.1

Six Reasons to Plan Your Estate

Estate planning is an easy thing to put off. Maybe you think it's too early; maybe you think your estate is too small. Here are six good reasons why you should plan your estate now.

With a Plan	Without a Plan
1. You decide who receives a share of your assets.	State laws determine who inherits your assets—they could pass to an estranged relative.
2. You decide how and when your beneficiaries will receive their inheritance.	The terms and timing are set by law. Your children could be left unfettered control of a sizable estate.
3. You decide who'll manage your estate (executor, trustee, etc.).	The court appoints administrators—administrators whose ideas may not be compatible with your own.
4. You can reduce estate taxes and administrative expenses.	Costs are usually greater, due to required administrative expenses and unnecessary taxes.
5. You select a guardian for your child.	The court appoints a guardian for your child.
6. You can provide for the orderly continuance or sale of a family business.	Financial loss and family hardships may result from an untimely forced sale.

Source: Practice Development Institute (PDI), Chicago. Reprinted with permission.

and other heirs receive substantially reduced amounts when the property is actually distributed. Estate planners cite numerous examples of substantial estate shrinkage because of lack of an estate plan or because of an improperly designed plan. Even the estates of famous people can experience substantial shrinkage after the celebrity dies (see Exhibit 17.2).

Estates can shrink because of the costs associated with the death itself, such as funeral expenses and uninsured medical expenses. There may also be outstanding installment debts, mortgage debt, and business claims against the estate that must be paid. The estate can also shrink because of legal costs of settling the estate, including attorney fees and administrator and executor fees. The fees are substantially higher if the estate is complex or the attorney must defend the estate in a contested claim.

Forced liquidation of property can also reduce the value of the estate. The estate may lack liquidity to pay federal and state death taxes, so property may have to be liquidated at reduced prices to obtain the needed cash. A profitable business may have to be sold as well to obtain the necessary cash. Finally, payment of the federal estate tax and state death taxes can substantially reduce the size of the estate before the property is distributed to the heirs.

Exhibit 17.2

Estates of Famous Persons

Name	Gross Estate	Settlement Costs	Net Estate	Percent Shrinkage
Stan Laurel	$91,562	$8,381	$83,181	9%
William Frawley	92,446	45,814	46,632	49%
"Gabby" Hayes	111,327	21,963	89,364	20%
Hedda Hopper	472,661	165,982	306,679	35%
Nelson Eddy	472,715	109,990	362,725	23%
Marilyn Monroe	819,176	448,750	370,426	55%
W.C. Fields	884,680	329,793	554,887	37%
Humphrey Bogart	910,146	274,234	635,912	30%
Dixie Crosby	1,332,571	781,953	550,618	59%
Erle Stanley Gardner	1,795,092	636,705	1,158,387	35%
Franklin D. Roosevelt	1,940,999	574,867	1,366,132	30%
Clark Gable	2,806,526	1,101,038	1,705,488	30%
Cecil B. DeMille	4,043,607	1,396,064	2,647,543	35%
Al Jolson	4,385,143	1,349,066	3,036,077	31%
Gary Cooper	4,984,985	1,530,454	3,454,531	31%
Henry J. Kaiser, Sr.	5,597,772	2,488,364	3,109,408	44%
Harry M. Warner	8,946,618	2,308,444	6,638,174	26%
Elvis Presley	10,165,434	7,374,635	2,790,799	73%
Alwin C. Ernst, CPA	12,642,431	7,124,112	5,518,319	56%
J.P. Morgan	17,121,482	11,893,691	5,227,791	69%
William E. Boeing	22,386,158	10,589,748	11,796,410	47%
Walt Disney	23,004,851	6,811,943	16,192,908	30%
John D. Rockefeller, Sr.	26,905,182	17,124,988	9,780,194	64%
Frederick Vanderbilt	76,838,530	42,846,112	33,992,418	56%

Source: *Your Estate Research Service* ©1990 by Dearborn Financial Publishing, Inc. Published by Dearborn/R&R Newkirk, a division of Dearborn Financial Publishing, Inc., Chicago. All rights reserved.

Federal Estate and Gift Taxes

We noted earlier that a fundamental objective of estate planning is to reduce or eliminate estate taxes and death taxes. These taxes include the federal estate tax, federal gift tax, and state death taxes.

Federal Estate Tax.   A federal estate tax is payable if the decedent's taxable estate exceeds $600,000. The federal estate tax starts at 37 percent on estates exceeding $600,000 and progressively increases to 55 percent on estates of $3 million or higher.

gross estate The total value of the property a person owns when he or she dies.

The **gross estate** includes the value of the property that you own when you die. The gross estate also includes one half of the value of property jointly owned with your spouse, life insurance death proceeds in which the insured has any incidents of ownership at the time of death, and certain other items (see Exhibit 17.3). Incidents of ownership in life insurance include the right to change the beneficiary, the right to borrow the cash value, and the right to select a settlement option.

taxable estate The amount of the estate on which taxes must be paid; it amounts to the gross estate less certain deductions.

The gross estate can be reduced by certain deductions in determining the **taxable estate.** Allowable deductions include funeral and administrative expenses, claims against the estate, debts owed at the time of death, casualty and theft losses that occur during the settlement of the estate, and contributions to charities. A marital deduction (discussed later) is also allowed, which can result in a substantial reduction or elimination of the taxable estate.

unified tax credit A tax credit that reduces dollar-for-dollar any federal estate or gift tax due.

A unified tax credit can be used to reduce any federal estate or gift tax that is payable. The **unified tax credit** is a tax credit that reduces dollar-for-dollar any federal estate or gift tax due. The maximum tax credit is currently $192,800. For example, assume that Pedro dies and has a gross estate of $700,000. Allowable deductions are $100,000. The federal estate tax on a taxable estate of $600,000 is $192,800. However, as a result of the unified tax credit of $192,800, the estate tax is zero. Exhibit 17.4 shows the federal and gift tax rates that apply at the time of this writing.

Exhibit 17.3

How Big Is Your Estate?

Cash	$ _____
Stock and bonds	$ _____
Notes and mortgages	_____
Annuities	_____
Retirement benefits	_____
Personal residence	_____
Other real estate	_____
Partnerships	_____
Insurance	_____
Automobiles	_____
Artwork	_____
Jewelry	_____
Other (furniture	_____
collectibles, etc.)	_____
Gross estate	$ _____

Source: Practice Development Institute (PDI), Chicago. Reprinted with permission.

Exhibit 17.4

Federal Estates and Gift Tax Rates (1993 and Beyond)

If Your Tax Base Is Over	But Not Over	Your Tax Is	+	%	On Excess Over
$0	$10,000	$0		18%	$0
10,000	20,000	1,800		20	10,000
20,000	40,000	3,800		22	20,000
40,000	60,000	8,200		24	40,000
60,000	80,000	13,000		26	60,000
80,000	100,000	18,200		28	80,000
100,000	150,000	23,800		30	100,000
150,000	250,000	38,300		32	150,000
250,000	500,000	70,800		34	250,000
500,000	750,000	155,800		37	500,000
750,000	1,000,000	248,300		39	750,000
1,000,000	1,250,000	345,800		41	1,000,000
1,250,000	1,500,000	448,300		43	1,250,000
1,500,000	2,000,000	555,800		45	1,500,000
2,000,000	2,500,000	780,800		49	2,000,000
2,500,000	3,000,000	1,025,800		53	2,500,000
3,000,000	10,000,000	1,290,800		55	3,000,000
10,000,000	21,040,000	5,140,800		60	10,000,000
21,040,000		11,764,800		55	21,040,000

Note: All rates are before the application of the unified credit or exemption equivalent. The actual tax credit for each unified credit is $192,800.

Source: *Estate Planning Made Easy,* David T. Phillips & Bill S. Wolfkiel, ©1994 by David T. Phillips and Bill S. Wolfkiel. Published by Dearborn Financial Publishing, Inc., Chicago. All rights reserved.

The federal estate tax is payable within nine months of the deceased's death unless an extension of time for filing has been granted. For this reason, liquidity is extremely important in estate planning because the necessary cash must be available.

At the time of this writing, federal legislation has been introduced that would change the federal estate tax. One proposal would increase the present exemption of $600,000 to $1 million over a period of years.

Federal Gift Tax.   A federal gift tax is payable if the gift exceeds a certain amount. However, the unified tax credit discussed earlier can be used to reduce the amount of the tax. Under present law, you can give a maximum gift of $10,000 annually to as many persons as you desire without incurring a federal gift tax on the transfer. If the spouse joins in the gift, a total of $20,000 can be given annually to each person. Certain gifts are not considered to be taxable gifts. They include gifts of $10,000 or less to any one person during a calendar year, payment of tuition or medical expenses, gifts to a spouse, gifts to charities, and certain other exceptions.

State Death Taxes.   The deceased's estate may also have to pay a state death tax. There are various types of state death taxes. First, some states levy a tax based on the federal credit for any death taxes paid to the state. Under federal law, the federal estate tax can be reduced by the tax credit allowed for any death taxes paid to the state, up to a certain maximum amount. The states have enacted laws that make certain that the state death tax will equal the maximum federal credit. Second, some states levy an inheritance tax that applies to the amount of property received by beneficiaries. Finally, a small number of states levy their own estate tax that is similar in structure to the federal estate tax.

Steps in Estate Planning

Estate planning is a process that involves certain steps. An estate attorney or financial planner typically performs the following steps, which are outlined in Exhibit 17.5:

- Obtain facts about the estate.
- Evaluate potential claims against the estate.
- Design an appropriate estate plan.
- Prepare the necessary legal documents.
- Periodically review and revise the plan.

The first step is to obtain relevant facts about the individual's estate. A detailed questionnaire must be filled out that shows the financial assets and real estate owned, names of family members, whether or not a will is in existence, business interests, estate plan objectives of the individual, the current estate plan, and other relevant information.

The second step is to evaluate potential claims against the estate. This includes an estimate of funeral and last illness expenses, attorney fees and probate expenses, the amount of federal estate and state gift taxes

Exhibit 17.5

Steps in Estate Planning

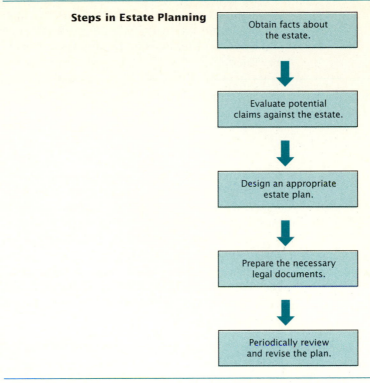

Obtain facts about
the estate.

Evaluate potential
claims against the estate.

Design an appropriate
estate plan.

Prepare the necessary
legal documents.

Periodically review
and revise the plan.

that may have to be paid, unpaid federal income taxes at the time of death, and other expenses that will be charged to the estate.

The third step is to design an appropriate plan. The estate attorney or financial planner designs a plan to meet the objectives of the individual and family. The plan design includes the judicious selection of various estate-planning tools, such as a will, marital deduction, gifts, trusts, and life insurance. We explain these tools in greater detail later in the chapter. The estate plan is then hypothetically tested to determine if the estate objectives will be accomplished.

The fourth step is preparation of the required legal documents by a competent attorney. An attorney usually drafts the legal documents such as a will or trust. The legal documents are complex and often include specific clauses and provisions to reflect the individual's estate-planning objectives. Thus, we do not advise using a do-it-yourself legal documents kit, such as those sold in book or software format.

Finally, the estate plan should be periodically reviewed and revised when necessary. The plan should be revised if there is a marriage or divorce; a child is born; a spouse or family member dies; a new business is acquired or an existing business is sold; the individual's financial position changes significantly; the individual moves to another state with a different estate tax; or the federal estate tax law is changed.

When an estate plan is drafted, certain pitfalls and mistakes should be avoided.

Tools of Estate Planning

An effective estate plan requires the use of certain estate-planning instruments. The basic tools of estate planning include a will, marital deduction, gifts, trusts, and life insurance.

Will

will A legal instrument by which property is disposed of in accordance with an individual's wishes on his or her death.

A will is a key tool in estate planning. A **will** is a legal instrument by which property is disposed of in accordance with the individual's wishes. It provides certain advantages in estate planning. A properly drafted will do the following:

■ Minimize legal and financial obstacles in distributing property to the heirs.

■ Speed up the estate settlement process.

■ Reduce family disputes among the heirs with respect to the distribution of valuable property, such as antiques and family heirlooms.

■ Name a guardian for any minor children.

■ Name a personal representative or executor to settle the estate.

■ Provide for the creation of trusts to attain your estate objectives.

■ Substantially reduce federal estate taxes and state death taxes.

intestate Without a will.

Many people die without a will. This is known as dying **intestate.** The property is then distributed according to the intestate provisions of state law where the individual lives. Dying intestate often results in property being distributed to people whom the deceased would not have wanted to receive the property. For example, in many states, if an individual with children dies without a will, the surviving spouse receives only one-third of the estate property, and the other two-thirds goes to the children. The deceased may have intended that the surviving spouse should receive all the property. In addition, if there are no children, part of the estate may pass to the parents. Thus, the surviving spouse may be deprived of needed financial assets for self-support.

Requirements of a Valid Will. To be valid, a will must meet certain legal requirements. First, in most states, the person who makes the will (testator) must be at least age 18. Although this is the general rule, some states have different minimum age requirements.

Second, the testator must be mentally competent. However, the law ordinarily requires less mental competency to make a will than to enter into a valid contract. A person can make a will even if he or she is aged, sick, weak, or has low mental capacity. In general, the testator must know (1) he or she is making a will, (2) the extent and character of the property to be distributed, and (3) the object of his or her bounty (those who will receive the property under the will). Finally, the will must be in writing, signed by the testator, and witnessed by at least two persons. Some states require three witnesses.

holographic will A will that you prepare yourself in your own handwriting.

Many states also recognize a holographic will. A **holographic will** is a will that you prepare yourself in your own handwriting. To be valid, the will must be in your own handwriting and must be signed by you and dated. The major difference between a holographic will and other valid wills is that the signature of witnesses is not required. As such, a holographic will is especially susceptible to forgery.

A holographic will may benefit a person who has little property to leave or cannot afford the expense of an attorney. However, it should not be used as a substitute for an attorney when the estate is large; an attorney can offer valuable suggestions for reducing estate taxes and for proper drafting of key will provisions.

Key Provisions. A properly drafted will contains several key provisions. It is beyond the scope of this text to discuss all provisions in a will. However, key provisions in a will should accomplish the following:

■ Identify the heirs and the property to be distributed to specific heirs

■ Name a guardian for any minor children

■ Provide for a marital deduction by which an unlimited amount of property can be passed to a surviving spouse free of estate taxes

■ Provide for the creation of trusts, if any, to attain certain estate objectives

■ Have a simultaneous death provision by which the spouse who dies simultaneously with you is presumed to have survived you; the purpose is to preserve the marital deduction for the testator by assuming that his or her spouse died last.

■ Name the personal representative or executor who will settle your estate

executor, or personal representative The person who is responsible for administering and settling the estate after your death.

This last provision names the **executor** or **personal representative** who is responsible for administering and settling the estate after your death. The executor can be a family member or a corporation, such as the trust department of a commercial bank. Many people name both an individual family member and a corporation as coexecutors (see Exhibit 17.6).

The executor has several major responsibilities, which include paying estate debts or expenses; collecting all life insurance proceeds and retirement plan benefits; making certain tax decisions; filing tax returns; paying any federal estate and state death taxes; and distributing the property to the designated heirs.

The executor should be selected with care. First, make certain that he or she is willing to serve. Second, provide for an alternative executor in the event the primary executor dies or becomes disabled. In addition, if the executor is a surviving spouse or close family member, your will should state that the executor can serve without posting a bond. Finally, the will is the foundation of your estate plan. As such, it should be drafted carefully because of its long-term impact on the family.

Changing a Will.   A will should be periodically reviewed and updated if necessary. A will may have to be changed because of a death, birth, marriage, divorce, relocation to another state, change in health or employ-

---

Exhibit 17.6

Selecting an Executor and Trustees

Advantages of a Corporate Executor/Trustee

1. Specialist in handling estates/trusts.
2. No emotional bias.
3. Impartial—usually free of conflicts of interest with the beneficiary.
4. Never moves or goes on vacation.
5. Never dies or gets sick.

Advantages of an Individual Executor/Trustee

1. More familiar with the family.
2. Administrative fees may be lower.

Source: Practice Development Institute (PDI), Chicago. Reprinted with permission.

codicil A supplement to a will that changes, modifies, or expands the original will.

ment, or change in the probate or tax laws. A codicil can be used to effectuate the change. A **codicil** is a supplement that changes, modifies, or expands the original will. To be valid, the codicil must be legally executed and witnessed with the same formalities as the original will. Because the codicil is an amendment, it should be attached to the original will so that it is not destroyed or lost.

A will does not become effective until death. The testator can revoke or modify the will any time prior to death. There are three methods for revoking a will. First, a new will may be drafted that revokes an earlier will. It is common to include a revocation provision in the new will, such as, "I hereby revoke all prior wills."

Second, the testator can revoke a will by burning, tearing, obliterating, or destroying the original will; the testator must also have the intention of revoking the will. The will should be destroyed if it no longer represents the last wishes of the testator.

Finally, depending on the state, certain circumstances, such as marriage and divorce, can revoke a will without the testator taking any action. For example, state law may specify that if the testator gets a divorce after making a will, the divorce will revoke any provision in the will passing property to the former spouse. Thus, the former spouse will receive nothing from the deceased person's estate.

living will A document that states your wishes concerning the medical care that will be provided to you if you should become mentally or physically disabled and cannot make a rational decision.

Living Will.   A living will is also used in estate planning. A **living will** is a document that states your wishes concerning the medical care that will be provided to you if you should become mentally or physically disabled and cannot make a rational decision. Some physicians provide extraordinary methods of care to keep a terminally ill patient alive, often at great cost to the family and little or no benefit to the patient. For example, a patient who is terminally ill often can be kept alive for an extended period by machines and new technology, such as new experimental surgery or drugs. However, a terminally ill patient who is unable to make a rational medical decision may prefer that only ordinary treatment should be provided—such as food, water, and pain relief—and that extraordinary methods of care should not be given. The patient's wishes can be specifically stated in a living will.

durable power of attorney for health care A legal document that authorizes someone to act on your behalf if you are incapable of making your own health-care decisions.

As an alternative to a living will, a durable power of attorney can be used. A **durable power of attorney for health care** is a legal document that authorizes someone to act on your behalf if you are incapable of making your own health-care decisions. For example, you may authorize your representative to permit or withdraw medical treatment on your behalf; allow pain-relieving drugs to be administered; gain access to your medical records and other personal information; employ and discharge physicians and other health-care providers; and protect your legal rights.

Marital Deduction

marital deduction A deduction of the value of property that is included in the gross estate but is passed on to the surviving spouse free of current estate taxes.

The marital deduction is a powerful estate-planning tool that can substantially reduce federal estate taxes. It applies when property is left to a surviving spouse. The **marital deduction** is a deduction of the value of the property that is included in the gross estate but is passed on to the surviving spouse. For example, assume that Miles dies and has a gross estate valued at $1.3 million. He leaves only $600,000 of property outright to his wife. In this case, the marital deduction is $600,000. Debts, administrative costs, and funeral expenses total $100,000. The taxable estate is $600,000, and the tentative federal estate tax is $192,800. However, as a result of the unified credit of $192,800, the federal estate tax is zero (see Exhibit 17.7).

If the estate is large, estate planners generally do not recommend leaving the entire estate outright to the surviving spouse by use of an unlimited marital deduction. Although all property would pass free of federal estate taxes to the surviving spouse, it would be subject to the federal estate tax when the surviving spouse dies. The federal estate tax payable at that time on the second estate generally is higher than that paid on the first since the second estate does not qualify for the marital deduction (unless the surviving spouse remarries). This can result in higher federal estate taxes and a shrinkage in the estate property that can be passed on to the heirs, such as children.

Exhibit 17.7

Illustration of Marital Deduction

Gross estate		$1,300,000
Less:		
Debts	$60,000	
Administrative costs	35,000	
Funeral expenses	5,000	
		−100,000
Adjusted gross estate		$1,200,000
Less:		
Marital deduction		−600,000
Taxable estate		$600,000
Tentative tax		$192,800
Less:		
Unified credit		−192,800
Federal estate tax		$0

Source: G. E. Rejda, *Principles of Risk Management & Insurance* 5/E (table 19.1, p. 409). © 1995 HarperCollins College Publishers. Reprinted by permission of Addison Wesley Longman, Inc.

Gifts

Gifts can be effectively used as an estate-planning tool since they can reduce the size of the taxable estate. However, a gift tax may have to be paid if the value of the gift exceeds $10,000 annually ($20,000 if the spouse joins in the gift). If a federal gift tax is payable, part or all of the unified tax credit can be used to defray the tax. However, any portion of the unified tax credit that is used to defray gift taxes is no longer available for reducing federal estate taxes.

Trusts

trust An arrangement by which property is legally transferred to a trustee, who manages the property for the benefit of named beneficiaries.

Trusts are also used as an effective estate-planning tool. A **trust** is an arrangement in which property is legally transferred to a trustee, who manages the property for the benefit of named beneficiaries. The trustee can be a bank, trust company, or an adult. A trust can provide security to the beneficiaries and insure competent management of estate property after an individual dies. Certain types of trusts can reduce estate taxes and probate costs in settling an estate. The saving in estate taxes is often substantial.

living *(inter vivo)* trust Trust into which property is placed while the individual who created the trust is still alive.

There are two broad categories of trusts: (1) living and (2) testamentary. In a **living *(inter vivo)* trust,** property is placed in the trust while the individual is still alive. If the creator of the trust has the right to revoke the trust and receive the property, this is known as a **revocable living trust.** A revocable living trust can be used to reduce probate costs and provide privacy if the trust is still in existence at the creator's death. In recent years, revocable living trusts have become increasingly popular as an estate planning tool.

revocable living trust Living trust that can be revoked by the creator.

irrevocable trust Trust that cannot be revoked by the creator.

If the creator of the trust gives up the right to receive the property, this is known as an **irrevocable trust.** An irrevocable trust can reduce estate taxes since property is taken out of the estate. Probate costs are also reduced. However, there are gift tax implications when property is placed in an irrevocable trust. A gift tax may have to be paid if it exceeds the amount of the unified tax credit.

testamentary trust Trust provided for in a will; it does not come into existence until the creator dies.

A second broad category of trusts is a testamentary trust. A **testamentary trust** is provided for in the will and does not come into existence until the creator dies. The testamentary trust can be used to protect minors, handicapped family members, or spendthrift heirs. This type of trust adds flexibility to the estate plan since the trustee can be granted discretionary powers to deal with the beneficiary's problems and needs as they arise.

Life Insurance

Life insurance is a widely used estate-planning tool to provide liquidity to the estate for the payment of probate expenses and the federal estate tax. In particular, a second-to-die life insurance policy (also called a sur-

second-to-die policy Life insurance policy that insures the lives of two people, such as a married couple; the death proceeds are paid on the death of the second spouse.

vivorship life policy) is widely used in estate planning to pay the federal estate tax. A **second-to-die policy** insures the lives of two people, such as a married couple, and the death proceeds are paid only upon the death of the second spouse. The death proceeds provide the necessary liquidity to the estate for payment of estate taxes. The cost of the second-to-die policy is substantially lower than two separate policies.

Life insurance has several advantages as an estate-planning tool. First, it provides estate liquidity. Cash is immediately available for funeral expenses, estate clearance costs, and death taxes. Thus, if the amount of life insurance is adequate, forced liquidation of property to raise the needed cash is unnecessary.

Second, life insurance proceeds paid to a named beneficiary are not subject to probate costs. The proceeds are paid immediately to the heirs without first having to go into a probate court.

Finally, life insurance can provide for the equitable treatment of heirs. For example, assume that a farmer has two sons, and that one son helps manage the farm. The farm is valued at $500,000 and is left to that son in the farmer's will. The farmer can then purchase a $500,000 life insurance policy and name the other son owner and beneficiary. Both children would be treated equally when the farmer dies.

Taxation of Life Insurance.   The advantages of life insurance as an estate-planning tool can be negated by unfavorable tax treatment if not properly planned. In the following paragraphs, we discuss briefly the taxation of life insurance.

incidents of ownership With regard to a life insurance policy, certain rights that evidence ownership, including the right to change the beneficiary, the right to borrow the cash value or surrender the policy, and the right to select a settlement option.

Federal estate tax. If the insured has any **incidents of ownership** in a life insurance policy at the time of death, the entire proceeds are included in the deceased's estate for federal estate tax purposes. Incidents of ownership include the right to change the beneficiary, the right to borrow the cash value or surrender the policy, and the right to select a settlement option. The proceeds are also included in the insured's gross estate if they are payable to the estate. They can be removed from the gross estate if the policyowner makes an *absolute assignment* of the policy to someone else and has no incidents of ownership in the policy at the time of death. However, if the assignment is made within three years of death, the policy proceeds will be included in the deceased's gross estate for federal estate tax purposes.

Federal income tax. Life insurance proceeds paid in a lump sum are generally received income-tax-free by the beneficiary. If the proceeds are periodically liquidated under the settlement options, the payments consist of both principal and interest. The principal is received income-tax-free. However, the interest income is taxable.

Premiums paid for individual life insurance policies generally are not deductible for income tax purposes. Dividends on life insurance policies are received income-tax-free unless the dividends are retained under the interest option, in which case the interest income is taxable to the policyowner. However, if the dividends are used to buy paid-up additions to the policy, the cash value of the paid-up additions accumulates income-tax-free. Thus, compared with the interest option, the paid-up additions option provides a small tax advantage.

In addition, the annual increase in cash value under a permanent life insurance policy is presently income-tax-free. However, if the policy is surrendered for its cash value, any gain is taxable as ordinary income. If the cash value exceeds the premiums paid less any dividends, the excess usually is taxable as ordinary income.

Strategies for Reducing the Federal Estate Tax

Certain strategies can be used to reduce the federal estate tax. They include a credit-shelter trust, annual gifts, irrevocable life insurance trusts, and charitable remainder trusts.

Credit-Shelter Trust

credit-shelter trust An irrevocable trust that is designed to make use of the $600,000 lifetime exemption that could be lost when the first spouse dies.

We noted earlier that under the marital deduction, an unlimited amount of property can be passed to a surviving spouse free of the federal estate tax. Although an entire estate can be left outright to a surviving spouse free of estate taxes, the property would be taxed when the surviving spouse dies, which may substantially increase the amount of tax payable. A credit-shelter trust (also called a bypass trust) can be used to deal with this problem. A **credit-shelter trust** is an irrevocable trust that is designed to make use of the $600,000 lifetime exemption that could be lost when the first spouse dies.

When the first spouse dies, $600,000 of estate assets goes into his or her credit-shelter trust rather than to the surviving spouse. The surviving spouse receives the trust income and can also withdraw a limited amount of the principal. Each year, the trust beneficiary is allowed to withdraw the higher of $5,000 or 5 percent of the principal without having the entire trust property included in his or her estate for federal estate tax purposes. Because of the trust language, the credit-shelter trust does not qualify for the marital deduction. Thus, the entire $600,000 is included in the taxable estate of the first spouse who dies; however, the unified tax credit of $192,800 is used to eliminate the federal estate tax on that amount. When the second spouse dies, the federal estate tax is substantially lower because of the credit-shelter trust (see Insight 17.1).

Insight

17.1 How to Reduce Federal Estate Taxes With a Credit-Shelter Trust

Scott and Jennifer are married and have adult children. Scott dies and has a taxable estate of $2 million. Because of the marital deduction, Jennifer receives $2 million, and Scott's taxable estate is zero. Shortly thereafter, Jennifer dies, leaving a taxable estate of $2 million. The first $600,000 is exempt from the federal estate tax because of the unified credit, but the remaining $1.4 million is subject to taxes of $588,000. *The problem is that the couple took advantage of the $600,000 lifetime exemption for only one estate, but not both.* This is summarized in the first chart to the right.

Now consider a more effective strategy. Both Scott and Jennifer establish credit-shelter trusts. Assume that Scott dies, and $600,000 goes into his credit-shelter trust. Jennifer receives income from the trust during her lifetime and has the right to withdraw limited amounts of principal. Because the trust does not qualify for the marital deduction, $600,000 is included in Scott's taxable estate. However, because of the unified credit, the estate tax on that amount is zero. The remaining $1.4 million goes to Jennifer under the marital deduction. When she dies, her taxable estate is only $1.4 million. The $600,000 credit-shelter trust is

No estate plan	
Scott and Jennifer's assets total $2 million.	
Scott dies	
Leaves everything to Jennifer	$2,000,000
Estate tax after marital deduction	0
Jennifer dies	
Leaves everything to her children	$2,000,000
Taxable estate	2,000,000
Tentative tax	780,800
Less: Unified credit	192,800
Estate tax	$588,000

With Credit-Shelter Trust	
Scott and Jennifer's assets total $2 million.	
Scott dies	
Tentative tax on $600,000 in credit-shelter trust	$192,800
Less: Unified credit	192,800
Tax on credit-shelter trust	0
Tax on $1.4 million passed to Jennifer	0
Jennifer dies	
Credit-shelter assets go to children	$600,000
Tax on credit-shelter assets	0
Estate of $1.4 million goes to children	1,400,000
Tentative tax on $1.4 million	512,800
Less: Unified credit	192,800
Estate tax	320,000
Estate tax saving	$268,000

not included in her estate because she does not own it. Thus, her estate is taxed only on $800,000 ($1.4 million less $600,000), which creates an estate tax of $320,000. Thus,

the credit-shelter trust saves $268,000 in federal estate taxes ($588,000 less $320,000). This is summarized in the second chart above.

Annual Gifts

Taking advantage of the annual gift tax exclusion is another method for reducing federal estate taxes. As we noted earlier, you can give as much as $10,000 annually to each donee without incurring a gift tax ($20,000 for a married couple). Thus, giving annual gifts to children, grandchildren, charities, or other parties can reduce the estate significantly over an extended period. Estate planners recommend a number of gift-giving strategies to take maximum advantage of current law (see Insight 17.2).

Irrevocable Life Insurance Trust

irrevocable life insurance trust A trust funded by life insurance; it is designed to restore shrinkage in the estate because of estate taxes or to replace for the heirs estate property gifted to charity.

Life insurance death proceeds are included in your gross estate if you have any incidents of ownership at the time of death. However, it is possible to get the life insurance proceeds out of your estate by an irrevocable life insurance trust. An **irrevocable life insurance trust** is a trust funded by life insurance; it is designed to restore shrinkage in the estate because of estate taxes or to replace for the heirs estate property gifted to charity. The trust owns the life insurance and is the beneficiary. The insured makes a gift of the premiums to the trust each year. When the insured dies, the life insurance proceeds are paid to the trust and are not included in the insured's gross estate. The trust can be structured to provide lifetime income to the surviving spouse and for ultimate distribution of the proceeds to the children.

The trust agreement cannot state that the life insurance proceeds must be used to pay estate taxes; if this were done, the death proceeds would be included in the insured's gross estate for federal estate tax purposes and defeat the purpose of establishing the trust. However, the trustee can be given authority to purchase estate property from the insured's estate or to make a loan to the estate. Thus, the insured's estate would have the liquidity to pay estate taxes and probate costs.

The insured can also transfer existing life insurance policies into the irrevocable life insurance trust by making an absolute assignment of the policies to the trust. However, as we noted earlier, if the insured dies within three years of the assignment, the death proceeds are included in the insured's gross estate for federal estate tax purposes.

In recent years, a second-to-die policy has become increasingly popular as a method of funding an irrevocable life insurance trust. The leveraging effect is powerful since a large estate tax can be paid by a relatively small premium payment. For example, a married couple both age 53 could make a single payment of $9,383 into an irrevocable life insurance trust, which would pay the tax of $153,000 on a $1 million taxable estate. This represents a return of 16.3 to 1 on the single premium paid (see Exhibit 17.8).

Insight 17.2 Strategies for Giving

Parents and grandparents frequently make substantial gifts to their loved ones, whether to help buy a home or business, to fund a college education or to pay for needed medical care.

Such gifts, however, should not be made without adequate consideration of all of the tax implications involved. The gift tax and the estate tax are part of a unified system. A gift tax is due from the donor at rates that are equal to the estate tax rates and the same $600,000 exemption that applies at death also applies to lifetime gifts. After the exemption is fully used, a tax is imposed. The rationale is to assure that individuals will not avoid the estate tax at death by simply giving their assets away while they are alive.

Does this mean there are no real advantages to making lifetime gifts? No. There are, in fact, a number of distinct advantages to making such gifts. Here are a few potential gift-giving strategies:

■ *Make use of the annual exclusion against the gift tax.* Each individual is permitted to make up to $10,000 of gifts to anyone else each year without eroding the $600,000 exemption. The number of donees is unlimited and there is no requirement that they be related to you. As part of a systematic gift-giving program, you could pass a substantial amount of wealth on to your heirs without the imposition of any gift or estate taxes.

■ *Benefit from the exclusion for medical payments.* You may pay an unlimited amount of medical expenses for the benefit of an another without any of those payments being classified as taxable gifts. This exclusion pertains only to direct payments made to medical care providers, however. Payments may not be made to reimburse someone for their medical care, or to pay their health insurance premiums. This exclusion is in addition to, and not in lieu of, the $10,000 annual gift tax exclusion.

■ *Use the exclusion for tuition payments.* A gift tax exclusion also applies to tuition payments made directly to an educational institution on behalf of a student. This exclusion applies to both full-time and part-time students but is limited to tuition. Expenditures for books, housing and meals, for example, do not qualify. This exclusion is also in addition to the $10,000 annual exclusion.

■ *Split gifts between spouses.* A husband and wife have the opportunity to treat all gifts made by one of them during a calendar year as being made one half by each of them. At first, this may not appear to be much of a benefit, but it actually is. Each spouse can use the $10,000 annual exclusion, as well as his or her own $600,000 estate and gift tax exemption. They can also each benefit from the graduation in gift tax rates from 37% to 55% on gifts of between $600,000 and $3 million in value.

■ *Give property with a high appreciation potential.* When you make a bequest at death, your heirs receive a tax basis for future capital gains tax purposes equal to the fair market value of the property at death. In the event of a lifetime gift, however, the recipient of the gift usually takes on the same tax basis as the donor. In many cases, the tax basis will merely be the original cost to the donor.

This lack of a "step up" in basis can be mitigated to a large extent by giving assets that have not yet appreciated in value, but may be expected to do so in the future. None of the appreciation in value after the date of the gift will be part of the donor's estate at death, and most of the capital gains tax will be attributed to an increase in the value of the property while in the recipient's hands.

■ *Make gifts to minors under the Uniform Gifts to Minors or Transfers to Minors acts.* Parents and grandparents often have a desire to make gifts to minor children or grandchildren. Because of their ages, however, minors are not deemed capable of managing their own financial affairs.

To prevent the necessity of having a guardian appointed to handle the property of a minor, all states have enacted uniform laws that facilitate the giving of cash, securities, life insurance policies and other assets through a custodian designated by the donor. The custodian holds title to the property on the minor's behalf and all of the income earned belongs to the minor. There is no need to set up a formal trust because the state has, in essence, already set one up.

Source: R. Mark Hochberg, *Financial World,* Vol. 164, No. 12, 5/23/95, p. 84. Reprinted with permission.

Charitable Remainder Trusts

A direct gift to a charitable institution is fully deductible for federal estate purposes. If you leave your entire estate to charity in your will, your estate would owe no federal estate tax. However, most people do not leave all of their property to charity since they wish to take care of their children and other heirs. A reasonable compromise is to leave part of the property to charity and the remainder to the heirs. A charitable remainder trust can be especially helpful in this regard.

A **charitable remainder trust** is a trust in which property or money is donated to a charity; the trust provides income to your beneficiaries for a stated period, after which time the property belongs to the charity. In return, the donor receives certain income and estate tax deductions.

For example, assume that you want to provide for your elderly mother after you die. A charitable remainder trust can be created. Income from the trust would be paid to your mother during her lifetime or for a stated period. After that time, the property passes to the designated charity. Since you are making a partial donation to charity at the time of your death, your estate can deduct a portion of the trust's value. Internal Revenue Service (IRS) tables determine the amount of the deduction based on a number of factors, including the value of the trust assets, the term of the trust, and income paid to the trust beneficiary.

charitable remainder trust A trust in which property or money is donated to a charity; the trust provides income to the creator's beneficiaries for a stated period, after which time the property belongs to the charity.

Exhibit 17.8

94% Discount on Your Estate Tax Cost

$9,383 transferred to an irrevocable trust
pays $153,000 tax on your $1,000,000 estate

Transfer
$9,383 or $2,182
yearly for 5 years

Gain
$143,617

16.3 to 1 return
$153,000

Note: The policy is a second-to-die policy for a married couple both age 53. The tax payable reflects application of the unified credit.

Source: Barry Kaye, *Save a Fortune on Your Estate Taxes: Wealth, Creation and Preservation* Business One Irwin, 1993, Chart 1, p. 73. Reprinted with permission of the McGraw-Hill Companies.

A charitable remainder trust can also be created during your lifetime. You are entitled to an income tax deduction based on government tables that determine the amount of the charitable gift. Thus, if the trust is created during your lifetime, you can reduce both federal income and estate taxes.

A charitable remainder trust is especially valuable if you donate assets that have appreciated substantially in value. For example, assume that you own a growth stock with a current yield of 1 percent. The current market value of the stock is $110,000, and your cost basis is $10,000. If you are in the 31 percent marginal tax bracket and sell the stock outright, you would pay $31,000 in federal income taxes. However, assume that you transfer the stock to a charitable remainder trust and that the trustee sells the stock and invests the proceeds in government bonds yielding 6 percent. Because the trust is a charitable trust, no capital gains are payable. The increased income can then be paid to the designated beneficiaries of the trust. There are other benefits as well (see Exhibit 17.9)

In summary, estate planning is a complex process. We have only touched the basic principles of estate planning in this chapter, and actual case situations can be extremely complicated. For this reason, estate planning is not a do-it-yourself activity, and you may need a team of highly competent professionals. A Chartered Life Underwriter (CLU), Chartered Financial Consultant (ChFC), or Certified Financial Planner (CFP) can make valuable suggestions but cannot give legal advice. Therefore, a competent attorney who can give legal advice and draw up the necessary legal documents is necessary. You may also need a tax accountant, especially if complex business interests must be considered. If a trust is required, a trust officer of a commercial bank or trust company can provide valuable advice on the conservation and investment of estate assets.

Finally, adult children should have a frank discussion with their parents concerning their financial affairs if one or both parents should die.

Exhibit 17.9

Benefits of a Charitable Remainder Trust
■ Annual income for a beneficiary or yourself
■ Current year tax deduction
■ No capital gains tax on assets used to fund the trust
■ Ability to increase your investment yield
■ Gift to your favorite charity

Source: Practice Development Institute (PDI), Chicago. Reprinted with permission.

Insight

17.3   Dear Mom and Dad: Here's Something That's Easier to Read Than to Discuss

My brothers and I recently discussed what would happen if either of our parents fell ill or died.

We agreed that we should talk to our folks about their wishes concerning things like nursing homes, life-support machines and funeral arrangements. We also agreed that we should push them to get some critical legal documents drawn up, including living wills and durable powers of attorney.

In fact, we agreed on a lot of things—everything, that is, except who is going to pick up the phone and have the big discussion. We still haven't agreed on that one.

Just how do you get the ball rolling? I put that question to Richard Kohan, an estate-planning expert at Price Waterhouse.

"Ask your parents what they would like to accomplish with their estate," he suggested. For instance, he said, there might be needy friends, political causes or favorite charities that your parents would like to benefit.

"If you put it in that context, it makes estate planning less morbid and it makes parents realize the importance of doing estate planning."

And just what does estate planning involve? At a minimum, each parent should have a will, a durable power of attorney and a medical power of attorney. A medical power of attorney designates somebody to make healthcare decisions for your parents, should they become too ill to do so themselves, while a durable power of attorney designates someone to handle their finances. Your parents may also want to draw up living wills, which state their wishes concerning life-prolonging medical procedures.

Even if your folks already have wills, they may need to update them--especially if they have moved to a different state, if there's been a change in federal or state tax law or if there's been a big change in the value of their estate. Also, encourage both of your parents to draw up a letter of instructions, which specifies who should receive their personal belongings.

Next, ask your parents whether their estate, including the value of their home and all investments, is likely to top $600,000. How come? Your parents can pass on their assets to one another without paying any federal estate taxes. But if either of them leaves more than $600,000 to their children, grandchildren and anybody else, federal estate taxes kick in at rates that start at 37% and rise rapidly.

What should parents do? A good estate-planning lawyer can suggest a variety of ways to save on estate taxes. But for starters, you might mention a couple of popular strategies.

Your parents may want to use a bypass trust, which would allow both of them to make full use of the $600,000 federal estate tax exemption. Here's how it might work. When the first parent dies, $600,000 goes into a trust earmarked for the kids, but the surviving spouse continues to get the income kicked off by the trust. That ensures that the first parent's $600,000 exemption gets used. On the death of the second parent, another $600,000 will be exempt, thereby sheltering a full $1.2 million from federal estate taxes.

Both of your parents could also shrink their estates by taking advantage of the annual $10,000 gift-tax exclusion. Every year, they could give a combined gift of $20,000 to each of their children, without triggering the gift tax.

Moreover, if your parents want to help with medical bills or a grandchild's college tuition, these gifts aren't counted toward the $10,000 annual exclusion, so long as the money is paid directly to the medical provider or college.

Of course, all these clever arrangements can be thrown into disarray if kids don't know where to find their parents' key documents. "You want to know the whereabouts of all estate-planning documents, all insurance policies, all collectibles, all brokerage accounts," said San Francisco investment adviser Malcolm Gissen. "You also want to know whether they're owed money or whether they owe it."

Mr. Gissen advises asking your parents what they plan to do if maintaining their home becomes too burdensome. They may be able to hire somebody to help with chores, or they could take in a lodger who does housework in lieu of rent. "But if you need somebody to look after your parents around the clock, it can get very expensive," Mr. Gissen said. The alternative? "There's a range of options, from senior housing to nursing homes to living with the children."

And if you've worked your way through all the other issues, you might as well finish the job. So go ahead, ask about funeral arrangements.

But it sure isn't easy to ask your parents whether they want to be buried or cremated. As a copout, you could simply send them this article. That's what my brothers and I plan to do.

Source: Jonathan Clements, "Dear Mom and Dad: Here's Something That's Easier to Read Than to Discuss," April 11, 1995. Reprinted by permission of *The Wall Street Journal*, ©19953 Dow Jones & Company, Inc. All Rights Reserved Worldwide.

This includes such things as a will, location and list of financial assets, durable power of attorney, health-care proxy, and funeral arrangements (see Insight 17.3).

SUMMARY

- Estate planning is a process for the conservation and distribution of a person's property and wealth.

- The objectives of estate planning include the following:

   Conserve estate assets both before and after death.

   Distribute property according to the individual's wishes.

   Minimize federal estate and state death taxes.

   Minimize income taxes.

   Minimize probate costs in the settlement of an estate.

   Provide liquidity to the estate.

   Provide for the family's financial needs or other special needs.

- Without an estate plan, the estate is exposed to substantial shrinkage. The shrinkage is due to administrative and probate expenses, federal estate and state death taxes, and forced liquidation of estate property.

- The federal estate tax applies to taxable estates over $600,000. A unified tax credit of $192,800 can be used to reduce the tax.

- Annual gifts of $10,000 can be given to as many persons as desired without incurring a federal gift tax on the transfer. If the spouse joins in the gift, a total of $20,000 can be given to each person. The unified tax credit can be used when a gift tax is payable.

- The estate-planning process involves the following steps: (1) obtain facts about the estate; (2) evaluate potential claims against the estate; (3) design an appropriate estate plan; (4) prepare the necessary legal documents; (5) periodically review and revise the plan.

- A will is a legal instrument by which property is disposed of in accordance with the individual's wishes. Dying without a will is known as dying intestate, in which case the state determines who will receive the property.

■ The marital deduction is a deduction of the value of the property included in the gross estate that is passed on to a surviving spouse. The marital deduction is unlimited. However, estate planners generally do not recommend leaving the entire estate to the surviving spouse because the $600,000 lifetime exemption would be lost when the first spouse dies.

■ A living trust is a revocable trust in which property is legally transferred to a trustee who manages the property for the benefit of named beneficiaries. A living trust is used to avoid probate costs. However, estate taxes are not reduced.

■ A second-to-die life insurance policy insures the lives of two persons, and the death proceeds are paid only upon the death of the second spouse. The proceeds are used to pay estate taxes or provide liquidity to an estate.

■ Life insurance proceeds are included in the gross estate if the insured has any incidents of ownership at the time of death.

■ Strategies that can reduce the federal estate tax include credit-shelter trusts, annual gifts, irrevocable life insurance trusts, and charitable remainder trusts.

■ A credit-shelter trust is an irrevocable trust that does not qualify for the unlimited marital deduction. It is designed to make use of the $600,000 lifetime exemption that could be lost when the first spouse dies.

■ Annual gifts can effectively be used as an estate-planning tool since they reduce the size of the taxable estate.

■ An irrevocable life insurance trust is a trust funded by life insurance. It is designed to restore shrinkage in the estate because of estate taxes or to replace for the heirs any estate property gifted to charity. The trust owns the life insurance and is the beneficiary. The death proceeds are paid to the trust and are not included in the insured's gross estate.

■ A charitable remainder trust is a trust in which property or money is donated to a charity that provides income to the beneficiaries for a stated period, after which time the property belongs to the charity. In return, the donor receives certain income and estate tax deductions.

KEY CONCEPTS AND TERMS

Charitable remainder trust
Codicil
Credit-shelter trust
Durable power of attorney for
   health care
Estate shrinkage
Executor, or personal represen-
   tative
Gross estate
Holographic will
Incidents of ownership
Intestate
Irrevocable life insurance trust

Irrevocable trust
Living *(inter vivo)* trust
Living will
Marital deduction
Probate
Revocable living trust
Second-to-die policy
Taxable estate
Testamentary trust
Trust
Unified tax credit
Will

QUESTIONS FOR REVIEW

1. Explain the basic objectives of estate planning.

2. Describe the factors that may contribute to shrinkage of an estate after an individual dies.

3. Briefly describe the unified tax credit that applies to both the federal estate and federal gift taxes.

4. Explain the five basic steps in the estate-planning process.

5. Briefly describe how the following can be effectively used in estate planning:
   a. Will
   b. Marital deduction
   c. Gifts
   d. Trusts
   e. Life insurance

6. With respect to the federal estate tax and federal income tax, briefly explain how life insurance is taxed.

7. Explain how a living trust can reduce probate expenses.

8. Explain how a credit-shelter trust (bypass trust) can reduce the federal estate tax.

9. Briefly explain how the following trusts can reduce federal estate taxes:
   a. Irrevocable life insurance trust
   b. Charitable remainder trust

PROBLEMS

1. Kelsey, age 32, owns a condominium with a current market value of $125,000; the remaining mortgage on the condominium is $75,000. She also owns the following: a $75,000 life insurance policy, mutual funds and a checking account in the amount of $25,000, and an automobile and other personal property with a current market value of $25,000. In addition, the current balance in her Section 401(k) plan is $40,000. Assume that Kelsey dies and funeral expenses and probate costs total $15,000. What is the amount of her taxable estate?

2. Betty and Ed are married and have a gross estate of $950,000. Ed's will specifies that upon his death, the estate property is to pass to the other spouse under the unlimited marital deduction provision. If Ed should die first, will his estate have any federal estate tax liability? Explain.

3. Helen, age 60, is a widow and has a gross estate of $800,000. Her will specifies that a local charity is to receive $100,000 upon her death. The remainder of the estate will pass to her two children in equal shares after all estate expenses are paid. If Helen should die and funeral expenses and probate costs are $25,000, will her estate have any estate tax liability? Explain.

INTERNET EXERCISES

1. The Nolo Press Self-Help Law Center at:

   http://www.nolo.com/

   provides information on wills and estate planning in its "Legal Encyclopedia" section. Browse to see what information is available.

2. LifeNet, cited in Chapter 16, also offers information on estate planning. Go to the site at:

   http://www.lifenet.com/

   and select "Estate Planning." See if you have enough information about your finances to use the calculators.

CASE APPLICATIONS

Case 1

Sam and Kathy, both age 60, are married and have adult children. They own the following assets and life insurance:

Joint ownership	
Residence	$150,000
Mutual funds, securities, and cash	650,000
Sam's property	
Private pension plan	700,000
Individual retirement account (IRA)	300,000
Life insurance	600,000
Kathy's property	
Private pension plan	100,000
Individual retirement account (IRA)	50,000
Life insurance	250,000

Sam and Kathy have separate wills. In his will, Sam bequeaths all of his property to Kathy if she is living and to the children if Kathy dies first. Kathy is the beneficiary of Sam's retirement plans and life insurance. The couple believes their estate plan should be updated. Sam would like to minimize probate expenses and federal estate taxes. Kathy would like to make a substantial bequest to her church.

Assume that you are a financial planner. Answer the following questions:

1. Explain to Sam how a living trust can reduce probate costs.

2. Assume Sam dies first. Administrative expenses, funeral expenses, and probate costs are $100,000. What is the amount of Sam's gross estate?

3. In the preceding example, does Sam's estate have any federal estate tax liability? Explain your answer.

4. What fundamental error in estate planning did Sam commit by leaving all of his property outright to Kathy?

5. Explain how a credit-shelter trust (bypass trust) would avoid the error identified in the preceding question.

6. Explain to Kathy the advantages of establishing a charitable remainder trust during her lifetime as a vehicle for making a charitable donation to her church.

Case II

Lorri is a widow, age 49. Her husband was recently killed in an auto accident by a drunk driver who failed to stop at a red light. Lorri received $550,000 in death benefits from her husband's private retirement plan. She also received $650,000 as beneficiary of her husband's life insurance policy. Lorri also owns individual securities and cash of $300,000. She would like to minimize payment of federal estate taxes and probate costs. Her estate planner recently suggested a program of lifetime gifts to reduce her taxable estate.

Assume that you are a financial planner. Explain to Lorri the gift tax implications of each of the following:

1. Lorri gave her niece a cash gift of $5,000 at Christmas.

2. Lorri paid $15,000 for college tuition for her daughter, age 20.

3. Lorri gave her son, age 25, $25,000 for a down payment on a house.

4. Lorri donated $50,000 to a nonprofit charity to build a shelter for the homeless.

5. Lorri is currently paying the medical bills for her elderly mother who has Alzheimer's disease and is confined to a nursing home. Annual costs are $35,000.

Case III

Sheldon and Hillary, both age 58, are married and have two adult children. After visiting their tax attorney, they were told they have a taxable estate of $2 million and that estimated federal estate taxes upon the death of the second spouse would be $588,000. They would like their children to receive that amount rather than the federal government. The attorney suggested that they establish an irrevocable life insurance trust because of the powerful leveraging effect of life insurance premiums on the federal estate tax.

1. Explain how an irrevocable life insurance trust can be used to pay federal estate taxes.

2. Can the trust agreement specifically state that the life insurance death proceeds must be used to pay the federal estate tax? Explain your answer.

3. What did the tax attorney mean when he said that "life insurance premiums have a powerful leveraging effect on the federal estate tax"?

SUGGESTIONS FOR ADDITIONAL READING

Estate Planning, 4th ed. Chicago, Ill.: Dearborn, R & R Newkirk, 1993.

Estate Planning Strategies for the 1990s. Practice Development Institute, n.d.

Kaye, Barry. *Save a Fortune on Your Estate Taxes: Wealth Creation and Preservation.* Homewood, Ill.: Business One Irwin, 1993.

Leimberg, Stephan R. et al. *The Tools & Techniques of Estate Planning,* 10th ed. Cincinnati, Ohio: The National Underwriter Company, 1995.

Phillips, David T. and Bill S. Wolfkiel. *Estate Planning Made Easy.* Chicago, Ill.: Dearborn Financial Publishing, Inc., 1994.

Pollan, Stephen M. and Mark Levine. "Die Broke," *Worth,* Vol. 4, No. 6 (July/August 1995), pp. 56–66.

Rejda, George E. *Principles of Risk Management and Insurance,* 6th ed. Reading, MA: Addison Wesley Longman, 1998, Chapter 19.

Roha, Ronaleen R. "An Estate-Planning Kit for Dawdlers." *Kiplinger's Personal Finance Magazine,* Vol. 49, No. 6 (June 1995), pp. 71–76.

Appendix A

99 Ways to Cut Costs Every Day

1. Use coupons. Using coupons does cut costs over time. When used for items that you will buy anyway, coupons are free money from the manufacturer. Never buy anything simply because you have a coupon for it.

2. Buy on sale. Never pay full price for anything that you can buy on sale. But beware: If you buy something just because it is on sale and you don't really need it, it's no bargain.

3. Buy generic. Buy store brands whenever possible. With most items, such as paper products, the only difference you'll notice is in your wallet.

4. Buy floor models. Look into buying the floor model when shopping for large appliances and furniture. Prices are often greatly reduced.

5. Avoid fashion trends. When shopping for your wardrobe, concentrate on clothing items that are timeless rather than those with a shorter wearing "life." Limit your trendy pieces to one or two a year. They may look cool this year, but next year they'll be hanging on the racks at the Salvation Army.

6. Buy clothing off season. Buy winter clothes at the end of winter and summer clothes at the end of summer. You'll hit the best bargains that way.

7. Eat at home. Save eating out for special occasions. (Or celebrate at home with a candlelit dinner.)

8. Plant a garden. Plant your own vegetables—they are less expensive and healthier than anything you could buy in a store. Besides, it's also relaxing to work in a garden.

9. Do not call directory assistance. Let your fingers do the walking through your white or yellow pages—it's just as fast as directory assistance, *and* it's free.

10. Call during discount hours. Familiarize yourself with the bargain calling times offered by your long-distance carrier, and make calls only during the least expensive times. (You may want to post a reminder of these times by the phone you use most.)

11. Write a letter. The 32-cent stamp is the best bargain in the country. Next time you go to pick up the phone to make a long-distance call, write that person a letter instead. You'll save a bundle, and you can be quite certain that the letter will be much appreciated.

12. Use e-mail. If you have it use it—you don't even need a 32-cent stamp.

13. Recycle. Returning those cans and bottles is good for the community and good for your wallet. Remember, you already paid a deposit, so get it back.

14. Stay healthy. Take care of your health—you are the most expensive item to repair and by far the hardest to replace.

15. Lose weight on your own. Do not pay clinics for what you ultimately will have to do on your own.

16. Use the YMCA or YWCA. You usually have excellent facilities and classes. Brand-name health clubs are just overpriced.

17. Don't smoke. Smokers easily spend more than $1500 a year on cigarettes and tobacco. Add to that the premiums that health, life, and home insurers charge smokers, and the cost is astronomical.

18. Refinish, repair, and remodel. All cost less than buying something new.

19. Buy a good used car. The quickest way to lose $2,000 is to drive a new car off the lot. There are many good used cars on the market; you simply need to be educated on what to look for and then go buy it.

20. If you are single, you probably do not need life insurance. Life insurance is designed to protect those who depend on you for financial support. If no one depends on you, then you don't need life insurance.

21. If you need insurance, consider term life insurance first. It is much less expensive than any other insurance policy. If your employer offers a group plan, use it. (It may even be included as a benefit.)

22. Shop around for life insurance. Prices greatly vary from company to company.

23. Raise your deductible. A higher deductible on your car or home insurance will greatly reduce your insurance costs—usually much more than the actual amount of the deductible.

24. Use your ATM card wisely. Withdraw as much cash as you have budgeted for yourself at the beginning of each week. Then leave the money access card at home the rest of the week.

25. Use credit cards for convenience, not credit. Never charge more than you can pay off each month.

26. Use fee-free credit cards. Get credit cards from companies that charge no annual fee. Consider applying for a card that offers you something for using the card, such as cash back bonuses, air miles, or a discount on a big-ticket item, like a car.

27. Shop at discount stores. Small shops and boutiques are grossly overpriced because they don't buy in volume.

28. Avoid convenience stores. Convenience is very expensive, and these stores charge a premium for it. Plan in advance, and you'll never be in too much of a hurry to shop wisely.

29. Find out when double-coupon day is at your local supermarket.

30. Join a buying club. Always buy things at the least expensive price possible. Watch out—you may be tempted to buy more than you need or could ever use.

31. Buy bulk only if you will use it. Buying in bulk is cheaper only if you need the items and a lot of them. Best bulk buys: paper products, cereal, frozen food.

32. Buy cereal in poly bags. There's less packaging to pay for.

33. Buy frozen juice. You can stock up when they're on sale without worrying about how long they'll last or how much space they'll take up in the refrigerator.

34. Shred cheese yourself. Packaged shredded cheese costs up to 30 percent more than cheese sold in chunks.

35. Buy white eggs. They're cheaper. Eggs are all the same inside—no matter whether they're brown or white.

36. Buy refills of window cleaner and other cleaning products.

37. Shop with a list. Always have a list and stick to it. You will save anything you might have spent on impulse purchases.

38. Never shop when hungry. Do not shop for food on an empty stomach. Everything looks good, and you'll be tempted to spend more than you'd intended.

39. Use public transportation whenever possible and convenient. Fare for a local bus or train is cheaper than the costs you incur driving your own vehicle (gas, wear and tear, parking).

40. Make a budget and follow it. It is the best way to keep tabs on yourself and plan ahead.

41. Conserve energy. Shut off lights, shut vents in unused rooms, buy energy-efficient appliances. Many electric companies will provide an efficiency inspection free of charge—call your local company to see if they offer such a service.

42. Buy quality. Buy the best that you can afford, and it will outlast brands of less quality.

43. Forget the extended warranty. These are usually offered by specialty department stores and car dealerships. If the extended warranty were not a very profitable venture for sellers, they wouldn't offer it. Almost always the warranty that comes with the product should be enough to protect you.

44. Don't lease anything. Use the money that you are paying out to build equity instead of just throwing it away.

45. Pay back student loans and mortgages biweekly instead of monthly. And ask that the extra monthly payment be applied toward your principal. The interest you can save with this method increases with the term of the loan.

46. Own a home. Owning builds equity and credit. You also have a capital investment with the potential to appreciate.

47. Own the best home that you can afford. Your home is an excellent investment.

48. Pay your mortgage off early. Overpaying your mortgage cuts the interest rate very quickly. On an 8 percent, $100,000 loan, you can save $62,400 by paying an extra $100 per month.

49. Buy and sell homes and cars privately. Any third party receives a part of the money that changes hands.

50. Insulate your home. The cost of adding extra insulation is less than paying the extra energy costs—even over just one winter.

51. Forget cable. It's cheaper to rent a movie every week.

52. Do not run the dishwasher or clothes washer unless full. Waiting until you have a full load will reduce the water consumption and use less electricity.

53. In warm weather, dry clothes on the line. It costs less, and your clothes will last longer.

54. Maintain everything. Learn how to repair everything that you possibly can; it is very expensive to pay someone else to do it.

55. Donate old clothes to charity. If you haven't worn it in two years, you'll probably never wear it again. Find a good local charity or thrift shop that will take your donations, and ask for a tax receipt.

56. Do not put money into savings accounts. Put extra money into bonds or mutual funds. You will earn more on the money you've saved.

57. Buy children's toys at garage sales. You can get some good-quality items at garage sales. (Remember to go to sales in neighborhoods that are wealthier than yours.)

58. Do your own taxes if they're relatively simple. The taxes for the average person are not nearly as difficult as your accountant would like you to believe.

59. Hire a professional tax preparer if your taxes are complex. If your financial situation is complicated, it is likely that you will benefit from having a professional complete them for you. A professional will be aware of the many changes in tax laws and may end up saving you as much as it cost to hire help.

60. Cut your taxes. Invest in tax shelters and tax-free bonds if you are in a high tax bracket and need to shelter some income.

61. Pay yourself first. If the first bill you pay every month is to yourself—for savings bonds, to a mutual fund, or simply to a savings account—the saving will be painless and certain.

62. Use automatic deductions for monthly bills. Have your bills and investments deducted from your bank account automatically. This ensures that you won't spend the money on other things first.

63. Car pool to work or school. It's much cheaper (and more fun) than driving alone.

64. Wash and wax your own car. Keeping your own car clean is simple, inexpensive, and good exercise.

65. Keep your cars longer. Cars are made to last at least ten years, so why not use them that long?

66. Pump your own gas. At most gas stations, you pay for the added convenience of full service.

67. Finance cars over three years instead of five. The interest savings is large, and you will be out from under your car payment sooner.

68. Turn off the lights when you leave a room. When you add up the amount of wasted electricity in an average home, and combine it with the amount that everyone else wastes, the dollar amount becomes huge.

69. Go on vacation off season. Resorts off season are much less expensive and less crowded.

70. Don't play the lottery. The chances of getting struck by lightening are much greater. The lottery is simply a tax on the uneducated.

71. Make your own lunch. Keep track of what it costs to buy your lunch every day, and you will see that you are wasting a lot of money.

72. Put on a sweater. And turn down the heat.

73. Change your furnace filters. Clean filters will extend the life of the furnace and air conditioner. It will also work more efficiently.

74. Buy a humidifier. Added humidity in the air will let you turn down the heat in the winter comfortably.

75. Remember: nothing is free. Most everything is done for a profit. If a deal looks too good to be true, it probably is.

76. Read labels. Follow storage and care instructions labels on your clothes, and they will provide you with years of wear.

77. Hand wash sweaters. They'll last longer, and it's cheaper than having them dry cleaned.

78. Use less detergent. The newest detergents are so effective that you really don't need to fill up to the line. Try using half as much as the manufacturer recommends. You'll notice your clothes get just as clean (and rinse better, too).

79. Take major vacations every other year. Take short three-day vacations closer to home on the off years. You'll also appreciate the major vacations more.

80. Make airline reservations well in advance. Take advantage of promotions and specials. Usually, the sooner you book, the cheaper it is.

81. On short trips, take the bus. Bus tickets are less expensive than airline tickets.

82. Visit your local library. Whenever you get an urge to buy a book or magazine, go to the library. Reading can be a very cheap form of entertainment.

83. Cancel magazines you don't read. If you don't read it, don't pay for it.

84. Buy a magazine subscription. Buy a subscription only for those magazines that you buy off the stand more than three times a year.

85. Rent recreational equipment. Very few people use boats, RVs, motorcycles, and so on enough to justify their cost.

86. Send packages third class. Third-class mail will usually get there just as fast as first class.

87. Use sponges or rags. They are durable and less expensive than paper towels.

88. Turn off the TV. If you want background noise, turn on the radio—it is cheaper to run and to replace.

89. Buy an average car. Insurance and taxes are much less expensive on average cars.

90. Shop around. Take the extra time to find that good deal.

91. Decide if it is worth it for both spouses to work. If you spend more on day care, house maintenance, additional dry cleaning, and so on than one spouse makes, the hassle and extra taxes may not be worth it. Be sure to factor in that spouse's benefits as well—life and medical insurance, retirement plans, bonus or profit-sharing plans, and the like.

92. Fix it under warranty. Get it checked out under warranty. You've paid for the warranty, so use it.

93. Fill your freezer. A full freezer retains cold better than a partially filled or empty one.

94. Cook from scratch. Cook instead of buying expensive stacks of frozen dinners.

95. Use your microwave less. And use your oven more.

96. Replace old doors and windows. Install insulated glass and good-quality doors. It is less expensive in the long run.

97. Clean your own home. Few people are too busy to clean up after themselves.

98. Adopt pets at an animal shelter. Most come paper-trained, spayed or neutered, and with all of their shots.

99. Move yourself whenever practical. Most people can pack and move themselves with a little effort and some help from friends. An obvious benefit is that you will naturally be more careful with your own things. If you are moving a long distance or have a abundance of belongings, it may pay to have someone do the dirty work for you.

Appendix B-1

Interest Rate of 1/2 Percent

N	Future value of a present amount	Present value of a future amount	Future value of an annuity	Annuity providing a future amount	Present value of an annuity	Annuity repaying a present amount	N
1	1.0050	.9950	1.0000	1.0000	.9950	1.0050	1
2	1.0100	.9901	2.0050	.4988	1.9851	.5038	2
3	1.0151	.9851	3.0150	.3317	2.9702	.3367	3
4	1.0202	.9802	4.0301	.2481	3.9505	.2531	4
5	1.0253	.9754	5.0503	.1980	4.9259	.2030	5
6	1.0304	.9705	6.0755	.1646	5.8964	.1696	6
7	1.0355	.9657	7.1059	.1407	6.8621	.1457	7
8	1.0407	.9609	8.1414	.1228	7.8230	.1278	8
9	1.0459	.9561	9.1821	.1089	8.7791	.1139	9
10	1.0511	.9513	10.2280	.0978	9.7304	.1028	10
11	1.0564	.9466	11.2792	.0887	10.6770	.0937	11
12	1.0617	.9419	12.3356	.0811	11.6189	.0861	12
13	1.0670	.9372	13.3972	.0746	12.5562	.0796	13
14	1.0723	.9326	14.4642	.0691	13.4887	.0741	14
15	1.0777	.9279	15.5365	.0644	14.4166	.0694	15
16	1.0831	.9233	16.6142	.0602	15.3399	.0652	16
17	1.0885	.9187	17.6973	.0565	16.2586	.0615	17
18	1.0939	.9141	18.7858	.0532	17.1728	.0582	18
19	1.0994	.9096	19.8797	.0503	18.0824	.0553	19
20	1.1049	.9051	20.9791	.0477	18.9874	.0527	20
21	1.1104	.9006	22.0840	.0453	19.8880	.0503	21
22	1.1160	.8961	23.1944	.0431	20.7841	.0481	22
23	1.1216	.8916	24.3104	.0411	21.6757	.0461	23
24	1.1272	.8872	25.4320	.0393	22.5629	.0443	24
25	1.1328	.8828	26.5591	.0377	23.3456	.0427	25
26	1.1385	.8784	27.6919	.0361	24.3240	.0411	26
27	1.1442	.8740	28.8304	.0347	25.1980	.0397	27
28	1.1499	.8697	29.9745	.0334	26.0677	.0384	28
29	1.1556	.8653	31.1244	.0321	26.9930	.0371	29
30	1.1614	.8610	32.2800	.0310	27.7941	.0360	30
31	1.1672	.8567	33.4414	.0299	28.6508	.0349	31
32	1.1730	.8525	34.6086	.0289	29.5033	.0339	32
33	1.1789	.8482	35.7817	.0279	30.3515	.0329	33
34	1.1848	.8440	36.9606	.0271	31.1955	.0321	34
35	1.1907	.8398	38.1454	.0262	32.0354	.0312	35
36	1.1967	.8356	39.3361	.0254	32.8710	.0304	36

N	Future value of a present amount	Present value of a future amount	Future value of an annuity	Annuity providing a future amount	Present value of an annuity	Annuity repaying a present amount	N
48	1.2705	.7871	54.0978	.0185	42.5803	.0235	48
60	1.3489	.7414	69.7700	.0143	51.7256	.0193	60
72	1.4320	.6983	86.4089	.0116	60.3395	.0166	72
84	1.5204	.6577	104.0739	.0096	68.4530	.0146	84
96	1.6141	.6195	122.8285	.0081	76.0952	.0131	96
108	1.7137	.5835	142.7399	.0070	83.2934	.0120	108
120	1.8194	.5496	163.8793	.0061	90.0735	.0111	120
132	1.9316	.5177	186.3226	.0054	96.4596	.0104	132
144	2.0508	.4876	210.1502	.0048	102.4747	.0098	144
156	2.1772	.4593	235.4473	.0042	108.1404	.0092	156
168	2.3115	.4326	262.3048	.0038	113.4770	.0088	168
180	2.4541	.4075	290.8187	.0034	118.5035	.0084	180
192	2.6055	.3838	321.0913	.0031	123.2380	.0081	192
204	2.7662	.3615	353.2311	.0028	127.6975	.0078	204
216	2.9368	.3405	387.3532	.0026	131.8979	.0076	216
228	3.1179	.3207	423.5799	.0024	135.8542	.0074	228
240	3.3102	.3012	462.0409	.0022	139.5808	.0072	240
252	3.5144	.2845	502.8741	.0020	143.0908	.0070	252
264	3.7311	.2680	546.2259	.0018	146.3969	.0068	264
276	3.9613	.2524	592.2514	.0017	149.5110	.0067	276
288	4.2056	.2378	641.1158	.0016	152.4441	.0066	288
300	4.4650	.2240	692.9940	.0014	155.2069	.0064	300
312	4.7404	.2110	748.0719	.0013	157.8091	.0063	312
324	5.0327	.1987	806.5469	.0012	160.2802	.0062	324
336	5.3431	.1872	868.6285	.0012	162.5688	.0062	336
348	5.6727	.1763	934.5392	.0011	164.7434	.0061	348
360	6.0226	.1660	1004.5150	.0010	166.7916	.0060	360
∞					200.0000	.0050	∞

Appendix B-2

Interest Rate of 3/4 Percent

N	Future value of a present amount	Present value of a future amount	Future value of an annuity	Annuity providing a future amount	Present value of an annuity	Annuity repaying a present amount	N
48	1.4314	.6986	57.5207	.0174	40.1848	.0249	48
60	1.5657	.6387	75.4241	.0133	48.1734	.0208	60
72	1.7126	.5839	95.0070	.0105	55.4768	.0180	72
84	1.8732	.5338	116.4269	.0086	62.1540	.0161	84
96	2.0489	.4881	139.8562	.0072	68.2584	.0147	96
108	2.2411	.4462	165.4832	.0060	73.8394	.0135	108
120	2.4514	.4079	193.5143	.0052	78.9417	.0127	120
132	2.6813	.3730	224.1748	.0045	89.6064	.0120	132
144	2.9328	.3410	257.7116	.0039	87.8711	.0114	144
156	3.2080	.3117	294.3943	.0034	91.7700	.0109	156
168	3.5089	.2850	334.5181	.0030	95.3346	.0105	168
180	3.8380	.2605	378.4058	.0026	98.5934	.0101	180
192	4.1981	.2382	426.4104	.0023	101.5728	.0098	192
204	4.5919	.2178	478.9183	.0021	104.2966	.0096	204
216	5.0226	.1991	536.3517	.0019	106.7869	.0094	216
228	5.4938	.1820	599.1727	.0017	109.0635	.0092	228
240	6.0000	.1664	667.8869	.0015	111.1450	.0090	240
252	6.5729	.1521	743.0469	.0013	113.0469	.0088	252
264	7.1894	.1391	825.2574	.0012	114.7876	.0087	264
276	7.8638	.1272	915.1798	.0011	116.3781	.0086	276
288	8.6015	.1163	1013.5375	.0010	117.8322	.0085	288
300	9.4084	.1063	1121.1219	.0009	119.1616	.0084	300
312	10.2910	.0972	1238.7985	.0008	120.3770	.0083	312
324	11.2564	.0888	1367.5139	.0007	121.4882	.0082	324
336	12.3123	.0812	1508.3037	.0007	122.5040	.0082	336
348	13.4673	.0743	1662.3006	.0006	123.4328	.0081	348
360	14.7306	.0679	1830.7435	.0005	124.2819	.0080	360
∞					133.3333	.0075	∞

N	Future value of a present amount	Present value of a future amount	Future value of an annuity	Annuity providing a future amount	Present value of an annuity	Annuity repaying a present amount	N
1	1.0075	.9926	1.0000	1.0000	.9926	1.0075	1
2	1.0151	.9852	2.0075	.4981	1.9777	.5056	2
3	1.0227	.9778	3.0226	.3308	2.9556	.3383	3
4	1.0303	.9706	4.0452	.2472	3.9261	.2547	4
5	1.0381	.9633	5.0756	.1970	4.8894	.2045	5
6	1.0459	.9562	6.1136	.1636	5.8456	.1711	6
7	1.0537	.9490	7.1595	.1397	6.7946	.1472	7
8	1.0616	.9420	8.2132	.1218	7.7366	.1293	8
9	1.0696	.9350	9.2748	.1078	8.6716	.1153	9
10	1.0776	.9280	10.3443	.0967	9.5996	.1042	10
11	1.0857	.9211	11.4219	.0876	10.5207	.0951	11
12	1.0938	.9142	12.5076	.0800	11.4349	.0875	12
13	1.1020	.9074	13.6014	.0735	12.3423	.0810	13
14	1.1103	.9007	14.7034	.0680	13.2430	.0755	14
15	1.1186	.8940	15.8137	.0632	14.1370	.0707	15
16	1.1270	.8873	16.9323	.0591	15.0243	.0666	16
17	1.1354	.8807	18.0593	.0554	15.9050	.0629	17
18	1.1440	.8742	19.1947	.0521	16.7792	.0596	18
19	1.1525	.8676	20.3387	.0492	17.6468	.0567	19
20	1.1612	.8612	21.4912	.0465	18.5080	.0540	20
21	1.1699	.8548	22.6524	.0441	19.3628	.0516	21
22	1.1787	.8484	23.8223	.0420	20.2112	.0495	22
23	1.1875	.8421	25.0010	.0400	21.0533	.0475	23
24	1.1964	.8358	26.1885	.0382	21.8891	.0457	24
25	1.2054	.8296	27.3849	.0365	22.7188	.0440	25
26	1.2144	.8234	28.5903	.0350	23.5422	.0425	26
27	1.2235	.8173	29.8047	.0336	24.3595	.0411	27
28	1.2327	.8112	31.0282	.0322	25.1707	.0397	28
29	1.2420	.8052	32.2609	.0310	25.9759	.0385	29
30	1.2513	.7992	33.5029	.0298	26.7751	.0373	30
31	1.2607	.7932	34.7542	.0288	27.5683	.0363	31
32	1.2701	.7873	36.0148	.0278	28.3557	.0353	32
33	1.2796	.7815	37.2849	.0268	29.1371	.0343	33
34	1.2892	.7757	38.5646	.0259	29.9128	.0334	34
35	1.2989	.7699	39.8538	.0251	30.6827	.0326	35
36	1.3086	.7641	41.1527	.0243	31.4468	.0318	36

Appendix B-3

Interest Rate of 1.00 Percent

N	Future value of a present amount	Present value of a future amount	Future value of an annuity	Annuity providing a future amount	Present value of an annuity	Annuity repaying a present amount	N
48	1.6122	.6203	31.2226	.0163	37.9740	.0263	48
60	1.8167	.5504	81.6697	.0122	44.9550	.0222	60
72	2.0471	.4885	104.7099	.0096	51.1504	.0196	72
84	2.3067	.4335	130.6723	.0077	56.6485	.0177	84
96	2.5993	.3847	159.9273	.0063	61.5277	.0163	96
108	2.9289	.3414	192.8926	.0052	65.8578	.0152	108
120	3.3004	.3030	230.0387	.0043	69.7005	.0143	120
132	3.7190	.2689	271.8959	.0037	73.1108	.0137	132
144	4.1906	.2386	319.0616	.0031	76.1372	.0131	144
156	4.7221	.2118	372.2091	.0027	78.8229	.0127	156
168	5.3210	.1879	432.0970	.0023	81.2064	.0123	168
180	5.9958	.1668	499.5802	.0020	83.3217	.0120	180
192	6.7562	.1480	575.6220	.0017	85.1988	.0117	192
204	7.6131	.1314	661.3078	.0015	86.8647	.0115	204
216	8.5786	.1166	757.8606	.0013	88.3431	.0113	216
228	9.6666	.1034	866.6588	.0012	89.6551	.0112	228
240	10.8926	.0918	989.2554	.0010	90.8194	.0110	240
252	12.2740	.0815	1127.4002	.0009	91.8527	.0109	252
264	13.8307	.0723	1283.0653	.0008	92.7697	.0108	264
276	15.5847	.0642	1458.4726	.0007	93.5835	.0107	276
288	17.5613	.0569	1656.1259	.0006	94.3056	.0106	288
300	19.7885	.0505	1878.8466	.0005	94.9466	.0105	300
312	22.2981	.0448	2129.8139	.0005	95.5153	.0105	312
324	25.1261	.0398	2414.6101	.0004	96.0201	.0104	324
336	28.3127	.0353	2731.2720	.0004	96.4680	.0104	336
348	31.9035	.0313	3090.3481	.0003	96.8655	.0103	348
360	35.9496	.0278	3494.9641	.0003	97.2183	.0103	360
∞					100.0000	.0100	∞

N	Future value of a present amount	Present value of a future amount	Future value of an annuity	Annuity providing a future amount	Present value of an annuity	Annuity repaying a present amount	N
1	1.0100	.9901	1.0000	1.0000	.9901	1.0100	1
2	1.0201	.9803	2.0100	.4975	1.9704	.5075	2
3	1.0303	.9706	3.0301	.3300	2.9410	.3400	3
4	1.0406	.9610	4.0604	.2463	3.9020	.2563	4
5	1.0510	.9515	5.1010	.1960	4.8534	.2060	5
6	1.0615	.9420	6.1520	.1625	5.7955	.1725	6
7	1.0721	.9327	7.2135	.1386	6.7282	.1486	7
8	1.0829	.9235	8.2857	.1207	7.6517	.1307	8
9	1.0937	.9143	9.3685	.1067	8.5660	.1167	9
10	1.1046	.9053	10.4622	.0956	9.4713	.1056	10
11	1.1157	.8963	11.5668	.0865	10.3676	.0965	11
12	1.1268	.8874	12.6825	.0788	11.2551	.0888	12
13	1.1381	.8787	13.8093	.0724	12.1337	.0824	13
14	1.1495	.8700	14.9474	.0669	13.0037	.0769	14
15	1.1610	.8613	16.0969	.0621	13.8651	.0721	15
16	1.1726	.8525	17.2579	.0579	14.7179	.0679	16
17	1.1843	.8444	18.4304	.0543	15.5623	.0643	17
18	1.1961	.8360	19.6147	.0510	16.3983	.0610	18
19	1.2081	.8277	20.8109	.0481	17.2260	.0581	19
20	1.2202	.8195	22.0190	.0454	18.0456	.0554	20
21	1.2324	.8114	23.2392	.0430	18.8570	.0530	21
22	1.2447	.8034	24.4716	.0409	19.6604	.0509	22
23	1.2572	.7954	25.7163	.0389	20.4558	.0489	23
24	1.2697	.7876	26.9735	.0371	21.2434	.0471	24
25	1.2824	.7798	28.2432	.0354	22.0232	.0454	25
26	1.2953	.7720	29.5256	.0339	22.7952	.0439	26
27	1.3082	.7644	30.8209	.0324	23.5596	.0424	27
28	1.3213	.7568	32.1291	.0311	24.3164	.0411	28
29	1.3345	.7493	33.4504	.0299	25.0658	.0399	29
30	1.3478	.7419	34.7849	.0287	25.8077	.0387	30
31	1.3613	.7346	36.1327	.0277	26.5423	.0377	31
32	1.3749	.7273	37.4941	.0267	27.2696	.0367	32
33	1.3887	.7201	38.8690	.0257	27.9897	.0357	33
34	1.4026	.7130	40.2577	.0248	28.7027	.0348	34
35	1.4166	.7059	41.6603	.0240	29.4086	.0340	35
36	1.4308	.6989	43.0769	.0232	30.1075	.0332	36

Appendix B-4

Interest Rate of 1.50 Percent

N	Future value of a present amount	Present value of a future amount	Future value of an annuity	Annuity providing a future amount	Present value of an annuity	Annuity repaying a present amount	N
1	1.0150	.9852	1.0000	1.0000	.9852	1.0150	1
2	1.0302	.9707	2.0150	.4963	1.9559	.5113	2
3	1.0457	.9563	3.0452	.3284	2.9122	.3434	3
4	1.0614	.9422	4.0909	.2444	3.8544	.2594	4
5	1.0773	.9283	5.1523	.1941	4.7826	.2091	5
6	1.0934	.9145	6.2296	.1605	5.6972	.1755	6
7	1.1098	.9010	7.3230	.1366	6.5982	.1516	7
8	1.1265	.8877	8.4328	.1186	7.4859	.1336	8
9	1.1434	.8746	9.5593	.1046	8.3605	.1196	9
10	1.1605	.8617	10.7027	.0934	9.2222	.1084	10
11	1.1779	.8489	11.8633	.0843	10.0711	.0993	11
12	1.1956	.8364	13.0412	.0767	10.9075	.0917	12
13	1.2136	.8240	14.2368	.0702	11.7315	.0852	13
14	1.2318	.8118	15.4504	.0647	12.5434	.0797	14
15	1.2502	.7999	16.6821	.0599	13.3432	.0749	15
16	1.2690	.7880	17.9324	.0558	14.1313	.0708	16
17	1.2880	.7764	19.2014	.0521	14.9076	.0671	17
18	1.3073	.7649	20.4894	.0488	15.6726	.0638	18
19	1.3270	.7536	21.7967	.0459	16.4262	.0609	19
20	1.3469	.7425	23.1237	.0432	17.1686	.0582	20
21	1.3671	.7315	24.4705	.0409	17.9001	.0559	21
22	1.3876	.7207	25.8376	.0387	18.6208	.0537	22
23	1.4084	.7100	27.2251	.0367	19.3309	.0517	23
24	1.4295	.6995	28.6335	.0349	20.0304	.0499	24
25	1.4509	.6892	30.0630	.0333	20.7196	.0483	25
26	1.4727	.6790	31.5140	.0317	21.3986	.0467	26
27	1.4948	.6690	32.9867	.0303	22.0676	.0453	27
28	1.5172	.6591	34.4815	.0290	22.7267	.0440	28
29	1.5400	.6494	35.9987	.0278	23.3761	.0428	29
30	1.5631	.6398	37.5387	.0266	24.0158	.0416	30
31	1.5865	.6303	39.1018	.0256	24.6461	.0406	31
32	1.6103	.6210	40.6883	.0246	25.2671	.0396	32
33	1.6345	.6118	42.2986	.0236	25.8790	.0386	33
34	1.6590	.6028	43.9331	.0228	26.4817	.0378	34
35	1.6839	.5939	45.5921	.0219	27.0756	.0369	35
36	1.7091	.5851	47.2760	.0212	27.6607	.0362	36

N	Future value of a present amount	Present value of a future amount	Future value of an annuity	Annuity providing a future amount	Present value of an annuity	Annuity repaying a present amount	N
40	1.8140	.5513	54.2679	.0184	29.9158	.0334	40
44	1.9253	.5194	61.6889	.0162	32.0406	.0312	44
48	2.0435	.4894	69.5652	.0144	34.0426	.0294	48
52	2.1689	.4611	77.9249	.0128	35.9287	.0278	52
56	2.3020	.4344	86.7975	.0115	37.7059	.0265	56
60	2.4432	.4039	96.2147	.0104	39.3803	.0254	60
64	2.5931	.3856	106.2096	.0094	40.9579	.0244	64
68	2.7523	.3633	116.8179	.0086	42.4442	.0236	68
72	2.9212	.3423	128.0772	.0078	43.8447	.0228	72
76	3.1004	.3225	140.0274	.0071	45.1641	.0221	76
80	3.2907	.3039	152.7109	.0065	46.4073	.0215	80
84	3.4926	.2863	166.1726	.0060	47.5786	.0210	84
88	3.7069	.2698	180.4605	.0055	48.6822	.0205	88
92	3.9344	.2542	195.6251	.0051	49.7220	.0201	92
96	4.1758	.2395	211.7202	.0047	50.7017	.0197	96
100	4.4320	.2256	228.8030	.0044	51.6247	.0194	100
104	4.7040	.2126	246.9341	.0040	52.4944	.0190	104
108	4.9927	.2003	266.1778	.0038	53.3137	.0188	108
112	5.2990	.1887	286.6023	.0035	54.0858	.0185	112
116	5.6242	.1778	308.2801	.0032	54.8131	.0182	116
120	5.9693	.1675	331.2882	.0030	55.4985	.0180	120
∞					66.6667	.0150	∞

Appendix B-5

Interest Rate of 1.75 Percent

Future value of a present amount	Present value of a future amount	Future value of an annuity	Annuity providing a future amount	Present value of an annuity	Annuity repaying a present amount	N
1.0175	.9828	1.0000	1.0000	.9828	1.0175	1
1.0353	.9659	2.0175	.4957	1.9487	.5132	2
1.0534	.9493	3.0528	.3276	2.8980	.3451	3
1.0719	.9330	4.1062	.2435	3.8309	.2610	4
1.0906	.9169	5.1781	.1931	4.7479	.2106	5
1.1097	.9011	6.2687	.1595	5.6490	.1770	6
1.1291	.8856	7.3784	.1355	6.5346	.1530	7
1.1489	.8704	8.5075	.1175	7.4051	.1350	8
1.1690	.8554	9.6564	.1036	8.2605	.1211	9
1.1894	.8407	10.8254	.0924	9.1012	.1099	10
1.2103	.8263	12.0418	.0832	9.9275	.1007	11
1.2314	.8121	13.2251	.0756	10.7395	.0931	12
1.2530	.7981	14.4565	.0692	11.5376	.0867	13
1.2749	.7844	15.7095	.0637	12.3220	.0812	14
1.2972	.7709	16.9844	.0589	13.0929	.0764	15
1.3199	.7576	18.2817	.0547	13.8505	.0722	16
1.3430	.7446	19.6016	.0510	14.5951	.0685	17
1.3665	.7318	20.9446	.0477	15.3269	.0652	18
1.3904	.7192	22.3112	.0448	16.0461	.0623	19
1.4148	.7068	23.7016	.0422	16.7529	.0597	20
1.4395	.6947	25.1164	.0398	17.4475	.0573	21
1.4647	.6827	26.5559	.0377	18.1303	.0552	22
1.4904	.6710	28.0207	.0357	18.8012	.0532	23
1.5164	.6594	29.5110	.0339	19.4607	.0514	24
1.5430	.6481	31.0275	.0322	20.1088	.0497	25
1.5700	.6369	32.5704	.0307	20.7457	.0482	26

N	Future value of a present amount	Present value of a future amount	Future value of an annuity	Annuity providing a future amount	Present value of an annuity	Annuity repaying a present amount	N
48	2.2996	.4349	74.2628	.0135	32.2938	.0310	48
60	2.8318	.3531	104.6752	.0096	36.9640	.0271	60
72	3.4872	.2868	142.1263	.0070	40.7564	.0245	72
84	4.2943	.2329	188.2450	.0053	43.8361	.0228	84
96	5.2882	.1891	245.0374	.0041	46.3370	.0216	96
108	6.5120	.1536	314.9738	.0032	48.3679	.0207	108
120	8.0192	.1247	401.0962	.0025	50.0170	.0200	120
132	9.8751	.1013	507.1507	.0020	51.3563	.0195	132
144	12.1606	.0822	637.7504	.0016	52.2439	.0191	144
156	14.9751	.0668	798.5761	.0013	53.3270	.0188	156
168	18.4409	.0542	996.6231	.0010	54.0442	.0185	168
180	22.7089	.0440	1240.5060	.0008	54.6265	.0183	180
192	27.9646	.0358	1540.8329	.0006	55.0995	.0181	192
204	34.4367	.0290	1910.6673	.0005	55.4835	.0180	204
216	42.4067	.0236	2366.0960	.0004	55.7954	.0179	216
228	52.2213	.0191	2926.9287	.0003	56.0486	.0178	228
240	64.3073	.0156	3617.5602	.0003	56.2543	.0178	240
252	79.1905	.0126	4468.0309	.0002	56.4213	.0177	252
264	97.5183	.0103	5515.3340	.0002	56.5569	.0177	264
276	120.0879	.0083	6805.0243	.0001	56.6670	.0176	276
288	147.8810	.0068	8393.1995	.0001	56.7564	.0176	288
300	182.1065	.0055	10348.9410	.0001	56.8291	.0176	300
312	224.2531	.0045	12757.3179	.0001	56.8880	.0176	312
324	276.1540	.0036	15723.0879	.0001	56.9359	.0176	324
336	340.0669	.0029	19375.2537	.0001	56.9748	.0176	336
348	418.7718	.0024	23872.6743	.0000	57.0064	.0175	348
360	515.6921	.0019	29410.9747	.0000	57.0320	.0175	360
∞					57.1429	.0175	∞

Appendix B-6

Interest Rate of 6.00 Percent

N	Future value of a present amount	Present value of a future amount	Future value of an annuity	Annuity providing a future amount	Present value of an annuity	Annuity repaying a present amount	N
1	1.0600	.9434	1.0000	1.0000	.9434	1.0600	1
2	1.1236	.8900	2.0600	.4854	1.8334	.5454	2
3	1.1910	.8396	3.1836	.3141	2.6730	.3741	3
4	1.2625	.7921	4.3746	.2286	3.4651	.2886	4
5	1.3382	.7473	5.6371	.1774	4.2124	.2374	5
6	1.4185	.7050	6.9753	.1434	4.9173	.2034	6
7	1.5036	.6651	8.3938	.1191	5.5824	.1791	7
8	1.5938	.6274	9.8975	.1010	6.2098	.1610	8
9	1.6895	.5919	11.4913	.0870	6.8017	.1470	9
10	1.7908	.5584	13.1808	.0759	7.3601	.1359	10
11	1.8983	.5268	14.9716	.0668	7.8869	.1268	11
12	2.0122	.4970	16.8699	.0593	8.3838	.1193	12
13	2.1329	.4688	18.8821	.0530	8.8527	.1130	13
14	2.2609	.4423	21.0151	.0476	9.2950	.1076	14
15	2.3966	.4173	23.2760	.0430	9.7122	.1030	15
16	2.5404	.3936	25.6725	.0390	10.1059	.0990	16
17	2.6928	.3714	28.2129	.0354	10.4773	.0954	17
18	2.8543	.3503	30.9057	.0324	10.8276	.0924	18
19	3.0256	.3305	33.7600	.0296	11.1581	.0896	19
20	3.2071	.3118	36.7856	.0272	11.4699	.0872	20
21	3.3996	.2942	39.9927	.0250	11.7641	.0850	21
22	3.6035	.2775	43.3923	.0230	12.0416	.0830	22
23	3.8197	.2618	46.9958	.0213	12.3034	.0813	23
24	4.0489	.2470	50.8156	.0197	12.5504	.0797	24
25	4.2919	.2330	54.8645	.0182	12.7834	.0782	25
26	4.5494	.2198	59.1564	.0169	13.0032	.0769	26
27	4.8223	.2074	63.7058	.0157	13.2105	.0757	27
28	5.1117	.1956	68.5281	.0146	13.4062	.0748	28
29	5.4184	.1846	73.6398	.0136	13.5907	.0736	29
30	5.7435	.1741	79.0582	.0126	13.7648	.0726	30
31	6.0881	.1643	84.8017	.0118	13.9291	.0718	31
32	6.4534	.1550	90.8898	.0110	14.0840	.0710	32
33	6.8406	.1462	97.3432	.0103	14.2302	.0703	33
34	7.2510	.1379	104.1838	.0096	14.3681	.0696	34
35	7.6861	.1301	111.4348	.0090	14.4982	.0690	35
36	8.1473	.1227	119.1209	.0084	14.6210	.0684	36

N	Future value of a present amount	Present value of a future amount	Future value of an annuity	Annuity providing a future amount	Present value of an annuity	Annuity repaying a present amount	N
40	10.2857	.0972	154.7620	.0065	15.0463	.0665	40
44	12.9855	.0770	199.7580	.0050	15.3832	.0650	44
48	16.3939	.0610	256.5645	.0039	15.6500	.0639	48
52	20.6969	.0483	328.2814	.0030	15.8614	.0630	52
56	26.1293	.0383	418.8223	.0024	16.0288	.0624	56
60	32.9877	.0303	533.1282	.0019	16.1614	.0619	60
64	41.6462	.0240	677.4367	.0015	16.2665	.0615	64
68	52.5774	.0190	859.6228	.0012	16.3497	.0612	68
72	66.3777	.0151	1089.6286	.0009	16.4156	.0609	72
76	83.8003	.0119	1380.0056	.0007	16.4678	.0607	76
80	105.7960	.0095	1746.5999	.0006	16.5091	.0606	80
84	133.5650	.0075	2209.4167	.0005	16.5419	.0605	84
88	168.6227	.0059	2793.7123	.0004	16.5678	.0604	88
92	212.2823	.0047	3531.3721	.0003	16.5884	.0603	92
96	268.7590	.0037	4462.3505	.0002	16.6047	.0602	96
100	339.3021	.0029	5638.3681	.0002	16.6175	.0602	100
104	428.3611	.0023	7122.6844	.0001	16.6278	.0601	104
108	540.7960	.0018	8996.5995	.0001	16.6358	.0601	108
112	682.7425	.0015	11362.3743	.0001	16.6423	.0601	112
116	861.9466	.0012	14349.1103	.0001	16.6473	.0601	116
120	1088.1877	.0009	18119.7958	.0001	16.6514	.0601	120
∞					16.6667	.0600	∞

Appendix B-7

Interest Rate of 8 Percent and Interest Rate of 12 Percent

Interest Rate of 12 Percent

N	Future value of a present amount	Present value of a future amount	Future value of an annuity	Annuity providing a future amount	Present value of an annuity	Annuity repaying a present amount	N
1	1.1200	.8929	1.0000	1.0000	.8929	1.1200	1
2	1.2544	.7972	2.1200	.4717	1.6901	.5917	2
3	1.4049	.7118	3.3744	.2963	2.4018	.4163	3
4	1.5735	.6355	4.7793	.2092	3.0373	.3292	4
5	1.7623	.5674	6.3528	.1574	3.6048	.2774	5
6	1.9738	.5066	8.1152	.1232	4.1114	.2432	6
7	2.2107	.4523	10.0890	.0991	4.5638	.2191	7
8	2.4760	.4039	12.2997	.0813	4.9676	.2013	8
9	2.7731	.3606	14.7757	.0677	5.3282	.1877	9
10	3.1058	.3220	17.6487	.0570	5.6502	.1770	10
11	3.4785	.2875	20.6546	.0484	5.9377	.1684	11
12	3.8960	.2567	24.1331	.0414	6.1944	.1614	12
13	4.3635	.2292	28.0291	.0357	6.4235	.1557	13
14	4.8871	.2046	32.3926	.0309	6.6282	.1509	14
15	5.4736	.1827	37.2792	.0268	6.8109	.1468	15
16	6.1304	.1631	42.7533	.0234	6.9740	.1434	16
17	6.8660	.1456	48.8837	.0205	7.1196	.1405	17
18	7.6900	.1300	55.7497	.0179	7.2497	.1379	18
19	8.6128	.1161	63.4397	.0158	7.3658	.1358	19
20	9.6463	.1037	72.0524	.0139	7.4694	.1339	20
21	10.8038	.0926	81.6987	.0122	7.5620	.1322	21
22	12.1003	.0826	92.5026	.0108	7.6446	.1308	22
23	13.5523	.0738	104.6029	.0096	7.7184	.1296	23
24	15.1786	.0659	118.1552	.0085	7.7843	.1285	24
25	17.001	.0588	133.3339	.0075	7.8431	.1275	25
26	19.0401	.0525	150.3339	.0067	7.8957	.1267	26
27	21.3249	.0469	169.6989	.0059	7.9426	.1259	27
28	23.8839	.0419	190.6989	.0052	7.9844	.1252	28
29	26.7499	.0374	214.5828	.0047	8.0218	.1247	29
30	29.9599	.0334	241.2237	.0041	8.0552	.1241	30
35	52.7996	.0189	431.6635	.0023	8.1755	.1223	35
40	93.0510	.0107	767.0914	.0013	8.2438	.1213	40
45	163.9876	.0061	1358.2300	.0007	8.2825	.1207	45
50	289.0022	.0035	2400.0182	.0004	8.3045	.1204	50
55	509.3206	.0020	4236.0050	.0002	8.3170	.1202	55
60	897.5969	.0011	7471.6411	.0001	8.3240	.1201	60
∞					8.3333	.1200	∞

Interest Rate of 8 Percent

N	Future value of a present amount	Present value of a future amount	Future value of an annuity	Annuity providing a future amount	Present value of an annuity	Annuity repaying a present amount	N
1	1.0800	.9259	1.0000	1.0000	.9259	1.0800	1
2	1.1664	.8573	2.0800	.4808	1.7833	.5608	2
3	1.2597	.7938	3.2464	.3080	2.5771	.3880	3
4	1.3605	.7350	4.5061	.2219	3.3121	.3019	4
5	1.4693	.6806	5.8666	.1705	3.9927	.2505	5
6	1.5869	.6302	7.3359	.1363	4.6229	.2163	6
7	1.7138	.5835	8.9228	.1121	5.2064	.1921	7
8	1.8509	.5403	10.6366	.0940	5.7466	.1740	8
9	1.9990	.5002	12.4876	.0801	6.2469	.1601	9
10	2.1589	.4632	14.4866	.0690	6.7101	.1490	10
11	2.3316	.4289	16.6455	.0601	7.1390	.1401	11
12	2.5182	.3971	18.9771	.0527	7.5361	.1327	12
13	2.7196	.3677	21.4953	.0465	7.9038	.1265	13
14	2.9372	.3405	24.2149	.0413	8.2442	.1213	14
15	3.1722	.3152	27.1521	.0368	8.5595	.1168	15
16	3.4259	.2919	30.3243	.0330	8.8514	.1130	16
17	3.7000	.2703	33.7502	.0296	9.1216	.1096	17
18	3.9960	.2502	37.4502	.0267	9.3719	.1067	18
19	4.3157	.2317	41.4463	.0241	9.6036	.1041	19
20	4.6610	.2145	45.7620	.0219	9.8181	.1019	20
21	5.0338	.1987	50.4229	.0198	10.0168	.0998	21
22	5.4365	.1839	55.4568	.0180	10.2007	.0980	22
23	5.8715	.1703	60.8922	.0164	10.3711	.0964	23
24	6.3412	.1577	66.7648	.0150	10.5288	.0950	24
25	6.8485	.1460	73.1059	.0137	10.6748	.0937	25
26	7.3964	.1352	79.9544	.0125	10.8100	.0925	26
27	7.9881	.1252	87.3508	.0114	10.9352	.0914	27
28	8.6271	.1159	95.3388	.0105	11.0511	.0905	28
29	9.3173	.1073	103.9659	.0096	11.1584	.0896	29
30	10.0627	.0994	113.2832	.0088	11.2578	.0888	30
35	14.7853	.0676	172.3168	.0058	11.6546	.0858	35
40	21.7245	.0460	259.0565	.0039	11.9246	.0839	40
45	31.9204	.0313	386.5056	.0026	12.1084	.0826	45
50	46.9016	.0213	573.7702	.0017	12.2335	.0817	50
55	68.9139	.0145	848.9232	.0012	12.3186	.0812	55
60	101.2571	.0099	1253.2133	.0008	12.3766	.0808	60
∞					12.500	.0800	∞

Appendix C

Homeowners 3 (Special Form) Policy

HOMEOWNERS POLICY

Declarations applicable to all policy forms

Policy Number

Policy Period: 12:01 a.m. Standard time   From: To:
              at the residence premises

Named Insured and mailing address

The residence premises covered by this policy is located at the above address unless otherwise stated:

Coverage is provided where a premium or limit of liability is shown for the coverage.

	Limit of Liability	Premium
SECTION I COVERAGES		
A. Dwelling		
B. Other structures		
C. Personal property		
D. Loss of use		
SECTION II COVERAGES		
E. Personal liability: each occurrence		
F. Medical payments to others: each person		

Total premium for endorsements listed below

Policy Total

Forms and endorsements made part of this policy:

Number	Edition Date	Title	Premium

[Special State Provisions: South Carolina: Valuation Clause (Cov.A) $
                        Minnesota Insurable Value (Cov.A) $
                        New York: Coinsurance Clause Applies ___Yes ___No]

DEDUCTIBLE - Section I: $
In case of a loss under Section I, we cover only that part of the loss over the deductible stated.

Section II: Other insured locations:

[Mortgagee/Lienholder (Name and address)]

Countersignature of agent/date   Signature/title - company officer

Ed.4/84

HOMEOWNERS 3
SPECIAL FORM

AGREEMENT

We will provide the insurance described in this policy in return for the premium and compliance with all applicable provisions of this policy.

DEFINITIONS

In this policy, "you" and "your" refer to the "named insured" shown in the Declarations and the spouse if a resident of the same household. "We," "us" and "our" refer to the Company providing this insurance. In addition, certain words and phrases are defined as follows:

1. "Bodily injury" means bodily harm, sickness or disease, including required care, loss of services and death that results.

2. "Business" includes trade, profession or occupation.

3. "Insured" means you and residents of your household who are:

   a. Your relatives; or

   b. Other persons under the age of 21 and in the care of any person named above.

   Under Section II, "insured" also means:

   c. With respect to animals or watercraft to which this policy applies, any person or organization legally responsible for these animals or watercraft which are owned by you or any person included in **3.a.** or **3.b.** above. A person or organization using or having custody of these animals or watercraft in the course of any "business" or without consent of the owner is not an "insured";

   d. With respect to any vehicle to which this policy applies:

   (1) Persons while engaged in your employ or that of any person included in **3.a.** or **3.b.** above; or

   (2) Other persons using the vehicle on an "insured location" with your consent.

4. "Insured location" means:

   a. The "residence premises";

   b. The part of other premises, other structures and grounds used by you as a residence and:

   (1) Which is shown in the Declarations; or

   (2) Which is acquired by you during the policy period for your use as a residence;

   c. Any premises used by you in connection with a premises in **4.a.** and **4.b.** above;

   d. Any part of a premises:

   (1) Not owned by an "insured"; and

   (2) Where an "insured" is temporarily residing;

   e. Vacant land, other than farm land, owned by or rented to an "insured";

   f. Land owned by or rented to an "insured" on which a one or two family dwelling is being built as a residence for an "insured";

   g. Individual or family cemetery plots or burial vaults of an "insured"; or

   h. Any part of a premises occasionally rented to an "insured" for other than "business" use.

5. "Occurrence" means an accident, including continuous or repeated exposure to substantially the same general harmful conditions, which results, during the policy period, in:

   a. "Bodily injury"; or

   b. "Property damage."

6. "Property damage" means physical injury to, destruction of, or loss of use of tangible property.

7. "Residence employee" means:

   a. An employee of an "insured" whose duties are related to the maintenance or use of the "residence premises," including household or domestic services; or

   b. One who performs similar duties elsewhere not related to the "business" of an "insured."

8. "Residence premises" means:

   a. The one family dwelling, other structures, and grounds; or

   b. That part of any other building;

   where you reside and which is shown as the "residence premises" in the Declarations.

   "Residence premises" also means a two family dwelling where you reside in at least one of the family units and which is shown as the "residence premises" in the Declarations.

HO 00 03 04 91   Copyright, Insurance Services Office, Inc., 1990   **Page 1 of 18**

HO 00 03 04 91

SECTION I – PROPERTY COVERAGES

COVERAGE A - Dwelling

We cover:

1. The dwelling on the "residence premises" shown in the Declarations, including structures attached to the dwelling; and

2. Materials and supplies located on or next to the "residence premises" used to construct, alter or repair the dwelling or other structures on the "residence premises."

This coverage does not apply to land, including land on which the dwelling is located.

COVERAGE B - Other Structures

We cover other structures on the "residence premises" set apart from the dwelling by clear space. This includes structures connected to the dwelling by only a fence, utility line, or similar connection.

This coverage does not apply to land, including land on which the other structures are located.

We do not cover other structures:

1. Used in whole or in part for "business"; or

2. Rented or held for rental to any person not a tenant of the dwelling, unless used solely as a private garage.

The limit of liability for this coverage will not be more than 10% of the limit of liability that applies to Coverage A. Use of this coverage does not reduce the Coverage A limit of liability.

COVERAGE C - Personal Property

We cover personal property owned or used by an "insured" while it is anywhere in the world. At your request, we will cover personal property owned by:

1. Others while the property is on the part of the "residence premises" occupied by an "insured";

2. A guest or a "residence employee," while the property is in any residence occupied by an "insured."

Our limit of liability for personal property usually located at an "insured's" residence, other than the "residence premises," is 10% of the limit of liability for Coverage C, or $1000, whichever is greater. Personal property in a newly acquired principal residence is not subject to this limitation for the 30 days from the time you begin to move the property there.

Special Limits of Liability. These limits do not increase the Coverage C limit of liability. The special limit for each numbered category below is the total limit for each loss for all property in that category.

1. $200 on money, bank notes, bullion, gold other than goldware, silver other than silverware, platinum, coins and medals.

2. $1000 on securities, accounts, deeds, evidences of debt, letters of credit, notes other than bank notes, manuscripts, personal records, passports, tickets and stamps. This dollar limit applies to these categories regardless of the medium (such as paper or computer software) on which the material exists.

   This limit includes the cost to research, replace or restore the information from the lost or damaged material.

3. $1000 on watercraft, including their trailers, furnishings, equipment and outboard engines or motors.

4. $1000 on trailers not used with watercraft.

5. $1000 for loss by theft of jewelry, watches, furs, precious and semi-precious stones.

6. $2000 for loss by theft of firearms.

7. $2500 for loss by theft of silverware, silver-plated ware, goldware, gold-plated ware and pewterware. This includes flatware, hollowware, tea sets, trays and trophies made of or including silver, gold or pewter.

8. $2500 on property, on the "residence premises," used at any time or in any manner for any "business" purpose.

9. $250 on property, away from the "residence premises," used at any time or in any manner for any "business" purpose. However, this limit does not apply to loss to adaptable electronic apparatus as described in Special Limits 10. and 11. below.

10. $1000 for loss to electronic apparatus, while in or upon a motor vehicle or other motorized land conveyance, if the electronic apparatus is equipped to be operated by power from the electrical system of the vehicle or conveyance while retaining its capability of being operated by other sources of power. Electronic apparatus includes:

    a. Accessories or antennas; or

    b. Tapes, wires, records, discs or other media;

    for use with any electronic apparatus.

11. $1000 for loss to electronic apparatus, while not in or upon a motor vehicle or other motorized land conveyance, if the electronic apparatus:

    a. Is equipped to be operated by power from the electrical system of the vehicle or conveyance while retaining its capability of being operated by other sources of power;

    b. Is away from the "residence premises"; and

    c. Is used at any time or in any manner for any "business" purpose.

    Electronic apparatus includes:

    a. Accessories and antennas; or

    b. Tapes, wires, records, discs or other media;

    for use with any electronic apparatus.

Property Not Covered. We do not cover:

1. Articles separately described and specifically insured in this or other insurance;

2. Animals, birds or fish;

3. Motor vehicles or all other motorized land conveyances. This includes:

    a. Their equipment and accessories; or

    b. Electronic apparatus that is designed to be operated solely by use of the power from the electrical system of motor vehicles or all other motorized land conveyances. Electronic apparatus includes:

       (1) Accessories or antennas; or

       (2) Tapes, wires, records, discs or other media;

       for use with any electronic apparatus.

       The exclusion of property described in **3.a.** and **3.b.** above applies only while the property is in or upon the vehicle or conveyance.

    We do cover vehicles or conveyances not subject to motor vehicle registration which are:

    a. Used to service an "insured's" residence; or

    b. Designed for assisting the handicapped;

4. Aircraft and parts. Aircraft means any contrivance used or designed for flight, except model or hobby aircraft not used or designed to carry people or cargo;

5. Property of roomers, boarders and other tenants, except property of roomers and boarders related to an "insured";

6. Property in an apartment regularly rented or held for rental to others by an "insured," except as provided in Additional Coverages **10.**;

7. Property rented or held for rental to others off the "residence premises";

8. "Business" data, including such data stored in:

    a. Books of account, drawings or other paper records; or

    b. Electronic data processing tapes, wires, records, discs or other software media;

    However, we do cover the cost of blank recording or storage media, and of pre-recorded computer programs available on the retail market; or

9. Credit cards or fund transfer cards except as provided in Additional Coverages **6.**

COVERAGE D - Loss Of Use

The limit of liability for Coverage D is the total limit for all the coverages that follow.

1. If a loss covered under this Section makes that part of the "residence premises" where you reside not fit to live in, we cover, at your choice, either of the following. However, if the "residence premises" is not your principal place of residence, we will not provide the option under paragraph **b.** below.

    a. **Additional Living Expense,** meaning any necessary increase in living expenses incurred by you so that your household can maintain its normal standard of living; or

    b. **Fair Rental Value,** meaning the fair rental value of that part of the "residence premises" where you reside less any expenses that do not continue while the premises is not fit to live in.

    Payment under **a.** or **b.** will be for the shortest time required to repair or replace the damage or, if you permanently relocate, the shortest time required for your household to settle elsewhere.

2. If a loss covered under this Section makes that part of the "residence premises" rented to others or held for rental by you not fit to live in, we cover the:

    Fair Rental Value, meaning the fair rental value of that part of the "residence premises" rented to others or held for rental by you less any expenses that do not continue while the premises is not fit to live in.

    Payment will be for the shortest time required to repair or replace that part of the premises rented or held for rental.

3. If a civil authority prohibits you from use of the "residence premises" as a result of direct damage to neighboring premises by a Peril Insured Against in this policy, we cover the Additional Living Expense and Fair Rental Value loss as provided under **1.** and **2.** above for no more than two weeks.

HO 00 03 04 91

The periods of time under **1.**, **2.** and **3.** above are not limited by expiration of this policy.

We do not cover loss or expense due to cancellation of a lease or agreement.

ADDITIONAL COVERAGES

1. Debris Removal. We will pay your reasonable expense for the removal of:

a. Debris of covered property if a Peril Insured Against that applies to the damaged property causes the loss; or

b. Ash, dust or particles from a volcanic eruption that has caused direct loss to a building or property contained in a building.

This expense is included in the limit of liability that applies to the damaged property. If the amount to be paid for the actual damage to the property plus the debris removal expense is more than the limit of liability for the damaged property, an additional 5% of that limit of liability is available for debris removal expense.

We will also pay your reasonable expense, up to $500, for the removal from the "residence premises" of:

a. Your tree(s) felled by the peril of Windstorm or Hail;

b. Your tree(s) felled by the peril of Weight of Ice, Snow or Sleet; or

c. A neighbor's tree(s) felled by a Peril Insured Against under Coverage C;

provided the tree(s) damages a covered structure. The $500 limit is the most we will pay in any one loss regardless of the number of fallen trees.

2. Reasonable Repairs. In the event that covered property is damaged by an applicable Peril Insured Against, we will pay the reasonable cost incurred by you for necessary measures taken solely to protect against further damage. If the measures taken involve repair to other damaged property, we will pay for those measures only if that property is covered under this policy and the damage to that property is caused by an applicable Peril Insured Against.

This coverage:

a. Does not increase the limit of liability that applies to the covered property;

b. Does not relieve you of your duties, in case of a loss to covered property, as set forth in SECTION I - CONDITION **2.d.**

3. Trees, Shrubs and Other Plants. We cover trees, shrubs, plants or lawns, on the "residence premises," for loss caused by the following Perils Insured Against: Fire or lightning, Explosion, Riot or civil commotion, Aircraft, Vehicles not owned or operated by a resident of the "residence premises," Vandalism or malicious mischief or Theft.

We will pay up to 5% of the limit of liability that applies to the dwelling for all trees, shrubs, plants or lawns. No more than $500 of this limit will be available for any one tree, shrub or plant. We do not cover property grown for "business" purposes.

This coverage is additional insurance.

4. Fire Department Service Charge. We will pay up to $500 for your liability assumed by contract or agreement for fire department charges incurred when the fire department is called to save or protect covered property from a Peril Insured Against. We do not cover fire department service charges if the property is located within the limits of the city, municipality or protection district furnishing the fire department response.

This coverage is additional insurance. No deductible applies to this coverage.

5. Property Removed. We insure covered property against direct loss from any cause while being removed from a premises endangered by a Peril Insured Against and for no more than 30 days while removed. This coverage does not change the limit of liability that applies to the property being removed.

6. Credit Card, Fund Transfer Card, Forgery and Counterfeit Money.

We will pay up to $500 for:

a. The legal obligation of an "insured" to pay because of the theft or unauthorized use of credit cards issued to or registered in an "insured's" name;

b. Loss resulting from theft or unauthorized use of a fund transfer card used for deposit, withdrawal or transfer of funds, issued to or registered in an "insured's" name;

c. Loss to an "insured" caused by forgery or alteration of any check or negotiable instrument; and

d. Loss to an "insured" through acceptance in good faith of counterfeit United States or Canadian paper currency.

HO 00 03 04 91

We do not cover use of a credit card or fund transfer card:

a. By a resident of your household;

b. By a person who has been entrusted with either type of card; or

c. If an "insured" has not complied with all terms and conditions under which the cards are issued.

All loss resulting from a series of acts committed by any one person or in which any one person is concerned or implicated is considered to be one loss.

We do not cover loss arising out of "business" use or dishonesty of an "insured."

This coverage is additional insurance. No deductible applies to this coverage.

Defense:

a. We may investigate and settle any claim or suit that we decide is appropriate. Our duty to defend a claim or suit ends when the amount we pay for the loss equals our limit of liability.

b. If a suit is brought against an "insured" for liability under the Credit Card or Fund Transfer Card coverage, we will provide a defense at our expense by counsel of our choice.

c. We have the option to defend at our expense an "insured" or an "insured's" bank against any suit for the enforcement of payment under the Forgery coverage.

7. Loss Assessment. We will pay up to $1000 for your share of loss assessment charged during the policy period against you by a corporation or association of property owners, when the assessment is made as a result of direct loss to the property, owned by all members collectively, caused by a Peril Insured Against under COVERAGE A - DWELLING, other than earthquake or land shock waves or tremors before, during or after a volcanic eruption.

This coverage applies only to loss assessments charged against you as owner or tenant of the "residence premises."

We do not cover loss assessments charged against you or a corporation or association of property owners by any governmental body.

The limit of $1000 is the most we will pay with respect to any one loss, regardless of the number of assessments.

Condition **1.** Policy Period, under SECTIONS I AND II CONDITIONS, does not apply to this coverage.

8. Collapse. We insure for direct physical loss to covered property involving collapse of a building or any part of a building caused only by one or more of the following:

a. Perils Insured Against in COVERAGE C - PERSONAL PROPERTY. These perils apply to covered buildings and personal property for loss insured by this additional coverage;

b. Hidden decay;

c. Hidden insect or vermin damage;

d. Weight of contents, equipment, animals or people;

e. Weight of rain which collects on a roof; or

f. Use of defective material or methods in construction, remodeling or renovation if the collapse occurs during the course of the construction, remodeling or renovation.

Loss to an awning, fence, patio, pavement, swimming pool, underground pipe, flue, drain, cesspool, septic tank, foundation, retaining wall, bulkhead, pier, wharf or dock is not included under items **b.**, **c.**, **d.**, **e.**, and **f.** unless the loss is a direct result of the collapse of a building.

Collapse does not include settling, cracking, shrinking, bulging or expansion.

This coverage does not increase the limit of liability applying to the damaged covered property.

9. Glass or Safety Glazing Material.

We cover:

a. The breakage of glass or safety glazing material which is part of a covered building, storm door or storm window; and

b. Damage to covered property by glass or safety glazing material which is part of a building, storm door or storm window.

This coverage does not include loss on the "residence premises" if the dwelling has been vacant for more than 30 consecutive days immediately before the loss. A dwelling being constructed is not considered vacant.

Loss for damage to glass will be settled on the basis of replacement with safety glazing materials when required by ordinance or law.

This coverage does not increase the limit of liability that applies to the damaged property.

HO 00 03 04 91

10. Landlord's Furnishings. We will pay up to $2500 for your appliances, carpeting and other household furnishings, in an apartment on the "residence premises" regularly rented or held for rental to others by an "insured," for loss caused only by the following Perils Insured Against:

a. **Fire or lightning.**

b. **Windstorm or hail.**

This peril does not include loss to the property contained in a building caused by rain, snow, sleet, sand or dust unless the direct force of wind or hail damages the building causing an opening in a roof or wall and the rain, snow, sleet, sand or dust enters through this opening.

This peril includes loss to watercraft and their trailers, furnishings, equipment, and outboard engines or motors, only while inside a fully enclosed building.

c. **Explosion.**

d. **Riot or civil commotion.**

e. **Aircraft,** including self-propelled missiles and spacecraft.

f. **Vehicles.**

g. **Smoke,** meaning sudden and accidental damage from smoke.

This peril does not include loss caused by smoke from agricultural smudging or industrial operations.

h. **Vandalism or malicious mischief.**

i. **Falling objects.**

This peril does not include loss to property contained in a building unless the roof or an outside wall of the building is first damaged by a falling object. Damage to the falling object itself is not included.

j. **Weight of ice, snow or sleet** which causes damage to property contained in a building.

k. **Accidental discharge or overflow of water or steam** from within a plumbing, heating, air conditioning or automatic fire protective sprinkler system or from within a household appliance.

This peril does not include loss:

(1) To the system or appliance from which the water or steam escaped;

(2) Caused by or resulting from freezing except as provided in the peril of freezing below; or

(3) On the "residence premises" caused by accidental discharge or overflow which occurs off the "residence premises."

In this peril, a plumbing system does not include a sump, sump pump or related equipment.

l. **Sudden and accidental tearing apart, cracking, burning or bulging** of a steam or hot water heating system, an air conditioning or automatic fire protective sprinkler system, or an appliance for heating water.

We do not cover loss caused by or resulting from freezing under this peril.

m. **Freezing** of a plumbing, heating, air conditioning or automatic fire protective sprinkler system or of a household appliance.

This peril does not include loss on the "residence premises" while the dwelling is unoccupied, unless you have used reasonable care to:

(1) Maintain heat in the building; or

(2) Shut off the water supply and drain the system and appliances of water.

n. **Sudden and accidental damage from artificially generated electrical current.**

This peril does not include loss to a tube, transistor or similar electronic component.

o. **Volcanic eruption** other than loss caused by earthquake, land shock waves or tremors.

The $2500 limit is the most we will pay in any one loss regardless of the number of appliances, carpeting or other household furnishings involved in the loss.

SECTION I – PERILS INSURED AGAINST

COVERAGE A - DWELLING and COVERAGE B - OTHER STRUCTURES

We insure against risk of direct loss to property described in Coverages A and B only if that loss is a physical loss to property. We do not insure, however, for loss:

1. Involving collapse, other than as provided in Additional Coverage 8.;

2. Caused by:

HO 00 03 04 91

a. Freezing of a plumbing, heating, air conditioning or automatic fire protective sprinkler system or of a household appliance, or by discharge, leakage or overflow from within the system or appliance caused by freezing. This exclusion applies only while the dwelling is vacant, unoccupied or being constructed, unless you have used reasonable care to:

(1) Maintain heat in the building; or

(2) Shut off the water supply and drain the system and appliances of water;

b. Freezing, thawing, pressure or weight of water or ice, whether driven by wind or not, to a:

(1) Fence, pavement, patio or swimming pool;

(2) Foundation, retaining wall, or bulkhead; or

(3) Pier, wharf or dock;

c. Theft in or to a dwelling under construction, or of materials and supplies for use in the construction until the dwelling is finished and occupied;

d. Vandalism and malicious mischief if the dwelling has been vacant for more than 30 consecutive days immediately before the loss. A dwelling being constructed is not considered vacant;

e. Any of the following:

(1) Wear and tear, marring, deterioration;

(2) Inherent vice, latent defect, mechanical breakdown;

(3) Smog, rust or other corrosion, mold, wet or dry rot;

(4) Smoke from agricultural smudging or industrial operations;

(5) Discharge, dispersal, seepage, migration, release or escape of pollutants unless the discharge, dispersal, seepage, migration, release or escape is itself caused by a Peril Insured Against under Coverage C of this policy.

Pollutants means any solid, liquid, gaseous or thermal irritant or contaminant, including smoke, vapor, soot, fumes, acids, alkalis, chemicals and waste. Waste includes materials to be recycled, reconditioned or reclaimed;

(6) Settling, shrinking, bulging or expansion, including resultant cracking, of pavements, patios, foundations, walls, floors, roofs or ceilings;

(7) Birds, vermin, rodents, or insects; or

(8) Animals owned or kept by an "insured."

If any of these cause water damage not otherwise excluded, from a plumbing, heating, air conditioning or automatic fire protective sprinkler system or household appliance, we cover loss caused by the water including the cost of tearing out and replacing any part of a building necessary to repair the system or appliance. We do not cover loss to the system or appliance from which this water escaped.

3. Excluded under Section I - Exclusions.

Under items **1.** and **2.**, any ensuing loss to property described in Coverages A and B not excluded or excepted in this policy is covered.

COVERAGE C - PERSONAL PROPERTY

We insure for direct physical loss to the property described in Coverage C caused by a peril listed below unless the loss is excluded in SECTION I - EXCLUSIONS.

1. **Fire or lightning.**

2. **Windstorm or hail.**

This peril does not include loss to the property contained in a building caused by rain, snow, sleet, sand or dust unless the direct force of wind or hail damages the building causing an opening in a roof or wall and the rain, snow, sleet, sand or dust enters through this opening.

This peril includes loss to watercraft and their trailers, furnishings, equipment, and outboard engines or motors, only while inside a fully enclosed building.

3. **Explosion.**

4. **Riot or civil commotion.**

5. **Aircraft,** including self-propelled missiles and spacecraft.

6. **Vehicles.**

7. **Smoke,** meaning sudden and accidental damage from smoke.

This peril does not include loss caused by smoke from agricultural smudging or industrial operations.

8. **Vandalism or malicious mischief.**

9. **Theft,** including attempted theft and loss of property from a known place when it is likely that the property has been stolen.

This peril does not include loss caused by theft:

a. Committed by an "insured";

b. In or to a dwelling under construction, or of materials and supplies for use in the construction until the dwelling is finished and occupied; or

HO 00 03 04 91

c. From that part of a "residence premises" rented by an "insured" to other than an "insured."

This peril does not include loss caused by theft that occurs off the "residence premises" of:

a. Property while at any other residence owned by, rented to, or occupied by an "insured," except while an "insured" is temporarily living there. Property of a student who is an "insured" is covered while at a residence away from home if the student has been there at any time during the 45 days immediately before the loss;

b. Watercraft, and their furnishings, equipment and outboard engines or motors; or

c. Trailers and campers.

10. **Falling objects.**

This peril does not include loss to property contained in a building unless the roof or an outside wall of the building is first damaged by a falling object. Damage to the falling object itself is not included.

11. **Weight of ice, snow or sleet** which causes damage to property contained in a building.

12. **Accidental discharge or overflow of water or steam** from within a plumbing, heating, air conditioning or automatic fire protective sprinkler system or from within a household appliance.

This peril does not include loss:

a. To the system or appliance from which the water or steam escaped;

b. Caused by or resulting from freezing except as provided in the peril of freezing below; or

c. On the "residence premises" caused by accidental discharge or overflow which occurs off the "residence premises."

In this peril, a plumbing system does not include a sump, sump pump or related equipment.

13. **Sudden and accidental tearing apart, cracking, burning or bulging** of a steam or hot water heating system, an air conditioning or automatic fire protective sprinkler system, or an appliance for heating water.

We do not cover loss caused by or resulting from freezing under this peril.

14. **Freezing** of a plumbing, heating, air conditioning or automatic fire protective sprinkler system or of a household appliance.

This peril does not include loss on the "residence premises" while the dwelling is unoccupied, unless you have used reasonable care to:

a. Maintain heat in the building; or

b. Shut off the water supply and drain the system and appliances of water.

15. **Sudden and accidental damage from artificially generated electrical current.**

This peril does not include loss to a tube, transistor or similar electronic component.

16. **Volcanic eruption** other than loss caused by earthquake, land shock waves or tremors.

SECTION I – EXCLUSIONS

1. We do not insure for loss caused directly or indirectly by any of the following. Such loss is excluded regardless of any other cause or event contributing concurrently or in any sequence to the loss.

   a. **Ordinance or Law,** meaning enforcement of any ordinance or law regulating the construction, repair, or demolition of a building or other structure, unless specifically provided under this policy.

   b. **Earth Movement,** meaning earthquake including land shock waves or tremors before, during or after a volcanic eruption; landslide; mine subsidence; mudflow; earth sinking, rising or shifting; unless direct loss by:

      (1) Fire;

      (2) Explosion; or

      (3) Breakage of glass or safety glazing material which is part of a building, storm door or storm window;

      ensues and then we will pay only for the ensuing loss.

      This exclusion does not apply to loss by theft.

   c. **Water Damage,** meaning:

      (1) Flood, surface water, waves, tidal water, overflow of a body of water, or spray from any of these, whether or not driven by wind;

      (2) Water which backs up through sewers or drains or which overflows from a sump; or

---

(3) Water below the surface of the ground, including water which exerts pressure on or seeps or leaks through a building, sidewalk, driveway, foundation, swimming pool or other structure.

Direct loss by fire, explosion or theft resulting from water damage is covered.

d. **Power Failure,** meaning the failure of power or other utility service if the failure takes place off the "residence premises." But, if a Peril Insured Against ensues on the "residence premises," we will pay only for that ensuing loss.

e. **Neglect,** meaning neglect of the "insured" to use all reasonable means to save and preserve property at and after the time of a loss.

f. **War,** including the following and any consequence of any of the following:

(1) Undeclared war, civil war, insurrection, rebellion or revolution;

(2) Warlike act by a military force or military personnel; or

(3) Destruction, seizure or use for a military purpose.

Discharge of a nuclear weapon will be deemed a warlike act even if accidental.

g. **Nuclear Hazard,** to the extent set forth in the Nuclear Hazard Clause of SECTION I - CONDITIONS.

h. **Intentional Loss,** meaning any loss arising out of any act committed:

(1) By or at the direction of an "insured"; and

(2) With the intent to cause a loss.

2. We do not insure for loss to property described in Coverages A and B caused by any of the following. However, any ensuing loss to property described in Coverages A and B not excluded or excepted in this policy is covered.

a. **Weather conditions.** However, this exclusion only applies if weather conditions contribute in any way with a cause or event excluded in paragraph 1. above to produce the loss;

b. **Acts or decisions,** including the failure to act or decide, of any person, group, organization or governmental body;

c. **Faulty, inadequate or defective:**

(1) Planning, zoning, development, surveying, siting;

(2) Design, specifications, workmanship, repair, construction, renovation, remodeling, grading, compaction;

(3) Materials used in repair, construction, renovation or remodeling; or

(4) Maintenance;

of part or all of any property whether on or off the "residence premises."

SECTION I – CONDITIONS

1. **Insurable Interest and Limit of Liability.** Even if more than one person has an insurable interest in the property covered, we will not be liable in any one loss:

a. To the "insured" for more than the amount of the "insured's" interest at the time of loss; or

b. For more than the applicable limit of liability.

2. **Your Duties After Loss.** In case of a loss to covered property, you must see that the following are done:

a. Give prompt notice to us or our agent;

b. Notify the police in case of loss by theft;

c. Notify the credit card or fund transfer card company in case of loss under Credit Card or Fund Transfer Card coverage;

d. Protect the property from further damage. If repairs to the property are required, you must:

(1) Make reasonable and necessary repairs to protect the property; and

(2) Keep an accurate record of repair expenses;

e. Prepare an inventory of damaged personal property showing the quantity, description, actual cash value and amount of loss. Attach all bills, receipts and related documents that justify the figures in the inventory;

f. As often as we reasonably require:

(1) Show the damaged property;

(2) Provide us with records and documents we request and permit us to make copies; and

(3) Submit to examination under oath, while not in the presence of any other "insured," and sign the same;

HO 00 03 04 91

g. Send to us, within 60 days after our request, your signed, sworn proof of loss which sets forth, to the best of your knowledge and belief:

(1) The time and cause of loss;

(2) The interest of the "insured" and all others in the property involved and all liens on the property;

(3) Other insurance which may cover the loss;

(4) Changes in title or occupancy of the property during the term of the policy;

(5) Specifications of damaged buildings and detailed repair estimates;

(6) The inventory of damaged personal property described in **2.e.** above;

(7) Receipts for additional living expenses incurred and records that support the fair rental value loss; and

(8) Evidence or affidavit that supports a claim under the Credit Card, Fund Transfer Card, Forgery and Counterfeit Money coverage, stating the amount and cause of loss.

3. **Loss Settlement.** Covered property losses are settled as follows:

a. Property of the following types:

(1) Personal property;

(2) Awnings, carpeting, household appliances, outdoor antennas and outdoor equipment, whether or not attached to buildings; and

(3) Structures that are not buildings;

at actual cash value at the time of loss but not more than the amount required to repair or replace.

b. Buildings under Coverage A or B at replacement cost without deduction for depreciation, subject to the following:

(1) If, at the time of loss, the amount of insurance in this policy on the damaged building is 80% or more of the full replacement cost of the building immediately before the loss, we will pay the cost to repair or replace, after application of deductible and without deduction for depreciation, but not more than the least of the following amounts:

(a) The limit of liability under this policy that applies to the building;

(b) The replacement cost of that part of the building damaged for like construction and use on the same premises; or

(c) The necessary amount actually spent to repair or replace the damaged building.

(2) If, at the time of loss, the amount of insurance in this policy on the damaged building is less than 80% of the full replacement cost of the building immediately before the loss, we will pay the greater of the following amounts, but not more than the limit of liability under this policy that applies to the building:

(a) The actual cash value of that part of the building damaged; or

(b) That proportion of the cost to repair or replace, after application of deductible and without deduction for depreciation, that part of the building damaged, which the total amount of insurance in this policy on the damaged building bears to 80% of the replacement cost of the building.

(3) To determine the amount of insurance required to equal 80% of the full replacement cost of the building immediately before the loss, do not include the value of:

(a) Excavations, foundations, piers or any supports which are below the undersurface of the lowest basement floor;

(b) Those supports in (a) above which are below the surface of the ground inside the foundation walls, if there is no basement; and

(c) Underground flues, pipes, wiring and drains.

(4) We will pay no more than the actual cash value of the damage until actual repair or replacement is complete. Once actual repair or replacement is complete, we will settle the loss according to the provisions of **b.(1)** and **b.(2)** above.

However, if the cost to repair or replace the damage is both:

(a) Less than 5% of the amount of insurance in this policy on the building; and

(b) Less than $2500;

we will settle the loss according to the provisions of **b.(1)** and **b.(2)** above whether or not actual repair or replacement is complete.

(5) You may disregard the replacement cost loss settlement provisions and make claim under this policy for loss or damage to buildings on an actual cash value basis. You may then make claim within 180 days after loss for any additional liability according to the provisions of this Condition 3. Loss Settlement.

4. Loss to a Pair or Set. In case of loss to a pair or set we may elect to:

a. Repair or replace any part to restore the pair or set to its value before the loss; or

b. Pay the difference between actual cash value of the property before and after the loss.

5. Glass Replacement. Loss for damage to glass caused by a Peril Insured Against will be settled on the basis of replacement with safety glazing materials when required by ordinance or law.

6. Appraisal. If you and we fail to agree on the amount of loss, either may demand an appraisal of the loss. In this event, each party will choose a competent appraiser within 20 days after receiving a written request from the other. The two appraisers will choose an umpire. If they cannot agree upon an umpire within 15 days, you or we may request that the choice be made by a judge of a court of record in the state where the "residence premises" is located. The appraisers will separately set the amount of loss. If the appraisers submit a written report of an agreement to us, the amount agreed upon will be the amount of loss. If they fail to agree, they will submit their differences to the umpire. A decision agreed to by any two will set the amount of loss.

Each party will:

a. Pay its own appraiser; and

b. Bear the other expenses of the appraisal and umpire equally.

7. Other Insurance. If a loss covered by this policy is also covered by other insurance, we will pay only the proportion of the loss that the limit of liability that applies under this policy bears to the total amount of insurance covering the loss.

8. Suit Against Us. No action can be brought unless the policy provisions have been complied with and the action is started within one year after the date of loss.

9. Our Option. If we give you written notice within 30 days after we receive your signed, sworn proof of loss, we may repair or replace any part of the damaged property with like property.

10. Loss Payment. We will adjust all losses with you. We will pay you unless some other person is named in the policy or is legally entitled to receive payment. Loss will be payable 60 days after we receive your proof of loss and:

a. Reach an agreement with you;

b. There is an entry of a final judgment; or

c. There is a filing of an appraisal award with us.

11. Abandonment of Property. We need not accept any property abandoned by an "insured."

12. Mortgage Clause.

The word "mortgagee" includes trustee.

If a mortgagee is named in this policy, any loss payable under Coverage A or B will be paid to the mortgagee and you, as interests appear. If more than one mortgagee is named, the order of payment will be the same as the order of precedence of the mortgages.

If we deny your claim, that denial will not apply to a valid claim of the mortgagee, if the mortgagee:

a. Notifies us of any change in ownership, occupancy or substantial change in risk of which the mortgagee is aware;

b. Pays any premium due under this policy on demand if you have neglected to pay the premium; and

c. Submits a signed, sworn statement of loss within 60 days after receiving notice from us of your failure to do so. Policy conditions relating to Appraisal, Suit Against Us and Loss Payment apply to the mortgagee.

If we decide to cancel or not to renew this policy, the mortgagee will be notified at least 10 days before the date cancellation or nonrenewal takes effect.

If we pay the mortgagee for any loss and deny payment to you:

a. We are subrogated to all the rights of the mortgagee granted under the mortgage on the property; or

b. At our option, we may pay to the mortgagee the whole principal on the mortgage plus any accrued interest. In this event, we will receive a full assignment and transfer of the mortgage and all securities held as collateral to the mortgage debt.

Subrogation will not impair the right of the mortgagee to recover the full amount of the mortgagee's claim.

HO 00 03 04 91

13. **No Benefit to Bailee.** We will not recognize any assignment or grant any coverage that benefits a person or organization holding, storing or moving property for a fee regardless of any other provision of this policy.

14. **Nuclear Hazard Clause.**

   a. "Nuclear Hazard" means any nuclear reaction, radiation, or radioactive contamination, all whether controlled or uncontrolled or however caused, or any consequence of any of these.

   b. Loss caused by the nuclear hazard will not be considered loss caused by fire, explosion, or smoke, whether these perils are specifically named in or otherwise included within the Perils Insured Against in Section I.

   c. This policy does not apply under Section I to loss caused directly or indirectly by nuclear hazard, except that direct loss by fire resulting from the nuclear hazard is covered.

15. **Recovered Property.** If you or we recover any property for which we have made payment under this policy, you or we will notify the other of the recovery. At your option, the property will be returned to or retained by you or it will become our property. If the recovered property is returned to or retained by you, the loss payment will be adjusted based on the amount you received for the recovered property.

16. **Volcanic Eruption Period.** One or more volcanic eruptions that occur within a 72-hour period will be considered as one volcanic eruption.

SECTION II – LIABILITY COVERAGES

COVERAGE E - Personal Liability

If a claim is made or a suit is brought against an "insured" for damages because of "bodily injury" or "property damage" caused by an "occurrence" to which this coverage applies, we will:

1. Pay up to our limit of liability for the damages for which the "insured" is legally liable. Damages include prejudgment interest awarded against the "insured"; and

2. Provide a defense at our expense by counsel of our choice, even if the suit is groundless, false or fraudulent. We may investigate and settle any claim or suit that we decide is appropriate. Our duty to settle or defend ends when the amount we pay for damages resulting from the "occurrence" equals our limit of liability.

COVERAGE F - Medical Payments To Others

We will pay the necessary medical expenses that are incurred or medically ascertained within three years from the date of an accident causing "bodily injury." Medical expenses means reasonable charges for medical, surgical, x-ray, dental, ambulance, hospital, professional nursing, prosthetic devices and funeral services. This coverage does not apply to you or regular residents of your household except "residence employees." As to others, this coverage applies only:

1. To a person on the "insured location" with the permission of an "insured"; or

2. To a person off the "insured location," if the "bodily injury":

   a. Arises out of a condition on the "insured location" or the ways immediately adjoining;

   b. Is caused by the activities of an "insured";

   c. Is caused by a "residence employee" in the course of the "residence employee's" employment by an "insured"; or

   d. Is caused by an animal owned by or in the care of an "insured."

SECTION II – EXCLUSIONS

1. **Coverage E - Personal Liability** and **Coverage F - Medical Payments to Others** do not apply to "bodily injury" or "property damage":

   a. Which is expected or intended by the "insured";

   b. Arising out of or in connection with a "business" engaged in by an "insured." This exclusion applies but is not limited to an act or omission, regardless of its nature or circumstance, involving a service or duty rendered, promised, owed, or implied to be provided because of the nature of the "business";

c. Arising out of the rental or holding for rental of any part of any premises by an "insured." This exclusion does not apply to the rental or holding for rental of an "insured location":

(1) On an occasional basis if used only as a residence;

(2) In part for use only as a residence, unless a single family unit is intended for use by the occupying family to lodge more than two roomers or boarders; or

(3) In part, as an office, school, studio or private garage;

d. Arising out of the rendering of or failure to render professional services;

e. Arising out of a premises:

(1) Owned by an "insured";

(2) Rented to an "insured"; or

(3) Rented to others by an "insured";

that is not an "insured location";

f. Arising out of:

(1) The ownership, maintenance, use, loading or unloading of motor vehicles or all other motorized land conveyances, including trailers, owned or operated by or rented or loaned to an "insured";

(2) The entrustment by an "insured" of a motor vehicle or any other motorized land conveyance to any person; or

(3) Vicarious liability, whether or not statutorily imposed, for the actions of a child or minor using a conveyance excluded in paragraph (1) or (2) above.

This exclusion does not apply to:

(1) A trailer not towed by or carried on a motorized land conveyance.

(2) A motorized land conveyance designed for recreational use off public roads, not subject to motor vehicle registration and:

(a) Not owned by an "insured"; or

(b) Owned by an "insured" and on an "insured location";

(3) A motorized golf cart when used to play golf on a golf course;

(4) A vehicle or conveyance not subject to motor vehicle registration which is:

(a) Used to service an "insured's" residence;

(b) Designed for assisting the handicapped; or

(c) In dead storage on an "insured location";

g. Arising out of:

(1) The ownership, maintenance, use, loading or unloading of an excluded watercraft described below;

(2) The entrustment by an "insured" of an excluded watercraft described below to any person; or

(3) Vicarious liability, whether or not statutorily imposed, for the actions of a child or minor using an excluded watercraft described below.

Excluded watercraft are those that are principally designed to be propelled by engine power or electric motor, or are sailing vessels, whether owned by or rented to an "insured." This exclusion does not apply to watercraft:

(1) That are not sailing vessels and are powered by:

(a) Inboard or inboard-outdrive engine or motor power of 50 horsepower or less not owned by an "insured";

(b) Inboard or inboard-outdrive engine or motor power of more than 50 horsepower not owned by or rented to an "insured";

(c) One or more outboard engines or motors with 25 total horsepower or less;

(d) One or more outboard engines or motors with more than 25 total horsepower if the outboard engine or motor is not owned by an "insured";

(e) Outboard engines or motors of more than 25 total horsepower owned by an "insured" if:

(i) You acquire them prior to the policy period; and

(a) You declare them at policy inception; or

(b) Your intention to insure is reported to us in writing within 45 days after you acquire the outboard engines or motors.

(ii) You acquire them during the policy period.

This coverage applies for the policy period.

(2) That are sailing vessels, with or without auxiliary power:

(a) Less than 26 feet in overall length;

(b) 26 feet or more in overall length, not owned by or rented to an "insured."

HO 00 03 04 91

(3) That are stored;

h. Arising out of:

(1) The ownership, maintenance, use, loading or unloading of an aircraft;

(2) The entrustment by an "insured" of an aircraft to any person; or

(3) Vicarious liability, whether or not statutorily imposed, for the actions of a child or minor using an aircraft.

An aircraft means any contrivance used or designed for flight, except model or hobby aircraft not used or designed to carry people or cargo;

i. Caused directly or indirectly by war, including the following and any consequence of any of the following:

(1) Undeclared war, civil war, insurrection, rebellion or revolution;

(2) Warlike act by a military force or military personnel; or

(3) Destruction, seizure or use for a military purpose.

Discharge of a nuclear weapon will be deemed a warlike act even if accidental;

j. Which arises out of the transmission of a communicable disease by an "insured";

k. Arising out of sexual molestation, corporal punishment or physical or mental abuse; or

l. Arising out of the use, sale, manufacture, delivery, transfer or possession by any person of a Controlled Substance(s) as defined by the Federal Food and Drug Law at 21 U.S.C.A. Sections 811 and 812. Controlled Substances include but are not limited to cocaine, LSD, marijuana and all narcotic drugs. However, this exclusion does not apply to the legitimate use of prescription drugs by a person following the orders of a licensed physician.

Exclusions **e.**, **f.**, **g.**, and **h.** do not apply to "bodily injury" to a "residence employee" arising out of and in the course of the "residence employee's" employment by an "insured."

2. Coverage E - Personal Liability, does not apply to:

a. Liability:

(1) For any loss assessment charged against you as a member of an association, corporation or community of property owners;

(2) Under any contract or agreement. However, this exclusion does not apply to written contracts:

(a) That directly relate to the ownership, maintenance or use of an "insured location"; or

(b) Where the liability of others is assumed by the "insured" prior to an "occurrence";

unless excluded in **(1)** above or elsewhere in this policy;

b. "Property damage" to property owned by the "insured";

c. "Property damage" to property rented to, occupied or used by or in the care of the "insured." This exclusion does not apply to "property damage" caused by fire, smoke or explosion;

d. "Bodily injury" to any person eligible to receive any benefits:

(1) Voluntarily provided; or

(2) Required to be provided;

by the "insured" under any:

(1) Workers' compensation law;

(2) Non-occupational disability law; or

(3) Occupational disease law;

e. "Bodily injury" or "property damage" for which an "insured" under this policy:

(1) Is also an insured under a nuclear energy liability policy; or

(2) Would be an insured under that policy but for the exhaustion of its limit of liability.

A nuclear energy liability policy is one issued by:

(1) American Nuclear Insurers;

(2) Mutual Atomic Energy Liability Underwriters;

(3) Nuclear Insurance Association of Canada;

or any of their successors; or

f. "Bodily injury" to you or an "insured" within the meaning of part **a.** or **b.** of "insured" as defined.

3. Coverage F - Medical Payments to Others, does not apply to "bodily injury":

a. To a "residence employee" if the "bodily injury":

(1) Occurs off the "insured location"; and

(2) Does not arise out of or in the course of the "residence employee's" employment by an "insured";

HO 00 03 04 91

b. To any person eligible to receive benefits:

  (1) Voluntarily provided; or

  (2) Required to be provided;

  under any:

  (1) Workers' compensation law;

  (2) Non-occupational disability law; or

  (3) Occupational disease law;

c. From any:

  (1) Nuclear reaction;

  (2) Nuclear radiation; or

  (3) Radioactive contamination;

  all whether controlled or uncontrolled or however caused; or

  (4) Any consequence of any of these; or

d. To any person, other than a "residence employee" of an "insured," regularly residing on any part of the "insured location."

SECTION II – ADDITIONAL COVERAGES

We cover the following in addition to the limits of liability:

1. Claim Expenses. We pay:

  a. Expenses we incur and costs taxed against an "insured" in any suit we defend;

  b. Premiums on bonds required in a suit we defend, but not for bond amounts more than the limit of liability for Coverage E. We need not apply for or furnish any bond;

  c. Reasonable expenses incurred by an "insured" at our request, including actual loss of earnings (but not loss of other income) up to $50 per day, for assisting us in the investigation or defense of a claim or suit; and

  d. Interest on the entire judgment which accrues after entry of the judgment and before we pay or tender, or deposit in court that part of the judgment which does not exceed the limit of liability that applies.

2. First Aid Expenses. We will pay expenses for first aid to others incurred by an "insured" for "bodily injury" covered under this policy. We will not pay for first aid to you or any other "insured."

3. Damage to Property of Others. We will pay, at replacement cost, up to $500 per "occurrence" for "property damage" to property of others caused by an "insured."

We will not pay for "property damage":

  a. To the extent of any amount recoverable under Section I of this policy;

  b. Caused intentionally by an "insured" who is 13 years of age or older;

  c. To property owned by an "insured";

  d. To property owned by or rented to a tenant of an "insured" or a resident in your household; or

  e. Arising out of:

    (1) A "business" engaged in by an "insured";

    (2) Any act or omission in connection with a premises owned, rented or controlled by an "insured," other than the "insured location"; or

    (3) The ownership, maintenance, or use of aircraft, watercraft or motor vehicles or all other motorized land conveyances.

    This exclusion does not apply to a motorized land conveyance designed for recreational use off public roads, not subject to motor vehicle registration and not owned by an "insured."

4. Loss Assessment. We will pay up to $1000 for your share of loss assessment charged during the policy period against you by a corporation or association of property owners, when the assessment is made as a result of:

  a. "Bodily injury" or "property damage" not excluded under Section II of this policy; or

  b. Liability for an act of a director, officer or trustee in the capacity as a director, officer or trustee, provided:

    (1) The director, officer or trustee is elected by the members of a corporation or association of property owners; and

    (2) The director, officer or trustee serves without deriving any income from the exercise of duties which are solely on behalf of a corporation or association of property owners.

This coverage applies only to loss assessments charged against you as owner or tenant of the "residence premises."

HO 00 03 04 91

We do not cover loss assessments charged against you or a corporation or association of property owners by any governmental body.

Regardless of the number of assessments, the limit of $1000 is the most we will pay for loss arising out of:

a. One accident, including continuous or repeated exposure to substantially the same general harmful condition; or

b. A covered act of a director, officer or trustee. An act involving more than one director, officer or trustee is considered to be a single act.

The following do not apply to this coverage:

1. Section II - Coverage E - Personal Liability Exclusion **2.a.(1)**;

2. Condition **1.** Policy Period, under SECTIONS I AND II - CONDITIONS.

SECTION II – CONDITIONS

1. **Limit of Liability.** Our total liability under Coverage E for all damages resulting from any one "occurrence" will not be more than the limit of liability for Coverage E as shown in the Declarations. This limit is the same regardless of the number of "insureds," claims made or persons injured. All "bodily injury" and "property damage" resulting from any one accident or from continuous or repeated exposure to substantially the same general harmful conditions shall be considered to be the result of one "occurrence."

   Our total liability under Coverage F for all medical expense payable for "bodily injury" to one person as the result of one accident will not be more than the limit of liability for Coverage F as shown in the Declarations.

2. **Severability of Insurance.** This insurance applies separately to each "insured." This condition will not increase our limit of liability for any one "occurrence."

3. **Duties After Loss.** In case of an accident or "occurrence," the "insured" will perform the following duties that apply. You will help us by seeing that these duties are performed:

   a. Give written notice to us or our agent as soon as is practical, which sets forth:

      (1) The identity of the policy and "insured";

      (2) Reasonably available information on the time, place and circumstances of the accident or "occurrence"; and

      (3) Names and addresses of any claimants and witnesses;

   b. Promptly forward to us every notice, demand, summons or other process relating to the accident or "occurrence";

   c. At our request, help us:

      (1) To make settlement;

      (2) To enforce any right of contribution or indemnity against any person or organization who may be liable to an "insured";

      (3) With the conduct of suits and attend hearings and trials; and

      (4) To secure and give evidence and obtain the attendance of witnesses;

   d. Under the coverage - Damage to Property of Others - submit to us within 60 days after the loss, a sworn statement of loss and show the damaged property, if in the "insured's" control;

   e. The "insured" will not, except at the "insured's" own cost, voluntarily make payment, assume obligation or incur expense other than for first aid to others at the time of the "bodily injury."

4. **Duties of an Injured Person - Coverage F - Medical Payments to Others.**

   The injured person or someone acting for the injured person will:

   a. Give us written proof of claim, under oath if required, as soon as is practical; and

   b. Authorize us to obtain copies of medical reports and records.

   The injured person will submit to a physical exam by a doctor of our choice when and as often as we reasonably require.

5. **Payment of Claim - Coverage F - Medical Payments to Others.** Payment under this coverage is not an admission of liability by an "insured" or us.

6. Suit Against Us. No action can be brought against us unless there has been compliance with the policy provisions.

No one will have the right to join us as a party to any action against an "insured." Also, no action with respect to Coverage E can be brought against us until the obligation of the "insured" has been determined by final judgment or agreement signed by us.

7. Bankruptcy of an Insured. Bankruptcy or insolvency of an "insured" will not relieve us of our obligations under this policy.

8. Other Insurance - Coverage E - Personal Liability. This insurance is excess over other valid and collectible insurance except insurance written specifically to cover as excess over the limits of liability that apply in this policy.

SECTIONS I AND II – CONDITIONS

1. Policy Period. This policy applies only to loss in Section I or "bodily injury" or "property damage" in Section II, which occurs during the policy period.

2. Concealment or Fraud. The entire policy will be void if, whether before or after a loss, an "insured" has:

a. Intentionally concealed or misrepresented any material fact or circumstance;

b. Engaged in fraudulent conduct; or

c. Made false statements;

relating to this insurance.

3. Liberalization Clause. If we make a change which broadens coverage under this edition of our policy without additional premium charge, that change will automatically apply to your insurance as of the date we implement the change in your state, provided that this implementation date falls within 60 days prior to or during the policy period stated in the Declarations.

This Liberalization Clause does not apply to changes implemented through introduction of a subsequent edition of our policy.

4. Waiver or Change of Policy Provisions.

A waiver or change of a provision of this policy must be in writing by us to be valid. Our request for an appraisal or examination will not waive any of our rights.

5. Cancellation.

a. You may cancel this policy at any time by returning it to us or by letting us know in writing of the date cancellation is to take effect.

b. We may cancel this policy only for the reasons stated below by letting you know in writing of the date cancellation takes effect. This cancellation notice may be delivered to you, or mailed to you at your mailing address shown in the Declarations.

Proof of mailing will be sufficient proof of notice.

(1) When you have not paid the premium, we may cancel at any time by letting you know at least 10 days before the date cancellation takes effect.

(2) When this policy has been in effect for less than 60 days and is not a renewal with us, we may cancel for any reason by letting you know at least 10 days before the date cancellation takes effect.

(3) When this policy has been in effect for 60 days or more, or at any time if it is a renewal with us, we may cancel:

(a) If there has been a material misrepresentation of fact which if known to us would have caused us not to issue the policy; or

(b) If the risk has changed substantially since the policy was issued.

This can be done by letting you know at least 30 days before the date cancellation takes effect.

(4) When this policy is written for a period of more than one year, we may cancel for any reason at anniversary by letting you know at least 30 days before the date cancellation takes effect.

c. When this policy is cancelled, the premium for the period from the date of cancellation to the expiration date will be refunded pro rata.

d. If the return premium is not refunded with the notice of cancellation or when this policy is returned to us, we will refund it within a reasonable time after the date cancellation takes effect.

6. Nonrenewal. We may elect not to renew this policy. We may do so by delivering to you, or mailing to you at your mailing address shown in the Declarations, written notice at least 30 days before the expiration date of this policy. Proof of mailing will be sufficient proof of notice.

7. Assignment. Assignment of this policy will not be valid unless we give our written consent.

HO 00 03 04 91

8. **Subrogation.** An "insured" may waive in writing before a loss all rights of recovery against any person. If not waived, we may require an assignment of rights of recovery for a loss to the extent that payment is made by us.

If an assignment is sought, an "insured" must sign and deliver all related papers and cooperate with us.

Subrogation does not apply under Section II to Medical Payments to Others or Damage to Property of Others.

9. **Death.** If any person named in the Declarations or the spouse, if a resident of the same household, dies:

a. We insure the legal representative of the deceased but only with respect to the premises and property of the deceased covered under the policy at the time of death;

b. "Insured" includes:

(1) Any member of your household who is an "insured" at the time of your death, but only while a resident of the "residence premises"; and

(2) With respect to your property, the person having proper temporary custody of the property until appointment and qualification of a legal representative.

Appendix D

Personal Auto Policy

Personal Auto Policy Declarations

POLICYHOLDER: David M. and Joan G. Smith
(Named Insured)   216 Brookside Drive
                   Anytown, USA 40000

POLICY NUMBER: 296 S 468211

POLICY PERIOD: FROM: December 25, 1994
                 TO: June 25, 1995

But only if the required premium for this period has been paid, and for six-month renewal periods if renewal premiums are paid as required. Each period begins and ends at 12:01 A.M. standard time at the address of the policyholder.

INSURED VEHICLES AND
SCHEDULE OF COVERAGES

	VEHICLE	COVERAGES	LIMITS OF INSURANCE	PREMIUM
1	1985 Toyota Tercel		ID #JT2AL21E8B3306553	
		Coverage A— Liability	$ 300,000 Each Occurrence	$ 101.50
		Coverage B—Medical Payments	$ 5,000 Each Person	$ 18.00
		Coverage C—Uninsured Motorists	$ 300,000 Each Occurrence	$ 30.90
			TOTAL	$ 150.40
2	1993 Ford Taurus		ID #1FABP3OU7GG212619	
		Coverage A—Liability	$ 300,000 Each Occurrence	$ 101.50
		Coverage B—Medical Payments	$ 5,000 Each Person	$ 18.00
		Coverage C—Uninsured Motorists	$ 300,000 Each Occurrence	$ 30.90
		Coverage D—Other Than Collision	Actual Cash Value Less $ 100	$ 20.80
		—Collision	Actual Cash Value Less $ 250	$ 115.50
			TOTAL	$ 286.70

POLICY FORM AND ENDORSEMENTS: PP 00 01, PP 03 06

COUNTERSIGNATURE DATE: December 1, 1994

AGENT: A.M. Abel

SAMPLE

PERSONAL AUTO POLICY

AGREEMENT

In return for payment of the premium and subject to all the terms of this policy, we agree with you as follows:

DEFINITIONS

A. Throughout this policy, "you" and "your" refer to:

1. The "named insured" shown in the Declarations; and

2. The spouse if a resident of the same household.

B. "We", "us" and "our" refer to the Company providing this insurance.

C. For purposes of this policy, a private passenger type auto shall be deemed to be owned by a person if leased:

1. Under a written agreement to that person; and

2. For a continuous period of at least 6 months.

Other words and phrases are defined. They are in quotation marks when used.

D. "Bodily injury" means bodily harm, sickness or disease, including death that results.

E. "Business" includes trade, profession or occupation.

F. "Family member" means a person related to you by blood, marriage or adoption who is a resident of your household. This includes a ward or foster child.

G. "Occupying" means in, upon, getting in, on, out or off.

H. "Property damage" means physical injury to, destruction of or loss of use of tangible property.

I. "Trailer" means a vehicle designed to be pulled by a:

1. Private passenger auto; or

2. Pickup or van.

It also means a farm wagon or farm implement while towed by a vehicle listed in 1. or 2. above.

J. "Your covered auto" means:

1. Any vehicle shown in the Declarations.

2. Any of the following types of vehicles on the date you become the owner:

   a. A private passenger auto; or

b. A pickup or van that:

   (1) Has a Gross Vehicle Weight of less than 10,000 lbs.; and

   (2) Is not used for the delivery or transportation of goods and materials unless such use is:

      (a) Incidental to your "business" of installing, maintaining or repairing furnishings or equipment; or

      (b) For farming or ranching.

This provision (J.2.) applies only if:

a. You acquire the vehicle during the policy period;

b. You ask us to insure it within 30 days after you become the owner; and

c. With respect to a pickup or van, no other insurance policy provides coverage for that vehicle.

If the vehicle you acquire replaces one shown in the Declarations, it will have the same coverage as the vehicle it replaced. You must ask us to insure a replacement vehicle within 30 days only if you wish to add or continue Coverage for Damage to Your Auto.

If the vehicle you acquire is in addition to any shown in the Declarations, it will have the broadest coverage we now provide for any vehicle shown in the Declarations.

3. Any "trailer" you own.

4. Any auto or "trailer" you do not own while used as a temporary substitute for any other vehicle described in this definition which is out of normal use because of its:

a. Breakdown;   d. Loss; or
b. Repair;   e. Destruction.
c. Servicing;

This provision (J.4.) does not apply to Coverage for Damage to Your Auto.

SAMPLE

PART A - LIABILITY COVERAGE

INSURING AGREEMENT

A. We will pay damages for "bodily injury" or "property damage" for which any "insured" becomes legally responsible because of an auto accident. Damages include prejudgment interest awarded against the "insured". We will settle or defend, as we consider appropriate, any claim or suit asking for these damages. In addition to our limit of liability, we will pay all defense costs we incur. Our duty to settle or defend ends when our limit of liability for this coverage has been exhausted. We have no duty to defend any suit or settle any claim for "bodily injury" or "property damage" not covered under this policy.

B. "Insured" as used in this Part means:

1. You or any "family member" for the ownership, maintenance or use of any auto or "trailer".

2. Any person using "your covered auto".

3. For "your covered auto", any person or organization but only with respect to legal responsibility for acts or omissions of a person for whom coverage is afforded under this Part.

4. For any auto or "trailer", other than "your covered auto", any other person or organization but only with respect to legal responsibility for acts or omissions of you or any "family member" for whom coverage is afforded under this Part. This provision (**B.4.**) applies only if the person or organization does not own or hire the auto or "trailer".

SUPPLEMENTARY PAYMENTS

In addition to our limit of liability, we will pay on behalf of an "insured":

1. Up to $250 for the cost of bail bonds required because of an accident, including related traffic law violations. The accident must result in "bodily injury" or "property damage" covered under this policy.

2. Premiums on appeal bonds and bonds to release attachments in any suit we defend.

3. Interest accruing after a judgment is entered in any suit we defend. Our duty to pay interest ends when we offer to pay that part of the judgment which does not exceed our limit of liability for this coverage.

4. Up to $50 a day for loss of earnings, but not other income, because of attendance at hearings or trials at our request.

5. Other reasonable expenses incurred at our request.

EXCLUSIONS

A. We do not provide Liability Coverage for any "insured":

1. Who intentionally causes "bodily injury" or "property damage".

2. For "property damage" to property owned or being transported by that "insured".

3. For "property damage" to property:

   a. Rented to;

   b. Used by; or

   c. In the care of;

   that "insured".

   This exclusion (**A.3.**) does not apply to "property damage" to a residence or private garage.

4. For "bodily injury" to an employee of that "insured" during the course of employment. This exclusion (**A.4.**) does not apply to "bodily injury" to a domestic employee unless workers' compensation benefits are required or available for that domestic employee.

5. For that "insured's" liability arising out of the ownership or operation of a vehicle while it is being used as a public or livery conveyance. This exclusion (**A.5.**) does not apply to a share-the-expense car pool.

6. While employed or otherwise engaged in the "business" of:

a. Selling;	d. Storing; or
b. Repairing;	e. Parking;
c. Servicing;	

   vehicles designed for use mainly on public highways. This includes road testing and delivery. This exclusion (**A.6.**) does not apply to the ownership, maintenance or use of "your covered auto" by:

   a. You;

   b. Any "family member"; or

   c. Any partner, agent or employee of you or any "family member".

     PP 00 01 06 94

SAMPLE

7. Maintaining or using any vehicle while that "insured" is employed or otherwise engaged in any "business" (other than farming or ranching) not described in exclusion **A.6.**

This exclusion (**A.7.**) does not apply to the maintenance or use of a:

a. Private passenger auto;

b. Pickup or van that:

(1) You own; or

(2) You do not own while used as a temporary substitute for "your covered auto" which is out of normal use because of its:

  (a) Breakdown; (d) Loss; or
  (b) Repair;   (e) Destruction; or
  (c) Servicing;

c. "Trailer" used with a vehicle described in a. or b. above.

8. Using a vehicle without a reasonable belief that that "insured" is entitled to do so.

9. For "bodily injury" or "property damage" for which that "insured":

a. Is an insured under a nuclear energy liability policy; or

b. Would be an insured under a nuclear energy liability policy but for its termination upon exhaustion of its limit of liability.

A nuclear energy liability policy is a policy issued by any of the following or their successors:

a. American Nuclear Insurers;

b. Mutual Atomic Energy Liability Underwriters; or

c. Nuclear Insurance Association of Canada.

B. We do not provide Liability Coverage for the ownership, maintenance or use of:

1. Any vehicle which:

a. Has fewer than four wheels; or

b. Is designed mainly for use off public roads.

This exclusion (**B.1.**) does not apply:

a. While such vehicle is being used by an "insured" in a medical emergency; or

b. To any "trailer".

2. Any vehicle, other than "your covered auto", which is:

a. Owned by you; or

b. Furnished or available for your regular use.

3. Any vehicle, other than "your covered auto" which is:

a. Owned by any "family member"; or

b. Furnished or available for the regular use of any "family member".

However, this exclusion (**B.3.**) does not apply to you while you are maintaining or "occupying" any vehicle which is:

a. Owned by a "family member"; or

b. Furnished or available for the regular use of a "family member".

4. Any vehicle, located inside a facility designed for racing, for the purpose of:

a. Competing in; or

b. Practicing or preparing for;

any prearranged or organized racing or speed contest.

LIMIT OF LIABILITY

A. The limit of liability shown in the Declarations for this coverage is our maximum limit of liability for all damages resulting from any one auto accident. This is the most we will pay regardless of the number of:

1. "Insureds";

2. Claims made;

3. Vehicles or premiums shown in the Declarations; or

4. Vehicles involved in the auto accident.

B. We will apply the limit of liability to provide any separate limits required by law for bodily injury and property damage liability. However, this provision (**B.**) will not change our total limit of liability.

C. No one will be entitled to receive duplicate payments for the same elements of loss under this coverage and:

1. Part **B** or Part **C** of this policy; or

2. Any Underinsured Motorists Coverage provided by this policy.

SAMPLE

OUT OF STATE COVERAGE

If an auto accident to which this policy applies occurs in any state or province other than the one in which "your covered auto" is principally garaged, we will interpret your policy for that accident as follows:

A. If the state or province has:

1. A financial responsibility or similar law specifying limits of liability for "bodily injury" or "property damage" higher than the limit shown in the Declarations, your policy will provide the higher specified limit.

2. A compulsory insurance or similar law requiring a nonresident to maintain insurance whenever the nonresident uses a vehicle in that state or province, your policy will provide at least the required minimum amounts and types of coverage.

B. No one will be entitled to duplicate payments for the same elements of loss.

FINANCIAL RESPONSIBILITY

When this policy is certified as future proof of financial responsibility, this policy shall comply with the law to the extent required.

OTHER INSURANCE

If there is other applicable liability insurance we will pay only our share of the loss. Our share is the proportion that our limit of liability bears to the total of all applicable limits. However, any insurance we provide for a vehicle you do not own shall be excess over any other collectible insurance.

PART B - MEDICAL PAYMENTS COVERAGE

INSURING AGREEMENT

A. We will pay reasonable expenses incurred for necessary medical and funeral services because of "bodily injury":

1. Caused by accident; and

2. Sustained by an "insured".

We will pay only those expenses incurred for services rendered within 3 years from the date of the accident.

B. "Insured" as used in this Part means:

1. You or any "family member":

   a. While "occupying"; or

   b. As a pedestrian when struck by;

   a motor vehicle designed for use mainly on public roads or a trailer of any type.

2. Any other person while "occupying" "your covered auto".

EXCLUSIONS

We do not provide Medical Payments Coverage for any "insured" for "bodily injury":

1. Sustained while "occupying" any motorized vehicle having fewer than four wheels.

2. Sustained while "occupying" "your covered auto" when it is being used as a public or livery conveyance. This exclusion (2.) does not apply to a share-the-expense car pool.

3. Sustained while "occupying" any vehicle located for use as a residence or premises.

4. Occurring during the course of employment if workers' compensation benefits are required or available for the "bodily injury".

5. Sustained while "occupying", or when struck by, any vehicle (other than "your covered auto") which is:

   a. Owned by you; or

   b. Furnished or available for your regular use.

6. Sustained while "occupying", or when struck by, any vehicle (other than "your covered auto") which is:

   a. Owned by any "family member"; or

   b. Furnished or available for the regular use of any "family member".

   However, this exclusion (6.) does not apply to you.

7. Sustained while "occupying" a vehicle without a reasonable belief that that "insured" is entitled to do so.

8. Sustained while "occupying" a vehicle when it is being used in the "business" of an "insured". This exclusion (8.) does not apply to "bodily injury" sustained while "occupying" a:

   a. Private passenger auto;

   b. Pickup or van that you own; or

   c. "Trailer" used with a vehicle described in a. or b. above.

9. Caused by or as a consequence of:

   a. Discharge of a nuclear weapon (even if accidental);

   b. War (declared or undeclared);

   c. Civil war;

   d. Insurrection; or

   e. Rebellion or revolution.

10. From or as a consequence of the following, whether controlled or uncontrolled or however caused:

    a. Nuclear reaction;

    b. Radiation; or

    c. Radioactive contamination.

       PP 00 01 06 94

SAMPLE

11. Sustained while "occupying" any vehicle located inside a facility designed for racing, for the purpose of:

    a. Competing in; or

    b. Practicing or preparing for;

    any prearranged or organized racing or speed contest.

LIMIT OF LIABILITY

A. The limit of liability shown in the Declarations for this coverage is our maximum limit of liability for each person injured in any one accident. This is the most we will pay regardless of the number of:

1. "Insureds";

2. Claims made;

3. Vehicles or premiums shown in the Declarations; or

4. Vehicles involved in the accident.

B. No one will be entitled to receive duplicate payments for the same elements of loss under this coverage and:

1. Part **A** or Part **C** of this policy; or

2. Any Underinsured Motorists Coverage provided by this policy.

OTHER INSURANCE

If there is other applicable auto medical payments insurance we will pay only our share of the loss. Our share is the proportion that our limit of liability bears to the total of all applicable limits. However, any insurance we provide with respect to a vehicle you do not own shall be excess over any other collectible auto insurance providing payments for medical or funeral expenses.

PART C - UNINSURED MOTORISTS COVERAGE

INSURING AGREEMENT

A. We will pay compensatory damages which an "insured" is legally entitled to recover from the owner or operator of an "uninsured motor vehicle" because of "bodily injury":

1. Sustained by an "insured"; and

2. Caused by an accident.

The owner's or operator's liability for these damages must arise out of the ownership, maintenance or use of the "uninsured motor vehicle".

Any judgment for damages arising out of a suit brought without our written consent is not binding on us.

B. "Insured" as used in this Part means:

1. You or any "family member".

2. Any other person "occupying" "your covered auto".

3. Any person for damages that person is entitled to recover because of "bodily injury" to which this coverage applies sustained by a person described in **1.** or **2.** above.

C. "Uninsured motor vehicle" means a land motor vehicle or trailer of any type:

1. To which no bodily injury liability bond or policy applies at the time of the accident.

2. To which a bodily injury liability bond or policy applies at the time of the accident. In this case its limit for bodily injury liability must be less than the minimum limit for bodily injury liability specified by the financial responsibility law of the state in which "your covered auto" is principally garaged.

3. Which is a hit-and-run vehicle whose operator or owner cannot be identified and which hits:

    a. You or any "family member";

    b. A vehicle which you or any "family member" are "occupying"; or

    c. "Your covered auto".

4. To which a bodily injury liability bond or policy applies at the time of the accident but the bonding or insuring company:

    a. Denies coverage; or

    b. Is or becomes insolvent.

However, "uninsured motor vehicle" does not include any vehicle or equipment:

1. Owned by or furnished or available for the regular use of you or any "family member".

2. Owned or operated by a self-insurer under any applicable motor vehicle law, except a self-insurer which is or becomes insolvent.

3. Owned by any governmental unit or agency.

4. Operated on rails or crawler treads.

5. Designed mainly for use off public roads while not on public roads.

6. While located for use as a residence or premises.

EXCLUSIONS

A. We do not provide Uninsured Motorists Coverage for "bodily injury" sustained:

1. By an "insured" while "occupying", or when struck by, any motor vehicle owned by that "insured" which is not insured for this coverage under this policy. This includes a trailer of any type used with that vehicle.

SAMPLE

2. By any "family member" while "occupying", or when struck by, any motor vehicle you own which is insured for this coverage on a primary basis under any other policy.

B. We do not provide Uninsured Motorists Coverage for "bodily injury" sustained by any "insured":

1. If that "insured" or the legal representative settles the "bodily injury" claim without our consent.

2. While "occupying" "your covered auto" when it is being used as a public or livery conveyance. This exclusion (**B.2.**) does not apply to a share-the-expense car pool.

3. Using a vehicle without a reasonable belief that that "insured" is entitled to do so.

C. This coverage shall not apply directly or indirectly to benefit any insurer or self-insurer under any of the following or similar law:

1. Workers' compensation law; or

2. Disability benefits law.

D. We do not provide Uninsured Motorists Coverage for punitive or exemplary damages.

LIMIT OF LIABILITY

A. The limit of liability shown in the Declarations for this coverage is our maximum limit of liability for all damages resulting from any one accident. This is the most we will pay regardless of the number of:

1. "Insureds";

2. Claims made;

3. Vehicles or premiums shown in the Declarations; or

4. Vehicles involved in the accident.

B. No one will be entitled to receive duplicate payments for the same elements of loss under this coverage and:

1. Part **A** or Part **B** of this policy; or

2. Any Underinsured Motorists Coverage provided by this policy.

C. We will not make a duplicate payment under this coverage for any element of loss for which payment has been made by or on behalf of persons or organizations who may be legally responsible.

D. We will not pay for any element of loss if a person is entitled to receive payment for the same element of loss under any of the following or similar law:

1. Workers' compensation law; or

2. Disability benefits law.

OTHER INSURANCE

If there is other applicable insurance available under one or more policies or provisions of coverage:

1. Any recovery for damages under all such policies or provisions of coverage may equal but not exceed the highest applicable limit for any one vehicle under any insurance providing coverage on either a primary or excess basis.

2. Any insurance we provide with respect to a vehicle you do not own shall be excess over any collectible insurance providing coverage on a primary basis.

3. If the coverage under this policy is provided:

a. On a primary basis, we will pay only our share of the loss that must be paid under insurance providing coverage on a primary basis. Our share is the proportion that our limit of liability bears to the total of all applicable limits of liability for coverage provided on a primary basis.

b. On an excess basis, we will pay only our share of the loss that must be paid under insurance providing coverage on an excess basis. Our share is the proportion that our limit of liability bears to the total of all applicable limits of liability for coverage provided on an excess basis.

ARBITRATION

A. If we and an "insured" do not agree:

1. Whether that "insured" is legally entitled to recover damages; or

2. As to the amount of damages which are recoverable by that "insured";

from the owner or operator of an "uninsured motor vehicle", then the matter may be arbitrated. However, disputes concerning coverage under this Part may not be arbitrated.

Both parties must agree to arbitration. If so agreed, each party will select an arbitrator. The two arbitrators will select a third. If they cannot agree within 30 days, either may request that selection be made by a judge of a court having jurisdiction.

B. Each party will:

1. Pay the expenses it incurs; and

2. Bear the expenses of the third arbitrator equally.

C. Unless both parties agree otherwise, arbitration will take place in the county in which the "insured" lives. Local rules of law as to procedure and evidence will apply. A decision agreed to by two of the arbitrators will be binding as to:

1. Whether the "insured" is legally entitled to recover damages; and

2. The amount of damages. This applies only if the amount does not exceed the minimum limit for bodily injury liability specified by the financial responsibility law of the state in which "your covered auto" is principally garaged. If the amount exceeds that limit, either party may demand the right to a trial. This demand must be made within 60 days of the arbitrators' decision. If this demand is not made, the amount of damages agreed to by the arbitrators will be binding.

       PP 00 01 06 94

SAMPLE

PART D - COVERAGE FOR DAMAGE TO YOUR AUTO

INSURING AGREEMENT

A. We will pay for direct and accidental loss to "your covered auto" or any "non-owned auto", including their equipment, minus any applicable deductible shown in the Declarations. If loss to more than one "your covered auto" or "non-owned auto" results from the same "collision", only the highest applicable deductible will apply. We will pay for loss to "your covered auto" caused by:

1. Other than "collision" only if the Declarations indicate that Other Than Collision Coverage is provided for that auto.

2. "Collision" only if the Declarations indicate that Collision Coverage is provided for that auto.

If there is a loss to a "non-owned auto", we will provide the broadest coverage applicable to any "your covered auto" shown in the Declarations.

B. "Collision" means the upset of "your covered auto" or a "non-owned auto" or their impact with another vehicle or object.

Loss caused by the following is considered other than "collision":

1. Missiles or falling objects;
2. Fire;
3. Theft or larceny;
4. Explosion or earthquake;
5. Windstorm;
6. Hail, water or flood;
7. Malicious mischief or vandalism;
8. Riot or civil commotion;
9. Contact with bird or animal; or
10. Breakage of glass

If breakage of glass is caused by a "collision", you may elect to have it considered a loss caused by "collision".

C. "Non-owned auto" means:

1. Any private passenger auto, pickup, van or "trailer" not owned by or furnished or available for the regular use of you or any "family member" while in the custody of or being operated by you or any "family member"; or

2. Any auto or "trailer" you do not own while used as a temporary substitute for "your covered auto" which is out of normal use because of its:

   a. Breakdown;
   b. Repair;
   c. Servicing;
   d. Loss; or
   e. Destruction.

TRANSPORTATION EXPENSES

In addition, we will pay, without application of a deductible, up to $15 per day, to a maximum of $450, for:

1. Temporary transportation expenses incurred by you in the event of a loss to "your covered auto". We will pay for such expenses if the loss is caused by:

   a. Other than "collision" only if the Declarations indicate that Other Than Collision Coverage is provided for that auto.

   b. "Collision" only if the Declarations indicate that Collision Coverage is provided for that auto.

2. Loss of use expenses for which you become legally responsible in the event of loss to a "non-owned auto". We will pay for loss of use expenses if the loss is caused by:

   a. Other than "collision" only if the Delcarations indicate that Other Than Collision Coverage is provided for any "your covered auto".

   b. "Collision" only if the Declarations indicate that Collision Coverage is provided for any "your covered auto".

If the loss is caused by a total theft of "your covered auto" or a "non-owned auto", we will pay only expenses incurred during the period:

1. Beginning 48 hours after the theft; and

2. Ending when "your covered auto" or the "non-owned auto" is returned to use or we pay for its loss.

If the loss is caused by other than theft of a "your covered auto" or a "non-owned auto", we will pay only expenses beginning when the auto is withdrawn from use for more than 24 hours.

Our payment will be limited to that period of time reasonably required to repair or replace the "your covered auto" or the "non-owned auto".

EXCLUSIONS

We will not pay for:

1. Loss to "your covered auto" or any "non-owned auto" which occurs while it is being used as a public or livery conveyance. This exclusion (1.) does not apply to a share-the-expense car pool.

2. Damage due and confined to:

   a. Wear and tear;
   b. Freezing;
   c. Mechanical or electrical breakdown or failure; or
   d. Road damage to tires.

   This exclusion (2.) does not apply if the damage results from the total theft of "your covered auto" or any "non-owned auto"

3. Loss due to or as a consequence of:

   a. Radioactive contamination;
   b. Discharge of any nuclear weapon (even if accidental);
   c. War (declared or undeclared);
   d. Civil war;

SAMPLE

e. Insurrection; or

f. Rebellion or revolution.

4. Loss to:

    a. Any electronic equipment designed for the reproduction of sound, including, but not limited to:

      (1) Radios and stereos;

      (2) Tape decks; or

      (3) Compact disc players;

    b. Any other electronic equipment that receives or transmits audio, visual or data signals, including, but not limited to:

      (1) Citizens band radios;

      (2) Telephones;

      (3) Two-way mobile radios;

      (4) Scanning monitor receivers;

      (5) Television monitor receivers;

      (6) Video cassette recorders;

      (7) Audio cassette recorders; or

      (8) Personal computers;

    c. Tapes, records, discs, or other media used with equipment described in **a.** or **b.**; or

    d. Any other accessories used with equipment described in **a.** or **b.**

This exclusion (**4.**) does not apply to:

    a. Equipment designed solely for the reproduction of sound and accessories used with such equipment, provided:

      (1) The equipment is permanently installed in "your covered auto" or any "non-owned auto"; or

      (2) The equipment is:

        (a) Removable from a housing unit which is permanently installed in the auto;

        (b) Designed to be solely operated by use of the power from the auto's electrical system; and

        (c) In or upon "your covered auto" or any "non-owned auto";

      at the time of the loss.

    b. Any other electronic equipment that is:

      (1) Necessary for the normal operation of the auto or the monitoring of the auto's operating systems; or

      (2) An integral part of the same unit housing any sound reproducing equipment described in **a.** and permanently installed in the opening of the dash or console of "your covered auto" or any "non-owned auto" normally used by the manufacturer for installation of a radio.

5. A total loss to "your covered auto" or any "non-owned auto" due to destruction or confiscation by governmental or civil authorities.

    This exclusion (**5.**) does not apply to the interests of Loss Payees in "your covered auto".

6. Loss to a camper body or "trailer" you own which is not shown in the Declarations. This exclusion (**6.**) does not apply to a camper body or "trailer" you:

    a. Acquire during the policy period; and

    b. Ask us to insure within 30 days after you become the owner.

7. Loss to any "non-owned auto" when used by you or any "family member" without a reasonable belief that you or that "family member" are entitled to do so.

8. Loss to:

    a. Awnings or cabanas; or

    b. Equipment designed to create additional living facilities.

9. Loss to equipment designed or used for the detection or location of radar or laser.

10. Loss to any custom furnishings or equipment in or upon any pickup or van. Custom furnishings or equipment include but are not limited to:

    a. Special carpeting and insulation, furniture or bars;

    b. Facilities for cooking and sleeping;

    c. Height-extending roofs; or

    d. Custom murals, paintings or other decals or graphics.

11. Loss to any "non-owned auto" being maintained or used by any person while employed or otherwise engaged in the "business" of:

    a. Selling;   d. Storing; or

    b. Repairing;   e. Parking;

    c. Servicing;

    vehicles designed for use on public highways. This includes road testing and delivery.

12. Loss to any "non-owned auto" being maintained or used by any person while employed or otherwise engaged in any "business" not described in exclusion **11.** This exclusion (**12.**) does not apply to the maintenance or use by you or any "family member" of a "non-owned auto" which is a private passenger auto or "trailer".

13. Loss to "your covered auto" or any "non-owned auto", located inside a facility designed for racing, for the purpose of:

    a. Competing in; or

    b. Practicing or preparing for;

    any prearranged or organized racing or speed contest.

       PP 00 01 06 94

SAMPLE

14. Loss to, or loss of use of, a "non-owned auto" rented by:

  a. You; or

  b. Any "family member";

if a rental vehicle company is precluded from recovering such loss or loss of use, from you or that "family member", pursuant to the provisions of any applicable rental agreement or state law.

LIMIT OF LIABILITY

A. Our limit of liability for loss will be the lesser of the:

  1. Actual cash value of the stolen or damaged property;

  2. Amount necessary to repair or replace the property with other property of like kind and quality.

However, the most we will pay for loss to any "non-owned auto" which is a trailer is $500.

B. An adjustment for depreciation and physical condition will be made in determining actual cash value in the event of a total loss.

C. If a repair or replacement results in better than like kind or quality, we will not pay for the amount of the betterment.

PAYMENT OF LOSS

We may pay for loss in money or repair or replace the damaged or stolen property. We may, at our expense, return any stolen property to:

  1. You; or

  2. The address shown in this policy.

If we return stolen property we will pay for any damage resulting from the theft. We may keep all or part of the property at an agreed or appraised value.

If we pay for loss in money, our payment will include the applicable sales tax for the damaged or stolen property.

NO BENEFIT TO BAILEE

This insurance shall not directly or indirectly benefit any carrier or other bailee for hire.

OTHER SOURCES OF RECOVERY

If other sources of recovery also cover the loss, we will pay only our share of the loss. Our share is the proportion that our limit of liability bears to the total of all applicable limits. However, any insurance we provide with respect to a "non-owned auto" shall be excess over any other collectible source of recovery including, but not limited to:

  1. Any coverage provided by the owner of the "non-owned auto";

  2. Any other applicable physical damage insurance;

  3. Any other source of recovery applicable to the loss.

APPRAISAL

A. If we and you do not agree on the amount of loss, either may demand an appraisal of the loss. In this event, each party will select a competent appraiser. The two appraisers will select an umpire. The appraisers will state separately the actual cash value and the amount of loss. If they fail to agree, they will submit their differences to the umpire. A decision agreed to by any two will be binding. Each party will:

  1. Pay its chosen appraiser; and

  2. Bear the expenses of the appraisal and umpire equally.

B. We do not waive any of our rights under this policy by agreeing to an appraisal.

PART E - DUTIES AFTER AN ACCIDENT OR LOSS

We have no duty to provide coverage under this policy unless there has been full compliance with the following duties:

A. We must be notified promptly of how, when and where the accident or loss happened. Notice should also include the names and addresses of any injured persons and of any witnesses.

B. A person seeking any coverage must:

  1. Cooperate with us in the investigation, settlement or defense of any claim or suit.

  2. Promptly send us copies of any notices or legal papers received in connection with the accident or loss.

  3. Submit, as often as we reasonably require:

    a. To physical exams by physicians we select. We will pay for these exams.

    b. To examination under oath and subscribe the same.

  4. Authorize us to obtain:

    a. Medical reports; and

    b. Other pertinent records.

  5. Submit a proof of loss when required by us.

C. A person seeking Uninsured Motorists Coverage must also:

  1. Promptly notify the police if a hit-and-run driver is involved.

  2. Promptly send us copies of the legal papers if a suit is brought.

D. A person seeking Coverage for Damage to Your Auto must also:

  1. Take reasonable steps after loss to protect "your covered auto" or any "non-owned auto" and their equipment from further loss. We will pay reasonable expenses incurred to do this.

  2. Promptly notify the police if "your covered auto" or any "non-owned auto" is stolen.

  3. Permit us to inspect and appraise the damaged property before its repair or disposal.

SAMPLE

PART F - GENERAL PROVISIONS

BANKRUPTCY

Bankruptcy or insolvency of the "insured" shall not relieve us of any obligations under this policy.

CHANGES

A. This policy contains all the agreements between you and us. Its terms may not be changed or waived except by endorsement issued by us.

B. If there is a change to the information used to develop the policy premium, we may adjust your premium. Changes during the policy term that may result in a premium increase or decrease include, but are not limited to, changes in:

1. The number, type or use classification of insured vehicles;

2. Operators using insured vehicles;

3. The place of principal garaging of insured vehicles;

4. Coverage, deductible or limits.

If a change resulting from A. or B. requires a premium adjustment, we will make the premium adjustment in accordance with our manual rules.

C. If we make a change which broadens coverage under this edition of your policy without additional premium charge, that change will automatically apply to your policy as of the date we implement the change in your state. This paragraph (C.) does not apply to changes implemented with a general program revision that includes both broadenings and restrictions in coverage, whether that general program revision is implemented through introduction of:

1. A subsequent edition of your policy; or

2. An Amendatory Endorsement.

FRAUD

We do not provide coverage for any "insured" who has made fraudulent statements or engaged in fraudulent conduct in connection with any accident or loss for which coverage is sought under this policy.

LEGAL ACTION AGAINST US

A. No legal action may be brought against us until there has been full compliance with all the terms of this policy. In addition, under Part A, no legal action may be brought against us until:

1. We agree in writing that the "insured" has an obligation to pay; or

2. The amount of that obligation has been finally determined by judgment after trial.

B. No person or organization has any right under this policy to bring us into any action to determine the liability of an "insured".

OUR RIGHT TO RECOVER PAYMENT

A. If we make a payment under this policy and the person to or for whom payment was made has a right to recover damages from another we shall be subrogated to that right. That person shall do:

1. Whatever is necessary to enable us to exercise our rights; and

2. Nothing after loss to prejudice them.

However, our rights in this paragraph (A.) do not apply under Part D, against any person using "your covered auto" with a reasonable belief that that person is entitled to do so.

B. If we make a payment under this policy and the person to or for whom payment is made recovers damages from another, that person shall:

1. Hold in trust for us the proceeds of the recovery; and

2. Reimburse us to the extent of our payment.

POLICY PERIOD AND TERRITORY

A. This policy applies only to accidents and losses which occur:

1. During the policy period as shown in the Declarations; and

2. Within the policy territory.

B. The policy territory is:

1. The United States of America, its territories or possessions;

2. Puerto Rico; or

3. Canada.

This policy also applies to loss to, or accidents involving, "your covered auto" while being transported between their ports.

TERMINATION

A. **Cancellation.** This policy may be cancelled during the policy period as follows:

1. The named insured shown in the Declarations may cancel by:

a. Returning this policy to us; or

b. Giving us advance written notice of the date cancellation is to take effect.

2. We may cancel by mailing to the named insured shown in the Declarations at the address shown in this policy:

a. At least 10 days notice:

(1) If cancellation is for nonpayment of premium; or

(2) If notice is mailed during the first 60 days this policy is in effect and this is not a renewal or continuation policy; or

b. At least 20 days notice in all other cases.

       PP 00 01 06 94

SAMPLE

3. After this policy is in effect for 60 days, or if this is a renewal or continuation policy, we will cancel only:

    a. For nonpayment of premium; or

    b. If your driver's license or that of:

        (1) Any driver who lives with you; or

        (2) Any driver who customarily uses "your covered auto";

        has been suspended or revoked. This must have occurred:

        (1) During the policy period; or

        (2) Since the last anniversary of the original effective date if the policy period is other than 1 year; or

    c. If the policy was obtained through material misrepresentation.

B. **Nonrenewal.** If we decide not to renew or continue this policy, we will mail notice to the named insured shown in the Declarations at the address shown in this policy. Notice will be mailed at least 20 days before the end of the policy period. If the policy period is:

1. Less than 6 months, we will have the right not to renew or continue this policy every 6 months, beginning 6 months after its original effective date.

2. 1 year or longer, we will have the right not to renew or continue this policy at each anniversary of its original effective date.

C. **Automatic Termination.** If we offer to renew or continue and you or your representative do not accept, this policy will automatically terminate at the end of the current policy period. Failure to pay the required renewal or continuation premium when due shall mean that you have not accepted our offer.

If you obtain other insurance on "your covered auto", any similar insurance provided by this policy will terminate as to that auto on the effective date of the other insurance.

D. **Other Termination Provisions.**

1. We may deliver any notice instead of mailing it. Proof of mailing of any notice shall be sufficient proof of notice.

2. If this policy is cancelled, you may be entitled to a premium refund. If so, we will send you the refund. The premium refund, if any, will be computed according to our manuals. However, making or offering to make the refund is not a condition of cancellation.

3. The effective date of cancellation stated in the notice shall become the end of the policy period.

TRANSFER OF YOUR INTEREST IN THIS POLICY

A. Your rights and duties under this policy may not be assigned without our written consent. However, if a named insured shown in the Declarations dies, coverage will be provided for:

1. The surviving spouse if resident in the same household at the time of death. Coverage applies to the spouse as if a named insured shown in the Declarations; and

2. The legal representative of the deceased person as if a named insured shown in the Declarations. This applies only with respect to the representative's legal responsibility to maintain or use "your covered auto".

B. Coverage will only be provided until the end of the policy period.

TWO OR MORE AUTO POLICIES

If this policy and any other auto insurance policy issued to you by us apply to the same accident, the maximum limit of our liability under all the policies shall not exceed the highest applicable limit of liability under any one policy.

SAMPLE

Appendix E

Determining the Rate of Return on Cash Value Policies

Most methods for determining the rate of return on a cash value policy are too complex for the average consumer to understand, or the necessary information is not readily available. One exception is the yearly rate-of-return method developed by Professor Joseph M. Belth, a nationally known consumer expert in life insurance.[1]

The yearly rate of return on the savings component of a cash value policy is based on the following formula:

$$i \quad + \quad \frac{(CV + D) + (YPT)(DB - CV)(.001)}{(P + CVP) - 1}$$

where

i = yearly rate of return on the savings component, expressed as a decimal

CV = cash value at end of policy year

D = annual dividend

YPT = assumed yearly price per \$1,000 of protection (see benchmark prices in the table)

DB = death benefit

P = annual premium

CVP = cash value at end of preceding policy year

The first expression in the numerator of the formula is the amount available in the policy at the end of the policy year. The second expression in the numerator is the assumed price of the protection component, which is determined by multiplying the amount of protection by an assumed price per \$1,000 of protection. Assumed prices per \$1,000 of protection for various ages are benchmarks derived from certain U.S. population death rates (see table). Finally, the expression in the denominator of the formula is the amount available in the policy at the beginning of the policy year.

For example, assume that Mark purchased a \$100,000 participating ordinary life policy at age 35. He is now age 42 at the beginning of the eighth year of the policy. The annual premium is \$1,500. The cash value in the policy is \$7,800 at the end of the seventh policy year and \$9,200 at

[1]Belth, Joseph M. *Life Insurance: A Consumer's Handbook,* 2nd ed. Bloomington: Indiana University Press, 1985, pp. 89-91, 208-209.

the end of the eighth policy year. The eighth-year dividend is $400. Since Mark is age 42 at the beginning of the eighth policy year, the benchmark price is $4 (see table below).

Based on the preceding information, the yearly rate of return for the eighth policy year is calculated as follows:

$$i = \frac{(9,200 + 400) + (4)(100,000 - 9,200)(.001)}{(1,500 + 7,800)} - 1$$

$$= \frac{(9,600) + (4)(90,800)(.001)}{(9,300)} - 1$$

$$= \frac{9,600 + 363}{9,300} - 1$$

$$= \frac{9,963}{9,300} - 1 = 1.071 - 1 = .071 = 7.1\%$$

The yearly rate of return for the eighth policy year is 7.1 percent, assuming that the yearly price per $1,000 of protection is $4 (see table below).

The major advantage of Belth's method is simplicity—you do not need a computer. The information needed can be obtained by referring to your policy and premium notice, or by contacting your agent or insurer.

Benchmark Prices

Age	Price
Under 30	$1.50
30–34	2.00
35–39	3.00
40–44	4.00
45–49	6.50
50–54	10.00
55–59	15.00
60–64	25.00
65–69	35.00
70–74	50.00
75–79	80.00
80–84	125.00

The benchmark prices were derived from certain U.S. population death rates. The benchmark figure for each five-year age bracket is close to the death rate per $1,000 at the highest age in that bracket.

Source: Adapted from Joseph M. Belth, *Life Insurance: A Consumer's Handbook*, 2nd ed. Bloomington: Indiana University Press, 1985, Table 9, p. 84. Reprinted by permission of the author.

Glossary

accelerated death benefits rider Provision allowing insured persons who are terminally ill or have certain catastrophic diseases to collect part or all of their life insurance before they die, primarily to pay for the care they require.

acceleration clause A clause in a loan agreement that specifies that if the borrower misses a scheduled installment payment, the entire debt automatically becomes payable at that time.

accumulation unit Units purchased by periodic premium contributions to a variable annuity. Value of each unit depends on market conditions.

actual cash value Value of property at the time of its damage or loss, determined by subtracting depreciation of the item from its replacement cost.

actual rate of return With regard to a bond investment, the amount the holder receives divided by the amount the holder has invested.

additional living expense In relation to homeowners insurance policies, the increase in living expenses required to maintain the household's normal standard of living when the insured dwelling cannot be used.

add-on method A method of determining interest charges under which interest is calculated based on the loan principal and added to the principal; installment payments are based on the sum of these values.

adjustable-rate mortgage (ARM) A mortgage in which the interest rate fluctuates over time.

adjusted-balance method A method of calculating finance charges in which finance charges are levied on the outstanding balance less any payments made during the period.

adjusted gross income Gross income less certain deductions.

affinity card Bank card issued to individuals who have some common bond. Educational, religious, civic, and other groups sponsor affinity cards and in return receive some percentage of the profits from the card.

agency bond A bond issued by a U.S. government agency, such as the Federal Housing Administration or the Government National Mortgage Association.

agent With regard to insurance, someone who represents the insurer and has the legal authority to act on the insurer's behalf.

aggressive growth fund Mutual fund whose investments are more speculative than those of long-term growth funds—for example, new companies that have just "gone public" and small companies that have yet to establish a record of performance.

all-risks basis Basis under which an insurance policy promises to cover all losses except those specifically excluded.

alternative minimum tax (AMT) A system for taxing upper-income taxpayers who have large itemized deductions or substantial amounts of tax-sheltered income.

annual fee With respect to credit cards, the yearly fee a cardholder pays for having the use of the card. Not all credit cards require payment of an annual fee.

annual percentage rate (APR) The actual rate of interest charged on an outstanding balance.

annual percentage yield (APY) The effective annual rate of return paid on an account.

annuitant Person who receives the periodic payments composing an annuity or whose life governs the duration of payments.

annuity A series of equal periodic payments that continues for a fixed period or for the duration of a designated life or lives.

annuity unit [[[AU: Please provide definition or delete as key term.]]]

appraisal fee A fee charged by an appraiser who sets a value on the property.

appraisal provision In a personal auto policy, a provision for handling disputes over a physical damage loss; the insurer and the insured each select an appraiser, and any difference between appraisals is settled by an umpire.

asset Item a person owns that has monetary value.

asset allocation The assignment of investment dollars to different types of investments.

asset allocation fund Mutual fund whose investment mix varies according to the fund manager's expectations; also called a *flexible portfolio fund*.

assumable mortgage A mortgage passed on to a purchaser of property from the seller of the property.

"at the money" Condition of an option that is at a break-even point; exercising it will produce neither a profit nor a loss.

audit An examination by the Internal Revenue Service of a tax return and the records that substantiate the various deductions, tax credits, and income items reported on the tax return.

automated adjustment A notice to a taxpayer from the Internal Revenue Service that the taxpayer owes more taxes or has made a mistake in the tax return.

automated teller machine (ATM) Computerized banking terminal that allows users to perform account transactions by inserting cards and entering personal identification numbers.

automatic premium loan provision Provision by which money can be automatically borrowed from a life insurance policy's cash value to pay an overdue premium after the grace period has expired.

average daily balance method A method of calculating finance charges in which the average outstanding daily balance is calculated and used as the basis for finance charges.

average tax rate The total tax paid divided by taxable income.

avoidance A method for handling potential losses by avoiding certain situations in which losses might occur.

back-end load A load levied at the time mutual fund shares are redeemed; also called *sales charge or redemption fee.*

balanced fund Mutual fund that combines the objectives of maintaining principal, generating income, and providing long-term growth.

balance sheet A financial statement that summarizes the value of a person's assets, liabilities, and net worth position on a specific date.

balloon payment A single large payment at the end of a series of smaller installment payments (such as mortgage payments).

bank card Open account card, issued by banks, other financial institutions, and some nonfinancial institutions, that allows the cardholder to charge goods and services wherever the card is accepted and also to receive cash advances.

beneficiary The party named in a life insurance policy to receive the death benefits.

beta A measure of risk that expresses the volatility of a security's or fund's returns in relation to the volatility of the market. A stock or fund with a beta of 1.0 has the same volatility as the market.

blackout period The period from the time that social security survivor benefits to a surviving spouse terminate, when the youngest child reaches age 16, to the time they are resumed when the surviving spouse reaches age 62 (or, for reduced benefits, at age 60).

blue-chip stock Stock that has exhibited a record of solid performance over time.

bond Interest-bearing debt instrument issued by a corporation or a government entity.

bond covenant The written agreement under which a bond is issued, setting forth maturity date, interest rate, and other terms; also called an *indenture.*

broker With regard to investments, an intermediary who links buyers and sellers and is paid a commission for arranging the exchange of the asset. With regard to insurance, someone who legally represents the insured.

budget A summary of projected income and expenses for a specified future period.

budget deficit Excess of expenses over income for a specific budget period.

budget surplus Excess of income over expenses for a specific budget period.

business risk Uncertainty associated with the characteristics of a particular industry.

buy-and-hold strategy Investment strategy in which an investor makes an investment and then holds (does not sell) the investment asset for a long period.

buy-down A financing arrangement through which a builder or seller pays points to lower the interest rate and the payments of the buyer.

buyer's agent A representative of prospective purchasers who assist them in locating suitable property and negotiating the terms of the purchase.

cafeteria plan A group benefit plan in which an employer provides a variety of benefits, including insurance benefits, and employees select those that best meet their financial needs.

calendar-year deductible Amount payable by an insured during a calendar year before a group or individual health insurance policy begins to pay for medical expenses.

callable preferred stock Preferred stock that the issuer may choose to retire by paying the owner a specified amount.

call option The right to purchase shares of stock at a given price during a specified period.

call provision A provision by which the bond issuer can retire the debt issue before the scheduled maturity.

capital asset Property a person owns and uses for personal purposes, pleasure, or investment.

capital gain A gain realized when a capital asset is sold or exchanged for an amount that exceeds the seller's adjusted cost basis in the property.

capital market A market that deals in the creation and transfer of long-term debt, common stock, and preferred stock.

cash advance With respect to credit cards, a cash loan made to a credit card holder through use of the credit card.

cash refund annuity Annuity that, if the annuitant dies before receiving total payments equal to the premium paid, makes a lump-sum payment to a beneficiary.

cash value Amount paid to a policyowner who surrenders the policy for its cash surrender value.

cash value life insurance A form of life insurance that provides a savings element in addition to life insurance protection.

catastrophic illness rider Provision allowing insured persons who have certain catastrophic diseases to collect part or all of the policy's face amount.

certificate of deposit (CD) An interest-bearing savings instrument requiring the holder to commit funds for a specified period.

Chapter 7 bankruptcy A legal remedy through which a debtor's assets are immediately liquidated, and the debtor is relieved of further obligations to his or her creditors.

Chapter 13 bankruptcy A legal remedy through which the debts of an individual are restructured according to a repayment plan.

charitable remainder trust A trust in which property or money is donated to a charity; the trust provides income to the creator's beneficiaries for a stated period, after which time the property belongs to the charity.

check A financial instrument written on an account that directs the financial institution to pay the party listed on the check a specified amount and to reduce the checking account balance by the same amount.

checking account An account at a deposit-type financial institution that permits deposits and withdrawals through negotiable instruments known as checks; also called a *demand deposit.*

closed-end fund A mutual fund that issues a fixed number of shares; after the shares have been sold, the fund is closed and will neither buy back shares nor issue additional shares.

closing A meeting at which all arrangements of the sale, including any payments due, are finalized and title is transferred to the new owner.

closing statement A statement summarizing all the costs (fees and prepayments) the buyer is to pay at closing.

codicil A supplement to a will that changes, modifies, or expands the original will.

coinsurance A provision in a health insurance policy that requires the insured to pay a certain percentage of the eligible medical expenses in excess of the deductible.

collateral Item of value pledged to secure a loan.

collateralized credit card Credit card that requires the cardholder to maintain a specified dollar deposit with the issuer as a condition for the issuance and use of the card; also called a *secured credit card.*

collateralized mortgage obligation (CMO) A bond issued against a pool of mortgage-backed securities.

collision With respect to a personal auto policy, the upset of a covered auto or nonowned auto or its impact with another vehicle or object.

commercial savings bank Deposit-type financial institution that offers individuals and businesses a complete range of financial services, including savings and checking accounts. Commercial banks are chartered by the federal government or the state.

commission A per-trade fee for service.

commodity A product or good—for example, corn, wheat, metals, and petroleum products.

common stock Stock representing ownership of a corporation.

compounding Converting the present value of a single amount into a future value.

comprehensive dental insurance An insurance plan that covers most dental services.

comprehensive major medical insurance A combination of basic health plan benefits and major medical insurance in one policy.

compulsory insurance law State law that requires the owners and operators of motor vehicles to carry liability insurance in certain minimum amounts in order for their vehicles to be registered or licensed.

condominium Individual ownership of a unit in a multiunit structure (such as an apartment building) or on land owned in common (such as a townhouse complex).

consolidation loan A loan taken out from a single source and used to repay other outstanding debts.

consumer borrowing Obtaining funds from a lender under specific loan provisions.

consumer credit Credit extended to a purchaser in advance of the purchase.

consumer finance company A lending business that does not accept deposits and offers small secured and unsecured loans to qualified individuals on an installment basis.

consumer loan Loan involving specific agreed-upon terms and a scheduled repayment plan.

contingent beneficiary Beneficiary entitled to death benefits if the primary beneficiary dies before the insured.

continuous premium whole life insurance Whole life insurance that provides lifetime protection to age 100 with level premiums; also called *ordinary life insurance and straight life insurance.*

contrarian investing Investment strategy involving investing in companies or industries that have fallen out of favor with other investors; also called *value investing.*

conventional mortgage A mortgage under which the lender assumes the risk of loss.

convertible bond Bond that can be exchanged for a specified number of shares of common stock of the issuing company.

convertible term insurance policy A term insurance policy that can be exchanged for a cash value policy without evidence of insurability.

cooperative A multiunit structure that is owned by a corporation and operated for the benefit of the shareholders who live in the units.

coordination-of-benefits provision A provision in a group health insurance plan that specifies the order of payment when an individual is covered under two group health insurance plans.

corporate bond Bond issued by a private company.

correlation With regard to investments, the degree to which the prices or returns of two investments move together, up or down, over time.

correspondence audit An audit conducted by mail.

cosigner One who signs a loan agreement along with the borrower and promises to repay the outstanding loan obligation if the borrower defaults.

cost-of-living rider Provision allowing the policyowner to purchase one-year term insurance equal to the percentage change in the consumer price index without evidence of insurability.

coupon rate The rate of interest designated on a bond certificate.

coverage for damage to your auto The part of a personal auto policy that provides coverage for physical damage to or theft of the insured's automobile.

covered auto As defined in the personal auto policy, (1) any vehicle shown in the declarations, (2) a vehicle acquired by the insured during the policy period, (3) a trailer owned by the insured, or (4) a temporary substitute auto.

covered call option A call option written on a stock that is already owned by the call writer.

credit bureau An organization that collects credit-related data about individuals and makes the data available to interested parties.

credit card insurance Insurance designed to provide coverage against unauthorized use of a credit card if the card is lost or stolen.

credit card statement A summary of credit card account activity during the previous billing period.

credit investigation A thorough review of data supplied by a credit applicant.

credit life insurance Insurance designed to pay the holder's credit card debt when the cardholder dies.

credit limit The maximum amount of credit provided.

credit report A detailed record of an individual's credit history.

credit scoring A system in which point values are assigned to responses to questions on the credit application; the results are used in deciding whether to approve an application and how much credit to grant.

credit-shelter trust An irrevocable trust that is designed to make use of the $600,000 lifetime exemption that could be lost when the first spouse dies.

credit terms The conditions under which credit is extended.

credit union Deposit-type financial institution owned by depositors who share a common bond, such as the same employer or the same occupation. They offer a number of services and are operated on a non-profit basis for the benefit of the members.

cumulative preferred stock Preferred stock on which any dividends not paid in previous periods must be paid in full before the company can pay dividends on common stock.

current account With respect to credit cards, an account on which the cardholder is not behind in his or her payments.

current assets Cash and cash equivalents.

current liabilities Short-term debts, such as short-term loans, credit card debt, and other debt for which repayment is due in one year or less; also called *short-term liabilities.*

currently insured Status of one who has earned at least six social security credits during the last 13 calendar quarters ending with the quarter of death, disability, or entitlement to retirement benefits.

current market value The price an asset would bring if sold on the open market at the present time.

current yield With regard to a bond, annual interest payment divided by current price.

cyclical stock Stock that moves in step with the business cycle.

dealer One who buys and sells assets and whose profit or loss is the difference between the price paid for the asset and the sales price.

debit card Specially coded card by which a user can automatically transfer funds from the user's account to another's account.

debt payments to income ratio The ratio of monthly debt payments, excluding mortgage debt, to monthly take-home pay.

debt service ratio The ratio of monthly debt payments to monthly gross income.

debt-to-asset ratio The ratio of total debt to total assets.

decreasing term insurance Term life insurance for which the face amount gradually declines.

defensive stock Stock that is immune or less susceptible than cyclical stock to economic fluctuations.

deferred annuity An annuity that provides income at some future date.

defined-benefit plan Pension plan in which the retirement benefit is known in advance, but the contributions vary depending on the amount necessary to fund the benefit.

defined-contribution plan Pension plan for which the contribution rate is fixed, but the retirement benefit is variable.

delayed retirement credit Social security credit available to workers who delay retiring beyond the normal retirement age.

demand deposit An account at a deposit-type financial institution that permits deposits and withdrawals through negotiable instruments known as checks; also called a *checking account.*

dependency exemption An amount an individual taxpayer may deduct from adjusted gross income for each eligible dependent.

dependency period A period following the breadwinner's death that follows the readjustment period and lasts until the youngest child reaches age 18.

deposit insurance Insurance provided by the federal government to protect depositors against the risk of financial loss associated with insolvency of the financial institution.

deposit-type financial institution A financial institution that accepts money from individuals who do not need the money for consumption or who wish to use the services of the institution to facilitate bill paying through checking accounts.

derivative A financial instrument that derives its value from another asset.

direct loss A financial loss that results from the physical damage, destruction, or theft of property.

direct response insurer An insurer that sells directly to the public; the insurer does not employ agents but sells through the mails or mass media.

direct transaction The purchase and sale of an asset without the use of an investment intermediary.

disability income insurance Insurance that provides periodic income payments to the insured when he or she is unable to work because of sickness or injury.

disability insured Status determined according to age and social security credits earned at the point of becoming disabled.

discount With regard to bonds, the amount by which a bond sells below its maturity value.

discount broker Broker that charges lower commissions than a full-service broker but offers fewer services.

discounting Determining the present value of a future amount.

discount method A method of determining interest charges under which interest is calculated based on the loan principal and then deducted from the principal; the borrower receives the remainder but repays the original principal amount.

disposable income Gross pay minus certain amounts that are withheld, such as taxes; net pay.

diversification Investment in a number of different financial assets.

dividend In the context of life insurance, a refund of part of the gross premium; payment of the dividend depends on the insurer's operating performance.

dividend options Ways in which life insurance dividends can be taken; they include cash, reduction of premiums, accumulation of cash at interest, paid-up additions, and in some companies, term insurance.

dividend reinvestment plan Plan by which an investor who owns common stock in a particular company can have dividends automatically used to purchase more stock in the company rather than receiving the dividends in cash; also called a DRIP.

dividend yield Annual dividend divided by market price per share.

dollar cost averaging Investment strategy involving investing a set amount at regular intervals with the goal of purchasing more shares at low prices than at high prices over the long term.

double indemnity rider Provision doubling the face amount of life insurance if death occurs as a result of an accident.

down payment A portion of the purchase price paid at the time of purchase.

durable power of attorney for health care A legal document that authorizes someone to act on one's behalf if one becomes incapable of making one's own health care decisions.

early retirement age The earliest age at which a worker can retire and receive a retirement benefit.

earned income credit A tax credit available to certain low-income persons who work.

earnest money A good-faith deposit demonstrating a prospective buyer's intent to purchase a particular home.

earnings per share (EPS) The net earnings available to common stockholders after taxes divided by the number of common shares outstanding.

earnings test Test by which monthly cash social security benefits are reduced or terminated if earned income exceeds the maximum annual limit; also called *retirement test.*

earthquake endorsement An endorsement to a homeowners insurance policy to cover earthquakes, landslides, volcanic eruption, and earth movement.

efficiency With regard to markets, the degree to which the prices of assets traded in a market reflects all relevant information.

electronic fund transfer (EFT) An electronic debit (decrease) or credit (increase) in a checking account.

elimination period Waiting period during which benefits are not paid.

emergency fund A reserve held in cash and cash equivalents to finance living expenses for a period in case of an emergency.

equity The difference between what property is worth and what is owed on the property.

equity REIT REIT that invests directly in real estate.

escrow account A savings reserve account established to hold funds designated to cover the cost of certain prepaid items, such as insurance and real estate taxes, when they come due.

estate clearance fund Fund to provide immediate cash following a person's death for burial expenses; uninsured medical bills; installment debts; estate administration expenses; and estate, inheritance, and income taxes.

estate shrinkage The decline in the value of an estate after an individual dies because of failure to develop an effective estate plan.

exclusive agent With regard to insurance, an agent who represents only one insurer or a group of insurers under common ownership.

exclusive provider organization (EPO) A plan that does not cover medical care received outside a network of preferred providers.

executor The person who is responsible for administering and settling one's estate after one's death; also called *personal representative.*

exemption An amount subtracted from adjusted gross income to determine taxable income.

expected inflation The anticipated increase in price levels.

expenses Cash outflows.

failure-to-file penalty Penalty for failing to file a tax return by the due date.

failure-to-pay penalty Penalty for failing to pay income taxes when they are due.

fair rental value Amount payable to an insured homeowner for loss of rental income due to damage that makes the premises uninhabitable.

family of funds A group of mutual funds with different objectives and asset compositions under the management of the same investment company.

federal crop insurance Insurance against unavoidable crop losses, including those resulting from hail, wind, excessive rain, and disease.

federal flood insurance A government insurance program that provides flood insurance at subsidized rates to property owners in flood zones.

FHA-insured loan A high loan-to-value mortgage that is guaranteed by the U.S. Federal Housing Administration.

FHLMC (Freddie Mac) The Federal Home Loan Mortgage Corporation, a government-chartered, publicly held corporation that buys mortgages and sells mortgage-backed securities.

field audit An audit conducted in the taxpayer's home or office or the tax professional's office if that person is qualified to practice before the Internal Revenue Service.

filing status A category that identifies a taxpayer based on marital and family situation. The categories are single, married filing jointly, married filing separately, head of household, and qualifying widow(er) with dependent child.

finance charges Interest payments on a loan.

financial asset Intangible asset (such as stocks or bonds) acquired in the hope of some future return.

financial market A market in which financial assets are created and transferred.

financial planning The process of developing a comprehensive plan that determines financial goals and objectives and the best strategies for obtaining them.

financial ratio A ratio that expresses the relationship between two financial values.

financial responsibility law State law that requires persons involved in automobile accidents under certain circumstances to furnish proof of financial responsibility up to a minimum dollar limit or face having their driving privileges revoked or suspended.

financial risk Uncertainty associated with a company's fixed financial obligations.

five Cs of consumer borrowing Five categories composing the factors lenders consider in evaluating loan applications. The five Cs are character, capital, capacity, collateral, and conditions.

fixed amount option A settlement option in which the beneficiary receives a fixed amount periodically; also called the *installment amount option*.

fixed annuity Annuity that makes payments of a guaranteed fixed amount during the annuitant's lifetime.

fixed expenses Expenses that remain the same over time, such as rent and installment loan payments.

fixed period option A settlement option in which the beneficiary receives the policy proceeds over some fixed period, such as 10, 20, or 30 years; also called the *installment-time option*.

fixed-rate loan A loan on which the interest rate remains constant over the life of the loan.

fixed-rate mortgage A mortgage in which the interest rate does not change over the life of the loan.

flexible portfolio fund Mutual fund whose investment mix varies according to the fund manager's expectations; also called an *asset allocation fund*.

flexible premium annuity A deferred annuity permitting purchase by use of flexible premiums.

flexible spending account Account established by an employer for an employee into which a certain amount of the employee's annual salary is paid, to be used for medical and dental bills or dependent care; contributions into the account are not included as taxable income.

float With respect to credit cards, the ability to use funds between the date of the purchase and the date payment is made.

FNMA (Fannie Mae) The Federal National Mortgage Association, a government-chartered, privately owned corporation that buys mortgages and sells mortgage-backed securities.

Form 1040 A complex tax form for reporting all types of income, deductions, and tax credits; it must be used by taxpayers who have taxable incomes of $50,000 or more or who wish to itemize their deductions.

Form 1040A A tax form designed for taxpayers with less than $50,000 in taxable income who do not itemize deductions but do claim exemptions for qualified dependents.

Form 1040EZ A simple one-page tax form for taxpayers with taxable incomes under $50,000 who do not itemize deductions or claim dependents.

fortuitous loss A loss that is unforeseen and unexpected and occurs as a result of chance.

front-end load A charge levied at the time of purchase.

full-service broker Broker that offers a complete range of services in addition to performing investment transactions.

fully insured Status of one who has earned at least 40 social security credits.

futures contract A contract providing for the delivery of a specified amount of a commodity on a certain day at a specified price.

garnishment Legal attachment of a debtor's earnings, directing the debtor's employer to withhold a portion of the debtor's earnings to be used to satisfy the outstanding debt.

Ginnie Mae fund Mutual fund that invests primarily in mortgage-backed securities issued by the Government National Mortgage Association (GNMA, or "Ginnie Mae") and in other mortgage-backed securities.

global bond fund Mutual fund that invests in debt securities issued by U.S. companies and foreign companies.

global equity fund Mutual fund that invests in the stock of U.S. companies and companies based in other nations.

GNMA (Ginnie Mae) The Government National Mortgage Association, a wholly owned U.S. government corporation, part of the Department of Housing and Urban Development (HUD), that buys mortgages and sells mortgage-backed securities.

government bond Bond issued by a governmental entity.

grace period With respect to life insurance, a provision that allows the policyowner 31 days to pay an overdue premium. With respect to credit cards, the period, starting at the statement closing date, during which the cardholder can pay the outstanding balance and not be assessed any finance charges.

gross estate The total value of the property a person owns when he or she dies.

gross income All income received from money, goods, property, and services that is not exempt from taxation.

gross pay The salary or total compensation earned for a given period.

group life insurance Life insurance that provides coverage to members of a group under a single master contract.

growth and income fund Mutual fund that combines the objectives of current income and capital appreciation.

growth fund Mutual fund that emphasizes capital appreciation rather than current income.

growth stock Stock issued by a company that has posted superior earnings growth; the stock is expected to provide above-average price appreciation.

guaranteed purchase option Option permitting the insured to purchase additional amounts of life insurance without evidence of insurability.

guaranteed renewable policy A policy that cannot be canceled and that the insurer guarantees may be renewed to some stated age; the insurer has the right to increase the premiums.

guaranteed replacement cost endorsement An endorsement to a homeowners insurance policy by which the insured agrees to insure a home to 100 percent of its replacement cost rather than 80 percent.

health insurance Insurance that pays benefits if the insured becomes sick or injured.

health maintenance organization (HMO) An organized system of health care that provides comprehensive services to its members for a fixed prepaid fee.

hedger In the futures market for a commodity, a trader who is an actual producer or user of the commodity and who engages in trading in an attempt to reduce the negative impact of possible future price changes.

high-yield (junk) bond fund Mutual fund that invests in debt securities rated BB or lower by Standard & Poor's and Ba or lower by Moody's.

holographic will A will that one prepares oneself in one's own handwriting.

home equity line of credit A home equity loan in which the homeowner is approved for the loan and then is allowed to borrow on an as-needed basis.

home equity loan A loan secured by the value of a principal residence.

Homeowners 2 A type of homeowners insurance that provides coverage on a named-perils basis on the dwelling, other structures, and personal property; personal liability is also covered.

Homeowners 3 A type of homeowners insurance that covers the dwelling and other structures on an all-risks basis against the risk of direct loss.

Homeowners 4 A type of homeowners insurance for tenants that covers the tenant's personal property against loss or damage and also provides personal liability insurance.

Homeowners 6 A type of homeowners insurance for the owners of condominium units; it provides coverage for personal property for the same named perils as Homeowners 2 and also provides coverage for personal liability.

Homeowners 8 A type of homeowners insurance designed for older homes; the dwelling and other structures are indemnified on the basis of repair cost using common construction materials and methods; personal liability is also covered.

hospital expense insurance Insurance that pays for medical expenses the insured incurs while in a hospital.

Hospital Insurance (Part A) Pays for inpatient hospital care and other medical expenses under Part A of Medicare.

human life value The present value of the family's share of the deceased breadwinner's future earnings.

hybrid REIT REIT that invests in both property and mortgages.

immediate annuity An annuity whose first payment is due one payment interval from the date of purchase.

incidents of ownership With regard to a life insurance policy, certain rights that evidence ownership, including the right to change the beneficiary, the right to borrow the cash value or surrender the policy, and the right to select a settlement option.

income Money received.

income and expense statement A financial statement that summarizes income received and expenses paid over a certain period, such as the previous month or the previous year.

income fund Mutual fund that emphasizes current income rather than capital appreciation.

income stock Stock that has relatively high dividend yield.

incontestable clause Clause in a life insurance contract stating that the insurer cannot contest the policy after it has been in force two years during the insured's lifetime.

indemnification A process by which an insured person who has suffered a loss is restored to his or her approximate financial position prior to the occurrence of the loss.

indemnity plan An approach by which hospital expense insurance pays for hospital room and board charges; actual room and board charges are paid up to some maximum daily limit.

indenture The written agreement under which a bond is issued, setting forth maturity date, interest rate, and other terms; also called a *bond covenant.*

independent agent With regard to insurance, an independent businessperson who represents several insurers.

index fund Mutual fund that attempts to match the performance of a known index by purchasing the same securities that compose the index in the same relative weights.

indirect loss A financial loss that results indirectly from the occurrence of a direct loss from physical damage or theft.

individual retirement account (IRA) A retirement plan that allows workers with earned incomes to make annual contributions up to certain limits; earnings from the IRA are not taxed until they are withdrawn.

inflation An overall increase in prices throughout the economy.

inflation-guard endorsement An endorsement to a homeowners insurance policy that increases the amount of insurance on the dwelling, other structures, and personal property by a specified annual percentage.

inflation risk Uncertainty associated with the loss of purchasing power due to inflation.

initial public offering (IPO) A corporation's first issue of common stock.

installment amount option A settlement option in which the beneficiary receives a fixed amount periodically; also called the *fixed amount option*.

installment loan a loan repaid through a series of equal periodic payments.

installment refund annuity Annuity that, if the annuitant dies before receiving total payments equal to the premium paid, continues to make payments to a beneficiary.

installment-time option A settlement option in which the beneficiary receives the policy proceeds over some fixed period, such as 10, 20, or 30 years; also called the *fixed period option.*

insurance The pooling of fortuitous losses by the transfer of pure risk to the insurer, who agrees to indemnify the insured for a covered loss.

interest A charge levied by a lender to compensate the lender for loss of the use of the loaned funds.

interest option A settlement option in which the policy proceeds are retained by the insurer and interest is periodically paid to the beneficiary.

interest rate The "price" of money; the rate required to compensate individuals or institutions for the use of their funds.

internal limit The maximum amount an insurer will pay for certain covered services.

international equity fund Mutual fund that invests all or almost all the fund assets in the stock of companies located in other countries.

***inter vivo* trust** Trust into which property is placed while the individual who created the trust is still alive; also called *living trust.*

intestate Without a will.

"in the money" Condition of an option that is capable of being exercised at a profit.

investment The commitment of funds for the purpose of achieving some long-term goal or objective; an asset acquired for the purpose of earning a return, such as stocks and bonds.

investment strategy An investment plan designed to bring about a desired investment result.

irrevocable life insurance trust A trust funded by life insurance; it is designed to restore shrinkage in the estate because of estate taxes or to replace for the heirs estate property gifted to charity.

irrevocable trust Trust that cannot be revoked by the creator.

itemized deductions Deductions from adjusted gross income for various types of personal expenses that are listed on Schedule A in Form 1040.

joint-and-survivor annuity Annuity based on the lives of two or more annuitants; payments are made until the death of the last annuitant.

junk bond Bond rated BB or lower by Standard & Poor's and Ba or lower by Moody's; junk bonds offer potentially higher returns than higher-rated bonds but also involve significantly higher risk.

Keogh plan A retirement plan that allows self-employed persons to make tax-deductible contributions to a qualified defined-contribution or defined-benefit pension plan.

late fee A fee assessed for late payment.

late retirement age Any age beyond the normal retirement age.

law of large numbers A principle stating that the larger is the number of exposure units, the more closely will the actual results approach the expected results.

lease A formal rental agreement between a lessee, the person who is leasing property, and a lessor, the owner of the property.

legal reserve Liability item on a life insurer's balance sheet representing the redundant, or excessive, premiums paid under the level-premium method during the early years.

liabilities The debts a person owes.

liability coverage The part of a personal auto policy that protects a covered person against a suit or claim involving bodily injury or property damages arising out of negligent operation of an automobile.

liability insurance Insurance that pays for losses arising out of the negligence of an individual that results in bodily injury or property damage to others.

lien A claim on property as security for a debt.

life annuity (no refund) Annuity that provides a lifetime income to the annuitant only during the annuitant's life.

life annuity with guaranteed payments Annuity that pays a life income to the annuitant with a certain number of guaranteed payments.

life-cycle fund Mutual fund that invests in a broad array of securities; the investment mix varies slightly in response to expected investment performance; similar to, but more conservative than, an asset allocation fund.

life income option A settlement option in which the policy proceeds are paid during the lifetime of the beneficiary.

life insurance Insurance that pays death benefits to designated beneficiaries when the insured dies.

life insurance policy loan A loan against the cash value of a life insurance policy.

limited-payment life insurance Whole life insurance for which premiums are paid for a specified period, after which time the policy is paid up. The insured has permanent protection.

limited policy A health insurance policy that covers only certain specified diseases or accidents, pays limited benefits, or places serious restrictions on the right to receive benefits. Examples include hospital indemnity policies, cancer policies, and accident-only policies.

liquidity The ability to meet short-term financial obligations with current assets.

liquidity ratio The ratio of current assets to current liabilities plus current payments for long-term liabilities.

liquidity risk Uncertainty associated with ability of the holder of an investment asset to buy or sell the asset at a reasonable price within a short period.

living trust Trust into which property is placed while the individual who created the trust is still alive; also called *inter vivo trust*.

living will A document that states one's wishes concerning the medical care that will be provided should one become mentally or physically disabled and incapable of making a rational decision.

loan extension An agreement increasing the duration of a loan, thereby providing the borrower with additional time to repay the loan.

loan maturity The duration of a loan; the period over which the money is borrowed.

loan origination fee A fee charged by the mortgage lender for making the loan.

loan principal The original amount of a loan, on which interest is paid.

loan roll-over A loan taken out to repay another loan.

loan-to-value ratio The ratio of a mortgage loan amount to the value of the property.

long-term care insurance Insurance that pays a daily or monthly benefit for medical or custodial care received in a nursing facility or hospital or at home.

long-term care rider Provision allowing insured persons who required long-term care to collect part of their life insurance.

long-term growth fund Mutual fund that invests in large, mature companies that are expected to perform well without undue risk to the purchaser.

long-term liabilities Debts for which repayment is due in more than one year.

long-term loan Generally, a loan with a duration of more than one year.

loss control Certain activities that reduce both the frequency and the severity of loss.

low-load life insurance Life insurance sold directly to the public through telephone representatives or fee-only financial planners.

major medical insurance An insurance plan that pays a large proportion of the covered expenses of a catastrophic illness or injury.

managed care A generic term describing medical expense plans that provide necessary medical care to covered persons in a cost-effective manner.

management fees With regard to a mutual fund, fees charged to compensate the professionals who make the investment decisions and also to cover the cost to the fund of securities transactions and basic overhead costs.

manufactured housing Housing constructed away from the location where the house will be used.

marginal tax rate In a progressive income tax system, the additional tax that must be paid divided by the additional amount of taxable income.

margin trade Transaction in which an investor borrows from the stock brokerage a portion of the funds necessary to buy stock, using the stock to secure the loan.

marital deduction A deduction of the value of property that is included in the gross estate but is passed on to the surviving spouse.

market A coming together of buyers and sellers for the purpose of making transactions.

market risk Uncertainty associated with price volatility of a firm's financial securities.

market timing Investment strategy in which an investor attempts to buy securities before a price increase and sell securities before a price drop.

maturity date With regard to a debt issue, the date on which the borrow must repay the maturity value.

maturity value With regard to a debt issue, the amount that must be repaid when the issue matures; also called *par value.*

Medicaid A joint state–federal welfare program that covers the medical expenses of low-income persons who satisfy a stringent means test.

medical payments coverage The part of a personal auto policy that covers reasonable medical and funeral expenses incurred by a covered person within three years from the date of an accident.

medical payments to others In regard to insurance, coverage that pays the reasonable medical expenses of someone who is accidentally injured on an insured location or by the activities of an insured, a resident employee, or an animal owned by or in the care of an insured.

Medicare A federal program that covers the medical expenses of the elderly age 65 and older and certain people with disabilities under age 65.

Medigap policy Insurance policy that pays part or all of the costs not covered by Medicare.

minimum payment With respect to credit cards, the lowest amount the cardholder is permitted to pay for the account to remain current.

mobile home Transportable dwelling constructed without a permanent foundation.

modified life insurance Whole life insurance for which premiums are lower for the first three to five years and higher thereafter.

monetary policy Policy utilized by the Federal Reserve to control the cost and supply of money.

money management The effective utilization of cash, cash equivalents, and money market savings instruments.

money market The market in which short-term debt instruments, such as Treasury Bills and certificates of deposit, are created and transferred.

money market deposit account (MMDA) A government-insured money market account offered through a deposit-type financial institution.

money market mutual fund (MMMF) A pool of money collected from savers and used to purchase short-term, high-quality debt obligations of commercial banks, government entities, and corporations. MMMFs are offered by mutual fund investment companies and insurance companies.

mortgage A written loan agreement for the purchase of real estate through which the real estate purchased is used to secure the loan and the purchaser agrees to repay the loan by making periodic payments (usually monthly) over the life of the mortgage.

mortgage-backed security Debt issue backed by a pool of mortgages.

mortgage contingency clause A clause in a purchase contract specifying that the agreement is void unless the buyer is able to arrange financing for the purchase.

mortgage REIT REIT consisting of a portfolio of real estate loans.

multiple-family dwelling A structure designed to accommodate more than one family.

municipal bond Bond issued by a city, state, county, or other political unit.

municipal bond mutual fund Mutual fund that purchases municipal bonds issued in states and cities across the country or specializes in municipal bonds issued by political subdivisions in a single state.

mutual fund n organization that pools funds from many investors through the sale of shares and uses the funds to purchase financial securities issued by corporations and government entities.

mutual insurer A private insurance corporation owned by the policy-owners; there are no stockholders.

mutual savings banks Deposit-type financial institutions similar to savings and loan associations. They are owned by their depositors and located primarily in Northeastern states.

needs approach An approach to determining how much life insurance to carry in which the financial needs that must be met after the family head dies are determined and, after consideration of other sources of income and financial assets, converted into specific amounts of life insurance.

negotiable order of withdrawal (NOW) account A checking account that earns interest provided the depositor satisfies any minimum deposit requirement imposed by the institution.

net asset value (NAV) The per unit price of a mutual fund—the price at which shares are purchased and redeemed.

net capital gain (or loss) The difference between capital gains and capital losses for a particular period.

net gain (or loss) The difference between total income and total expenses. A positive value is a net gain, and a negative value is a net loss.

net pay Gross pay minus certain amounts that are withheld, such as taxes; disposable income.

net payment cost index Method of measuring the cost of an insurance policy to an insured if death occurs at the end of some specified period. The time value of money is taken into account.

net worth The difference between assets and liabilities.

no-fault insurance A type of insurance providing that after an automobile accident, each party collects from his or her own insurer regardless of fault.

no-load mutual fund Mutual fund that does not charge purchase fees.

nominal interest rate The rate of interest observed in an economy.

noncancellable policy A policy that cannot be canceled and that the insurer guarantees may be renewed to some stated age; the insurer cannot increase the premiums.

nonforfeiture value The cash surrender value of a cash value life insurance policy.

noninsurance transfers Methods other than insurance by which a pure risk and its potential financial consequences are transferred to another party other than an insurance company.

nonowned auto A private passenger auto, pickup, van, or trailer not owned by or furnished or made available for the regular use of the named insured or family member, while it is in the custody of or is being operated by the named insured or family member.

nonparticipating policy A policy that does not pay dividends.

normal retirement age The age at which a worker can retire and receive a full, unreduced benefit.

office audit An audit conducted in an office of the Internal Revenue Service.

Old-Age, Survivors, Disability, and Health Insurance (OASDHI) An insurance program of the U.S. government, commonly known as social security, that provides retirement benefits, survivor benefits, disability income benefits, and Medicare benefits to eligible beneficiaries and family members.

open account credit Credit extended to a credit card holder before any purchases are made.

open-end fund A mutual fund that stands ready to repurchase shares and to issue new shares.

option The right to buy or sell an asset at a given price during a specified period.

optional methods of settlement The ways in which death benefits are payable other than in a lump sum; also called *settlement options.* They include the interest option, the fixed-period option, the fixed amount option, and the life income option.

ordinary life insurance Whole life insurance that provides lifetime protection to age 100 with level premiums; also called *continuous premium whole life insurance and straight life insurance.*

other-than-collision loss Loss that may be covered by a personal auto policy; such losses include all physical damage losses except collision losses and other, specified losses.

"out of the money" Condition of an option whose exercise would produce a loss.

overdraft A check written for more than the balance in the checking account.

overdraft protection An arrangement between a depositor and a financial institution through which the institution automatically covers the excess amount of an overdraft.

over-the-counter (OTC) market A secondary market dealing in securities not listed or traded on the regular exchanges (the New York Stock Exchange and the American Stock Exchange).

participating policy A policy that pays dividends.

par value With regard to a debt issue, the amount that must be repaid when the issue matures; also called *maturity value.*

passbook account An interest-bearing account at a deposit-type financial institution that permits deposits and withdrawals; also called *savings account or time deposit.*

past due amount A payment not made in time.

pawnshop A business that extends single-payment loans for short periods at high interest rates, with the amount of the loan based on the value of property that is pledged as collateral for the loan.

Pension Benefit Guaranty Corporation (PBGC) Federal corporation that guarantees the payment of vested benefits up to a specified monthly amount if a private pension plan is terminated.

peril In terms of an insurance policy, the cause of loss.

period of limitations A limited period after which no legal action can be taken against a taxpayer with respect to a given tax return; usually three years from the date the return is filed or two years from the date the tax is paid, whichever is later.

perpetual annuity (perpetuity) An annuity that provides a constant stream of payments with no maturity date; also called a *perpetuity.*

personal auto policy (PAP) Standard automobile insurance policy drafted by the Insurance Services Office and widely used throughout the United States; major coverages are liability coverage, medical payments coverage, uninsured motorists coverage, and coverage for damage to your auto.

personal bankruptcy A legal declaration that an individual is unable to repay amounts owed.

personal exemption An amount each individual taxpayer may deduct from adjusted gross income.

personal liability insurance Insurance that protects the insured against a claim or suit for damages arising from bodily injury or property damage caused by the insured's negligence.

personal property All property other than real property.

personal property replacement-cost endorsement An endorsement to a homeowners insurance policy that provides replacement cost coverage on personal property, carpets, domestic appliances, and outdoor equipment with no deduction for depreciation.

personal representative The person who is responsible for administering and settling one's estate after one's death; also called *executor.*

personal risk Risk that directly affects an individual.

personal risk management The identification and evaluation of pure risks faced by an individual or family and the selection of the most appropriate techniques for treating such risks.

personal umbrella policy Insurance policy designed to provide protection against a catastrophic lawsuit or judgment; coverage generally ranges from $1 to $10 million.

physicians' visit insurance Insurance that pays a benefit for nonsurgical care by an attending physician other than a surgeon.

PITI Principal, interest, taxes, and insurance—the four components of a mortgage payment.

point-of-service (POS) plan A hybrid managed care plan that combines the characteristics of HMOs and PPOs; members pay little or nothing out of pocket for care by providers in the network but pay substantially higher deductibles and copayments for care by providers outside the network.

points Fees paid to the lender when a borrow closes a loan.

policy loan provision Provision in a life insurance policy that allows the policyowner to borrow the cash value.

pooling The spreading of losses incurred by the few over the entire group so that, in the process, average loss is substituted for actual loss.

portfolio A collection of financial assets held by an individual or company.

portfolio composition The combination of financial assets in a portfolio.

portfolio turnover With regard to a mutual fund, the amount of financial securities sold by a mutual fund in one year versus the total assets of the fund.

precious metals mutual fund Mutual fund that invests directly or indirectly in precious metals, including gold, silver, and platinum.

predetermination of benefits A provision, widely used in dental insurance policies, under which the provider submits a plan of treatment to the insurer when the cost of treatment exceeds a certain amount.

preexisting condition A medical condition diagnosed or treated during the six months prior to the effective date of coverage of a health insurance policy.

preferred provider organization (PPO) A plan that contracts with health care providers to provide medical services to members at reduced fees.

preferred risk A person whose health history, weight, occupation, and habits are more favorable in terms of mortality risk than the average.

preferred stock Stock that entitles the holder to a fixed dividend that must be paid before any dividend is paid on common stock. Preferred stock is often called a hybrid security because it has characteristics of both common stock and debt.

premature death The death of a family head with outstanding unfulfilled financial obligations, such as dependents to support, children to educate, or a mortgage or other installment debts to be paid off.

premium With respect to bonds, the amount by which a bond's selling price exceeds its maturity value. With respect to options, the price the buyer pays for the option and the price the seller receives.

prepayment penalty A charge paid by a buyer who repays a mortgage early to compensate the lender for lost interest income.

prestige card Bank card that provides high credit limits and various other benefits to the cardholder.

previous balance method A method of calculating finance charges in which finance charges are levied on the outstanding balance at the end of the previous period.

price/earnings (P/E) ratio The ratio of share price to earnings per share.

primary beneficiary The beneficiary who is first entitled to death benefits when the insured dies.

primary insurance amount (PIA) The social security benefit paid to a worker at the normal retirement age or to a disabled worker.

primary market Market in which securities are sold by the issuing corporation.

prime rate The rate banks charge their most creditworthy customers.

private mortgage insurance (PMI) Insurance that protects a portion of the loan, typically 20 to 25 percent, against default by the borrower.

probate The process of proving the validity of a will in a court of law and executing its provisions under the supervision of the court.

profit-sharing plan A defined contribution plan in which an employer contributes part of its profits to eligible employees.

progressive income tax An income tax system in which the effective tax rate increases as taxable income increases.

property Tangible objects that a person owns.

property insurance Insurance that pays for losses to the insured person's home, auto, boat, or other personal property brought about by fire, windstorm, vandalism, theft, or other causes.

prospectus A disclosure document describing the operations of a mutual fund, including important financial data about the fund.

purchase contract A contract reflecting the details of an agreement between a buyer and a seller.

pure risk Risk present in a situation in which the only possibilities are loss and no loss.

put option A right to sell shares of stock at a given price during a specified period.

rate cap A limitation on the amount by which an adjustable mortgage rate can increase.

readjustment period A one- or two-year period following the breadwinner's death.

real average weekly earnings Weekly earnings adjusted for inflation.

real estate agent A representative of sellers of real estate who assists prospective purchasers by helping them locate suitable property.

real estate investment trust (REIT) Closed-end investment company that uses borrowed funds and equity funds from investors to purchase properties or mortgages on property.

real income Money income adjusted for inflation.

real interest rate The interest rate necessary to compensate other parties for the use of their funds.

real property Land and permanent attachments to the land (primarily buildings).

redemption fee A load levied at the time mutual fund shares are redeemed; also called *sales charge or back-end load.*

reentry term Term life insurance for which renewal premiums are based on lower rates if the insured periodically demonstrates evidence of insurability.

refinancing Replacing an existing mortgage loan with a new loan at more favorable terms.

regular checking account Noninterest-bearing checking account.

reinsurance Assumption by one insurer of all or part of a risk undertaken by another insurer.

reinvestment load A fee charged by a mutual fund for the reinvestment of dividends or capital gains distributions.

renewable term insurance policy A term insurance policy that can be renewed for additional periods without evidence of insurability.

replacement cost In regard to homeowners insurance policies, the amount necessary to repair or replace the dwelling with material of like kind and quality at current prices.

required rate of return The minimum acceptable rate of return that a saver or investor is willing to accept for a given savings or investment alternative.

residual claimant Shareholder in a corporation, also called *residual owner.* Residual owners' claims on the corporation's assets are good only after all other obligations have been met.

residual disability benefit A pro rata disability income benefit paid to an insured who returns to work but has a reduction in earnings.

residual owner Shareholder in a corporation, also called *residual claimant.* Residual owners' claims on the corporation's assets are good only after all other obligations have been met.

retail credit card Credit card issued by a retail establishment that can be used to purchase goods and services from that establishment.

retention A method for handling potential losses by retaining part or all of a loss if it should occur.

retirement annuity A deferred annuity intended to accumulate a sum of money for retirement purposes.

retirement test Test by which monthly cash social security benefits are reduced or terminated if earned income exceeds the maximum annual limit; also called *earnings test.*

revocable living trust Living trust that can be revoked by the creator.

risk Uncertainty concerning the occurrence of a loss; in the context of investment, the variability of investment outcomes.

risk averse Having a dislike for risk; tending to seek to avoid or minimize risk.

risk tolerance Level of comfort with uncertainty.

risk transfer A process in which a pure risk is transferred to the insurer, who typically is in a stronger financial position to pay the loss than the insured.

Rule of 78s A widely used method of determining how much interest should be charged on an installment loan if the loan is repaid early; the rule favors lenders.

sales charge A load levied at the time mutual fund shares are redeemed; also called *redemption fee or back-end load.*

sales finance company An organization that assists consumers with the purchase of high-priced assets by purchasing loans from the sellers.

saving Using money and interest-bearing cash equivalents that emphasize safety of principal to achieve some short-term goal.

savings Disposable income not used for current consumption.

savings account An interest-bearing account at a deposit-type financial institution that permits deposits and withdrawals; also called *passbook account or time deposit.*

savings and loan associations Deposit-type financial institutions that offer a range of services similar to those offered by commercial banks. They may be organized as mutual or stock organizations and are chartered by the federal government or the state.

savings ratio The ratio of net gain or net loss to total income after income taxes and social security taxes.

schedule In relation to homeowners insurance policies, a list of covered property with specific amounts of insurance designated.

scheduled personal property endorsement An endorsement to a homeowners insurance policy that provides coverage for items specifically listed, such as jewelry, furs, and paintings.

secondary market Market in which securities are traded among investors; the issuing companies receive none of the proceeds.

second mortgage A loan against the equity in a home that is subordinate (secondary) to the first mortgage on the property in case of default.

second-to-die life insurance Life insurance (usually whole life) that insures two or more lives and pays the death benefit upon the death of the second or last insured.

Section 401 (k) plan A plan in which part of an eligible employee's pay is invested rather than being paid as cash; taxes on the contributions and the investment earnings are paid only as funds are withdrawn.

sector fund Mutual fund that concentrates investment in a single area (or sector) of the economy.

secured credit card Credit card that requires the cardholder to maintain a specified dollar deposit with the issuer as a condition for the issuance and use of the card; also called a *collateralized credit card*.

secured debt debt for which specific assets have been pledged as collateral.

secured loan A loan that requires the pledge of collateral.

self-insured plan With regard to health insurance, a plan by which the employer pays part or all of the cost of providing health insurance to employees.

self-insured retention A provision in a personal umbrella policy whereby, when a loss is covered by the umbrella policy but not by any underlying insurance policy, the insured must retain, or pay, a certain amount of the loss.

service benefits An approach by which hospital expense insurance pays for hospital room and board charges; the full cost of a semiprivate room is paid up to a maximum number of days.

settlement options The ways in which death benefits are payable other than in a lump sum; also called *optional methods of settlement*. They include the interest option, the fixed-period option, the fixed amount option, and the life income option.

share account A savings account at a credit union.

share draft account A checking account at a credit union.

short-term liabilities Short-term debts, such as short-term loans, credit card debt, and other debt for which repayment is due in one year or less; also called *current liabilities*.

short-term loan Generally, a loan with a duration of one year or less.

simple interest method A method of determining interest charges under which interest is charged on the outstanding loan balance.

SIMPLE plan Plan that allows eligible employees to contribute a percentage of salary up to a certain limit; the employer may either match each employee's contribution or provide a flat-rate contribution for all eligible employees. SIMPLE stands for Savings Incentive Match Plan for Employees.

simplified employee pension (SEP) A plan by which an employer contributes to an IRA for each covered employee.

single limit With respect to liability coverage in a personal auto policy, a provision by which the total amount of insurance applies to the entire accident without a separate limit for each person and without a distinction between bodily injury and property damage liability.

single-payment loan A loan requiring the borrower to pay the entire loan principal at the maturity of the loan.

single-premium deferred annuity A deferred annuity purchased with a lump sum.

social choice mutual fund Mutual fund that restricts investments to companies their investors deem socially good.

Social Security credit Credit toward Social Security eligibility based on a certain amount of covered earnings in a calender quarter.

solvency The ability to pay all one's debts.

solvency ratio Net worth as a percentage of assets.

"special" whole life insurance Whole life insurance with a reduced rate that requires purchase of a minimum amount of insurance or is sold only to preferred risks.

speculative Involving great uncertainty.

speculative risk Risk present in a situation in which either profit or loss is possible.

speculative stock Risky stock; the stock of a new, unproven company or a company out of favor with investors.

speculator In the futures market for a commodity, a trader who is neither a producer nor a user of the commodity but who engages in trading in an attempt to profit from commodity price movements.

split limits With respect to liability coverage in a personal auto policy, a provision by which the amounts of insurance for bodily injury and property damage liability are stated separately.

spot price The price today of a commodity.

spousal IRA An IRA established for a nonworking spouse.

standard deduction A specific amount deducted from adjusted gross income by taxpayers who do not itemize their deductions.

standard of living The goods, services, and luxuries that a person can purchase.

stock dividend A dividend paid in the form of additional stock, stated as a specified percentage of stock already held.

stock insurer A private insurance corporation owned by stockholders, who participate in the profits and losses of the corporation.

stock option A contract that permits its owner to buy or sell 100 shares of stock at a specified price during a specified period.

stock repurchase Buyback of stocks by the issuing company.

stock split A division of the existing shares of a corporation's stock into a greater number of shares so that the value of each share is proportionately reduced.

stop-loss limit A provision in a health insurance policy by which, once the insured's out-of-pocket expenses exceed a certain amount, all remaining covered medical expenses are paid in full.

straight life insurance Whole life insurance that provides lifetime protection to age 100 with level premiums; also called *ordinary life insurance* and *continuous premium whole life insurance.*

strike price, or exercise price The price per share at which stock can be bought or sold under an option.

suicide clause Clause in a life insurance contract stating that if the insured commits suicide within two years after the policy has been issued, the face amount of insurance will not be paid.

Supplementary Medical Insurance (Part B) Pays for physicians and surgeons' fees and other medical expenses under Part B of Medicare.

surgical expense insurance Insurance that pays physicians' fees for surgery.

surrender cost index Method of measuring the cost of an insurance policy to an insured if the policy is surrendered at the end of some specified period. The time value of money is taken into consideration.

taxable estate The amount of the estate on which taxes must be paid; it amounts to the gross estate less certain deductions.

taxable income The actual amount of income subject to taxation for a given year.

tax avoidance A planned strategy of legally minimizing tax liability.

tax credit A credit that reduces dollar for dollar the actual income tax due.

tax-deferred retirement plan Retirement plan that receives favorable income tax treatment.

tax load A built-in tax liability that is part of a mutual fund's net asset value; it consists of realized but not yet distributed capital gains and unrealized capital gains.

tax loss switching Practice of selling securities at a capital loss and reinvesting the proceeds in other securities that are not substantially identical.

tax rate schedules Schedules for determining taxes based on filing status and income; tax rate schedules must be used by taxpayers with taxable incomes of $100,000 or more.

tax table A table that shows the amount of tax for taxable incomes up to $100,000.

teaser rate A low-interest rate charged for an initial period, offered to entice a borrower to accept a mortgage. Also, a low-interest rate offered by a credit card issuer so as to attract new cardholders.

temporary substitute auto A nonowned auto or trailer that the insured is temporarily using because of mechanical breakdown, repair, servicing, loss, or destruction of a covered vehicle.

terminal illness rider Provision allowing insured persons with life expectancy of six months to one year to receive part or all of the face amount of their insurance.

term insurance Life insurance providing protection for a temporary period, such as 1, 5, 10, or 20 years or up to age 65.

term to age 65 policy Term life insurance that provides protection to age 65, at which time the policy expires.

testamentary trust Trust provided for in a will; it does not come into existence until the creator dies.

thrift plan A defined contribution plan to which eligible employees voluntarily contribute; the employer contributes in an amount that is typically some fraction of the employee's contribution.

time deposit An interest-bearing account at a deposit-type financial institution that permits deposits and withdrawals; also called *savings account or passbook account.*

time value of money The value of money when interest earned over time is taken into consideration.

title Evidence of ownership of a property.

title insurance Insurance coverage that guarantees clear and unencumbered title to the property; it protects the homeowner against unknown defects in the title.

total disability As defined by insurers, (1) the complete inability of the insured to perform each and every duty of his or her own occupation; or (2) the complete inability of the insured to perform the duties of any occupation for which he or she is reasonably fitted by education, training, and experience; or (3) the inability of the insured to perform the duties of any gainful occupation. Many insurers use a combined definition whereby the first definition applies for an initial period, after which the second definition applies.

total rate of return With regard to a mutual fund, the rate of return generated through dividend payments, capital gains distributions, and price appreciation.

traditional net cost method Traditional method of determining the cost of a life insurance policy to an insured; the total dividends received and cash value at the end of a period are subtracted from the total premiums paid during that period.

travel and entertainment card Credit card that can be used to charge travel- and entertainment-related expenses, such as airline tickets, hotel rooms, and meals at restaurants.

Treasury bond A long-term debt security issued by the U.S. government.

Treasury note An intermediate-term debt security issued by the U.S. government.

trust An arrangement by which property is legally transferred to a trustee, who manages the property for the benefit of named beneficiaries.

12(b)-1 fee A fee that may be assessed by a mutual fund to cover the cost of advertising and promoting the fund.

two-cycle balance calculation method A method of calculating finance charges in which finance charges are based on the sum of average daily balances for the present and previous billing periods.

unemployment insurance Insurance provided by state governments that pays weekly cash benefits to eligible workers who experience short-term involuntary unemployment.

unified tax credit A tax credit that reduces dollar-for-dollar any federal estate or gift tax due.

uninsured motorists coverage The part of a personal auto policy that covers bodily injury (and property damage in some states) caused by an uninsured motorist, by a hit-and-run driver, or by a negligent driver whose company is insolvent.

unit investment trust A pool of bonds or mortgage-backed securities assembled by a brokerage house.

universal life insurance Flexible-premium life insurance that can provide lifetime protection under a contract that unbundles the protection and savings elements.

unsatisfied judgment fund A fund established by a state to compensate accident victims who have exhausted all other means of recovery.

unsecured loan A loan that does not require the pledge of collateral.

U.S. savings bond Financial instrument representing a long-term, tax-advantaged loan to the federal government made in exchange for a promised future payment.

U.S. Treasury bill (T-bill) Financial instrument that represents a short-term loan to the federal government.

usual, reasonable, and customary charges An approach by which medical expense plans reimburse physicians; reimbursement is based on the physician's usual fee as long as the fee is considered reasonable and customary.

usury rate The maximum interest rate that lenders are permitted to charge under state law.

VA guaranteed loan A loan available to qualified armed services veterans that is backed up to a specified amount by the U.S. Department of Veteran's Affairs.

value investing Investment strategy involving investing in companies or industries that have fallen out of favor with other investors; also called *contrarian investing.*

value mutual fund Mutual fund that purchases financial securities of companies that are experiencing financial difficulty, new and unproven companies, and companies in depressed industries; also known as *vulture funds.*

variable annuity Annuity that makes payments that vary in amount depending on investment performance.

variable expenses Expenses that vary over time, such as expenses for food and clothing.

variable life insurance Life insurance in which the death benefit and the cash surrender value vary according to the investment experience of a separate account maintained by the insurer.

variable-rate loan A loan on which the interest rate may change over time to reflect current market rates.

variable universal life insurance Life insurance similar to universal life, with two major exceptions: (1) the policyowner has a variety of options for investment of the cash value, and (2) there is no minimum guaranteed interest rate.

vesting An employee's right to the benefits attributable to the employer's contributions if employment is terminated prior to retirement.

waiver of premium A provision in a disability income policy stating that if the insured is totally disabled for 90 days, future premiums will be waived as long as the insured remains disabled.

waiver-of-premium provision Provision by which, if the insured becomes totally disabled from injury or disease before some stated age, all premiums coming due during the period of disability are waived.

wash sale Transaction in which securities are sold at a loss and substantially identical securities are bought within a certain period.

wetlands Swamps, marshes, bogs, and other areas that are subject to saturation by water.[[[AU: Does this term and definition belong here?]]]

whole life insurance Life insurance that provides lifetime protection; a stated amount is paid to a designated beneficiary when the insured dies, regardless of when the death occurs.

will A legal instrument by which property is disposed of in accordance with an individual's wishes on the individual's death.

workers' compensation insurance Insurance that pays medical bills and disability income benefits for workers who have job-related accidents or disease or pays death benefits to the dependents of employees whose deaths are job-related.

workers' compensation laws State laws that require covered employers to provide workers' compensation benefits to employees who have job-related accidents or disease.

wraparound mortgage A new mortgage that incorporates the existing mortgage.

writing an option Selling an option to a buyer. **yearly renewable term insurance** Term life insurance that is issued for a one-year period and can be renewed for successive one-year periods to some stated age without evidence of insurability.

yield curve Relationship between rate of return and length of investment, as shown on a graph.

yield to maturity With regard to a bond, the rate of return that will be earned by a bondholder who purchases the bond, holds it until it matures, and receives all the payments (interest and maturity value) associated with the bond.

zero coupon bond Bond that does not provide a periodic interest payment to the holder.

zoning restriction Local limitation placed on the usage of property for a certain purpose.

Index

Personal Financial Planning Software Templates

The accompanying CD-Rom contains a very special set of 39 Personal Financial Planning student templates that supplements the text material. These templates are compatible with Excel 5, Excel 7, and Excel 97. The following list of templates help solve your personal financial planning problems that range from setting financial goals to allocating your invested assets. Each application utilizes a custom toolbar that helps you navigate through the Excel workbook, use a Windows calculator, review examples, print a report, and even visit relevant World Wide Web personal finance sites.

Chapter 1: Introduction to Financial Planning

■ PERSONAL FINANCIAL GOALS
Use this template to list several of your financial goals.
■ PERSONAL FINANCE CHECK-LIST
Use this template to prepare a check-list that could help identify personal finance areas in need of improvement.
■ WHERE DOES YOUR MONEY GO?
Use this template to set a personal disposable income goal.

Chapter 2: Tools of Financial Planning

■ BALANCE SHEET
Use this template to create a "snapshot" of your financial condition.
■ INCOME AND EXPENSE STATEMENT
Use this template to summarize how much you earned and spent during a particular time period.
■ PERSONAL BUDGET
Use this template to prepare a summary of your projected income and expenses for a specified future period.
■ ASSET LOCATION
Use this template to record the location of such important papers as wills, mortgages, deeds, titles, banking and investment records.
■ TIME VALUE OF MONEY
Use this template to work with the four basic time value of money calculations: present value of a future amount, present value of an annuity, future value of a present amount, and future value of an annuity.

Chapter 3: Money Management

■ FUNDING A COLLEGE EDUCATION
Use this template to begin a college funding plan for one or more children.
■ CD SWITCH ANALYSIS
This template helps answer the question: "Do I take the interest penalty on a CD or wait?"

Chapter 4: Credit Management

■ TIME IT TAKES TO PAY OFF CREDIT CARD DEBT
Use this template to calculate the number of months it will take to pay off a credit card balance.

Chapter 5: Borrowing and Debt Management

■ CONSUMER DEBT MANAGER
Use this template to control your consumer debt of personal loans, credit cards, and other personal obligations other than your home mortgage.
■ CONSUMER DEBT CONSOLIDATION
Use this template to examine the impact of consolidating your consumer loans into one home equity loan.
■ BUY VS. LEASE AUTOMOBILE
Use this template to analyze whether to buy or lease a car.
■ MAXIMUM LOAN AMOUNT
Use this template to calculate the maximum loan you can afford for a car and the purchase price you can pay based on financing options.

Chapter 6: Tax Planning

■ GAIN ON THE SALE OF A HOME
Use this template to calculate the capital gains tax that may be due on the sale of a personal residence.
■ YEAR-END TAX PLAN
Use this template to plan federal income tax payments and to look for opportunities to reduce taxable income.
■ INCOME PLANNING WORKSHEET
Use this template at or near the beginning of the year to lay out an overall strategy for the coming year.

Chapter 7: The Housing Decision

■ HOME RENT OR BUY ANALYSIS
Use this template to compare renting versus buying your own home.
■ HOW MUCH CAN YOU BORROW?
Use this template to calculate your affordable monthly mortgage payment.
■ CLOSING COST ANALYSIS
Use this template to help estimate closing costs when you buy a home or condo unit.
■ MORTGAGE AMORTIZATION
This template creates a loan amortization schedule.
■ WILL IT PAY TO REFINANCE?
This template provides the analysis to make an informed refinancing decision.

Chapter 8: Risk Management and Insurance

■ PERSONAL RISK EXPOSURE
Use this template to think about and identify all the potential losses that can create serious financial problems for you.

Chapter 9: Life Insurance

■ HOW MUCH LIFE INSURANCE DO YOU NEED?
Use this template to calculate how much life insurance that you need.

Chapter 10: Health Insurance

■ HOW MUCH DISABILITY INSURANCE DO YOU NEED?
Use this template to estimate the amount of disability income insurance that you need.

Chapter 11: Property and Liability Insurance

■ AUTOMOBILE INSURANCE SHOPPER'S WORKSHEET
Use this template to shop for automobile insurance coverage.
■ PROPERTY INVENTORY FORM
Inventory your household possessions on this template for insurance purposes.

Chapter 12: Fundamentals of Investing

■ REAL RATE OF RETURN ON INVESTMENT
This template calculates the real rate of return on investments.
■ PORTFOLIO ALLOCATION
This template offers two allocation models and takes your risk tolerance and tax situation into consideration.

Chapter 13: Investing in Stocks and Bonds

■ INVESTMENT RECORD
This template serves as a review and inventory of your current investments.

Chapter 14: Investing in Mutual Funds

■ MUTUAL FUND LOAD ANALYZER
Use this template to understand the true cost of a front-end load.
■ MUTUAL FUND COST COMPARISON
This template calculates the total cost of investing in mutual funds.

Chapter 16: Retirement Planning

■ RETIREMENT INCOME PLAN
Use this template to arrive at a rough approximation of your retirement investment plan.
■ RETIREMENT BUDGET
Use this template to estimate your retirement needs for income and the potential sources of that income.
■ RETIREMENT PLAN CONTRIBUTIONS
This template can help self-employed individuals calculate the maximum contribution they can make to a retirement plan.
■ 401K PLANNER
Use this template to forecast the growth in value of your 401K plan and to project the monthly income you will receive from the plan upon retirement.

Chapter 17: Estate Planning

■ HOW BIG IS YOUR ESTATE?
Use this template to estimate the size of your estate.
■ ESTATE LIQUIDITY ANALYSIS
This template allows you to forecast the liquidity of your estate at death.